ESSAYS ON CHINA'S LEGAL TRADITION

Studies in East Asian Law
Harvard University
Sponsored by the Subcommittee on Chinese Law of the Joint Committee on Contemporary China of the Social Science Research Council and the American Council of Learned Societies

CONTRIBUTORS

Derk Bodde
Rosser H. Brockman
Fu-mei Chang Chen
Jerome Alan Cohen
Herrlee Glessner Creel
R. Randle Edwards
Dan Fenno Henderson
Marinus J. Meijer
Ichisada Miyazaki
William Shaw

ESSAYS ON CHINA'S LEGAL TRADITION

Edited by Jerome Alan Cohen
R. Randle Edwards
and
Fu-mei Chang Chen

PRINCETON UNIVERSITY PRESS
PRINCETON, NEW JERSEY

The Harvard Law School, in cooperation with Harvard's East Asian Research Center, the Harvard-Yenching Institute, and scholars from other institutions, has initiated a program of training and research designed to further scholarly understanding of the legal systems of China, Japan, Korea, and adjacent areas. A series of publications has been established in conjunction with this program. A list of the *Studies in East Asian Law* appears at the back of this book.

Published by Princeton University Press, Princeton, New Jersey
In the United Kingdom: Princeton University Press, Guildford, Surrey

Library of Congress Cataloging in Publication Data will be found on the last printed page of this book

Publication of this book has been aided by the Whitney Darrow Publication Reserve Fund of Princeton University Press

This book has been composed in VIP Bembo

Clothbound editions of Princeton University Press books are printed on acid-free paper, and binding materials are chosen for strength and durability

Printed in the United States of America by Princeton University Press, Princeton, New Jersey

This volume is dedicated to the memory of
HSÜ DAU-LIN
(1906-1973)
a distinguished legal historian of China
whose works in three languages advanced
our understanding of a great tradition.

CONTENTS

Review the past to understand the present.

THE CONFUCIAN ANALECTS

I

INTRODUCTION

Jerome Alan Cohen

Writing in 1954, the late Étienne Balazs claimed that no justification is needed to study Chinese legal history.[1] His fellow sinologists and historians would undoubtedly agree that, apart from the intrinsic satisfaction of mastering a complex aspect of one of the world's great civilizations, the contribution of the legal system to that civilization makes it an important subject of inquiry for those who seek to understand China's past.

But what of those who wish to understand China today? Should they be interested in China's legal tradition? It is a tendency of lawyers to be contemporary-minded activists, relevance mongers whose interest in legal history is limited to its impact upon the present. Of course, that impact is significant in most modern societies, even those that have developed through revolution as well as evolution. One is reminded of Frederick Maitland's famous phrase *à propos* English civil procedure: "The forms of action we have buried, but they still rule us from their graves."[2] As Oliver Wendell Holmes put it: "The life of the law has not been logic: it has been experience."[3] Of all the major nations of the world, however, China has undergone the most profound political, economic, and social transformation. In these circumstances, is knowledge of law in imperial China likely to offer insights into the contemporary legal system?

As the People's Republic of China (PRC) has become more clearly differentiated from the Soviet Union, students of Chinese affairs have begun to take history more seriously. Yet historians have not been unanimous in asserting the importance of their subject to contemporary understanding. When I started to study Chinese law, several historian friends cautioned me against being seduced by those of their brethren who tended to see People's China as imperial China in proletarian garb. That unfortunate breed, whom my friends often lumped with sinologists—a group they plainly regarded as antiquarians—failed to comprehend that the Chinese Communists had made a sharp break with tradition and that knowledge of the past was largely unimportant to contemporary understanding. It was said that, in order to avoid ob-

0-691-09238-9/80/000003-23$01.15/1 For copying information, see copyright page

solescence, these historians of the "eternal China" school and their sinologist allies would have to "reform themselves into new men," as the Communists might put it, and don fresh spectacles. Otherwise, it was predicted, they would persist in viewing Mao Tse-tung's China through distorting lenses because of their predilection for seeking, finding, and magnifying evidence of continuity with the past.

It seemed sound then and seems so now to resist the notion that the contemporary regime is really another dynasty. It hardly follows, however, that in no respect is the impact of the past significant. Rather than debate in "either/or" terms that require a sweeping answer to the large and complex question of continuity and change, it would seem more useful to engage in particularistic analysis. Certain aspects of contemporary Chinese life may reveal a high degree of continuity with the past, while many others may reveal none whatever.

If we are to get on with the task of examining the impact of the past upon specific aspects of Chinese life, we cannot omit the law.[4] Even in countries like China that have traditonally held law in relatively low regard, its role has been and continues to be of considerable importance. As I have noted elsewhere,[5] both in basic assumptions and in institutions and practices judicial administration in contemporary China displays some striking resemblances to its predecessor under the Chinese empire. Indeed, Max Weber's characterization of the administration of justice in traditional China as "a type of partriarchal obliteration of the line between justice and administration"[6] might also be applied to the contemporary system.

In certain respects even contemporary Chinese spokesmen have encouraged the belief that tradition is relevant to an understanding of the PRC's unique legal system. In mid-1974, after almost a year of an incessant nationwide campaign against Confucius and his latter-day emulators allegedly led by Lin Piao and Liu Shao-ch'i, the *People's Daily*, the newspaper that voices the views of the Central Committee of the Chinese Communist Party, stated: "Both Liu Shao-ch'i and Lin Piao were worshippers of the Confucian school and opponents of the Legalist school, and so are the Soviet revisionists. Facts in class struggle, and the struggle between the two lines tell us that the struggle between the Confucian and Legalist schools over the last 2,000 years and more still has its impact today and has in fact continued to this day. Its impact will be felt in the future too."[7] In reviving the millennial debate over the better philosophy of law and government,[8] the Communist Party demonstrated its ability to alter its assessment of the current importance of China's tradition. In the early 1960s Confucius had been regarded as ideologically irrelevant rather than as a persisting reactionary influence, and it had even been possible to note that in his day certain elements in his thought had been "progressive." Indeed, as of 1961 the Party had yet to endorse the

Legalist cause, which had been discredited by Confucian historians ever since the first Chinese emperor used Draconian Legalist methods to unify the country in the third century B.C.[9]

To be sure, before the Cultural Revolution of 1966-1969 suspended scholarly publication, most Chinese writers who discussed the problem of the extent to which China's pre-Communist heritage should be viewed as influencing contemporary legal development emphatically rejected the idea of the "inheritability" of the old law. (Soviet scholars still react strongly against the suggestion that Soviet law is importantly influenced by Russian history.) Yet some Chinese publications did indicate interest in Chinese legal history, and found traces of continuity between past and present. More particularly, in seeking to justify the PRC's departure from the Soviet model of criminal justice,[10] some writers argued that slavish application of Soviet criminal procedure in a country with "different national characteristics, historical conditions, class relations and revolutionary experience" would constitute dogmatism.[11]

During the same period, Party judicial spokesmen offered similar explanations to foreign visitors who expressed surprise at the sudden disappearance of "people's lawyers," the Soviet-style advocates who had begun to be active in China's cities in the mid-1950s. In Peking in 1959, for example, a group of Japanese lawyers and scholars met with the late Wu Te-feng, a frequent greeter of delegations of foreign lawyers. In this interview Mr. Wu, who subsequently became vice-president of the Supreme People's Court, attributed the demise of professional lawyers in the PRC primarily to an historical factor that he said was not common to the history of all socialist countries. This was the extremely bad reputation of lawyers in "the old China." Traditionally, lawyers were thought to be servants of the exploiting classes, who were cynical, mercenary, and dishonest. Because of this, he said, following the Communist liberation of China, the people could not bring themselves to consult lawyers, and this had hindered development of the bar.[12] In 1963 another group of Japanese lawyers received a similar explanation of why lawyers did not defend accused criminals.[13]

When this Communist regime that has committed itself to smashing China's "semifeudal" heritage defends its administration of justice by an appeal to history and to the low regard that Chinese are said traditionally to have held for lawyers, does this suggest that even one of the world's most totalitarian governments is forced to take into account habits and attitudes that have become deeply ingrained over centuries? Or are the Communists cynically invoking the Muse as an excuse for adopting a system of criminal procedure better suited to enhance their political power? Even if the latter is the case, is not the contemporary Chinese view of the criminal process itself the product of China's authoritarian tradition as well as more immediate political pressures?

Those Chinese officials who attempted to attribute the absence of lawyers to the impact of tradition may have chosen an explanation that was likely to have especial appeal to their Japanese visitors. After all, during Japan's Tokugawa era (1603-1868) unauthorized suit solicitors called *kujishi* "conducted a marginal practice with frequent cases of bribery and swindling."[14] Their activities, which were proscribed by law, unfairly gave a bad name to the innkeepers who were officially authorized to aid litigants in various ways but who were confused by the public and by modern Japanese historians with the disreputable *kujishi*. Because of this confusion, even the legitimate precursor of the contemporary Japanese lawyer has had a low reputation, and scholars have noted this as a factor that may have retarded the growth of the Japanese legal profession.[15] Premodern China, like Tokugawa Japan, had no professional bar and generally did not allow an accused to be represented by anyone at trial. There was in China, however, a rough counterpart to the *kujishi*. This was the *sung-kun* or "litigation trickster." Unlike the *tai-shu* or scrivener, who was authorized to draw up accusations and pleadings to aid the illiterate and unsophisticated, the *sung-kun* operated surreptitiously in giving advice and drafting documents outside the courtroom. These "tricksters" were often punished as persons who stirred up controversy for their own gain and corrupted human relations, and it is true that they were often poorly regarded by the people as well as the government.[16]

It is also true that, after the last of the imperial dynasties was replaced by the Republic of China (ROC) in 1912 and a professional lawyer class was allowed to develop as part of the paraphernalia of modernization, its earliest members tended to vindicate the traditional belief that lawyers destroy rather than support community values. By 1922 China was so overrun by ill-trained, self-aggrandizing practitioners that a convention of important educators urged the abolition of all government law colleges, on the ground that they produced "disorderly graduates" and "case-multiplying lawyers." Such a radical measure was not taken, but for a period during 1922-1923 the government refused to issue lawyers' licenses except to those who had studied abroad and a few others, and it increased the license fee twentyfold.[17] After Chiang Kai-shek's Nationalist Party came to power in 1928, it improved legal education and imposed higher standards for admission to the bar.[18] But neither on the mainland prior to 1949 nor after Chiang's flight to Taiwan can it be said that many of the tightly controlled lawyers of supposedly "Free China" have earned popular esteem by vigorously defending the rights of accused, and their profitable efforts to settle disputes and to facilitate economic transactions have only gradually improved their social status. We know too little about litigation tricksters and Republican lawyers, but what we do know suggests that the Communist regime has not fabricated their unpopularity out of whole cloth.

It is far from clear, however, that the paucity of contemporary "people's lawyers" should be attributed to this historical factor. Contemporary Japan has made great progress toward developing a vigorous, independent bar, despite a tradition that is similar to China's. Moreover, although in China, as in Japan, the traditional attitude toward lawyers undoubtedly carried over into the present era, there is evidence that the Communists could have overcome it, had the political will to do so existed. Certainly the Chinese press of the mid-1950s reported popular acclaim for the legal advisory offices being established in the cities.[19] And in interviews in Hong Kong two lawyers who practiced in China during the period immediately preceding the "antirightist" campaign asserted that the Communist experiment with the bar had proved a popular success. They reported that on many occasions criminal accused who had initially mistrusted their counsel expressed satisfaction with his efforts at the conclusion of the public trial. Also, the masses who attended such trials were often enthusiastic about having someone able and willing to present the plight of a hapless accused and the views of the common people, especially in cases when they felt the prosecution was acting in a one-sided and high-handed fashion. Because their help to the public elicited warm appreciation, those who served as lawyers were developing a sense of mission and professional self-esteem. As one ex-lawyer told me with pride, "every day people formed lines to see us." Although the evidence is slight, it suggests that, like urban Russians, urban Chinese might have made good use of the new, inexpensive people's lawyers if they had been allowed to flourish.

It is in a continuity of governmental rather than popular attitudes that history appears to play a more significant role in this case. When, during the 1957 antirightist movement, the PRC abandoned its experiments with Soviet-style trials in favor of exclusive resort to inquisitorial methods of adjudication that necessarily excluded participation by defense counsel, it was building on deep roots. This, after all, is the way in which criminal justice had traditionally been dispensed in China. For example, during the last of the imperial dynasties, the Ch'ing or Manchu (1644-1911), although trials were usually public, the accused was entirely at the mercy of the magistrate. Trial consisted of interrogation by the magistrate, who was legally authorized to torture the accused in court if he refused to confess. The tendency to use torture was reinforced by the rule that the accused could not be convicted unless he confessed. Forced to kneel abjectly before the magistrate's high bench, flanked by guards wielding bamboo staves, whips, and other instruments, precluded from presenting his own witnesses, and denied the services of a professional advocate, the accused had no meaningful opportunity to defend himself.[20]

This Ch'ing procedure reflected the view that law and legal institutions serve principally as instruments for maintaining the power of the state rather than enhancing the sense of security of its citizens. In the traditional Chinese value system the interests of the state dwarfed those of the individual, and this value preference was expressed in the criminal process. Thus, it was assumed that the administration of justice was the exclusive preserve of the state and that no independent actors such as defense counsel should be allowed to intrude.

This basic assumption and the concomitant absence of professional advocates suggest similarities with the criminal process not only in the PRC but also, albeit to a lesser extent, in the Republic of China now on Taiwan. Although there lawyers do play a role in the criminal process, it is a limited one compared to that of judges, prosecutors, and police, and the lawyers' ability to defend political offenders is especially circumscribed by what remains an essentially inquisitorial system.

How should we interpret these similarities? Certainly one cannot say that there is a causal connection between the traditional system of administering justice and the contemporary systems. Yet it seems clear that the past does not conflict with, but rather reinforces, contemporary Chinese attitudes toward the criminal process. Can it be said to do more? Does it create a predisposition toward handling cases in the inquisitorial way? Does it constitute an unconscious barrier to the development of an independent legal profession?

One can infer that this does seem to be an aspect of contemporary Chinese affairs in which there is a significant degree of continuity with the past. Perhaps one can also say that there may be a predisposition to maintain this continuity despite the intervention of other influences. Nevertheless, it seems unlikely that tradition would constitute a barrier to a regime that genuinely sought to overcome it. Why the Communists, and to some extent their Nationalist rivals on Taiwan, have refused to make the effort, why they and many other modernizing governments in both East and West see an independent legal profession and the achievement of national goals as mutually exclusive, deserves our further consideration, but surely tradition ought to be considered a contributory factor. The PRC's recently renewed program to create a formal legal system assures us that this topic will continue to warrant the attention of both Chinese and foreigners.

The Contribution of This Volume

As the above discussion suggests, at least at this early stage of scholarship on Chinese law, the subject of continuity and change is itself too broad a topic. We know far too little about all fields of law and all eras. Moreover, there may be much continuity in one field and little in another. In these circumstances it seemed desirable as a first step in assessing the relevance of tradition to convene a conference of interested historians and lawyers who would add to our knowledge of the traditional legal system itself. The conference, it was hoped, would stimulate an exchange of ideas and perhaps lead to cooperation among people from different countries, universities, and academic disciplines in providing a more solid basis for a subsequent evaluation of the changes wrought by "modernization."

Accordingly, the Subcommittee on Chinese Law of the Joint Committee on Contemporary China of the American Council of Learned Societies and the Social Science Research Council sponsored a meeting on August 7-14, 1969, at the Rockefeller Foundation's Villa Serbelloni in Bellagio on Italy's Lake Como. Seventeen scholars from Europe, Japan, the ROC, and the United States attended. These experts were asked to describe and analyze previously neglected aspects of the traditional system. Although it is premature to undertake a comprehensive study of the growth of Chinese law and legal institutions through the major dynastic periods, a number of the papers submitted did offer fresh information and interpretation and, after appropriate revision, seemed to warrant publication. This volume presents these essays, together with several by other scholars who have more recently joined the gradually expanding group. Its painstaking labors will ultimately make possible an overall appraisal of traditional Chinese justice and its impact upon the contemporary systems of the mainland and Taiwan. The following brief comments do not by any means do justice to these essays or even summarize them, but merely introduce the authors and suggest the dimensions of their contributions.

Herrlee Glessner Creel, Professor of History, Emeritus, at the University of Chicago, begins the volume by searching the extant records of China's earliest civilization for the development of legal institutions. Professor Creel offers an account of ancient law that should be of broad general interest. Students of other legal systems will note that as early as 3,000 years ago Chinese were making contracts, litigating disputes, and enlisting others as advocates of their causes. Although there is no evidence of the growth of a professional class of legal representatives during the Chou dynasty (1122-256 B.C.), at least one source indicates that many people studied the techniques of trying cases.

Those familiar with contemporary Chinese law will be struck by many aspects of Professor Creel's essay. Not the least of these is the impressive continuity of certain Chinese legal language throughout the millennia. Terms such as *sung* ("to litigate"), *kao* ("to accuse") and *hsün* ("to interrogate") retain their original meaning today on both sides of the Taiwan Strait.

Students of Chinese legal history will find much that is new in Professor Creel's contribution. For example, he challenges the view that China had no promulgated laws until the sixth century B.C. and that Chou rulers sought to keep their laws secret. He also points out what some scholars have overlooked—that, although law in China was not attributed to divine origin, the chief deity, Heaven, was thought to scrutinize the administration of justice, and that the Chou believed the failure of the previous dynasty, the Shang, to do justice was one of the reasons why it had lost the Mandate of Heaven. Thus, it is difficult to attribute the low regard that the Chinese came to have for law to a lack in their experience of anything resembling the associations between law and the divine that one frequently finds in the early stages of Western cultures.

Professor Creel's essay was written before the 1973-1974 attack upon Confucius by the PRC, but his comments take on added meaning in view of that Communist effort to depict the Sage as the spokesman for a waning aristocracy that was vainly seeking to perpetuate a "slave society" based upon subjugation of the humble. Confucius, according to Creel, actually worked to destroy, not sustain, the barriers between the rich, powerful, and educated and the poor, helpless, and illiterate. Although Confucius wished to maintain the social order, states Creel, he did not envisage it as one in which the nobility was deemed exempt from legal regulation and the common people were deemed undeserving of moral education. He was a frequent critic of those in authority and a teacher of the humble, and reinterpreted the aristocratic ethical terminology of his day in a way that made it applicable to all classes. Scholars who have regarded the introduction of principles of social inequality into the laws of the Han dynasty (206 B.C.-220 A.D.) as "the Confucianization of Chinese law" have done an injustice to the Sage, Creel maintains.

Communist Chinese writers of the early 1970s will find Creel's portrait of the Legalists closer to their own. Like them, for example, he sees the Legalists as preaching a philosophy conducive to the construction of a centralized government over widely dispersed and diverse peoples who had yet to become a nation; the Legalists were pragmatic modern men, not captives of tradition, and they marshaled new ideas to meet new needs. Yet Creel brings out aspects of the Legalists that are muted in the PRC, particularly their emphasis upon the publication of detailed, clear legislation that is to be consistently and equally applied to all persons, and their endorsement of information gathering through a network of spies and informers. He does not defend the totalitarian repression practiced by that arch-Legalist statesman, the first Chinese emperor, who, according to PRC apologists, only burned books that were offensive and only buried scholars who were subversive.[21]

The Chou dynasty claims our attention because it gave birth to China's legal institutions and formulated the two major philosophies of law and government that have contended, coexisted, and interacted down to the present. Yet, at least at this stage of research, it is difficult to speak of a legal system existing even at the end of the Chou, in the third century B.C. Not only is the evidence of law scattered but what it reveals was unsystematized and in certain respects primitive. Creel reminds us, by way of illustration, that some lawsuits were decided by archery contests.

How different the situation became under centralized imperial rule is made clear by the essay on the administration of justice during the Sung dynasty (960-1279), by Ichisada Miyazaki, Professor of History, Emeritus, of Kyoto University. Over a thousand years of development since the Chou enabled the Sung to inherit from the T'ang dynasty (618-906) a comprehensive and sophisticated body of legislation and an impressive legal system that furnished a model not only for subsequent Chinese dynasties but also for the early rulers of Korea, Vietnam, and Japan. Westerners already know a good deal about the initial stages of this achievement, during the Han dynasty (206 B.C.-220 A.D.), from A.F.P. Hulsewé's *Remnants of Han Law*.[22] The works of Balazs,[23] Karl Bünger,[24] and others[25] have permitted those who cannot read the formidable Chinese and Japanese language scholarship on the subject to learn much about the formative era that began with the Sui dynasty (581-618) and culminated in the T'ang. Professor Miyazaki's essay gives us the first broad portrait of Sung justice in the English language. It shows that Sung statesmen modified T'ang legislation to meet the demands of their increasingly commercial and populous society. Such was the complexity of this legislation and the multitude of reported judicial decisions applying it that by the twelfth century the Sung had compiled for the use of officials both a compendium of the various laws, classified according to subject matter, and a compilation of case precedents. According to Professor Miyazaki, these aids were designed to enhance the efficiency of the judicial process and to facilitate its response to the growing pressures for uniformity and predictability in adjudication.

The judicial process was an important responsibility of a highly articulated, centralized bureaucracy that was staffed by officials generally selected on the basis of merit demonstrated in passing examinations that tested knowledge of the Confucian classics and literary skill. Although the division of labor at the higher reaches of government permitted certain officials to develop legal expertise, at every level officials charged with judicial administration were assisted by clerks who, while lacking the broad education of officialdom, were specialists better versed in legal technicalities and documentation.

Perhaps the most significant aspect of Sung adjudication was its concern for developing institutional restraints in the interest of assuring a fair trial. Professor Miyazaki emphasizes the exclusion from the judicial process of those who served as police and would receive a reward following conviction. Also, although in major cases confession by the accused was essential to a finding of guilt and torture could be used to obtain it from him, he was given an opportunity to recant the confession on the ground of coercion, and in such cases a different group of interrogators was ordered to conduct a reinvestigation. These procedures were part of an elaborate process of review, deriving from the T'ang, that was tailored to the seriousness of the proposed sentence. Officials who were found to have committed transgressions in the course of administering justice suffered administrative and other sanctions.

One of the most fascinating points in Professor Miyazaki's essay is his discussion of the attempt by some high officials to gain acceptance for the idea of the independence of judicial decision makers from political interference. One hopes that future researchers will explore not only the extent to which this concept developed in China during the subsequent millennium but also other efforts to restrict the exercise of imperial discretion through legal regulation.

Given the role of advocates in litigation during the Chou, and given the sophistication of the legal system by Sung times, one might have expected to witness the corresponding emergence of a legal profession. Yet none developed. To be sure, Sung officials involved as parties to a litigation were allowed to send assistants to represent them in court, and female and elderly male litigants occasionally could have kinsmen serve as representatives. But in the hope of restraining an increasingly litigious populace, the general use of advocates was prohibited, and judicial officials were expected to take account of the interests of all parties without the prompting and assistance of advocates. Because of the illiteracy of the common people, however, the authorities had to acknowledge the need for the services of scriveners, private persons who were skilled in the writing of the complaints required to initiate judicial proceedings. These scriveners were licensed and subjected to continuing scrutiny by the government.

Sung judicial proceedings were closed to the public. Moreover, although the public was required to respect the law as the will of the emperor, it was not permitted to obtain copies of the prevailing legislation, which was for the exclusive guidance of officials. As Professor Miyazaki points out, this latter policy reflected a traditional fear (which he, unlike Professor Creel, traces to certain Chou statesmen), that if the people knew the law in detail they would circumvent it, manipulate it to their advantage, engage in litigation, and act obstreperously rather than behave like moral persons. In view of this attitude—very different from that of the Ming dynasty (1368-1644), which encouraged popular knowledge of, as well as respect for, the law—it is surprising that the Sung allowed civil litigation to go on seemingly without end, a toleration that caused much hardship to disputants and consumed an undue amount of bureaucratic resources. It is also surprising that the government did not move more vigorously to stamp out efforts to teach the common people litigation techniques, especially after such activity was made illegal in 1086.

During the brief period of his influence, the famed reformer, Wang An-shih, succeeded in easing the Sung prohibition against the dissemination of legislative norms. Wang, whom students of law should find one of the most interesting figures in Chinese history, also made a gallant effort to revive legal education both for those who staffed the bureaucracy and those who aspired to it. He also tried to meet the perennial problem of widespread corruption among the officials' clerks by offering not only the stick of strict punishment but also the carrot of higher salaries.

Having surveyed both the earliest traces of Chinese law and the sophistication that the administration of justice had attained by the T'ang-Sung era, our volume turns to the legal system as it operated during the Ch'ing or Manchu dynasty (1644-1911). The Ch'ing constituted the most complete expression of China's legal tradition and the baseline from which twentieth-century modernization proceeded. It also left us more extensive documentary deposits than did previous dynasties, thus permitting detailed examination of various aspects of its legal system. For these reasons most of the essays in this volume deal with the Ch'ing.

At least since 1810, when Sir George Staunton, the British trader-sinologist, published a translation of the basic provisions of the penal code called *Ta Ch'ing lü-li*,[26] Anglo-American interest in Chinese law has tended to focus on the role that this principal Ch'ing Code played in the government of imperial China. The Code, which closely resembled that of the preceding Ming dynasty first enacted in 1397, was only part of a vast body of norms promulgated to guide the administration of the empire.[27] It was preeminently an instrument for state building and the preservation of the social order, being essentially a compendium of rules, directed to district magistrates and their superiors, for the punishment of persons who hindered the operation of government. Thus, it slighted matters of "private law" that have been the principal focus of European legislators beginning with the Roman Empire.[28] The provisions that it did contain pertaining to what we call civil law problems were limited, incomplete, and designed to punish certain kinds of antisocial acts. They merely added some specific rules to a broader body of norms that derived from customary rather than official sources.

Rosser H. Brockman's study of contract law in nineteenth-century Taiwan demonstrates the Code's particular irrelevance to most commercial activity. Indeed, Mr. Brockman, a lawyer and historian who practices law in Seattle and Tokyo and is an adjunct lecturer at the Law School of the University of Washington, also emphasizes the highly restricted role of Ch'ing courts in generating legal principles to guide the conduct of merchants. Drawing upon the valuable research of Japanese colonial authorities into the customary law that had evolved in Taiwan under the Ch'ing prior to Japan's annexation of the island in 1895, he shows that resort to the magistrate's tribunal was an infrequent last resort for businessmen in a society that regarded litigation as bad form. Disputes that did reach the magistrate were often settled through informal mediation. Those that were not disposed of through mediation were generally decided by the magistrate on the basis of local customary law rather than legislative prescriptions, sometimes even when custom contravened an explicit statutory provision. In any event, the magistrate's decision rarely gave the aggrieved party complete satisfaction but tended, rather, to compromise his claim. Brockman's portrait of traditional judicial practice, one of the fullest we have had, suggests that, at least on Taiwan, magistrates acted much more flexibly in commercial cases than in criminal cases.

The fact that the government played a very limited role with respect to commercial contracts did not mean that there was no need for such contracts or for rules, techniques, and processes to foster and regulate them and to settle disputes arising from them. Brockman shows that the reluctance of businessmen to go to court did not reflect a lack of "rights consciousness" or of appreciation for contractual skills. By the end of the nineteenth century, he points out, Taiwanese merchants operated in a complex, large, and impersonal market that required a variety of sophisticated rules and contractual devices to meet the demands of trade in many different products. Given the limited scope of informal norms and social controls, traditional village, lineage, and guild organizations could not meet those demands. But the broader commercial community did develop the requisite norms and forms into an unofficial, yet binding, customary law of contract that spelled out the rights and obligations of the parties and enhanced their incentives to fulfil their promises.

Focusing especially on sales contracts, Brockman analyzes the types of contracts in use for different lines of business or different kinds of transactions. He notes the largely successful efforts of merchants to draft documents that dealt with many of the legal questions that are handled by legislation and case law in Western countries today, such as who bears the risk of sudden changes in the market price, when is the seller responsible for defects in the goods, what are the obligations of the buyer, and how is loss allocated in case of calamity. In order to minimize a party's need to go to court or to invoke the assistance of other institutions in case of the other party's nonperformance, self-enforcement mechanisms, such as advance deposits that would be forfeited for nonperformance, were written into contracts whenever possible. Of course, the contracting parties did not have to spell out all of the rules governing their transaction, since they and their contracts functioned within the context of the well-understood customs and practices of their community and line of business, and these customs and practices would be recognized as applicable in the absence of specific provisions to the contrary.

Brockman describes what was essentially an impressive private legal system that sought to realize expectations and avoid disputes by defining rights precisely, according to rules that were as clear, simple and well known as possible; by linking legal consequences to the occurrence of objective acts, such as payment or physical delivery of the goods; and by developing contract terms that maximized the parties' incentives to perform.

To the traditional Chinese, however, "law" was what was prescribed in the Ch'ing Code. One of the Code's most interesting features was the inclusion of many explicit provisions that required magistrates and their superiors, when determining the gravity of various offenses and the appropriate degree of punishment, to take careful account of the offender's individual circumstances, such as his social status, sex, age, physical condition, and relation to the victim of his offense. Thus, both officials and slaves were to be held to different standards from commoners as well as each other, a father who assaulted his son was to be punished much less severely than a son who assaulted his father, and theft within the family was to be dealt with more leniently than theft from a stranger. In his contribution to this volume, Derk Bodde, Professor Emeritus of Chinese at the University of Pennsylvania, calls this principle of legalized inequality "probably the most conspicuous single Confucian influence on imperial Chinese law." His essay traces the actual application of some of these statutory strictures by the Ch'ing legal bureaucracy and thereby sheds light upon the relation between legislation and adjudication in traditional China.

Professor Bodde selects for his study the complex body of statutes, substatutes and official commentary that required reduction in punishment for certain categories of very old, very young, or physically disabled persons who committed designated types of offenses. After analyzing the relevant legislation and the humanitarian policy that underlay it, he examines forty case records in an effort to ascertain the extent to which the decisions of the Board of Punishments, the central agency with principal responsibility for the adjudication of criminal-type cases, were governed by legislatively prescribed factors.

This study shows how, by and large, the Board sought to impose patterns upon facts and to manipulate undefined statutory terms, such as "unreasonable," "abusive," and "vicious," in order to arrive at results that would be consonant with the major assumptions and values of the legislative scheme and the Ch'ing legal system. The essay offers insights into the Board's inner processes, its relation to inferior, local tribunals and to the emperor and other agencies in Peking, and its treatment of its own prior decisions. Although "precedent" was cited only in a minority of the cases reviewed, the Board generally appeared to appreciate the importance of continuity in its decision making. Nevertheless, it did not shy away from an occasional explicit rejection of a precedent as "too old" or "wrongly decided."

Professor Bodde recognizes that, despite the statutory mandates, the Board inevitably possessed broad discretion in determining whether a case should be deemed to fall within one of the privileged categories that authorized leniency and, if so, whether in the circumstances the particular offenders should be allowed to benefit. He strives mightily to find explanations for those cases in which the Board does not appear to have followed the applicable statutes. In some instances, it seems to have given greater weight to other Ch'ing policies than those embodied in this humanitarian legislation. For example, the strong official antipathy toward those who stir up lawsuits is reflected in the Board's refusal to grant the prescribed commutation of punishment to a "litigation trickster." It preferred instead to rid society of his socially destructive activities by requiring him to serve out his sentence in exile, despite his advanced age. Although Bodde concedes that certain other decisions seem to be the product of ignorance, prejudice, or misunderstanding, he concludes that, on the whole, the Board was quite successful in applying the relevant statutes in a reasoned and systematic manner.

In carrying out this difficult task, the Board of Punishments was able to consult a number of private commentaries on the Ch'ing Code. These commentaries, the works of learned men who had both absorbed the Confucian classics and become acquainted with the judicial process through periods of service as legal secretaries, stand out as principal examples of traditional China's modest legal scholarship. The private commentaries were designed to assist officials and their legal secretaries in the complex process of construing a host of overlapping and frequently archaic and elliptical statutes and substatutes, amid all the permutations and combinations of fact situations spawned by Chinese society.

Despite the obvious interest that these commentaries hold for students of comparative law, virtually nothing about them has been published in the West. The essay by Mrs. Fu-mei Chang Chen, a legal historian trained both in Taiwan and the United States and a coeditor of this volume, rectifies this situation. Focusing on the most influential and frequently cited of the Ch'ing commentaries—Shen Chih-ch'i's *Chi-chu*—her study analyzes the use that reported court decisions made of the 1715 publication and subsequent revised editions.

Mrs. Chen, who is a Research Fellow at the Hoover Institution, notes that only 21 of the more than 9,000 cases she examined actually contain quotations from Shen's work. Yet, she points out, this statistic hardly reflects the work's importance. Indeed, her analysis of those decisions that do refer to it by name reveals that, although the Board of Punishments gradually developed a policy forbidding provincial judicial officials to rely explicitly on any of the private commentaries, that policy was not consistently enforced; and that in any event, the Board could not prevent local magistrates from consulting the commentaries so long as their opinions did not reflect the fact.

Interestingly, the Board itself pursued a "do as I say, not as I do" policy in this respect. Officials of its constituent units in Peking not only were free to rely on the private commentaries but also were even encouraged to do so. According to Mrs. Chen, there were several reasons why the Board allowed officials in the capital such latitude while denying it to those in the provinces. For one thing, in their decision making, provincial officials, as inferior members of the governmental hierarchy, were not supposed to be guided by any other sources than the legislative commands of the emperor. It was feared that reference to the interpretations and recommendations of private commentators might subvert the enforcement of the law. The Board of Punishments, by contrast, not only stood at the apex of the judicial system, working closely with the emperor in the administration of justice, but it also enjoyed major responsibility for the legislative process, recommending new laws and revisions of the existing ones on the basis of its intimate involvement in the judicial system. It thus seemed appropriate for the Board to take advantage of whatever assistance was available for improving the quality of justice.

Moreover, as Mrs. Chen emphasizes, Board officials were more sophisticated about law than were those in the provinces, and, because of their close working relationship with the emperor, they were less likely to misinterpret his legislative purposes. Thus, there seemed to be less danger in their consulting private commentaries. Probably in order to avoid the appearance of inconsistency, Board officials only referred to books such as Shen's in the internal documents they circulated in Peking and eliminated these references in documents disseminated in the provinces.

Mrs. Chen's essay, like Professor Bodde's, sheds considerable light upon the Board's internal operations. It reveals the frequent use made of the Statutes Commission to provide the directorate with another expert opinion in difficult cases. It also provides further confirmation of the extent to which decision makers at various levels of the bureaucratic hierarchy sought guidance in pertinent precedents.

The Ch'ing legal system described in these essays was in many ways an impressive achievement. Yet it was very different from anything the nationals of the Western maritime powers had ever experienced before. As Westerners came to China in growing numbers, their contacts with the host country came to be increasingly marred by disputes that reflected the dramatic differences between the two cultures in legal institutions and practices and in underlying assumptions and values. Many of those disputes arose because of Western resistance to the assertion of Chinese criminal jurisdiction over the sailors and traders from Europe and the United States who came to Canton and Macao. Westerners balked at submitting to a system that imposed collective responsibility and that failed to exonerate an accused who acted in self-defense; to procedures that denied the accused an opportunity to make a meaningful defense; to standards of proof that permitted arbitrary convictions; and to punishments that seemed disproportionately inhumane. In an original and thoughtful reappraisal of two centuries of Ch'ing efforts to cope with this problem until the outbreak of the Opium War in 1839, Professor R. Randle Edwards of the Columbia Law School shows how the imperial government, recognizing the peculiar difficulties of enforcing Chinese law against the distinctive and powerful "outer barbarians" from the West, adapted to the new situation the traditional "tribute system" that had been designed to deal with more familiar foreigners.

Making extensive use of Chinese as well as Western sources, Professor Edwards, a coeditor of this volume, details Ch'ing efforts to develop special jurisdictional policies and trial procedures for the Western seafarers. His research confirms what some had controverted: that in principle the imperial government claimed the right to punish all foreigners for crimes committed in China. But it also makes clear that, as a matter of policy, the Ch'ing decided to exercise jurisdiction over only those aliens who were thought to have committed homicide against Chinese subjects. In cases where aliens could have been charged with lesser offenses against Chinese, or any offense against other aliens, it was the general policy of the government, with only occasional departures in practice, not to exercise jurisdiction but to turn the case over for handling by the leadership of the foreign community. Moreover, according to Edwards, in an effort—often not understood or appreciated—to accommodate the foreigners, the government also created special abbreviated procedures for those cases in which it did take jurisdiction. The procedures developed for trying Portuguese subjects in Macao provided for a significant degree of participation by the Portuguese authorities and, although

Chinese substantive law was applied in those proceedings, they afforded the accused a greater opportunity to defend himself than he would have enjoyed under the regular Chinese system.

Portugal in the eighteenth century was less powerful than Great Britain and, being land-based in Macao, was more vulnerable to Chinese pressures than were the sea-based British in Canton. One should also recall that by this time legal developments in Britain had outstripped those in Portugal in offering accused an opportunity for a fair trial, and this may have stiffened British resistance to surrendering suspects to the seemingly capricious mercies of the Chinese. Furthermore, the truncated procedures that the Ch'ing devised for handling the cases of aliens accused of homicide in Canton, unlike those applied to foreign accused in Macao, simply provided for foreign authorities to identify and question the suspect before surrendering him for an exclusively Chinese trial. Whatever the reasons, Edwards emphasizes the extent to which the British rejected the example of the compliant Portuguese and instead stubbornly resisted China's jurisdiction, even while recognizing the zeal with which the Ch'ing punished all Chinese who committed homicide and most other crimes against the foreign community.

There are many ironies, of course, in the long Anglo-Chinese struggle over criminal jurisdiction. Edwards shows that the British, while demanding that China not only move swiftly and harshly against Chinese who killed foreigners but also execute Frenchmen who killed British subjects, nevertheless refused to tolerate China's exercise of jurisdiction over British subjects who killed either Chinese or Frenchmen. Had China not denied Britain permission to try British subjects in China, a number of them who killed Chinese might not have gone unpunished, and relations between the two countries would have suffered less damage. Had their concern for what they deemed to be pertinent international law not led some British judges and members of Parliament to frustrate the efforts of their government to establish a tribunal for British subjects in China in the absence of China's consent, they might have eliminated one of the major tensions that led to British aggression in the Opium War, which current observers would regard as a far graver violation of international law than the unilateral establishment of a tribunal on foreign territory. Of course, this example of Britain's fastidiousness about international law also seems ludicrous when contrasted with her flagrant disregard of China's efforts, supported by international law, to prevent British subjects from illegally importing massive quantities of opium into China.

Unlike the Western nations, the countries that shared China's Confucian heritage found the traditional Chinese legal system to be not only impressive but also useful in their own development. As early as the eighth century, the Japanese imported the legal system of China's T'ang dynasty to meet the needs of their emerging nation-state. Less well known is the extent to which the feudal and supposedly autochthonous regime of Tokugawa Japan (1603-1868) borrowed and assimilated traditional Chinese legal ideas and institutions, especially during the eighteenth century. This is the subject of Dan Fenno Henderson's essay. It reveals the modest Chinese impact upon specific legal institutions of the central domain that was governed by the Shogunate in Edo (Tokyo) and the substantial weight that Shogunal decision makers attached to China's jurisprudence. It also emphasizes the significant influences of Chinese law upon the codes of a few leading *han*, the outlying fiefs that owed allegiance to the Shogun but enjoyed substantial autonomy in the making and application of law.

According to Professor Henderson, Director of the Asian Law Program at the University of Washington and a well-known specialist on Japan, to eighteenth-century Japanese law reformers Chinese law usually meant the Ming Code and the legal thought associated with it. This did not wholly exclude influences from the ancient T'ang or the contemporaneous Ch'ing system, but the former was generally regarded as too remote, and the latter, insofar as it was known to the law reformers of the early 1700s, was as yet barely distinguishable from the Ming.

Henderson shows that some Tokugawa codifiers looked to Ming law for guidance in formulating penal legislation, and he illustrates the point by detailing similarities between portions of the Ming Code and the penal codes drafted by five main *han* that were influenced by the Chinese model. To be sure, most of Japan's approximately 265 *han* did not codify their law; most of those that did followed Shogunal legislation; and even those few that to differing degrees did selectively make use of the Chinese model adapted it to Japanese conditions, values, and techniques. Yet this limited experience proved valuable in 1868, when the radical reformers of the Meiji Restoration, after overthrowing the Shogunate, briefly sought to create a national criminal law by drafting a penal code along traditional Chinese lines.

The Ming Code, and Chinese law generally, exercised much greater influence upon Korea's Yi dynasty (1392-1910), as William Shaw's contribution to this volume demonstrates. The Chinese model furnished Korea's kings with a comprehensive body of legislative norms for centralizing their realm as well as institutions for applying and revising those norms and for checking upon the conduct of the bureaucracy and even of the kings themselves. Shaw, a legal historian who specializes in the comparison of East Asia's traditional systems, emphasizes the utility of law as an instrument of Korean state building that gave form and structure to the entire range of governmental activity. Law reinforced and spread the centrally endorsed Confucian ethical and social practices in ways that were designed to overcome diverse local customs and other disunifying forces. For example, Shaw points out that, although scholars frequently note the extent to which legislation reflected the Confucian preoccupation with class status, they seldom recognize the extent to which legislation actually limited the importance of class status in the administration of justice, moderating what might otherwise have been even more substantial inequality.

The essay by Shaw, a Research Associate at the Harvard Law School, suggests that Korean officialdom was more law-minded than is commonly supposed. Legal learning was important to the work of many officials. Moreover, they developed a sense of duty to adhere to statutory provisions even when the outcome prescribed by statute seemed at variance with Confucian values. Law was considered to be the command of the sovereign, and hence deserving of respect. Indeed, to some extent, legal, institutional, and ideological restraints even inhibited the king himself from altering the law according to whim.

Of course, by the late nineteenth century the Korean legal system, like the Chinese, was beginning to be judged by new standards and had become the target of law reformers seeking to strengthen their country's institutions in order to meet the challenge of the West and Japan. Shaw concludes his study by focusing on the proposals of one of these innovators, Pak Yŏng-hyo, who regarded such familiar features as collective responsibility, cruel punishments, coerced confessions, and sovereign intervention in the judicial process as inconsistent with a modern state. Although Pak's ideas were inspired by foreign contacts and pressures, Shaw finds that most of these ideas had been anticipated in the writing and practice of earlier Korean reformers long before the barriers of the Hermit Kingdom had been breached. In this sense, despite the obvious need for significant changes in the administration of justice, Korea's legal heritage can be said to have contained modern elements and, had Korea been permitted to pursue her own course, this might have facilitated her transition into the contemporary world.

The Ch'ing legal system itself changed markedly during the dynasty's final decade, as desperate efforts were made to halt the deterioration that threatened not only the empire but also China's very viability. The abolition of slavery was one of many demands made by reformers who were bent upon modernizing the country and ridding it of social evils. Like opium smoking, foot binding, prostitution, and gambling, the buying and selling of human beings was considered to be an intolerable manifestation of China's backwardness. To be sure, the Ch'ing had earlier enacted certain measures in an attempt to mitigate some of the worst abuses of slavery; by the twentieth century, male slavery had virtually disappeared, and changing circumstances were gradually undermining all traditional social classes. Yet many wealthy families as well as Manchu and Chinese officials continued to purchase slave girls as servants. Thus, as shown by the contribution to this volume of Dr. Marinus J. Meijer, a distinguished Dutch scholar and retired diplomat, efforts to abolish slavery met with opposition despite the compelling humanitarian and political reasons for this reform.

Dr. Meijer, whose books on the modernization of Chinese criminal law and family law[29] are well known, devotes the first part of his study to the distinctive aspects of traditional Chinese slavery. He contrasts the legal provisions pertaining to public slavery, which was imposed by the state as a punishment, with those governing private slavery, into which individuals were either born or sold. He spells out the technical differences between the so-called red and white contracts used for the sale of human beings and the legal consequences of choosing one or the other of these documents, or none at all, for the transaction. He also deals with the complicated legislation delineating the circumstances in which persons could be sold as slaves, and he discusses the practical problems of enforcing these laws as, for example, against impoverished parents who sold their children into bondage when no other means existed of keeping the children alive. Meijer also analyzes the manifold legal ramifications of the relations between the master and his family and the slave and his family, including what were, in effect, principles of vicarious liability governing the scope of the master's responsibility for acts of his servant outside the household.

After thus laying the groundwork for our appreciation of the significance of the abolition of slavery, Meijer, who has held high positions in Dutch diplomatic missions in China, Japan, Korea, and Hong Kong, then turns our attention to the process by which abolition was accomplished on the very eve of the Ch'ing dynasty's downfall. He discusses the proposals submitted to the throne by the leading reformers, the supporting arguments they mustered, the practical problems that had to be confronted and the solutions finally endorsed. This chapter, like Meijer's other work, makes clear the eminent desirability of a comprehensive research effort into the entire range of law reforms attempted during the last years of the Ch'ing, when China belatedly and self-consciously began to adapt Western legal ideas and institutions to national needs. That, however, will have to be the subject of another volume. It will be enough if this volume succeeds in stimulating interest in China's legal tradition.

NOTES

1. Étienne Balazs, tr., *Le Traité juridique du "Souei-chou"* (Leiden, 1954), p. 1.
2. F. W. Maitland, *Equity; also The Forms of Action at Common Law* (Cambridge, 1913), p. 296.
3. Oliver Wendell Holmes, *The Common Law*, ed. Mark DeWolfe Howe, (Cambridge, Mass., 1963), p. 5.
4. For discussion of the evolution of Western scholarship in the field of Chinese law, see the Introduction to Jerome Alan Cohen, ed., *Contemporary Chinese Law* (Cambridge, Mass., 1970), pp. 1-9.
5. See Jerome Alan Cohen, *The Criminal Process in the People's Republic of China, 1949-1963: An Introduction* (Cambridge, Mass., 1968), pp. 50-51.
6. Max Weber on *Law in Economy and Society*, trs. and eds. Edward Shils and Max Rheinstein (Cambridge, Mass., 1954), p. 264.
7. "Train a Contingent of Theoretical Workers in Struggle," *People's Daily* editorial, June 18, 1974, tr. in *Peking Review*, Vol. 17, No. 26 (June 28, 1974), pp. 5-6.
8. For a sample of the 1974 writing of Party-approved publicists on the subject, see Yang Jung-Kuo, "Struggle Between Two Lines in the Ideological Sphere During the Spring and Autumn Period and the Warring States Period," *Peking Review*, Vol. 17, No. 8 (Feb. 22, 1974), pp. 4-7; and *ibid.*, Vol. 17, No. 9 (March 1, 1974), pp. 12-15; Lo Ssu-ting, "Struggle Between Restoration and Counter-Restoration In the Course of Founding the Chin Dynasty," *ibid.*, Vol. 17, No. 17 (April 26, 1974), pp. 7-10; and Shih Ting, "Clarifying 'Burning Books and Burying Confucian Scholars Alive,' " *ibid.*, Vol. 17, No. 19 (May 10, 1974), pp. 25-28. After the overthrow of the "Gang of Four" in October 1976, many of the views expressed in the above essays were repudiated.
9. Cf. Joseph R. Levenson, "The Place of Confucius in Communist China," *The China Quarterly*, No. 12 (Oct.-Dec. 1962), pp. 1-18.
10. For a detailed study of the distinctive development of criminal justice in the PRC, see Cohen, note 5 above.
11. Jen Chen-to and Ho En-t'ao, "How to Establish China's New System of Criminal Litigation," *Chi-lin ta-hsüeh jen-wen k'o-hsüeh hsüeh-pao* [Kirin University Journal of Humanistic Sciences], Vol. 2 (1959), p. 123.
12. See Kawasaki Mitsunari, "The Attorney System," in *Chūgoku no hō to shakai* [Chinese Law and Society] (Tokyo, 1960), p. 80.
13. Tadasuke Torio, "Chinese Lawyers," in *Horitsuka no mita Chūgoku* [China as Seen by Lawyers] (Tokyo, 1965), pp. 216-217.
14. Dan Fenno Henderson, *Conciliation and Japanese Law* (Seattle and Tokyo, 1964), p. 169. Henderson's discussion, pp. 167-169, is well worth reading.
15. See, e.g., Takaaki Hattori, assisted by Richard W. Rabinowitz, "The Legal Profession in Japan: Its Historical Development and Present State," in Arthur Taylor von Mehren, ed., *Law in Japan* (Cambridge, Mass., 1963), pp. 111, 112, 117.
16. See Derk Bodde and Clarence Morris, *Law in Imperial China* (Cambridge, Mass., 1967), pp. 189, 143; Sybille van der Sprenkel, *Legal Institutions in Man-*

chu China (London, 1962), pp. 66, 69; John R. Watt, *The District Magistrate in Late Imperial China* (New York and London, 1972), pp. 220-224.

17. See W. W. Blume, "Legal Education in China," *The China Law Review*, Vol. 1 (1922-1924), pp. 305, 308-310.
18. See Yü-Chüan Chang, "The Legal Practitioner in China," *The Chinese Social and Political Science Review*, Vol. 22 (1938-1939), pp. 146-184.
19. See, e.g., "This Year There Are Over 3,000 Lawyers Serving the Masses," *Kuang-ming jih-pao* [Enlightenment Daily], Jan. 14, 1957; tr. in Cohen, note 5 above, at p. 440.
20. See Cohen, note 5 above, at pp. 5-7. For an excellent recent study of the administration of justice under the Ch'ing, see Shuzo Shiga, "Criminal Procedure in the Ch'ing Dynasty," *Memoirs of the Research Department of the Tōyō Bunko* (Tokyo), No. 32 (1974), and No. 33 (1975).
21. See, e.g., Shih Ting, note 8 above.
22. A.F.P. Hulsewé, *Remnants of Han Law* (Leiden, 1955).
23. See note 1 above for reference to Balazs' translation of and commentary on the Sui "Legal Treatise."
24. Karl Bünger, *Quellen zur Rechtsgeschichte der T'ang-Zeit* (Monumenta Serica Monograph 9; Peiping, 1946).
25. See the works cited in Bodde and Morris, note 16 above, at p. 572.
26. George Thomas Staunton, tr., *Ta Tsing Leu Lee; Being the Fundamental Laws . . . of the Penal Code of China* (London, 1810).
27. Although scholars' attention to Ch'ing law has thus far focused mainly on the most important Ch'ing Code, the Penal Code, Ch'ing legislation was hardly limited to that Code. Ch'ing law was basically administrative in nature, that is, it prescribed norms to guide the operations of the complex bureaucracy. Because administrative functions were divided among diverse offices in the capital, different offices were allocated principal responsibility for applying different laws. Thus, among the six administrative boards that constituted the core of the central government, the Board of Punishments was chiefly responsible for the application of the Penal Code. But in each of the other boards, there was a set of rules governing the affairs that fell under the jurisdiction of that board. These laws were usually, but not always, called *tse-li*. For example, the *ch'u-fen tse-li* were the regulations on administrative punishment that were designed to maintain discipline in the Chinese civil bureaucracy. The special problems of punishing those with official status were so important and complicated that they necessitated a separate body of legislation that was closely related to, but separate from, the Penal Code itself. Unlike the Code, these regulations were the responsibility of the Board of Civil Officials, not the Board of Punishments, and they provided for administrative sanctions to be meted out to officials for offenses relating to government affairs. The regulations, which punished acts of omission as well as acts of commission, were intended to curb corruption, extravagance, favoritism and other deviant official conduct. Major misconduct by an official could also lead to the imposition of regular criminal sanctions, following his dismissal from office under the regulations. For a subtle and innovative sociological exploration of this long-neglected aspect of Ch'ing law, see Thomas A.

Metzger, *The Internal Organization of the Ch'ing Bureaucracy: Legal, Normative and Communication Aspects* (Cambridge, Mass., 1973), pp. 235–417.

28. See the interesting article by William C. Jones, "Studying the Ch'ing Code—The Ta Ch'ing Lü Li," *American Journal of Comparative Law*, Vol. 22 (1974), pp. 330–359.
29. See M. J. Meijer, *The Introduction of Modern Criminal Law in China* (Batavia [Jakarta], 1949); and *idem, Marriage Law and Policy in the Chinese People's Republic* (Hong Kong, 1971).

11

LEGAL INSTITUTIONS AND PROCEDURES DURING THE CHOU DYNASTY

Herrlee Glessner Creel

New Light on Ancient China

It is only in the twentieth century that it has become possible to achieve some degree of real understanding of China's cultural institutions before the founding of the Han dynasty in 206 B.C. This is not to denigrate the invaluable contributions made by scholars over the past 2,000 years, but they worked under three handicaps. First, the documents were few. Second, genuine documents were mixed almost inextricably with others that were false, or very seriously misdated. Finally even the genuine documents were rendered, in any true sense, almost unintelligible, by the interpretation that became almost inseparable from them. Commentators of Han and later times "elucidated" the documents by reading into them, in somewhat idealized replica, the ideas and institutions of their own day.

New documents have become available during every decade of the twentieth century, from the first publication of squeezes of Shang inscriptions in 1903 to the continuing discovery of inscribed bronzes to the present day—a single cache unearthed in 1961 yielded, for example, fifty-three Western Chou bronzes. No less important is the research that has been carried on, chiefly in China but elsewhere as well, little by little revealing the ancient culture in its true colors. Inscriptions have been deciphered, great strides have been made in separating the genuine from the false among the transmitted documents, and ancient documents have been reinterpreted and retranslated in light of the new discoveries. Yet all this does not mean, of course, that we have arrived at complete understanding. As each new plateau is reached, all of us who work in this field realize that we have made mistakes. It would be fatuous to suppose that we could avoid them completely in the future. We may hope, however, that we are gradually moving nearer to the truth.

The advances have been very uneven. Most of them have been achieved by specialists in various fields, who have been inadequately informed of each other's work. It is only very slowly that the specialists' results are applied to the elucidation of the history of the culture as a whole, or even to various aspects of it. Nowhere does this lag show more clearly than in the study of legal institutions and procedures of the Chou dynasty (1122-256 B.C.).[1] This is especially true of the early centuries of this period.

There has been a general tendency to suppose that in early Chou times legal institutions were very deficient, if they existed at all. Henri Maspero wrote that until the third century B.C. "there was no code and custom alone reigned."[2] Others deduce, from the passage in the *Tso-chuan* that says the state of Cheng cast its laws in bronze in 536 B.C., that before this time there were no written laws, or at least no laws that were openly promulgated.[3]

In 1935 Maspero published a paper entitled "Le Serment dans la procédure judiciaire de la Chine antique."[4] He undertook to describe juridical procedures on the basis of a number of bronze inscriptions of the Western Chou period (1122-771 B.C.). The fact that the decipherment of inscriptions had not at that time progressed to the degree that it has now was an unavoidable limitation, but an even more serious handicap, in my opinion, was the approach that he used. He began by drawing a picture of juridical procedure derived from works such as the *Ritual of Chou*, which Maspero himself, like other critical scholars, recognized to have been compiled centuries after the end of Western Chou.[5] He then used the inscriptions to fill some details into this picture. It was a courageous pioneering effort, but it did not add to our knowledge of Western Chou legal institutions to the extent that might have been hoped.[6]

This approach, putting the new wine into old bottles, has commonly been followed by both Chinese and Western scholars. It could be justified only if we were assured that the old conception of ancient China was in all of its essentials accurate. But the new materials cry out that—especially as regards Western Chou—the prevailing conceptions, whether those of the Chinese tradition or of modern critical scholarship, have been grossly wrong in important respects.

Not long ago I completed a reexamination, which occupied some years, of the history and institutions of the Western Chou period. I tried to base it, in the first instance, exclusively on primary source materials: all of the literature, subjected to rigorous critical scrutiny, and 184 carefully selected bronze inscriptions.[7] My attempt has been to derive a picture of the period from these sources alone. That having been done, I have used traditions embodied in later works to supplement the sources, in those cases in which the traditions do not conflict with the sources. This gives a picture—attested alike by newly discovered bronze inscriptions and by reinterpretation of documents that have been transmitted to us from antiquity—that is in important respects new. Since this is the setting against which legal institutions must be understood, it is necessary to describe it briefly.

Western Chou Government

The power of the Western Chou kings has been conceived as being effectively limited to a "royal domain," beyond which the land was ruled by feudal lords. The king, it was thought, could not interfere in the affairs of the feudal states. Being without a standing army, or a financial system that permitted effective control, he did not, it has been supposed, rule a centralized regime but exercised, beyond the "royal domain," only very limited authority, which depended chiefly upon the prestige that he derived from his kinship with the feudal lords and upon his religious status.

In fact, however, the Western Chou kings exercised very powerful control over a remarkably broad territory. At that time there was no "royal domain,"[8] and the king and his officials could and sometimes did intervene in the affairs of feudal states. Royal officials made visits of inspection to vassal states, and it appears that in some states at some times the king had resident inspectors as his representatives. There was a financial system, with taxation and the auditing of accounts. The Western Chou kings, unlike later Chinese emperors, were not remote figures, seldom seen. They maintained strong personal control of the government and traveled about inspecting the realm and meeting their subjects. The kings also led their own armies in a great many cases. There were fourteen royal standing armies, housed in garrisons, as well as other guard posts, and principal roads were patrolled by royal troops. Major military threats, such as barbarian revolts or incursions, were countered by the armies of the king, not by feudal lords. Bronze inscriptions and the transmitted literature alike show that the king was seldom obliged to use military power to enforce his authority against a vassal—in strong contrast to the frequent wars between medieval European rulers and their vassals.[9]

The social situation in Western Chou was not, as has commonly been supposed, like that of the Spring and Autumn period.[10] The large and powerful aristocratic class that was dominant in Spring and Autumn times does not appear to have existed at the beginning of Western Chou. Apparently it developed gradually during that period, just as the nobility of medieval Europe appeared well after the beginning of the feudal age.[11] Similarly, the code of aristocratic conduct known as *li* (one aspect of which was "chivalry" in war), does not appear in the sources, though no doubt it, too, was coming into being during Western Chou.[12]

Early Evidence of Codes

The Chou were by no means without institutions of their own, but their culture was in some respects less advanced than that of the Shang, whom they conquered in 1122 B.C. The nature of the Shang inscriptions that remain to us is such that it is not likely that legal institutions would be mentioned in them; if there is such mention, I am unaware of it. Yet it is evident that there were Shang laws, which the Chou took over at least to some extent. The conqueror, King Wu, says to his brother: "You should set forth the items of the law,[13] and follow those laws of Yin [an alternative name for Shang] that have good principles. . . . Take for punishments and verdicts the norms of the Yin. Use their just punishments and just killings."[14]

It is unlikely that, as some scholars contend, these laws were not written down; we know that the Chou were, in fact, addicted to the making of written records. The character *tien*, which is a pictograph of a book lying on a table, is repeatedly used to mean "lawful."[15] Whether there was a "code," or codes, is perhaps a matter of definition. One document speaks of the "regular punishments" for each of a list of offenses by soldiers, which seems to imply the existence of a code of military law.[16] Probably there were codes, but we have no specific information about them.

The principal source of Western Chou law, as of other law, appears to have been tradition. There seems to be only one case in which an individual is named as a legislator: that in which King Wu says that familial offenses should be dealt with "according to the punishments made by King Wen," who was Wu's father.[17] No specific laws are ascribed to divine origin, but the chief deity, Heaven, was conceived as supervising the administration of justice. Failure to do justice was listed as one of the reasons for which Heaven withdrew its mandate to rule from the Shang and ordered the Chou to replace them. And King Wu took upon himself the responsibility for the administration of justice throughout his realm, declaring: "If there is any fault, Heaven will punish and kill me, and I shall not resent it."[18]

The Administration of Justice

The "Announcement to K'ang," in the *Documents*, is the oldest Chinese work extant that discusses justice. It is a charge by King Wu, the conqueror, to his younger brother K'ang Shu. The *Tso-chuan* says that K'ang Shu was appointed *Ssu-k'ou* (literally director of crime, a title often rendered as "minister of justice").[19] This "Announcement" may embody the king's instructions to his brother upon the latter's assumption of this office.

King Wu describes the "primary evildoers" as "robbers and thieves and villains and traitors, who kill and destroy and go for spoil, and are forceful and do not fear death." However, even these, he says, are to be deplored less than "the son who does not serve his father with respect, but greatly wounds his father's heart; the father who cannot love his son, but hates him; the younger brother who does not think of Heaven's brightness, and cannot be respectful to his elder brother; the elder brother who feels no compassion for his tender younger brother, and treats him coldly." All these must be punished without pardon.[20] This familial motif was to continue throughout the next 3,000 years, but it is noteworthy that here, in contrast with later Chinese practice, the father and the elder brother are held equally responsible with the son and the younger brother for upholding the norms of relations between kin.

King Wu's advice makes manifest another strain that was to develop in the Chinese legal system—law in the service of government administration: "All those who are insubordinate should be greatly regulated. How much more then . . . the administrators and the various minor officers. When they depart [from the course prescribed for them] and promulgate innovations . . . you should speedily, in accord with justice, put them to death."[21] A.F.P. Hulsewé has commented upon the manner in which, in the later Han law, regulations for the administration of the government are found intermixed with penal statutes.[22] Karl Bünger has pointed out that, whereas law regulating governmental administration was little developed in the Roman Empire, China very early had a body of such law "of astonishing completeness" such as did not appear in Europe until a late date.[23]

Other offenses are mentioned in the literature and the inscriptions. These include failure to pay taxes, whether by Chinese or by subject barbarians. Alleged breach of contract was adjudicated by royal officials. Failure to go to war, apparently in defiance of royal orders, was prosecuted. At the beginning of the dynasty severe penalties were prescribed for those who drank intoxicating liquor in groups, unless they were taking part in a sacrificial ceremony. But this seems to have been an expression of early Chou puritanism, which soon diminished.[24]

For such drinking, King Wu prescribes the penalty of death. We have seen that he also says that officials who depart from the prescribed course and "promulgate innovations" are to suffer death. In fact, he says, even small offenses, if they have been committed intentionally, must be punished with death. King Wu even threatens one of his brothers with death if he does not rule his fief well. There is little mention of the death penalty in Western Chou after the opening years, but this may be due to the uneven nature of our sources. Mutilation, cutting off the nose or the legs, is only mentioned in Wu's "Announcement to K'ang."

In a case of breach of contract there was no penalty, but the ruling was that the contract must be carried out. When grain was stolen, the culprit was ordered not only to make restitution but to pay to the plaintiff an equal amount as punitive damages, and the whole debt was to be doubled if not paid within a year. It was adjudged that men who had failed to "follow the king" to war should pay a fine, but the sentence was reduced when they could not pay it. Banishment as a punishment was known, but not actually imposed in any case on record.[25] There were evidently jails for the detention of persons under arrest, but there is no mention of imprisonment as a punishment.

The administration of justice was conceived, as we have seen, to be formally the responsibility of the king. With regard to those who drink together, King Wu says, "Send them to Chou [the capital] and I will kill them."[26] Wu seems to have been fanatical on the subject of liquor, and there is no other indication that the king claimed the right to execute or review sentences. The king was the natural arbiter over the feudal lords, and we see them taking various disputes to his court for justice. We have seen that King Wu threatened one of them, his own brother, with death. And a tradition which, though found only in works later than Western Chou, may be valid, says that in 892 B.C. King I "caused the feudal lords to boil Duke Ai of Ch'i in a caldron."[27]

It is not easy to determine whether any Western Chou officials were specifically and exclusively charged with the administration of justice. Even the title director of crime, commonly considered equivalent to "minister of justice," occurs only in two bronze inscriptions, and even there the context does not make the nature of the office clear. Sometimes those we see administering justice hold the title of secretary, but in most cases they are merely named, with no indication of the office they held.

There are two probable reasons for this. One is that it is likely that the function of administering justice was diffused, discharged as only one of the duties of the officials who undertook it; this has been normal in later Chinese history. Secondly, it is characteristic of Western Chou government that it is difficult to derive a "table of organization" of those who perform functions of any category. We find secretaries sometimes leading armies, and commanders occasionally performing civil functions. This was a personal government, in which the king commonly assigned functions to individuals on the basis of their capacities and performance, often without regard to the titles they held.[28]

Trial Procedure

In the "Announcement to K'ang," King Wu repeatedly emphasizes the necessity of proceeding with the utmost caution in prosecutions, to avoid miscarriage of justice. "Having tried a case, deliberate on it for five or six days, or as much as ten days or a season, before deciding. . . . Take for punishments and verdicts the norms of the Yin. Use their just punishments and just killings. Do not use them so as to accord with your own wishes."[29] The character *i* that is here translated as "just" has, more strictly, the sense of "appropriate."

It is clear that, in the process of reaching a verdict, attention was supposed to be paid not only to the law but also to equity, in the sense of "a liberal and humane application of the law." In various documents and bronze inscriptions we find emphasis on the necessity of caution with regard to punishment, and on justice and even clemency. There is no reason to question the sincerity of these sentiments, but they were also counseled by prudence. At the beginning of their reign, in particular, the Chou needed to follow—as they did—a policy of conciliation toward their conquered subjects. Thus, we find King Wu warning: "Now the people are not quiet, they have not yet settled their minds. . . . Be careful! Do not create resentment. . . . May your verdicts be correct, and such as to inspire confidence."[30] This concern appears to have borne some fruit, for Chinese tradition represents Western Chou as, on the whole, a time of unusual tranquillity and justice.

We have no complete description of a Western Chou trial, but it is clear from the use of the term *yao-ch'iu* that careful consideration was given to evidence. *Ch'iu* is a pictograph of a man in an enclosure; it means a jail and also the case of one who is under arrest. *Yao*, as an extension of its sense of "important," means a précis, summarizing important points. In the *Tso-chuan*, it is used to mean a brief, which summarizes the evidence for a contender in a lawsuit.[31] Thus, *yao-ch'iu* has the sense of putting in order all the points in connection with a prosecution, that is, trying the case.[32] Both King Wu and his brother the Duke of Chou use this term. The duke, even when he is obviously trying to frighten the conquered Shang people into submission, does not threaten them with summary execution; he says that he will *yao-ch'iu*, arrest them and bring them to trial.[33]

Another term that has the sense of "to bring to trial" is *hsün*, which has the basic sense of "to inquire, to interrogate." In three bronze inscriptions it clearly refers to judicial inquiry. There is no indication that torture was prescribed to accompany judicial interrogation; indeed, one passage in the *Documents* appears to condemn torturers, along with "traitors and villains."[34]

Perhaps the most commonly encountered term for legal action is one that has continued in use to modern times: *sung*. Meaning "to sue, to litigate," it apparently refers to cases in which one individual lays information against another and requests judicial action.

A few bronze inscriptions give us glimpses of the judicial process at work. One of these, dating from early in Western Chou, was cast by (that is, of course, for) Commander Ch'i. He relates that a group of his subordinates (probably men living on his fief) failed to follow the king—as they had presumably been ordered to do—on a certain military expedition. Ch'i therefore caused his colleague, Hung, to accuse them before Po Mou Fu (a royal official).[35] His verdict was that they should pay a fine of 300 *lieh* of silk(?).[36] They were unable, however, to pay the fine. Po Mou Fu then issued an order saying: "In accord with justice [*i*, "appropriateness"] they should be banished for failing to follow their leader to war, but if they are not banished then they should make a payment to Commander Ch'i." Hung informed a secretary of this decision and asked him to record it. Ch'i, the inscription concludes, also recorded it on a sacrificial vessel.[37]

This incident has interesting features. First, Hung acted throughout as advocate for Ch'i. Second, this is a case of the administration of justice by a royal officer within what was almost certainly a fief. The defendants were definitely humble men, and Commander Ch'i was almost certainly a vassal of the king.

Another inscription dated to late in Western Chou briefly records a litigation between two men of status. It says that when the king was in the capital, in a certain great hall, Kuo Ts'ung spoke to him, accusing Yu Wei Mu. The dispute concerned certain lands, but its nature is obscure. The king ordered that the matter be investigated. A royal official resolved the case by ordering Yu Wei Mu to swear to give satisfaction to Kuo Ts'ung. The latter celebrated his triumph by casting a record of the event on a bronze.[38]

One of the most interesting of all bronzes, for the study of law, describes two different legal proceedings in independent sections of its inscription. The vessel was cast by a man named Yao who lived about 900 B.C. and who eventually (probably after this bronze was cast) rose to very high office.[39] One section relates that in a year of famine twenty men, subordinates of K'uang Chi, stole 10 *tzu*[40] of grain belonging to Yao. Yao laid a complaint against K'uang Chi with Tung Kung, a royal official. Tung Kung then said to K'uang: "Control your men! If you cannot, you will be punished severely." K'uang acknowledged to Yao that he was at fault and offered him, as redress, five fields and four men, whose names are given. K'uang also made a statement, of which the sense is not clear, minimizing his guilt. But Yao again complained to Tung Kung, pointing out that his stolen grain had not been restored. Tung Kung then ordered: "Give back to Yao 10 *tzu* [of grain], and another 10 *tzu*, making [a total of] 20 *tzu*. If restitution is not made by the coming year, then [your liability will be] doubled, to 40 *tzu*." K'uang then offered Yao two more fields and one more man. It would appear that settlement was not made until the following year, when 40 *tzu* would have been due. But in consideration of the other payments,

Yao agreed to be content with only the restitution of the 10 *tzu* that had been stolen.

Another section of this inscription relates that Yao caused his subordinate, Yün, to bring suit against (*sung*) a royal official, Hsien. The suit was judged by a high royal officer, Ching Shu. This is an involved case of alleged breach of contract. Yao had paid over to an agent of Hsien the agreed price—one horse and a roll of silk—for the purchase of five men. The bargain was not fulfilled, and the return of the purchase price was therefore promised. However, Hsien's agents then made another proposal. Its nature is not wholly clear, but they undertook to do something—possibly to enter into a new contract written on wooden tallies—at the "Royal Comparison Office." This is my own translation, admittedly hypothetical.[41] Yet, however the characters are translated, it seems clear that what was involved was the examination of a contract written on wood—probably in duplicate—after which the piece of wood was split down the middle making two "tallies" which could be matched as proof of authenticity.[42] There is a good deal of basis for believing there may have been a royal office in Western Chou at which contracts could be registered with the government, as deeds to land are registered today. A number of bronze inscriptions mention tallies used as evidence of agreements of various sorts, and in some cases royal officials seem to act as guarantors of agreements.[43]

This very early concern with private contracts is quite surprising as compared with later practice. Jean Escarra wrote that in China formal law has traditionally been little concerned with such matters as "a sale, a rental, a contract of whatever sort," and Karl Bünger states: "The law concerning daily business, law regulating debt and commerce, developed late and only in rudimentary fashion. . . . The field was left to usage and custom."[44]

Law in Later Chou Times

The foregoing treatment of legal institutions and procedures of Western Chou times is based on an analysis of all of the available, relevant sources. For the remainder of the dynasty, the years from 770 to 256 B.C., there is far more material. Works that purport to inform us of that time are voluminous, but with some of them the problems of authenticity are extremely complex. To treat the remainder of the dynasty adequately would require a book, and not a small one. Here I can give only brief consideration to a few facets of the problem.

Despite the standard theory that law codes first appeared only in 536 B.C., it is clear that these were in existence continuously during the Spring and Autumn period. This is evident from the *Tso-chuan*. Certainly, that great historical work was compiled, as critical scholarly opinion agrees, only around 300 B.C. and contains some late passages.[45] But, as is also generally agreed, it consists largely of valid historical records. It relates that in 621 B.C. an officer who took charge of the government of the state of Chin "rectified the laws concerning crime and regulated [the procedures for] trial and punishment."[46] This work and others contain numerous references to law, some of it certainly written, ascribed to dates both before and after 536 B.C.[47]

This law is ascribed to various origins. We find "the laws of King Wen" appealed to in 535 B.C., six centuries after his time.[48] And in 484 B.C. it is said that "the statutes of the Duke of Chou"—Wen's son—are still in existence.[49] It appears probable that, in China as elsewhere, new codes were principally revisions of old ones. The revision of codes was commonly a part of the general renovation of a government; this was the setting for the revision in the state of Chin in 621 B.C. In 597 B.C. a new chief minister in Ch'u "selected among the administrative statutes." As part of another reform of the administration of Chin, in 573 B.C., the duke ordered the revision of "the laws of Shih Wei" and "the laws of Fan Wu-tzu."[50] Shih Wei lived during the first half of the seventh century; Fan Wu-tzu, his grandson, flourished around 600 B.C. Both were officials.

The Code of 536 B.C. has been so persistently emphasized by those who write on Chinese law that we must examine the account with care. The *Tso-chuan* records:

> The men of Cheng cast legal writings [i.e., a code, in bronze]. Shu-hsiang [of Chin] sent a letter to Tzu-ch'an [who controlled the government of Cheng] saying: "At first I thought well of you, but that is finished. Anciently the former Kings discussed matters in order to decide them, and did not establish [definite] punishments, for fear that the people would have a contentious spirit that could not be controlled. . . . When the people know the penalties they will not fear their superiors, but will all have a contentious spirit, seeking to prove [their contentions] by the written word, hoping by good fortune to succeed. It cannot be done! When the government of the Hsia dynasty fell into confusion the Code of Yü was made. When the government of the Shang dynasty fell into confusion, the Code of T'ang was made. When the government of Chou fell into confusion the [Code called the] 'Nine Punishments' was made. These three codes all arose in periods of decline."[51]

The first part of this passage is constantly quoted by those who contend that codes began only in 536 B.C., but they almost never quote, or mention, the latter portion. This makes it quite clear that the author of the passage did not pretend that this was the earliest code—far from it.

Actually, this whole passage is highly suspect. Yü was the reputed (in fact legendary) founder of the Hsia dynasty, and T'ang the founder of the Shang. Why would codes composed after their governments had "fallen into confusion" have borne the names of these founders? As for the code known as the "Nine Punishments," it is nowhere mentioned in the Western Chou sources, and only once (aside from this passage) in the *Tso-chuan*. In that case it is referred to in what purports to be a speech by the Duke of Chou.[52] But the Duke of Chou lived at the beginning of Chou, in its most flourishing period. How, then, could this code have been written after the Chou government "had fallen into confusion"? The man who concocted this passage was a slipshod scholar. But Shu-hsiang, the alleged author of this letter, was famous as one of the most brilliant and learned men of his time.

This passage is rendered even more dubious by its implication that it was the usual practice to keep the laws secret. Much has been made of this. T'ung-tsu Ch'ü writes: "When the people were kept from knowing the law, the ruling class could manipulate it as it saw fit. Its words were the law—and a law that the people could neither doubt nor question. . . . Not until the sixth century B.C. were the laws of the various states revealed to the general public."[53] Such secrecy is also implied in one other passage in the *Tso-chuan*—which is also highly suspect, as will be shown in the next section. Aside from these two passages, I know of nothing else in the sources suggesting that laws were kept secret. There is much to indicate that they were not.

Certainly there was no such secrecy in Western Chou. King Wu directed that "the items of the law" were to be "set forth"; the character used here means literally "to display," "to publish." When the Duke of Chou reproached the conquered Shang people with doing that which was "not lawful," the character meaning "lawful" was *tien*, a pictograph of a book. He was accusing them of not acting in accord with the statutes—a meaningless reproach if they were kept in ignorance of them. Again, a duke haranguing his army before a battle listed various offenses, and warned that one who violated each would incur "the regular punishment" for it. His soldiers, men so humble that they were expected to provide fodder, posts, and so forth, were assumed to know what was the regular punishment for each of these crimes.[54]

In the Spring and Autumn period, when the king no longer exercised effective power, it is probable that the administration of justice in some states fell to a low ebb. Certainly we see many cases of what appears to be arbitrary punishment without legal process, and those guilty of this might well have preferred that law not be emphasized. However, we have seen that officials of a number of states did produce codes well before 536 B.C. That these codes were made only to be locked away seems improbable, and I know of no indication that they were so treated. In a conversation in 632 B.C., King Hsiang is quoted as saying that it is unacceptable "having proclaimed the law, not to act in accord with it."[55] An officer of Ch'u is quoted as saying, around 550 B.C., that his state's "laws and punishments are in the hearts of the people, and kept in the King's repository."[56] Everything seems to indicate that laws were normally made public.

Before leaving the subject of codes, it is necessary to mention the *Fa-ching* or *Classic of Law*, supposed to have been written around 400 B.C. by Li K'uei. Eminent scholars, both Chinese and Western, have supposed this work to have provided the base upon which subsequent codifications have rested. But the earliest reference to it seems to appear about a thousand years later than the date of its supposed composition, and it has been abundantly shown that the existence of any such work in antiquity is, to say the least, highly doubtful.[57]

Confucius and the Law

The second passage in the *Tso-chuan* that discusses secrecy in connection with law is dated to 513 B.C. It says that the state of Chin in that year cast a code of laws on tripods. Again there was a remonstrance, as follows:

> Chung-ni [Confucius] said: "Chin is going to ruin. It has lost its [proper] measures. Chin should keep the regulations that T'ang-shu [its first ruler] received for keeping its people in order. If the ministers and great officers would, each in his proper place, preserve them, the people would therefore be able to honor the noble and the noble would be able to preserve their inheritance. Neither noble nor humble would err; this is what is [properly] called regulation. For this reason Duke Wen instituted offices of various ranks and the laws of Pei-lu, and thus came to preside over the covenants [between the states]. Now when they abandon those regulations, and make tripods [inscribed with] laws, the people's [attention will be fixed] on the tripods. Why will they honor the noble? How will the noble be able to maintain their inheritance? If the noble and the humble are not distinguished, how can the state be governed?"[58]

This passage is clearly a part of the Confucian *apocrypha*. The name of Confucius, like that of many another famous and influential man, was borrowed for almost every purpose, and attached to statements of even the most anti-Confucian character. The *Chuang-tzu* repeatedly quotes Confucius as denouncing his own principles and speaking as a convinced

Taoist; the *Han-fei-tzu* represents him as a Legalist zealot who defends the practice of cutting off a man's hand for throwing ashes in the street.[59]

Critical scholars are agreed that the best and the only reliable source for the thought of Confucius is the *Analects*.[60] If we compare the passage quoted above from the *Tso-chuan* with the *Analects*, it is clear that it does not contain the words of Confucius. Some of the evidence is obvious. In that statement, the characters that have been translated as "noble" and "humble" are *kuei* and *chien*; in this brief passage the former occurs six times and the latter twice. But in the whole of the *Analects* neither Confucius nor anyone else ever uses either of these terms to denote a class. The only time either of them is applied to a person, even as an adjective, is when Confucius says of himself: "When I was young, I was humble [*chien*]."[61]

The Confucius of the *Analects*—the real Confucius—simply did not talk in terms of an upper class and a lower class, or of the necessity that the latter be kept in their proper place, or in ignorance. He said, "To put people to death without having instructed them is cruelty."[62] He spoke of the wealthy and powerful, but almost always in terms of criticism. He told the men in power that they could secure the adherence of the people only by setting them an example of moral conduct—which, he usually implied, they signally failed to do.[63]

Certainly Confucius did believe that social order should be maintained, and that respect should be given where it was due. But more than any other person he worked to destroy arbitrary barriers between classes. The term *chün-tzu* usually meant, before his day, a man of noble birth; he redefined it as meaning a "true gentleman," having nobility of character. *Hsiao-jen*, "little man," had meant a plebeian; Confucius transformed it into "mean man," one lacking nobility of character, whatever his birth. Confucius took as his students men of humble origin, and gave them education such as then had previously been enjoyed only by the well born; some of his pupils rose to high office.

Li is important in this connection. In Western Chou times, it had almost exclusively the sense of "sacrifice" or "religious ritual." In Spring and Autumn times, this term was used to denote a code of aristocratic conduct, analogous to the *courtoisie* of medieval Europe. Confucius universalized it, making it the code of proper conduct for all men, as well as the just and benevolent methods by which government should be conducted. And he taught *li* to his students, from all walks of life.

The derivation of the concept of *li* (like that of our word "courtesy") from an aristocratic code is perhaps an important part of the reason why so many writers on Chinese law have supposed that the principle of inequality before the law, and of legal privilege for persons of superior status, was a "Confucian" tenet. The introduction of such inequality, in

Han times, is said to have been "the Confucianization of Chinese law."[64] But the appropriateness of this term is questionable.[65]

Some of those who write on Chinese law have given quite undeserved emphasis to a statement that occurs, almost at random, in the *Book of Rites* (*Li-chi*). This work, compiled in Han times, undoubtedly contains some material that is somewhat older, but the pedigree of any particular passage is very hard to establish. The one in question says: "*Li* does not extend down to the common people; punishments do not extend up to *tai-fu*."[66] Although *tai-fu* is conventionally translated as "great officer," these were in fact the lowest rank of the officers of a feudal state. This saying has been widely misinterpreted as being Confucian and as meaning that the aristocracy was at some time governed only by its code of etiquette, while punishments were applied only to plebeians.

We have already seen that Confucius taught *li* to all of his students, some of whom came from the humblest origins. In the *Analects*, 2.3, he said, in direct contradiction of the above passage, that the common people should be kept in order by means of *li*, rather than by punishments. As for the proposition that there was ever a time when punishments were not applied to officials and aristocrats, this seems to find no support in the sources. On the contrary, we see men of the rank of *tai-fu* and higher being punished constantly and put to death with great frequency and sometimes in numbers. In 650 B.C. nine such men were executed at one time, and in 552 B.C., ten. Men of rank were sometimes subjected to the most humiliating and painful deaths, being publicly executed and even torn to pieces by chariots. After death their corpses were sometimes publicly exposed, or even made into pickle.[67] The controversial passage in the *Book of Rites* was thus no doubt written by some official as an expression of hope.

Appraisals of the attitude of Confucius toward law, when based upon the numerous and often contradictory apocryphal sayings, are understandably unsatisfactory; but if we concentrate on the *Analects* alone, it is possible to derive a consistent and comprehensible picture. It is a part of Confucius' general conception of the state: ideally a cooperative commonwealth, in which the ruler and his officials are dedicated to the welfare of the people, and the people in turn render loyalty and willing obedience to those above them. The most potent force for causing the people to be good, Confucius repeated over and over, was proper example set for them by the rulers.[68] The people should be positively motivated by *li*, to do that which they ought; if they are intimidated by fear of punishment they will merely strive to avoid the punishment, but will not be made good. To render justice in lawsuits is all very well, but the important thing, Confucius said, is to bring about a condition in which there will be no lawsuits.[69]

Obviously, these were utopian views. Yet Confucius was not so totally impractical as to suppose that legal procedures could be abolished immediately. He said, " 'If good men governed a state for a century, it would then be possible to eliminate violence and do away with capital punishment.' True indeed is this saying."[70] Thus, Confucius cannot be said to have been wholly antilegal, but his attitude toward legal institutions was perhaps somewhat like the attitude toward the state in Marxist philosophy: under ideal conditions they would be unnecessary, and simply cease to exist.

Legal Procedure in Later Chou Times

In general, legal procedures during the remainder of the dynasty seem to have had a good deal of resemblance to those of Western Chou. We see more of such things as the bribery of judges, and extreme punishments—like that of dismemberment by four chariots—but this may only be because we have a great deal more information.

In various states we find a Director of Crime (*Ssu-k'ou*). One passage appears to indicate that in the state of Chin he alone was empowered to impose the sentence of death.[71] For the most part, however, those that we find administering justice are officials, or rulers, who discharge other administrative duties as well. Thus, we read that the administrator of a local district in the state of Chin, being unable to decide a case, forwarded it to the capital, where it was dealt with by the chief minister. The dispensing of justice was a function of rulers of states. In 684 B.C. the Duke of Lu, in enumerating his claims to virtue, stated: "In trying cases, whether small or great, even though I am not capable of great penetration, I always [render judgment] in accord with the facts." During the time when the Duke of Chin was in fact the most powerful man in China, we find him rendering a verdict even in a lawsuit that had been brought against the king.[72]

There are many accounts of lawsuits during this time. Perhaps the most complete one concerns a case that was heard in 563 B.C. Two of the king's ministers, Wang Shu and Po Yü, were contending for control of the royal government and brought suit (*sung*) against each other. The Duke of Chin (who then controlled China, though nominally a vassal of the king) sent an envoy, who heard the case in the king's court. Wang Shu and Po Yü were represented, each by one of his retainers who acted as his advocate and argued on his behalf. Wang Shu's advocate said that Po Yü was a low fellow who insulted his superiors. Po Yü's advocate said that his principal held office by virtue of an ancient pact between the royal house and his family. Furthermore, he noted, since Wang Shu had become chief minister, bribery had been rampant and the government had become entirely corrupt. The envoy of Chin then ordered the two men to present briefs of their evidence. Wang Shu, however, could not do so, and fled. In the upshot, control of the royal government went to neither litigant, but to a third party.[73]

Here again, as in some Western Chou cases, we see the parties represented at the trial by advocates. This seems to have been fairly common in Spring and Autumn times.[74] In most cases, however, there is no indication as to the basis on which these advocates were chosen. Neither does there seem to be any evidence that particular individuals made a regular practice of acting as advocates, as happened in ancient Rome.

We do read, however, of one man who is said to have taught a great many people the techniques of litigation. The *Tso-chuan* says that in 501 B.C. the chief minister of the state of Cheng, Ssu Ch'uan, "put to death Teng Hsi and yet used his laws written on bamboo."[75] The *Lü-shih ch'un-ch'iu*, compiled in the middle of the third century B.C., elaborates on this case:

> When Tzu-ch'an governed the state of Cheng [as chief minister], Teng Hsi worked to make difficulties for him. He contracted with those involved in legal proceedings; if the case was important [he received] a garment, if unimportant a jacket and trousers. Those among the people who gave him such presents and studied [the art of carrying on] lawsuits were more than could be counted. They held wrong to be right and right to be wrong, so that there was no standard of right or wrong and the proper and improper changed every day. Those that [Teng Hsi] wished to win [their cases] won; those he wished found guilty were convicted. The state of Cheng was thrown into great confusion, and the people clamored and wrangled. Tzu-ch'an was distressed by this, and put Teng Hsi to death and exposed his corpse. The people's hearts were then quieted, right and wrong were established, and law prevailed.[76]

Elsewhere we find Teng Hsi described as a sophist.[77] The truth concerning him is difficult to determine. The passage just quoted says that for teaching people to circumvent the law he was put to death by Tzu-ch'an, who died in 522 B.C. The *Tso-chuan* on the other hand, as we have seen, makes him the author of a code of law, and says that he was killed by Ssu Ch'uan in 501 B.C.

Whatever the activities of Teng Hsi may have been, it is clear that during much of the Chou period parties to legal proceedings were often represented by advocates. This stands, of course, in sharp contrast to the situation in later times, when advocates were rigidly excluded from legal proceedings.[78] This is by no means the only difference. Derk Bodde, commenting on the translations by Henri Maspero of Western Chou bronze inscriptions involving litigation, writes: "The give-and-take spirit apparent in these disputes distinguishes them sharply from the vertically oriented court procedures of imperial times and suggests a society closer in spirit to Western society than was later possible when Chinese government became bureaucratized."[79] The degree to which bureaucratization was the cause may be debated. But the difference between the administration of justice, and the whole philosophy underlying it, throughout most of the Chou period as contrasted with later dynasties, was great indeed.

Law and the Order of Nature

Jean Escarra, in his pioneering work on Chinese law, began his discussion of the conceptions underlying it as follows: "One of the most ancient guiding principles of the Chinese spirit is the belief in the existence of an order of nature and in the efficacy of an accord between it and the social order." In describing this "order of nature" he discussed such conceptions as the positive and negative principles called *yin* and *yang*; the so-called five elements and the way in which phenomena are catalogued in many different series of five (five metals, five virtues, five punishments, etc., etc.) and other numerological arrangements; and the manner in which man and nature are conceived to interact (so that, for instance, injustice by the ruler produces excessive rain).[80]

Certainly this conception of the order of nature, and its correlation with human activities, has been basic in Chinese legal thinking for the past 2,000 years. Many have supposed that this was, in China, a "primitive" conception. In fact, it might with greater accuracy be called relatively modern. Not one of the specific ideas mentioned above, from *yin* and *yang* to the preoccupation with numbers and the detailed correlation of human actions with the weather, was present until late in the Spring and Autumn period, and such conceptions did not begin to be pervasive until the time of the Warring States.[81] Bodde, who calls the introduction of such ideas the "naturalization" of law, says that it occurred gradually during the last two centuries before China was reunified by Ch'in in 221 B.C.[82]

This shift was not, of course, limited to the domain of legal affairs. It was part of a thoroughgoing—and as yet but little studied or understood—transformation that took place in Chinese thought, from the fifth century to the third century B.C. It is easy to recognize, but hard to characterize. Perhaps it can be described as movement from analysis of the universe, and of man's place in it, in personal terms, to an analysis in mechanical or protoscientific terms. For instance, in the early period from

Shang times on, rain was sought by personal means, prayers or sacrifices to spirits. But in the Han period, Tung Chung-shu wrote that it was not spirits that brought rain. "Those who understand this, wishing to produce rain, will stimulate the *yin* [the negative principle]." Therefore, he said, "one produces rain by means of the dragon," a symbol of *yin*. Another Han writer said that, in order to attract rain, Tung Chung-shu "set up a dragon [fashioned of] clay."[83]

In a universe so conceived, some alteration in the role of law was inevitable. During most of the Chou dynasty the objectives of legal procedures appear to have been, chiefly, to uphold the power and prestige of the government and to maintain order and tranquillity in society. Bodde points out that with the new conception, "a disturbance of the social order really meant, in Chinese thinking, a violation of the total cosmic order because, according to the Chinese world-view, the spheres of man and nature were inextricably interwoven to form an unbroken continuum." This cosmic order, as well as the social order, was disrupted by "acts of moral or ritual impropriety or of criminal violence." When these occurred, it was necessary that "punishment be inflicted to exact retribution from their doer." Thus, Bodde says, in all of the imperial codes "their treatment even of administrative and other noncriminal matters usually follows a standard formula: 'Anyone who does *x* is to receive punishment *y*.' "[84]

A principal theme, then, became the effort to make "the punishment fit the crime." This is the chief preoccupation of the treatise in the *Documents* called the "Punishments of Lü." It describes a trial as follows: "When both parties have appeared fully prepared, the court assessors listen to the five kinds of pleading. When by this means they have ascertained and verified the guilt, they attribute to it one of the five punishments. If the five punishments do not meet the case, they attribute to it one of the five redemption-fines. If none of these meets the case, they attribute it to one of the five cases of error."[85] The composition of the "Punishments of Lü" was traditionally ascribed to the reign of King Mu (1001-947 B.C.) of the Western Chou, and Escarra placed it in the year 952 B.C.[86] In fact, the "five punishments," around which it is constructed, do not seem to appear before the Warring States period,[87] and a number of criteria seem to date the "Punishments of Lü" to that time.[88]

The "Legalists"

The philosophy known as Legalism was developed, beginning in the fourth century B.C., by men of whom a number, at least, were practicing officials.[89] It advocated strict totalitarian regimentation, with emphasis on agriculture to make the state rich, and on warfare to make it invincible. The people and the officials alike were to be controlled by two means: reward and punishment.

The Legalist philosophy played an important role in the totalitarian organization of the far western state of Ch'in. That organization enabled Ch'in to conquer the rest of China and thereby extend Legalist rule over the whole country during the short-lived Ch'in dynasty (221-207 B.C.). The succeeding dynasty, the Han, continued many of the governmental institutions of the Ch'in, and Legalism undoubtedly had great influence on the subsequent development of China's legal institutions.

The early Legalist thinkers consistently decried the tendency to follow tradition and declared that they were men with new measures for new times.[90] "There is no constant method for governing the people. . . . If the laws change with the times, there is good order."[91] Han-fei-tzu said, "The sage does not seek to follow [the ways of] antiquity, nor to conform to any constant standard; he is able to examine the affairs of his own time, and devise measures appropriate to it."[92] It would seem reasonable to expect, then, that the thought patterns of the early Legalist works would differ greatly from those of Western Chou and even of Spring and Autumn times, and would be more in accord with those of the late Warring States period—when they were produced—and perhaps of Han times. When we examine these books closely, however, they prove surprising.

The earliest and most important of the Legalist works are the *Book of Lord Shang* and the *Han-fei-tzu*; these may fairly be considered to present the Legalist philosophy in its early form.[93] In them, it is only very rarely that we find reference to the peculiar qualities of the special conception of the order of nature that became current in the time of the Warring States and later: *yin* and *yang*, the "five elements," and other numbered categories.[94]

Neither of these works seems to have been affected by what Bodde calls the "naturalization" of law. There is no suggestion in either of them that a criminal offense is "a violation of the total cosmic order." There is little emphasis, like that found in the "Punishments of Lü," on making the punishment fit the crime.[95] Neither work makes any mention of the five punishments.

This is not to say that there is nothing whatever that is new in these Legalist books. There is an insistence that the law is to be made comprehensible and made known to the people, such as is only rarely found earlier.[96] We have seen, however, that there is little reason to suppose that law was kept secret in earlier times. We can only speculate whether this new note is a reaction against such secrecy that may have been practiced by some of the despotic regimes of the Warring States period.

Two techniques that they advocate seem relatively new, though both had been suggested somewhat earlier by the philosopher Mo-tzu.[97] One is the use of reward as well as punishment, though there is far less emphasis on the former than on the latter. The *Book of Lord Shang* prescribes that "in a well-governed country punishments are many and rewards few."[98] Another innovation is the practice—which is, however, only rarely mentioned—of compelling the people, under heavy penalties, to spy upon and inform against their relatives and neighbors.[99]

Far more surprising than their relative lack of novelty is another characteristic of these Legalist texts. Together, their volume is considerable; in English translation, the *Book of Lord Shang* and the *Han-fei-tzu* total well over 200,000 words. Much of their content is anecdotal and the range of subject matter is wide, but there is usually some reference to law or Legalism. Yet in all of this large body of material, detailed reference to legal institutions and procedures is minimal.

Law is mentioned constantly, but it is only very occasionally that there is allusion to particular statutes or specific penalties. And very little is said about the way in which the law is to be enforced. The impression is constantly given that the mere existence of law is all that is necessary. "If laws are equable, there is no wickedness on the part of the officials."[100] "If the laws are detailed and clear, the 'worthy' cannot overcome the 'unworthy,' the strong cannot encroach upon the weak, the many cannot violate the few." "That which produces order is law, that which produces disorder is selfishness. When law has been established, no one is able to act selfishly."[101]

It might almost seem that a magical efficacy was ascribed to the law, but a more mundane explanation is probable. The *Han-fei-tzu* says that the people must be "terrified with punishments,"[102] and the necessity of severe punishment is constantly stressed. The *Book of Lord Shang* says that punishment must be applied to those who merely intend to transgress, and that all, high or low, who do not obey the king's commands, or who violate the official prohibitions, or who rebel against the regulations of their superiors, must be put to death without pardon.[103] The purpose of all this, we are told again and again, is not to multiply executions but to bring about a condition in which the people will not dare to break the law.[104]

If this happy state were achieved, there would be little need, of course, for prosecutions. This is perhaps the reason why, in this large body of Legalist writings, there is only rarely any mention of anything like a trial.[105] The statement is made, from time to time, that the innocent should not be punished, but only a small amount of attention is given to the matter of evidence and its evaluation. In some cases the manner in which legal decisions are reached seems almost frivolous. A judge, unable to decide a case, gives the decision to the last litigant to stop arguing. In the state of Wei it is decreed that lawsuits shall be decided by archery contests, with the decision going to the best archer. An official hears a woman crying over the death of her husband, and notes that her cries sound fearful; he arrests and interrogates her, and determines that she has murdered her husband.[106]

For the Western Chou period our sources are very sparse, and yet it is possible to obtain from them some conception, however sketchy, of the legal institutions and procedures of that time. It is scarcely possible to derive a comparable picture from the early Legalist texts, even though they come to us from a much more recent and better-known period. But the underlying philosophy of these late texts does have a good deal in common with the approach to law that is found in Western Chou.

The purpose of legal procedures, in Western Chou times, appears to have had nothing to do with maintaining cosmic harmony; they were designed, rather, to uphold the authority of the government and to maintain order and tranquillity among the people. These were also the ends that law, as conceived by the Legalists, was calculated to achieve. The *Book of Lord Shang* says: "For benefiting the people there is nothing greater than order. Nothing makes order so firm as establishing the ruler. No method of establishing the ruler is so effective as causing law to prevail."[107] Both that work and the *Han-fei-tzu* tell us constantly that the ends of law are to support the ruler and to maintain order.[108]

The *Book of Lord Shang* praises the founder of Chou, saying: "King Wu seized [the empire] as a rebel, yet he prized obedience; he contended for the empire and yet exalted compliance; he took it by means of force, but held it by means of justice."[109] In fact, there is more than a little resemblance between the ideas of King Wu on justice, as we find them in the *Documents*, and those of the early Legalists. We have seen that Wu was inclined toward frequent use of the death penalty, and that he admonished his younger brother that if officials should dare to disregard their orders and promulgate innovations "you should speedily, in accord with justice, put them to death." The *Book of Lord Shang* similarly recommends that "if, among officials who have charge of the law and of governmental functions, there are those who do not follow the king's regulations, their guilt [requires the penalty of] death without pardon."[110] Again, King Wu says that even small offenses, if they have been committed intentionally, must be punished with death. When the law is enforced in this way, he says, "the people will completely abandon their errors . . . and become tranquil and orderly." The *Book of Lord Shang* agrees: "Punish light offenses heavily; if light offenses do not appear, heavy offenses will not occur. This is what is called using punishment to abolish punishment." The Legalist works repeat this idea many times.[111]

Such similarities between the attitudes of King Wu and those of the Legalists are not wholly surprising, for they found themselves in comparable situations. King Wu was trying to establish a centralized government over a large and heterogeneous territory, and, in fact, he and his immediate successors achieved some success in this difficult task. Likewise, a major concern of the Legalists was to establish centralized administration after the extreme fragmentation of the Spring and Autumn period. Wu was trying to weld into an obedient nation the various peoples he had conquered in north China, many of whom were decidedly hostile to him; therefore, some of his measures were Draconian. The Legalists were attempting, in similar manner, to mold the populace of their states—made turbulent by the ferment and strife of the Warring States period—into bodies responsive to the wills of their rulers; their tool was totalitarian regimentation.

A great deal of research remains to be done before we can thoroughly understand the history of legal institutions and procedures during the Chou dynasty. It is clear, however, that in many ways they differed considerably from those existing in Han times and later. It might be argued, therefore, that this early history is irrelevant to the study of the main body of the history of Chinese law. Yet nothing can be fully understood without understanding its origins. As our knowledge of the early history increases, it is reasonable to hope that it will shed useful light on the nature and the development of China's legal institutions and procedures of later times.

NOTES

1. 1122 B.C. is the traditional date for the beginning of the Chou dynasty. I am well aware that numerous other dates—1027, 1050, 1111, and still others—have been proposed. However, like a number of other scholars I do not find, after careful examination, that the evidence adduced for any one of these is wholly convincing. For this reason, I continue to use the traditional date as a convention, while recognizing that it may involve a factor of error. For further discussion of this problem, see Herrlee G. Creel, *The Origins of Statecraft in China*, Vol. 1, *The Western Chou Empire* (Chicago, 1970), pp. 487-491.
2. Henri Maspero, "Le Régime féodal et la propriété foncière dans la Chine antique," in Maspero, *Mélanges posthumes sur les religions et l'histoire de la Chine*, 3 vols. (Paris, 1950), Vol. 3, p. 139.
3. *Tso-chuan* [History of Tso (?)], compiled around 300 B.C. on the basis of earlier records, tr. James Legge, *The Chinese Classics*, Vol. 5 (Hong Kong, 1960), p. 609.
4. *Mélanges chinois et bouddhiques*, Vol. 3 (1934-1935), pp. 257-317.

5. He ascribed it to the fourth century B.C. See Henri Maspero, "Contribution à l'étude de la société chinoise à la fin des Chang et au début des Tcheou," *Bulletin de l'École Française d'Extrême-Orient*, Vol. 46 (1954), p. 335.
6. If Maspero had started, rather than ended, with the Western Chou source material, it is doubtful that he would have chosen the oath as his subject. For while oaths became very important in the Spring and Autumn period, they are very rarely mentioned either in the literature or the inscriptions from Western Chou. Of the six inscriptions with which Maspero principally dealt in this paper, only two contain any mention of an oath.
7. I consulted the following Western Chou sources. (1) The text (excluding the commentaries called the "Ten Wings") of the *I-ching* [Book of Changes]. (2) twelve sections of the *Shu-ching* [literally Document Classic, often called the "Book of History," which I refer to as the *Documents*]; these are: "Ta Kao," "K'ang Kao," "Chiu Kao," "Tzu Ts'ai," "Shao Kao," "Le Kao," "To Shih," "Chün Shih," "To Fang," "Ku Ming," "Wen Hou chih Ming," and "Pi Shih." (3) The *Shih-ching* [Poetry Classic, which I refer to as *Poetry*]. These poems are generally accepted as having been composed between, roughly, 1122 and 600 B.C. Some of them can be dated as having been composed later than 771 B.C. and therefore excluded, but it is in most cases very difficult to date individual poems certainly. (4) 184 bronze inscriptions. These are only a fraction of the known inscriptions that have been alleged to date from Western Chou times. I believe, however, that they include the great majority of the relatively long inscriptions that yield significant information concerning government, which is the focus of my study. All of these inscriptions have been studied, and accepted as genuine, by at least one scholar—in some cases many scholars—in whose competence I have confidence. The evidence on the basis of which I accept these materials, and exclude others, is set forth in Creel, *The Origins of Statecraft in China*, Vol. 1, pp. 444-486.
8. This does not mean that the king did not have his private estates; undoubtedly he did. But there was not in Western Chou, as has traditionally been supposed, a *Wang ch'i*—a "royal domain" to which the direct administrative authority of the king and his officers was limited.
9. Detailed evidence for these various statements about the Western Chou period will be found in Creel, *The Origins of Statecraft in China*, Vol. 1.
10. The "Spring and Autumn period," as I use the term, is dated 770-464 B.C. I use the term "Warring States period" to refer to 463-222 B.C. This usage differs from that of some other scholars. My reasons for this are explained in Creel, *The Origins of Statecraft in China*, Vol. 1, p. 47, notes 18 and 19.
11. Cf. Marc Bloch, *Feudal Society*, tr. L. A. Manyon (Chicago, 1961), pp. 283-285. The *Tso-chuan*, which deals with the Spring and Autumn period, is filled with references to aristocratic kinship groups, called *shih* (sometimes translated as "clan"). But in Western Chou sources there seems to be no single case in which *shih* is the name of a kinship group, and there is little reference to kinship groups under any other name.

12. The character *li* is quite rare in the Western Chou sources, and seems never to be used to denote a code of aristocratic conduct. The absence of the motif of chivalry from the *Poetry* is noted in Magdalene von Dewall, *Pferd und Wagen im frühen China* (Bonn, 1964), p. 186. It is also lacking in the other sources, including the bronze inscriptions. See Creel, *The Origins of Statecraft in China*, Vol. 1, pp. 331-342.
13. Cf. Bernhard Karlgren, "Glosses on the Book of Documents (1)," *Bulletin of the Museum of Far Eastern Antiquities*, Vol. 20 (1948), p. 290.
14. "The Book of Documents," tr. Bernhard Karlgren, *Bulletin of the Museum of Far Eastern Antiquities*, Vol. 22 (1950), p. 40 (hereinafter cited as *Documents*). Here, as in other quotations from translations that will be cited, I have made such alterations in the translation as seem to me justified; references should be considered, therefore, to relate primarily to the Chinese text rather than to the translation.
15. *Documents*, pp. 40 and 65.
16. *Documents*, p. 80.
17. *Documents*, p. 42
18. *Documents*, pp. 42, 45, and 64.
19. *Tso-chuan*, p. 754. Legge's translation reads "T'ang Shu," but this is an obvious typographical error.
20. *Documents*, p. 42.
21. *Documents*, p. 42. My translation of this passage differs greatly from that of Karlgren. The character I have translated as "justice" is *i*, literally "appropriateness."
22. A.F.P. Hulsewé, *Remnants of Han Law*, Vol. 1 (Leiden, 1955), pp. 4-9.
23. Karl Bünger, "Die Rechtsidee in der chinesischen Geschichte," *Saeculum*, Vol. 3 (1952), p. 211.
24. For documentation on all of these points, see the chapter on "Justice" in Creel, *The Origins of Statecraft in China*, Vol. 1, pp. 161-193.
25. After a great rebellion of the conquered Shang people, many of them were removed to locations distant from their former homes, but this seems to have been a political expedient to prevent future dissidence rather than judicial punishment in the ordinary sense. Banishment as punishment is mentioned, though not imposed, in two inscriptions. See Kuo Mo-jo, *Liang-Chou chin-wen tz'u ta-hsi t'u-lu k'ao-shih* [Inscribed Bronzes of Western and Eastern Chou] (1958), 26a, and 127a.
26. *Documents*, p. 46.
27. Wang Kuo-wei, *Ku-pen chu-shu chi-nien chi-chiao* [A Collated Collection of Passages from the Ancient Text of the Bamboo Annals], in *Wang Chung-ch'io Kung i-shu* [Collected Works of Wang Kuo-wei] (1927-1928), *San-chi* (Third Collection), 8a.
28. It must be noted that while students of Western Chou, including myself, have held that offices were commonly hereditary, careful study of the evidence shows that this is not true. If there was hereditary office at all in Western Chou, its role was extremely limited. See Creel, *The Origins of Statecraft in China*, Vol. 1, pp. 396-400.

29. *Documents*, pp. 40–42.
30. *Documents*, pp. 42–43.
31. *Tso-chuan*, p. 449.
32. Cf. Bernhard Karlgren, "Glosses on the Book of Documents (2)," *Bulletin of the Museum of Far Eastern Antiquities*, Vol. 21 (1949), p. 142.
33. *Documents*, p. 65; cf. also pp. 40 and 64.
34. *Documents*, p. 46.
35. The term here rendered as "accuse" is *kao*, which normally means "to tell." It appears repeatedly in the inscriptions with the sense of "to lay a complaint against."
36. The *lieh*, originally a weight, became a unit of value. Whether the commodity named here is silk has been much debated, but silk was used as currency in China from an early time. See Creel, *The Origins of Statecraft in China*, Vol. 1, pp. 144–151.
37. This inscription and its problems have been discussed by many scholars. I have principally followed the interpretation in Chou Fa-kao, *Chin-wen ling-shih* [Miscellaneous Comments on Bronze Inscriptions] (Taiwan, 1951), pp. 38–88.
38. Kuo, *Liang-Chou chin-wen tz'u ta-hsi t'u-lu k'ao-shih* [Inscribed Bronzes of Western and Eastern Chou], 127a.
39. *Ibid*., 96b-97b. This inscription involves many difficult problems, which are discussed in Creel, *The Origins of Statecraft in China*, Vol. 1, pp. 180–184. Maspero discusses it, with interpretations sometimes differing from mine, in "Le Serment dans la procédure judiciaire de la Chine antique," pp. 272–280. One problem is the name of the maker, which Maspero reads as "Hou," a French transcription equivalent to Hu, while I render it as Yao.
40. A *tzu* is said to have been equivalent to 200 handfuls.
41. The Chinese is *Wang ts'an men*. I have given complete details concerning this translation in Creel, *The Origins of Statecraft in China*, Vol. 1, pp. 183–185.
42. Maspero, in "Le Serment dans la procédure judiciaire de la Chine antique," p. 275, reads the inscription at this point quite differently from the way I do, but he translates: "que le roi fasse une enquête [et fasse examiner] la tablette de bois."
43. Kuo, *Liang-Chou chin-wen tz'u ta-hsi t'u-lu k'ao-shih* [Inscribed Bronzes of Western and Eastern Chou], 26a, 40b, 81b, 96b, 124b-125a, 127a, 129b-131a, and 144b. Chou, *Chin-wen ling-shih* [Miscellaneous Comments on Bronze Inscriptions], pp. 64–72. Concerning the use of tallies, see Creel, *The Origins of Statecraft in China*, Vol. 1, pp. 185–188.
44. Jean Escarra, *Le Droit chinois* (Peking, 1936), p. 79; cf. also Derk Bodde and Clarence Morris, *Law in Imperial China* (Cambridge, Mass., 1967), p. 4, and Karl Bünger, "Die Rechtsidee in der chinesischen Geschichte," p. 212.
45. For instance, *Tso-chuan*, p. 244, refers to what are evidently written codes of law, but the passage must be regarded with some skepticism, because it is preceded by the statement *chün-tzu yüeh*, "the 'true gentleman' would say." Such remarks, inserted at various places in this text, are clearly editorial comments that may date from a time as late as that of its compilation. For a

summary of scholarly opinion concerning the dating of the *Tso-chuan*, see Creel, *The Origins of Statecraft in China*, Vol. 1, pp. 475-477.

46. *Tso-chuan*, pp. 243-244. The characters that I have translated as "laws concerning crime" are *fa-tsui*, literally "legal guilts."
47. *Tso-chuan*, pp. 317, 409, 609, 616, 711, 732, 772, and 802. *Kuo-yü* [Discourses of the States] (*Ssu-pu pei-yao* ed.), 2:6a, 3:7a, and 14:4b. *Chan-kuo ts'e* [Stratagems of the Warring States] (*Ssu-pu pei-yao* ed.), 14:10b.
48. *Tso-chuan*, p. 616.
49. *Tso-chuan*, p. 826.
50. *Tso-chuan*, pp. 243-244, 317, and 409.
51. *Tso-chuan*, p. 609.
52. *Tso-chuan*, p. 282.
53. T'ung-tsu Ch'ü, *Law and Society in Traditional China* (Paris and The Hague, 1961), p. 170.
54. *Documents*, pp. 40, 65, and 80.
55. *Kuo-yü*, 2:6a. This incident is dated in *Tso-chuan*, p. 212.
56. *Kuo-yü*, 17:3a. The point in question has to do with sacrifices to the officer's father. The father is last mentioned in *Tso-chuan*, p. 469, under the year 557 B.C., and the son's name first appears in *ibid.*, p. 496, under the year 551 B.C. The "King's repository" mentioned here is that of the ruler of Ch'u.
57. Timoteus Pokora, "The Canon of Laws by Li K'uei—A Double Falsification?" *Archiv Orientalni*, Vol. 27 (1959), pp. 96-121. Hulsewé, *Remnants of Han Law*, Vol. 1, pp. 28-30.
58. *Tso-chuan*, p. 732.
59. *The Writings of Kwang-zze* (Chuang-tzu), tr. James Legge, in *Sacred Books of the East*, Vols. 39-40 (London, 1891), Vol. 1, pp. 203-210, 354-362; Vol. 2, pp. 144-145 and 192-201. *Complete Works of Han Fei Tzŭ*, tr. W. K. Liao, 2 vols. (London, 1939, 1959), Vol. 1, pp. 293-294.
60. This does not mean that the *Analects* is free from interpolations, but it is relatively so. For textual criticism of the *Analects*, see H. G. Creel, *Confucius, the Man and the Myth* (New York, 1949), pp. 291-294.
61. *Analects*, 9.6.
62. *Analects*, 20.2.3. I suspect that this passage, while reporting a statement of Confucius, underwent some alteration of form before being placed in the canon.
63. *Analects*, 1.15.1; 2.19, 20; 3.3; 4.13; 6.3.2; 8.2.2, 13; 11.16; 12.9, 17-19; 13.4.3, 6, 11, 13, 15, 20; 14.23, 44; 19.19; and 20.2.3.
64. Ch'ü, *Law and Society in Traditional China*, pp. 267-279; Étienne Balazs, *Le Traité juridique du "Souei-chou"* (Leiden, 1954), pp. 9-18. Hulsewé, *Remnants of Han Law*, Vol. 1, p. 5.
65. It is true that most of those involved in this activity were called, among other things, Confucians. After students of other philosophies were barred from government service in 140 B.C. it became customary for almost all officials to be nominal Confucians. It is true that such Confucians as Mencius and, especially, Hsün-tzu, gave far more emphasis to class distinctions than did Confucius, but it is doubtful that even they would have espoused

lighter punishment, for the same crime, for those of superior status. In fact, they might well have urged that their punishment should be heavier, in view of their privileges and responsibilities. Although the meaning of the appellation "Confucian" becomes doubtful from Han times on, it is clear that those who have been considered most genuinely Confucian have usually been ranged on the side of the poor and humble against the rich and powerful. For instance, in 81 B.C. the emperor called upon a group of Confucians—many of whom were poor and humble men—to state the "rankling grievances" of the common people against the government; cf. Huan K'uan, *Discourses on Salt and Iron*, tr. Esson M. Gale (Leiden, 1931), Vol. 1, pp. 76-77, 103-105, and 121.

It is doubtful that one needs to look to any ideology—Confucian or any other—to explain the insistence of officials under the Han dynasty that they should have privileged status before the law. In Han times, especially under Emperor Wu, it was extremely dangerous to be an official, even of the highest rank. Homer Dubs writes: "From 121 to 88 B.C., a period of thirty-three years, during which there were seven Lieutenant Chancellors, only Shih Ch'ing died a natural death; the others were all condemned for some crime or other." Cf. Pan Ku, *The History of the Former Han Dynasty*, tr. Homer H. Dubs, 3 vols. (Baltimore, 1938-1955), Vol. 2, p. 9. Men living in such peril, claiming privileged status before the law, need have been prompted by no philosophy—unless that of *sauve qui peut*!

66. *Lî Kî*, tr. James Legge, in *Sacred Books of the East*, Vols. 27-28; Vol. 27, p. 90 (F. Müller ed., 1885).
67. *Tso-chuan*, pp. 17, 71, 79, 89, 92, 95, 97, 121, 142, 157, 169, 186, 195, 208, 212, 226, 310, 322, 374, 404, 405, 417, 490, 495, 535, 604, 637, and 656; *Kuo-yü*, 3.9b; 92.b; 7b-8a; 12.5a; 14.2b, and 15.1a; *Chan-kuo ts'e*, 3.1b and 14.8a.
68. *Analects*, 2.19-20; 12.17-19; 13.4.3, and 13.13.
69. *Analects*, 2.3; 12.13. No mention has been made of *Analects*, 13.3, which quotes Confucius as speaking of punishments, because this passage is obviously a late interpolation. I believe that Arthur Waley was the first to point this out. See Creel, *Confucius, the Man and the Myth*, pp. 221 and 321-323.
70. *Analects*, 13.11.
71. *Kuo-yü*, 15.1a; *Tso-chuan*, p. 728.
72. *Tso-chuan*, pp. 86, 376, and 728.
73. *Tso-chuan*, pp. 448-449.
74. *Tso-chuan*, pp. 212, 267, 355, 376, and 448.
75. *Tso-chuan*, p. 772.
76. *Lü-shih ch'un-ch'iu* [Mr. Lü's Spring and Autumn Chronicle] (*Ssu-pu pei-yao* ed.), 18.8b-9a.
77. *Hsün-tzu* (*Ssu-pu pei-yao* ed.), 2.1b, 3.9a, 4.3b, and 20.1b. The book called *Teng Hsi-tzu*, traditionally attributed to him, is believed to be a forgery.
78. Bodde and Morris, *Law in Imperial China*, pp. 4 and 28; Escarra, *Le Droit chinois*, pp. 255 and 326.
79. Bodde and Morris, *Law in Imperial China*, p. 48, note 95.
80. Escarra, *Le Droit chinois*, pp. 7-11.

81. Li Han-san, *Hsien-Ch'in Liang-Han chih yin-yang wu-hsing hsüeh-shuo* [Theory of Yin-yang and the Five Elements in the Pre-Ch'in and Han Periods] (Taipei, 1967), pp. 47-49; Bodde and Morris, *Law in Imperial China*, pp. 43-44; Arthur Waley, *The Way and Its Power* (London, 1934), pp. 109-110; Creel, *Confucius, the Man and the Myth*, pp. 198-200, 203, and 317-319.
82. Bodde and Morris, *Law in Imperial China*, pp. 43-44.
83. Tung Chung-shu, *Ch'un-ch'iu fan-lu* [Abundant Dew from the Spring and Autumn Annals] (*Ssu-pu pei-yao* ed.), 13:3b; Wang Ch'ung, *Lun-heng* [Disquisitions] (*Ssu-pu pei-yao* ed.), 16:1a.
84. Bodde and Morris, *Law in Imperial China*, pp. 4 and 28.
85. *Documents*, p. 77.
86. Jean Escarra, "Law, Chinese," *Encyclopaedia of the Social Sciences* (New York, 1933), Vol. 9, p. 251.
87. I have found no reference to the "five punishments" in any bronze inscription, or in any other of the Western Chou sources. It does not occur in the *Tso-chuan*, in the *Analects*, or even in a work as late as the *Mencius*. The earliest datable work in which it appears would seem to be the *Mo-tzu*, coming from a time not earlier than the latter half of the fifth century B.C. It is true that the *Discourses of the States* has a lengthy discussion of the "five punishments" in a conversation attributed to 632 B.C. (*Kuo-yü*, 4.4b-5a). But that work can hardly have been compiled before late Warring States times. And when we find in it passages like this one, which seem to reflect the thinking of that period but to be quite out of context in the earlier time to which they are dated, we cannot accept them as being unquestionably contemporary records from the earlier date.
88. Not only the "five punishments" but an almost innumerable series of other fives, as well as numerous threes, stamp the "Punishments of Lü" as coming from not earlier than Warring States time. Ch'i Ssu-ho said that it was probably written at the beginning of the Warring States period; cf. Ch'i Ssu-ho, "Hsi-Chou shih-tai chih cheng-chih ssu-hsiang," *Yen-ching she-hui k'e-hsüeh* [Yenching Journal of Social Sciences], Vol. 1 (1948), p. 32. Bodde says that the fact that the "Punishments of Lü" is quoted and mentioned by name in the *Mo-tzu* "of the fourth century B.C. provides us with at least a *terminus ante quem*"; cf. Bodde and Morris, *Law in Imperial China*, p. 13.
89. The term Legalism, as denoting a school of Chinese philosophy, is in my opinion commonly misused. It is employed as a translation of the term *fa-chia*. But the *fa-chia* was in fact a combination of two schools; for details see H. G. Creel, "The Fa-chia: 'Legalists' or 'Administrators'?", *Bulletin of the Institute of History and Philology, Academia Sinica*, Extra Vol. 4 (1961), pp. 607-636. One of these schools was founded by Shen Pu-hai, who died between 340 and 337 B.C., and was not concerned with law at all, but with administrative technique. The other, founded by Shang Yang, who died in 338 B.C., may properly be called Legalist. As the term is used in this paper, "Legalist" refers to the Legalist wing of the *fa-chia*. For an exposition of the philosophy of Shen Pu-hai, see Herrlee G. Creel, *Shen Pu-hai, A Chinese Political Philosopher of the Fourth Century B.C.* (Chicago, 1974).

90. *Book of Lord Shang*, tr. J.J.L. Duyvendak (London, 1928), pp. 167-175 and 225-233; *Complete Works of Han Fei Tzŭ*, Vol. 1, pp. 154-155; Vol. 2, pp. 252, 275-280, 316-317, and 328.
91. *Complete Works of Han Fei Tzŭ*, Vol. 2, p. 328.
92. *Ibid*., p. 276. This passage occurs in one of the small number of sections which, by common consent, are agreed to have very probably been written by Han-fei-tzu himself.
93. While the *Book of Lord Shang* is traditionally attributed to the authorship of Shang Yang, there seems to be no definite evidence that he wrote any part of it, and the work is certainly composed of materials from a number of hands. J.J.L. Duyvendak concluded that its most original portions might preserve some material from the fourth century B.C., while much of it was composed in the third century and some portions might be even later; cf. *Book of Lord Shang*, pp. 131-159. The *Han-fei-tzu* is attributed to the philosopher of that name, and it undoubtedly does contain some chapters written by him. But it is an extremely composite work which also included sections written well after the time of Han-fei-tzu, who died in 233 B.C., and some that are not Legalist at all.

    A third book which has commonly been called Legalist is the *Kuan-tzu*. Twelve of its chapters are translated in *Kuan-tzu*, tr. W. Allyn Rickett (Hong Kong, 1965). In his Foreword to this book, Derk Bodde says that "only some of its chapters are wholeheartedly Legalistic, while many others stem from a variety of other schools. . . . On the basis of the available evidence—admittedly not always too decisive—Dr. Rickett's conclusion is that most of the chapters probably belong to the third century B.C., though a few may possibly be as early as the late fourth century, and others may have been added during the second or even the first century B.C." (*ibid*., p. x). Certainly, the *Kuan-tzu* contains important material from the Legalist school, but it is not of the same importance, as an early Legalist work, as the *Book of Lord Shang* and the *Han-fei-tzu*.
94. I find no references to *yin* and *yang* in the *Book of Lord Shang*, and only four in the *Complete Works of Han Fei Tzŭ* (Vol. 1, pp. 52, 55, and 173; Vol. 2, p. 168). The "five elements" seem to be mentioned in neither work, though W. K. Liao interprets another term occurring once as their equivalent; cf. *ibid*., Vol. 1, p. 192. Numbered categories occur with somewhat greater frequency, but not often as compared with many other works of Warring States time.
95. There is mention, in each work, of punishments that accord with the crime committed: *Book of Lord Shang*, pp. 327-328, and *Complete Works of Han Fei Tzŭ*, Vol. 1, p. 272; Vol. 2, p. 158. But this is not a dominant theme; the emphasis is usually on making punishment so severe and so certain that people will be afraid to commit any crime whatsoever.
96. *Book of Lord Shang*, pp. 188, 237, and 327-335. *Complete Works of Han Fei Tzŭ*, Vol. 2, pp. 188, 283-284, and 288.
97. *Ethical and Political Works of Motse*, tr. Yi-pao Mei (London, 1929), pp. 30-77.
98. *Book of Lord Shang*, p. 230. Cf. also *Complete Works of Han Fei Tzŭ*, Vol. 2,

pp. 325 and 326. Such rewards as offices, titles, and gifts had, of course, been used as stimuli as early as Western Chou.

99. *Complete Works of Han Fei Tzŭ*, Vol. 2, pp. 265-269 and 331-332.
100. *Book of Lord Shang*, p. 252; cf. also pp. 223 and 325.
101. *Complete Works of Han Fei Tzŭ*, Vol. 1, p. 267; Vol. 2, p. 235; cf. also Vol. 2, pp. 117, 240, 254, 322, and 330.
102. *Complete Works of Han Fei Tzŭ*, Vol. 2, p. 317.
103. *Book of Lord Shang*, pp. 231 and 278-279.
104. *Book of Lord Shang*, pp. 203, 209, and 212, and *passim; Complete Works of Han Fei Tzŭ*, Vol. 1, p. 295; Vol. 2, pp. 244-245 and 325.
105. In the *Book of Lord Shang* I find nothing of the kind. In the *Han-fei-tzu*, there are some references to trials and trial procedures but no real description of a trial; cf. *Complete Works of Han Fei Tzŭ*, Vol. 1, pp. 123, 144, 285, and 301; Vol. 2, pp. 39, 67, 182, and 265-267.
106. *Complete Works of Han Fei Tzŭ*, Vol. 1, p. 301; Vol. 2, pp. 39 and 182. For other references to the consideration of evidence, cf. *ibid.*, Vol. 1, pp. 285 and 310; Vol. 2, pp. 62 and 265-267.
107. *Book of Lord Shang*, pp. 232-233.
108. *Ibid.*, pp. 168, 223, 230, 260, 278-279, and 325. *Complete Works of Han Fei Tzŭ*, Vol. 1, pp. 38 and 122-124; Vol. 2, pp. 117, 124, 235, 254, 326, 328, and 330.
109. *Book of Lord Shang*, p. 228.
110. *Documents*, p. 42. *Book of Lord Shang*, p. 279.
111. *Documents*, p. 40. *Book of Lord Shang*, pp. 203, 209, 212, 233, 258-259, 275, 285, and 288. *Complete Works of Han Fei Tzŭ*, Vol. 1, p. 295; Vol. 2, pp. 244-245 and 325.

III

THE ADMINISTRATION OF JUSTICE DURING THE SUNG DYNASTY[1]

Ichisada Miyazaki

Life in China during the Sung dynasty (960-1279) became increasingly urbanized and sophisticated. Interregional commerce grew greatly and became more specialized. The need to meet the demands of a more prosperous and populous society led to the training of a larger and more expert body of civil servants for a bureaucracy whose foundations had been laid during the T'ang dynasty (618-906). Officials were recruited and promoted primarily according to the merit principle. Although they were heavily indoctrinated in Confucian ethics and the traditional literary classics, the effective conduct of government depended upon their faithful execution of comprehensive and universal norms promulgated by the emperor and his authorized representatives. One of the chief functions of Sung officialdom, as with any government, was the administration of justice—mainly the settlement of disputes and the imposition of criminal sanctions against offenders. This chapter will briefly describe Sung laws, judicial processes, and legal training. It will show how the Sung employed supplementary legislation and adjudication to modify the received T'ang Code in order to respond to contemporary political, economic, and social developments.

Legal Norms

There were four distinct categories of legal compilations prepared under the official auspices of the Sung court: (1) the Sung Code and subordinate rules and regulations; (2) collections of imperial edicts; (3) classified compilations of all laws in force; and (4) collections of case precedents. Let us first look at the *Sung hsing-t'ung* (Sung Code). It was promulgated in 963, the fourth year after the founding of the new dynasty, and was modeled on the *T'ang-lü shu-i* (T'ang Code with Commentary) of 737. Rather than enact a new code of its own, the Sung government preserved the T'ang Code in its entirety, merely attaching new provisions to various sections. These new provisions took precedence over those adopted from the T'ang.[2] One result of these changes was that the punishments prescribed in the Sung Code were less severe than those prescribed by the T'ang Code for similar offenses.

In addition to the Code, the T'ang had promulgated various rules and regulations: *ling* ("administrative statutes"), *ko* ("regulations"), and *shih* ("ordinances"). Although its Code was virtually the same as that of the T'ang, the Sung did not retain these supplemental T'ang provisions but instead enacted its own, at times quite different, administrative statutes, regulations, and ordinances. Given the differences between each dynasty's subordinate legislative provisions it is even more difficult to understand why the founder of the Sung decided to preserve the basic T'ang Code intact. Why did he not simply delete those provisions that conflicted with Sung legislation and incorporate the new provisions directly into the body of the Code? Perhaps because the T'ang Code was considered a great achievement and was widely respected and copied, even in Japan and in Korea, the Sung refrained from major revision of the Code itself. An analogy can be drawn to the Ming and the Ch'ing practice, where the *lü* (original statutes promulgated at the beginning of each dynasty) were considered in theory to be supreme and immutable for the duration of the dynasty but in fact were modified whenever necessary, without actual repeal, by the addition of new substatutes, the *li*.

The Sung was a transition period. Changes in the social, economic, and bureaucratic structure dictated changes in the realm of law. While the T'ang Code had hardly touched on the area of commercial regulation, Sung finances relied primarily on income from monopolies on merchandise of daily use, such as salt, tea, and wine, and the Sung government soon found it necessary to issue new laws (in the form of imperial edicts called *ch'ih*) to protect its economic interests. Edicts of this type were periodically compiled into separate works and called *pien-ch'ih* ("collection of edicts"). Approximately twenty such compilations were produced during the dynasty.[3] The edicts in effect—though not in form—superseded many provisions of the Sung Code. Like the *ling*, *ko*, and *shih* of the T'ang, they rendered obsolete the adopted T'ang Code provisions. This was the basis for the observation by Chu Hsi (1130-1200), a famous Sung philosopher, that the Sung Code had been replaced by the imperial edicts.[4]

A third major category of legal compilations was called *t'iao-fa shih-lei* ("classified laws") and was first introduced during the Ch'un-hsi reign (1174-89).[5] In an attempt to aid its judicial officials to find the law applicable in each case, the government selected and rearranged by subject matter the important edicts, statutes, regulations, and ordinances and published them in a single work. Several of these compilations of current legislation were compiled by various Sung emperors. The only one extant dates from the Ch'ing-yüan period (1195–1200), and only half of that text has survived.[6]

A fourth type of legal compilation comprised collections of judicial precedents called *tuan-li* ("examples of judgment"). Experienced legal clerks, who were familiar with past court decisions, supplied the judges with precedents applicable to the case at hand. The imperial court frequently warned officials not to give precedents more weight than the relevant statutes. Eventually the government compiled the important precedents for the use of both officials and clerks because there was no other means to expedite judicial business and to make rulings consistent. By utilizing the *t'iao-fa shih-lei* and the *tuan-li*, judgments could be arrived at by reference to the classified statutes and the collections of precedents; searching through all the laws and decisions was unnecessary.

Although no official collection of precedents has survived, we can learn about Sung case judgments from the study of a type of literary work called *p'an* ("judgments"). Because the judge was usually a literary man, he tended to compose judgments in a *belles lettres* style. In 1203 a book entitled *Ch'ing-ming chi* [Pure Clear Collection] was published. As the title indicates, it is a collection of judgments written by "pure-hearted and clear-sighted" judges.[7]

The Sung authorities prohibited private individuals both from printing or copying any laws and from possessing any code provisions.[8] According to an imperial edict collected in the *Ch'ing-yüan t'iao-fa shih-lei*, whoever privately printed the penal code, statutes, regulations, ordinances, or classified statutes was to be punished by 100 blows of the heavy bamboo (converted to 20 blows on the buttocks). Furthermore, if a person reported this offense to the authorities, he would be rewarded with 50 strings of cash, each containing about 1,000 copper coins.[9] The philosophy of the Sung rulers was that the laws belonged exclusively to the emperor and were never to be made accessible to the people. The theory was that, if the people knew the law, they could devise means to circumvent it. The people's duty was simply to obey the doctrines of Confucianism and to fear violation of the sacred laws of the supreme emperor. In fact, when we examine the *Ch'ing-ming chi*, we often find that a space just above the legal terms remains blank as a mark of respect for the emperor, since the law was synonymous with the imperial will.

During the dominance of the Reform Party led by Wang An-shih (1021-1086), the prohibition on the private possession of law books was relaxed.[10] At other times, however, the laws were printed only by the government, and were distributed solely for the use of government offices, where they were indispensable for administration.

The Sung government's policy of keeping the laws from the people is reminiscent of the famous incident of the sixth century B.C. in which Tzu-ch'an, prime minister of the state of Cheng, was strongly criticized for publicly promulgating its penal code. The critic contended that after learning the exact content of the penal law (*hsing*) the people would never again be bound by the principles of correct social behavior (*li*) but would have constant recourse to litigation.[11] These assumptions contrasted sharply with those underlying the approach of Ming T'ai-tsu, the founder of the Ming dynasty (1368-1644), who instituted a program of disseminating knowledge of the law for the guidance of the people.[12]

Trial in the District

Under the Sung, the lowest-level court was part of the basic administrative unit, the district (*hsien*), and was presided over by a magistrate. The district court was open to all litigation except during the farming season from planting until after harvest, when the court would not hear minor disputes which would interfere with people working in the fields; for example, those involving property, contract, trade, family quarrels, and beatings.[13] This policy had certain drawbacks: a clever individual could purposely commit a "minor" crime just before the busy season, and not face prosecution for a considerable time. During the long period of waiting the complainant might succumb to the pressure to accept an inequitable money settlement. In one recorded case, a farmer brought into the court a mortgagee who had refused to return mortgaged land. The mortgagee had cleverly succeeded in avoiding trial from the beginning until the end of the busy season. Finally, the magistrate sentenced him to 100 blows of the heavy bamboo under a code provision that prohibited any mortgagee from using such a tactic.[14]

On the district level, even without a complaint, police and military officials had the power to arrest anyone suspected of a crime. Moreover, any individual could bring a criminal complaint, or even capture an offender in the act of committing a crime in order to obtain the reward offered.

The district magistrate functioned both as chief judge of the lowest court and as head of the *hsien* administration. In a book published in 1117, a conscientious district magistrate named Li Yüan-pi gave a detailed account of how he conducted judicial matters.[15] We can use his experience as one example of the inner workings of a magistrate's court in Sung China.

As the first stage, litigation required a written complaint to be presented to the court. If a peasant decided to present a complaint in a civil or criminal-type case and was unable to write it himself, he went to a scrivener's shop (*shu-p'u*). Scriveners were licensed by the municipal government, and only those with licenses were allowed to carry on this trade. When a scrivener was approached by a client, he examined the case to decide whether it was worth litigating. If he rejected a case with merit, or accepted one without merit, he was subject to official reprimand. When this occurred frequently, his license was revoked.[16]

Each district *yamen* ("office") had six main sections, and it was the punishment section (*hsing-fang*) that was in charge of receiving complaints. In his writings, Magistrate Li recorded that he ordered all complaints to be deposited in the complaint box by early morning. Each complaint was then examined by the punishment section to determine whether there was a valid cause of action. If so, it was handed over to the magistrate. The magistrate then dictated to clerks a summons for each person concerned, including the plaintiff, the defendant, and the witnesses. All were required to arrive at the *yamen* by mid-morning on the appointed day.[17] A special practice applied to holders of official rank, who could be represented by proxies chosen from among the people in their employ. Plaintiffs, especially if they were women or old men, sometimes had kinsmen act in their place. Men above 70 years old and pregnant women could not be chief plaintiffs because they were legally exempt from the punishment of beating (the penalty for submitting a false statement).[18] Prior to the day appointed for trial, if it was feared that the accused or the suspect might run away, the magistrate might order him confined in the detention house (*yü*), or instruct his kinsmen or a village headman to watch his actions. In all cases of serious offenses, the suspect was detained in a cell with shackles on his hands and feet.

The nature of this detention requires further elaboration. The Chinese word *yü* meant a detention house where an accused was confined pending trial and sentencing, or where a sentenced criminal awaited the execution of his sentence; it did not mean a prison where a convicted offender was incarcerated as a punishment. Thus, the term *yü-k'ung* ("the detention house is vacant") did not mean that no serious criminal had appeared in the district, but that the magistrate was so diligent that no one was forced to wait a long time in the detention house.[19] When such a condition continued for a long period, the magistrate's meritorious performance was recorded in his personal history.

The judge, of course, shared the credit for this achievement with the personnel of the various bureaus under his control. The punishment section dealt with civil and criminal-type suits for the entire district. Serving in this section were many clerks, including the chief clerk (*ya-ssu*), the second clerk (*lu-shih*), ordinary clerks (*shou-fen*), and apprentice clerks (*t'ieh-ssu*). Attached to the section were two departments—the detention house (*yü*) and the archives (*pien-lu-ssu*). The former was staffed by a chief warden (*chu-tien*), an assistant warden (*chieh-chi*), jailers (*yü-tzu*), and whippers (*chang-chih*); and the latter by a law clerk (*pien-lu ssu*, same name as the bureau) and apprentice law clerks (*hsi-hsüeh jen*).

The process of judgment comprised two stages: first, the investigation of facts; second, the application of law. The magistrate presided over both stages. The defendant was questioned by the magistrate sitting with two of his colleagues—the assistant magistrate (*hsien-ch'eng*) and the record keeper (*chu-pu*). The police commissioner (*hsien-wei*) was never present at the interrogation. He did not participate because his major duty was the apprehension of criminals. During the trial he might unjustly exert pressure on the defendant, in anticipation of a reward for a conviction.[20] Unlike those of earlier dynasties, the more sophisticated Sung legal institutions recognized the advantage of separating police and judicial functions.

Yet in major cases the actual fact of a completed offense was established by the criminal's confession, and not by the material evidence or the testimony of witnesses.[21] Even when material evidence existed, if the accused did not acknowledge it, guilt could not be legally established. However, when despite a substantial showing of evidence the accused refused to confess, the magistrate could have him tortured. All that was required procedurally was the consent of the assistant magistrate and the record keeper. The magistrate would issue a writ ordering a certain number of blows, obtain the signature of his colleagues signifying their assent, and show the writ to the chief clerk and the runner on duty. The runner then carried out the beating in the presence of the officials and clerks.[22]

The accused could of course deny the charge, while the complainant could challenge the accused's version of the facts. Each party inevitably disputed the other's account, but it was the duty and the right of the presiding officials to act as both defense lawyer and prosecutor. In Ming-Ch'ing times, the court was open to the public, and anyone could attend the trial; but, during the Sung, only those involved were allowed to be present.

When the accused admitted his offense, the clerk transcribed his confession word by word. He then read it to the accused and requested his signature (or the trace of the length of the middle finger in the case of an illiterate criminal defendant).[23] When the accused signed the letter of confession, the material facts were considered to be completely established (*yü-ch'eng*). As we shall see, for serious charges the accused retained the right to repudiate his confession and ask for a retrial at a later stage.

The second stage was the application of the law (*chien-tuan*). At this stage the clerk of the archives played a major role.[24] First he examined the law code and assembled the relevant articles with the aid of the classified laws. Then, after consulting the compilation of major precedents, he listed all applicable precedents. Utilizing this material, the magistrate consulted with his colleagues and issued a judgment (*p'an*) which he wrote in the literary style. The judgment gave a brief outline of the case, stated the reasons for the decision and, if necessary in a civil-type case, determined the rights and obligations of plaintiff and defendant. When the punishment was less than 100 blows it was carried out immediately, and a report sent to the prefect. It should be noted that 100 blows was in fact only 20 blows on the buttocks, because of the reduction of punishment instituted by the Sung Code.[25] If the magistrate thought the crime deserved a more severe punishment, he had to propose a preliminary judgment using the appropriate formula, and send the parties concerned and all relevant documents to the prefecture for further proceedings. As a matter of principle, civil-type cases were supposed to be concluded at the *hsien* level because of their relative unimportance. In practice, however, an aggrieved party was permitted to seek appellate review of serious errors committed at the original trial. In criminal cases, if the accused repudiated his confession at the trial level, the case was supposed to be automatically retried by other officials. Moreover, the accused or his family could appeal directly to higher authorities for review of any injustice committed by the *hsien* officials.

Trial in the Prefecture

During the Sung period the prefecture (*chou*) was, in theory, under direct control of the central government, and the prefect was answerable to the emperor himself. The circuit (*lu*), which stood between the prefecture and the central government, was not an administrative but a supervisory division. A supervisor was appointed for each of four concerns: finance (*chuan-yün shih*), military (*an-fu shih*), punishment (*t'i-tien hsing-yü*) and agriculture (*t'i-chü ch'ang-p'ing*). These positions were mutually independent; each supervisor was separately dispatched by imperial mandate to perform a special duty. The supervisor of punishments was charged with supervision of legal affairs in the prefectures belonging to his circuit.

The prefectural government was comprised of several bureaus (*ts'ao*), each staffed by specialized personnel. Under the prefect, there was the assistant prefect (*t'ung-p'an*), the secretary-general (*lu-shih ts'an-chün*), and sometimes advisors without fixed office (*p'an-kuan, t'ui-kuan*). The bureau of punishments (*hsing-ts'ao*) had three main branches: the "left inquiring office" (*tso t'ui-k'an ssu*), the "right inquiring office" (*yu t'ui-k'an ssu*), and the law office (*fa-ssu*). The bureau chief (*ts'an-chün*) and the three office heads (*yüan*) were all appointed by the central government. Officials serving in this bureau were selected from among those well versed in the law. The subordinate clerks were also required to have practical experience in legal affairs.

Each of the two inquiring offices (*t'ui-k'an ssu*) at the prefectural *yamen* had a separate detention house. Moreover, the prefectural *yamen* at times established a third inquiring office, also with its own detention house.[26] The reason for having two or three inquiring offices was to make possible a change in personnel during an investigation should that prove necessary. For example, when toward the close of the prefectural proceedings the accused was asked to sign his confession in the presence of all the prefectural legal officials, he could repudiate it on the ground that he had been forced to acknowledge the offense because of threats or torture. His case would then be transferred to the other inquiring office for a new investigation.

The law office had a separate function. After a case had reached the prefectural *yamen* (either on appeal by the accused or by referral from the *hsien* magistrate, who considered that the offence warranted a heavier punishment than he was authorized to administer directly), it was the duty of the law office to examine the code and to assemble all existing regulations concerning the alleged offense. This process is described in the record of an actual case inscribed on a stone found in Kiangsu province. In the year 1228, the director of the Soochow prefectural school charged a man named Ch'en Cho with misappropriating land belonging to the school. The law office, in processing the case, selected the following legal provisions:[27]

(1) From the Code [*lü*]: Whoever clandestinely ploughs and sows land belonging to another or to the government shall be punished in proportion to the extent of the land illicitly cultivated; when not exceeding one *mou* [6.6 *mou*=1 acre], [he shall be punished] with 30 strokes, and one degree more severely in proportion to each additional 5 *mou*, . . .

(2) From the Code: Whoever unlawfully appropriates and sells land belonging to another or to the government shall be punished in proportion to the extent of the land unlawfully sold; when not exceeding one *mou*, with 50 strokes, . . .

(3) From the imperial edicts [*ch'ih*]: Whoever cultivates or sells government land clandestinely shall be punished as provided in the Code, . . .

(4) From the administrative statutes [*ling*]: Whoever cultivates or sells government land clandestinely, . . . shall indemnify the government by an amount equivalent to the rent and the loss in taxation to the government. This amount should not exceed the amount accruing in a ten year period. . . .

(5) From the regulations [*ko*]: Whoever accuses and brings to conviction an offender who has clandestinely cultivated or sold government lands . . . will receive five per cent of the indemnity as a reward.
(6) From the administrative statutes: A reward for which no rightful claimant exists shall be forfeited to the state.

The examination of the law was carried out by an expert clerk of the law office under the instructions of the office head. The classified law compilations were utilized, but the articles concerned had to be quoted as if they had been taken directly from the original lawbooks. The officials and clerks of the inquiring office, and those of the law office, worked entirely independently of each other, for the separation of the inquiry into the facts from the inquiry into the law was a basic principle of Sung legal institutions and was given even more explicit institutional recognition at the prefectural level than at the district level.[28]

The prefect, after receiving the reports on the facts and the law from the above two offices, drafted a possible sentence and called upon all prefectural legal officials to adjudicate the case together (*chü-lu*).[29] A clerk would ask the accused to repeat his earlier confession in order to ascertain whether his present statement and his previous confession were identical. A second clerk would then read the original confession and ask the accused to sign it. It was at this point that the accused could repudiate his confession, proclaim his innocence, and condemn the improper actions of the clerks and wardens who had handled his case (*fan-i*).[30] To avoid this possibility and conclude cases speedily, some officials and clerks apparently resorted to such abuses as stuffing rags into the accused's mouth, or reading the confession quickly and unintelligibly.[31] If the accused did sign his confession, the prefect showed his draft sentence to the officials present and requested them to countersign to indicate their accord.

Whereas the accused could contest only the facts, the prefectural legal officials could, by withholding their signatures, protest either the finding of facts or the application of the law, or both. When the prefect considered the protest reasonable, he either transferred the case to the other inquiring office, or modified the proposed sentence. He could, however, persist in his sentence despite the objection of his colleagues. If afterwards the sentence was found to be unduly severe or unduly light, the prefect and those who supported his decision would be subject to administrative sanctions while those dissenters who had advocated the correct ruling would be free from any liability.[32]

It was the duty of the head of the second inquiring office to correct any mistakes committed by the first office. When an official succeeded in clearing an innocent person of a grave charge (*p'ing-fan*), he received both a reward and public acclamation.[33] Not only could the defendant make his own accusation of improper treatment but his kinsmen could also petition the prefect or circuit supervisor to investigate the misfeasance of the presiding officials.

If the defendant was sentenced to no more than penal servitude, his case would not go beyond the prefectural level, but disposition of the case was subsequently reported to the circuit supervisor. By contrast, if a sentence of exile or capital punishment was handed down by the prefect, the case record had to be submitted for the immediate review of the circuit supervisor. The supervisor then directed the prefect to execute the sentence, to modify it, or to transfer the case to the second office of inquiry. In the last situation, the circuit supervisor sometimes sent his personal representative to the prefecture to preside over the retrial. However, he took that step only if he decided that there was no suitable official attached to the prefectural *yamen* to try the case. The circuit supervisor had a strong staff of experts, officials as well as clerks, but no detention house for confining suspects pending his inquiry into a case. Therefore, he had to order any necessary retrial to take place at the prefectural *yamen*.

Cases incurring the death penalty were divided into two categories: one category did not have to be reported to the emperor (*pu-ying-tsou*); regarding the other category, notification to the emperor was mandatory (*ying-tsou*). In the latter group of cases, where appropriate facts existed, the subordinate officials might submit an additional document, a plea for clemency, to the emperor. But when the facts of the case were clear, when there was no doubt about the application of the law and the offender himself agreed that he deserved the death penalty, there was no need to bring the case to the emperor's attention. In such cases, the prefect simply sent a report and the case record to the supervisor of the circuit. Upon the latter's approval, the offender would be executed at the prefectural level.[34]

Yet, if there existed even the slightest doubt about which article of the law should be applied (for example, where there was no pertinent law governing the situation, or where the sanction provided by the applicable law was considered either too severe or too lenient for the crime under consideration), or if extenuating circumstances existed, a report and the case record had to be submitted to the central government through the circuit supervisor's office.

For a convict under final sentence of exile or death, there remained one more opportunity to protest his innocence.[35] If, when he was granted a moment's opportunity to take leave of his kinsmen or friends—either at the gate of the city just before his departure into exile or at the market place where he was to be put to death—he proclaimed his innocence, a retrial had to be conducted. However, the retrial was restricted to questions of fact and did not concern itself with the application of the law.

If an offender sent up from trial at the district level was ultimately sentenced at the prefecture to a beating on the buttocks only, a punishment ordinarily carried out at the district level, he would be punished immediately at the prefectural *yamen* in order to avoid having to return him to the district under police escort. In certain cases, such as those involving property, the prefect could place an offender on probation. The scope of the prefect's discretionary power to grant probation is illustrated by a case arising in 1265, in which a woman named Hsü was accused by a municipal school of unlawfully occupying the latter's land. The prefect, after sentencing her to 100 strokes, granted a stay of execution on condition that she acknowledge her offense. She obstinately requested a retrial, however, and was again found guilty. Because she was a woman, the prefect placed her once more on probation, though he could have deprived her of the privilege as a result of her obstinate and dishonest conduct.[36]

A civil-type case often continued for many years because appeal to the central government was not allowed, such cases being deemed relatively unimportant, and because no lower court was empowered to give a final decision. When either the plaintiff or the defendant was not content with the decision of the prefect, he or his kinsmen could present a demand for review not only to the circuit's supervisor of punishments but also to any of the other supervisors. But the supervisors, having neither a court nor detention house, could only examine the documents and warn the prefect to perform his duty impartially. No court in the province was empowered to give final decisions in civil-type cases, so they passed back and forth between the prefectural and circuit levels. Thus, a famous magistrate in the Southern Sung confessed: "Some people have carried on their pleas as long as several years, never content with any judgment. Naturally, there were those who persisted obstinately in their wrongful views in the hope that the case would eventually die out. But in some cases the officials were at fault. For example, in property and marriage disputes they failed to apply the law and did not take human feeling into consideration. As a result, the aggrieved parties went through all the judicial *yamen* in a vain attempt to secure justice. This phenomenon of repeatedly going to the court must not necessarily be condemned as a vice, for those people sometimes had good reason for doing so."[37]

Review by the Central Government

During the T'ang era, the death penalty had been imposed exclusively by the Supreme Court of the central government. Prior to execution, imperial assent had to be given three times to a repeated recommendation of capital punishment submitted by the imperial advisers. This regulation was abolished by the central government during the Five Dynasties period that followed the T'ang and preceded the Sung, and the local military governments began to execute criminals arbitrarily. The Emperor T'ai-tsu, founder of the Sung dynasty, seeking to revive the policy of taking great care in imposing the death penalty, allowed every criminal under sentence of death who requested review of his case to come to the capital for an imperial review. Most had their lives spared after the emperor revised their sentences. Moreover, to avoid the difficulties of long travel, central government officials began to review capital cases on the basis of the documents alone.

The Sung central government had three *yamen* that dealt with legal affairs: the Supreme Court (*Ta-li ssu*), the Board of Punishments (*Hsing-pu*) and the Counsellors' Committee (*Shen-hsing yüan*). Early in the Sung period, although the Supreme Court retained the prestigious name of the Han and T'ang eras, it became nothing more than the first court of revision. Similarly, the role of the Board of Punishments was not of chief importance in the early Sung and many of its functions were actually performed by the Counsellors' Committee. Later, as a result of one of the reform measures promulgated by the Emperor Shen-tsung, the Board of Punishments absorbed the Counsellors' Committee. The two became the second and the third courts of revision under the Sung system.

When there was a difference of opinion among the officials of the three legal *yamen*, the emperor sent the matter to certain of his special advisers (*Liang-chih*),[38] to an ad hoc committee of scholar officials, and ultimately to the ministers of the cabinet (*Chung-shu*). It was, however, the emperor himself who made the final decision in capital cases.

In the year 1068, the prefect of Tengchou (Honan) reported the following case: a woman was compelled to become engaged to a youth whom she hated because of his ugliness. She finally attempted to murder him, but succeeded only in wounding him. She was arrested by police and brought to court, where she readily confessed the offense. The prefect then reported the case to the Supreme Court, recommending commutation of the death penalty because she had confessed prior to the beginning of the inquiry. The Supreme Court, however, proposed the death penalty for the offense of attempted murder. The prefect objected to the decision and requested the emperor to grant the accused a two-degree reduction in punishment in accordance with the law on confession. However, the Supreme Court and the Counsellors' Committee ignored the issue and submitted a joint report to the emperor, recommending instead a one-degree reduction in punishment by imperial clemency on the ground that the offender had been unlawfully compelled to become engaged during the period of her mother's mourning. In other words, they considered the issue of confession irrelevant, apparently because the woman confessed to the authorities only after she had been arrested and brought to the court. The emperor then sought the opinion of the Board of Punishments, whose answer agreed with that of the Supreme Court. But the prefect was not satisfied and requested the emperor to send the case to other officials for deliberation. Two eminent secretaries, Wang An-shih and Ssu-ma Kuang, were selected to review the case together. Unfortunately these men came to different conclusions on the matter and submitted opposite recommendations. Wang An-shih supported the prefect, whereas Ssu-ma Kuang endorsed the position taken by the Supreme Court. The emperor then summoned an ad hoc committee of secretaries to argue for or against the two opinions. They all spoke in favor of the two-degree reduction, the position taken by Wang An-shih and the prefect. The emperor agreed. He then issued two edicts in quick succession, declaring the correctness of Wang's opinion. If the emperor intended to resolve the question by this act, his plan was thwarted. Immediately, strong opposition arose among some officials against the issuance of such executive directives to judges presiding in pending cases. The emperor had no choice but to take the matter back under consideration. He next asked the advice of the ministers of the cabinet, the majority of whom had supported him in his original edicts.

The issue then shifted. The emperor's request for advice touched off a debate on the proper role of the imperial ministers. Some of the ministers argued against the propriety of rendering advice on the question. The independence of the judicial function was greatly esteemed by some statesmen who maintained that, because they were administrators and not judicial officials, the ministers of the cabinet should not interfere with a judgment. However, Wang An-shih, himself one of the ministers, answered this argument by saying that the ministers had a duty to help the emperor, who decided all controversies, whether judicial or administrative. Strictly for purposes of aiding the emperor, the ministers should be able to deal with judicial questions and yet not exceed their proper role. To support the legitimacy of the union of judicial and administrative functions, Wang pointed out that although there was a procedural separation between the inquiry into the facts and the application of the law at the district and prefectural levels, the district magistrate and the prefect each possessed both functions, and they were no more than agents of the emperor. Whether Wang's argument was entirely persuasive or not, it apparently concluded the immediate dispute. At this point we may note that the discussion of a single peasant woman's case had occupied the Sung officialdom for well over a year—probably the most unusual example of the judicial process in the world at that date.[39] Clearly more than legal principle was involved in this case, which obviously reflected the political struggle between Wang An-shih and his opponents. Nevertheless, it is significant that political conflict in China a millennium ago could take the form of a debate over the proper disposition of an appellate case.

There were numerous occasions for use of this review process. The Sung records tell us that there were usually about 2,000 criminals sentenced to death every year.[40] Yet in the year 1085, of 264 felons whose case records were forwarded to the central government for review, only 25 were actually put to death. The others were spared, although they had been sentenced to capital punishment in the prefecture. Moreover, imperial decrees of total or partial amnesty for convicts were issued so frequently during the Sung period that political commentators of the time occasionally criticized the evil consequences of the practice. In one recorded case, a landlord was killed by a tenant farmer and his family during a visit to the tenant's house. After being freed by an imperial amnesty decree, the tenant killer went to see the landlord's family, boasting of his good health and asking: "Why doesn't the master come once more to my house to collect rent?"[41] Such flagrant failure to administer proper punishment must surely have been a source of unrest and distrust of the legal process.

Legal Training

As mentioned above, there were no advocates or lawyers permitted in Sung courts. There were, however, others who became involved in the administration of justice. These were classified into three categories according to social rank: officials, clerks, and commoners.

The most educated and select group was the officials. Ranking officials usually achieved their position through the narrow path of the literary examination for academic degrees (*k'o-chü*) in which knowledge of the law was never tested. Before they were appointed officials, however, another examination was held by the Board of Appointment. The four T'ang subjects of examination—physical appearance, speech, calligraphy, and "judgment-writing" (*shen, yen, shu, p'an*)—continued to be tested in the Sung appointment examination, although their significance gradually changed. In Sung times judgment-writing was thought of as a literary rather than a judicial skill. Tests in the other three subjects were largely nominal, since candidates for official appointment in Sung had already been tested by the emperor in the final step of the literary examination and the assumption was that they were qualified in the areas necessary for official status. Prospective officials in the Sung thus made little effort to become really competent in any of the four subjects in which they were examined prior to appointment.

An important exception to the above situation should be noted, however. In the time of the Emperor Shen-tsung, (r.1067-1085) the need for officials to possess legal knowledge and judicial ability was keenly felt by the statesmen of the progressive party led by Wang An-shih. To alter the trend evident in the Sung examination practice, they drafted new laws that promoted the spread of judicial knowledge among officials.[42] Their first step was the initiation of examinations in jurisprudence for lower officials who otherwise had little chance of early promotion. Successful candidates were to be given priority in appointment to posts in the Supreme Court, in the *yamen* of the circuit supervisor of punishments, and in the law offices of the prefectures. The second step was the requirement that all newly accredited scholars take a similar examination in law as part of the literary examination held prior to their appointment to governmental posts. The antagonists of Wang An-shih opposed these measures, claiming that the study of law would make the literati cruel minded.

Despite opposition, a third step was taken by Wang An-shih to promote judicial knowledge among the officials. The law college, which had fallen into ruin at the end of the T'ang, was restored and reopened. Students were divided into two groups for the separate study of legal philosophy and the techniques of adjudication. Wang An-shih also reorganized the Imperial University for the purpose of having it replace the examination system in the future. Students of the university could take the tests of the law college in order to gain the same privileges as those bestowed by the college, such as appointment to government positions requiring knowledge of the law.[43]

All these reforms were abolished by the conservative party after the death of the Emperor Shen-tsung. Nevertheless, the examination in law was restored after only a short lapse and continued through the Southern Sung (1127-1279).

The second group of individuals who functioned as administrators of Sung justice consisted of the clerks. They were required to be more skilled in handling the law than the ranking officials since their tasks were more closely connected with the people's daily activities. Wang An-shih actively encouraged the study of law by clerks who served in posts concerned with judicial affairs, establishing a special law examination for clerks. Those who passed were appointed chief clerks in the bureaus or offices with judicial functions. The examination consisted of hypothetical cases, and the questions tested only the clerk's mastery of adjudication procedures. These tests never involved legal philosophy, a discipline considered to be beyond the comprehension of individuals who had not mastered the classics of Confucianism.[44]

In connection with these policies, Wang An-shih relaxed the prohibition against the possession of lawbooks. Books were obviously indispensable for learning the law required in the examinations. Applicants were granted special permission to buy from the authorities any statute book printed by government authorities.[45]

Since officials and clerks served both a prosecutorial and a judicial function, the government had to consider how to prevent them from accepting bribes and distorting the law. The clerks were particularly vulnerable because, unlike the officials, whose high-ranking position was worth preserving, their status was very low, and they had little to lose by improper behavior. One of the reforms of Wang An-shih was a special regulation called the heavy salary act (*Chung-lu fa*), by which some clerks with important duties, such as those connected with judicial inquiry, received relatively high salaries. These clerks were to be severely punished if they accepted any donations or bribes, however small.[46] Ordinary clerks, by contrast, continued to make a living on the irregular income of small donations contributed by the people. The danger posed by their acceptance of money was considered less threatening to the judicial apparatus.

Despite the Sung government's attempts to retain exclusive control over legal materials, the people did manage to acquire some knowledge of the law and manifested an increasing willingness to involve themselves in litigation. In Kiangsi province, particularly in Chi and Ch'ien prefectures, whose inhabitants were not known for their refinement or sophistication, legal techniques were taught in the village schools from a textbook called the *Teng Ssu-hsien*.[47] In 1086 the government prohibited such teaching and continued to issue edicts against it, yet it apparently persisted throughout the Southern Sung.[48] For example, a second textbook, entitled *Ssu-yen tsa-tzu* (*The Four Character Proverb*), was published later, in the Southern Sung period.[49] Contemporary officials and intellectuals deplored this development and denounced the popularization of the law. A report written by a Southern Sung statesman commented on the people's harassment of a magistrate by a charge that his decision was contrary to the emperor's rescript.[50] The significance of this report is somewhat ambiguous. On the one hand, it might be construed as indicative of the central government's toleration and even tacit encouragement of the development; on the other hand, and this is probably the more likely view, it might indicate that the development was regarded with disfavor as being contrary to the Confucian values and a sign of rebelliousness and disrespect for the paternalistic bureaucracy.

CONCLUSION

Sung legal institutions are noteworthy for the relatively thorough appellate review they provided and for the effort, reflected in their organization, to insure a separation of judicial from police functions. Reinforcing these positive characteristics was a systematic attempt by the central government, through supplementary legislation modifying the T'ang Code and through judicial practice, to mitigate punishments and to impose the death penalty only in extreme cases. To realize these significant changes, the Sung improved legal training and countered corruption at all levels of the legal administration.

Yet the Sung reforms did not cope with all of the problems of litigation in Chinese society. Most notable was the failure to institute a final judgment rule. The interminability of litigation, especially in civil cases, was a negative aspect of the appellate system. Expeditious conclusion of lawsuits was perhaps rendered even more difficult during the Sung than in earlier eras as the populace became more sophisticated and urbanized and less timorous about resort to the courts. Indeed, the Sung's own reforms may have contributed to a new spirit of litigiousness by making the courts less forbidding than before.

NOTES

1. This paper is a development of my article (in Japanese) entitled "Sō-Gen jidai no hōsei to saiban kikō" [Law and Judicial System in the Sung-Yuan Period], which appeared in the *Tōhō gakuhō* [Journal of Oriental Studies] Vol. 24 (1954), pp. 115-225, and which was later reprinted in my *Ajiashi kenkyū* [Studies in Asian History], Vol. 4 (Kyoto, 1964), pp. 179-305.
2. For example, in the section on punishments, the T'ang version stipulated that there be three grades of banishment: to 3,000, 2,500 and 2,000 *li*, respectively. However, in the Sung appendix to that section it is stated that banishment to 3,000 *li* was to be changed to three years of penal servitude plus 20 blows on the back; banishment to 2500 *li* was to be changed to two and a half years of penal servitude plus 18 blows; and banishment to 2,000 *li* was to be changed to two years plus 17 blows. *Sung hsing-t'ung* [Compendium of Penal Laws of the Sung Dynasty], 963 A.D. (Peking, 1918 reprint; reprinted Taipei, 1964), Vol. 1, pp. 1 and 5-6.
3. Yang Hung-lieh, *Chung-kuo fa-lü fa-ta shih* [The History of Chinese Legal Development] (Shanghai, 1930, 1st ed.; reprinted Taipei, 1967), pp. 571-574.
4. Chu Hsi, *Chu-tzu yü-lei* [The Classified Analects of Master Chu] (Chu-bun shuppan-sha ed., Kyoto 1970), 128:4936.
5. Yang, *Fa-ta shih*, pp. 568-569.
6. In 1968, this work was reprinted in lithography in Japan, using the manuscript preserved in the Seikado library in Tokyo. It now consists of eighty

chüan (chapters). Most scholars believe the eighty *chüan* work is complete, but I suspect that this book represents less than half of the original text.

7. This work was reprinted in Tokyo in 1954, using the world's only existing Sung edition, which carries a preface dated 1261. This edition is kept in the Seikado library in Tokyo.
8. See my article "Shokin to kinsho" [Prohibition on books and prohibited books], *Ajiashi kenkyū*, Vol. 2 (Kyoto, 1959), pp. 232-254.
9. *Ch'ing-yüan t'iao-fa shih-lei*, pp. 244-245.
10. *Ajiashi kenkyū*, Vol. 4, p. 238. See text at notes 47-50 for discussion of the spread of legal knowledge among the common people and the increase in litigation noted in the late eleventh century.
11. Derk Bodde and Clarence Morris, *Law in Imperial China* (Cambridge, Mass., 1967), pp. 16-17.
12. For a discussion on the legal institutions established by Ming T'ai-tsu, cf. Frank Münzel, "Some Remarks on Ming T'ai-tsu," *Archiv Orientalni*, Vol. 37 (1969), pp. 377-399.
13. *Sung hui-yao kao* [Draft Summary of Sung Governmental Institutions], "Hsing-fa" (Penal Law Section), 3:48b; *Sung hsing-t'ung*, Vol. I, pp. 434-436. Cf. also Hsü Dau-lin, "Sung-ch'ao te hsien-chi ssu-fa" [Administration of Justice at the District Level During the Sung Dynasty], *Tung-fang tsa-chih fu-k'an* [Eastern Miscellany—New Series], Vol. 5, No. 9 (1971), pp. 19-28.
14. *Ch'ing-ming chi* (Tokyo, 1954), pp. 355-359. Because of his advanced age, the defendant was exempted from suffering the penalty.
15. Li Yüan-pi, *Tso-i tzu-chen* [Self-exhortations of a Magistrate] (original Preface dated 1117; Ssu-pu ts'ung-k'an hsu-pien ed., Shanghai, 1934).
16. *Ibid.*, 12b. With regard to the *shu-p'u*, cf. also *Sung hui-yao kao*, 6:73b.
17. Li, *Tso-i tzu-chen*, p. 9b.
18. *Ibid.*, p. 40b.
19. *Sung hui-yao kao*, "Hsing-fa," 4:85-92.
20. *Sung hui-yao kao*, "Chih-kuan" [Officials], 5:48. For a detailed study of the evolution of the separation between fact finding and law finding, cf. Hsü Dau-lin, "Chü-yen fen-ssu k'ao" [Note on the Separate Function of Investigation and Decision], *Tung-fang tsa-chih fu-k'an*, Vol. 5, No. 5 (1971), pp. 40-45.
21. But cf. Hsü Dau-lin, "Sung-lü chung te shen-p'an chih-tu" [The Sung Trail System as Prescribed in the Fundamental Statutes of the Sung], *Tung-fang tsa-chih fu-k'an*, Vol. 4, No. 4 (1970), 18-28, at p. 19. Hsü states that during both the T'ang and Sung periods it was not always necessary to obtain the accused's confession before convicting him of the offense charged.
22. Li, *Tso-i tzu-chen*, p. 26.
23. Niida Noboru, *Chūgoku Hōseishi Kenkyū*: *Tochihō, Torihikinō* [A Study of Chinese Legal History-Law of Land and Law of Transactions] (Tokyo University Press, 1960).
24. *Ch'ing-yüan t'iao-fa shih-lei*, pp. 492-494.
25. *Sung hsing-t'ung*, Vol. 1, p. 7.
26. It was called *Tang-chih ssu*. Cf. *Sung hui-yao kao*, "Hsing-fa," 3:54b-55a.
27. *Chiang-su chin-shih chih* [Stone Inscriptions of Kiangsu Province] (Chiang-su

t'ung-chih chu, 1927) 15:31b-32a. Cf. an inscription dated 1228. The two *lü* provisions cited here are found in *Sung hsing-t'ung* , Vol. 1, pp. 425–426.

28. This principle was established during the second half of the eleventh century. This principle was also discussed in a memorial submitted by Chou Lin to the Kao-tsung emperor (r. 1127-1162). Cf. *Li-tai ming-ch'en tsou-i* [Memorials Submitted by Famous Officials of the Various Dynasties], 217:4b-5a. Cf. also *Sung hui-yao k'ao*, "Chih-kuan," 48-14.
29. Ma Tuan-lin, *Wen-hsien t'ung-k'ao* [Compendium of Historical Institutions], 167:37 (a memorial of 1168).
30. *Sung hui-yao kao*, "Hsing-fa," 5:48 (a memorial of 1221). Cf. also, Hsü Dau-lin, "Fan-i pieh-k'an k'ao" [A Study of the Principle of Repudiation of Confession and New Trials], *Tung-fang tsa-chih fu-k'an*, Vol. 6, No. 2 (1972), pp. 20–28. Hsü presents a detailed and amply documented account of the many changes in this principle from its first introduction under the T'ang in 653 A.D. He points out that there were always limitations on the number of new trials as well as punishment for a defendant making groundless allegations of error.
31. In 1148 the officials and clerks of two prefectures were found to have unlawfully stuffed rags into the mouths and ears of suspects, and completely blindfolded them—apparently to prevent denial of guilt. This led to two separate cases of misidentification of offenders, with the result that in one case an offender was mistakenly executed instead of banished. In another case, an offender was erroneously banished instead of sentenced to the less severe punishment of blows of the heavy bamboo. An edict was issued to the effect that henceforth, prior to execution, offenders should be accompanied by their relatives so as to assure that no similar errors took place. Cf. Ma, *Wen-hsien t'ung-k'ao* 167:33b-34b. Also see note 29 above, and *Ch'ing-yüan t'iao-fa shih-lei*, p. 500.
32. *Sung hui-yao kao*, "Hsing-fa," 4:73. In 1033 the prefect of Ch'i-chou and many other officials were degraded because they imposed too severe a sentence upon an offender. Only an official named Liu Huan was permitted to retain his position, apparently because he had submitted a letter of protest during the adjudication (even though he had supported the prefect in the final decision).
33. *Ibid.*, 4:93a-94b.
34. Ma, *Wen-hsien t'ung-k'ao*, and *Sung hui-yao kao*, "Hsing-fa," 4:57.
35. Note 29, above.
36. *Liang-che chin-shih chih* [Inscriptions on Stone and Metal in the Province of Chekiang] (Che-chiang shu-chü, 1890) 13:12a-17b (a stone inscription of 1264 A.D.).
37. *Ch'ing-ming chi*, pp. 200–201.
38. *Liang-chih* means two types of secretaries, of upper and lower rank, who advised the emperor when requested.
39. Ma, *Wen-hsien t'ung-k'ao* 170:6b-8. Cf. also Hsü Dau-lin, *Chung-kuo fa-chih-shih lun-lüeh* [Brief Discussion of Chinese Legal History] (Taipei, 1953), pp. 73–79, for a detailed discussion of this case.
40. The number of criminals sentenced to death was 800 in 1004, 2,436 in 1025,

2,560 in 1060, 1,683 in 1062, and 1,832 in 1065. Cf. Ma, *Wen-hsien t'ung-k'ao*, 166:38b; 167:2a-b; 167:5b; and 167:6.

41. Hung Mai, *Jung-chai san-pi* [The Third Volume of Jung-chai's Collected Essays], a Sung work, *chüan* 16, an article entitled "To-she chang-o" [Evils Resulting from Overly Frequent Amnesties].
42. See my article entitled "Ōanseki no rishi gōtsu saku" [Wang An-shih's Policy of Combining Officials and Clerks], *Ajiashi kenkyū*, Vol. 2 (Kyoto, 1957), pp. 311-364.
43. Li T'ao, *Hsü tzu chih t'ung-chien ch'ang-pien* [Detailed Supplement to the Comprehensive Mirror for Aid in Government] (Che-chiang shu-chü, 1881), 244:2, 334:17b.
44. *Ibid., 264:6.*
45. See note 8 above.
46. See note 39 above.
47. The book was named for one Teng Ssu-hsien who is said to have taught the art of litigation in his village school. Cf. Chen Kua, *Meng-hsi pi-t'an* (Ssu-pu ts'ung-k'an hsü-pien ed., Shanghai, 1934), 25:7a.
48. *Hsü tzu-chih t'ung-chien ch'ang-pien*, 374:21b.
49. *Sung hui-yao kao*, "Hsing-fa," 3:26.
50. *Chien-yen i-lai hsi-nien yao-lu* [Brief Chronological Record of Events Dating from the Chien-yen Reign] (Kuang-ya ts'ung-shu ed., Canton, 1920), 126:11a.

I V

COMMERCIAL CONTRACT LAW IN LATE NINETEENTH-CENTURY TAIWAN

Rosser H. Brockman

This chapter seeks to examine traditional Chinese contract law. Taiwan in the late nineteenth century was selected because of the unique quality of the materials compiled by the Survey Commission established by the Japanese colonial authorities in Taiwan to study the indigenous customary law.[1] On the theory that the purely contractual aspects of transactions would be revealed most clearly where contracts were used on a regular basis between knowledgeable parties and where the goods in question did not have great cultural significance and were not subject to a high level of governmental regulation, contracts involving land and other forms of real property were largely avoided. Instead, primary emphasis has been placed in this chapter on the ordinary types of commercial transactions that merchants commonly engaged in during their regular course of business.[2] Contracts involving personal property, loans unsecured by pledges of real property, services, partnerships and other forms of traditional contracts have been discussed elsewhere.[3] Formal codified law and court procedure are treated to the extent they are relevant.

Taiwan in the Nineteenth Century

Taiwan in the nineteenth century shared many basic characteristics with the rest of Chinese society, but it also possessed several distinctive features.[4] The most striking difference, of course, was that Taiwan is an island, located ninety miles from the southern Chinese mainland at the closest point. The Taiwan Strait which separates it from Fukien province on the mainland is a treacherous body of water, and crossing it was a difficult and dangerous undertaking. As a result, the settlement of Taiwan occurred later than the opening of the rest of South China. Permanent settlements began only in the late Ming dynasty after 1573,[5] but by the early nineteenth century more than two million Chinese had migrated to the island[6] and by 1892, the population totaled more than 2.5

0-691-09238-9/80/000076-61$03.05/1

million, and by 1905, 3 million.[7] Although virtually all of this emigration was from the Southern Chinese provinces of Fukien and Kwangtung across the Strait, there was a great deal of diversity among the settlers. On the mainland, people felt strong attachments to their native areas and those from the same place tended to maintain close mutual associations wherever they went.

In the early settlement of Taiwan the population was composed of four distinct groups: the people from Ch'üan-chou in Fukien, from Chang-chou in the same province, from Ch'ao-chou in Kwangtung, and the Hakkas from the hill country along the Fukien-Kwangtung border.[8] These people were all ethnically Chinese but spoke different dialects and to some extent followed different customs. Most of them felt stronger ties to their native areas across the Strait than they did to each other.

The late settlement of Taiwan meant that frontier conditions prevailed there until well into the nineteenth century. Chinese officials sent from the mainland to Taiwan reported that the society there was wild and lawless. Numerous conflicts between the four major groups of immigrants occurred and the general state of disorder was reflected in the common description of Taiwan: "every three years an outbreak, every five years a rebellion."[9]

In part, this was due to a lack of concern by the government in Peking. Taiwan was far away and the emperors of the Ch'ing Dynasty (1644-1911) appeared to be more interested in the military campaigns they conducted from time to time in Central Asia. With the necessity of a dangerous sea passage and the prevailing social disorder, Taiwan was not considered a choice official post and the bureaucrats assigned there were said to be less competent and often more corrupt than most.[10]

However, by the period relevant to this study, the late nineteenth century, the worst aspects of social disorder had subsided and the Chinese government had made efforts to incorporate Taiwan completely into the empire and to improve administration of the island. The development of sea trade along the China coast in the nineteenth century increased the importance of Taiwan, which was situated in the middle of the trade routes. In 1874 a Japanese military expedition landed in the southeast of Taiwan and occupied part of the island in retaliation for the deaths of 54 Ryūkyūan sailors who had been killed by aborigines[11] on the east coast of Taiwan in 1871.[12] By this time the Ch'ing government had realized the strategic importance of the island, carried out an administrative reorganization there and began a program of "self-strengthening" under the energetic Governor Liu Ming-ch'uan.[13] In 1884 Taiwan was threatened by the French fleet during the Sino-French War of that year. After this, Taiwan reached the peak of its importance to the Chinese government. Before, the island had been administered as part of Fukien province. But in 1886, it was granted full provincial status and the self-strengthening program proceeded apace.[14] Any benefit of the progress made was lost to China, however, in 1895 when Taiwan was ceded to Japan as part of the Treaty of Shimonoseki.

The important point here is that during the period relevant to this study, Taiwan was thoroughly Chinese. There were distinctive features about Taiwan, to be sure, but regional variations existed throughout China. If any one place can be considered typical of a country as large and diverse as China, then Taiwan was probably as typical a representative of the whole as any other province. This does not mean that every custom found in Taiwan was also present throughout the rest of China. Very few customs were uniform in every part of the country. But it does mean that the practices there can be taken as typical of Chinese practices in general.

Chinese Legal Ideology

Traditional Chinese legal ideology and thought, and especially the central concepts of *li* and *fa*, have been discussed in various places at length.[15] Yet none of these discussions focuses on the aspect of traditional legal thought most relevant to the subject of this paper: The attitude taken by individual Chinese toward the rights and obligations which flow from formal contractual relationships. It should be emphasized that the following discussion does not concern the political concept of rights enjoyed by the individual *vis-à-vis* the state or the society. Instead it is confined to the narrower topic of contractual rights and obligations created between individuals by their own voluntary acts.

In the literature, much has been made of the Chinese predisposition toward compromise, and it is said that in Chinese society "rights consciousness" was not well developed.[16] This is supposed to be in stark contrast with the modern Western countries in which people are said to be acutely aware of their "rights" and anxious to assert them. However, in the area of concern to this study, this generalization seems to be greatly exaggerated on both sides. In contracts, and especially in commercial transactions, legal scholarship in the United States has indicated that among American businessmen, at least, there is a greater predisposition to compromise contract disputes than to assert rights to the full extent that the law allows.[17] Although it might seem surprising in a country that glorifies the "sanctity of contract," the fact remains that very few contract cases are brought to court in the United States.[18]

In traditional China, on the other hand, people who dealt regularly with business contracts, especially merchants and moneylenders, were far more conscious of their rights and anxious to protect them than the usual stereotype would lead one to believe. It is important to distinguish two aspects of this problem: awareness of one's rights and willingness to compromise. Chinese merchants, much as American businessmen, may have been willing to compromise when involved in disputes, but this does not mean that they were unaware of the obligations owed to them under the contracts they created and did not expect that those obligations would be performed in full in the everyday course of business. It will be shown below that in the creation of contracts in traditional China, rights were very well defined. The parties were careful to specify their reciprocal rights and obligations in the contracts themselves. In addition, there were generated out of trade practices and usages a number of well developed and relatively precise rules which provided for a determination and allocation of the rights and obligations of the parties on the occurrence of certain contingencies. These contextual rules provided for such things as the shifting of risks, responsibility of the seller for defects in the goods, and the distribution of loss on the occurrence of a calamity. Moreover, the parties were very concerned with protecting their rights. This was especially difficult in the absence of easy access to a judicial system which regularly enforced contracts, and the parties went to great lengths to provide for ways to insure that performance would be completed in the terms and structures of the contracts they created. As far as commercial transactions were concerned, the level of "rights consciousness" in traditional Taiwan was no obstacle to the creation and effective use of contracts. When a contract was breached or an unanticipated event affected the performance of that contract, the consequences that would ordinarily ensue for the parties were well known. Each party was aware of where the losses would fall, what rights he possessed, and what duties he owed. The parties did not enter the contract on the basis of some ill-defined promise of good faith with later disputes to be settled on the basis of a mutual sense of natural justice.

Contract Law and Custom

Custom as a Source of Substantive Law and an Instrument for Enforcement

Discussions of contract law in the United States typically focus on enforcement. What promises should be enforced? What events will excuse performance? How should enforcement take place?[19] This preoccupation with enforcement tends to overlook the first function of any system of contract: to provide a framework within which people can reach agreements, make bargains, carry out transactions and in general order their affairs.

Contract law provides such a framework by performing a number of functions which can be roughly classified into the following categories:

1. The communicative function: Contracts provide a form and a language which communicates, as unambiguously as possible, the terms of an agreement to the immediate parties and other interested persons who may not have taken part in the bargaining process. This language must be understandable during the preliminary negotiations, when the agreement is put in final form, and later in time and at distant locations where the contract may be implemented or a dispute may arise. As a result, contract language tends to become stereotyped, as certain terms and phrases are developed and conventionally accepted over the years as expressing and producing unambiguous legal results. Creative drafting techniques are discouraged and the equivalent of contract form books come into use. Problems in mutual understanding exist everywhere but were perhaps even more intense in traditional China where local dialects and widely varying levels of literacy made clear communication all the more difficult.[20]

2. The policing function: Contract law allows a society to determine what types of agreements will not be permitted in that society, whether for reasons of tradition, prevailing concepts of morality, feelings of fairness or natural justice, or considerations of public policy.

3. The instrumental function: Contract law determines what types of agreements can be freely made in practice. By directing the attention of the parties to the provisions in frequent use, contract law indicates the proper subject matter for bargaining by them.

4. The prescriptive function: Contract law may prescribe some of the terms of an agreement, by making them either compulsory or presumptive. In this way a whole series of terms may automatically become part of the contract unless specifically altered or denied by the parties. These may include in the case of sales, for example, where delivery is to take place and by what means, who bears the risk of loss before delivery is made, and whether the seller is responsible for latent defects which appear after the buyer has received delivery of the goods. Acceptance of these prescribed terms becomes common for most transactions because it is simpler and easier for the parties to fix the primary terms—price, quantity, time of delivery—by negotiation and allow the usual commercial practices to govern the other terms of the contract.

As can be seen from the above, most of the ways in which contract law shapes and channels private agreements into certain molds draw directly from trade and commercial practices. Moreover, custom influences the restorative and corrective rules which are applied by courts when contract cases are brought before them. Karl Llewellyn has pointed out that there is inevitably a tension between statutory and case law, which of necessity must be rigid and consistent, and commercial customs and expectations, which are by their nature dynamic and evolve over time.[21]

When legal and nonlegal norms diverge too widely, pressure will be brought to reform the laws and to bring them closer into conformity with the prevailing practices, either through legislation or judicial interpretation.

In addition to being rigid, law is of necessity incomplete since it is impossible to anticipate and provide rules in advance for the almost infinite variety of fact situations which may give rise to disputes. These cases falling into the "interstices" of the law may be dealt with only through analogy or judicial creativity, which draw on the prevailing trade practices and customary usages of the society, whether this is openly admitted, as it is in the U.S. Uniform Commercial Code,[22] or not.

If custom is important in the formation of substantive contract law rules, it is also important in the enforcement of contracts once made. As mentioned above, few contract cases are brought to court in the United States. The overwhelming majority of contracts which are entered into and performed every day are not enforced through the judicial machinery. It is possible that respect for contractual obligations in many cases may result from fear of the possible legal consequences, but it is likely that most are performed simply because performance is expected by the society. As Max Weber has pointed out, "The broad masses of participants (in a rational legal order) act in a way corresponding to legal norms, not out of obedience to a legal obligation, but either because the environment approves of the conduct and disapproves of its opposite, or merely as a result of unreflective habituation to a regularity of life that has engraved itself as a custom."[23]

Custom as a Source of Contract Law in Taiwan

In traditional Taiwan, custom was far more important in the formation of contract law than it is in the United States, both in the creation of substantive rules and enforcement. There was no relevant legislation, which meant that the rules in use were taken almost entirely from the social practices and customary usages of the people. Moreover, the courts in Taiwan did not generate rules for the law of contract as common law courts did. When contract cases were brought before the local magistrate (and very few ever made it beyond him to the appellate level), he would not attempt to formulate law. Rather he would deliberately decide the case in accordance with local custom. His task was confined to the establishment of the facts of the case, the determination of the local custom, and the application of the latter to the former. In determining the local customs, the magistrate could turn to a number of different sources of information—his local assistants, village headmen, guild leaders, and other prominent persons in the community. In addition, the magistrate would frequently require that the parties first submit to mediation and would hold a formal trial only if mediation failed to produce a settlement. In mediated cases, local custom was likely to be just as or more important than in formal trials, because the mediators were very often the same people the magistrate depended on as sources of information about custom, especially the local headmen.

The actual influence of local custom, however, was even more dramatic than its use in the courts would suggest because very few contract cases were ever brought to the magistrate at all. David Buxbaum has attempted to show that the official legal system in China was more receptive to civil suits, than has previously been thought.[24] But, as will be shown below, the local courts were not effective as instruments of contract enforcement or as sources of contract rules. Buxbaum's own figures indicate that few contract cases were brought to court.[25] Moreover, the nature of judicial treatment of contracts made it unlikely that parties would perceive the legal system as an imminent threat that would hold them to the terms of their bargain if they failed to perform. The courts favored the same type of mediation that was available outside the judicial system and contract claims that did reach final judgment were compromised with only partial performance being required.

To an extent, the enforcement of these contracts depended on the types of informal community pressures and social controls that have been shown to operate in cohesive communities in the absence of a formalized legal system.[26] However, the difficulty with exclusive dependence on this type of enforcement for contract has been well stated by Llewellyn:

> These types of sanctions [i.e. informal pressures and long-run mutual dependence] fail in a society mobile as to institution, mobile as to residence, mobile as to occupation; they fail increasingly as the market expands spatially and in complexity. They fail, in a word, as to long-run, long-range, impersonal bargains, as also in cases where death, or transfer of rights, removes from the relation what may at the outset have been a personal aspect.[27]

Yet commerce in Taiwan was carried on in a very complex market. Rice, sugar, and camphor, to mention only the most prominent commodities, were purchased from all over the island by large merchants in the coastal cities and exported in huge quantities to the Chinese mainland. Large amounts of goods were also imported from the mainland and elsewhere and then distributed throughout the island. Most of the transactions in this large-scale trade were "long-run, long-range, impersonal bargains." Moreover, even on the local level the extent to which guilds, clans, and village organizations could effectively exercise control was limited. The basic difficulty they faced was that of jurisdiction. Guilds, for example, could control their own members through sanctions ranging up to expulsion. But most of the guilds were organized by trades, and the only disputes likely to occur among the members of the same trade would relate to maintenance of their monopoly, disputes over prices charged, debts among members, and so forth. Any transactional disputes, on the other hand, as between supplier and purchaser, would typically be between members of different guilds or between a guild member and one not associated with any guild. In this situation, the guild had no controlling authority. It may have had an interest in settling the dispute, especially when relations with another important guild were at stake, and it could seek to influence the parties; but it could not use any of its sanctions against the nonmember and dictate the outcome of the case. Clans and village organizations also faced this problem when disputes arose with nonmembers. So, even on the local level, many transactions were not subject to the type of group pressure seen by Llewellyn as essential in the absence of formal legal enforcement.

Thus, commerce in Taiwan was not restricted to local areas or to members of the same social communities as one might expect from the lack of easy access to the courts and effective enforcement from the formal legal system. A high level of "impersonal" commerce existed, both locally and at long range. This was made possible not by the use of the judicial system nor by dependence on informal social controls but rather by the development of contract forms and substantive contract rules which incorporated mechanisms of self-enforcement and self-execution directly into the contracts themselves. The prominent role played by third-party guarantors in loan contracts in China has been noted before.[28] But other devices, such as advance deposit payments and provisions for simultaneous performance, were equally important. Moreover, other contract rules, such as the allocation of the risk of fortuitous loss and the responsibility of the seller for defects after the buyer had accepted delivery of the goods, were designed to strengthen these self-enforcing features.

This self-enforcement was by no means total or perfect. There were some situations in which it did not work at all and others where it was weak. But the self-enforcing and self-executing provisions written into these contracts enabled their use and made them effective in a much wider range of circumstances than would have been otherwise possible. Moreover, it allowed contract to develop into a very flexible and useful tool. It might be thought that the absence of meaningful legal enforcement would restrict the contract forms to simple types of limited use. But, to the contrary, the contracts in use were very sophisticated and well adapted to the uses they secured. For example, the rice merchants were able to devise contracts which provided these self-enforcing safeguards and at the same time allowed them to contract for future goods and to shift the risk of price changes between themselves at will.

The fact that the formal legal system did not adequately provide for the enforcement of contract did not mean that a vigorous system of contract was prevented nor did it merely transfer the problem into the hands of local and less effective groups. Rather, contracts continued to be used effectively, all the more so because their provisions for self-enforcement allowed them to be used largely independent of both the demands of the formal legal system and the pressures of local social organizations.

Formal Legal Regulation of Civil Cases in Taiwan

The Basic Level Court

The official legal system in China during the Ch'ing period coincided, more or less, with the governmental administrative system. Cases were first heard by the lowest-level government official, the district magistrate. Appeals could be made to the provincial level government and from there to the central government in Peking. At the latter two levels, legal matters were handled by specialized personnel who devoted their entire efforts to their judicial tasks, but at the district level, legal matters were only part, although a very important part, of the magistrate's general administrative duties. His staff was composed both of retainers who formed part of his own entourage and traveled with him from post to post and of assistants from the local area who remained at one district office or *yamen* and aided the magistrates assigned there. The magistrate received no formal legal training and was forced to depend on advice from the members of his staff who specialized in the law ("legal secretaries" and "financial secretaries"),[29] administrative handbooks, and his own wits.

Moreover, the scope of his legal duties was extremely broad. He received complaints, investigated them, arrested and interrogated criminals, heard cases in courts, passed judgment, and administered punishment. The magistrate was, then, at the same time policeman, detective, district attorney, judge, and jury. In addition, since there were no authorized advocates to represent defendants in court, the magistrate also performed the role of protecting the defendants' rights (to the extent they were protected at all). Thus, without the benefit of a legal education, the magistrate was forced to perform a vast variety of legal duties while at the same time carrying out what were perhaps even more vital administrative tasks—collecting taxes, keeping order, public works, and all the rest. This precluded the development of specialized expertise or even familiarity with any but the most common legal problems for all but the most gifted and conscientious magistrates.[30]

The main body of law to be administered by the basic level magistrate was to be found in the *Ch'ing Code (Ta Ch'ing lü-li)* which was revised periodically, but the legal jurisdiction of the magistrate was not limited to the topics treated in the Code. His authority extended to all disputes within his district whether dealt with in the Code or not. Indeed, in most of the cases used in this study the Code was never even mentioned. Without this extended jurisdiction, the magistrate would have been confined within very narrow limits because the Code was primarily concerned with what today would be classified as criminal law and neglected most of the topics that are now considered civil law, especially in the area of commercial activity.

Treatment of Civil Law in the Ch'ing Code

The Ch'ing Code dealt almost exclusively with criminal matters. There were statutes concerning such traditionally civil matters as land law and marriage law, but very few of these Code provisions were directed at the ordinary, nonpenal regulation that is usually associated with civil as opposed to criminal law.[31] For example, of the eleven statutes in the Code section dealing with land, six actually concerned forms of theft: Article 90, fraudulent evasion of the land tax; Article 93, fraudulent sales of land and tenants; Article 96, cultivation of lands belonging to others; Article 98, destruction of tools and crops; Article 99, taking fruit from orchards without permission; and Article 100, misappropriation of boats and carriages belonging to the government. The marriage statutes also dealt primarily with the criminal aspects of marriage: Article 102, selling one's wife; Article 105, marriage under forbidden circumstances such as during the legally imposed period of mourning following the death of a parent; and Article 112, the abduction and forced marriage of a woman from a respectable family.[32] Heavy penalties were provided for violations of all of these. The criminal nature of these provisions should be apparent.

The general neglect of civil law in the Code is even more evident in the area of greatest importance to this paper: commercial affairs. Of the 436 statutes in the Code, only eight dealt at all with what is usually called commercial law. The following is a summary of the full extent of commercial regulation found in the Ch'ing Code:[33]

Article 149: Usury. Interest on a loan may not exceed 3 percent of principal per month. On repayment, the total interest may not exceed the amount of the principal. Punishment for violation shall be 40-100 blows in proportion to the amount of illegitimate interest charged. A debtor who fails to pay a valid debt when due shall be punished with 10-60 blows depending on the amount due and the period the debt has remained unpaid. The debt shall remain lawfully due.

A creditor who himself violently seizes the property of a defaulting debtor in satisfaction of the debt shall be punished with 80 blows. A creditor who accepts the wives or children of his debtor as security shall be punished with 100 blows.

Article 150: Bailment. A bailee who misappropriates the property of another shall be liable for a maximum penalty of 90 blows and two and one-half years' banishment. The bailee shall not be responsible if he can establish that the loss was due to fire or other natural causes. A bailee who refuses to acknowledge that he was entrusted with property shall be deemed guilty of fraud. Should he turn over the property to another who misappropriates it, each shall be guilty of theft in an amount equal to the value of the property.

(Substatutes.) If pawned property is destroyed by fire, the pawnbroker must indemnify the owner full value if the fire originated on the premises and 80 percent of full value if the fire originated outside. If pawned property is stolen, the pawnbroker must indemnify the owner for 75 percent of full value if the robbery was committed by force of arms and full value in all other cases. The value of a pawned article for these purposes shall be twice the amount loaned on it. In each case, the interest due on the loan may be deducted.

The owner of a dyeshop must report to the local authorities all articles in his shop destroyed by fire. The authorities will fix a value for them and the dyer must indemnify the owners 50 percent of the fixed value, if the fire originated in the shop, and 30 percent of the fixed value, if the fire originated outside.

Article 151: Lost Property. A finder of lost property must deliver it to the government authorities within five days. Failure to do so will be considered theft.

Article 152: License of Commercial Agents. The government shall authorize a commercial agent for each city, public market, and village district, who shall keep a register of ships and merchants. Anyone who acts in this capacity without license shall be punished with 60 blows and shall forfeit to the government his profits therefrom.

Article 153: Valuation of Merchandise. The commercial agent shall value merchandise at a fair level. Any agent who deviates from this standard shall be punished in proportion to the gravity of the offense.

Article 154: Monopolizers and Unfair Traders. Anyone who realizes an exorbitant profit through monopoly or other undue influence in the market or who, in collusion with a commercial agent or otherwise, manipulates prices to his own advantage shall be punished with 80 blows and shall be deemed guilty of theft in the amount of the excess profit.

Article 155: False Weights, Measures and Scales. Anyone who makes, procures, or uses false weights, measures, or scales in the public market or who alters those issued or sanctioned by the government shall be punished with 60 blows.

Article 156: Substandard Manufacture. Anyone who manufactures goods of lower quality than he represents them to be or lower than the established or customary standard shall be punished with 50 blows.

From the above, it is evident that the Code regulation of commercial activities was very limited in scope. Little of what is ordinarily considered commercial law today is mentioned at all. And what is mentioned is dealt with almost entirely in penal terms. There are no nonpenal remedies available. The only action that can be taken against a defaulting debtor is to apply a criminal punishment, flogging. There is no process by which the magistrate may force the debtor actually to pay. He cannot seize the debtor's assets or force his employer to pay over his wages to satisfy the debt. In addition, the creditor's own self-help is discouraged. He cannot act on his own but must appeal to the magistrate and hope that the threat of punishment will be enough to induce payment. The Code provisions are phrased in terms of the criminal law. Certain activities are punished because they amount to fraud or are the equivalent of theft. The extraction of usurious interest or monopoly profit is considered larceny and punished accordingly. The use of false weights and measures is fraud and criminally wrong. Duress is an important element in these offenses. A creditor cannot seize a debtor's property or family members. Monopolizers cannot use "undue influence" in the market. The only instance where compensation is paid without a clear finding of the defendant's culpability and is not accompanied by penal sanctions is in the bailment context, where pawnbrokers and dyers must pay those whose property was lost in a fire that was not due to the shopkeeper's negligence or intent. But even there the fault principle is not completely absent. The shopkeeper must pay more if the fire started inside his shop than if it spread there from neighboring property. There seems to be a suggestion that he is more "responsible" or "culpable" for a fire originating on the premises, and accordingly must pay a larger sum.

Thus, while some aspects of commercial law were dealt with in the Code, if the distinction between civil and criminal depends, as Buxbaum seems to suggest,[34] on whether a criminal penalty is provided, then the Code treatment of these aspects of commercial law is certainly not civil as that term is commonly understood today. However commercial law cases were actually dealt with in the courts, in the Ch'ing Code they were viewed as criminal offenses and punished as crimes.

Application of the Code to Civil Matters in Taiwan

In addition to the incompleteness of the Code in regard to commercial matters, in Taiwan at least the laws that did exist in the Code were not uniformly applied even where they were directly relevant. For example, the usury statute seems to have been a dead letter. Pawnshops on Taiwan regularly charged more than the 3 percent per month or 36 percent per year allowed by Article 149 of the Code. The regulations of the Tainan pawnshop organization contained a fee schedule that reached 8 percent per month for loans of 10 *ch'ien* to 1 *yüan*; 6 percent per month for loans of 1 *yüan* to 5 *yüan*; 5 percent for 5 to 15 *yüan*; and 4 percent for 15 to 30 *yüan*. The posted rates did not reach as low as the legally prescribed maximum until the loan exceeded 30 *yüan*.[35] Loans made in high-risk situations commanded equally high rates. Shipping goods across the Taiwan Strait was very dangerous, and commercial loans to ships involved in trade with the mainland commanded such high rates that there was a special name for it: "interest sent to sea" (*fang-shui li*). This type of interest was calculated on the basis of a round trip and both the duration of the loan and the rate varied according to the port of destination. Interest charged for a round trip to Foochow across the Strait from Taipei, which usually took one month, was 7 percent. Up the mainland coast to Chenhai and back to Taipei was 15 percent for a four-month trip. A voyage all the way to Tientsin near Peking and back took six months and bore an interest rate of 20 percent per trip.[36] These high rates were due entirely to the riskiness of the voyage. These were loans to substantial businessmen. Similar loans to merchants in Taipei would probably have commanded interest rates of no more than 1.5 percent a month.

Another custom of long standing in Taiwan which was not overruled by the district magistrates even though it was directly contradicted in the Code concerned the time limit during which *tien*, which has been called a mortgage or pledge but which was really a type of sale of real property with a retained right of redemption, was effective. Under the terms of *tien*, real property was transferred in return for a sum of money. The property could be redeemed by the seller at any time on repayment of the original sum.[37] The Ch'ing Code provided that if the right of redemption was not exercised within thirty years, it lapsed and the sale became permanent. Despite this, in Taiwan redemption could be made long after the thirty-year period. In 1902 the Appeals Court of the Japanese colonial government determined that *tien* redemption had long been allowed in Taiwan beyond the period specified in the Code and, because it was the policy of the Japanese government to honor local customs in cases involving local citizens, upheld the right of redemption beyond the thirty-year period in the case at bar.[38]

Other provisions of the Code were observed in some places but not others. Article 149 provided that interest collected on a debt at the time of repayment could not exceed the amount of the principal. The Japanese Appeals Court found that this was, in fact, the custom in the area around Tainan[39] and in Taipei but that this was not true of the island as a whole.[40] Interestingly, the Japanese considered this so irrational that it was one of the few local customs to be specifically overruled in the colonial courts.[41]

Civil Cases in the Courts

If the Code treatment of commercial law was restricted in scope, the opportunities to apply what few laws existed were also rare. Despite Buxbaum's effort to prove that many of the cases actually taken to court involved civil law matters, a close examination of his own data show that commercial cases were very rarely brought to court. About 70 percent of the civil cases heard by the Tanshui and Hsinchu magistrates concerned land, which was subject to a high degree of government regulation through the land registries and the land tax. Only about 5 percent of the cases examined by Buxbaum involved debts, and the commercial transaction cases numbered 3 over a period of 106 years for an insignificant 0.2 percent.[42]

In addition to the failure of the Code to deal comprehensively with commercial affairs and the infrequency with which such cases appeared in the courts, the impact of the legal system on local commerce was further limited by a general tendency in Chinese legal administration to be flexible in the application of existing laws. It was felt that achieving justice in the circumstances of an individual case was more important than rigid adherence to the letter of the law. This general tendency can be seen clearly in *Tso-chih yao-yen* [Precepts for Local Administrative Officials] written in 1785 by Wang Hui-tsu, a legal secretary who worked for many years for a number of district magistrates. In a passage that would horrify American judicial advocates of the doctrine of *stare decisis* but might please a practicing lawyer who seeks to distinguish a difficult case, Wang advises against a rigid application of the law.

> DO NOT QUOTE PRECEDENT TOO READILY
>
> Precedents are like traces of writing in ink: they indicate only a pattern and an outline, and that is all. If you insist on quoting one as a standard to be followed, this is like making a mark on a moving ship to show where to recover a sword that has been dropped over the side into the river. There is rarely one which exactly matches. . . . Human nature is infinitely varied and there never is a case which is exactly the same as one that has been decided before. If only to a small degree, there are differences, but this means you will have to ponder them at length. In doing this lies the way of saving life: in failing to do so lies equally the reason for sending in a mistaken report. . . .
>
> YOU MUST RESPECT LOCAL CUSTOMS
>
> The primary study for a legal secretary is to know the Code, but skill in its application depends still more on being in sympathy with the ways of the people. Now as customs often vary from place to place, it is essential to find out all about them, without preconception, and make it your chief concern to abide by them. If you never act on a penal law or an edict without first seeing that it does not conflict with what local custom values, then there will be harmony between *yamen* [district magistrate's office] and people, the magistrate's fame will spread, and his secretary's prestige will increase accordingly, whereas applying the law rigidly on every occasion would probably give rise to much dissatisfaction and complaint. There is an old saying: only by common consent can you promote good and dispel evil. This has stood the test of experience and should be borne in mind.[43]

The question of whether legal cases should be decided by the strict application of law or in accord with a sense of natural justice is, of course, an extremely important issue in the development of jurisprudence. Perhaps the most celebrated discussion of this issue is to be found in the writings of Max Weber, who distinguished "Khadi" justice, where the judge decides entirely on the basis of his own sense of what is right without reference to any rules or principles outside the instant case, from "formal rational" justice, in which cases are decided exclusively by strict adherence to a comprehensive set of man-made laws.[44] Weber's distinction has not been adequately discussed with reference to Chinese law.[45] But, as these passages from Wang's administrative handbook show, there was at least a strain of "Khadi" justice present in Chinese jurisprudence.

Furthermore, Wang was referring to the criminal law. In commercial law matters, this tendency was even more pronounced. There was a reasonably comprehensive body of criminal law while none existed for commercial affairs, and the government had much less direct interest in the legal regulation of commerce than it did in the suppression of crime and the maintenance of local order. For these reasons the magistrate was free to deal with the civil law, and especially commercial affairs, much more flexibly than he could with the criminal statutes.

A final factor which limited the impact of the legal system was the passive role in law making played by the basic level judges, the district magistrates. Unlike common law judges, they did not seek to generate legal rules through careful analysis of policy questions, estimations of the future effect of present rulings, and the establishment and observation of precedent. Instead, the magistrates would turn to local custom rather than statutory or case law as a source of rules.

In determining the content of the local customs, the magistrate, not himself a native of the area, was forced to depend on local sources of information—his assistants, local community leaders, wealthy gentry, guild leaders, rich merchants, and so forth. Of course, it would be possible for his "findings of fact" concerning custom to develop into the sort of law-generating activity that common law judges engage in. This was an uncertain business at best and a magistrate might be psychologically more inclined to select as the local practice something that appealed to his own sense of justice or reason, especially when his sources of information were in conflict and he had to choose between two or more alternatives. Once recognized as the prevailing custom in one case, it might well be applied to others, especially by the same magistrate, and might thus tend to acquire at least some of the force of binding precedent. But the difference in theory was clear: a custom was applied not because the magistrate thought it just or because it had been earlier recognized, but because it was in fact the local custom at the time of the suit. This theoretical distinction made a practical difference as well. There was no system of appellate review whereby higher level courts made their findings of law or fact binding on the district magistrates under their jurisdiction. The magistrates did not perceive their own previous findings as binding and they could easily depart from earlier decisions if they chose to. Most importantly, no litigant was bound by an earlier holding, and if he could show that a different local custom currently prevailed, the earlier decision would be disregarded.

Despite the very limited concern of the official legal system with commercial affairs, there did not arise a separate set of commercial courts independent of the government which could make and enforce their own rules. To a limited extent, guild tribunals handled disputes between guild members[46] but their jurisdiction did not extend beyond the narrow confines of their own trade. There were no courts with jurisdiction over all merchants doing business in a specific area that might be compared with the development of the "law merchant" in the cities of Europe during the Middle Ages,[47] or even with the more limited self-regulation of the urban merchant communities in Japan during the Tokugawa period (1603-1868).[48] The legal jurisdiction of the traditional Chinese state extended to all persons and disputes within its boundaries. Delegation of legal authority did occur, but only on an informal and always on a revocable basis. The Chinese government was very jealous of its control and would tolerate the exercise of power from other sources only if it felt that no real challenge to its own authority existed.

Consequently, commercial matters were, for the most part, effectively barred from any courts. The official legal system was not receptive to them, and no independent courts could develop. The types of regulation that did emerge had to be self-contained. They could not depend on the external compulsion of a tribunal for their effectiveness.

Civil Procedure

In order to appreciate the role played by custom in the official legal system and why that system was ineffective as a source of substantive contract law or an instrument of contract enforcement, it is important to understand the procedures that were applied to those few cases actually brought to court.

The Trial Process

Suits in respect to civil matters could be brought to the magistrate only on certain days. None at all could be brought during the period of greatest agricultural activity—the fourth through the seventh lunar months—and during the rest of the year they were to be received only on six specified days during each month.[49] The magistrate had to accept all pleas presented to him and was subject to a punishment of 80 blows for failure to do so. He could reject pleas which were of improper form or which failed to state a case or contained some obvious untruth, but all rejected pleas were posted on a public bulletin board outside the *yamen* with the reasons for rejection attached. Petitioners were allowed to revise and resubmit them freely.[50]

These pleas could be drafted by the parties themselves, but each *yamen* had an authorized scrivener who would compose them on request. Whether it was written by him or not, the plea had to have the scrivener's seal before the magistrate would receive it. For this service the scrivener charged a fee of 1 to 100 *yüan* depending on the wealth of the individual. In return for this fee, the scrivener performed limited guarantor functions. He guaranteed that the status[51] of the petitioner was stated correctly on the plea, and if the petitioner disappeared while the case was being considered, the scrivener was obliged to make a reasonable effort to find him. This was doubly useful to the magistrate. Not only were these services valuable, but also imposing these responsibilities on the scrivener encouraged him to make preliminary inquiries about the petitioners. This served as a screening procedure to keep out the more obvious charlatans and "litigation tricksters"[52] even before the plea had been presented to the magistrate. The requirement of having the scrivener's seal and thus his guarantee was waived for members of the gentry, the educated and economic elite. The magistrate already had access to information about them and since most of the gentry owned land that was registered with the *yamen*, it was more difficult for them to flee with their possessions and escape the magistrate's jurisdiction.[53]

On acceptance of a plea, the magistrate would send *yamen* "runners" (a group of *yamen* servants who performed various tasks such as guarding the magistrate and carrying messages) to investigate the facts of the case.[54]

After the investigation, a date would be set for trial and the plaintiff, the defendant, and any witnesses requested by them or the magistrate would be summoned to appear.[55] Questioning of all witnesses at the trial was done by the magistrate himself. The rules of evidence were very flexible. The magistrate was not confined to the information presented to him. He could collect evidence on his own and he could hear and consider any facts he felt relevant to the case. Torture was used to extract confessions in criminal cases, but apparently not in civil suits.[56]

Although the Ch'ing Code provided criminal penalties for civil-type cases as well as criminal ones, Sybille van der Sprenkel's statement that ". . . the unavoidable consequences of a legal case once started was punishment for at least one person. It could end in punishment for the accused, if judged guilty; if he were not, punishment would be assigned to the unjustified accuser . . ."[57] seems clearly unwarranted, as Buxbaum points out,[58] at least for civil cases in Taiwan. The cases examined in this study indicate that rarely if ever was criminal punishment applied in a case involving civil matters. If a debtor refused to pay a money judgment entered against him, flogging might be used to force him to do so. But a defendant was not punished simply because he was found to be in default of a debt. Nor was an unsuccessful plaintiff ever punished as a false accuser in the civil suits here examined.

The plaintiff did run a risk in bringing suit. Once the case had been submitted to the magistrate, the plaintiff lost all control over it. He could not restrict the magistrate to the issues or the facts raised in his plea. He could try to spur the magistrate to action by submitting additional pleas, but beyond this the conduct of the case was taken entirely out of his hands. A civil suit was not so much an adversarial process between the plaintiff and defendant as between the parties on the one hand and the magistrate on the other.

The magistrate could consider any relevant evidence and, if he felt the facts compelled it, could order the plaintiff to pay the defendant instead of the other way around. For example, in a suit in Heng-ch'un *hsien* in 1893, Ch'en Liang brought suit against Yü Yüan to recover 39 *yüan* which Yü allegedly owed him for credit purchases from Ch'en's butcher shop. However, on examination, the magistrate discovered that actually Yü had lent 700 *yüan* to Ch'en and his stepson Wang Neng. The meat had been taken by Yü as interest on the loan. After attempts at mediation had failed, the magistrate ordered Ch'en to repay the loan immediately.[59] Yet no criminal punishments were administered in this case and in most civil cases the defendant would only be directed to pay his debt or fulfill whatever obligation he had to the plaintiff with no penal sanction.

In addition, at any point in the proceedings the suit could be withdrawn at the request of the parties if they reached a private settlement,[60] whether this was done on their own accord, through the intervention of a third party, or at the direction of the magistrate. The Ch'en Liang-Yü Yüan case mentioned above included a dispute over a loan that Yü Yüan had made to his kinsman Yü Chiang. The magistrate directed the local headman (*tsung-li*) to mediate both disputes. Yü was unable to agree with Ch'en, but the disagreement with Yü Chiang was settled, the parties requested that the suit be dropped and the magistrate complied.[61] This practice was known as *ho-hsi*, "agreement and settlement." The magistrate would inscribe these characters on the plea to indicate that the case had been withdrawn before decision.[62]

If the parties reached a private settlement, they were left to arrange between themselves how its provisions were to be carried out, although a court-directed mediated settlement could be given the force of a court order. When the magistrate decided the case, the parties could appeal if they wished. If not, they had to sign a consent bond, *kan-chieh-chuang*, agreeing to obey the magistrate's order, usually to pay a sum of money. If it appeared that the defendant was unlikely to pay, because of a lack of resources or a reputation for recalcitrance, the magistrate, probably at the insistence of the plaintiff, could require a guaranty bond, *pao-chieh-chuang*, signed by a third party who agreed to pay if the defendant did not.[63]

If the defendant refused to sign the consent bond or refused to pay after signing it, the magistrate had few ways to execute the judgment. As noted above, the Code did not permit direct judicial seizure of the assets of a debtor and apparently the magistrates did not develop this technique on their own. They were restricted to the use of indirect coercive means, imprisonment, or the flogging provided for debtors in Article 149 of the Code.[64]

A literal reading of Article 149 gives the impression that a failure to pay one's creditor was itself a punishable offense and anyone found guilty would be flogged. However, actual legal practice in Taiwan shows that Article 149 was used only to enforce a court judgment. In the course of the trial, the debt itself was not considered criminal and was not punished as a crime. Criminal sanctions were used in the administration of the civil law, but only as a way to force payment of a debt. This is similar to some types of contract remedies in the United States today, such as specific performance where a court cannot compel performance directly but must rely on imprisonment or a fine for contempt of court to force performance indirectly.

It is unclear how much influence the creditor had in the application of this punishment to a debtor who refused to obey a court order. In the rest of the trial process the magistrate took complete control and the creditor could do little to affect the course of events besides agree to a private settlement. However, at least in civil suits, the general tendency was for the magistrate not to act unless prodded by one of the parties, so it was probably unlikely that the magistrate would punish the debtor (or even be aware of his failure to pay) unless asked to do so by the creditor. But even then the magistrate would not act automatically. Instead, he would examine the circumstances, hear the debtor, and then decide whether the punishment should be applied.

The Case of Hsü Ting

The following documents are from a case in Heng-ch'un *hsien* in 1883 and give some idea of the court procedures used in civil cases. A shopkeeper, Hsü Ting, brought suit against a customer, Wang Chin-kao, to collect for sales made to him on credit.

The plaintiff's request for a trial is written on a *chuang-shih-chih*, the most common type of document used for this purpose.[65] It was sold to him by the *yamen* scrivener, who also composed the plea for the illiterate plaintiff. It is a rectangular piece of paper folded over. The plaintiff's name and the scrivener's seal are on the outside while the text of the plea is on the inside of the document. The outside is arranged in vertical rows:

Petitioner
Hsü Ting

Representative
(blank)

Age
33

Runner Clerk
(blank) (blank)

Residence
this city [Heng-ch'un]

Seal of the Scrivener with the Magistrate's Signature
Scrivener: Sung Huan-wen

Text of the plea:

The petitioner, the shopkeeper Hsü Ting, seeks to recover a debt not yet repaid. He implores you to exercise your compassion and examine [the case], recover [the debt] and quiet this incident among the people. Until now, [Hsü] Ting has earned his living by selling opium. Since the seventh year of the Kuang-hsü reign [1881], he has had transactions with Wang Chin-kao, a soldier in the Heng-ch'un garrison. Among these have been a number of credit sales which amount to a total of 38 *yüan* 3 *chiao* and 1 *ch'ien* in *fo-yin* [Mexican dollars]. There is indisputable proof of this in the records of the store. [Hsü] has repeatedly dunned him for repayment. No due date was set; the credit was extended month by month. [Hsü] appealed to him urgently during the first part of this month because [Hsü's] business took a turn for the worse, with creditors pressing him on all sides. Unexpectedly, [Wang Chin-]kao dared to fabricate stories and claimed that [Hsü] Ting owed him more than 160 *yüan*. [Wang Chin-] kao saw profit and forgot propriety. To come out ahead he neglected humanity. He sought to avoid repayment by making use of the soldiers' [fierce] reputation. This was clearly an attempt to intimidate [Hsü] Ting. He has been put in an unmanageable position and is slipping and falling to the right and to the left. How can this go on? [Hsü] asks that you, in your goodness, investigate and pursue [this case]. It is approaching winter and it will be hard for him to eat. How can his heart rest easy? [Hsü] begs for your sympathy and requests that you order the soldier Wang Chin-kao to come to court, be examined, and return [the money]. [In this way] the weak will achieve heaven, the masses [of people] will be strong, and the evil [ones] will be warned. Hard-earned capital will be returned and the good [*kung*] will last 10,000 generations. [This petition] is respectfully submitted.

Rescript of the Heng-ch'un *hsien* magistrate and manager of pacification:

The soldier Wang Chin-kao [is accused of] owing more than 30 *yüan* which has not been repaid. To the contrary he has fabricated confused accounts which say that he is owed 160 *yüan*. Whether this [accusation] is right or wrong, we transmit [this] to the Heng-ch'un garrison to have the soldier Wang Chin-kao sent to the *yamen* to submit his evidence [so we can] investigate and decide.

Kuang-hsü 9th year, 11th month, 13th day.[66]

The rescript above was written by the magistrate directly on the plea document. Next the magistrate issued an investigation warrant to a *yamen* runner.

Warrant

From the Heng-ch'un *hsien* magistrate:

In order that this affair be investigated. On the 13th day of the eleventh month this year, it was said by the shopkeeper Hsü Ting of this city that in his sales of opium he had had repeated dealings with the soldier Wang Chin-kao of the Heng-ch'un garrison beginning in [1881]. Altogether Wang owed him 38 *yüan*. Whenever they had dealings [Hsü] asked him to repay. [It went like this] from month to month. The first part of this month when [Hsü] pressed him for the debt, Wang Chin-kao unexpectedly claimed that he was owed 160 *yüan* [by Hsü]. Because of the soldiers' reputation [Hsü] cannot manage it himself. He asks that we investigate. So aside from having the soldier Wang Chin-kao questioned as ordered in the rescript, by this warrant, I order the runner to investigate this accusation by Hsü Ting to see whether it is right or wrong that Wang Chin-kao owes money which has not been repaid and that he falsely claims Hsü owes him 160 *yüan*. If this is true, make a report based on the facts and send a copy to the plaintiff, Hsü Ting. Bring the report to the *yamen* to use as evidence in the questioning and judgment. Go without delay. This is urgent. Kuang-hsü 9th year [1883], 11th month, 26th day.

Runner: Wu Fa
To be done today.[67]

SEAL OF THE *Yamen*

The runner investigated, Wang was questioned and judgment was entered for the plaintiff. A record of the judgment was kept at the *yamen* in a document called a *ming-tan*, literally "name list," which also includes a summary of the testimony of the parties and relevant witnesses.

Judgment

Runner: Wu Fa

Plaintiff: Hsü Ting
Defendant: Wang Chin-kao

We have heard the accusation of Hsü Ting that Wang Chin-kao has not repaid him; that he has repeatedly sold opium to Wang Chin-kao since [1881] and is still owed by him 38 *yüan*. Wang Chin-kao charged that Hsü owed him 160 *yüan*. Hsü disagreed. [I] questioned Hsü Ting, who said that Wang Chin-kao has repeatedly bought opium from him since [1881] and still owes him 38 *yüan*. He has presented a bill of account to Wang and has records of this for proof. Moreover, he appealed to Huang Tung-sheng and others to have Wang Chin-kao pay him 30 *yüan*. Wang Chin-kao, when examined, only denied [Hsü's testimony] in general. He did not point to specific facts. He said that two times last year Hsü borrowed from him a total of 48 *yüan* at 8 percent interest per month. But if so there should be documents as proof and there is no proof at all. This is an attempt to injure [Hsü]. I examined the receipts that Wang gave to Hsü. They matched Hsü Ting's accounts perfectly [and confirm his words]. Wang refused to pay on a pretext. This should be condemned. [It is necessary] to be lenient in these cases, but crafty [practices] should not develop. [People should] willingly and honestly recognize their debts. I order Wang Chin-kao to pay Hsü Ting 20 *yüan* to be repaid in three parts: on the 28th of the first month and the 28th of the 2nd month, 7 *yüan* will be repaid, and on the 28th of the 3rd month the remaining 6 *yüan* will be repaid. When repayment is complete, both parties will obey [this decree] and consider the case finished. It is so decreed.

11th month 28th day[68]

Wang and Hsü then signed consent bonds agreeing to the terms of the judgment. This is the one Hsü signed accepting 20 yüan repayment in 5 months in full satisfaction of his claim for 38 yüan.

Written bond of consent. Hsü Ting of this city today undertakes [this obligation]

Before the magistrate, [Hsü] Ting accused the soldier Wang Chin-kao of borrowing money and not repaying it. This case has been investigated and decided today. It is ordered that Wang Chin-kao pay 20 *yüan* to [Hsü] Ting: 7 *yüan* on the 28th of the 1st month [of next year] and 7 *yüan* on the 28th of the 2nd month. On the 28th of the third month, he must repay the remaining 6 *yüan*. These three payments will be accepted in complete satisfaction [of Wang's debt]. [Hsü] Ting will obey the law in conformity with this consent bond.

[-Sealed-]

Kuang-hsü 9th year, 11th month, 28th day.

[This is] consented to in writing: [Hsü Ting] thumb-print.[69]

This case is interesting for several reasons. The sum of money involved in the claim is relatively small. This was not a large transaction between business suppliers, but simply advances of credit by a retailer to a regular customer. This is the sort of case that might be handled in Small Claims Courts in the United States today. Moreover, the case was decided with remarkable speed. Only fifteen days lapsed from the filing of the plea to the issuing of judgment. This is very fast, even when compared to the statistics Buxbaum cites to show the usual swiftness of the traditional judicial machinery. Only 4 percent of his civil cases were settled in as few as fifteen days.[70] Of course, this was a simple case. The facts were uncomplicated and the parties were readily available so there was no cause for delay. Nevertheless, the dispatch with which it was handled is impressive. Finally, no penal sanctions were invoked against the defendant even though his debt and default were proved beyond doubt and even though his counterclaim was found to be entirely without merit, thus making him liable for punishment as a false accuser. Penal sanctions would be used only if the defendant failed to pay according to the terms of the consent bond.

All of this goes to support Buxbaum's view that traditional Chinese legal procedure was not as draconic as it has usually been portrayed and that there were few formal obstacles that would inhibit plaintiffs from bringing civil suits. But this case does not support the conclusion that, in fact, they readily did so. This is a good example of a dispute in which the parties did not fall within the "jurisdiction" of any of the social organizations in Chinese society. There was no guild or clan or village organization which commanded the loyalty of both and could apply social sanctions to force a settlement. Both of the parties—a soldier and an opium seller—were probably considered unsavory characters who would not be responsive to the moral suasion of community leaders. Perhaps this is why the magistrate did not direct the local headman to try mediation. In any event, this dispute was beyond the reach of informal group pressures and thus a likely candidate for litigation from the start. Moreover this was a case where social and business relations had been permanently disrupted. The defendant, Wang, had indicated by his counterclaim that he intended not to pay. As is stated in the judgment but not in the original plea, Hsü, the plaintiff, had already attempted to have a third party, Huang Tung-sheng, intercede for him and had offered to settle the debt at discount of 25 percent.[71] He probably turned to the court only because it seemed clear that otherwise he would not collect anything. He, also, must have been confident that Wang's counterclaim was so unfounded in fact that there was no danger of its being upheld.

But even with all this, Hsü still felt it necessary to justify his taking the case to court. He stressed the fact of his business being in trouble, with his creditors on the doorstep. Winter was coming and Hsü would have trouble finding enough to eat. He said, and the magistrate accepted this in the investigation warrant issued to the runner, that there was no way he could handle this himself because of the fierce reputation of the soldiers, the implication being that under other, more manageable circumstances he would not have brought suit. This is typical of the cases studied for this paper. The plaintiffs would usually go to great lengths to rationalize bringing suit with reasons that were totally irrelevant to the merits of the case. This suggests that an appeal to litigation was seen as bad form and had to be explained and justified to one's peers.

Finally, despite the magistrate's recognition that the full claim of 38 *yüan* was valid as entered in Hsü's accounts, he settled the debt for 20 *yüan*, nearly 50 percent less than the amount that had been completely proved. This was hardly an inducement for plaintiffs to bring their civil claims to court. This case does suggest that if all alternatives failed, a creditor could go to the magistrate and expect at least a partial recovery.

This case is also interesting for what it reveals of Chinese court procedure. As soon as the plea had been submitted, the magistrate took over the direction of the case. In a rescript written directly on the plea document, he, or an assistant in his name, characterized the facts and directed the preliminary investigation. Thus, the character of the case and the direction it would take were determined from the start not by the plaintiff's plea but by the magistrate. Because of his active role in investigation, the burden of presenting evidence did not fall exclusively on the parties in civil suits. The magistrate directed his runner to make an independent investigation, which was probably weighted more heavily than the information the parties presented.

At trial, the magistrate placed much importance on documentary proof. Wang's counterclaim failed because he could not produce a loan contract, while apparently the critical pieces of evidence submitted by Hsü were the receipts signed by Wang which were found to match Hsü's accounts. There is no indication that torture was used to force Wang to confess or sign the consent bond as commonly occurred in criminal trials. As the magistrate handled the case, it was entirely a factual inquiry. There were no doctrinal discussions or decisions about points of law. He was interested only in whether the sales or the loans actually took place and not in such issues as what constitutes a sale or whether the seller warrants the quality of the goods. It could be that no such issues were raised here but a reading of this case and others indicates that unlike criminal suits, where there were often lengthy and intricate discussions of statutory interpretation, analogical reasoning, and ways to insure that the punishment matched the crime,[72] in civil suits magistrates did not attempt to generate doctrine by analogy or otherwise. In Hsü Ting's case, the Code was never even mentioned. In civil cases, decisions about points of law were not reached by reference to the Code or to precedent. The magistrate's function was not to create law but only to decide if the facts of the case fit the local custom and to reach a decision accordingly.

The flexibility of court procedure was evident in Hsü Ting's case. The defendant was allowed freely to make his counterclaim and submit testimony to support it. The magistrate considered evidence that his runner had gathered as well as that entered by the parties. Finally, he exercised great discretion in granting a remedy. He reduced the award from 38 to 20 *yüan* despite his finding that the full 38 *yüan* debt was valid, and he allowed payment in three monthly installments.

Mediations as an Integral Part of Formal Court Procedure

A further indication of the flexibility of the judicial process was the extent to which mediation (*tiao-ch'u*) was incorporated into the formal court procedure. Mediation could arise through the efforts of the parties to a dispute or at the direction of the magistrate, who would usually refer the dispute to the local headman (*tsung-li*).[73] This was often done before formal investigation had started but it could occur at any stage in the proceedings.

Jerome A. Cohen has pointed out that the Ch'ing Code strictly forbad private settlements once cases had been brought before the magistrate,[74] but he also noted that in spite of this, "Magistrates themselves favored extrajudicial adjustments and sometimes referred cases to appropriate nongovernmental mediators."[75] For Taiwan, this seems to be an understatement. In civil cases, the magistrates referred disputes to the *tsung-li* for mediation as a matter of course. The cases in which this did not occur, like Hsü Ting's case above, were more the exception than the rule.

Buxbaum reports that 15 percent of the cases examined by him were concluded by mediated settlements.[76] Actually, 36 percent of the civil cases in his data which reached final decision at the district level were settled through mediation.[77] Even this figure probably understates the frequency of occurrence, since it does not reflect the cases where mediation may have been tried unsuccessfully or the cases which were successfully mediated but were reported as withdrawn or lapsed without decision.

The great majority of cases examined for this chapter involved some type of reference to or attempt at mediation. Even Hsü Ting, as reported above, attempted on his own to have a third party intercede with the debtor, Wang Chin-kao. Where a court-ordered mediation was successful, it was typically enforced by the magistrate as if it were his own decision. If mediation was not successful, the mediator normally submitted to the magistrate a report which was very influential in the final disposition of the case. For example, in the 1893 case of Ch'en Liang and Yü Yüan mentioned briefly above, midway in the court proceeding the magistrate ordered the *tsung-li* to mediate two disputes involved in that case. He failed to reach a settlement in one of the disputes, but in the other his efforts were successful. The *tsung-li* submitted a report[78] to the magistrate and the two parties each signed a consent bond agreeing to the terms of the mediated settlement and requesting that the magistrate dismiss their case.[79] The magistrate approved, the case was dismissed, and the consent bonds became just as enforceable as a court order would have been.[80]

In another case in 1894, the *tsung-li* had attempted mediation before the case was brought to trial. Although the attempt was unsuccessful, it figured prominently in the final decision of the case. There the defendant had broken through the dike of an irrigation ditch and allowed water to run into his field. The plaintiff repaired the dike and blocked off the water, which precipitated an altercation with the defendant. The dispute was submitted to the *tsung-li* who decided that the defendant had no right to the water and that he should pay damages to the plaintiff. The defendant refused and the case was brought before the Heng-ch'un magistrate. The *tsung-li* submitted a statement setting forth his views which the magistrate accepted completely. The court decision directed the defendant to leave the dikes alone and to pay damages.[81]

It can be seen from this case that the *tsung-li* did more than merely encourage the parties to settle the case between themselves. Here he in effect made a decision on the case that was later enforced by the magistrate. This does not mean that the *tsung-li*'s decision was binding, only that it was given great probative weight by the court. The magistrate would be free to reject the *tsung-li*'s conclusion if he cared to. But as this case shows, the *tsung-li* played a very important role, as a mediator and as a type of preliminary hearing officer. His mediated settlements were given the force of law and even in those cases where the parties failed to reach agreement the findings and recommendations of the *tsung-li* helped to determine the final result.

Even without mediation, plaintiff's claims were rarely awarded in full. For example, in Hsü Ting's case translated above, his claim was reduced by almost 50 percent even though it had been proved in full. Unfortunately, it is unexplained why the magistrate granted the plaintiff only partial recovery. It may have been out of sympathy for the circumstances of the defendant or a feeling that disputes like this should reach a compromise settlement. If the parties themselves did not seek mediation or refused to cooperate with a mediator, the magistrate may have felt justified in imposing a settlement that compromised the claim. But in any event, it is clear that formal adjudication was not a "zero-sum game" in which each party either won or lost the full amount at issue. Rather the decisions reached a "minimax" solution, with each party being forced to relinquish part of his claim. As such it produced a calculation by potential plaintiffs greatly different from that used in the United States. American plaintiffs are willing to compromise claims to avoid the large "transaction costs" necessary to collect the full amount—primarily legal fees and delay.[82] But there is a floor below which they will not compromise. That floor is determined by the amount of the claim minus the expected transaction costs.

In Taiwan on the other hand, plaintiffs could not be confident that they would be awarded their full claims by the courts. In fact, they could be quite sure that they would not. Consequently, there was a much greater incentive to reach an informal settlement or to submit any disputes to extra-judicial mediation than to go to court. It was unlikely that a lawsuit could produce a greater recovery than mediation and it was sure to produce greater expenses and difficulties.[83] Mediated settlements once reached were highly favored by the magistrates and were usually accepted and enforced by them in full. Moreover, even if the case was taken to court, the magistrate would quite likely refer it to mediation anyway and then enforce the mediator's decision if it was resisted. In this way, a variety of pressures converged to lead potential plaintiffs to look to mediation rather than the formal court system as the preferred forum for the settlement of their claims.

Sales Contracts in Taiwan

Contract forms

In nineteenth-century Taiwan, contracts were used widely in a variety of different circumstances. The popularity of their use was reflected in a local adage, *kuan yu cheng-t'iao, min yu ssu-yüeh*, "the officials have their regulations, the people have private contracts [to govern their relationships]."[84] There were three different types of documents which were used as written contracts: the *ch'i-yüeh*, the *p'iao*, and the *tan*.[85]

Ch'i-yüeh was the general term used for contract, and this form was closest to the freely composed voluntary agreement that is usually thought of as a contract in the classic sense. Indeed, this term is used today to mean contract in the modern legal systems of the Republic of China in Taiwan, the People's Republic on the mainland, and in Japan where it is pronounced *keiyaku*. The original meaning of *yüeh* was "to bind together,"[86] and it came to mean contract in the sense of people being bound to each other by mutual agreement. *Ch'i* originally referred to lines scratched on bamboo or wood to record events before the invention of writing. Later it was used to mean proof, and when combined with *yüeh* meant proof of the contract. By the end of the seventeenth century, *ch'i* had been used so frequently in this sense that it had come to be virtually synonymous with *yüeh*.[87] In combination the two together meant a document serving as proof of a binding agreement or relationship. The character *tzu*, meaning written character and hence document, was also used to mean contract and a number of terms developed, using the characters *ch'i*, *yüeh*, and *tzu* alone and in various combinations of themselves and sometimes with other characters such as *ch'i-tzu*, *yüeh-tzu*, *ho-yüeh-tzu*, and *yüeh-chü*, all of which referred to the basic *ch'i-yüeh* contract form. This type of contract was frequently used for the sale of land and several of these terms, especially *ch'i* and *ch'i-tzu*, also came to mean land deed. But it was not confined to land sales and was also used for sales of personal property, loans, employment contracts, and so on.

The term used for the second category of contracts, *p'iao*, had the basic meaning of ticket or certificate and was used for short, standardized form contracts which were freely transferable and were issued in large numbers. A *tang-p'iao* was a pawn ticket. *Chin-p'iao* (gold certificate) and *yin-p'iao* (silver certificate) were types of privately issued paper money which could be exchanged for gold or silver on demand. Mere possession was enough for this exchange; no endorsement was needed. *Hui-p'iao* was the term used for an instrument similar to a bill of exchange. It was a money order which circulated freely when endorsed. This term was a vivid one. *Hui* meant whirlpool and the term *hui-p'iao* indicated a money order floating and circulating around and around.[88]

The third contract form, the *tan*, was used in a wide variety of situations. The basic meaning of the character *tan* was memorandum or receipt and the primary use of the *tan* document was to provide proof of payment or notice of delivery. Many of the *tan* in use resembled the form contracts used by commercial buyers and suppliers in the United States. For example, a *ts'ai-huo-tan* (literally, select goods *tan*) was an order form; a *hui-tan* (return *tan*) was sent by a buyer to his seller to acknowledge delivery of goods; and a *p'ei-huo-tan* (shipped goods *tan*) was a general invoice. Others were used as receipts for payment—a *wan-tan* (final *tan*) was a receipt given a debtor by his creditor when repayment had been made in full; a *shou-tan* (received *tan*) was given to a tenant farmer when he paid the rent. A *ju-chan-tan* (enter warehouse *tan*) was a warehouse receipt given to the owner of goods when they were placed in storage. It is significant that warehouse recepts were *tan* and not *p'iao*. *Tan* were used only as proof of the receipt of money or goods. They never represented ownership of the goods themselves and they could not be freely negotiated as the *p'iao* were and as warehouse receipts and bills of lading are in the present day. A system of documentary sales of goods was never developed in traditional Taiwan.

Other *tan* represented intricate, detailed agreements which were the products of free bargaining by the parties. These *tan*, like the others, began as receipts issued to serve as proof of partial performance by one side. Since there was additional performance to occur in the future, they were used as proof of the future obligation as well as the past performance. Ultimately, they came to contain all the terms of the agreement and became full-fledged contracts. For example, a *chieh-tan* (loan *tan*) was at first given to the lender by the borrower to acknowledge receipt of the loaned sum. The rate of interest and time of repayment would be recorded on the receipt. Additional terms were added until, finally, the *chieh-tan* contained conditions precedent and subsequent, liquidated damage clauses, third-party guarantor terms, and all the other contract devices that agile minds have been able to devise over the years. In the same way, the *hsü-tui-tan* (promise to hand over *tan*) was a receipt used for both partial delivery of goods and advance deposit payments which became a full-fledged contract of sale.[89]

Thus, the *tan* form of contract was used for both standardized form contracts like the *p'iao* and individualized, detailed, freely bargained ones like the *ch'i-yueh* and to some extent overlapped with both.

Sales Contracts

The law of sales is an immensely complicated body of law. In the United States, Article II of the Uniform Commercial Code, which deals specifically with sales, contains almost 200 pages of some of the most technical language that one could have the misfortune of reading,[90] and this is not to mention other parts of the U.C.C. that are also relevant to sales. Nor is this enormous statute sufficiently detailed to handle all the transactions that arise, as the emerging case law shows.[91] Indeed, one may wonder whether it is possible to construct a systematic, coherent body of law that would do so. As two eminent legal scholars have lamented, "It has been said that the law of sales of goods is barely adequate to deal with the transfer in a local market, for cash, between seller and buyer who meet face to face, of such uncomplicated objects as horses and haystacks."[92] The point here is that even in the United States, which is commercially and legalistically oriented to what sometimes seems to be an extreme degree, the law of sales cannot be a hard-and-fast set of concrete rules. Rather, it is a collection of general principles and norms which are sometimes incomplete and mutually contradictory.

The difficulties of dealing with sales law in Taiwan in the nineteenth century are even more acute than trying to understand present law in the United States. There were no statutes of any kind, however incoherent. The case law was underdeveloped and, in any event, had no binding force. The sales law that did exist was generated, instead, by the commercial practices and trade usages that developed over many hundreds of years. It was the joint product of individual traders, guild regulations, and local customs. It depended for adherence not on the enforcement power of the state, although the official judiciary almost invariably deferred to trade customs and practices in commercial cases, but rather on its acceptance by the merchants and the public as a framework within which commercial intercourse could take place. Because there was no national or even regional body to legislate rules, the trade practices tended to be localized geographically and to specific trades. For example, in Taiwan there were different retailing customs in the north and the south of the island. The rice trade, with its island-wide network, tended to follow the same practices everywhere, but these differed from those of the sugar trade and the camphor trade, which were also island-wide operations. As a result, generalization is difficult if not impossible. Furthermore, the available sources of information leave much to be desired. One is forced to depend on the testimony of the Survey Commission's informants and inferences which can be drawn from the available sales contracts of that period. Nevertheless, it is possible to reach some conclusions. The following is not intended to be a comprehensive description of the law of sales in Taiwan in the late nineteenth century, but rather an analysis of several of the most important features of sales contracts: their formation and binding force, shifting of the risk of loss, responsibility of the seller for the quality of goods, and remedies available to the injured party on breach.

Types of Sales Contracts. There were a number of different types of sales which were recognized as distinct and referred to with different terms. A *hsien-ch'ien chiao-kuan* was a sale for cash, with the money and the item sold exchanging hands at the same time. A sale on credit was called a *kua-mai*, "suspended sale" or *she-chang*, "credit account." *Mai-fu-shui*, literally "purchase of swimming [goods]," was a sale of imported goods while they were still in transit from the mainland. *Tai-mai*, "substitute sale," was a sale on consignment. *Mai-huan-huo*, "purchase of delayed goods," indicated present payment for future goods not yet in existence. This was used primarily for sales of agricultural commodity futures, such as the various grains grown in Taiwan, fruit, sugar, hemp, and so forth, but it was also used for manufactured products to be made in the future.[93]

Sales contracts could be oral or written. Little distinction as to enforceability was made between them and, especially among merchants, contracts involving large sums of money were often made without written documents.[94] There was no Statute of Frauds as in Anglo-American law to require that certain types of contracts be in writing or under seal. Nor were there required any specific formalities, as in the civil law system, or rituals as in the so-called stipulation of Roman law where in a ritual recitation the promisee would ask, "Do you promise so-and-so?" and the promisor would reply, "I promise."[95]

Purely executory contracts, with performance from both sides to occur in the future, were practically unknown in Taiwan. Oral executory contracts were unenforceable. The Survey Commission's informants said that putting a contract in writing was enough without more to make it binding,[96] but none of the contracts examined in this study were purely executory. All of them were drawn up and signed at the same time as partial or full performance was taking place, usually delivery or the payment of a deposit. It is possible that an executory contract would have been enforced if taken to court, but it would seem that if executory contracts were used at all they were very infrequent and were certainly not favored. For all practical purposes, contracts became binding only on partial or full performance by one party. Until the contract was partially performed, it could be revoked at will by either side. The payment of a deposit was sufficient and was the most common way of assuring the enforceability of future performance.

(1) *Ch'i-yüeh*. The *ch'i-tzu* or *ch'i-yüeh* form of sales contract was rarely used for ordinary commercial sales. It was largely reserved for infrequent sales of very valuable items, primarily real property—hence, its acquired meaning of "deed." However, the *ch'i-tzu* was sometimes used for movable property as in the following sale of a boat.

> The persons who have drawn up this unconditional [*chin-ken*][97] contract of sale are Li Yen-fan and Li Yen-yung who live at No. 163 on Tzu Street in An-p'ing. They have inherited a Chinese-style boat from their grandfather who purchased it himself. Now they need the money for other purposes so they have employed a middleman to sell it to the *Hsieh-hsing-lung* store, No. 13, *Pei-ch'i-heng* Street in Tainan. The price was fixed at 560 *yüan* in silver of 73 percent purity, which today has been paid to the middleman. The boat has been inspected to see that all equipment is there and has been transferred to the buyer for his permanent use. It is guaranteed that this boat is the one the Li brothers inherited from their grandfather who bought it himself. Their brothers are all in agreement and do not oppose the sale. There is no mortgage or other encumbrance on the boat. If there is any encumbrance that has not been revealed, the Li brothers will accept responsibility for it so the

buyer will not be disturbed. This [sales contract] is created mutually, willingly and without regret. Since spoken words cannot be relied upon, this unconditional sales contract has been jointly created as proof.

This is to verify that today [we] together with the middleman received 560 *yüan*.
Meiji 32 [1899], 9th month, 10th day.

[Signed] *Middleman* Ch'en Fen-sao
Sellers Li Yen-fan
Li Yen-yung
Scrivener Li Yen-yung wrote it himself.[98]

The most striking feature of this contract is the resemblance it bears to sales of real property. There is an emphasis in the text of the contract on the legitimacy of the seller's title and lawful acquisition (from their grandfather who also acquired it legitimately) and a clear implication that there might be other claims on the boat which would survive the sale. For ordinary commercial goods, such a warranty of title was unnecessary. A bona fide purchaser without notice of other claims had complete ownership, good against all claims even by someone who had previously purchased and paid for them.[99] There is also the interesting note that the sellers' brothers did not oppose the sale. Sellers of land in China were supposed to give their relatives right of first refusal and it was said that without this sales of land could be successfully challenged even after a long period of time.[100] It would seem that the reference in this contract was an attempt to prevent a similar claim being made here. It is unclear whether relatives could actually challenge a boat sale in these circumstances or whether this was just an empty formality taken over from contracts for the sale of real property. But in any event, it would appear from this contract that in sales, boats were considered much more similar to real property than to ordinary personal property or commercial goods.[101]

This is understandable in view of the economic importance of a boat to the local society. It was income-producing in much the same way as agricultural fields were, whether it was used for fishing or shipping. Moreover, there was not a rapid turnover in the ownership of boats. They became a relatively permanent part of the community. Boats were also more valuable than most types of personal property and more likely to receive detailed attention than less expensive goods in the ordinary course of business.

(2) *Tan*. Most sales of ordinary goods used the *tan* form of sales contract. As noted above, the *tan* were originally receipts which came to contain all the elements of a contract. Yet they retained their original func-

tion as receipts and were usually issued at the time money or goods changed hands. Thus a loan contract, *chieh-tan*, was issued when the loan was actually made and the contract indicated receipt of the loaned sum. Sales contracts were similar. A *hsü-tui-tan*, (promise to hand over *tan*), was issued in two situations: to acknowledge receipt of a deposit with the rest of the purchase price to be paid on delivery of the goods and to acknowledge delivery of all or part of the goods with payment to follow at a future date.

The following is an example of a typical *hsü-tui-tan*. It was on white paper about six inches long and three inches wide. The writing was on one side only, in two long vertical columns with the date and signatures in a third column on the left. Chinese is a terse language and the text of the contract was much more concise than its English translation may indicate.

> [With this] *tan* as evidence, I promise to sell 55 packages of *ch'iang-huang* [a dyeing material] at the fixed price of 33 *yüan* per 100 catties net weight [i.e. without the packing material]. As a deposit, 200 *yüan* in silver of 68 percent purity has been received. It is agreed that the *ch'iang-huang* will be handed over at the end of this month. No delay is possible. Since spoken words cannot be relied on, we jointly create this *hsü-tui-tan* [which is] transferred as proof [of the transaction].
> The honorable *Sen-ch'in* store [received] the year of *Yi-yu*
> [1885]; 11th month, 7th day
> [Seal] *Yi-chi* [store][102]

This was issued by the seller, the *Yi-chi* store, to the buyer, the *Sen-ch'in* store. It was both a receipt for the deposit and an expression of the terms of the contract.

Several features of this contract should be noted. Both the seller and buyer were indicated by the names of their stores (*tien-hao*) rather than their personal names. It was a practice of long standing in Taiwan for merchants to deal with each other, the public, and the government using their store names. These firms were often partnerships but sole proprietors also followed this practice.

Many different types of money were in circulation in Taiwan and the parties were careful to specify which kind they intended. The money used here was called 6-8 silver to indicate its true rather than face value. Theoretically, a *yüan* coin should have been equal to one ounce (*liang*) of silver. But debasement became a regular feature of Chinese coinage. One-tenth of an ounce of silver was a *ch'ien* and one-tenth of a *ch'ien* was a *fen*. A *yüan* coin worth 6 *ch'ien* 8 *fen* or 0.68 of an ounce of silver was called a 6-8 silver *yüan*. There were also *yüan* of other values, such as 7-3 silver *yüan*, and Mexican silver dollars in circulation.[103]

At the end of this contract there appeared a series of stock phrases which appeared frequently in sales and loan contracts in this period and had been used in Taiwan contracts as early as 1788.[104] The use of these phrases suggests the formula incantations so often seen in Anglo-American common law contracts such as "for full consideration had and received" and "in full accord and satisfaction" and the use of boilerplate in general. Their use was probably stimulated in part by the same effort of contract draftsmen to use standardized terminology which had been successfully used in the past to produce the desired legal result and which was widely understood and accepted. In Taiwan there was added incentive to utilize this sort of stereotyped language. Even in the few contract cases that were brought to court, the magistrates rarely made an effort to interpret contract language or to inquire into the nature of the obligation. There was no accumulated body of approved principles of textual interpretation. Under such conditions, it was even more essential than it is in the United States to make the intent of the parties as clear and unambiguous as possible through the use of language that had the widest possible acceptance.

Moreover, through the use of these stock phrases the draftsmen tried, within the confines of the contract, to deal with many of the legal issues handled by statutory and case law in modern Western legal systems.

In common law countries, the Statute of Frauds requires that certain types of contracts must be written to be valid. Among other reasons, this is intended to ease problems of proof. Several of the phrases in Taiwan contracts were used to show that parties intended the written contract to serve as proof of the agreement. One of the most frequently appearing phrases was *k'ung-k'ou wu-feng*, literally "empty mouths cannot be depended upon," indicating that the contract was reduced to writing to avoid the difficulties of proving the existence and terms of an oral agreement. *Fu-chih ts'un-chao*, "to hand over as proof," was almost invariably the last phrase in every loan contract and appeared in many sales contracts as well. It indicated that the document itself was proof of the agreement and was transferred to the promisee for his use as evidence of the promisor's obligation. *Chin yü yu p'ing*,[105] "now [we] wish there to be proof [of our agreement so we have created this written document]," expressed a similar intent.

Another feature of common law contracts is the parol evidence rule which forbids oral testimony to alter any of the terms of a written contract. The stock phrases used in Taiwan contracts included several which were intended to produce the same result. A slightly extended version of the "empty mouth" phrase mentioned above, *hou-jih k'ung-k'ou wu-p'ing*,[106] literally "empty words on a later day will have no effect," was a type of self-imposed parol evidence rule. Its intent was that the obligations expressed in the written document could not be changed by mere spoken words. Other frequently used phrases with similar meanings included *pu te i-yen*,[107] "[he] shall not [speak] different words [than the ones here]" and *chüeh pu shih-yen*,[108] "[he] definitely will not eat [his] words [i.e. take them back]."

The concept of duress plays an important role in modern contract law. The whole idea of a binding contract is an agreement entered freely and voluntarily by the parties. The exercise of force or undue influence by one party over the other invalidates the contract from the start. In Taiwan, duress was also viewed as illegitimate, and parties often included language in their contracts to indicate the willingness of both sides: *erh-pi kan-yüan*,[109] "both parties are willing and honest"; *ko wu fan-hui*,[110] "each is without regrets"; *liang wu tiao-nan*,[111] "neither side is obstructive"; *jen-i chiao-kuan*, "this is a just transaction"; and *wu-i-le* and *wu-p'o-le*,[112] "[this transaction is] without coercion."

It is, of course, uncertain how seriously disclaimers of duress should be taken. After all, anyone who could force other terms on an unwilling party could presumably force a duress disclaimer as well. The important point here is that this, together with the written contract and parol evidence considerations mentioned above, were recognized as important to the process of contract and were dealt with in the contract language as an attempt to impose a sort of internal regulation on contracts which were not effectively regulated by the official legal system.

The use of these formalistic expressions to produce certainty and clarity had an additional effect on the development of contract in Taiwan. The great need to communicate contract terms discouraged the use of original, inventive drafting techniques and tended to force contracts into standard patterns. As a result, almost all contracts of a given type would follow the same formula. This may have decreased any ambiguities in the contracts but it also prevented the flexible use of the same contract forms from one situation to another. Consequently, a variety of contract forms developed, each with its own specific formula which would be confined to a specific type of transaction.

Despite the emphasis on formalities in contract language in regard to these legal issues mentioned above, for the actual content of the contract there was a tendency to state only the primary terms of the bargain. For example, an important feature of the *hsü-tui-tan* translated above is its brevity and what it leaves unsaid. There is no indication of what quality goods will be delivered or even where or how delivery will take place and at whose cost. Nothing is said about the risk of loss or when it shifts from seller to buyer. And no effort is made to assign responsibility for latent defects or to anticipate any of the other contingencies that might occur. It says no delay is possible, but is silent as to what would happen if that impossible delay did come about. This may seem paradoxical in view of the effort to achieve certainty noted above. But there the effort was to establish the obligation and those terms of the contract that were primary and bargained for. The contextual terms, the secondary duties and obligations which made up the framework within which bargaining could take place, were assumed by the parties and implicitly incorporated into the contract. The secondary terms could be and frequently were altered at will. For example, the usual terms of delivery could be changed or a quality of goods that was higher or lower than usual could be indicated. But in the absence of explicit provisions, the customs and practices that were established in the trade as being an integral part of this form of contract were assumed.

The failure to state explicitly the duties and rights which arose from these practices does not mean that they were unimportant. To the contrary, the very fact that they were left unstated indicates that they were widely known and adhered to. If it was not clearly understood what these general rules were, it would have been necessary to specify all of them in the contract document.

The plethora of contract forms in use and the variety of trade practices which attached to them would have been confusing to anyone forced to master the full range of contracts in use, but most lines of trade used only a few different types. The rice merchants, for example, used mainly futures, purchase, and delivery contracts. The large importers and wholesalers in the coastal cities used delivery, supply, and "swimming goods" contracts. The retailers used ordinary purchase and sales contracts with their suppliers and customers. Each of these developed sufficient familiarity with the contract forms that were specifically relevant to his line of commerce to be fully informed not only of the obligations expressed in the language of the document but also of the trade usages and practices which supplied the framework of rights and obligations within which the contracts were formed.

Formation of a Binding Sales Contract. Not all of the *tan* in circulation were binding contracts. Even the binding ones were also issued as receipts for a deposit paid on partial or full delivery of goods. Moreover, some of the *tan* were mere inquiries or order forms. Typically, where the buyer and seller were in different towns or for some other reason did not discuss the sale face to face, there would be a series of inquiries, offers, and counteroffers as in the following exchange between rice merchants.

> Would you please inform me whether at present there is grain in your warehouse, either *lo-mi* or *wan-mi*, when you would sell it and what the price would be? If you are able [to sell at] current prices, please let me

know by courier or by telegraph. I wish to buy at the current price the day my order arrives. This will be extremely fortunate. It is only this that I present [for your consideration]. Other aspects [of the transaction] will be discussed later. May you be prosperous and peaceful.
Gentlemen of the Ta-ho store [received] The year of Ting-wei [1907]
4th Month, 11th day
[seal] Ho-ch'ang Store

The seller replied by telegram. And the buyer again inquired.

Yesterday I read your communication in which you said that you only have in your granary 1,000 *shih* of *lo-mi* of which the price is 5 *yüan* per *shih*. But as to the details of the transaction, I do not know if you are able to reduce [the price]. If so I would like to order 2,000 *shih*. If you agree, please inform me. I do not know how you would like the money transferred, through a bank or by having one of my employees bring it over. If you wish to ship it, select inspected [by the rice merchants association] high quality grain. It is important that [the grain] be fresh. Replied.
Ta-ho store; [received]

1907, 4th month, 12th day
[Seal] Ho-ch'ang Store

To this the seller replied:

For your information, yesterday I inspected the grain at my place. You want to buy 2,000 *shih*. I only have 1,000 *shih* in my granary for sale. The price is not expensive. It is firmly 5 *yüan* per *shih*. Only at that price can I sell. It is difficult to reduce the price even a penny. So I only have 1,000 *shih* to sell at 5 *yüan* per *shih*. [Your] reply should be sent quickly by telegram or by bringing it personally. The 1,000 *shih* of grain is already packed. Please let me know soon whether it is to be sent by boat or train, so I can load it. Replied.
Gentlemen of the Ho-ch'ang Store [received]

1907, 4th month, 12th day
[Seal] Te-ho Store[113]

There is a certain resemblance between these *tan* and the form contracts used by business suppliers and purchasers in the United States. Each specifies the terms which that party wishes to include in the bargain and each is anticipatory in that its tone seems to assume that it will be accepted by the other side. However, unlike the contracts used in the "Battle of the Forms" in the United States, none of these communications were contracts by themselves, and even if the buyer replied to the seller's final offer and accepted all his terms, a binding contract would not have been formed. Offers could be revoked at any time, even after written acceptance by the offeree, unless there had been partial or full performance by one side, usually payment of a deposit or delivery of the goods.[114]

The acceptance of an offer, whether written or oral, created a situation in which each party to a bilateral contract was placed in the position of an offeree of a unilateral contract in American law. Each party could, by performing his side of the agreement in whole or in part, make the contract binding on the other party.

Making enforceability dependent on an objective act instead of subjective acceptance of an offer had several advantages under the legal conditions that prevailed in Taiwan. Defining with precision when and how a valid acceptance of a valid offer occurs is extremely difficult, as is shown by the whole range of problems that the common law has encountered trying to describe a "meeting of the minds." To use such a concept in Taiwan would have required an active legal system capable not only of generating such doctrine but also of enforcing it. Partial performance, on the other hand, offered a clear, unambiguous, objective indication that acceptance had occurred and the contract made binding. Moreover, the requirement of partial performance decreased the problems of enforceability by introducing an element of self-enforcement into the contract. After one party had paid a deposit, he could avoid performance only by forfeiting it. The deposit was a form of security for his performance.

If partial performance had the effect of binding the other party, it did not fully bind the party who performed. For example, if *A* agreed to sell grain to *B* at a future date, *B* could make *A*'s obligation binding by paying to him part of the purchase price as a deposit. But even then *B* would not be obliged to accept the full amount of grain in the contract. He could, by forfeiting his deposit, refuse delivery with impunity. He could not, however, compel delivery of the amount covered by the deposit and refuse the rest. Delivery and payment would take place at the same time and the seller could withhold delivery of any goods until full payment by the buyer. Likewise, if, in the above example, *A* delivered part of the grain to *B* before any money changed hands, *B* was bound to pay for that much, but *B* could not force *A* to deliver the rest of the grain.

This became very important when unexpected events caused sharp changes in the market price. Traders could anticipate seasonal prices from year to year and often they contracted for grain at a price to be determined by the prevailing market at the time of delivery. But unless a contract at a specified price was made binding by payment of a deposit, either the seller or the buyer could freely abandon it when it was to his advantage to do so. As one of the Survey Commission's interviews revealed:

Question: When the market price falls and the buyer refuses to take delivery [because he can buy at the new lower price], for example if the price falls from 50 *yüan* to 45 *yüan*, is the seller compensated for his loss?

Answer: Perhaps it is reasonable to provide compensation, but in transactions today he is not compensated and is in the position of crying himself to sleep.[115]

In most transactions among grain merchants this problem was avoided by making the deposits very large in proportion to the sales price. These deposits would run as high as 60 percent or 80 percent of the contract price[116] and were in part forms of short-term credit.

It should be emphasized that these were not purchases of grain directly from the peasants who cultivated the fields. The purchasing and financing arrangements among them were complicated by the existence of a very intricate system of landholding, leasing, and subleasing. Suffice it to say that most credit advanced to peasant-farmers was on a seasonal basis, keyed to the harvest. The contracts involved here, on the other hand, were purely commercial contracts between grain merchants on different levels of the distribution system. Large grain wholesalers in the cities and exporters on the coast would contract with middle-level grain purchasers and advance them large deposits or loans, which would in turn be used by the middle-level dealers to buy up grain through their purchasing agents or from other suppliers.[117]

These credit-purchase contracts took two forms. Some of them specified sale at a discount from the expected market price to provide a return on the prepaid capital as in the following contract issued by a grain merchant in Lu-kang, a prominent port in the nineteenth century. The lines of the text presented horizontally here were vertical in the original, so to achieve the proper visual effect this page should be turned on its side.

I have received from your hand 350 *yüan* [as a deposit]
The Te-ho Store, on the 26th day of the 5th month of 1906, contracts to sell 100 *shih* of inspected *hua-lo-mi* [a type of grain] at 5.37 *yüan* [per *shih*]
It is agreed that the grain will be transferred at the ferry boat at *Fan-tzu-kou* [a place name] on the 3rd or 4th of the 7th month.[118]

Other credit-purchase contracts specified sale at the market price with a provision for interest.

> The Ch'üan-fa store on the 10th day of the 3rd month, 1907, borrowed 400 *yüan*.
> [It] contracts to sell 200 *shih* of grain on the 15th of the 5th month at the prevailing market price. For each 100 *yüan* there will be 5 *ch'ien* interest per day [i.e. 150 *ch'ien* or 1.5 percent a month]. When the grain is delivered, both the principal and interest will be calculated as part of the purchase price. This will serve as evidence.[119]

Such large deposits made it unlikely that the buyer would forfeit and refuse to pay the rest of the grain price. For example, in the first credit-purchase contract listed above, the price of grain would have to fall below 1.87 *yüan* per *shih* to make it economically profitable for the buyer to breach and purchase at the market price. Such a drop, to 30 percent of the projected market price was possible but probably unlikely. In the second credit-purchase contract, which was pegged to the market price, the buyer would be bound to accept delivery, as a practical matter, no matter how low the price fell. If it declined to 2.06 *yüan* per *shih*, the buyer-lender would break even. The combined principal and interest over two months would be equal to the market price of 200 *shih*, 412 *yüan*. If the price fell below that, the buyer would be forced to accept grain worth less at the market than the deposit he had advanced plus interest. But no matter how far the price declined, the buyer would accept delivery. His only alternative would be complete forfeiture of the money he had already paid, and acceptance of partial repayment would be better than none at all.

The major advantage of the market price plus interest credit-sale contract to the seller, however, was that it allowed him to reap the entire benefit of an upside price shift. In fact, under this arrangement the risk of all price shifts, up and down, were on the seller unless the price fell below the level necessary to cover the loan, in the case of the contract mentioned immediately above, 2.06 *yüan* per *shih*. Thus, this type of transaction assured the seller of a minimum price for his grain. The buyer assumed all risk of prices falling below that level and the seller received all the profit or assumed all the loss of price changes above that minimum.

Credit-purchase contracts which specified a fixed price for the grain to be delivered one to two months later provided for a more equal allocation of the risks and benefits resulting from changes in price levels. In the first example above, if the market price five weeks later had risen above 5.37 *yüan* per *shih*, the entire benefit of that rise would go to the buyer and the seller would lose the profit he would have had in the absence of the contract. On the other hand, all price shifts below 5.37 *yüan* would result in losses to the buyer, because he otherwise would have been able to purchase grain below the contract price in the market. This would remain true until the price declined to a level below 1.87 *yüan*. At that point, the buyer would forfeit his deposit and purchase elsewhere at the market price. This would shift part, but not all, of the loss to the seller. To illustrate how this works, it is necessary to imagine several hypothetical price changes. Using the first credit-purchase contract above as an example, if, on the 3rd of the 7th month the market price was 5.50 *yüan* per *shih* the parties would be even. The buyer would get 100 *shih* worth 550 *yüan* for 537 *yüan*. This would allow interest of 13 *yüan* for an effective rate of 3.7 percent for the loan of 350 *yüan* for five weeks. This rate is typical of short-term commercial credit at the time and will be assumed in the examples below. If the market price rose in those five weeks to 7.5 *yüan*, the buyer would get grain worth 750 for 550 (including interest) for a windfall profit of 200. If the price fell to 3.5 *yüan*, the buyer would still be bound to pay 550, so he would lose 200. In both of these examples, the seller would lose what the buyer gained and vice versa. If the price fell to 1.5 *yüan* per *shih*, the situation is slightly more complicated. The buyer would forfeit his deposit and buy 100 *shih* at the market, thus expending his deposit of 350 plus 150 purchase price for a total of 500. His loss would be 350 (he would pay 500 for grain worth 150) rather than the 400 he would lose at the contract price. Symmetrically, the seller would get 500 for his grain (150 from whomever he could sell to in the market plus the 350 deposit) rather than 550. In this way, the loss of 400 *yüan* due to the declining market price would be distributed as 350 to the buyer and 50 to the seller. If the price fell further to 0.5 *yüan*, the same calculation would produce the same 350 *yüan* deficit to the buyer, with the additional 100 *yüan* loss falling to the seller.

It should be noted that, in this situation, the larger the deposit the more the risk of all price changes shifted to the buyer, resulting in the extreme in complete prepayment of the contract price, which shifted the complete risk of all price changes entirely to the buyer.

Thus, even in the absence of enforceable executory contracts, the grain merchants in Taiwan were able, through a combination of credit and purchase arrangements, to devise a system whereby the risks of changes in price levels could be effectively shifted between buyer and seller to whatever degree they desired. At one extreme, a pure loan with no connected sale left the entire risk on the seller. At the other extreme, complete prepayment of the contract price shifted that risk entirely to the buyer. Allocation of risks to both parties anywhere between these two extremes could be effected by tying the sale to a loan (or a deposit, which was really the same thing) and varying its size. The larger the deposit, the more risk shifted to the buyer.

In this manner, the grain merchants were able to arrange their affairs and allocate business risks between themselves as they pleased. In effect, this was a functional substitute for the system of enforceable executory contracts that achieves the same objective in the United States today.

Shifting the Risk of Loss. If sales contracts did not become binding on the seller or the buyer until partial payment or delivery, the risk of damage to or loss of the object of the sale did not shift from the seller to the buyer until actual delivery was made. Here, three aspects of this type of risk will be examined: (1) loss due to fraud; (2) fortuitous loss due to wholly accidental and unpreventable causes; and (3) loss due to defects in the goods.

The general rules regarding these types of losses are revealed in the following interview conducted by the Survey Commission.

Question: If, where the buyer has paid for the goods but has not received them and the seller still has them in his possession, the goods are destroyed by fire, on whom does the loss fall?

Answer: It does not matter whether the price has been paid or not; as long as the goods have not changed hands, the loss is the seller's.

Question: What happens if after the goods have been received (by the buyer) they are found to be insufficient or to be defective?

Answer: It is the responsibility of the buyer. After he has accepted delivery there is nothing he can do.

Question: If the seller has with bad intent deceived the buyer as to the weight (quantity) of the goods delivered or has delivered inferior goods, should the responsibility still fall on the buyer?

Answer: This is a difficult problem. For example, the seller may contract to sell 80 chests of tea and send 1 chest ahead as a sample which is accepted by the buyer. If when the rest are delivered only 5 or 6 of the other 79 are inspected because it is too much trouble, then the buyer is being negligent. If he accepts them all and later discovers an insufficiency, the responsibility should still rest with him because he could have inspected and used his own scales.

Question: What happens if the person who does the weighing is deceitful and misrepresents the weight?

Answer: I have not heard of such a situation, but I would think that since the buyer can inspect the weighing equipment and since the weighing is done in front of him, there should be no problem.

Question: What happens if someone sells an object that is gold-plated (instead of solid gold) and later it is discovered?

Answer: In this case, he should be able to seek compensation from the seller. Especially in this situation the penalty should be heavy.[120]

Question: Can one seek compensation for defects [in the goods]?

Answer: That depends on whether they can be detected by the purchaser.

Question: You said earlier that losses occurring after delivery would not fall to the seller. Is it necessary that the delivery be an actual one? For example, if tea deposited in a warehouse is sold and the seller hands over the warehouse receipt and notifies the warehouseman, and if the tea is then lost in a fire, to whom does the loss fall? That is to say, can there be oral (or constructive) delivery rather than actual delivery?

Answer: The loss still goes to the seller, the buyer would not have seen the goods and no delivery would have actually taken place.

Question: What happens if the buyer goes to the warehouse, sees the goods and consents to the sale.

Answer: This is not a delivery, on this island that would be equivalent only to presenting a sample for approval.[121]

Thus, there were two very strict rules regarding damage to the goods. First, all loss which occurred while the goods were still under the control of the seller fell to him even if payment had been made and a binding contract created and even if the seller was in no way responsible for the loss. The risk of loss accompanied possession and not ownership or title.

Every system of commercial intercourse has to provide some point at which the risk of fortuitous loss which is wholly accidental and not due to the intent or negligence of either party shifts from the seller to the buyer. Various solutions have been tried in different systems. The United States has tried two different solutions. Under the early Uniform Sales Act the risk of fortuitous loss passed to the buyer when "ownership" of the goods became his regardless of who had possession at that point.[122] The Uniform Commercial Code, which has superseded the earlier Act, changed this and now, interestingly enough, U.S. law produces the same result that prevailed in Taiwan.[123] Risk of loss passes to the buyer on delivery to him or a carrier. The only point on which U.S. law diverges is where the goods are held by a bailee, e.g., a warehouse. The system of documentary sales in the United States allows delivery to occur on the transfer of a warehouse receipt or other negotiable documents, while in Taiwan actual physical removal from the bailee's possession was necessary.

The result reached in Taiwan, to pass the risk of loss with possession rather than ownership or title, would seem to be a solution particularly well adapted to the legal conditions there. There was no well-developed body of statutory or case law to determine the passage of such abstract rights as ownership or legal title. Also, easy access to the judicial machinery that would have been necessary to enforce those rights was lacking. Passage with possession had the advantage of being relatively definite and clear. Except for the inevitable borderline situation,[124] the physical passage of the goods was an overt act that would be obvious to all. In addition, commercial insurance was underdeveloped among Chinese traders in Taiwan,[125] and making the possessor responsible for any loss probably served to protect the goods, because the possessor could be expected to be more careful in protecting his own interests than in caring for goods held for another who would suffer any loss incurred.

Moreover, this solution reduced the complexity of the issues involved. If ownership had passed to the buyer but loss had occurred while the goods were held by the seller, the buyer could charge inadequate care, which would raise very difficult problems of proof. The same difficulty would result if the loss occurred after delivery of the goods to the buyer if abstract ownership for some reason remained with the seller. By allowing the loss to stay with the possessor, the adequacy of his care became entirely irrelevant as a legal issue.

This result produced simplification and self-execution in another way as well. The possessor had to absorb the loss. In most commercial sales, the purchase price, except for any deposit that may have been paid, was handed over at the time of delivery. Allocating the loss to the possessor made it unnecessary in most situations for one party to seek compensation from the other. The only case where this would not be true was where the buyer would seek recovery of his prepaid deposit, which for grain sales was quite large, but which was usually about 10 percent of the purchase price of most goods. The largest part of the price would pass at the same time as possession, and no recovery of that would be necessary.

This again is an example of how commercial customs and rules were arranged in Taiwan to incorporate methods of self-enforcement and to avoid the necessity of appealing to a tribunal.

In determining when possession passed, the crucial factor was control by the seller, or his agents, as in the warehouse case, not the actual possession or exercise of control over the goods by the buyer. Delivery was considered accomplished when the goods passed out of the hands of the seller and were handed over to a carrier, and the risk of fortuitous loss passed to the buyer when the carrier loaded them. This was quite important to Taiwan merchants because many of the goods they handled were imported from or exported to the mainland. This required a perilous journey across the Taiwan Strait, and often ships and cargo were lost at sea. The rule in this situation was that the risk had passed and the loss went to the buyer in the absence of contrary provisions.[126] This general rule could be altered by the parties, either directly in the contract or by changing the nature of the transaction. One way in which the large wholesale importers in the coastal cities on Taiwan avoided the risk of loss at sea was to operate strictly on a commission basis, usually 2 percent. This left ownership and all risk of loss with the seller of the goods.

Although the rule which allocated the risk of loss at sea to the buyer seems to have developed out of the shipping trade with the mainland, it was also used in coastwise shipping on Taiwan. Later, it was used by analogy when goods were shipped by train.[127] Unless otherwise agreed by the parties, the rule was applied quite rigidly. Delivery was considered made to the buyer when the goods were loaded, regardless of whether the ship was owned by the buyer, the seller, or an independent carrier.[128] This contrasted with local deliveries in Taiwan, where agency principles were recognized. Delivery made by an employee of the seller was completed at the buyer's place of business; if the buyer sent his employees after the goods, delivery was complete when they picked them up.[129] The rigidity of the shipping rule seems to have been an attempt at establishing a rule of certainty. There were risks involved in the passage across the Strait. From the point of view of the parties it did not matter where those risks fell as long as they fell consistently in the same place. Then the parties to the transaction could adjust the price terms between themselves in consideration of who would incur any possible loss. The seller would offer and the buyer would get a lower price knowing that the buyer would bear the risks of sea passage. There was also a consideration of convenience. Except for the large wholesalers and importers who kept running accounts with firms on the mainland, cargo would not be shipped until it had been paid for. To transfer money across the Strait was difficult, whether by shipment of specie or by bank transfer. Once this had been done, it would have been wasteful to hold the seller to the loss and force him to retransfer the purchase price back across the water. Of course, this rule, or any rule for that matter, could not prevent the perplexing borderline case. For example, in An-p'ing harbor a boat partially loaded with sugar intended for the Chinese mainland overturned and all the sugar was lost. In that case, two-thirds of the loss was assumed by the seller and the buyer took the remaining one-third.[130] Apparently, the theory here was that incomplete loading passed some but not all risk to the buyer.

The Buyer's Duty of Inspection. The second rule was as strict against the buyer as the first was against the seller. If the seller was responsible for all loss even after the goods had been sold and paid for while still in his possession, once goods had been delivered to the buyer, the seller retained virtually no responsibility for them. As the adage in Taiwan had it, *ch'u-men wu-jen-huo*, "once the goods are out the door, they are no longer recognized."[131] The Survey Commission scholars report that several hundred years before, sellers in Taiwan were responsible for all defects and all sales of goods in which defects appeared were void.[132] If so, that would suggest a development similar to the change from *caveat venditor* to *caveat emptor* that occurred in the West.[133] But no sources are cited for this point and it is hard to evaluate the statement. In any event, by the nineteenth century, a form of *caveat emptor* had developed. As indicated in the interview quoted above, the buyer was expected to exercise a great deal of care in inspecting the goods when they were delivered. Later the buyer could not complain about defects that he could have discovered by inspection. Even intentional deceit by the seller such as using inaccurate scales or deliberately misreporting the weight, could not be protested later since the buyer had had the opportunity to inspect the scales and supervise the weighing. In sales where the goods were shipped by boat or train, inspection could not occur until the goods reached the buyer. In that case, inspection has to take place promptly within several days after arrival. Defects not discovered for twenty or thirty days, no matter how obvious, could not be asserted against the seller.[134] So even though the seller had no responsibility for any fortuitous loss that might occur during the trip, he could be held for any defects that might show up during the buyer's examination.

Although this principle was applied strictly in most situations, there were a few exceptions. A general exception was made for latent defects which were not discoverable in a careful examination.[135] The seller remained liable for such defects as the internal rotting of wood in lumber sales, defects in cloth where it was impractical to inspect each square yard of a huge roll, and moisture and impurities in bulk grain sales where adequate inspection and sampling had been made.[136] This, of course, was a logical and consistent qualification of the usual rule. If the reason that sellers could escape responsibility was that buyers were expected to make a careful examination of the goods on receipt, it would have been illogical to make the buyer responsible for defects he could not discover in such an examination. But even here, the seller's responsibility did not extend indefinitely. The latent defects had to be discovered and brought to the seller's attention within a "reasonable" time, which was nowhere specified but which was at most several weeks.

A special custom was in effect for the sale of pigs which illustrated the limited nature of the seller's warranty against latent defects.

Question: If a water buffalo or a pig is sold but not delivered and it dies who bears the loss?

Answer: The seller, but there is a special custom for the purchase of a pig. If the pig dies (of natural causes) within three days after delivery, the buyer does not have to pay any more but he cannot recover the deposit or price already paid.[137]

Even though this was a special rule for use in pig sales, it shows quite clearly the presumptions made by contract practices for sales. It was assumed that the pig might have some latent infirmity or illness that was not obvious to the eye and for which the seller should remain responsible. If that defect or illness became manifest and resulted in death within three days after delivery, this was assumed to be the natural result of a condition that started and developed while the pig was still in the hands of the seller and thus should be considered his responsibility. On the other hand, if the condition resulted in death more than three days after delivery, it was considered likely to have developed entirely or primarily while the pig was in the possession of the buyer and the presumption that it had was established. But even this three-day limit did not allocate risks absolutely. If the pig died within three days, part of the loss was passed on to the buyer by the refusal to allow recovery of any partial or full payment he had made. Risk passed to the buyer *pro tanto*. As can be seen, within these rules the parties involved in a pig sale could freely allocate the risk that the pig would die during the three-day period between themselves by varying the amount of the deposit. If no deposit was made all risk stayed with the seller while full prepayment would shift it entirely to the buyer.

Thus, there was not full-fledged *caveat emptor* in the strict sense in late nineteenth-century Taiwan. Buyers did not take goods "as is" with all defects obvious or not. There was recourse to be had against sellers for defects that did not show up in a careful examination. But this recourse was strictly limited to a rather short period after delivery, and the overall situation was far closer to strict *caveat emptor* than to the virtually absolute warranty of goods to which manufacturers are held under present American law.[138]

Max Gluckman, in his study of Barotse jurisprudence, has associated the development of *caveat emptor* with the growth of commerce.[139] *Caveat venditor*, which Gluckman sees as prior and more basic, places too many restrictions in the way of trade and must give way before unfettered commerce can emerge.

Without knowing more about the development of commerce in Taiwan, and the earlier history there of the allocation of responsibility for defective goods, it is impossible to confirm Gluckman's theory. But the existence of *caveat emptor* in Taiwan suggests indirect support for it. *Caveat venditor* is a difficult doctrine to enforce because it requires a substantial amount of legal activity. Someone must decide if the goods are defective and whether the buyer is responsible for the defects through misuse or negligence. Most difficult of all, someone must calculate the amount of any compensation due and ensure that such compensation is taken from the responsible party and given to the other. These are very difficult tasks for even an alert, active, and responsive judicial system. They are even more difficult in the absence of such a system unless the community is cohesive enough to enforce the result entirely through informal social sanctions. Apparently Barotse society, the subject of Gluckman's study, was cohesive enough for these purposes.

Here I would associate *caveat emptor* with judicial capacity rather than the development of commerce. The return to *caveat venditor* principles in modern American law suggests that vigorous commerce can coexist with it if there is appropriate enforcement. Without the relevant commercial activities occurring entirely within a close-knit, cohesive community and without an extensive and effective legal system, the main requirement is simplicity, and *caveat venditor* is too complex to work well. *Caveat emptor* is both simple and precise. Transactions can occur smoothly without the necessity of later readjustments or judicial interference.

Remedies on Breach. The remedies available to an injured party for breach of a sales contract were strictly limited. If a buyer refused to accept delivery of goods, the seller had no recourse other than to keep any partial payment the buyer might have made. Since no buyer could be forced to take goods he had not paid for, sellers usually required the payment of deposits, typically about 10 percent of the purchase price of ordinary goods,[140] which they could then retain as security for the sale. If the buyer breached and refused delivery, the amount of the deposit was the only compensation the seller could receive. Since this measure of his compensation was not determined by the actual losses or damages that resulted from the breach, its adequacy was largely problematic. If the seller was forced to unload the goods at a distress price, the amount of the deposit could have covered only a small part of an extensive loss. On the other hand, if the seller could find a ready alternative market for his goods, the deposit could be entirely a windfall profit. In any event, the deposit served as a fairly satisfactory approximation. Experienced traders could develop some idea of what damages might result from a breach and vary the size of the deposit they required from buyers accordingly. In American legal terms, this was a way of building in a liquidated damage clause that was self-executing and did not require the machinery of judicial enforcement.

Remedies on the buyers' side were almost as limited. A buyer who had prepaid partially or fully was theoretically entitled to full delivery of the goods. This was the weakest point of self-enforcement in traditional Taiwan contracts. The prepaying buyers possessed no security or leverage to exert pressure on the seller. The only way in which the contract itself could encourage the seller to perform was for the prepayment to act as a sort of security in reverse. For the seller to refuse delivery and retain the prepayment as well was tantamount to theft, a far more serious offense than refusal to perform a contract obligation. This would elicit greater condemnation and probably more severe sanctions from the community and from the legal system. At very least, the defaulting seller would probably attempt to return any prepayment that had been made. The buyer might be able to refuse to accept this attempt or, if his money was tied up, the seller might find it less convenient to return the money than to perform. But if the seller insisted that the prepayment be returned, the buyer could do little more than depend on community pressures, long-term business relationships, and self-interest to induce the seller's performance.

Other problems developed when the seller could not perform because the goods had been destroyed or damaged or were for some other reason unavailable. If the goods were unique and could not be replaced, the buyer was out of luck. His only remedy was to recover whatever part of the purchase price he had paid.[141] He was not entitled to the type of compensation usually called "consequential damages" in American law. For example, if the buyer had arranged for a resale transaction at a profit, or if he had incurred large expenses in preparation for receiving the goods, under American law he could recover the profit he would have received as his "expectation interest" and the money he had expended "in reliance" on the contract. In late nineteenth-century Taiwan, no such recovery was allowed. The buyer in Taiwan was placed in the position he occupied before the contract was made, not the one he would have occupied had the contract been completely performed, which is the solution sought under American law.

There was a different result where the destroyed goods were fungible commodities or could otherwise be replaced. There, the seller was held to the contract terms and required to replace the goods and deliver them to the buyer. If a large price shift caused substantial hardship to a seller forced to replace goods at a higher price, the price might be renegotiated but this was a concession to be granted at the discretion of the buyer. The seller's duty was to deliver at the price in the contract, and often the seller would merely pay the buyer the difference between the contract price and the market and the buyer would make his own market purchase.[142] This is very similar to the "market-contract formula" used to calculate damages under the Uniform Commercial Code.[143] But although a limited "expectation interest" was allowed here, this was merely for replacement of the destroyed goods, no provision for lost profit was made and, as above, no "reliance interest" damages could be collected.

Where the seller's breach was not failure to deliver but delivery of nonconforming goods, similar restrictions on the available remedies prevailed. The buyer was limited, first of all, as to the time within which he could request any remedy at all. For most goods, if the buyer failed to notice a nonconformity at the time of delivery, he could not assert it later. Latent defects could be raised after delivery only during the first few weeks. Even if these nonconforming features were discovered and reported within these narrow time limits, the available remedies were limited to replacement of the nonconforming goods, reduction of the price, or refund of the purchase price paid.[144] As in the case above, no consequential damages were available.

The net effect of the strict inspection requirement imposed on the buyer and the limitation of the available remedies on breach was to confine the legal consequences of a transaction to a very short period of time centered on the moment of delivery of the goods. Defects appearing later, even latent defects after several weeks, would not be compensated. The only damages deemed to be recoverable on breach were those associated with the transaction. This forced the buyer to anticipate any future disputes and seek to prevent them by as careful an inspection as he could manage. Any part of the purchase price paid could be recovered or the goods could be replaced if a nonconformity was discovered in time, but there was no provision for the recovery of damages suffered by the injured party outside the narrow confines of the transaction itself. Any damages not directly related but consequential to the exchange, such as long profits or costs incurred in anticipation of receiving the goods, would not be collected. This may seem unfair to the buyer who might suffer substantial consequential losses, but it should be remembered that remedies were confined to the time of delivery before the consequences of the transaction could have proceeded very far. The consequential damages suffered then would probably not be as large as six months or a year later. Confining compensation in time to delivery served to restrict the size of necessary compensation as well.

This also was related to the parties' inability to appeal effectively to the official legal system. Just as having the risk of loss travel with possession rather than ownership avoided the difficulty of forcing the parties to compensate each other when the loss did not fall to the appropriate person, limiting the available remedies in time to the transfer of the goods and in scope to the transaction itself avoided the problems of proof and enforcement that would arise if compensation for defects and for damages suffered outside these narrow limits was sought. Self-enforcement could work only within a narrow range and the rules were kept accordingly simple. As long as the rules were definite, the parties were not greatly disadvantaged. Sellers learned to take deposits. Buyers learned to inspect closely and not to expend large sums in reliance unless they were relatively certain of the seller's performance. Just as the inadequacies of any legal system are taken into account by those who must operate under it, all of these factors were taken into consideration as business risks along with the large number of other factors considered in any business decision.

Conclusion

Legal conditions in Taiwan in the late nineteenth century were seemingly not favorable for the development of an extensive body of contract law. There was no accessible and effective system of courts to be used for purposes of contract enforcement and for the generation of legal rules. The official legal system was not receptive to contract cases, did not provide uniform enforcement, and did not create contract law. In addition, there were no independent commercial courts with jurisdiction over all merchants to perform these tasks.

Yet there developed in Taiwan an effective and sophisticated system of contract that supported a high level of commerce both within the island of Taiwan and across the Taiwan Strait with the mainland Chinese provinces. This was achieved in two ways: by creating a variety of contract forms to be used in various types of transactions and by relying for enforcement not on external coercion but on the provisions and rules of the contracts themselves.

The contracts that were used in Twaiwan were very highly developed. There were a number of different types designed for different commercial situations. Some were strictly sales contracts. Others were loans. Still others combined sales with extensions of short-term credit. A variety of specialized contracts emerged such as warehouse receipts and bills of exchange to serve commercial purposes. These various contract forms used distinctive formulas and formalized language to provide certainty for the terms of the obligations and to supply convenient forms for the creation of binding promises. Moreover, a sophisticated framework of contract rules developed to determine the rights and obligations of the parties on the occurrence of such contingencies as damage to the goods, the appearance of defects, or any of the other things that might occur in the course of an ordinary commercial transaction.

Without effective access to the legal system and with commerce spread far beyond the cohesive local communities where social pressures could control, merchants in Taiwan had to rely on the contracts themselves to insure performance. This was achieved not only by structuring the terms of the contract to provide different types of security but also by shaping the contextual contract rules to encourage performance as much as possible and decrease the need for appeal to a tribunal. For this self-contained process to work efficiently, three vital elements were necessary: (1) the contract rules had to be simple; (2) they had to refer to objective acts and not to abstract principles; and (3) there had to be self-enforcing mechanisms included within the contract terms.

The relevant contract rules had to be simple to work well, both in the sense of being easily understood and in the sense of reducing the complexity of the issues to be considered, thus keeping the necessary legal activity to a minimum. There were no courts to decide difficult legal questions. To gain compliance, the rules had to be unambiguous and straightforward. Moreover, they had to involve as little remedial activity as possible, because there was no judicial machinery to direct it. The primary emphasis was not placed on correction after the fact but on preventing the necessity of later remedies. For example, the risk of loss in a sales contract passed to the buyer with possession, not ownership. This was a perfectly straightforward rule that was easily understandable. It eliminated the need to determine if the possessor had rendered adequate care, since the loss was his regardless. And because payment, with the exception of the prepaid deposit, usually was made at the same time as delivery, it was not necessary to force one party to transfer compensation to the other after the goods had been damaged or lost. The single exception to this was the deposit which might have to be returned, but this was usually about 10 percent of the price, so it was not a large exception. There was no need for a high level of legal activity.

Imposing a strict duty of inspection on the buyer at the time of delivery served the same purposes. It made questions of care irrelevant and established the buyer's right to reject the goods before most of the purchase price had been transferred and would have to be recovered.

Related to this need for simplicity in the rules was the practice of having legal consequences attach to objective acts and not to abstract principles. This, too, was a result of the ineffective rule of the courts. There was no tribunal to determine when abstract rights like ownership were transferred or to answer such questions as how many "incidents of ownership" were retained or how the "bundle of rights" was divided. These are difficult issues for the most well-developed judicial systems. Overt acts like the delivery of the goods were much more concrete. They were visible and they were definite. Physical possession of the goods passed or it did not. Ambiguities and borderline situations were reduced to a minimum.

This was also true of having contracts become binding on the occurrence of partial or full performance and not acceptance of an offer or a "meeting of the minds." Partial performance, usually payment of a deposit, was clear and definite. It was paid or it was not. The only question would be one of fact and not of an abstract principle of law.

All of these rules served to reinforce the self-executing devices that were built into the terms of the contracts themselves. In the absence of a legal system that readily and uniformly enforced the contracts that came before it, contracts in Taiwan were structured in a way to encourage performance by the force of their own terms. Prepaid deposits, which were forfeited if the buyer failed to pay completely, were commonly used and ranged from 10 percent of the purchase price for ordinary goods to as high as 80 percent for grain sales. These deposits acted as security for performance and, on a buyer's breach, as liquidated damages for the seller, all without the intervention of a court. Apart from this type of deposit, the remaining terms of a sales contract were normally arranged so that there would be simultaneous performance. The goods would be paid for at the same time they were being transferred. Each side could effectively withhold his own performance to force the other.

In loan contracts, third-party guarantors played a vital role. In addition to agreeing to pay, partially or fully, if the debtor did not, the guarantor gave publicity to the transaction, served as a sort of credit reference, and was expected to do everything he could to encourage the debtor to repay. The use of guarantors allowed loans to be made among strangers, enabled bad credit risks to get loans, and, as security provisions do everywhere, lowered the cost of money by allowing lower interest rates than would otherwise be necessary.

This self-enforcement did not work perfectly. Buyers could always choose to forfeit their deposits, and sometimes the amount of the deposit was not enough to cover the seller's losses. Simultaneous performance prevented one party from backing out after the other had performed, but it did not assure performance of a purely executory contract by either; each side could refuse at the last minute. The weakest point of all was that very little effective leverage was given to the buyer of goods who had prepaid a deposit. The seller was bound to deliver, but there was no mechanism built into the contract to force him to do so. The buyer could only try to resist a return of the deposit or hope that the seller would be too inconvenienced to return it.

Despite these weaknesses, the achievement of the highly developed, sophisticated system of contract that did exist is impressive. It allowed commerce to flourish through the use of long-range, impersonal bargains which did not require extensive external coercion to assure performance. Studies of the impact of Western legal systems on Taiwan and China in general in the twentieth century and the resulting "legal modernization" will have to take full account of the vitality of the traditional legal forms.

Whether Western contract law has fully superseded these indigenous forms is a question that remains to be answered. But it may be that the "legal modernization" which has taken place in China and Taiwan owes its success as much or more to the strength of the traditional institutions as to any contributions made by Western law.

NOTES

1. Sources for this study are chiefly taken from the work of the Temporary Commission for the Survey of Traditional Customs in Taiwan (*Rinji Taiwan kyūkan chōsakai*; hereinafter Survey Commission), established in 1901 by the Japanese colonial government-general. The Survey Commission collected materials and conducted extensive research on a wide variety of subjects. The major publication in the area of customary law was *Taiwan shihō* [The Private Law of Taiwan] (1910), a six-volume work which reprinted and analyzed documents pertaining to land law, family law, personal property and commercial law (hereinafter cited as *TWSH*), with seven volumes of reference materials entitled *Taiwan shihō furoku sankōsho*. The Survey Commission's monthly magazine *Taiwan kanshū kiji* [Articles on the Customs of Taiwan], published from 1901 to 1907, contains a substantial amount of additional information. Another useful Survey Commission publication for contracts is *Keiji oyobi shokan bunruishu* [A Collection of Contracts and Documents] (1916).
2. In this paper I have tried to avoid technical definitions of legal terms and concepts and instead have used these terms in their ordinary, "commonsense" meanings intelligible to most readers. I use "law" to refer to the whole body of rules which are binding on members of a society and which are enforced through sanctions of any kind from any source. "Formal" or "written law" is prescribed by the state and enforced through its sanctioning apparatus. "Customary law" is not prescribed by the state but may be enforced through state legal institutions or by the application of informal social sanctions. "Customs," "practices," and "usages" are used to indicate forms of behavior usually found and expected in a society but in respect to which violations will not be punished. Customs or practices may become customary law through an increase in the expectations of a society to the point where a failure to conform to that expectation will be punished, formally or informally, or through a process of restatement by a formal legal institution, as discussed in P. Bohannan, "Law and Legal Institutions," *Int'l. Encyc. Soc. Sci.*, Vol. 9 (New York, 1968), p. 75. "Adjudication" or "litigation" is a process of dispute settlement in which a third party decides the outcome and imposes it on the parties to the dispute. "Mediation," on the other hand, requires the assent of both parties to the result and may not be imposed from the outside. I have also tried to limit my use of terms frequently used in the legal system of the United States. The reader should keep in mind that such terms are used here in a descriptive and general way and not in their technical legal sense.

3. See Rosser H. Brockman, "Customary Contract Law in Late Traditional Taiwan" (unpublished Ph.D. Thesis, Cambridge, Mass., 1973).
4. For a general introduction to Chinese society and government in late Ch'ing times, cf. J. Fairbank, E. Reischauer, and A. Craig, *East Asia, The Modern Transformation* (Boston, 1965). More detailed coverage of selected aspects of Chinese law and administration may be found in Hsiao Kung-chuan, *Rural China: Imperial Control in the Nineteenth Century* (Seattle, 1960); Derk Bodde and Clarence Morris, *Law in Imperial China* (Cambridge, Mass., 1967); and Ch'ü T'ung-tsu, *Local Government in China under the Ch'ing* (hereinafter cited as Ch'ü, *Local Government*) (Cambridge, Mass., 1962). Works of special usefulness as background to the present study include William Skinner, "Marketing and Social Structure in Rural China, Part I," *Journal of Asian Studies*, Vol. 24, No. 1 (1969), pp. 3-43; R. Tawney, *Land and Labor in China* (London and New York, 1932); Ino Yoshinori, *Taiwan bunka shi* [Cultural History of Taiwan], Vol. 2 (Tokyo, 1929); H. Lamley, "The Taiwan Literati and Early Japanese Rule, 1895-1915" (hereinafter cited as Lamley) (unpublished Ph.D. Thesis, Seattle, 1964); G. Barclay, *Colonial Development and Population in Taiwan* (hereinafter cited as Barclay) (Princeton, 1954); and Huang Ching-chia, *Jih-chü shih-tai chih T'aiwan chih-min-ti fa-chih yü chih-min t'ung-chih* [The Colonial Legal System and Colonial Control of Taiwan during the Period of Japanese Occupation] (Taipei, 1960).
5. Lamley, p. 32.
6. *Ibid.*, at p. 44.
7. Barclay, p. 13.
8. Lamley, p. 52.
9. *Ibid.*, at p. 55.
10. *Ibid.*, at p. 59.
11. The aborigines were few, and lived primarily in the interior mountains. There was little interaction between the Chinese settlers and the aborigines, and for the purposes of this study the aborigines are largely irrelevant. In 1905 the aborigines made up 2.7 percent of the total population. Barclay, at p. 16.
12. J. Davidson, *The Island of Formosa* (London and New York, 1903), pp. 123-169.
13. W. Speidel, "Liu Ming-ch'uan in Taiwan, 1844-1891" (unpublished Ph.D. Thesis, New Haven, 1967).
14. Lamley, at pp. 37-41.
15. See, for example, Bodde and Morris, note 4 above; Ch'ü T'ung-tsu, *Law and Society in Traditional China* (Paris and The Hague, 1961); and especially Benjamin Schwartz, "On Attitudes Toward Law in China" in Jerome A. Cohen, *The Criminal Process in the People's Republic of China, 1949-1963: An Introduction* (Cambridge, Mass., 1968), pp. 62-70.
16. For example, cf. the statement by C. H. Peake quoted in J. Fairbank, *The United States and China* (rev. ed., 1958), p. 96. "Likewise the characteristics of Chinese customary law with its emphasis on human rights over property rights, on duty over right, on individual and group responsibility for the social consequences of all acts, stand in marked contrast to the significant characteristics of Western law."

17. S. Macauley, "Non-Contractual Relations in Business," *Am. Sociolog. Rev.*, Vol. 28 (1968) (hereinafter cited as Macauley), pp. 55-67.
18. In 1961, only 2,779 of the 58,293 civil suits filed with U.S. District Courts involved private contracts. *Ibid.*, at p. 62.
19. Most major contracts case books in the United States follow this pattern. A typical example is the excellent L. Fuller and R. Braucher, *Basic Contract Law* (St. Paul, 1964) (hereinafter cited as Fuller and Braucher). The tendency to stress what happens after a dispute occurs is not limited to contract law. Legal scholarship in general shows an inclination to stress the restorative or corrective aspects of law and to neglect the prescriptive and instrumental features of the law.
20. Stereotyped contract language also serves to make it easier for inexperienced persons—"legal amateurs"—to make use of the legal system. In the United States, for example, any person can purchase legally effective contract forms and other documents from a legal stationer without having specific legal knowledge or going to the expense of having the documents drafted independently. In Taiwan, stereotyped contract language performed a similar service. By using these phrases, a "legal amateur" could create what he knew would be recognized as a binding agreement.
21. K. Llewellyn, "What Price Contract?," *Yale L.J.*, Vol. 40, No. 5 (1931), pp. 712-714.
22. Many sections of the Uniform Commercial Code either provide that elements of the transaction will be determined directly by commercial custom or allow custom to alter the prescribed terms of the bargain. For example, Section 2-316 (3) (c) provides that "an implied warranty may also be excluded or modified by course of dealing or course of performance or usuage of trade." An entire section, 1-205, is devoted to definitions of these terms.
23. Rheinstein, ed., *Max Weber on Law in Economy and Society*, tr. Shils and Rheinstein (1954) (hereinafter cited as Rheinstein), p. 12.
24. D. Buxbaum, "Some Aspects of Civil Procedure and Practice at the Trial Level in Tanshui and Hsinchu from 1789 to 1895," *J. Asian Studies*, Vol. 30 (1971) (hereinafter cited as Buxbaum), p. 255.
25. See discussion at note 42, below.
26. R. Schwartz, "Social Factors in the Development of Legal Control: A Case Study of Two Israeli Settlements," *Yale L.J.*, Vol. 63 (1954), p. 470.
27. Llewellyn, note 21 above, at pp. 720-721.
28. Most notably by Niida Noboru, *Chūgoku hōseishi Kenkyū: Tochihō, Torihikihō* [A Study of Chinese Legal History: Law of Land and Law of Transaction] (Tokyo, 1960-1964), pp. 477-643.
29. Apparently the "financial secretaries" served as advisers for civil cases while the "legal secretaries" confined themselves primarily to criminal cases. Cf. *TWSH*, Vol. 6 (1910), p. 467.
30. Ch'ü, *Local Government*, p. 127.
31. Buxbaum to the contrary, note 24 above, at p. 262.
32. The statute numbers used here and below are taken from G. Staunton, *Ta Tsing Leu Lee* (hereinafter cited as Staunton) (London, 1810).

33. Full translations may be found in Staunton, pp. 160–165 and G. Jamieson, *Chinese Family and Commercial Law* (Shanghai, 1921), pp. 110–112.
34. Buxbaum, note 24 above, at p. 264.
35. 5 *TWSH*, note 1 above, at pp. 73–74. A *yüan* was a Chinese coin that was in theory worth one ounce of silver, but which was actually worth about 70 percent of the value of an ounce of silver.
36. *Ibid.*, p. 322.
37. H. McAleavy, "Dien in China and Vietnam," *J. Asian Studies*, Vol. 17 (May 1958), pp. 403–415.
38. Civil Appeal Case No. 56 (1902) in *Taiwan kanshū kiji* [Articles on the Customs of Taiwan], Vol. 2 (1902) (hereinafter cited as *KSKJ*), p. 691.
39. Civil Appeal Case No. 293 (1902), *ibid.*, pp. 951-952.
40. Civil Appeal Case No. 270 (1900), in *KSKJ*, Vol. 3, p. 534.
41. Civil Appeal Case No. 20 (1901), in *KSKJ*, Vol. 4, p. 18.
42. Buxbaum, note 24 above, at p. 271. Buxbaum's data tables are difficult to use. They contain minor inconsistencies and the only tables where the general categories criminal and civil are broken down into subdivisions are apparently complicated by double counting. The percentages given above are approximations.
43. Tr. in S. van der Sprenkel, *Legal Institutions in Manchu China* (London, 1962), pp. 149–150.
44. Rheinstein, note 23 above, at p. 213, n. 48.
45. Buxbaum says that by Weber's standards Chinese law during the Ch'ing "does not fare badly." Buxbaum, note 24 above, at p. 272. He gives as a reason for this the existence of a Code. Yet for his primary concern, civil law, the Code was mostly irrelevant. Additional analysis is necessary before the Chinese legal system can be graded using Weber's criteria.
46. D. J. MacGowan, "Chinese Guilds or Chambers of Commerce and Trade Unions," *J. of the China Branch, Royal Asiatic Society*, Vol. 21 (Shanghai, 1886), pp. 140–141.
47. F. R. Sanborn, "Law Merchant," *Encyc. Soc. Sci.*, Vol. 9 (1933), pp. 270–274.
48. J. H. Wigmore, ed., "Materials for the Study of Private Law in Old Japan," *Transactions of the Asiatic Society of Japan, Supplement 1*, Vol. 20 (1892), p. 157.
49. The 3rd, 8th, 13th, 18th, 23rd, and 28th days of each month. Ch'ü, *Local Government*, p. 274, n. 13.
50. *TWSH*, Vol. 5, p. 465.
51. This would typically include an individual's age, address, marital status, occupation and so on.
52. This was the colorful term, *sung-kun*, used for litigious troublemakers.
53. *TWSH*, Vol. 6, pp. 460–462.
54. Ch'ü, *Local Government*, pp. 56–73.
55. *TWSH*, Vol. 6, p. 467.
56. *Ibid.*, p. 471.
57. van der Sprenkel, note 43 above, at p. 69.
58. Buxbaum, note 24 above, at p. 268.
59. Rinji Taiwan kyūkan chōsakai [Temporary Commission for the Survey of

Traditional Customs in Taiwan] *Taiwan shihō furoku sankōsho* [Supplementary Reference Materials for the Private Law of Taiwan] (hereinafter cited as *Reference Materials*), Vol. 3 Part 1, pp. 234-241.

60. *TWSH*, Vol. 6, p. 463.
61. *Reference Materials*, Vol. 3, Part 1, pp. 239-240.
62. *TWSH*, Vol. 6, p. 463.
63. *Ibid.*, p. 474.
64. *Ibid.*, p. 476-477.
65. There were two other plea forms which were used less frequently: *hung-pin* or "red petition," which could be used by the gentry, and *pai-pin* or "white petition," which could be used by the common people. *Ibid.*, p. 458.
66. *Ibid.*, p. 459-460.
67. *Ibid.*, p. 465.
68. *Ibid.*, p. 472-473.
69. *Ibid.*, p. 475.
70. Buxbaum, note 24 above, at p. 269.
71. This apparently came up in the oral testimony because the magistrate refers to it in the judgment without its having been mentioned in any of the other documents.
72. For example, cf. the cases translated in Bodde and Morris, note 4 above.
73. The *tsung-li* headed the government-sponsored organizations called *li* and *pao* which were composed of subsidiary street and village organizations. He was chosen by the local elders and officially authorized by the *yamen*. "The Old Village Customs Regarding Civil Mediation," *KHKJ*, Vol. 3 (1901), p. 56.
74. Cohen, "Chinese Mediation on the Eve of Modernization," *Calif. L. Rev.*, Vol. 54, No. 2 (Aug. 1966) (hereinafter cited as Cohen), p. 1209.
75. *Ibid.*, p. 1210.
76. Buxbaum, note 24 above at p. 276.
77. *Ibid.*
78. *Reference Materials*, Vol. 3, Part 1, pp. 239-240.
79. *Ibid.*, p. 240.
80. *Ibid.*, pp. 240-241.
81. *Ibid.*, pp. 232-234.
82. Cf. A. A. Leff, "Injury, Ignorance and Spite—The Dynamics of Coercive Collection," *Yale L.J.*, Vol. 80, No. 1 (Nov. 1970), p. 1.
83. Cohen, pp. 1214-1215.
84. *TWSH*, Vol. 5, p. 344.
85. For a general discussion of contracts in China, cf. Richard Pfeffer, *Understanding Business Contracts in China, 1949-1963* (Cambridge, Mass., 1973).
86. It is defined as *ch'an-shu* (to bind together) in the *K'ang-hsi T'zu-tien* (hereinafter cited as *Kangsi Dictionary*).
87. *Kangsi Dictionary*. A discussion of these terms can be found in *TWSH*, Vol. 5, pp. 344-346.
88. *TWSH*, Vol. 5, p. 360.
89. *Ibid.*, pp. 360-363.
90. American Law Institute, *Uniform Commercial Code*, 1962, Official Text with Comments.

91. For example, see the cases in E. A. Peters, *Commercial Transactions: Cases, Text and Problems on Contracts Dealing with Personality, Realty and Services* (Indianapolis, 1971).
92. G. Gilmore and C. Black, *The Law of Admiralty* (New York, 1957), p. 93.
93. *TWSH*, Vol. 5, pp. 384-386.
94. *Ibid.*, p. 395.
95. Fuller and Braucher, p. 151.
96. *TWSH*, Vol. 5, p. 338.
97. The term translated as "unconditional" is literally "exhaust the root" and means without reserve, or total.
98. Rinji Taiwan kyūkan chōsakai [Temporary Commission for the Survey of Traditional Customs in Taiwan], *Keiji oyobi shokan bunruishū* [A Collection of Contracts and Documents] (Tokyo, 1916), pp. 73-74.
99. Interview, *KSKJ*, Vol. 5, p. 401.
100. E. Kroker, "The Concept of Property in Chinese Customary Law," *Transactions of the Asiatic Society of Japan, 3rd Series*, Vol. 7 (1959), p. 138.
101. McAleavy, note 37 above, at p. 405, notes that boats could be mortgaged (*tien*) just as land could.
102. *TWSH*, Vol. 5, p. 399.
103. Rinji Taiwan kyūkan chōsakai [Temporary Commission for the Survey of Traditional Customs in Taiwan], *Taiwan kanshū taiyō* [An Outline of Old Customs in Taiwan] (Tokyo, n.d.).
104. *Reference Materials*, Vol. 3, Part 1, pp. 184-185.
105. *TWSH*, Vol. 5, pp. 457-458.
106. *Reference Materials*, Vol. 3, Part 1, pp. 190-191.
107. *Ibid.*, pp. 194-195.
108. *Ibid.*, p. 192.
109. *TWSH*, Vol. 5, pp. 457-458.
110. *Ibid.*
111. *Reference Materials*, Vol. 3, Part 1, p. 187.
112. *TWSH*, Vol. 5, p. 344.
113. *TWSH*, Vol. 5, pp. 397-398.
114. *Ibid.*, p. 396.
115. *KSKJ*, Vol. 5, p. 401.
116. *TWSH*, Vol. 5, p. 420.
117. This type of purchasing system conforms very well with the system projected by Skinner, note 4 above.
118. *TWSH*, Vol. 5, p. 401.
119. *Ibid.*, p. 405.
120. The mention of a penalty for fraud suggests that criminal concepts retained some vitality in customary contract ideas.
121. *KSKJ*, Vol. 5, pp. 401-403.
122. Uniform Sales Act, Section 22.
123. Uniform Commercial Code, Section 2-509.
124. These also exist in American and, indeed, any law. They involve questions such as whether a gangplank is an extension of the boat or the dock.
125. Insurance, especially maritime insurance, was used by Western traders.
126. Question: When a wholesaler on this island orders goods from a guild on

the mainland and there are no special contract terms and the goods are lost at sea through no one's fault, who bears the loss?
Answer: The wholesaler on this island who ordered the goods. *TWSH*, Vol. 5, p. 374.

127. *Ibid.*, p. 374.
128. *Ibid.*, p. 437.
129. *Ibid.*
130. *Ibid.*, p. 445.
131. *Ibid.*, p. 374.
132. *Ibid.*, p. 439.
133. W. Hamilton, "The Ancient Maxim Caveat Emptor," *Yale L.J.*, Vol. 40, No. 8 (June 1931), p. 1133.
134. *TWSH*, Vol. 5, p. 444.
135. *Ibid.*, p. 441.
136. *Ibid.*, pp. 441-442.
137. *Ibid.*, p. 375.
138. Cf. Peters, note 91 above, at pp. 346-353.
139. M. Gluckman, *Ideas in Barotse Jurisprudence* (New Haven, 1965), pp. 202-203.
140. *TWSH*, Vol. 5, p. 419.
141. *Ibid.*, p. 446.
142. *Ibid.*
143. That is, a defaulting buyer would pay the seller the difference between the contract price and the market price. E. A. Peters, "Remedies for Breach of Contracts Relating to the Sale of Goods under the Uniform Commercial Code: A Roadmap for Article Two," *Yale L.J.*, Vol. 73, No. 2 (Dec. 1963), pp. 253-254.
144. *TWSH*, Vol. 5, p. 444.

V

AGE, YOUTH, AND INFIRMITY IN THE LAW OF CH'ING CHINA[1]

Derk Bodde

Introduction

Probably the most conspicuous single Confucian influence on imperial Chinese law is the principle of legalized inequality. Prior to the revolution of 1911, Chinese law endlessly differentiated its treatment according to individual rank, relationship, and specific circumstance. Entire social groups—notably the officials—enjoyed special legal privileges differentiating them from the great mass of commoners. Punishments were carefully graduated according to the social status of the wrongdoer and his victim. Especially within the family, hierarchy was highly stressed: an offense by a junior family member against a senior was punished more severely than the same offense committed outside the family, and *much* more severely than the same offense committed by a senior family member against a junior.[2]

In the world of today, although the disastrous consequences of forced social inequality remain only too apparent, the *theory* at least of legalized inequality is no longer openly espoused save in a few countries. By saying this, I mean in no way to suggest that instances of sanctioned inequality never occur, even today, in Western law systems. Of course they do, as, for example, in laws of the sort providing harsher punishment for killing a policeman or other upholder of state authority than for an ordinary homicide. Nowhere as much as in pre-Republican China, however, has the principle of legalized differentiation according to rank, relationship, and specific circumstance been so deliberately, systematically, and conspicuously enshrined. This fact is not surprising in view of the enormous emphasis on hierarchical differentiation which has always characterized Confucian social thinking.

Before congratulating ourselves, however, we should remember that there is a second side to the Confucian coin of hierarchy: Confucian particularism, when coupled with Confucian humanitarianism, leads to special legal provisions concerning weaker members of society who are

0-691-09238-9/80/000137-33$01.65/1 For copying information, see copyright page

guilty of crime. These are notably women, the aged, the young, and the infirm. In the codes of successive dynasties, women are discussed separately from the rest, and we shall not consider them in this study except for a few brief remarks in the concluding section. The other three categories, however, have been treated as a single unit in the codes since the earliest surviving T'ang Code of A.D. 653 and probably before. This makes it appropriate for us to study them jointly; the more so as apparently no comprehensive study of all three of them has previously been made.[3] Our study will be restricted to the Ch'ing dynasty (1644–1911), focusing on the Ch'ing Code of 1740, and on forty relevant Ch'ing legal cases (the great majority belonging to the early decades of the nineteenth century).

The Statutes

As arranged in the Ch'ing Code, the major laws dealing with the aged, the young, and the infirm comprise a single statute and nine substatutes under section 22 ("Monetary Redemption Permitted to the Aged, the Young, and Infirm"), followed in section 23 ("Wrongdoing Committed Prior to Becoming Aged or Infirm") by one more statute without substatutes. Both statutes (but not the substatutes) are accompanied by an imperially sponsored and therefore equally authoritative Official Commentary. Translations of the statutes, of the Official Commentary for the first statute but not the second, and of four out of the nine substatutes (the rest being irrelevant for our purpose), will be found in Appendix 5.1.

This appendix also provides dates of origin for each item. The statutes themselves, with only minor verbal changes, date back to the T'ang Code of 653, and their Official Commentary conforms closely to the corresponding passages of commentary found in the Ming Code of 1397 (the dynastic code immediately preceding the Ch'ing). As for the nine substatutes, the earliest (number 3) ultimately derives, with some verbal changes, from a passage of commentary in the corresponding section in the T'ang Code; the next earliest (number 1) is a replica of a substatute in the Ming Code; the remaining seven are all Ch'ing creations, variously dating from 1673 to 1818.

Of the nine substatutes, only the seventh (especially the second paragraph, dealing with homicide committed by children aged 11-15) is cited frequently enough in the forty cases discussed below to render it a really significant Ch'ing addition to legal theory on age, youth, and infirmity.[4] The fifth substatute[5] has some importance in that it restricts, for the period following its promulgation in 1745, the scope of legally defined "infirmity." For the most part, however, the Ch'ing jurists, like their predecessors, rely primarily for their handling of age, youth, and infirmity cases on what the all-important initial statute says on this subject.

In the statute and its commentary, age and youth are each discussed under three levels or grades. Arranged in ascending order of importance, the levels begin with ages 70-79 (first degree of age) and 11-15 (first degree of youth); then come 80-89 (second degree of age) and 8-10 (second degree of youth); followed by 90 and above (third degree of age) and 7 and below (third degree of youth). For physical impairment there are only two levels or degrees. The first, "infirmity" (*fei-chi*), is the correlate of the first degrees of age and youth, while the second, "incapacity" (*tu-chi*), is the correlate of the higher two degrees of age and youth lumped together.

The extent of privilege granted to an offender varies not only according to his age or infirmity level but also according to the seriousness of his offense. For certain major crimes—notably rebellion and treason—no privilege at all is accorded (save possibly for children of 7 years or less; the text is not explicit on this point). In most instances, however, the offender is permitted to substitute a payment of money (monetary redemption) for the statutory punishment. The sums involved (unspecified in this section of the Code) are relatively trifling: only 0.525 taels (ounces of silver), for example, for a capital offense. In certain instances, exemption from punishment is granted without the need for monetary redemption at all. However, as we shall see in detail later, the according of these privileges is by no means invariable or automatic, but has to be individually determined in each case. In capital cases it almost always requires either the submission of a special petition to the throne for clemency or, less frequently, favorable judgment at the autumn assizes held annually in Peking.[6]

Why did the Chinese thus single out the aged, young, and infirm for special legal treatment? Two possible answers, the one pragmatic, the other moralistic, emerge from the 40 legal cases whose analysis will form the main body of this study.[7] In case 18 (dated 1792) the following practical justification for granting clemency to aged wrongdoers is found: "Their powers have already declined so that they are not in a position to repeat their offense. Hence clemency is especially applied to them." In case 21 (dated 1827), on the other hand, the special kinds of treatment accorded to the three categories of wrongdoers are described as "all of them examples of extralegal humanity" (*jen*). By extralegal the writer certainly does not mean that the special kinds of treatment are in any way illegal; rather, they are exceptions to ordinary legal procedure, being determined by a special group of laws whose promulgation has been motivated by considerations of humanity. He would not deny that within the particular social sphere covered by these particular laws, they operate just as regularly and legally as do the laws not motivated by such special considerations.

That Confucian humanitarianism was in fact the dominant and original reason why, long before the Ch'ing dynasty, the Chinese promulgated special laws on age, youth, and infirmity, becomes apparent as soon as we compare the Ch'ing Code's major statute on the subject (section 22) with its earliest surviving legal counterpart, that in the T'ang Code of 653. We at once see that whereas the texts of the two statutes themselves are almost identical, word for word, the officially compiled commentary on the T'ang statute is considerably longer than the corresponding Ch'ing Code's Official Commentary. In part, the reason for the T'ang commentary's greater length is that, unlike its Ch'ing counterpart, it goes to some pains to explain *why* monetary redemption may properly be granted to wrongdoers who are aged, young, or infirm. In so doing, it repeatedly introduces the words "compassion" (*chin*) and "love" (*ai*) into its discussion. But the decisive point—one that takes the humanitarian concept all the way back to classical Confucianism—is the fact that the T'ang commentary supports its argument by quoting the following passage from the opening chapter of the *Li Chi* or *Book of Rites*: "A person of eighty or ninety is called a venerable greybeard (*mao*). A person of seven is called a child deserving of pity (*tao*). A child deserving of pity or a venerable greybeard, even though they may have committed a crime, are not to be subjected to punishment." This *Li Chi* passage, as cited by the T'ang commentary, is made even stronger by deliberately changing the *Li Chi*'s original phrase, "committed a crime," into "committed a capital crime."[8]

The Cases

The great advantage of working with Ch'ing law, and the reason why that dynasty is the subject of our inquiry, is that its law can be checked against a large body of actual cases. Most notable of the Ch'ing casebooks is the *Hsing-an hui-lan* or *Conspectus of Penal Cases*.[9] The three component divisions of the *Conspectus* (the *Hsing-an hui-lan* or *HAHL* proper, the *HAHL First Supplement*, and the *HAHL Second Supplement*) contain reports of over 7,600 cases that came to the Board of Punishments in Peking from lower judicial levels and were adjudicated by the Board. Their time span is 1736-1885, though more than three-quarters of them belong to the first three decades of the nineteenth century.

Within this huge body of cases covering the entire gamut of the Ch'ing Code, forty are relevant to our interest. Thirty-eight of them appear in section 14 of the *Conspectus* (entitled, like its Code counterpart, "Monetary Redemption Permitted to the Aged, the Young, and the Infirm"), followed by two more in section 15 ("Wrongdoing Committed Prior to Becoming Aged or Infirm"). A list of the entire forty, with full data about source, date, and locale, will be found in Appendix 5.2.[10] The total time span is 1788-1881, but thirty-two of the cases belong to the 29-year period, 1809-1837. Geographically, the cases cover all of the provinces of China proper except Kansu. In addition, they cover Mukden and Heilungkiang in Manchuria, Chahar in Inner Mongolia, and Urumchi in Sinkiang—all areas of greater China.

Among the forty cases, fifteen involve youth, nine involve the aged, and another fifteen concern infirmity. The single remaining case[11] does not really belong to this section at all—its concern is not the killer but his youthful victim—but it is of great importance for all the cases involving age because it establishes definitive legal criteria for measuring human age. Therefore it can logically begin our discussion.

The case is one in which the murderer, an adult, strangled the small son of a neighbor on a date corresponding to March 6, 1810. This was less than ten full years after the birth date of the victim, which was November 7, 1800. The governor-general who reported the case to Peking therefore made the almost unprecedented suggestion that the killer, on the basis of this reckoning, should be sentenced to immediate decapitation, this being the statutory penalty for the premeditated murder of a child of 10 or less.

I say almost unprecedented because, as we shall see in the concluding section, the governor-general based his recommendation upon a single earlier case. According to traditional Chinese reckoning, an individual begins his life at the moment of conception and therefore, as is well known, is conventionally considered to be 1 year old at birth. Furthermore, for the sake of convenience in maintaining the official population records (based on a lunar and therefore a fluctuating calendar), the individual is said to become 2 years old at the first lunar New Year following his birth; thereafter he, like everyone else, acquires an additional year with each successive New Year.

For the murder victim of our case this means that, for purposes of vital statistics, he became 2 years old on February 13, 1801, this being his first New Year, and that on the New Year of 1810, which that year fell on February 4, he became 11 only a little over a month prior to his death on March 6 of that year. This is the reckoning used by the Board of Punishments to reject the governor-general's proposed judgment. For the murderer the difference was of crucial importance, for by changing the victim's official age from less than 10 to barely 11, it also changed the murderer's penalty from immediate decapitation to decapitation after the assizes, thereby making possible (though by no means certain) further reduction of penalty at the autumn assizes to a sentence of life exile.

The Board argued that if, as suggested by the governor-general, permission were given to correlate the precise solar-based ages of individuals with the fluctuating lunar calendar, endless confusion would result. The emperor, in an imperial rescript, further supported the Board's ruling with a sociological argument. If, he wrote, the governor-general's decision were followed, "it is to be feared that offenders would participate in deliberate deception and embellishment, and that officials would shift high and low ages around and give increase to corrupt practices."[12]

The governor-general, as part of his argument, had pointed out that a legal year, as defined in the Code, has 360 days,[13] and that this definition seriously conflicts with age reckoning based on the lunar calendar. To this the Board replied that the 360-day year is legally used only to calculate relatively short-term time spans such as the deadline set for arresting a criminal or for paying a tax. Never is it used to calculate human age, for which the only basis of reckoning is the date in the lunar-based 60-year cycle under which an individual's birth is recorded in the population and tax registers of his local district. The governor-general should in fact have known as much, because the Board was merely citing at this point the statement contained in the statute that defined the legal year.

This case illustrates how complexities were constantly creeping into the Chinese bureaucratic system—caused in this instance by the need to reconcile a fluctuating lunar calendar with a fixed solar reckoning. It also illustrates the need of the Chinese state—no doubt psychological as well as actual—to deal institutionally with individual differences by subsuming them under a universal bureaucratic model. Finally, the case is important for our understanding of the composition of Chinese age groups as legally defined, for we see from it that, legally speaking, people in China passed from childhood to adulthood (Chinese age 16), and from adulthood to old age (Chinese age 70) anywhere from a year to two years earlier than did their counterparts in the West.

Thus, the Chinese system of reckoning gave Chinese society a smaller proportion of "young" people and a larger proportion of "old" than would have been possible under Western reckoning. The net result is that the laws on youth and age, although ostensibly designed to protect the two age groups equally, actually applied to, and therefore were important for, a relatively broad sector of aged people as against a relatively narrow sector of the young, legally defined. No doubt this fact harmonized well with the traditional Confucian veneration of age and emphasis on filial piety. No doubt, too, it provided a psychological counterbalance to the biological forces of high rates of birth and early death which, in China, as in other preindustrial societies, favored the development of a predominantly youthful population.

Treatment of the Young

Of the fifteen cases having to do with the young,[14] all but the final two are based on the important seventh substatute in section 22 of the Code: the first eleven cases on its second paragraph, the next two on its first. What makes the seventh substatute significant is that, with respect to young persons guilty of homicides punishable by death, it widens the scope of allowable clemency as defined in the main statute under section 22. Under the statute itself, only those capital offenders who belong to the two higher degrees of youth, age, or infirmity are eligible for clemency. The substatute, however, lays down circumstances under which capital offenders belonging to the first degree of youth (but not to the first degrees of age or infirmity) also become eligible. The importance of this provision is shown by the fact that homicide is a primary factor in all of the youth cases to be discussed, but in only about a fourth of the age and infirmity cases.

The seventh substatute states, under its vital second paragraph, that if a child of 11-15 (first degree of youth) has been provoked by a person four or more years older than himself into fighting that person and thereby killing him, he may have a petition submitted to the throne on his behalf requesting clemency for his offense of killing in an affray, the normal penalty being strangulation after the assizes. (Once submission of the petition has been approved by the Board of Punishments, approval of the petition itself is normally routine.) The precedent justifying this substatute is the Ting Ch'i-san case of 1732. Ting was a boy of 14 who, while carrying baskets of earth, was bombarded with earth clods by another boy four years his senior until, under provocation, he threw clods back, one of which hit and killed the other boy. Ting's trial resulted in his being accorded imperial clemency, and in the end he was permitted monetary redemption. (Incidentally, it is somewhat curious that this case precedent had to wait more than four decades before finally becoming enshrined as a substatute in 1779.)

Among the first eleven cases, several not only cite the prototype case of Ting Ch'i-san but also cite and state the essential facts of several later case precedents. Putting together the cases proper and the precedent cases cited therein, we find an even balance between cases in which clemency is accorded and cases in which it is not—eight of each.[15]

The wording of substatute 7, coupled with what is said in the cases, makes it evident that for a youthful killer to be accorded clemency, he must have been provoked by the behavior of his subsequent victim (his elder) in a way deemed by the court to be "unreasonable" (*li-ch'ü*), "abusive" (*ch'i* and compounds of this word), or "vicious" (*ch'eng-hsiung*).[16] The foregoing terms, despite frequent mention in the cases, are nowhere explicitly defined. Therefore, we have to deduce their meaning from the objective facts narrated in the cases.

The first term, *li-ch'ü* ("unreasonable"), serves to describe the initial act of the older person (the person who is later killed) in response to the initial act of the child who later kills him. In all of these cases it is always the child who initiates the chain of action leading to tragedy. Never is it his victim. The meaning of *li-ch'ü* becomes clear in cases 4 and 6. In the latter, a boy of 14, in order to catch a fish, drains the water from an irrigation ditch which he shares with a much older man. The older man objects and a quarrel ensues in which the older man raises his hand to strike the boy. Before he can actually do so, however, the boy runs off, with the older man in pursuit. As he runs, the boy picks up a stone and throws it at the older man, killing him. The Board finds that the older man's reviling of the boy and his attempt to halt the boy's action were motivated by a reasonable fear that the irrigation ditch would dry up. Thus, it did not constitute "unreasonable" (*li-ch'ü*) conduct. The Board therefore denies clemency to the boy.

In case 4, a youth of over 19 tries unsuccessfully to borrow money for wine from a boy of 14. The two quarrel, and the youth dies. The Board finds that this quarrel, being limited to verbal wrangling, did not constitute unreasonable (*li-ch'ü*) conduct on the part of the victim. It therefore denies clemency to his killer. (We shall discuss shortly the actions that followed the initial verbal wrangling.)

Li-ch'ü is essentially a negative term; it tells us only that the victim's initial reaction was (or was not) "unreasonable." To get a more positive picture of how the victim then and later acted, we must turn to a second group of interrelated terms. They are "abusive" (*ch'i*), "abusive and insulting" (*ch'i-wu*), and "abusive and bullying" (*ch'i-ling*). The idea basic to all of them is that the older person takes advantage of his seniority to browbeat, bully, oppress, ridicule, or cheat the child.

The central word *ch'i* is well illustrated in case 9 where, during the teacher's absence, a schoolboy of 12 plays a game of hitting fists with a classmate of 16. By hiding a bamboo sliver in his hand, he hurts the older boy's finger. An altercation ensues in which the older boy first strikes and hurts the younger boy's shoulder and then, by holding the younger boy from behind, forcibly covers the latter's mouth to prevent him from making an outcry. The younger boy seizes a paper-knife with which he stabs and kills the older one. In its judgment, the Board holds that the older boy, by striking the younger one and then covering his mouth from behind, was guilty of taking advantage of his own age to abuse (*ch'i*) the younger boy. It therefore grants the latter monetary redemption.

The third term, "vicious conduct" (*ch'eng-hsiung*), is close to *ch'i* and its compounds (it could easily have replaced *ch'i* in the case just cited), but its emphasis is upon the act of physical violence per se rather than, as with *ch'i*, upon the fact that the act is directed against a younger person. Its meaning emerges clearly in case 11, where a boy of 14, working as a farmhand, asks his employer for his wages. The latter refuses, and in the resulting altercation he seizes and twists the boy's queue in order to strike him; the boy, out of fear, draws a knife with which he kills the older man. The Board adjudges the seizing of the queue to constitute vicious conduct (*ch'eng-hsiung*) and so allows the boy to petition for clemency.

In all the cases, clemency is granted only when the victim had committed actual physical violence against his youthful killer; mere reviling of him and the like is insufficient cause in itself. The pattern becomes less clear, however, in those cases that deny clemency. In several of them the Board indulges in what, to some, may seem like judicial hairsplitting to prove that what appears to be violent behavior is really not, and therefore does not justify clemency.

In case 2, for example, the older person (aged 21) asks the younger one (aged 14) for some of his sugarcane and is refused, whereupon the older strikes the younger on the left arm. The Board explains that the blow was made only in sport (*hsi*), and therefore does not constitute abuse and insult (*ch'i-wu*). Accordingly clemency is refused to the boy for his act of killing the older person.

In case 3, a boy of 15 becomes angered at a man (age not given but obviously mature) who, on hearing the boy's widowed mother lamenting the difficulty of living as a widow, suggests remarriage. In the resulting quarrel between the boy and the older man, the latter attacks the boy with a stool but is persuaded by a bystander to stop before he actually inflicts injury. The boy then kills the would-be suitor. The Board holds that the older man's acts did not constitute abuse and bullying (*ch'i-ling*)—presumably, though we are not told so, because his use of the stool inflicted no actual injury. Therefore, the Board rules that the case is not analogous to that of Ting Ch'i-san and that the boy does not deserve clemency.

In case 4 (the case involving a dispute over money for wine, mentioned above), the older youth, following the initial verbal wrangling, pushes the boy to the ground and then, upon the latter's getting up and cursing him, picks up a stone. Before he can use it, however, the boy stabs him with a knife. The Provincial Court of Kuangsi, from which the case originates, thinks that the two acts of pushing to the ground and picking up a stone constitute vicious conduct (*ch'eng-hsiung*). It therefore recommends clemency. The Board of Punishments, however, in what may seem to some an arbitrary ruling, rules that inasmuch as no concrete injury resulted from either act, and the situation was not really dangerous, no actual "viciousness" was evident.

Finally, in case 5, a boy goes to glean what is left of tea growing on the mountain plot of another person. He encounters the owner and a quarrel follows during which the owner seizes the boy with the intent of stripping him of his clothes. However, the owner does not actually strike the boy, and when the latter tries to tear himself away, the older man falls and loses his life. The Board, because the victim did not strike the boy, refuses to find that his conduct was either abusive and insulting (*ch'i-wu*) or vicious (*ch'eng-hsiung*) and thus denies clemency to the boy. The circumstances here seem at first sight very similar to those in case 1, in which a boy who is gleaning soybeans likewise becomes embroiled with the bean grower, who chases, catches, and beats him. Thereupon the boy fatally stabs the grower with a sickle. Contrary to its judgment in the tea case, however, the Board finds the bean grower's treatment of the boy to have been both vicious, and abusive and insulting. Therefore, it accords clemency to the boy.

A possible clue to these different holdings may lie in a statement made in case 1 that the gleaning of soybeans by poor people is a recognized practice, as against the absence of a comparable statement in the other case, where, instead, the Board charges the youthful tea gleaner with having violated propriety. Probably more decisive, however, is the act of beating in case 1 as against its absence in case 5. In the latter, the Board obviously does not regard the attempt to strip the boy of his clothes as comparable to a beating. The net result is a judgment of clemency in case 1 and its denial in case 5.

In all of these cases except the one discussed first (case 2, in which the older person is said to have struck his later killer in sport only), the intent of the victim is ignored and judgment rests entirely or at least heavily upon a narrow definition of the physical act performed by the subsequent victim. This mechanistic approach runs counter to the concern with intent found in other categories of cases—for example, in the numerous homicide cases not involving age differences in which careful distinction is made between premeditation, intent, negligence, and so on.

Four of our cases are of special interest because they involve a problem of measuring or balancing: how to adjudicate a situation in which a minor kills a person who is either aged, infirm, or a woman and who, therefore, like himself, enjoys a privileged status, though one different in category from his own. Two such situations are presented jointly in case 10, in which the victims are respectively a woman and a man, "the latter over 70." In both instances, despite these circumstances, clemency is allowed because each of the victims struck his or her killer. In case 6, on the other hand, clemency is denied to the killer of a man of 76 not because of the man's age but because the man raised his hand with intent to strike but, inasmuch as the boy ran away, was unable to effectuate the blow. Finally, in case 7, the Board angrily rejects the suggestion of a provincial court that a boy who killed a blind man (the details are not given) should be accorded clemency. The implications of these and other examples of what I call "balancing" cases will be examined further in the concluding section.[17]

So far we have been discussing the eleven cases whose judgment invokes the second paragraph of substatute 7. Two other cases (12 and 13) have to do with the first paragraph of the same substatute, in which a petition for pardon is to be allowed for a child of 7 or under who is guilty of homicide. In case 12, originating in northern Manchuria, a Manchu boy of 6 quarrels with another Manchu boy of 9 and kills him with a knife. The substatute granting petition for pardon is held applicable. Case 13, probably the most tragic of all our youth cases, concerns a boy of 7 who, carrying a pair of scissors, runs out on the street to play. His married sister calls him to bring them back and he, probably in a fury (though this is not stated), throws them toward her. By mischance (*wu*), he hits and kills a boy of 6 who just then is running toward the sister.[18] The offender's father, tortured by fear that his only son might have to pay with his life (*ti ming*) for the other boy's death, hangs himself. Again the Board holds the substatute to be applicable, so that the son receives no punishment for either of the homicides.[19]

Treatment of the Aged

Among the nine cases involving the aged,[20] the first four (together with two precedent cases cited in case 14) concern men belonging to the second or higher age level (80–89) who are guilty of homicide. Unlike the youth cases, in which none of the killings was premeditated, some of the murders committed by the older men are quite lurid affairs. In each instance, nevertheless, the relevant statute (section 22 of the Code) permits reduction of punishment first from the statutory death penalty to exile and then, by means of monetary redemption, from exile to no penalty at all. Perhaps the most striking is case 17, in which the offender induces several persons to join together to murder a distant nephew, then encourages a member of his clan falsely to accuse an outsider of the crime, and finally flees before he can be arrested. On being captured three years later, his sentence is increased because he fled, from decapitation after the assizes (the standard penalty for his offense) to immediate decapitation. A general imperial amnesty at this time, however, reduces the added punishment once more to decapitation after the assizes. Then the fact that he is 80 (we are not told whether he had just become 80 or was already so at the time of his crime) enables him to escape punishment completely through redemption.

Two other cases, 15.1 and 15.2, are based upon the principle that wrongdoers who become aged or infirm only after their offense comes to light are to be judged in the same manner as if they had already been aged or infirm at the time of the offense. This principle is formulated in general terms in section 23 of the Code and, with special reference to offenders sent to Peking for trial, in substatute 2 of the preceding section. In case 15.1, a licentiate is sentenced to military exile for having written a composition on behalf of his son at the civil service examinations; by the time he is ready for exile, he has reached the age of 70. In case 15.2, the instigator of a fatal group affray is sentenced to exile. Though only 67 at the time of the offense, delay in deciding the case, caused by the Board's reversal of the provincial sentence, brings him to 70 by the time he is ready for exile. Both he and the licentiate of the preceding case are allowed monetary redemption.

The three remaining cases indicate that age is by no means an invariable protection against punishment. Case 19, perhaps the most poignant in the age category, is based upon substatute 8 in section 22, under which redemption may not be accorded a second time for a deliberate offense to any aged, young, or infirm person who has already been granted it for an earlier offense. The case concerns a man who, in 1754, when he was 43, was convicted of theft. His sentence included, as is normal in theft cases, tattooing of the word "thief" on his right forearm. An imperial amnesty released him, however, before he had completed his sentence, and allowed the tattoo then to be removed. Decades later, in 1781, he was again convicted of theft, and this time, having become 70, was permitted redemption. This enabled him to escape all usual punishment on this second occasion, including reimposition of the tattoo. Then in 1788, when he was 77, poverty forced him to come to Peking in search of relatives. Failing to find them but seeing a bin of rice outside a grain shop, he stole several pints and was caught.

The Board of Punishments begins its judgment by admitting that his act, being motivated by poverty and suffering, differed from those of "thieves who bore holes and scale walls" (professional thieves). Nevertheless, continues the Board, the act was deliberate. Hence, under the substatute, the redemption enjoyed by the offender in 1781 may not be repeated. The redemption of that year had canceled out the punishment for that particular theft, thus enabling the new theft of 1788 to be counted as calling for a second rather than a third punishment. The thief should now be sentenced, as if for a second punishment, to the wearing of the cangue and reimposition of the tattoo. The Board further warns that yet another theft will be considered a third offense and will incur the appropriate increased punishment.

Though the humanity and effectiveness of this judgment may be questioned, it at least rests firmly on statutory law. The next two cases, on the other hand, run counter to the literal wording of the primary statute that persons of 70 "are to be given monetary redemption" for offenses punishable by exile or less. This counterindication strongly suggests that, at least as far as the Board was concerned, this statute functioned more as a sanction for discretionary lenience than as an absolute imperative.

In case 26, dated 1809, a district magistrate of over 70 has been found guilty of juggling government funds to the tune of 18,000 taels, the penalty for which is military exile. The Board cites a precedent case of 1804 in which a district magistrate, sentenced to penal servitude for an unspecified offense, was, although over 70, denied redemption on the ground that he was still "basically flourishing" (*pen jung*), that is, he was still in good physical health. The present case is held by the Board to be sufficiently similar to the 1804 precedent to justify a similar denial of redemption. Nevertheless, an unexpected quirk enables the juggler of 18,000 taels to enjoy a happier fate than that of the stealer of several pints of rice in the just mentioned case 19. The Board points out that the juggler's offense was committed prior to a New Year's Day proclamation of imperial clemency of the present year. The net result is that the denial of redemption, though inherently correct, has now lost its validity and therefore, the Board concludes, the sentence should be revised (that is, clemency should be granted).

The last and perhaps most arbitrary of the Board's rulings in cases of this category is case 18, concerning a man of 70 sentenced to exile for having incited litigation. This crime was regarded with particular horror by the authorities.[21] The persons who indulged in it (stigmatized as "litigation tricksters") were men of some education who prepared legal petitions or otherwise helped illiterate or semiliterate persons in rural areas in legal matters. In a Confucian society possessing no formal legal profession, which traditionally regarded the growth of litigation as a symptom of moral decay, these men were apparently viewed as enemies of social stability. Concerning the offender in case 18, the Board writes: "Although old in years, his mental capacities (*chih-lü*) have not declined, so that if permitted monetary redemption and the good fortune of escaping punishment, he would still remain able to stir up the ignorant country folk. This is not the way to give warning to rascally agitators or to bring cessation to litigation."[22] The Board goes on to say that occasional precedents (which it does not specify) are known in which aged persons guilty of crimes entailing either military or ordinary exile have been denied redemption. Similar denial should therefore be made in the present case.[23]

Treatment of the Infirm

The fifteen cases in this section are not easy to discuss, because several of them do not fall into readily discernible legal patterns. A few, because they involve obscure procedural technicalities, will be excluded from the discussion.[24] The atmosphere of the section differs sharply from that of the two other categories owing to the large number of noncommoners who figure in it: officials in six cases, a provincial military graduate in another, and a Mongol bannerman in yet another.[25] One almost wonders whether, in the legal world, infirmity was not predominantly an upper-class phenomenon.

The infirmities themselves are few in kind. Those of the leg or foot, with nine cases, are by far the most common; we read about frozen feet, numbed legs, cramps in the legs, paralysis of the legs, or simply inability to use the legs; some of the medical terms are hard to identify.[26] The next largest group is of partial or total blindness, with four cases (28, 29, 32, and 36). Then come hand injuries (cases 20, 35, 37), dumbness (case 20), and a peculiar but unexplained "frequent state of incapacity" (case 34, conceivably epilepsy).

The limited variety of infirmities reflects the limited range allowable in the Ch'ing Code. Two grades or degrees are defined in the statute under section 22. The first or lower degree is *fei-chi*, translated here "infirmity" to distinguish it from the higher degree that follows. The Official Commentary defines it as "blindness in one eye or loss of one limb and the like." The second and higher degree is *tu-chi*, "incapacity," which the Official Commentary defines as "blindness in both eyes or loss of two limbs and the like." "And the like" does not, as we shall see presently, greatly extend the allowable varieties of infirmity or incapacity.[27] In fact, substatute 5, promulgated in 1745, nullifies the Official Commentary's inclusion of blindness in one eye under infirmity by explicitly denying that such blindness can actually serve as a legal ground for claiming redemption.

The Official Commentary's definitions of infirmity and incapacity reproduce without change the corresponding definitions in the commentary on the Ming Code of 1397. Both sets of definitions, in their very restricted enumeration of possible varieties of infirmity and incapacity, represent a sharp break with earlier dynastic codes, all heavily dominated by the T'ang legal tradition. This becomes apparent if we compare the Ming and Ch'ing definitions with the much broader formulations found both in the T'ang Code of 653 and in the lesser regulations of the same dynasty known as *ling* ("ordinances").[28]

The T'ang legal definition for infirmity (*fei-chi*), as given in these two bodies of law, does not restrict the term to the Ming-Ch'ing requirement of loss of a single limb. It also lists the breaking of a thigh-bone or a vertebra, as well as dumbness and dwarfishness. The only respect, in fact, in which the Ming-Ch'ing definition is broader than the T'ang is the former's inclusion under infirmity of blindness in one eye. The absence of this item from the T'ang definition may conceivably have encouraged the Ch'ing jurists, after having initially accepted the Ming "one-eye" definition for their own Official Commentary, to add later in 1745 a substatute nullifying this provision. On the other hand, irrespective of T'ang precedent, the promulgation of the substatute accords well with a later tendency, discernible in some of the cases discussed below, to restrict the scope both of infirmity and incapacity.

Concerning the second degree, incapacity (*tu-chi*), the T'ang legal sources not only define it as loss of two eyes or two limbs (the Ming-Ch'ing definition) but also mention "loathsome disease" (nature unspecified but probably leprosy), severing of the tongue, which renders speech impossible, and destruction of the male or female generative organs, which prevents procreation. In addition, loss of all ten fingers is accounted incapacity because it prevents the victim from holding things and therefore is comparable to the loss of two limbs.[29]

Quite remarkable is the T'ang legal recognition not merely of physical but also of mental ailments as valid criteria for determining infirmity and incapacity. Indeed, two degrees are specified by the legal sources: "feeblemindedness" (*ch'ih*) under infirmity, and "insanity" (*tien-k'uang*) under incapacity.[30] Dr. Bünger has demonstrated that in T'ang times the feebleminded and the insane were not held legally responsible for their actions, and that this situation apparently persisted at least through the Sung dynasty (960–1279).[31]

With the narrowing of the stipulated criteria for infirmity and incapacity in the Ming and Ch'ing Codes, however, the terms for feeblemindedness (*ch'ih*) and insanity (*tien-k'uang*) disappeared entirely from these codes. The complete absence in our cases of any mention of mental illness confirms the conclusion that the Ch'ing Code's clauses on infirmity and incapacity were intended to deal only with physical and not mental ills.[32] In the Ch'ing Code, to be sure, insanity continues to be discussed in a single section under homicide. No crimes other than homicide are considered, and less stress is laid on the insane person himself than on the responsibility of his family or the local authorities to confine him if he is dangerous. In contrast to the T'ang distinction between feeblemindedness (*ch'ih*) and insanity (*tien-k'uang*), the Ch'ing Code employs a single generalized term, *feng-ping* ("mental illness"). Yet, despite this reduced concern with insanity, the Code still gives some very limited support to Dr. Bünger's general thesis that lunatics were not held responsible for their acts in classical (by which he really means pre-Republican) Chinese law. Thus, for an insane person guilty of a single homicide, the Code provides no punishment other than confinement by his relatives or the local authorities; in addition, a monetary payment must be made by the relatives to the victim's family for funeral expenses. However, should the homicide be of two or more persons, the Code then somewhat inconsistently shifts its stand by sentencing the insane killer to strangulation (or sometimes decapitation) after the assizes.[33]

How the Ch'ing jurists restricted the legal scope of infirmity is illustrated by case 20, in which a governor recommends monetary redemption for unspecified offenses committed by two offenders, one of them dumb since infancy, the other lacking his left hand. The Board recognizes the latter as infirmity but rejects dumbness on the ground that it does not interfere with movement and therefore cannot be compared to loss of a limb. In so doing, the Board runs counter not only to the governor but also to what is said in the Shen Chih-ch'i private commentary of 1715 on the Code. There, as we have seen,[34] dumbness appears in a list of named infirmities, most of them (including dumbness) going back to the T'ang Code. Of course, the Board has good statutory justification for its action. Dumbness is nowhere named as an infirmity in the text proper of the Code, and Shen Chih-ch'i's commentary, influential and widely read though it was, remained a privately written and therefore necessarily nonauthoritative work.

The limitations found in three other cases seem more arbitrary. In case 37, a district magistrate suffers paralysis after being sentenced to exile, but the Board finds that the paralysis affects only the offender's left hand and foot and concludes that this is not enough to support a plea of infirmity (*fei-chi*). The judgment seems clearly at variance with the definition in the Official Commentary ("loss of one limb and the like"). It should be noted that the word "loss" (*che*), though narrowly definable as "to snap, to break off," should not on that account be understood as referring here solely to a broken or amputated limb. In the context of the statute it plainly includes any injury or illness that renders the limb unusable. This is confirmed by case 27, where the Board rules that a cramp in the left leg that prevents walking is to be accounted infirmity.

In case 32 an uncle sentenced to penal servitude for beating an alcoholic nephew to death has suffered partial blindness in both eyes for more than ten years. The Board concludes that such blindness, not being total, is not enough to constitute incapacity (*tu-chi*). Fortunately for the offender, however, it *is* enough to be accounted infirmity, which is all he needs in order to be granted redemption for his particular crime.

The third example is case 34, involving a provincial military graduate's son who is subject to a "frequent state of incapacity" (*tu-chi*), possibly epilepsy, as suggested earlier. This son joins the father in committing vicious acts against two other men, apparently including acts of sadism toward the men's wives and daughters. When the two criminals are given military exile, the Board firmly denies redemption to the son, pointing out that his incapacity is only sporadic and thus in no way excuses his vicious behavior between seizures.

Four of the official cases (27-29 and 38) illustrate the fact that the procedures that normally favor officials over commoners in legal proceedings may on occasion serve to their detriment. In each of the four, the circumstances are such that, if the officials had been commoners, they would have been permitted immediate redemption. As officials, however, all the various steps involved in their trial and sentence require imperial ratification. This means that redemption may not be granted except through a special petition to the throne. The end result is, of course, the same as it would have been for a commoner, but it requires longer time.

Case 21 is interesting because it raises the question of something like double jeopardy—or perhaps it would be better to term it double punishment. A man who has been sentenced to military exile for plundering is granted redemption on grounds of incapacity (*tu-chi*) because rheumatism has deprived him of the use of both legs. Following his release, however, medication by his father proves so effective that he regains the ability to walk as before. The question now raised is whether, as someone no longer incapacitated, he should at this point be sent into exile. The Board's reply is to cite the analogy of the wrongdoer who, as the only adult son of aged parents, has had his sentence commuted from exile to bambooing and wearing of the cangue for a set period so that he may thereafter remain at home to care for his parents.[35] The Board points out that such a wrongdoer, even should his parents die, does not on that account go into exile. The fact that he has worn the cangue for the stipulated period means that the law of the nation (*kuo-fa*) has been applied to him. Hence, there is no further offense for which he has to be punished. By the same token, a person who has been granted redemption on grounds of incapacity, even should the incapacity subsequently be cured, may not properly be subjected a second time to restraint by the law (*sheng i fa*). The thinking and phraseology in this case of 1827 have a remarkably modern ring.

Case 31, which involves an offender who is *both* aged and incapacitated, illustrates the greater importance attached to the second degree of infirmity (incapacity) as against the first degree of age (70). It also demonstrates (as do cases 18-19 and 26 in section 3) that the granting of redemption on grounds of age is by no means automatic or invariable. The offender, a man of 70, has been sentenced to exile for having induced another man to plunder. Despite his age, redemption is initially denied him on the stated grounds that he has been guilty of leading many people into capital crimes. While in prison awaiting final judgment, however, he suffers cramps in both legs, which reduce him to a state of incapacity. Therefore the same governor who had initially recommended against redemption now speaks in its favor. In both statements he is actually ignoring the relevant statute in section 22, one clause of which prescribes redemption for persons of 70 who have been sentenced to life exile or less, while another clause prescribes complete exemption from punishment, without the need for monetary redemption at all, for any incapacitated person whose offense is neither capital, nor an act of robbery, nor the infliction of physical injury upon another.[36] The Board, nevertheless, goes along with the governor's recommendation. Its reasoning is that the offender deserves strict treatment, and that the governor has correctly upheld such treatment by first opposing redemption when it was theoretically possible and then recommending it when in fact it was no longer necessary.

In case 35 there is the problem of weighing one kind of incapacity against another: a man kills someone who is incapacitated in both legs, and then himself becomes incapacitated by suffering burns on both hands. Because the two kinds of incapacity are of equal weight, the Board allows redemption despite the fact that the incapacity caused by burning took place only after the crime.[37]

Finally, case 36 is probably the most pathetic of the infirmity group, even though not legally important. A member of the Bordered Red Mongol Banner who has been a guard at one of the city gates of Peking wounds his superior gate captain in a quarrel. For this heinous crime he is sentenced to deportation as a slave, but an imperial rescript reduces the sentence to lifetime wearing of the cangue while uninterruptedly patrolling the nine city gates of Peking. After twelve years of this, the Board is informed that the man has become completely blind and can no longer patrol. The case, presumably because it concerns a Mongol guard, is passed by the Board without judgment to the Court of Revision. Though we are not told the outcome, it seems probable that clemency was granted.

Conclusion

We have said nothing so far about the social composition of the cases, other than noting the high incidence of officials in infirmity cases. Social origins are rarely specified in cases from the *HAHL* unless they involve officials, monks, bannermen, or other special groups. Often, however, deduction is possible. For example, when we are told in case 6 that two persons shared an irrigation ditch, it is reasonable to suppose that both were peasants. Even so, however, fifteen of our cases are peopled by social "unknowns."[38] Officials constitute the largest identifiable category, with seven cases—all of them infirmity cases except for one (case 26), which falls under age.[39] Socially close to the officials are the nonofficial members of the gentry, who appear in five cases.[40] A single case (11) concerns a dispute between a rural landlord and his agricultural worker. With the latter may be grouped six peasant cases, four of which fall under youth and the others under age.[41] The remaining groups are those of urban dwellers (cases 13, 19, 32), Manchus and Mongols (12, 30—also an official case—and 36), and women involved in treason (case 23). Keeping in mind that the great bulk of the fifteen "unknown" cases probably concern ordinary people precisely because their social composition is unspecified, we may conclude that officials and gentry probably constitute little more than one-third of all participants.

If we turn to questions of judicial technique revealed in the cases, we see that out of the forty, no less than eight, or 20 percent, cite earlier cases as precedents.[42] This very high percentage contrasts with the just over 8 percent of translated cases in *Law in Imperial China* in which precedents are cited.[43] The disparity suggests that sharp variations in the citation of precedents may be expected in different sections of the *HAHL*.

Two precedent citations are of particular interest because of the way the Board rejects them after they have been submitted from lower judicial levels. In case 15.1, dated 1821, the reporting governor cites a precedent case of 1743 involving a Buddhist monk. The Board of Punishments, in its reversal of the governor's decision, rejects the precedent out of hand as too old and therefore "unsuitable to cite as a basis." Again, in case 25 (dated 1811), which we have discussed previously,[44] the governor-general proposed that the age of a murdered boy be calculated according to his actual date of birth instead of by conventional cyclical dating. He justified this unusual suggestion by citing another murder case of 1802 in which, apparently, the Board had actually accepted this unorthodox procedure for determining the age of the victim. The Board in the 1811 case, replying somewhat impatiently to the governor-general, makes a surprising admission. The 1802 case, it says, "was previously wrongly judged and may not be adduced for comparison."

A higher court that invariably, or almost invariably, left unchanged the decisions appealed to it from lower courts might quite properly be accused of judicial slackness. Evidence of the conscientiousness with which the Board of Punishments approached its work lies in its high percentage of reversals of provincial decisions: ten out of the forty cases.[45] In another three cases (8, 15, 24), the Board's own judgments as reached at the departmental or lowest level are in turn reversed at higher levels within the Board (the Board's Directorate or the Statutes Commission).

Besides rejecting unsuitable precedents, the Board does not hesitate to correct factual errors made on the provincial level. In case 20, it corrects the governor when the latter attributes to the Code's Official Commentary a statement actually deriving from the unofficial Shen Chih-ch'i commentary of 1715. In case 35, the governor vaguely attributes to "the statutes and substatutes" a passage reading: "A petition for clemency may not be filed for a totally blind person who kills another totally blind person." The Board, while supporting the governor's general recommendation of monetary redemption, points out that no such passage exists in the Code. However, even the Board seems to be remiss in another (largely procedural) case (23), where it fails to adduce any quoted statute or substatute to back up its decision.

Seven cases, all discussed earlier, are of interest because in each of them the offender and his victim are both members of privileged (though usually differing) groups. In sections 22 and 23 of the Code, only the legal treatment of aged, young, or infirm *wrongdoers* is discussed; nothing is said about the situations in which *victims* as well as wrongdoers happen to hold privileged status. In view of the strong Chinese penchant for the quantification of justice, however, one might suspect that in such cases the court would implicitly take into account, and mutually balance, the respective degrees of privilege of offender and victim. This assumption is in fact supported by the findings in our seven "balancing" cases. The general principle emerging from them is that, granted the objective circumstances are such as would otherwise justify an appeal for clemency, then clemency is to be accorded to an offender only if his privileged status equals or exceeds that of his victim.

The principle is most clearly discernible when both parties belong not only to the same category of privilege but to the same degree within that category, or at least to adjoining degrees. Thus in cases 12 and 13, clemency is granted to a child of 6 (third degree of youth) who kills a child of 9 (second degree of the same), and also to a child of 7 who kills a child of 6 (both degree 3). The same thing happens in case 35, where the killer and his victim, though suffering from different kinds of incapacity, both belong to the same degree within that category (two burned hands as against two incapacitated legs); this balance permits the killer to receive clemency.

In the next case (10), despite differences in category, the degrees within the two categories balance. This case actually involves two separate but parallel cases. In one of them, a boy whose age is unspecified but obviously, in view of the context, belongs to the 11-15 age group (first degree of youth), kills a man who is a little over 70 (first degree of age). The even balance between the degrees permits clemency for the boy.

The other part of case 10 is more complex because it concerns a boy 13 who kills a married woman of unspecified age. The legal status of women as against that of the aged, young, and infirm is not spelled out in the Code, where women are discussed in a separate section. However, the most important statement in the Code that throws light on this point (hedged, to be sure, by some exceptions) is that women, if guilty of offenses punishable by exile or less, are eligible for monetary redemption. The same provision, of course, applies to the first degrees of youth (11-15), age (70-79), and infirmity.[46] Moreover, the Code's redemption fees for women are generally roughly equivalent to those specified for the other three categories. It is evident, therefore, that women guilty of less than capital crimes are, in the Code, implicitly regarded as comparable in status to persons belonging to the first degrees of the three categories.[47] It logically follows that the boy who has killed the woman in our case 10 is granted redemption.

Case 7 is a single but dramatic example of what happens when the statuses of killer and victim fail to balance. A boy belonging to the first degree of youth has slashed to death a man blind in both eyes (second degree of infirmity). On the grounds that the boy has suffered abuse and insult (*ch'i-wu*) from the older man, the provincial court recommends clemency. The Board, however, sharply rejects the recommendation, remarking that the victim's incapacity, that of total blindness, eliminates any reason for showing compassion toward his killer.

The one possible exception to the principle of balance in our seven cases—and even it is not a true exception—is case 6. This is the irrigation-ditch case previously discussed, in which a boy of 14 (first degree of youth) kills a man of 76 (first degree of age). Despite the balance, clemency is denied because, in the Board's opinion, it is not justified by the other circumstances of the case. It will be remembered that the Board adjudges the old man's conduct to have been not "unreasonable" (*li-ch'ü*) on grounds that he merely raised his hand to strike the boy but before he could deliver the blow the boy had run away. This judgment, though no doubt technically correct, raises the question whether the Board may not have been subconsciously influenced in favor of the old man by the traditional Chinese respect for age.

This is one of several hairsplitting decisions which may seem to some to be closer to the letter of the law than to its spirit. Others in the youth category occur in case 2, in which the blow given by the later victim (a youth of 21) to his later killer (a boy of 14) is said to have been delivered in sport only and therefore not to constitute vicious conduct (*ch'eng-hsiung*); case 3, in which the older man attacked the boy with a stool but did not actually inflict injury; case 4, in which the older man did in fact push the boy to the ground but likewise inflicted no injury; and case 5, in which the tea owner tried to strip the younger boy of his clothes but did not actually strike him and therefore was adjudged innocent of vicious conduct.[48] In all these cases clemency is denied. The same is true of old-age case 19, where the Board refuses clemency to the improverished thief of 77 on the technically correct but morally dubious ground that he had already been accorded clemency for a theft seven years earlier.

Four other cases seem demonstrably at odds with the Code or with other cases. In case 26, we find clemency being denied to a man over 70 on the sole stated ground that, despite his age, his physical condition was still "basically flourishing." This argument, of course, has no statutory basis. In case 18, clemency is similarly denied to a "litigation trickster" of 70 on the ground that, as demonstrated by his activities, he is still too mentally vigorous, and therefore dangerous, to deserve clemency. In case 31, a man of 70 is at first denied redemption in a situation where he is eligible for it, and then, when he becomes incapacitated, is allowed redemption although, as an incapacitated person, redemption is no longer needed in order to free him from punishment. Finally, in case 37, it is denied that paralysis affecting both the left foot and the left hand constitutes infirmity, although, according to statute, "loss" of merely *one* foot or hand constitutes infirmity. As we have already seen,[49] the word "loss" in this context has a broad connotation, which would certainly include paralysis.

As against these decisions, which seem to err on the side of overseverity, there are occasional judgments that seem to lean the other way. Notable is case 17[50] in which a man of 80, guilty of having induced others to murder a distant nephew, and then of having instigated someone to make a false accusation, and finally of having been a fugitive from justice for three years, is saved by the fortuitous occurrence of an imperial amnesty. After the amnesty, because of his age, he is permitted to escape all remaining punishment through monetary redemption.

Whether we agree with these decisions or not, they clearly confirm the observation made earlier that the Board of Punishments enjoyed considerable discretion in deciding how and why the laws on age, youth, and infirmity were to be applied. Despite the seemingly categorical wording of the laws, there was nothing automatic in their functioning. Their purpose was to provide fixed legal guidelines by which favorable legal treatment could be extended in a controlled manner to certain categories of wrongdoers deemed by Confucian morality to be especially deserving of such treatment. In every individual instance, however, it remained the task of the courts, and especially the Board of Punishments, to determine whether or not a given wrongdoer did in fact fit into one of the privileged categories and, if he did, whether his own motivation and the circumstances of his case justified extending to him personally the special legal treatment intended for his category. It was in making these individual assessments that the courts, even when holding to the letter of the law as they usually tried to do, could on occasion reveal what seems to us to be ignorance, prejudice, or misunderstanding.

Some degree of whim and error is inevitable in every legal system. On the whole the Board of Punishments, once we recognize its frame of reference, seems to have been reasonably successful in applying to these forty cases a Confucian humanity directed within legal channels. By compiling all instances of granting or denying clemency as recorded not only in the cases proper but in the precedent cases cited in many of them, we arrive at the figures in the table:[51]

Category of cases	*Clemency granted*	*Clemency denied*
Youth	11	8
Age	8	4
Infirmity	10	4
Totals	29	16

Thus, clemency is granted in nearly two-thirds of the 45 instances in which either granting or withholding it is in question.[52] In the modern world such a proportion would probably be regarded by many as inadequate, but in the still relatively stable Chinese society of the early nineteenth century it could be pointed to as a reasonable example of the triumph of juridically controlled Confucian benevolence over Legalist sternness. I think these cases confirm on the whole the favorable evaluation of Ch'ing legal procedure made by my colleague Clarence Morris in commenting on the 190 cases translated in *Law in Imperial China*. "The few cases in our collection," he writes, "that can be viewed as instances of judicial whim are not surprising. More significant is the general conclusion that Ch'ing penal procedure was systematic, reasoned, and an ongoing effort to effectuate a few important policies; only rarely were these policies ignored."[53]

Appendix 5.1
The Ch'ing Code's Articles on Age, Youth, and Infirmity

Section 22.[54] Monetary Redemption Permitted to the Aged, the Young, and the Infirm

Statute[55]

All offenders aged 70 or above or 15 or below, or suffering from an infirmity (*fei-chi*) [*Official Commentary*: blindness in one eye or loss (*che*) of one limb and the like] are, if guilty of an offense punishable by life exile or less, to be given monetary redemption. [*Official Commentary*: This statute does not apply to persons guilty of a capital offense, nor to those deserving of exile because of their vicarious responsibility in cases of rebellion or treason, nor to those who, being guilty of preparing magic poison, or dismembering a living person, or killing three members of a single family, have had their punishment (of death) reduced to exile because of an amnesty. Monetary redemption will be allowed to all other persons, they being guilty of injuring someone's person or property. It applies equally to those guilty of offenses punishable by military exile or by ordinary exile.]

Persons aged 80 or above or 10 or below, or who are incapacitated (*tu-chi*) [*Official Commentary*: through blindness in both eyes or loss (*che*) of two limbs and the like], if guilty of a homicide [*Official Commentary*: premeditated, intentional, or committed in an affray] for which the punishment is death [*Official Commentary*: either decapitation or strangulation], will have a recommended sentence for their offense submitted to the throne and await judgment. [The usual result is a reduction from death to a lower punishment. *Official Commentary*: This statute does not apply to those guilty of rebellion or treason.] If they have committed robbery or have injured someone [*Official Commentary*: but are not guilty of a capital offense], they too are to be given monetary redemption. [*Official Commentary*: This means that, inasmuch as they have inflicted injury or loss upon another person, they are not to be wholly exempted from punishment. Nevertheless, they are still to be permitted redemption.] For all offenses other than the foregoing, they are not to be held responsible at all. [*Official Commentary*: This means that, aside from those homicides which call for capital punishment, for which a petition is submitted to the throne, or aside from robbery or physical injury, for which there is to be monetary redemption, they are not to be judged guilty of any other offense.]

Persons aged 90 or above or 7 or below, even though guilty of a capital offense, are not to suffer any punishment. [*Official Commentary*: This statute does not apply to persons of 90 or above who are guilty of rebellion or treason.] If these persons have been instigated by someone, the instigator will be tried for the offense. If there is property to be restored, he who has received the property is to restore it. [*Official Commentary*: This means that persons of 90 or above or 7 or below are all deficient in their mental powers and physical strength. Thus if they have been instigated by someone, it is the instigator who is to be tried for the offense. Or if there has been a robbery and another person has received and made use of what has been taken, it is that other person who is to make restitution. If, however, the aged or young person has himself made use of it, it is from him that restitution is to be demanded.]

Substatute 1.[56] [Concerning exemption of the aged, young, or infirm, once they have been granted redemption, from wearing the cangue or undergoing bambooing.]

Substatute 2.[57] If, either at the capital or in the provinces, among those offenders currently on trial whose cases do not require to be memorialized [via the Board of Punishments to the throne for final judgment], there are persons who are aged, young, or infirm, they are always to be adjudicated [at the lower judicial level] in accordance with the statute [on the aged, young, and infirm]. If, among the cases which are tried in the provinces and *do* require to be memorialized [to the throne for final judgment], some of the offenders are actually aged, young or infirm, the governors-general or governors of the said provinces are carefully to examine and receive the certified and sealed statement from their subordinate local official and, on its basis, to submit a memorial asking for monetary redemption according to statute. If in reality, however, the offenders are not aged, young, or infirm but, because of favoritism, their cases have been memorialized [to Peking] with a request for exemption from punishment, the officials who have thus memorialized and the governor-general or governor are then [to have the facts of their involvement in the affair] transmitted to the Board [of Civil Office] for judgment. But if, among offenders arriving [from the provincial courts] to the Board [of Punishments] for adjudication, there are some who declare that they are [now] aged or that, while en route, they became infirm, and if examination indicates that they actually are aged or infirm, they are then to be permitted monetary redemption.

Substatute 3.[58] [Concerning persons who instigate a child of 7 to strike his parents or a man of 90 to kill his child or grandchild.]

Substatute 4.[59] [How cases of the aged, young, or infirm are to be handled at the Autumn and Court Assizes.]

Substatute 5.[60] Any person who has lost the sight of one eye, if he has committed an offense punishable by military or ordinary exile, penal servitude, or bambooing, will in none of these instances be permitted monetary redemption on grounds of infirmity. He who, by beating another person, causes him to lose the sight of one eye, will be punished according to statute.

Substatute 6.[61] [Classification at the Autumn Assizes of incapacitated persons who are guilty of a capital offense.]

Substatute 7.[62] A child of 7 or below, if he has killed someone, is permitted, according to statute, to have a petition presented to the throne for remission of punishment. A child of 8-10, if during an affray he has committed homicide, is permitted the same privilege provided the victim is four or more years older than the offender. But if the age difference is only three years or less, the sentence will, as in ordinary cases, be that of strangulation after the assizes, without the privilege of submission to the throne of a special request for clemency.

If a child of 11-15, on being abused (*ch'i*) and insulted (*wu*) by someone older than himself, strikes that person and thereby causes his death, it should then be determined whether the deceased was four or more years older than the offender and, if this be the case, whether the deceased had displayed unreasonable (*li-ch'ü*) or vicious (*ch'eng-hsiung*) conduct toward the offender, or whether the latter's homicidal act had been done unintentionally in sport. If one or the other be so, a petition may then be submitted to the throne requesting clemency, in accordance with the holding in the case of Ting Ch'i-san.

Substatute 8.[63] All offenders aged 70 or above or 15 or below, or suffering from an infirmity are, if guilty of an offense punishable by life exile or less, to be permitted monetary redemption on a single occasion; their exercise of this privilege will be noted in the record made of the case. If after this first redemption they again commit an offense, at this point, provided the offense was committed deliberately, and aside from cases in which they have been only indirectly or by mistake involved in the offense, for which redemption will still be permitted, they will then be subjected to full punishment as provided by statute, without being permitted monetary redemption a second time.

Substatute 9.[64] [Concerning false accusations made by persons who are aged or infirm.]

Section 23.[65] Wrongdoing Committed Prior to Becoming Aged or Infirm

Statute[66]

Any offender who was not yet aged or infirm when he committed his offense but who has become aged or infirm by the time the offense comes to light, will be tried according to the laws on age and infirmity. The same principle will apply if he becomes aged or infirm in the course of undergoing penal servitude. [I.e., he will be permitted redemption for the term of penal servitude still remaining to be served.]

Any offender who was an infant or a youth when he committed his offense but has attained adulthood by the time the offense comes to light, will be tried according to the laws on infancy and youth.

APPENDIX 5.2
Table of *Hsing-an hui-lan* Cases on the Aged, the Young, and the Infirm[a]

Section 14. Monetary Redemption Permitted to the Aged, the Young, and the Infirm

Case No.	*Date*	*Locale*	*Type of Case*	*Source HAHL*
1	1826	Kiangsu	Memorandum	4.4/1a-b
2	1814	Kiangsi	Memorandum	4.4/1b
3	1812	Szechuan	Memorandum	4.4/1b-2a
4	1816	Kuangsi	Memorandum	4.4/2a-b
5	1817	Kiangsi	Memorandum	4.4/2b
6	1803[b]	Kuangsi	Memorandum	4.4/2b-3a
7	1813	Shensi	Leading Case	4.4/3a
8	1830	Kuangtung	Memorandum	4.4/3a-b
9	1798	Szechuan	Memorandum	4.4/3b-4a
10	1812	Chihli	Memorandum	4.4/4a-b
11	1812	Szechuan	Memorandum	4.4/4b
12	1812	Heilungkiang	Memorandum from the Department for Mukden	4.4/4b
13	1823	Honan	Leading Case	4.4/4b-5a
14	1804	Mukden	Memorandum	4.4/5a
15	1820	Chihli	Memorandum	4.4/5a-b
16	1815	Shantung	Leading Case	4.4/5b
17	1822	Fukien	Leading Case	4.4/5b
18	1792	Kueichou	Memorandum	4.4/5b-6a
19	1788	Peking	Memorandum	4.4/6a
20	1794	Yunnan	Memorandum	4.4/6a-b
21	1827	Shantung	Memorandum	4.4/6b-7a
22	1820	Kiangsi	Memorandum	4.4/7a
23	1815	Urumchi	Memorandum from the Department for Shensi	4.4/7a-b
24	1799	Kiangsi	Memorandum	4.4/7b-8a
25	1811	Chihli	General Circular	4.4/8a-9b
26	1809	Yunnan	Memorandum	4.4/9b-10a
27	1818	Yunnan	Memorandum	4.4/10a
28	1828	Kuangsi	Memorandum	4.4/10a-b
29	1829	Kiangsu	Memorandum	4.4/10b
30	1830	Chahar	Memorandum from the Department for Shansi	4.4/10b-11b

APPENDIX 5.2 (*Cont.*)
Section 14 (*Cont.*)

Case No.	*Date*	*Locale*	*Type of Case*	*Source*
31	1832	Hunan-Hupei	Memorandum	4.4/11b-12a
				HAHL Supplement
32	1824	Peking	Leading Case from the Department for Mukden	29.2/13a
33	1827	Anhui	Leading Case	29.2/13a-b
34	1830	Kueichou	Leading Case	29.2/13b
35	1837	Shantung	Memorandum	29.2/13b
36	1836	Peking	Memorandum from the Department for Kuangtung	29.2/13b-14a
37	1834	Kueichou	Memorandum	29.2/14a
				HAHL New Supplement
38	1881	Shensi	Leading Case	37.2/2b

Section 15. Wrongdoing Committed Prior to Becoming Aged or Infirm

				HAHL
1	1821	Kiangsu	Memorandum	4.4/12a-b
2	1826	Chekiang	Memorandum	4.4/12b

[a] Only 270 of the 436 sections of the Ch'ing Code are represented by cases in the *Hsing-an hui-lan* (*HAHL*). This is why sections 14 and 15 of the *HAHL* above correspond, despite the differences in numbering, to sections 22 and 23 of the code in Appendix 5.1. In the right-hand column above, the annotation *HAHL* 4.4/1a-b means that the case in question occurs in the fourth *ts'e* (volume) of the *HAHL* proper, at pp. 1a-1b of the fourth *chuan* (part or book).

[b] The date of case 6 (1803) is surely in error because the case cites as a precedent another case which it dates 1812 and which is the same as case 10, wherein the date of 1812 is confirmed. Possibly the erroneous date for case 6—of the eighth year of Chia-ch'ing (1803)—is a misprint for eighteenth year (1813).

NOTES

1. An earlier version of this chapter was published in the *University of Pennsylvania Law Review*, Vol. 121, No. 3 (Jan. 1973), pp. 437-470.
2. For a detailed discussion, see D. Bodde and C. Morris, *Law in Imperial China* (1967), pp. 29-38. (Full bibliographical data for this and other cited writings will be found in the Bibliography at the end of this volume.)
3. Special legal provisions for the treatment of the aged and the young existed already during the Han dynasty (206 B.C.-220 A.D.), and have been examined in A. Hulsewé, *Remnants of Han Law*, Vol. 1 (1955), pp. 1-16. As for

treatment of the infirm, see Karl Bünger, "The Punishment of Lunatics and Negligents According to Classified Chinese Law," *Studia Serica*, Vol. 9 (1950), pp. 1-16.

4. The implications of this substatute are analyzed in detail at text accompanying notes 13-18 below.
5. See text following note 27 below.
6. In addition to sections 22 and 23 of the Ch'ing Code, which are by far the most important pronouncements on the legal status of the aged, the young, and the infirm, there are a very few, relatively minor, further statements occurring elsewhere in the Code. They include provisions: (1) that persons belonging to the second degree of age, youth, or infirmity, and by extension, the third degrees of age and youth, may not, except in cases of treason and a very few other major listed crimes, personally bring accusations to court against other people, though relatives may be delegated to do so on their behalf; *Ta Ch'ing lü-li hui-t'ung hsin-tsuan* [Comprehensive New Edition of the Great Ch'ing Code] (Taipei ed. 1964) (hereinafter cited as *Code*), p. 3021; *Ta Tsing Leu Lee; Being the Fundamental Laws . . . of the Penal Code of China* (Taipei ed., G. Staunton tr., 1966) (hereinafter cited as Staunton), section 339; *Le Code annamite, nouvelle traduction complète* (Taipei ed., P.L.F. Philastre tr., 1967), Vol. 2 (hereinafter cited as Philastre), p. 445; *Manuel du code chinois* (Shanghai ed., Guy Boulais tr., 1924) (hereinafter cited as Boulais), section 1511; (2) that prisoners belonging to the first degrees of age, youth, or infirmity (and by extension those of the higher degrees as well) are to have their fetters regularly washed and their sleeping mats aired, and to be supplied with warm beds in winter and cooling drinks in summer, *Code*, p. 3550; Philastre, Vol. 2, pp. 650-651; and (3) that prisoners belonging to the first (or higher) degrees of age, youth, or infirmity are not to undergo judicial torture, and those belonging to the second (or higher) degrees are not to be accepted as witnesses, *Code*, p. 3561; Staunton, section 404; Philastre, Vol. 2, p. 656; Boulais, section 1681. It should be noted that the work by Philastre, despite its title, is actually a translation of much of the Ch'ing Code, because the Annamite Code which it covers is very largely a word-for-word reproduction of the edition of the 1740 Ch'ing Code then current.
7. See note 10 below and accompanying text.
8. Cf. *T'ang-lü shu-i* [Official Commentary to the Tang Code], Vol. 2, bk. 4, art. 2, pp. 2-5 (Taipei ed., 1955) (hereinafter cited as *T'ang Code*). The *Li Chi* quotation, the translation of which has been modified by the author, may be found in J. Legge, *The Lî Kî* [Book of Rites], *The Sacred Books of the East*, Vol. 27, p. 66 (F. Müller ed. 1885).
9. The *Conspectus* is analyzed in Bodde and Morris, note 2 above, pp. 144-159. 190 cases from the *Conspectus* have been translated in *ibid.*, pp. 203-489.
10. No doubt the 40 could be supplemented by a few others if one were willing to search for all references to the subject that may be scattered among the more than 7,600 other cases in the *Conspectus*. I doubt, however, that such enormous effort would markedly alter the picture provided by the main body of 40 cases. Among these, those belonging to section 14 of the *Conspectus* should, strictly speaking, be designated as cases 14.1, 14.2, 14.3, etc., but

for reasons of simplicity they will be referred to merely as cases 1, 2, 3, etc. To distinguish the two in section 15, these will be referred to in full as cases 15.1 and 15.2. It should be noted that sections 14 and 15 of the *Conspectus* are identical in title and subject matter with sections 22 and 23 in the Ch'ing Code (see Appendix 5.1), despite the differences in numbering. The discrepancy arises from the fact that only 270 out of a total of 436 sections in the Code are covered by cases in the *Conspectus*, plus the fact that in the present study, as in Bodde and Morris, note 2 above, the sections in the *Conspectus* have been numbered consecutively and therefore differently from their counterparts (also consecutively numbered) in the Code.

11. This is case 25. The case has already been discussed more briefly in Philastre, Vol. 1, p. 271.
12. Cf. case 25.
13. For this statute, cf. *Code*, p. 553; Staunton, section 41; Philastre, Vol. 1, p. 271.
14. They are cases 1-13, 22, and 24. The first of them, under the designation of case 14.1, has already been tr. in Bodde and Morris, note 2 above, pp. 229-231.
15. Clemency is accorded in cases 1, 8-9, 10 (twice, because two separate though parallel cases are involved), and 11, as well as in two precedents cited in case 10. Clemency is denied in cases 2-7, as well as in two precedents cited in case 4.
16. A further clause in the same substatute provides clemency if the homicide has been committed unintentionally in sport, but, strangely enough, none of the cases invokes this clause.
17. See text accompanying notes 46-47 below.
18. The word *wu* has the technical meaning of intending to injure or kill a particular person and by mischance injuring or killing someone else instead. See Bodde and Morris, note 2 above, p. 197. Use of the word here probably means that the culprit was trying to hit his sister with the scissors.
19. Two other youth cases, 22 and 24, will be omitted from our exposition because they are largely procedural and have little legal interest.

    Incidentally, the term used in describing the father's act in this case—*ti-ming*, "to requite life"—has considerable philosophical interest. As a technical term, it probably reflects the ancient Chinese belief that the taking of life disrupts the balance of the universe, and that therefore another life must be exacted or requited in return in order to restore this balance. See Bodde and Morris, note 2 above, p. 182.
20. Cases 14-19, 26, 15.1, and 15.2.
21. Cases 203.2, 203.4-5, and 203.7 in Bodde and Morris, note 2 above, pp. 413-417.
22. This is the same case in which the Board, as quoted at text following note 7 above, justifies redemption for the aged on the ground that "their powers have already declined so that they are not in a position to repeat their offense." This pragmatic explanation is probably a distortion of the original motivation.
23. This case, dated 1792, is almost surely the unmentioned precedent for the

equally arbitrary denial of redemption to the aged "litigation trickster" who appears in case 203.5, dated 1820, in Bodde and Morris, note 2 above, pp. 415-416. It should be noted that in all of the translated "trickster" cases, note 21 above, the statutory punishment of military exile is at least reduced to three years of penal servitude, in contrast to its retention (for unexplained reasons) in the present case.

24. The fifteen are cases 20-21, 23, and 27-38. The excluded cases are 23, 30, and 33.
25. The six official cases are 27-30 and 37-38. The provincial military graduate appears in case 34 and the Mongol bannerman in 36.
26. Cf. cases 21, 23, 27, 30-31, 33, 35, 37-38.
27. Cf. text accompanying notes 33-34 below.
28. Cf. *T'ang Code*, note 8 above, Vol. 2, bk. 22, art. 13, p. 102, and Vol. 4, bk. 29, art. 6, p. 74. Both passages are actually citations of a single definition contained in the ordinances. Cf. Niida Noboru, *Tōryō Shūi* [The T'ang Ordinances Re-Collected] (Tokyo, 1933), p. 228.
29. Cf. *T'ang Code*, note 8 above, Vol. 3, bk. 21, art. 2, p. 82; Vol. 3, bk. 21, art. 4, p. 84; Vol. 3, bk. 22, art. 13, p. 102; Niida Noboru, note 28 above.
30. For *ch'ih*, *T'ang Code*, note 8 above, Vol. 4, bk. 29, art. 6, p. 74, and, for *tien-k'uang*, Niida Noboru, note 28 above. Bünger, note 3 above, p. 4, interprets *ch'ih* in the *T'ang Code* passage as combining with the next word in the text, *ya*, to form a compound, *ch'ih-ya*, which he translates "imbecility" (my "feeble-mindedness"). This is surely wrong, for *ch'ih* by itself means feeble-mindedness, while *ya* is an entirely separate word meaning "dumbness." Shen Chih-ch'i, in his 1715 commentary on the Ch'ing Code (comment on statute in section 22, *Code*, pp. 409-410), reproduces the major T'ang definition of infirmity and at the same time suggests some items of his own such as *lung*, "deafness." Of course, as a private commentator, his interpretation of the Ch'ing Code remained suggestive only and did not, like the Official Commentary, carry any judicial authority. Significantly, Shen groups *ya* with *lung* in his list, and in so doing places it before rather than after *ch'ih*. Thus, there is no doubt that he regards *ch'ih* and *ya* as two separate ailments.
31. Bünger, note 3 above, pp. 4-5.
32. The author cannot readily agree with Dr. Bünger, therefore, when he says, concerning this radical change, that "the alterations did not touch the basic principle of exempting lunatics from punishment." Cf. Bünger, p. 7.
33. For the several Ch'ing substatutes on insanity, cf. *Code*, pp. 2535-2542; Philastre, Vol. 2, pp. 226-227; Boulais, sections 1287-1290. The corresponding section in the *Conspectus*, see note 9 above and accompanying text, contains 43 cases on insanity which would be well worth studying. They occur in *Hsing-an hui-lan* [Conspectus of Penal Cases], Vol. 15, bk. 32, pp. 20b-28b (Shanghai ed., 1886) (42 cases); *Hsu-tseng hsing-an hui-lan* [*HAHL*, First Supplement], Vol. 33, bk. 9, p. 10b (1886) (one case).
34. Note 30 above.
35. For cases exemplifying this injection of filial piety into law, see Bodde and Morris, note 2 above, pp. 223-227.
36. See Appendix 5.1.

37. This and similar "balancing" cases will be discussed further in the concluding section to this paper. See text accompanying notes 46-47 below.
38. Cases 2, 4, 7-8, 10, 14-15, 17, 20-22, 25, 31, 33, 35.
39. Cases 26-30, 37-38.
40. Cases 9, 18, 24(?), 34, 15.1.
41. Cases 1, 3, and 5-6 (all youth); 16 and 15.2 (age). It is conceivable, though improbable, that 15.2, which concerns the reclamation of alluvial land, should be classed as landlord rather than peasant.
42. The distribution of precedents is: *youth cases*, nos. 4, 6, 10; *age cases*, nos. 14-15, 26, 15.1. A precedent is also cited in case 25 (the case on determining age, separately discussed at text accompanying notes 11-13 above). Excluded from this calculation are the six youth cases (1-3, 5, 7-8) that cite the Ting Ch'i-san precedent, because this citation does not represent their own words but is an integral part of the relevant substatute (no. 7 in section 22) they are quoting.
43. See Bodde and Morris, note 2 above, pp. 179-80.
44. See text accompanying notes 11-13 above.
45. They are cases 4-5, 7, 20, 25, 29-30, 37, 15.1, and 15.2.
46. For the laws on women, cf. *Code*, pp. 383-89; Staunton, section 20; Philastre, Vol. 1, pp. 172-176; Boulais, sections 127-130.
47. When it comes to capital cases the situation changes: no monetary redemption is then normally available to women in contrast to its availability for the first degree of youth, within limitations laid down in the seventh substatute under section 22. Among the cases translated from the *Hsing-an hui-lan* in Bodde and Morris, note 2 above, there are five in which women receive death sentences with no indication of redemption being permitted. They are 160.15 (death by slicing?); 224.22 and 262.3 (immediate decapitation); 172.4 (immediate strangulation); 159.3 (decapitation after the assizes).
48. In this last case, as already seen (text preceding note 17 above), another factor was possibly present as well; but the failure to strike was probably decisive.
49. Text following note 34 above.
50. Text accompanying note 20 above.
51. The breakdown into specific cases is as follows:

    Clemency granted: (a) *youth cases*: 1, 8, 9, 10 (two main cases and two cited precedents), 11-13, 22; (b) *age cases*: 14 (main case and two cited precedents), 15-17, 15.1, 15.2; (c) *infirmity cases*: 20, 21, 27-29, 31-33, 35, 38.

    Clemency denied: (a) *youth cases*: 2, 3, 4 (main case and two cited precedents), 5-7; (b) *age cases*: 18, 19, and one cited precedent each in 26 and 15.1; (c) *infirmity* cases: 20, 30, 34, 37.
52. It is not always easy to decide whether a case really supports clemency or not. In case 26, for example, the Board, after stating that clemency is inherently inappropriate, points to an imperial New Year's proclamation as bringing a change into the situation. The unstated implication is that, because of this extraneous factor, the sentence will in fact be changed. In view of this ambiguity, I have excluded the case from the statistics.
53. Bodde and Morris, note 2 above, p. 541. What the policies were is summarized by Professor Morris in the subsequent paragraphs.

54. One statute and nine substatutes. Square brackets are used to enclose the comments of the Official Commentary on the statute, as well as any additional phrases inserted by the translator for greater clarity. Only substatutes relevant to the present study have been translated. Others are briefly summarized within square brackets. The dates of promulgation provided below for each statute and substatute are based on Hsüeh Yün-sheng, *Tu-li ts'un-i* [Concentration on Doubtful Matters While Perusing the Substatutes], bk. 4 at 1a-10a (1905).
55. *Code*, pp. 409-410; Staunton, section 22; Boulais, section 131; Philastre, Vol. 1, pp. 185-186. The main text goes back unchanged to the Ming Code of 1397, and with only slight changes to the T'ang Code of 653. The Official Commentary—first published in 1646 and revised in 1740—is a slight modification and rearrangement of that in the Ming Code.
56. *Code*, p. 412; Boulais, section 132; Philastre, Vol. 1, p. 187. Initially taken from a substatute in the Ming Code; revised in 1740.
57. *Code*, pp. 412-413; Philastre, Vol. 1, p. 187. Initially promulgated in 1673; revised in 1725 and 1740.
58. *Code*, p. 413; Philastre, Vol. 1, pp. 187-188. Derived in the first instance from a private commentary on the Ming Code, but, with slight changes, going back from it to the Official Commentary on the T'ang Code of 653.
59. *Code*, p. 413; Philastre, Vol. 1, p. 188. Promulgated in 1740.
60. *Code*, pp. 413-414; Boulais, section 133; Philastre, Vol. 1, p. 188. Promulgated in 1745.
61. *Code*, p. 414; Philastre, Vol. 1, p. 188, with considerable changes. Initially promulgated in 1774; revised in 1803.
62. *Code*, pp. 414-415; Boulais, section 134; Philastre, Vol. 1, p. 188. Based on a case of 1732; initially promulgated in 1779; revised in 1806.
63. *Code*, pp. 415-416; Boulais, section 135; Philastre, Vol. 1, pp. 188-189. Initially promulgated in 1759 for insertion in section 404 of the Code; transferred to the present section in 1788.
64. *Code*, p. 416; briefly mentioned in Philastre, Vol. 1, p. 189. Promulgated in 1818.
65. One statute and no substatutes. The main text goes back unchanged to the Ming Code of 1397 and from there to the T'ang Code of 653. The Official Commentary has been left untranslated because it is lengthy and adds nothing significant.
66. *Code*, p. 419; Staunton, section 23; Boulais, section 136; Philastre, Vol. 1, pp. 191-192.

VI

THE INFLUENCE OF SHEN CHIH-CH'I'S *CHI-CHU COMMENTARY* UPON CH'ING JUDICIAL DECISIONS

Fu-mei Chang Chen

Introduction: Background and Development of the *Chi-chu*

In 1646, two years after the founding of the Ch'ing dynasty, the first Ch'ing Code was promulgated. It borrowed extensively from the preceding Ming Code of 1585. Like the Ming Code, it adhered to the tradition of honoring the *lü* ("statute") as sacred and immutable. In fact, almost all of the Ch'ing *lü* were identical with those in the Ming Code of 1397.[1] Although some of the *lü* provisions were modified in subsequent code compilations under the Yung-cheng (r. 1723-1735) and Ch'ien-lung (r. 1736–1795) emperors, a great majority of the *lü* remained unchanged throughout the dynasty.

When the last Ming Code and the first Ch'ing Code are compared, one notes that the latter has greatly increased the *hsiao-chu*, the so-called official interlinear commentary or "small commentary," which in small print is irregularly interspersed among the phrases and clauses of the *lü*. A handful of the *hsiao-chu* were directly inherited from the Ming Code, but most of them were incorporated into the Ch'ing Code by compilers who had taken them from a few private Ming Code commentaries.[2] In view of the function that it came to play, we should recognize that the Ch'ing *hsiao-chu* served as more than a commentary; not only did it make the literary, laconic, and archaic text of the *lü* easier to comprehend but in some instances it also contained substantive changes which were treated as an integral part of the *lü* text.

Despite the addition of the *hsiao-chu*, however, the meaning of many provisions of the *lü* still remained ambiguous and difficult to understand. Thus, in 1695 the K'ang-hsi emperor (r. 1662-1722) commissioned Chang Yü-shu (1642-1711), a Grand Secretary who concurrently served as the director of the Statutes Commission of the Board of Punishments, and several other high-ranking officials to produce an official commentary explaining the meaning of all the *lü*.[3] According to Chang's memorial, such a commentary was earnestly requested by many officials. Furthermore, the famous example of the official *T'ang-lü shu-i* (The

T'ang Code with Commentary) of 653 A.D. constituted an historical precedent for this undertaking by the government. The final product, known as *tsung-chu* ("general commentary"), was presented to the K'ang-hsi emperor in 1707, but for some unknown reason was not adopted. Not until 1723 was it resubmitted to the Yung-cheng emperor and, after some revision, finally incorporated into the body of the new 1725 Code.[4]

This official "general commentary" enjoyed a life span of only fifteen years. In the Code of 1740, promulgated by the succeeding Ch'ien-lung emperor, those portions of the commentary deemed valuable were enacted as *li* ("substatutes") or incorporated into the *hsiao-chu*.[5] The rest of the general commentary was removed from the Code on the ground that it was either misleading or superfluous. It never reappeared in any of the subsequent Ch'ing Codes issued by the government.

The *li*, the third component of the official Code, witnessed a sustained growth during the Ch'ing dynasty. Their number increased from 449 articles in 1646 to 1,892 in 1870.[6] The *li* did not require explanatory interlinear commentaries because they could simply be revised or replaced if they were considered ambiguous or obsolete.

The Ch'ing court's long delay in producing an official general commentary and its subsequent decision to delete it created an environment in which private commentaries could flourish. During the Ch'ing dynasty some twenty commentaries were produced by various scholars learned in law, although those jurists and their works remain largely unknown.[7]

Among these private commentaries, Shen Chih-ch'i's *Chi-chu*, originally published in 1715, was very highly regarded by Ch'ing readers and seems to have exerted the greatest influence upon the development of Ch'ing law. This work contained Shen's own "general" as well as "upper" commentary. His general commentary, a phrase-by-phrase exposition of the statutes, appeared between the statutes and the substatutes of each section of the Code reproduced in Shen's volume. If Shen felt the essence of a statute was still unclear, he further elaborated on it and presented his own interpretations in the upper commentary, a series of comments printed on the upper portion of a page. The gist of many relevant substatutes also appeared in this upper commentary.

In 1745 Hung Hung-hsü revised and adapted Shen's work in light of the third Ch'ing Code, the Ch'ien-lung Code of 1740, and published it as Shen's revised *Chi-chu*. The basic content was not tampered with in this undertaking.[8] Around 1763 another scholar, Wan Wei-han, again revised it and published it under his own name with a new title, *Chyi-chu*.[9] In the process of revision Wan, unlike Hung, took the liberty of adding a substantial number of his own opinions. In the early nineteenth century, however, an effort was made to restore Shen's work to its pristine state.[10] From then until the downfall of the dynasty, almost all private commentaries bore Shen's name as the original author, and kept both his general commentary and a large portion of his upper commentary, merely adding whatever contributions the later commentators considered necessary. The supremacy of Shen's work became unchallenged.

There are two principal ways to ascertain the role private commentaries played in shaping the development of Ch'ing law. One is to examine the legislative history of particular provisions to determine how the commentaries influenced new legislation. The other is to search through court decisions to see whether private commentaries were invoked as a source of law or as an aid to ascertaining and applying the law and, if so, in what manner. The second method is the one adopted in this chapter. In view of the fact that Shen's *Chi-chu* was considered the most authoritative private commentary by Ch'ing scholars and its opinions were most frequently cited in court decisions, I shall limit my discussion to this work.

My research is based on an examination of nearly 9,000 entries from the *Hsing-an hui-lan* [Conspectus of Penal Cases] by Chu Ch'ing-ch'i and Pao Shu-yün, published in 1834, and three of its supplements, one by the same authors and two by others.[11] Most of these cases are either internal documents directly taken from the archives of the Board of Punishments (e.g., *shuo-t'ieh*, "memorandum") or documents issued by the same Board to provincial officials (e.g., *t'ung-hsing*, "general circular"). In addition, I have also read several hundred cases in various works of similar nature,[12] although I have not researched these sources as systematically as the material in the *Hsing-an hui-lan* and its supplements.

This extensive search has revealed only eighteen cases that explicitly quoted Shen's *Chi-chu*.[13] However, in a number of other cases the opinions of this commentary may have been influential. On some occasions, judicial officials appear to have made use of the *Chi-chu* without acknowledging it; naturally this is difficult to detect. Although I have thus far identified only one such instance,[14] it was probably a rather common practice. In other cases opinions identified as coming from Wan Weihan's *Chyi-chu* actually orginated with Shen. Since the titles of these two works possess the same pronunciation and a similar meaning and since the works have similar content, it must have been easy to confuse them. Indeed, even the Board of Punishments, whose staff was generally more expert than that of the lower tribunals, was vulnerable to this type of mistake. In one case, the Board cited the two works interchangeably as if they were the same.[15] There are seven cases containing quotations allegedly coming from Wan's *Chyi-chu*.[16] In two of these, the quotations are identical to passages in Shen's *Chi-chu* and in the remaining five the quotations are very close to the Shen version.[17] In order to ascertain the indirect as well as direct influence exerted by Shen's *Chi-chu* upon judicial decisions, I might properly include all seven cases in my discussion. But, since I do not have access to Wan's *Chyi-chu* and am unable to determine exactly how Wan borrowed from or improved on Shen's original opinions, I have decided to eliminate the five borderline cases that did not have the exact quotations from Shen's *Chi-chu*.

Thus, I have found twenty-one cases that reveal the direct influence of the *Chi-chu* commentary in some way: eighteen quoted this work explicitly, one did so without credit and two did so by way of Wan's *Chyi-chu*. Those twenty-one cases were decided between 1763 and 1868. Among them, two distinctive groups can be discerned. The first group consists of eight cases that came to the Board of Punishments for review after provincial or local officials had invoked the *Chi-chu* in their recommendations for appropriate sentences. In most of these instances, the Board expressed its disapproval of the way the lower officials' decisions had relied upon a private commentary and discussed the weight to be accorded it. In the second group, consisting of thirteen cases, the *Chi-chu* was consulted by members of one of the Board's subordinate departments or its Statutes Commission when they prepared memoranda to be submitted to the directorate of the Board for the latter's review of sentences recommended by provincial judicial authorities.[18] Here the *Chi-chu* was used without restriction and no one was ever criticized for relying upon its opinions. In fact, when confronted with a thorny problem the directorate sometimes ordered its subordinates to search for an answer in various private commentaries[19] and in one instance, the *Chi-chu* and an earlier commentary, the *Chien-shih* (*Explanatory Notes*) of Wang K'en-t'ang, were even designated by name.[20] Occasionally, when the Department or the Commission members were not able to provide a satisfactory solution to such a problem, they defended themselves by arguing that even the private commentators were silent on this issue.[21]

In the first part of this chapter I will discuss the provincial usage of the *Chi-chu*—the invocation of this work by judicial officials outside Peking. The eight cases in this category are arranged chronologically in an attempt to discern the evolution of the central government's attitude toward the question of the proper weight to be accorded to the *Chi-chu* by provincial authorities. In the second part I examine how use of the *Chi-chu* was initiated in the capital—its application by officials of the Board of Punishments in preparing memoranda for the directorate. The thirteen cases are first classified by the function served in invoking the *Chi-chu* commentary and second by the nature of the offense involved.

Although the primary purpose of this chapter is to show the influence of a private Code commentary on Ch'ing judicial decisions, my discussion of the twenty-one cases that contained *Chi-chu* quotations also serves the important subsidiary purpose of illustrating the methods of construing legislation and the inner workings of Ch'ing judicial organs, especially at the Board level.

USE OF THE *Chi-chu Commentary* BY PROVINCIAL JUDICIAL OFFICIALS

In Re Ch'en Hsiang-li

The earliest judicial opinion I have found that cites the *Chi-chu* is a Kiangsu case of 1763.[22] In 1756 Ch'en Chia-tan unsuccessfully attempted to arrange a marriage between his son, Hsiang-li, and his landlord's daughter. Five years later, Ch'en conspired with his son and a group of relatives and friends to kidnap the daughter. At that time, Ch'en was no longer a tenant. He visited his former landlord's wife and asked her permission to stay overnight. That evening he enabled the group led by his son to enter the girl's room and kidnap her. The girl steadfastly refused to marry the son. He thereupon tied, beat, and sexually violated her. Subsequently, upon the complaint of the girl's mother, the participants in this episode were all arrested and tried. The elder Ch'en died of illness during the course of the trial.

The governor of Kiangsu reported the case to the Board of Punishments, proposing that the son and two other participants be punished with 100 blows of the heavy bamboo and banishment to 3,000 *li* as accessories to the deceased's offense of violently seizing the wife or daughter of a respectable family and carrying her away as one's wife in order to have sexual relations. This punishment represented a one degree reduction from strangulation after the assizes, which was prescribed for the principal.[23] The Board overruled the governor's decision and remanded the case to him, stating that the statute in question could be applied only if the marriage had been consummated; otherwise, Ch'en Hsiang-li should be punished for raping the victim, which was a capital offense.[24] The governor insisted on his original ruling, quoting a passage from the *Chi-chu* to support his stand:

> In punishing an offender the Code considers his intention in committing the offense to be of prime importance. The judge must always first ascertain the original intention of an offender. If the offender forcibly seizes a woman for the purpose of sleeping with her, he shall be punished as a rapist; but, if he seizes her in order to make her his wife or concubine, he shall be punished in accordance with the statute on violently seizing the wife or daughter of a respectable family and carrying her away as his wife in order to have sexual relations.[25]

The governor felt that the punishment of banishment meted out to Ch'en was sufficiently severe in view of the fact that the statute on forcibly seizing a woman as wife also stipulated that if the seized woman was given to the offender's son as wife, the father alone should bear the entire responsibility.[26] In its second review opinion the Board countered the governor's argument with the same quotation on the offender's intention:

> The governor quoted the *Chi-chu*, saying that the Code considers an offender's intention in committing the offense to be of prime importance and that in adjudicating cases the original intent of the offender must first be ascertained. That is the case here. Since Ch'en Hsiang-li originally intended to carry the woman away as his wife to have sexual relations with her, he should be punished [by death as the principal offender] in accordance with the statute on forcibly seizing a woman as wife, etc.[27]

Instead of insisting on punishing Ch'en with the offense of rape, this time the Board came around to the governor's view that the applicable statute was the one on seizing a woman as wife. The quotation from the *Chi-chu* invoked by the governor seems to have been instrumental in effecting the change of opinion. However, the Board pointed out that the son would be exempted from punishment only if he had not participated in the act of forcibly taking his future bride. This was obviously not the case, for Ch'en Hsiang-li not only actively participated in the kidnapping but also violated the woman. Although the abduction plot originated with the father, the Board was of the opinion that Ch'en Hsiang-li should be treated as the principal offender. Thus, the Board again remanded the case.

Subsequently, there was a change in provincial administration and a new governor assumed the post. He was probably eager to close the case, for he adopted the Board's opinion, treating the son as the principal offender and the deceased father as an accessory. In 1763, the Board's memorial sentencing Ch'en Hsiang-li to strangulation after the assizes was approved by the emperor, thus concluding the case. It is interesting to speculate on what would have happened had the first governor remained in office. Would he still have insisted on his original view after being rebuked by the Board, thus risking administrative sanction for making an erroneous decision?[28]

In Re Chu K'un-jong

In 1794 the governor-general of Szechwan reported to the Board of Punishments on the case of Chu K'un-jong, who fled from the place where he was serving a sentence of penal servitude and later surrendered voluntarily.[29] According to a Code provision, if a person escaped from a place of penal servitude and was subsequently arrested, he was to suffer 100 blows of the heavy bamboo, be returned to his original place of punishment, and his period of servitude was to recommence, with no credit extended for time already served.[30] However, in this case, since Chu surrendered himself to the authorities, the governor-general recommended that Chu's punishment be reduced by two degrees from 100 blows of the heavy bamboo to 80 blows, in accordance with another Code provision allowing such a reduction in punishment when a person who had fled or deserted the country returned, voluntarily or involuntarily.[31] Quoting the opinion of the *Chi-chu* commentary, the governor-general further recommended that the offender's sentence be permitted to continue rather than begin anew. The pertinent section of the *Chi-chu* stated:

> When an offender [serving the punishment of penal servitude or banishment] escapes and later surrenders himself to the authorities, he shall be exempted from punishment for the offense of fleeing from custody, and shall be returned to the original place where he served his sentence. If the offender was serving penal servitude prior to the escape, his period of servitude will not recommence, and he shall be given credit for time served.[32]

In reviewing the governor-general's recommendations, the Board pointed out that he had erred by recommending, in effect, that the offender be punished twice for the same offense (*i-tsui liang-ni*). If, because of his voluntary surrender, the offender was exempted from punishment for the offense of fleeing from a place of penal servitude, not only should he be allowed to continue his original sentence but he should also be exempted from the 80 blows of the heavy bamboo. The Board then criticized the governor-general for following the *Chi-chu*. "With regard to the passage cited from the *Chi-chu* commentary by the governor-general in his report, since the *Chi-chu* is not an established substatute enacted through [the proper legislative process of] memorializing by our Board to the emperor, it is inappropriate to apply it."[33]

The governor-general did not need *Chi-chu* in order accurately to decide on the exact period of penal servitude to be served by the offender: a statute on voluntary surrender clearly ordered that whoever committed an offense and voluntarily surrendered before his offense was otherwise discovered by the authorities was to be exempt from punishment.[34] In Chu's case the offense was fleeing from a place of penal servitude. Apparently, the governor-general was overwhelmed by the authoritative nature of the *Chi-chu* so he adopted its opinion and suggested that the offender need only finish his original sentence. However, because the *Chi-chu* was silent on the question of the proper number of blows to be administered, the governor-general was probably at a loss. He ended up by citing the statute on granting a two-degree reduction in sentence to an offender who escaped from his own country to a foreign land and then returned.

In another case collection published a few years before the *Hsing-an hui-lan*, the same case was reported without reference to either the *Chi-chu* quotation or the discussion establishing its weight by the Board of Punishments.[35] The significance of such an omission in terms of the applicability of the *Chi-chu* is not altogether clear. Nevertheless, it is relatively certain that even without the support of the *Chi-chu* opinion the decision could still stand on its own feet.

In Re Ch'e Lao-pa

In 1794 the governor of Yunnan province asked the Board of Punishments for some guidance on redemption of punishment.[36] He noted that two offenders from that province whose capital punishment had been reduced to banishment seemed to warrant special consideration. Both of them were mildly disabled (*fei-chi*, rather than seriously disabled, *tu-chi*): Hsiang Lao-erh had a broken arm and Ch'e Lao-pa was dumb by birth. According to a statute of the Code, a person with mild disability should be allowed to redeem a punishment of banishment or less. By way of illustration the official interlinear commentary pointed out that loss of one limb and blindness of one eye constituted mild disability.[37] The governor invoked a *Chi-chu* opinion which enumerated more examples of *fei-chi*: in addition to the two examples given by the official commentary it added deafness and dumbness to the list.[38] Perhaps inadvertently, the governor referred to Shen's opinion simply as "the commentary" (*chu*) which was the term ordinarily used to refer to the official interlinear commentary (*hsiao-chu*). Thus, intentionally or unintentionally, he falsely identified the opinion he relied upon.

In reply the Yunnan Department of the Board pointed out that the official interlinear commentary on mild disability had already been partly superseded by a substatute. According to the latter, a person who was blind in one eye could not be classified as *fei-chi*, so that the privilege of redemption was to be denied.[39] This was because a person with one good eye would not be affected in his ability to carry on normal activities. Likewise, aside from being unable to speak, a dumb man was in no way hindered in conducting his daily affairs. A deaf mute was equally capable of managing his affairs. Thus, the practice heretofore had been to deny the special privilege of redemption to both the deaf and the dumb. The Department concluded that both deaf mutes and dumb persons should continue to be excluded from the privileged group.

In its discussion, the Department did not explicitly criticize the governor for relying on the *Chi-chu* commentary. Instead, it merely stated: "The governor mentioned in his report that the commentary specified deafness, dumbness, and loss of a limb as *fei-chi*. Although we have thoroughly examined the official interlinear commentary of the current code, we cannot find such a quotation."[40] It is not clear whether the Department was genuinely puzzled over the origin of the governor's quotation or was deliberately avoiding the issue of the appropriateness of the lower court's reliance on a private commentary. Probably the Department officials never looked into the source of the quote and simply brushed it aside upon discovering that it varied from the official interlinear commentary. In any event, the Department's ruling was issued by the Board as a general circular to all the provinces. Although the name of *Chi-chu* was not mentioned explicitly in the circular, in effect that portion of the *Chi-chu* opinion that conflicted with the official Code was declared erroneous.

In Re Chang Chün

In 1801 the governor of Shantung reported a homicide case in which a man named Chang Chün had tried to force the deceased to commit sodomy.[41] When the latter refused, Chang killed him. Chang's brother reported the case to the authorities on his behalf.[42] According to a statute in the Code, a person who committed a sex offense was not allowed any mitigation of punishment for surrendering voluntarily.[43] Otherwise Chang would have been punished under the law on ordinary homicide rather than for the aggravated offense of a killing resulting from attempted sodomy. The punishment for ordinary intentional homicide was decapitation after the assizes;[44] the punishment for the more serious offense of homicide resulting from attempted sodomy was immediate decapitation.[45]

The governor of Shantung quoted the *Chi-chu* commentary in support of his argument that those guilty of attempted sex offenses should be allowed some mitigation of punishment for voluntary surrender. The pertinent *Chi-chu* opinion reads as follows: "In cases involving a sex offense, once accomplished, [the damage inflicted by] the offense cannot be undone. Therefore, even if the offender voluntarily surrenders himself, he shall nevertheless be punished. Such offenses are not covered by the statute on voluntary surrender."[46] On the basis of this quotation, the governor concluded that the denial of the privilege of voluntary surrender was limited to completed sex offenses and did not cover attempts. Consequently, he recommended that the Board disregard Chang Chün's antecedent causal offense of attempted sodomy and proposed punishing him with decapitation after the assizes in accordance with the statute on intentional killing. The Board, in its review of the case, noted that the reason the law did not allow a sex offender mitigation for voluntary surrender was that a completed sex offense ruined the reputation of the victim. Such an injury was truly "irreparable" and was so described in the Code.[47] On the other hand, robbers and thieves were not denied the privilege of voluntary surrender because the property taken could be recovered. In this case, since the attempted sodomy had not ruined the deceased's reputation, the governor correctly disregarded Chang Chün's antecedent causal offense. The Board approved the proposed sentence, saying that the governor's reasoning reflected respect for both the statutory words and the principle behind them. It further declared:

> Although the *Chi-chu* is not an established substatute that is currently applicable (*hsien-hsing ting-li*), it can be cited with discretion, provided that there exists a gap in the Code which can be filled by the opinions of the *Chi-chu* without contradicting [the Code's basic principles]. . . . Because the passage from the *Chi-chu* quoted by the governor in no way contradicts the statutory provisions on voluntary surrender, it seems a confirmatory reply should be issued."[48]

In this case the Board of Punishments in effect reversed its statement of 1794, *In Re Chu K'un-jong*, on the injunction against citing the *Chi-chu* in provincial case reports,[49] and authorized its application where no pertinent Code provision was available. However, the significance of the Board's authorization of conditional application of the *Chi-chu* is far from clear. The reply was directed towards a particular governor who had submitted the case for review and, unlike a general circular, probably did not reach a large number of judicial officials in the provinces. Moreover, the present ruling seems to have been the only instance in which reliance on the *Chi-chu* by provincial officials was explicitly approved by the Board. It may have reflected the particular view held by the Board members who prepared one document in question. Perhaps for this reason the compilers of the popular *Hsing-an hui-lan* decided not to include the case in its materials.

It might be added parenthetically that the principle upheld in this case (i.e., an unsuccessful sex offender shall be allowed to benefit from voluntary surrender) was in effect overruled by the Chia-ch'ing emperor's intervention in a similar criminal case four years later in 1805.[50] However, since the original case report submitted by the provincial authorities for the 1805 case is not available, it is not clear whether it invoked *In Re Chang Chün* as a precedent.

An Advisory Opinion for the Yen-chou Prefect

In 1815 the governor of Shantung forwarded to the Board a request for a statutory interpretation on behalf of the prefect of Yen-chou.[51] The prefect had doubts about the correct application of a substatute in the Code section entitled *Tou-ou chi ku-sha-jen* ("Killing in a fight and killing with intent") which dealt with the criminal responsibilities of offenders involved in a group fight in the course of which death ensued.[52] According to that substatute, if two or more people contrived to fight another person and inflicted multiple wounds resulting in death, it became essential to allocate the responsibilities so that only one of the offenders would receive capital punishment. After providing that, whether or not the deceased died instantly, the combatant who inflicted either the last mortal wound or the most serious wound would be deemed the principal perpetrator, the substatute went on to state: "In cases where the fight is carried out in a confused manner and it is impossible to determine the order of infliction of wounds or to ascertain the degree of severity of those wounds, the person who originated the idea shall be punished [with death]. If there was no single original contriver, the offender who strikes first shall be punished [with death]."[53] The prefect noted that the opinion of Shen Chih-ch'i's *Chi-chu* contradicted this passage: "In a group fight where the participants fight each other indiscriminately, if it is not clear who inflicted the mortal wound, the original contriver shall pay the death penalty, provided that he participated in the fight; otherwise, the person who strikes first shall pay the death penalty."[54]

It is worth noting that in his *Chi-chu* Shen was actually expanding on a statute that dealt with a group fight in which the person who inflicted the wound could be identified. On the other hand, the substatute in question was enacted in 1740,[55] some twenty-five years after Shen published his work; it is clear that Shen's opinion could not have been directed toward this substatute. In any event, the prefect wanted to know how to decide a case where the original contriver had not participated in the fight, the participant who struck first only inflicted a light wound, and it was impossible to determine which of the remaining participants had inflicted the mortal wound. According to the substatute of the Code, the original contriver should be punished with death in spite of the fact that he did not take part in the fighting. But the *Chi-chu* commentary said that in these circumstances the offender who struck first should be executed. Although the prefect considered the principle adopted by the Code more reasonable than that of the *Chi-chu*, he was not sure which to follow. He was so impressed by Shen's opinion that, even though it contradicted a Code provision, he felt quite uneasy about setting it aside. I am not sure how representative this particular local official's attitude toward the *Chi-chu* is; nevertheless, it is interesting that the provincial governor did not want to assume the responsibility for advising his subordinate to ignore this private commentary.

In his request for an opinion from the Board of Punishments the prefect stated: "The established substatute and the *Chi-chu* commentary contradict each other on this point. Because the outcome of the decision involves life and death for the offenders, I dare not propose a sentence lightheartedly. Please kindly give us guidance."[56] Apparently, the prefect was confronted with an actual criminal case, though the names of the parties were withheld from the report. Instead of proposing a sentence, he filed an eleventh-hour request for instructions from his superior officials on how to make an accurate decision. The Board replied that the pertinent legal provisions were quite clear and should be applied in this and in future similar cases.[57] After discussing the various statutory elements of the pertinent substatute, it then criticized the prefect for being swayed by the *Chi-chu* opinion. The Board continued:

> As long as there is a substatute clearly regulating the matter under consideration, why should [the prefect] be concerned about the *Chi-chu* commentary that has never been invoked? Furthermore, the Code is issued by the Board of Punishments, whereas the *Chi-chu* is circulated by private bookstores. How can he abandon an officially promulgated code and instead rely on a work produced by private sources, thereby causing confusion and misunderstanding? The governor should be ordered to notify [the prefect] that henceforth, should a similar situation occur, it shall be handled in accordance with the established substatute [rather than the *Chi-chu*]."[58]

The Board's reply could indicate a general ban on the *Chi-chu*, but it could also mean that the ban was applicable only when the *Chi-chu* contradicted the Code. Whichever interpretation is correct, the Board's ruling was circulated only to the small number of officials directly involved in the present case and was not communicated to the judicial authorities throughout the country. Thus, the ruling probably had little immediate impact beyond the borders of Shantung province.

Despite the existence of an earlier 1801 Board ruling (*In Re Chang Chün*) approving the application of the *Chi-chu* in a case involving the voluntary surrender of an offender,[59] in the present case the Board bluntly asserted that the *Chi-chu* commentary had never been applied (by provincial judicial authorities). The possible oversight is surprising in view of the fact that the Board's reply to the prefect's inquiry presumably was drafted by the Shantung Department that also produced the 1801 ruling.

In Re Wang En-chang

In 1822 the Tartar general and military governor of Ili reported a case of accidental death to the Board of Punishments.[60] Ho Yün, riding on horseback, passed under the eaves of Wang En-chang's secondhand clothes shop. Wang happened to be using a pronged stick to take down some clothes hung beneath the eaves. Suddenly the rope holding up a bar on which the clothes were hung broke, and the bar fell on the head of the horse. Startled, the horse began to gallop, throwing Ho to the ground. The frightened animal then ran up against Cheng Hsiang, a criminal from Fukien province who was serving his sentence of deportation to Ili, thereby causing his death. The general held both Ho and Wang liable for killing by accident. According to the Code, all persons who killed others purely by accident were permitted to redeem themselves by the payment to the family of the deceased of a redemption fee of 12.42 silver taels.[61] On the basis of a *Chi-chu* opinion, the general ruled that, since in this case there were two offenders against one victim, each of them should be required to pay 12.42 silver taels. One share was to be given to the victim's family for funeral expenses while the other would be confiscated by the Commissary Office of the government. Moreover, according to a substatute, the redemption fee could be converted into 80 blows of the heavy bamboo if the offender was too poor to pay.[62] Thus, the general requested the Board's permission to let Ho Yün receive the blows in lieu of the payment. The borrowed horse was to be returned to the original owner.

The Board concluded that the death of Cheng was indeed occasioned by Wang En-chang, who accidentally caused the bar to hit the horse. Ho, the horse rider, could not possibly have foreseen that his horse would kill Cheng after being startled. Wang, therefore, was held solely responsible for Cheng's death and was ordered to pay the redemption fee to Cheng's family. Ho was completely exonerated. The Board, however, was concerned about the quotation from *Chi-chu* given by the general. The Board stated that when two people were involved in the purely accidental killing of another person, such cases had always been handled by requiring the offenders jointly to pay the stipulated sum of money to the victim's family. Although the Code was silent on the point of allocation of liability between two people who jointly caused an accidental death, it was clear that the sum of 12.42 silver taels was exacted to pay expenses for the funeral of the deceased.[63] In nature it was different from an ordinary redemption fee or fine which, according to law, was to be confiscated by the government. It would be inappropriate to give twice the stipulated sum to the victim's family, but it was equally wrong for the government to confiscate the additional sum. The Board went on to declare:

> In this case the general of Ili justifies his decision to give one share [of the redemption fee] to the relatives of the deceased and to confiscate the other share on behalf of the Commissary Office by quoting the *Chi-chu*. We note that the *Chi-chu* is not the Code issued by the Board of Punishments. Any precedent from a remote period [*yüan-nien ch'eng-an*] cited in such a [private] work has heretofore been barred from being invoked [as a judicial precedent]. . . . From now on when adjudicating cases [judges] may not apply the *Chi-chu*; otherwise, mistakes cannot be avoided.[64]

The Board's ruling on the *Chi-chu* and the redemption fee was issued as a general circular which supposedly circulated throughout the country. The currently available sources show that in 1822 Shantung,[65] Kiangsi,[66] and Chekiang[67] provinces received the circular; it also reached Shansi[68] province the following year. It can be assumed that judicial officials throughout the country were notified of the ban on citing the *Chi-chu*.

Several questions may be raised in the light of the Board's ruling. Was this a prohibition against invoking Shen Chih-ch'i's *Chi-chu* (1715) alone, or did it also apply to all of its revisions—for example, to the revised *Chi-chu* (1745) of Hung Hung-hsü and to Wan Wei-han's *Chyi-chu* (1766) which was modeled after Shen's work? What about quotations from Shen's *Chi-chu* which by this time (1822) appeared extensively in a dozen other private commentaries on the Code? Should this ruling be interpreted to mean that other private commentaries, such as Wang K'en-t'ang's *Chien-shih*, were likewise not to be cited? What was the significance of the passage criticizing the error of relying on "a precedent from a remote period" contained in the *Chi-chu*—did it mean that it was permissible to apply only recent precedents, or did it simply mean that the Board of Punishments disapproved of reliance upon cases cited in the *Chi-chu* commentary but implicitly approved the use of *Chi-chu*'s statutory interpretations? To answer these inquiries, we can first examine the controversial *Chi-chu* quotation cited by the Tartar general and then, on the basis of later developments, formulate a tentative conclusion about the scope of the 1822 Board ruling. This quotation reads: "If two people kill a person by accident, both of them are required to pay the redemption fee. One of these fees shall be confiscated by the government."[69] I searched for this quotation in vain in the *Chi-chu* originally published by

Shen Chih-ch'i in 1715. The closest reference I have found is: "If two people kill a person by accident, no distinction of principal and accessory shall be made between these two offenders. This is because an accident occurs unexpectedly; in such circumstances there is indeed no meaningful way to distinguish a principal from an accessory. Both offenders shall together pay [*t'ung-ch'u*] the redemption fee."[70]

It is clear that Shen never advocated the theory that in cases of joint causation of accidental death an additional redemption fee should be confiscated by the government. Rather, this idea was introduced by Hung Hung-hsü, a later commentator who revised Shen's work in 1745.[71] This is a good illustration of how under the rubric of "Chi-chu" Shen was sometimes blamed for views of subsequent commentators who revised his work. Of course, he also enjoyed the benefit of the improvements made by those people. Rightly or wrongly, all opinions in any edition of the *Chi-chu* tended to be attributed to him.

Although the Board referred to the *Chi-chu* passage on confiscation of redemption fees by the government as a "precedent from a remote period," strictly speaking it was not a precedent but a private commentator's opinion. Perhaps Hung had extracted a rule from an actual case decision; even so, the rule so extracted was far from an ordinary precedent in the common parlance. In any event, the problems concerning the development of case precedents and their widespread usage in Ch'ing decisions, as well as Ch'ing emperors' attempts to regulate this situation, are interesting but too complicated to be handled thoroughly here. In 1811, eleven years prior to the 1822 ruling, the Chia-ch'ing emperor reiterated an earlier ban (issued in 1738) against invoking precedents which had not been adopted as substatutes of the Code or which had not been communicated to judicial authorities by a general circular.[72] As a result of this imperial command, many judicial decisions in the next ten or twenty years contained a passage discrediting the reliance on either recent or remote precedents.[73] It seems, then, that the 1822 ruling was concerned not with the age of a precedent but with the principle that materials contained in a private commentary, such as precedents and annotations, which are neither established substatutes nor general circulars, should not be relied upon in judicial decisions.

Logically, the conclusion to be drawn from the foregoing discussion is that neither the *Chi-chu* nor other private commentaries were to be invoked in judicial decisions. The reason the *Chi-chu* was singled out for mention was its prominence among private commentaries. However, the effectiveness of the government's policy in this regard is another matter. As we shall see in the next two cases, *Chi-chu* opinions continued to creep into provincial judicial decisions.

In Re Wang Feng

In 1833 the governor-general of Shensi reported a theft case to the Board of Punishments.[74] Wang Feng twice stole articles of silver from Chao Ming-yü. The first time he took articles worth 80 silver taels and the second time less than that amount.[75] The two incidents were separated by a couple of months, and in neither case was Chao aware of the stealing. The governor-general pointed out that where the Code provision stipulated that, "Theft offenders shall be punished in proportion to the amount of the largest sum stolen from any one property owner, and the punishment shall be estimated by the aggregate of all shares in the plunder,"[76] it was referring to a theft of property from two or more families. He quoted the *Chi-chu* commentary to the effect that when a person twice stole from the same family, the larger sum should be taken as the basis for his punishment.[77] However, since the Code was silent on how to punish a thief who was guilty of multiple thefts against a single property owner, the governor-general requested an opinion from the Board.

The Board replied that the official interlinear commentary of the Code provision in question clearly stated that when the aggregate of stolen goods was taken as the basis for determining the offender's criminality, that provision was dealing with the situation where several offenders jointly stole from one household.[78] On the other hand, the Code did not specify on what basis—the aggregate or the larger of the two sums—an offender should be punished if he committed mulitiple thefts against one household. The Board then repeated the quotation from the *Chi-chu* contained in the original request, and stated: "What the *Chi-chu* means is that in the case of a repeated theft offense by one person against one family, the offender shall be punished according to the scale pertaining to the larger of the two sums of his illegally acquired property. The *Chi-chu* quote is rather unequivocal in this regard."[79]

Therefore, the Board ruled that Wang Feng should be punished with 90 blows of the heavy bamboo and two and a half years of penal servitude in accordance with the statute which prescribed such punishment for a thief who had taken 80 silver taels worth of property.[80]

In Re Sung Mao-tzu

In 1840 the governor-general of Chihli reported a homicide case to the Board of Punishments.[81] Sung Mao-tzu used to play jokes with Mrs. Wang, née Chang, by hiding her five-month-old baby and letting her look for it. One day he saw the baby sleeping in the front yard of Mrs.

Wang's house. He hid the baby underneath a stack of hay beside a pig pen in the back yard and returned to work in the front yard. Unexpectedly, the baby woke up, fell into the pig pen, and was drowned in the water accumulated in the pen. The governor-general recommended that Sung be held responsible for accidental killing and be permitted to redeem his punishment.[82] The Board overruled the governor-general's recommendation, arguing that Sung was guilty of killing during roughhousing, for which no redemption was to be granted.[83]

Instead of submitting a new proposal, the governor-general requested an advisory opinion from the Board. After carefully studying the Code provisions governing accidental homicide and killing by roughhousing, the governor-general came to the conclusion that the law on accidental killing was more pertinent to the case under consideration. However, since he did not want to ignore the Board's opinion and since there was no express language in the Code dealing with a similar case, he decided to seek guidance from the Board.

In his request, the governor-general contended that the defendant had no intent to kill the baby, and the death occurred quite unexpectedly. On the other hand, he said, the Code provision dealing with killing during roughhousing governed the situation where people play together and death ensues immediately; the official interlinear commentary on this provision noted that when two people play with their fists, with a stick, or in any such manner as is likely to cause death, and in the course of action death does occur, the offender is to be punished with strangulation after the assizes.[84] The governor-general also consulted the *Chi-chu* commentary to clarify his thinking concerning the exact meaning and coverage of the law on killing during roughhousing. He stated:

> The *Chi-chu* says that the meaning of "killing during roughhousing" is that two people know an act is dangerous enough to cause grave consequences but nevertheless are willing to engage in it. If death occurs later, the offender shall be punished with strangulation after the assizes, as in the case of killing in a fight. In the present case, however, Sung Mao-tzu was playing practical jokes with Mrs. Wang; he was not playing with the baby. Moreover, placing an infant near a pig pen is normally not likely to kill him. This seems to have been a clear case of accidental death. If Sung were to be punished in accordance with the statute governing killing during roughhousing, it would not seem to be in conformity with the true meaning of that provision.[85]

The Board again disputed the governor-general's view. It declared that it was correct to say that Sung Mao-tzu did not intend to drown the baby, but it was inaccurate to assert that Sung did not know the water accumulated in the pig pen was sufficient to kill him. The official interlinear commentary on killing during roughhousing gave playing with the fists and with a stick as examples of what constituted roughhousing. Apart from these two, however, there were other ways through which killing could occur under this category. In this case, Sung's act of playing practical jokes with Mrs. Wang by hiding the baby was tantamount to roughhousing with the baby. The Board asserted that the defendant's act, in causing the baby's death by a spontaneous prank, was very similar to the case where one man occasionally became involved in competing with someone else in physical strength and thus caused the latter's death.

The most interesting part of the Board's reply lay in its criticism of the quote from the *Chi-chu* given by the governor-general. The Board issued the following rebuke:

> The *Chi-chu* commentary insisted that an [important] element of the offense of killing during roughhousing was that two people had willingly engaged in a dangerous act. Just think how unreasonable it is to expect a man who killed his playmate by chance to have come to an earlier agreement with the victim for engaging in that particular act! How can the governor-general go so far as to say that the Code provision punishing by strangulation the offense of killing during roughhousing is inferior to or less reliable than the *Chi-chu*?[86]

In all fairness, the governor-general did not build his contention solely on the *Chi-chu* opinion. His argument for convicting the defendant of accidental killing seems to be rather convincing. But after having been charged with honoring a private commentary more than the official Code provision, the governor-general would have had a hard time if he had decided to maintain his original position. Surprisingly, the Board did not reiterate the 1822 ruling which prohibited the use of the *Chi-chu* in judicial decisions.

Although the Board did not explicitly invoke the principle of "constructive intent" to bring about the unfortunate result in this case, the language it employed in condemning Sung's prank of hiding the baby near a pig pen and its argument that Sung should have known the water in the pig pen could kill the infant, indicate that the Board was tacitly applying such a principle.

Use of the *Chi-chu Commentary* as a Reference Tool by Members of the Board of Punishments

At least three different reasons for referring to the *Chi-chu* can be discerned among the thirteen cases in which it was initially invoked by members of the Board of Punishments in their review memoranda.[87] In the overwhelming majority (ten cases), the *Chi-chu* was consulted to ascertain the true meaning of the Code provision in question, or to determine the applicability of a particular provision; those ten cases can be further divided by subject matter into three groups: homicide (three cases), theft and related property offenses (five cases), and enticement of women (two cases). The remaining three cases illustrate two other reasons for using the *Chi-chu*. In one, in the absence of an applicable Code provision, it was treated as a source of law. In the other two, it was used simply as an ornament of the board's erudition. I shall began with the three latter cases.

In the Absence of Directly Applicable Statutory Provisions, a Chi-chu *Opinion Is Treated as a Source of Law*

In Re Liang T'ien-chao. In 1800 the Hukwang Department of the Board of Punishments reviewed the case of Liang T'ien-chao, who struck his son-in-law and frightened him so much that he committed suicide.[88] The Code provided that any person who alarmed a senior relative of the first degree of mourning with violent threats, as a consequence of which the relative killed himself, should be punished with strangulation after the assizes. For a similar offense against a senior relative of a more remote degree, the punishment was to be reduced by one degree.[89] The relationship between a father-in-law and a son-in-law would have fallen into the "more remote degree" category.[90] The Code, however, did not provide for the case where the death of a junior was occasioned by threats from a senior relative. The governor of Hunan sentenced Liang to 80 blows of the heavy bamboo in accordance with the statute on "doing what ought not to be done."[91] When reviewing the case, the Department quoted a passage from the *Chi-chu* to confirm the sentence. The passage reads:

> The reason why the Code does not provide any regulation in the case of a senior relative occasioning a junior's death by violent and fearful threats is that the latter owes certain obligations toward the former. Whatever the senior relative does to the junior, the latter must endure the hardship; indeed, it is improper to talk about being threatened with violence or frightened by a senior relative. Should death be occasioned, a senior relative in the first degree of mourning shall not be punished at all; a senior in the more remote degree of mourning may be dealt with in accordance with the law on doing what ought not to be done.[92]

The Department of the Board of Punishments concluded that, since the governor's proposed sentence was in accord with the *Chi-chu* opinion, a confirmatory reply should be granted.

Chi-chu *Is Quoted to Show the Erudition of the Members of the Board*

In Re Mrs. Chao, née Ch'en. In 1789 the case of Mrs. Chao, née Ch'en, who voluntarily surrendered to the authorities after having illicit sexual relations with a man, was reported to the Board of Punishments.[93] The available record of this case in the *Hsing-an hui-lan* is very brief, and several points of fact and procedure are omitted. The memorandum was probably prepared by the Statutes Commission, which affirmed the Chihli Department's order reversing the provincial governor's proposal *to exempt her from punishment because of voluntary surrender.*[94] After noting that sex offenses were not covered by the statute on voluntary surrender,[95] the Commission went on to discuss another statute which stipulated that in punishing sex offenders no distinction should be made between principals and accessories.[96] To support the latter point, the Commission quoted the *Chi-chu* commentary: "There is no distinction between principal and accessory in sex offense cases because each participant has personally violated the law."[97]

The punishment for both parties for the offense of adultery was 100 blows of the heavy bamboo in addition to wearing the cangue for two months;[98] both Mrs. Chao and her paramour were to receive the same punishment. Surely, even without the citation from the *Chi-chu* commentary, the Code provision would have sufficed to guide the judges to the proper conclusion in the case of Mrs. Chao. This type of *Chi-chu* quotation in a judicial opinion was largely ornamental.

On Violation of the Tomb. In 1865 the subdirector of the Court of Revision and several censors submitted a memorial to the throne requesting an increase in punishment for the offense of violating a tomb.[99] They were concerned about the rapid rise in the incidence of that crime and proposed to stem the tide by resorting to Draconian measures. It is well known that, to the Chinese, prying open a coffin and stealing therefrom was not a simple property offense; the disturbance of the corpse itself was punishable.[100] The Code section on violation of tombs contained numerous detailed statutes. The severity of the punishments varied in accordance with the offender's relationship to the deceased as well as the degree of disturbance caused to the corpse.[101] The memorialists felt that the punishments meted out in the Code were not severe enough. They wanted to revise the law to treat violation of tombs as armed robbery, a charge which carried a stiff penalty and also disregarded the principal-accessory distinction.[102]

The T'ung-chih emperor ordered the Board of Punishments to deliberate on this memorial. In a detailed reply, the Board agreed that a revision increasing the penalty was needed in order to warn and discourage future violators. However, it pointed out that there were ways to achieve this goal without applying the armed robbery provision. In other words, the Board was of the opinion that it was inappropriate to use the analogy of armed robbery. To bolster its claim, the Board quoted a passage from Shen's *Chi-chu*, saying that "the opinion of an earlier writer is quite accurate." The passage reads: "Though a tomb is located in an open field, digging up the coffin and prying it open (to steal therefrom) is not the same as committing armed robbery; likewise, if a man is already dead, to mutilate or discard his corpse cannot be viewed as murder."[103] The Board went on to propose a general increase in the penalty for the offense of violating tombs, carefully preserving the principal-accessory distinction as well as the stipulation on the relationship between the offenders and the corpse. The emperor endorsed the Board's view. An imperial order was later issued and circulated throughout the empire.[104] What interests us here is the fact that the Board could have reached the same conclusion without resorting to the *Chi-chu*. It is clear, then, that in this case Shen's work was cited also primarily for show.

This case is unique among the cases discussed in this essay: the *Chi-chu* was cited by the board in its reply to the emperor. Moreover, in the imperial order circulated throughout the country, the board's opinion, together with the *Chi-chu* quotation, was kept intact. The government was apparently not concerned about possible implications of preserving a quotation from a private code commentary in its official circular because, from the context, it was crystal clear that Shen's opinion was by no means the crucial point in the Board's reply and had nothing to do with the concrete case.

Chi-chu *Is Quoted to Elaborate the Meaning of Key Terms or to Determine the Applicability of a Code Provision*

In Re Mrs. Wang, née Han. In 1790 Mrs. Wang, née Han, from Honan killed her son from a former marriage.[105] According to a statute, if a parent kills a child who is not guilty of disobedience, the parent shall be punished with 60 blows of the heavy bamboo and one year of penal servitude.[106] The question confronting the Honan department of the Board of Punishments, which handled the case, was whether or not the remarriage of Mrs. Wang would affect the mother-child relationship with the deceased. According to the mourning chart, the relationship between a son (born to a secondary wife) and his father's principal wife or his stepmother was much more intimate than that between the son and his own mother who was divorced or remarried.[107] In the statute mentioned earlier, it was also provided that if a son was killed by his father's principal wife (other than his own mother) or by his stepmother, the punishment of 60 blows of the heavy bamboo and one year of penal servitude was to be increased by one degree.[108] The foregoing indicates that since Mrs. Wang was remarried and her relationship to the son became more remote than that of a stepmother to him, her punishment should have been increased by at least one degree. However, the Honan Department, without explaining its reasons, held that an increase was not necessary.

In reviewing the case, the Statutes Commission of the Board of Punishments confirmed the Department's ruling by quoting the *Chi-chu*. The opinion reads:

> Where a person's mother is divorced by his father, or remarries after the death of his father, the mother-son relationship still persists in spite of the fact that the woman has broken the matrimonial connection with the father. She is still considered a mother to the son. On the other hand, if the divorced or remarried woman is a stepmother, or the father's principal wife (whereas the son was born to a secondary wife), the mother-son relationship will cease to exist as soon as the matrimonial connection is broken."[109]

By relying on the *Chi-chu*, the Board prevented an increased punishment in Mrs. Wang's case.

In Re Mrs. Liu, née Tseng. In 1802 a case which occurred in Hunan province was reviewed by the Board of Punishments.[110] Mrs. Liu, née Tseng, had a son named Liu Nan, who was a loafer. He committed a theft and was arrested by the authorities. Mrs. Liu decided to poison him after being ridiculed by other people for having such a bad son. She mixed arsenic into flour with which she made six pieces of cake, and asked a friend to deliver them to him. Liu Nan ate one piece and gave another piece to Lo Lung-tzu, a prison mate, at the latter's request. Soon both men fell ill. Liu vomited the poisonous stuff and so he was saved; but Lo died. The governor of Hunan proposed to punish Mrs. Liu with banishment (to 3,000 *li* and 100 blows of the heavy bamboo) which was a one degree reduction from the death penalty.[111]

The Hukwang Department of the Board, which reviewed the case, noted that there was no express language in the Code on how to punish an offender who had intended to murder his own son but through error killed another person. It quoted a passage from the *Chi-chu* in an attempt to solve the problem:

> There is a statute governing death occasioned by a mistake in object which occurred in the course of committing an offense of premeditated homicide, intentional killing, or killing in a fight.[112] However,

> this provision deals exclusively with ordinary people who are not related. If, in an attempt to kill an ordinary person, a relative is instead killed by mistake, or vice versa, or if the mistake in object occurs between senior and junior relatives, the matter shall be handled by consulting pertinent Code provisions that govern the offenses committed by senior relatives against juniors, or junior relatives against seniors. The nature of the offense and other relevant circumstances should be taken into consideration [in determining the offender's guilt].[113]

Although the *Chi-chu* opinion did not furnish any specific guidance on how to adjust the proper amount of punishment when relatives became involved in the mistake in object in a homicide case, the message imparted by the *Chi-chu* seems to be clear. That is, the punishment prescribed for ordinary people should be reduced or increased to suit the particular circumstances of each case. The statute brought up by the *Chi-chu* provided that whoever contrived to murder a particular person but by mistake killed another, was to be given the same punishment as in the case of intentional killing. In turn, the offense of intentional killing was punishable by decapitation after the assizes.[114] The Hukwang Department observed that in the present case, if Mrs. Liu had successfully poisoned her unruly son, her punishment would have been 100 blows of the heavy bamboo;[115] however, she killed someone else by mistake. If her life was to be taken to pay for the death of the victim, her punishment would not seem to constitute a correct application of the law to the circumstances of the case. It would be a pity if, at the age of over 80, Mrs. Liu should be given a death penalty for an offense resulting from mistake. Since the governor of Hunan recommended that Mrs. Liu's sentence be reduced from the death penalty to banishment (at a distance of 3,000 *li* and 100 blows of the heavy bamboo), he seemed to have weighed the circumstances and handled the case accordingly. Therefore, the Department proposed to give a confirmatory reply to the governor.

The directorate of the Board, however, took issue with the Department's opinion. It suggested that, since Mrs. Liu was an ignorant woman, she probably could not have foreseen that someone else would share those poisonous cakes with her son. Thus, Mrs. Liu should have been held responsible for accidental killing and permitted to redeem her punishment. The directorate then referred this case to the Statutes Commission for further deliberation.

The Commission disagreed with the directorate's view. It pointed out that Mrs. Liu's offense was not accidental killing, because she had contemplated all along the idea of killing a person. Moreover, the dangerous nature of arsenic was probably known to everyone; it was hard to argue that Mrs. Liu could not have foreseen that someone other than her son might be poisoned.[116] The Commission then discussed two case precedents.[117] One was especially pertinent: it involved the death of a third person resulting from a father's attempt to poison a disobedient son.[118] The father was held liable for the offense of intentional killing and sentenced to decapitation after the assizes. However, the Commission agreed that in the case under consideration the death penalty was too severe for Mrs. Liu, who deserved compassion because of her age and her motivation in committing the crime. Hence, it supported the review opinion of the Hukwang Department and likewise recommended approval of the governor's proposed sentence.

In Re Mrs. Huang, née Wei. In 1811 a case which resembled the case of Mrs. Liu was submitted by the governor of Kwangsi for review. Mrs. Huang, née Wei, tried to kill her disobedient son by putting poison into his wine. Unaware of the poison, the son exchanged the wine with a friend for some food. The friend took the wine home and enjoyed it with his wife, with the result that both died.[119] The governor recommended that Mrs. Huang be held responsible for accidental killing and permitted to redeem her punishment.[120]

The Kwangsi Department of the Board of Punishments, which reviewed the case, took issue with the governor's finding.[121] It noted that in this case, if the exchange of the wine and the food had not taken place and the son had been poisoned, Mrs. Huang would have been given 100 blows of the heavy bamboo as punishment. But, since her plan had failed and two innocent people were killed instead, she was held liable for intentional killing.[122] Furthermore, in this case the punishment for intentional killing was to be increased from decapitation after the assizes to immediate decapitation plus the display of the offender's head (as a warning to the public), because killing two members of the same family constituted an aggravating circumstance.[123] However, the Kwangsi Department declared that both law and compassion required that Mrs. Huang be spared from such an excessively harsh punishment.

The Department first quoted the same *Chi-chu* opinion discussed in the 1802 case of *In Re Mrs. Liu, née Tseng* to justify the need to adjust the punishment stipulated for the offense of intentional killing in accordance with the particular circumstances of each case.[124] Then it went on to discuss the 1802 precedent and asserted that in the present case Mrs. Huang should be punished the same as Mrs. Liu: one degree reduction from the death penalty prescribed for the offense of intentional killing, thus resulting in the punishment of banishment to 3,000 *li* and 100 blows of the heavy bamboo. Although Mrs. Huang's guilt was considerably greater than that of Mrs. Liu, the Department deemed it unnecessary to increase the punishment from banishment to deportation to the frontier as a soldiers' slave.[125]

It seems that in the present case it was not necessary to cite the *Chi-chu* passage—the discussion of the 1802 precedent would have sufficed since it cited the same passage. Probably the authors of the present memorandum decided to include the *Chi-chu* quotation in the hope of making its recommendation more persuasive, knowing that the directorate of the Board might very well neglect to look into the content of the precedent in question.

In Re Ying Liang. In 1789 Ying Liang and his followers, defendants in this case, had stolen five head of cattle and two horses from Cha Mien; two of the cattle and one of the horses managed to return to their owner.[126] According to the Code, if cattle stealing took place in Outer or Inner Mongolia, as it did here, the severity of punishment was to be determined by the number of cattle stolen.[127] Thus, it was important to determine whether, within the meaning of the Code, the offenders had technically "stolen" the three animals that eventually returned to the owner. The governor of Shansi felt that the returned animals should not be classified as stolen and, as a result, the offenders were only liable for the four animals that they actually had taken with them. He proposed to sentence Ying and his gang in accordance with a substatute which prescribed that if three to five head of cattle or horses had been stolen, the principal offender was to be deported to Hukwang or some other adjacent province.[128] Under the same provision, the accessories were to be sent to Shantung or Honan province. Upon review, the recommendation was overruled by the Shansi Department of the Board of Punishments. The more severe punishment ordained for the theft of six to nine cattle was imposed on the offenders.[129] The Department considered all seven of the animals stolen. It referred to a statute which covered the theft of horses, cattle, and other domestic animals. Once the animals were taken out of the stable, the crime was consummated.[130] Afterwards, the Department's opinion was sent by the directorate of the Board to the Statutes Commission for deliberation.

In affirming the governor's original ruling, the Statutes Commission turned to the *Chi-chu* for support:

> Where a thief abandons in the street an article he has stolen and someone other than the owner has acquired the article, it is deemed that the thief has successfully stolen the property. This is because the property owner has already sustained loss, even though the thief has not acquired the booty. However, if the owner has retrieved the stolen arti-

cle, the offense of theft will not be deemed to have been carried out successfully."[131]

The Commission pointed out that, when the Code provision prescribed that theft was completed once domestic animals were taken out of the stable, its comment was restricted to the situation where the property owner immediately became aware of the incident. If the theft was discovered sometime later, the actual loss sustained by the property owner was to be used in measuring the amount taken by the thief. The Commission went on to say that since the governor's proposed sentence was in accord with the *Chi-chu*, it should be affirmed. Presumably, the directorate of the Board accepted the Commission's opinion.

In the absence of the *Chi-chu* opinion, the governor's proposed sentence would have been deemed erroneous because it seemed to contradict the statute governing the theft of domestic animals. By relying on the *Chi-chu*, the Statutes Commission of the Board of Punishments was able to introduce a new element into a relatively unequivocal Code provision and finally secured a lighter punishment for the defendant.

In Re Han Pang-fu. In 1790 the Chihli Department of the Board of Punishments deliberated on a bribery case.[132] Han Pang-fu had been involved in a criminal case and had been afraid that he would be severely punished. He confided his fear to Ch'ien K'e-ts'ung, an acquaintance of his and a runner at the local government office. Ch'ien assured him that by pumping money into the magistrate's *yamen*, a speedy trial with light punishment could be achieved. Ch'ien and a collaborator of his, another runner, each succeeded in getting 50 silver taels from Han, although it is not clear whether the amounts were delivered jointly or separately. Later the matter came to light and all three of the participants were charged with offering and accepting bribes.

The available record is too brief to indicate what was contained in the lower court's finding as reviewed by the Board. The Board's memorandum began with the applicable statutory provisions and the following quotation from Shen's *Chi-chu*: "In the case of dealing with bribes, whether for a lawful or unlawful purpose, the punishment for each offender shall be determined according to the amount which he himself appropriated."[133] The Board did not elaborate on the citation and never discussed the relevance of Shen's opinion to the case under consideration. However, it appears that there was some question whether the offenders should be punished jointly for the total amount received (100 taels) or separately for the sum appropriated by each individual (50 taels). The Code section on officials and clerks accepting bribes had an elaborate scale by which the severity of punishment was set according to the amount of property taken.[134] This provision prescribed that, in the case where an offender received bribes from more than one person, he was to be punished for the entire amount taken;[135] it was silent, however, on the method of calculation where joint offenders accepted a bribe from a single victim. The choice between using 50 taels or 100 taels as the basis for calculation was of crucial importance to the offenders. Accepting a bribe of 50 silver taels for the purpose of twisting the law was punishable by 100 blows of the heavy bamboo and banishment to 2,500 *li*.[136] But, if the amount was over 80 taels, the punishment became strangulation after the assizes.[137] Since the person who offered the bribe was given the same punishment as the bribe taker,[138] the determination of the method of calculation was also crucial to Han.

In this case, the two runners could have been charged with "fraudulently obtaining public or private property,"[139] instead of being charged with "officials and clerks accepting bribes."[140] Whereas punishment for the latter is calculated as described above, punishment for the former offense of fraud is calculated in accordance with the scale prescribed in the theft statutes. If theft was committed against more than one property owner, the highest amount of property taken was to be used as the basis for the punishment to be imposed; if joint offenders were involved in stealing from one property owner, the total loss of the victim was to be adopted as the basis for calculation, regardless of the manner in which the offenders divided up the booty.[141]

The explanation given by Shen Chih-ch'i for the different criteria used in theft and bribery regulations was that the former sought to protect the property owner, but the latter aimed at the punishment of greedy officials. Shen further explained that, in the case of accepting bribes, since each offender was judged by the amount of property he had taken, the principle of punishing the accessories one degree less than the principal offender would not be applicable.[142]

Apparently, the governor general held Ch'ien K'e-ts'ung responsible for accepting a bribe of 50 silver taels for the purpose of twisting the law.[143] Since Ch'ien was not a salaried official, he was eligible for a one degree reduction, resulting in the punishment of 100 blows of the heavy bamboo and three years of penal servitude.[144] Moreover, in the Code section governing fraudulently obtaining public and private property, a substatute provided that if a government runner sought a bribe allegedly for maneuvering in the *yamen* and if he was sentenced to penal servitude or a higher punishment for that offense, the punishment should be increased to military banishment to the near frontier.[145] Therefore, the governor-general recommended that Ch'ien be punished accordingly. Presumably, Ch'ien's collaborator was given the same punishment of military banishment. The recommendation was approved by the Board of Punishments.

Han, the bribe giver, was punished with 100 blows of the heavy bamboo and three years of penal servitude. Here the Board objected to what it deemed the governor-general's misapplication of law.[146] However, since the *Chi-chu* opinion was not relevant for determining Han's sentence, the Board's discussion of Han shall be omitted here.

The principle advocated by Shen and upheld by the Board of Punishments on the method of determining the responsibility of a bribe taker in this 1790 case was again articulated in an 1870 case.[147] In this later case, which also involved the acceptance of a bribe by joint offenders, the acting governor of Kweichow proposed to punish the offenders by totaling the amount of money received. Then he applied the principle of joint offense to mete out the punishment for the principal perpetrator and his accessories. The Board overruled the lower court's opinion, stating that it was a serious mistake on the part of the acting governor to ignore the rule that each bribe taker should be dealt with individually in accordance with the actual amount of money he had received. Although the Board did not quote Shen's *Chi-chu* specifically, it seems to have followed the earlier precedent in which Shen's opinion was quoted.

In Re Liang Fen-yung. In 1806 an embezzlement case was reported to the Board of Punishments by the governor of Shansi province.[148] Liang Fen-yung, a treasury janitor (*k'u-shu*), had stolen 299 silver taels from the provincial treasury. Although the facts and procedure of this case are only briefly reported in the *Hsing-an hui-lan* and are not too clear, the issue in the case apparently was whether Liang Fen-yung's act constituted embezzlement rather than theft of public property.[149]

The governor applied a substatute stating that when persons lawfully entrusted with public property or money deposited in government treasuries and storehouses of the government embezzled more than 100 but less than 330 silver taels, they were to be punished by 100 blows of the heavy bamboo and banishment to 2,000 *li*. According to the same provision, if the embezzled sum was returned within one year, the offender was exempt from punishment.[150] The governor recommended that Liang be exempted, since he had already returned the total amount taken.

When the case was submitted for review, the Shansi Department of the Board disagreed with the governor's opinion, arguing that Liang had committed theft of public property rather than embezzlement, so that exemption from punishment should not be granted even if the stolen property had been completely recovered. When the Department's recommendation was forwarded to the directorate for approval, the latter decided to send the case to the Statutes Commission for further deliberation.[151]

The Commission threw its support to the governor's view, quoting passages from both the *Chi-chu* and Wang K'en-t'ang's *Chien-shih*. It conceded that in the present case the offender's act in stealing 299 silver taels was distinguishable from *ch'in-k'uei*, the fraudulent appropriation to one's own use of property or money entrusted to him by the government. In other words, Liang was not officially in charge of the stolen property. However, the Commission held that if a treasury janitor stole any property or money deposited in the treasury, he should still be punished in accordance with Code provisions on embezzlement since it was his duty to safeguard the entire premises. All this accorded with the view stated in the *Chien-shih*. The Statutes Commission also noted that, according to the *Chi-chu* commentary, if the janitor took a thief into the treasury to steal any property or money, the janitor should be punished for the offense of embezzlement, while the thief should be punished for the theft of the same amount.[152] The conclusion drawn from these two commentaries was that a treasury janitor was to be sentenced according to the embezzlement statute.

Although the citation from the *Chi-chu* commentary did not directly govern the issue in this case, it helped to determine whether the substatute on embezzlement was correctly applied to Liang.

On Theft. A memorandum on theft submitted in 1865 by the Chihli Department of the Board of Punishments to the directorate of the Board was unusual in that it contained lengthy and abstract discussions on two aspects of law governing ordinary theft offenses, rather than recommendations on how to deal with a concrete case under consideration.[153] Unlike other memoranda, neither the names of the parties involved nor the facts of the case were given. In this memorandum, by citing and elaborating on pertinent Code provisions as well as on private commentators' views, the Department first showed how to distinguish between attempted and consummated thefts. Then it invoked four precedents to illustrate the exact meaning of the term *tao-so* ("the scene of the theft") in connection with substatutes governing thieves injuring or killing a property owner inside or outside the *tao-so*.

To answer the first inquiry, the Department discussed a Code provision entitled "What constitutes a theft or robbery, and what constitutes only an attempt."[154] Then it quoted passages from the *Chi-chu* and the *Chien-shih*. We have already encountered the pertinent *Chi-chu* passage in the 1789 case of *In Re Ying Liang*;[155] in essence it stated that if a thief dropped his stolen goods while fleeing and the goods were retrieved by the property owner, the act of stealing was not deemed to have been consummated; but if someone other than the owner obtained the goods, the theft was considered to have been completed. Moreover, according to the *Chien-shih*, if a thief was caught in the act of stealing on the owner's premises, whether he was to be punished for an attempt or for completed theft should be determined by the nature of the goods taken. If pearls, precious stones, or other small and valuable articles were found in the hands of the thief, theft was considered completed; but items such as strings of copper coins, bolts of cloth, and utensils had to be taken from the premises in order to constitute a completed theft.[156]

In Re Liu Ssu. In 1868 the Shantung Department of the Board of Punishments adjudicated a theft case originating in the city of Peking.[157] The chief issue was whether the offense of stealing public property should be regarded as an ordinary theft offense for the purpose of applying several substatutes governing recidivists in the Code section dealing with theft offenses. One of those substatutes provided that for a second offense the offender was to be given an additional punishment of wearing the cangue for twenty to forty days and then to be subjected to local control under guarantee.[158] Another substatute provided that, depending on the value of the stolen goods, the punishment for a third offense ranged from the minimum of banishment to 3,000 *li* and 100 blows of the heavy bamboo to the maximum of strangulation after the assizes (for stealing goods worth 50 silver taels or more).[159] If the recidivist statutes were construed narrowly so as to cover only ordinary theft offenses and not other similar offenses such as the theft of public property, then the accused in this case would obviously benefit. The Department officials adopted this narrow construction, and their conclusion was sent by the directorate to the Statutes Commission for review.

The Commission noted that there was no express language on this point in any provision of the Code. It also failed to find a precedent. Therefore, it turned to the *Chi-chu* commentary for an answer. The *Chi-chu* prescribed:

> The offenses of picking pockets[160] and ordinary theft shall be calculated cumulatively for the purpose of applying the Code provisions governing a [theft] recidivist. This is because exactly the same punishment is imposed upon these two types of offenses. On the other hand, embezzlement, theft of public property,[161] and unarmed robbery[162] shall not be taken into consideration while applying a recidivist statute for an ordinary theft offense. This is because their punishments are different from that prescribed for an ordinary theft offense.[163]

The *Chi-chu* opinion did not elaborate on how the last mentioned three offenses differed from ordinary theft. The Commission commented that:

"No doubt there are some foundations to this assertion made by an earlier writer," referring to Shen Chih-ch'i.[164] With that remark, the Commission went on to explore the difference between ordinary theft and theft of public property. In order to illustrate how the Commission's decision was influenced by the *Chi-chu*, a substantial part of the Commission's lengthy statutory interpretation deserves our attention.

The Commission emphasized that theft of public property was punished more severely than ordinary theft. For example, ordinary theft of goods worth less than 1 silver tael was punished by 60 blows of the heavy bamboo; where the goods were worth 80 silver taels, the punishment was two and a half years of penal servitude and 90 blows of the heavy bamboo.[165] On the other hand, the corresponding punishments for theft of public property were 70 blows of the heavy bamboo for less than 1 silver tael, and a nominal sentence of strangulation, automatically reduced to five years of penal servitude, for 80 taels.[166] Moreover, the Commission noted, a more lenient standard was adopted for ordinary theft in calculating the value of stolen goods. Where property was stolen from more than one owner, the thief's punishment was to be calculated according to the value of the property taken from the person who had suffered the greatest loss.[167] But, since the state was the only victim in the case of theft of public property, the basis for calculating the thief's punishment was the cumulative value of the total amount of property stolen from various government treasuries or granaries.[168]

The Commission further pointed out that, if the recidivist provisions for ordinary theft were applied to people who stole public property, as a result of the cumulative rule such offenders would become liable to the death penalty sooner than ordinary thieves. Thus, a person charged with stealing more than 50 taels worth of public property from several government warehouses after being twice convicted for ordinary theft would be punished with strangulation after the assizes if the recidivist statutes were applied to his case.[169] But if the third offense was an ordinary theft and the offender had stolen from several families, with no single victim losing as much as 50 taels, the offender would not receive the death penalty even though the total amount might be far beyond 50 taels. This discrepancy in treatment was deemed unjust by the Statutes Commission.[170]

The Commission then discussed the difference between ordinary theft and unarmed robbery, a difference stressed by the *Chi-chu* commentary. At first glance this comparison between theft and unarmed robbery may not seem meaningful, but in the Ch'ing Code these two offenses were closely related in several respects. First, the punishment of unarmed robbery was partly determined by reference to a property-value scale prescribed in the basic theft statute. An unarmed robber was ordinarily punished by three years of penal servitude and 100 blows of the heavy bamboo. However, if the value of the property taken was high, it had to be evaluated and the punishment would be determined by adding two degrees of severity to that prescribed by statute for theft of that amount. If the punishment thus calculated was greater than the three years of penal servitude and 100 blows of the heavy bamboo prescribed for unarmed robbery, the more severe punishment was to be applied.[171] Second, just as with ordinary theft, the Code section governing unarmed robbery contained a substatute governing recidivism—a third-time offender was punished by immediate strangulation.[172]

The Commission noted that in 1826 it had been requested by one of the departments of the Board of Punishments to give guidance on the correct method of calculation in the cases where a person was first convicted of unarmed robbery and then afterwards received a conviction for theft, or vice versa. The Commission answered that since these two offenses were different in nature, they should not be combined in order to impose an increased punishment upon a recidivist. In other words, theft should be calculated with theft and robbery with robbery, except as stipulated in the above-mentioned substatute. This opinion was approved and placed on record for future reference.[173]

After having discussed the relationships between ordinary theft and unarmed robbery, the Commission reverted to the original problem of stealing public property. It admitted that this offense differed from unarmed robbery, but the same method of calculating the booty's value was used to punish both offenses. In other words, unlike ordinary theft, the total property loss of all the victims involved in an unarmed robbery was adopted as the basis for determining the offender's punishment.[174] The Commission argued that, since unarmed robbery should not be combined in deciding the number of one's repeated ordinary theft offenses, it would seem to be appropriate also to exclude the offense of stealing public property from the purview of the recidivist statutes for ordinary theft. The Commission's opinion was approved by the directorate and circulated among the departments of the Board for guidance. The passage from Shen's *Chi-chu* quoted above seems to have influenced the decision of the Statutes Commission to construe the theft recidivist statutes narrowly.

In Re Shih Ta-p'eng. In 1792 in Kiangsi province Mrs. Yang, née Liao, was kicked out of her home after quarreling with her husband.[175] Mrs. Yang intended to return to her parents' home for temporary refuge but lost her way while walking. After asking various people for directions, she spotted an old neighbor, Shih Ta-p'eng. Mrs. Yang asked him to guide her to the home of her parents. Shih decided to take advantage of the circumstances and to sell the woman for profit. He took her to his home on the pretext that the time was late and the night unfit for travel, promising her that the trip would be resumed the following day. The next day, after they had been on the road for some distance, Shih began to urge remarriage as a solution to her problems. For some reason, Mrs. Yang felt compelled to agree. Shih, pretending that Mrs. Yang was his widowed sister-in-law, finally sold her into marriage.

The governor of Kiangsi proposed to punish Shih with two and one-half years of penal servitude and 90 blows of the heavy bamboo in accordance with the statute covering the sale of a lost woman as wife or concubine.[176] Shih should have turned Mrs. Yang over to the authorities for proper treatment. The governor further suggested that Mrs. Yang as a victim should be exonerated in compliance with the same statute. The Board of Punishments reversed the sentence and ordered the governor to submit another. It reached its decision by applying a different Code provision, which prescribed a harsher sentence for the offense of enticing a good woman.[177]

In reply, the governor requested the Board to uphold his original finding. To support his argument he cited a precedent *In Re Huang Hsüeh-hsien*, dated 1782.[178] The decision had been rendered in the same province and involved a beggar woman who had become lost and had sought shelter from a man who then sold her into marriage. In that case, the offender had been punished for selling a lost woman, and the victim had not been punished at all.

The Board of Punishments again disagreed with the decision below. It declared that the Code provision dealing with the sale of a lost woman was inapplicable in this case. A quotation from the *Chi-chu* was cited in support, the essence of which was that, if one deceived a lost woman and sold her into marriage, the offender should be held liable for abduction or enticement rather than for the sheltering and sale of a lost woman.[179] With aid from the *Chi-chu* quotation, the Board distinguished the present case from the 1782 precedent. First, unlike the beggar woman, Mrs. Yang was not a "lost" person without any home to which she could return. Even if Shih did not know the location of the home of Mrs. Yang's parents, he at least knew her husband's whereabouts. Second, in the precedent, the beggar woman had gone directly to the defendant's house to seek shelter, whereas in this case Shih came upon Mrs. Yang in the street and there conceived the idea of selling her for profit. Shih took advantage of the fact that she was lost. He deceived her, counseled her, and finally forced her consent to the remarriage. The Board held that under these circumstances Shih should be punished with military banishment to the extreme frontier. The distance was to be 4,000 *li*, which was the decreed punishment for the enticement of a good woman when the woman willingly submitted to the enticement.[180] As the enticed person, Mrs. Yang was given three years of penal servitude and 100 blows of the heavy bamboo, which was a one degree reduction from the punishment of Shih.[181] The penal servitude could be redeemed by the payment of a stipulated sum of money, but the blows were to be actually administered.[182] After the punishment, Mrs. Yang was to be returned to her husband.

The Board's final ruling substantially increased Shih's penalty. Since the statutory language did not provide clear guidelines as to which of the two offenses more neatly corresponded to the defendant's conduct, the Board resorted to the *Chi-chu* interpretation for assistance in reaching the proper conclusion.

In Re Mrs. Chu, née Li. Another case, decided in 1796, involved the following facts.[183] Ch'iu A-san had illicit sexual relations with Mrs. Chu, née Li, who agreed to run away with him. Ch'iu soon sold her to another man as a wife. Runners were dispatched to arrest Mrs. Chu upon the complaint of her original husband. Ashamed of her own behavior, Mrs. Chu committed suicide by hanging herself.

The governor of Chekiang sentenced Ch'iu to military banishment in accordance with a substatute covering the enticement of a woman who willingly runs away with a man.[184] The governor further declared that Mrs. Chu should have been sentenced to strangulation (after the assizes) in accordance with the statute prescribing the punishment for a woman who contracted marriage with another man after running away from her husband,[185] but since she had already died, no further deliberation was necessary.

The Chekiang Department of the Board of Punishments ordered the governor to correct his report on Mrs. Chu. It argued that the deceased was enticed away by Ch'iu, that she had not run away on her own initiative, and so it would have been more appropriate to punish her by (three years of) penal servitude (and 100 blows of the heavy bamboo), which was a one degree reduction from the punishment of the principal offender, Ch'iu. The case was then sent by the directorate of the Board to the Statutes Commission for review.

The Commission supported the Department's view in correcting the sentence. Shen's *Chi-chu* was quoted to determine the meaning of the above-mentioned statute, which prescribed death for a wife who remarried after deserting her original husband. The *Chi-chu* quotation reads:

> The statutory term "deserting her husband" refers to a wife who runs away for the sole purpose of leaving her mate rather than for any other purpose. The Code considers the intention of an offender of prime im-

> portance. Therefore, in punishing such a woman, the Code is extremely harsh. If, on the other hand, the wife is enticed by a man and then willingly runs away with him, she flees for fear of punishment. This situation is distinguishable from the earlier case where the wife intends to leave her husband for that purpose and none other.[186]

Shen Chih-ch'i seems to have assumed that, if a wife runs away with another man in response to his enticement, she flees only for fear of punishment—not for the purpose of deserting her husband. This, of course, is not necessarily the case. Apparently, the statute in question was designed to discourage a wife from remarrying on her own initiative. For example, it further provided that in the absence of a second marriage such an estranged woman would only be punished with 100 blows of the heavy bamboo.[187] The Statutes Commission pointed out that in the present case Mrs. Chu was involuntarily sold into a new marriage by her lover. This is distinguishable from a freely chosen remarriage. Consequently, a punishment reduced by one degree from that prescribed for her lover would be appropriate. This treatment also conformed to past practice in such offenses.

One striking feature of this case is the great emphasis placed on the appropriate punishment for a deceased offender. It is not uncommon to find in judicial decisions a nominal sentence for a dead offender; usually such a sentence is accompanied by a statement to the effect that since the offender has already died the matter need not be deliberated further.[188] It is rare, however, for the Board to devote a lengthy discussion to a deceased offender's proper punishment and then order the lower court to correct the original sentence.

Conclusion

Since the Ch'ing Code was written in a terse and archaic style, it was difficult for Ch'ing magistrates and legal secretaries to comprehend the meaning of many Code provisions, even with the aid of an official interlinear commentary. Thus, in applying the Code to concrete cases, Ch'ing officials frequently faced dilemmas of statutory construction. The private code commentaries were written to aid judicial officials in dealing with these problems. Shen Chih-ch'i, the most highly regarded of the private commentators, stated in the preface to his popular *Chi-chu* of 1715 that his chief purpose in compiling the work was to help judicial officials understand and apply the Code provisions.[189]

In attempting to ascertain the contribution of private code commentaries to the development of Ch'ing law, I have confined my inquiry to the use of Shen's *Chi-chu* by officials in the provinces and within the

Board of Punishments. It is striking that my extensive investigation of more than 9,000 cases, decided during one and a half centuries (1736-1885), reveals only twenty-one cases containing actual quotations from Shen's *Chi-chu*. If one were to conclude that the *Chi-chu*'s influence was limited to these twenty-one cases, the role played by this private code commentary would have been negligible; however, for several reasons this statistic is of questionable weight. One relates to the inherent defects in the case-reporting system. A large number of cases contained in the various compendia that I have read are merely case summaries, and these may very well have omitted references to Shen's *Chi-chu* that appeared in the original case reports. Moreover, the cases selected for a particular compendium may reflect the compiler's personal preference or bias. Had I not gone beyond the *Hsing-an hui-lan* and its three supplements I would not have discovered the case that revealed that at one time the Board of Punishments sanctioned the use of Shen's *Chi-chu* by provincial officials under conditions specified by the Board (*In Re Chang Chün*, 1801). Another reason why the reported cases probably do not fully reflect the *Chi-chu*'s influence upon Ch'ing judicial decision making is that magistrates, being aware that the Board of Punishments generally disapproved of explicit citations of the *Chi-chu*, might well have consulted it but avoided express mention of the fact. Thus, quantitative analysis alone is misleading. I have therefore concentrated upon a qualitative analysis of the influence of Shen's work on the above-mentioned twenty-one cases.

The Ch'ing Code did not explicitly prescribe whether private commentaries could be used as a source of law, as an aid for ascertaining the meaning of rules of law, or not at all. In the course of time, however, a clear policy seems to have developed. At the beginning of the Ch'ien-lung reign, the Ch'ing court apparently tolerated or acquiesced in the use of a private commentary as a source of law in provincial judicial decisions. Thus, in our first case, when the governor of Kiangsu quoted a *Chi-chu* opinion in his recommended sentence, the Board in its reply not only failed to object to reliance on this private commentary but also even favorably discussed the passage in question (*In Re Ch'en Hsiang-li*, 1763). Gradually, however, the Board began to criticize invocation of the *Chi-chu* in judicial decisions submitted for review by the provincial judicial authorities. The language used in the Board's criticism was at first rather mild. Later the attacks became more open and vehement. By 1822 (*In Re Wang En-chang*) provincial officials throughout the country were ordered never to rely on the *Chi-chu* in rendering their judicial decisions.

The full effect of this 1822 ruling is difficult to evaluate. However, post-1822 developments suggest that the Ch'ing government did not rigorously enforce the prohibition. References to Shen's *Chi-chu* continued to creep into decisions drafted by officials in the provinces. On one occasion when the Board caught such a reference, without reiterating the 1822 ban it simply asked rhetorically how the lower court could consider a Code provision as "inferior to or less reliable than" a *Chi-chu* opinion (*In Re Sung Mao-tzu*, 1840). In another case, after a governor general called to the Board's attention a *Chi-chu* opinion that directly governed the situation under consideration, the Board consented to its use without raising any objection (*In Re Wang Feng*, 1833).

In contrast to the policy against allowing officials in the provinces to invoke Shen's *Chi-chu* in their judicial decisions, the members of various departments and the Statutes Commission of the Board of Punishments were themselves always free to rely upon this work when preparing their review opinions in the form of memoranda for the directorate of the Board. Not only were they not restrained by the directorate from using the *Chi-chu* but they were even actually encouraged to do so.

The type of guidance rendered by this commentary varied from case to case. At one end of the spectrum, the *Chi-chu* laid down specific rules for the application of statutes, in passages such as: "Ordinary theft and theft of public property may not be calculated together for the purpose of theft recidivist statutes" (*In Re Liu Ssu*, 1868); "[For the purpose of punishment,] the mother-son relationship will not be terminated when the mother remarries" (*In Re Mrs. Wang, née Han*, 1790); and "If two or more people jointly committed the offense of receiving bribes, each offender shall be punished in accordance with the scale pertaining to the amount he received, not the aggregated sum" (*In Re Han Pang-fu*, 1790). Yet other directons given by the *Chi-chu* were broad and general; for example, when the Board was confronted with the problem of mistake in object in a homicide case involving relatives, the inspiration the Board members got from Shen's work was contained in a simple statement that the punishment prescribed for ordinary people (i.e., nonrelatives) should be increased or reduced to suit the particular circumstances of each case (*In Re Mrs. Liu, née Tseng*, 1802). Between these two extremes, the *Chi-chu* served, among other things, the important function of elucidating key terms and key concepts of the Code in order to lead the officials to an accurate application of law.

I would hazard an explanation for the contrast between the authorized free use of the *Chi-chu* by members of the Board and the policy of prohibiting provincial officials from using the same work. The Board of Punishments embodied the ultimate legal power of the throne. Apart from being the highest judicial organ directly assisting the emperor in his dispensation of justice, the Board also helped the emperor exercise legislative power. The Board's Statutes Commission was entrusted with the duty of carrying out the periodic revisions of the Code, during which it prepared new laws for enactment and scrutinized existing laws for revision or abrogation. In fact, the cases decided by the Board provided a major source of new legislation.

Thus, it was only natural for the Board, in its role as the highest regular court of review, to criticize officials in the provinces for relying upon a private commentary that had not been officially sanctioned as a source of law. Yet in conducting their own judicial work, it was perfectly appropriate for officials of the Board to utilize Shen's *Chi-chu* and other private commentaries, for the Board was endowed with power to provide authoritative interpretations of existing legislation and to make proposals for new laws, drawing upon various sources for information and inspiration.

There were several other possible reasons to allow free use of private commentaries by Board members. First, because the work of the Board was subjected to the emperor's close scrutiny, it was highly unlikely that the imperial legislative purpose would be misconstrued. Second, the professional quality of the Board members was much higher than that of members of the provincial courts. Third, the Board memoranda that contained the *Chi-chu* quotations were internal documents; when, on the basis of these documents, the Board prepared a reply to be issued to the provinces, references to the *Chi-chu* were eliminated.[190]

Of course Shen's *Chi-chu* was only one of many Ch'ing private commentaries. In my search through judicial decisions for references to Shen's work, I discovered that Wang K'en-t'ang's *Chien-shih* was cited in twelve cases,[191] and Wan Wei-han's *Chyi-chu* was cited in seven cases.[192] Two of the cases citing Wan's work were discussed above.[193] Of the remaining cases, only one discussed the weight to be accorded a private commentary when invoked by officials in the provinces (*In Re Tsou Chin-tien*, 1791). There the Board stated that "Since Wan's *Chyi-chu* is not an established substatute, it is inappropriate to apply it."[194] Thus, Shen's *Chi-chu* was not the only private commentary to draw fire from the Board. It was the eminence of Shen's work that accounted for the larger number of cases in which reliance on this private commentary by provincial officials was disapproved. This also explains why the 1822 ruling singled out Shen's *Chi-chu* as an undesirable source of law. The very fact that Shen's *Chi-chu* was the only commentary cited by most judicial officials from the provinces attested to its popularity.

Was the role of private Ch'ing Code commentators in any way similar to that of commentators in Western legal systems? Because the civil law system of continental Europe developed in a way that accorded preeminence to legislative codes rather than to case law and because commentators came to play an important part in the application of those codes, it may be useful to seek analogies in the European experience. The closest analogies that I can find are the glossators of medieval Italy.

When adjudicating cases, courts of various legal systems usually consult the literature of legal scholarship, such as treatises, code commentaries, and essays. The extent to which courts consult scholarly opinions varies from country to country and from period to period. To be sure, judicial officials consulted the expert opinions of both Italian glossators and Ch'ing commentators. Yet comparison between the glossators and the private Ch'ing Code commentators suggests more differences than similarities.

The glossators' duty was to expound the *Corpus Juris* of 535 A.D., the product of an authoritarian society of a much earlier age, whose ultimate judge had been the emperor. In the centuries following the destruction of the Roman empire, the society that had spawned the *Corpus Juris* had undergone drastic changes. For example, by the early twelfth century, towns and communes of northern and central Italy had acquired a large degree of autonomy. The glossators were not unaware of these changes, but they accepted from the *Corpus Juris* a theory of political absolutism and a conception of law as emanation of the sovereign's will. At the start of the twelfth century, glossators began to teach Roman law at the Bologna school, where thousands of students would eventually earn the degree of doctor of law. The glossators great learning was thus transmitted to a large group of disciples who in turn helped to propagate it. Besides teaching, they continued to write short treatises on law and to comment on specific legal issues. As a result, the glossators' influence was increasingly felt. Both the judiciary and the legal practitioners became more and more dependent on the glossators and the juris doctors to solve the difficult questions of law for them. Consequently, within 100 years the doctrines derived by the glossators from the *Corpus Juris* were well accepted in Italy.[195]

On the whole, Ch'ing commentators' opinions were consulted by judicial officials much less than the glossators' opinions were consulted by Italian judges. The commentators set about the task of elucidating the archaic *lü* provisions of the Ch'ing Code, most of which had originated in the Ming Code of 1397. To be sure, there were some differences between the Ming and Ch'ing societies, but the changes in the political structure were more in terms of degree than of kind. Unlike the glossators, the commentators were operating in a unified system under close control by the government; they did not have much freedom to innovate. It is true that learned men were needed to make the *lü* intelligible to the officials as well as to the commoners. Yet, unlike the glossators, the commentators through their interpretations did not have to construct an entirely new system to respond to vast social changes. In other words, the Ch'ing commentators were confronted with a less difficult problem. They were largely concerned with what the law "is," not what the law "ought to be." Knowledge of Confucian classics plus some degree of on-the-job training as legal secretaries sufficed to prepare the commentators for the task undertaken; they did not apparently feel the need to band together to discuss and exchange opinions on difficult or doubtful points. This may have constituted one of the reasons why a center of legal learning such as Bologna never evolved in Ch'ing China. Of course, the absorption of the energies of talented young men who tried to pass cumulative literary examinations in order to enter officialdom and the traditional distaste for law were probably more important reasons for the failure of legal science to advance in China.

One is tempted to compare Shen Chih-ch'i and his *Chi-chu* commentary with Accursius (d. *ca.* 1260 A.D.) and his *Great Gloss*.[196] Both were great synthesizers: Accursius availed himself of the works of earlier glossators of one and a half centuries, and Shen likewise drew heavily from the wisdom of Ming commentaries. The analogy fails, however, in one major respect. The Accursian *Gloss* acquired an authority of its own because it condensed into more usable form the new "common law" currently emerging on Italian soil. The *Gloss* did not replace the *Corpus Juris*, but it was treated as self-sufficient by later practitioners. Shen's *Chi-chu*, on the other hand, was more subservient to the Ch'ing Code and never challenged its authority. This is understandable because Ch'ing emperors were extremely powerful, whereas the emperors of medieval Italy led only a shadowy existence in terms of public influence.

NOTES

1. Derk Bodde and Clarence Morris, *Law in Imperial China*, (Cambridge, Mass., 1967), p. 65 (hereafter cited as Bodde and Morris). Also see, Fu-mei Chang, "The Emergence of the *Li* in the Ming Code" (unpubl. seminar paper, Harvard University, May 1965), which discusses the immutability of the *lü* provisions in the Ming Code.
2. Hsüeh Yun-sheng, *Tu-li ts'un-i* [Concentration on Doubtful Matters while Perusing the Substatutes of the Ch'ing Code] (Peking, 1905); 5:3, 14:19, 21:29, 29:1, 34:45, 35:2b, 41:19, 41:20 and 42:47. Cf. also Shen Chia-pen, *Shen Chi-i hsien-sheng i-shu, chia-pien* [Bequeathed Writings of Mr. Shen Chi-i, 1st Series] (Peking, ca. 1929; repr. Taipei, 1964). Shen states that the commentary of a late Ming official named Yao Ssu-jen was adopted as the *hsiao-chu*; Vol. 2, p. 789.
3. Cf. memorial dated 1697 by Chang Yü-shu in the official 1725 Yung-cheng Code, available in the Harvard-Yenching Library, entitled *Ta Ch'ing-lü chi-chieh fu-li* [The Great Annotated Ch'ing Code, with Substatutes Appended], Vol. 1, *tsou-shu* (memorials), 10–11b. With regard to the Statutes Commission, cf. Bodde and Morris, pp. 128 and 130.

4. *Ta Ch'ing-lü chi-chieh fu-li*, 6–8; cf. a memorial by Chu Shih (1665–1736), the chief compiler of the 1725 official Code.
5. Yao Yü-hsiang and Hu Yang-shan, ed., *Ta Ch'ing lü-li hui-t'ung hsin-tsuan* [Comprehensive New Edition of the Ch'ing Code] (Peking, 1873; repr. Taipei: Wen-hai Publishing Co., 5 vols., with consecutive pagination), Vol. 1, p. 80 (hereinafter cited as *Ch'ing Code*); *Ta Ch'ing lü-li an-yü* [Compilers' Notes on the Ch'ing Code] (Canton, 1847), 33:5b, 33:20b, 31:65b and 47:6b; Hsüeh, *Tu-li ts'un-i*, 4:3b–4b.
6. Yang Yüeh-k'un, ed., *Ta Ch'ing-lü tsuan-hsiu t'iao-li an-yü ts'e-kao* [A Collection of Compilers' Notes on Substatutes of the Ch'ing Code] (1807), Preface, 1b; Kuo-wu-yüan fa-chih-shih yen-chiu-shih [Legal History Research Office, Bureau of Legal Affairs, Council of State] *Ch'ing-shih-kao hsing-fa-chih chu-chieh* ["Legal Treatise" from the Ch'ing Draft History with Annotations] (Peking, 1957), p. 23.
7. See Fu-mei Chang Chen, "Private Code Commentaries in the Development of Ch'ing Law (1644–1911)" (unpubl. Ph.D. thesis, Cambridge, Mass., 1970). Cf. also a brief account on Ch'ing Code commentaries in Bodde and Morris, pp. 71-73.
8. Cf. Hu Chao-k'ai and Chou Meng-lin's preface to the 1814 and 1822 editions of the *Ta Ch'ing lü-li t'ung-tsuan chi-ch'eng* commentary, available in the Harvard-Yenching Library. Later editions of the same work also contain this preface, but neither Hu's nor Chou's name appears.
9. Cf. Wan's first preface (*ch'ien-hsü*), dated 1766, for his *Ta Ch'ing lü-li chi-chu ("chyi-chu")* [Collected Commentaries on the Ch'ing Code] (Chekiang, 1766; 2nd ed., 1769), Vol. 1. Actually, Wan named his commentary *Chi-chu*, which in Chinese is pronounced the same as Shen's *Chi-chu* and also has a similar meaning even though a different character is used for *chi*. To distinguish the two I have Romanized Wan's work *Chyi-chu*.
10. Hu Chao-k'ai and Chou Meng-lin, two legal secretaries from Chekiang, tried to restore Shen's work.
11. The three supplements are: (1) Chu Ch'ing-ch'i and Pao Shu-yün, *Hsü-tseng hsing-an hui-lan* (1840) (the first supp.); (2) P'an Wen-fang and Hsü Chien-ch'üan, *Hsin-tseng hsing-an hui-lan* (1886) (the second supp.); (3) Wu Ch'ao and Ho Hsi-yen, *Hsing-an hui-lan hsü-pien* (1900) (the third supp.). Cf. Bodde and Morris, pp. 147-148 and 564. Also see Fu-mei Chang Chen, "Review of Bodde and Morris, *Law in Imperial China*," *Harvard Journal of Asiatic Studies*, Vol. 29 (1969), p. 276, n. 2.

   In 1886 the *Hsing-an hui-lan* proper and the first two supplements were published together in a pocket-size edition in Shanghai by the T'u-shu chi-ch'eng Publishing Co. It was reprinted in Taipei in 1968 by Ch'eng-wen Publishing Co. in 11 volumes, with consecutive pagination. I have used the reprint for this chapter and cited it as *HAHL*. For the third supplement I have used the original 1900 edition and cited it as *HAHLHP*. (This was reprinted in Taipei in 1970 by Wen-hai Publishing Co. in 10 volumes, also with consecutive pagination.)

   The *Hsing-an hui-lan* and its three supplements contain some 9,300 entries. While reading them I have concentrated on the entries that are considered criminal or civil "cases" in the narrow sense. Some entries that are purely statutory or political in nature, such as rules of imperial amnesty (*HAHL*, Vol. 1, pp. 141-223) and a memorial calling for judicial reforms (*HAHL*, Vol. 11, p. 5129) have been excluded. Furthermore, some overlappings are found between the second and the third supplements, as well as within the second supplement itself (e.g., *HAHL*, Vol. 11, pp. 4868-4870, and *HAHLHP* 7:31b-33b; *HAHL*, Vol. 11, pp. 4981-4983 and 5101-5103). Therefore, the total number of entries in this group that I have read for this chapter is slightly less than 9,000.

12. Such as (1) Ch'üan Shih-ch'ao, comp. *Po-an hsin-pien* [A New Collection of Reversed Cases] (hereafter cited as *PAHP*) (Preface dated 1784; repr. Taipei, 1968, in 8 vols., with consecutive pagination); (2) Ma Shih-lin, comp., *Ch'eng-an so-chien chi* [Collection of Seen Cases], 1793; (3) Ch'ing-nien, compiler, *Shuo-t'ieh chai-yao ch'ao-ts'un* [Copying Essential Memoranda from the Board of Punishments] (K'ai-feng, Honan; 1831); and (4) Wang Chin-chih, comp., *Shuo-t'ieh pien-li* [Analyzing Substatutes of the Code Through the Study of Memoranda] (1836).
13. The eighteen cases are: *In Re Ch'en Hsiang-li* (1763), *PAHP* 4:32-40; *In Re Mrs. Chao, née Ch'en* (1789), *HAHL*, Vol. 1, p. 455; *In Re Mrs. Wang, née Han* (1790), *HAHL*, Vol. 6, pp. 2744-2745; *In Re Han Pang-fu* (1790), *HAHL*, Vol. 7, p. 3127; *In Re Chu K'un-jong* (1794), *HAHL*, Vol. 8, p. 3622; *In Re Mrs. Chu, née Li* (1796), *HAHL*, Vol. 3, p. 1401; *In Re Liang T'ien-chao* (1800), *HAHL*, Vol. 5, p. 2223; *In Re Chang Chün* (1801), Wang, *Pien-li* 5:50a-b (cf. also Ch'ing-nien, *Chai-yao*, 63-64b); *In Re Mrs. Liu, née Tseng* (1802), *HAHL*, Vol. 5, pp. 2074-2076; *In Re Liang Fen-yung* (1806), *HAHL*, Vol. 3, p. 955; *In Re Mrs. Huang, née Wei* (1811), *HAHL*, Vol. 5, pp. 2076-2078; An advisory opinion for the Yen-chou prefect (1815), *HAHL*, Vol. 5, pp. 1961-1963; *In Re Wang En-chang* (1822), *HAHL*, Vol. 5, pp. 2045-2046; *In Re Wang Feng* (1833), *HAHL*, Vol. 9, p. 4188; *In Re Sung Mao-tze* (1840), *HAHLHP* 19:4-5b; "On theft" (1865), *HAHLHP* 12:84-87b; "On violation of the tomb" (1865), *HAHL*, Vol. 11, pp. 4946-4949; and *In Re Liu Ssu* (1868), *HAHLHP* 10:68-70b.
14. *In Re Ch'e Lao-pa* (1794), *HAHL*, Vol. 1, pp. 417-418.
15. *In Re Mrs. Liu, née Tseng* (1802), *HAHL*, Vol. 5, pp. 2074-2076. The Hukwang Department of the Board of Punishments began its memorandum with a quote from Wan's *Chyi-chu*. Later, referring to the same quote, it is attributed to Shen's *Chi-chu*. This confusion is also found in another compendium which contains the case, indicating that the mistake is probably not the result of scribal error. Cf. *Yü-chih hsing-lü shuo-t'ieh* [The Memoranda on the Penal Code, Published under Imperial Auspices], in the volume dated 1802 (no pagination), a handwritten copy available at Harvard Law School.
16. The seven cases are: *In Re Mrs. Wu, née Wang* (1787), *HAHL*, Vol. 4, p. 1618; *In Re Ying Liang* (1789), *HAHL*, Vol. 3, pp. 1259-1260; *In Re Wu Hsüeh-k'uei* (1789), *HAHL*, Vol. 5, p. 2343; *In Re Tsou Chin-tien* (1791), *HAHL*, Vol. 9, p. 3853; *In Re Shih Ta-p'eng* (1792), *HAHL*, Vol. 3, pp. 1406-1407; *In Re Chiang Shih-chen* (1792), *HAHL*, Vol. 7, pp. 3168-3170; and *In Re Kan Ch'i-wei* (1796), *HAHL*, Vol. 5, pp. 2145-2146.
17. *In Re Ying Liang* and *In Re Shih Ta-p'eng* contain identical quotes from

Shen's *Chi-chu*, see note 16 above. Cf. Shen Chih-ch'i, *Ta Ch'ing-lü chi-chu* [Great Ch'ing Code with Collected Commentaries] (1715) (hereinafter cited as *CC*), 18:27b and 4:10b; the rest have passages very similar to Shen's versions. Cf. *CC*, 19:21a-b; 20:3; 19:6; 1:58b-59, and 22:22b.

18. The Board of Punishments was one of the six boards (ministries) of the central government. The directorate of the Board consisted of six members: two presidents, and two senior and two junior vice-presidents. Below the directorate there were seventeen departments whose territorial jurisdiction corresponded to the province whose name they bore. Excluding offenses punishable with penal servitude or less, which according to law were to be disposed of at the provincial level, the Board was required to deal with all the remaining serious offenses. Here the Board's important role was to review the sentences recommended by the provincial judicial authorities. The review opinion, or memorandum, drafted by the officials of a Department was submitted to the directorate for approval. The latter often sought advice from the Statutes Commission of the same Board if it was not satisfied with the Department's opinion and, occasionally, the recommended sentences from the provinces were directly handled by the Commission without first going through the departments. In these two situations the Statutes Commission also prepared memoranda for the directorate. Cf. Bodde and Morris, pp. 122-131.
19. *In Re Chia Ta* (1790), *HAHL*, Vol. 5, pp. 2044-2045.
20. *In Re Li Hsiu-liu-erh* (1797), *HAHL*, Vol. 3, pp. 1189-90. The *Chien-shih* of Wang K'en-t'ang was one of the most popular commentaries in the late Ming and early Ch'ing dynasties, before the *Chi-chu* appeared.
21. *In Re Han Kuang-ch'üan* (1796), *HAHL*, Vol. 9, pp. 3864-3866; *In Re Hao Ch'üan-tze* (1827), *HAHL*, Vol. 5, pp. 2372-2373.
22. *PAHP*, 4:32-40.
23. *Ch'ing Code*, Vol. 2, p. 1061; George T. Staunton, tr., *Ta Tsing Leu Lee; Being the Fundamental Laws . . . of the Penal Code of China* (London, 1810), p. 117; Gui Boulais, tr., *Manuel du code chinois* (Shanghai, 1924), p. 287, section 606; under the Code section entitled "Ch'iang-chan liang-chia ch'i-nü" [Abduction of women of a respectable family].
24. *Ch'ing Code*, Vol. 4, p. 3197; Staunton, p. 404; Boulais, p. 681, section 1582; under the Code section entitled "Fan-chien" [Sex offenses]. Rape was punishable by strangulation after the assizes.
25. *CC*, 6:16, *PAHP*, 4:36a-b.
26. Note 23 above.
27. *PAHP*, 4:37b.
28. The Ch'ing law on appellate review by the Board of Punishments is quite complicated. The general rule is that in capital cases, if the Board desired to reduce the punishment proposed by the governor, it could do so without remanding the case. However, if it desired to increase the punishment, the case had to be sent back to the province. When the Board remanded the case, the governor could choose to retain his view up to three times. After the third rebuke, if the Board decided that the proposed sentence was erroneous, the governor would then be subject to administrative sanction for his error in adjudication. Cf. *Ch'ing Code,* Vol. 5, p. 3743 under the Code

section entitled "Tuan-tsui pu-tang" [Improper execution of sentence] and p. 3614, under the Code section entitled "Kuan-ssu ch'u-ju jen tsui" [Officials imposing unduly light or unduly severe punishment].

29. *HAHL*, Vol. 8, p. 3622.
30. *Ch'ing Code*, Vol. 4, p. 3401; Staunton, p. 423; Boulais, p. 708, section 1664; under the Code section entitled "T'u-liu jen t'ao" [Escaping from a place where one serves the punishment of penal servitude or banishment].
31. *Ch'ing Code*, Vol. 1, p. 446; Staunton, p. 28; Boulais, p. 69, section 117; under the Code section entitled "Tan-tsui tzu-shou" [Voluntary surrender of offenders].
32. *CC*, 27:7b; *Ch'ing Code*, Vol. 5, p. 3401, middle section; *HAHL*, Vol. 8, p. 3622.
33. *HAHL*, Vol. 8, p. 3622.
34. *Ch'ing Code*, Vol. 1, p. 445; Staunton, p. 27; Boulais, p. 68, section 115.
35. Ch'ing-nien, *Chai-yao*, 63a-b. The offender's name was reported as Chu Ch'i-jong rather than Chu K'un-jong.
36. *HAHL*, Vol. 1, pp. 417-418; *Ch'ing Code*, Vol. 1, p. 409; Staunton, p. 23; Boulais, p. 75, section 131; under the Code section entitled "Lao-shao fei-chi shou-shu" [Redemption of punishment for offenders who are old, young or mildly disabled]. Cf. also Professor Bodde's contribution to this volume: "Age, Youth and Infirmity in the Law of Ch'ing China."
37. *Ch'ing Code*, Vol. 1, p. 410, middle section. In the T'ang dynasty, the dumb, dwarfs, and persons with a broken backbone were all considered "mildly disabled." Cf. Tai Yen-hui, *T'ang-lü t'ung-lun* [A General Treatise on the T'ang Code] (Taipei, 1965), pp. 304-305, quoting an ordinance.
38. *CC*, 1-38a-b.
39. *Ch'ing Code*, Vol. 1, pp. 413-414; Boulais, p. 75, section 133.
40. *HAHL*, Vol. 1, p. 418.
41. Wang, *Pien-li*, 5:50a-b; Ch'ing-nien, *Chai-yao*, 63-64b.
42. *Ch'ing Code*, Vol. 1, pp. 445-444; Staunton, p. 27; Boulais, p. 68; section 11.
43. *Ch'ing Code*, Vol. 1, p. 447; Staunton, p. 28; Boulais, p. 69, section 118.
44. *Ch'ing Code*, Vol. 4, p. 2497; Staunton, p. 311; Boulais, p. 559, section 1269; under the Code section entitled "Tou-ou chi ku-sha-jen" [Killing in a fight and killing with intent].
45. *Ch'ing Code*, Vol. 4, p. 3203; Boulais, p. 682, section 1588. Although both offenses were punishable by death, the decapitation after the assizes might be reduced to banishment.
46. *CC*, 1:49.
47. The text of the Code provision in question reads, "*sun-shang yü jen, yü wu pu-k'o p'ei-ch'ang*" [literally, "Injury to the person or property cannot be repaid by restitution or compensation," or, simply "The damage is irreparable"] *Ch'ing Code*, Vol. 1, pp. 446-447; Staunton, p. 28; Boulais, p. 69, section 118.
48. Note 41 above.
49. Note 29 above.
50. *In Re Ch'eng Hsiao-chu* (1805), *HAHL*, Vol. 1, pp. 453-455; *Ch'ing Code*, Vol. 1, pp. 453-455, middle section.
51. *HAHL*, Vol. 5, pp. 1961-1963.

52. *Ch'ing Code*, Vol. 4, p. 2503; Boulais, pp. 559-560, section 1272.
53. *Ibid.*
54. *CC*, 19:17; *HAHL*, Vol. 5, p. 1961.
55. *Ta Ch'ing lü-li an-yü* 57:3a-b. This substatute originated in the deleted official General Commentary of 1725.
56. *HAHL*, Vol. 5, p. 1962.
57. *HAHLHP*, 32:71a-b (1843), a memorandum of the Shantung Department of the Board of Punishments. In this opinion, the Board articulated its fear of "*Tzu-ni tzu-ho*" [Reviewing an opinion which the Board itself had drafted on behalf of a lower court].
58. *HAHL*, Vol. 5, p. 1963.
59. Note 41 above.
60. *HAHL*, Vol. 5, pp. 2045-2046; *Ch'ing Code*, Vol. 4, pp. 2559-2562, middle section.
61. *Ch'ing Code*, Vol. 4, pp. 2527-2528 and 2530-2531; Staunton, p. 314; Boulais, p. 565, section 1285; under the Code section entitled "Hsi-sha wu-sha kuo-shih sha-shang-jen" [Killing or wounding during roughhousing, by error, or by accident].
62. *Ch'ing Code*, Vol. 4, p. 2534. This substatute provided that an offender who was too poor to pay the redemption fee was to receive 80 blows of the heavy bamboo in accordance with the Code section governing the offense of "doing what ought not to be done." For the latter offense, cf. *ibid.*, Vol. 4, p. 3331; Staunton, p. 619; Boulais, p. 704, section 1656; the Chinese title for the section is "Pu-ying wei."
63. *Ibid.*, Vol. 4, pp. 2530-2531.
64. *HAHL*, Vol. 5, p. 2046.
65. *Pan-fa t'iao-li* [Regulations Issued by the Government] (Shantung, 1874), Vol. 2, no pagination. Shantung received the circular on April 26, 1822.
66. *Nieh-ssu ting-li hui-pien* [A Collection of Established Regulations by the Provincial Judicial Commissioner's Office] (Kiangsi, 1905), 69:6-9. Kiangsi province received the circular on June 11, 1822.
67. *Ch'ing Code*, Vol. 4, pp. 2559-2562, middle section. The circular was received on July 4, 1822, but the name of the province which received it was not available. Since Chekiang was the center for the publication of private Code commentaries, the recipient of this circular was probably Chekiang. Cf. also *ibid.*, Vol. 3, p. 2478, middle section.
68. *Ko pu-yüan t'iao-li ts'e* [A Compilation of Regulations Issued by Various Boards and Departments] (Shansi, 1871), Vol. 69, no pagination. Shansi province received the circular on February 6, 1823.
69. *HAHL*, Vol. 5, p. 2046.
70. *CC*, 19:22.
71. Hung's revised *Chi-chu* (1755) 19:28.
72. With regard to the 1738 ban, cf. *Kao-tsung Shih-lu* [The Veritable Records of the Ch'ien-lung Emperor], 79:12b (December 7, 1738); Hsüeh, *Tu-li ts'un-i*, 49:92b-93; *Ta Ch'ing lü-li an-yü*, 68:113; *Ch'ing Code*, Vol. 5, p. 3718; and P.L.F. Philastre, *Le Code annamite* (Paris, 1909), Vol. 2, p. 712. The Chia-ch'ing emperor's edict of 1811 is found in *Jen-tsung Shih-lu* [The Veritable Records of the Chia-ch'ing Emperor], 248:25a-b.

73. For example: *In Re Miu Erh* (1811), *HAHL*, Vol. 5, p. 2059; *In Re Hsieh Chang-lai* (1811), *HAHL*, Vol. 1, p. 424. *In Re Wang Ta* (1812), *HAHL*, Vol. 9, p. 3851; *In Re Wu Ju-p'an* (1816), *HAHL*, Vol. 1, p. 430; *In Re Wang Hua-i* (1816), *HAHL*, Vol. 6, p. 2797; *In Re Tan Pa* (1821), *HAHL*, Vol. 3, p. 1195; *In Re Yang Ts'ai* (1822), *HAHL*, Vol. 6, p. 2564; and *In Re Ch'eng Hsiao-no* (1833), *HAHL*, Vol. 2, p. 808.
74. *HAHL*, Vol. 9, p. 4188. The compilers of this book noted that "This case had been approved by the Statutes Commission of the Board of Punishments" (*An, chiao-kuan ho-kuo*).
75. The amount of the second theft was not specified in the case record.
76. *Ch'ing Code*, Vol. 3, p. 2069; Staunton, p. 284; Boulais, p. 503, section 1117. The governor-general was quoting a statute under the Code section entitled "Ch'ieh-tao" (Theft). Note that in the Code the terms "one property owner" (*i-chu*) and "one family" (*i-chia*) are used interchangeably.
77. This quote is not from Shen's *Chi-chu* of 1715. The opinion was probably added by Hung Hung-hsü in 1745 or later. Cf. also *Ch'ing Code*, Vol. 3, p. 2070, middle section.
78. *Ch'ing Code*, Vol. 3, p. 2069; Staunton, p. 284; Boulais, p. 503, section 1117.
79. *HAHL*, Vol. 9, p. 4188.
80. *Ch'ing Code*, Vol. 3, p. 2070; Staunton, p. 285; Boulais, p. 504, section 1119.
81. *HAHLHP*, 19:4–5b.
82. *Ch'ing Code*, Vol. 4, p. 2527; Staunton, p. 314; Boulais, p. 565, section 1285.
83. *Ch'ing Code*, Vol. 4, p. 2527; Staunton, p. 313; Boulais, p. 564, section 1283.
84. *Ch'ing Code*, Vol. 4, p. 2527; Staunton, p. 313.
85. *HAHLHP*, 19:4b; *CC*, 19:21.
86. *HAHLHP*, 19:5a-b.
87. The 1865 case on the violation of the tomb seems to be the exception. In that case, the *Chi-chu* was cited in a memorial submitted by the Board of Punishments to the emperor. Cf. *HAHL*, Vol. 11, pp. 4946–4949.
88. *HAHL*, Vol. 5, p. 2223.
89. *Ch'ing Code*, Vol. 4, p. 2593; Staunton, p. 321; Boulais, pp. 577-578, section 1324; under the Code section entitled "Wei pi-jen chih-ssu" [Causing the death of an individual by violent and fearful threats].
90. *Ch'ing Code*, Vol. 1, p. 207, "Fu-chih" [The system of mourning]; cf. also *ibid.*, p. 181. The father-in-law stands in the fifth degree mourning relationship to his son-in-law.
91. Note 62 above.
92. *CC*, 19:29a-b; *HAHL*, Vol. 5, p. 2223. The punishment for this offense consisted of either 80 blows of the heavy bamboo or 40 of the light bamboo.
93. *HAHL*, Vol. 1, p. 455.
94. It is possible that the memorandum was written by the Chihli Department, recommending the directorate of the Board of Punishments to affirm the revised opinion newly submitted to the Department by the governor-general of Chihli.
95. *Ch'ing Code*, Vol. 1, p. 447; Staunton, p. 28; Boulais, p. 69, section 118. The *Chien-shih* commentary was quoted to elaborate this point. *HAHL*, Vol. 1, p. 455.
96. *Ch'ing Code*, Vol. 1, p. 484; Staunton, p. 33; Philastre, Vol. 1, p. 232; under

the Code section entitled "Kung-fan-tsui fen shou-ts'ung" [Distinguishing principals and accessories].

97. *CC*, 1:57b; *HAHL*, Vol. 1, p. 455.
98. *Ch'ing Code*, Vol. 4, p. 3409; Boulais, p. 682, section 1590.
99. *HAHL*, Vol. 11, pp. 4946-4948.
100. *Ch'ing Code*, Vol. 3, pp. 2241-2278; Staunton, pp. 293-297; Boulais, pp. 532-534, section 1191-1194; under the Code section entitled "Fa-chung" [Violation of the tomb].
101. For example, if a slave dug up his master's coffin but did not expose the corpse, he was punishable by either immediate strangulation as a principal or strangulation after the assizes as an accessory. In the absence of any relationship, where the coffin was dug up and a slit was made in it by sawing a hole through which valuables were pulled out, the corpse was considered unexposed, and the principal offender was punishable only by deportation to the near frontier, and the accessory by three years of penal servitude plus 100 blows of the heavy bamboo. *HAHL*, Vol. 11, p. 4946.
102. *Ch'ing Code*, Vol. 3, p. 1953; Staunton, p. 280; Boulais, p. 482, sec. 1061; under the Code section entitled "Ch'iang-tao" [Armed robbery].
103. *HAHL*, Vol. 11, p. 4947; *CC*, 18:44b.
104. (1) *Nieh-ssu ting-li hui-pien*, Vol. 119, 113:10-20b. Kiangsi province received the circular on May 26, 1866. (2) *Shang-yü t'iao-tsou* [A Collection of Imperial Orders and Memorials], pp. 32-43. (3) *Ko-pu-yüan t'iao-li ts'e*, Vol. 110: 1-13, (1866). Shansi province received the circular on May 5, 1866.
105. *HAHL*, Vol. 6, pp. 2744-2745.
106. *Ch'ing Code*, Vol. 4, p. 2817; Staunton, p. 347; Boulais, p. 617, section 1420; under a Code section entitled "Ou tsu-fu-mu fu-mu" [Striking grandparents or parents].
107. *Ch'ing Code*, Vol. 1, p. 182, "San-fu pa-mu t'u" [The mourning chart for 3 types of fathers and 8 types of mothers]; also *ibid.* pp. 195-196, "Fu-chih" [The system of mourning]; Staunton, pp. lxxv-lxxvi, "Degree of relationship, and of mourning"; Boulais, pp. 17-18. A son mourned his father's principal wife and his stepmother for three years; but only one year for his remarried or divorced mother. It is to be noted that this point was not brought up in the case record.
108. *Ch'ing Code*, Vol. 4, p. 2817; Staunton, pp. 347-348; Boulais, p. 617, section 1420.
109. *CC*, 20:29; *HAHL*, Vol. 4, p. 2744.
110. *HAHL*, Vol. 5, pp. 2074-2076.
111. From the available records it is not clear what law the governor invoked to punish Mrs. Liu. She was probably given a one-degree reducton from the punishment of decapitation after the assizes for intentional killing. *Ch'ing Code*, Vol. 4, p. 2497; Staunton, p. 311; Boulais, p. 559, section 1269.
112. *Ch'ing Code*, Vol. 4, p. 2527; Staunton, p. 313; Boulais, p. 564, section 1283.
113. *CC*, 19:21b; *HAHL*, Vol. 5, pp. 2074-2075.
114. Note 112 above.
115. *Ch'ing Code*, Vol. 4, p. 2817; Staunton, p. 347; Boulais, p. 617, sec. 1420.
116. I have omitted a lengthy discussion of *In Re* [*Mrs. Li*], *née P'an*, a case prec-

edent decided in 1737. In this case Miss P'an angrily threw a stone at her disobedient son from a former marriage. Another person, coming out from behind a door, was hit and killed. Miss P'an was allowed to redeem her punishment for accidental killing. The Hukwang Department distinguished this case from the case under consideration. The directorate of the Board felt that Mrs. Liu should be accorded the same treatment as Miss P'an, if not more favorable treatment. However, the Statutes Commission threw its support to the Department and argued against applying *In Re Miss P'an*. *HAHL*, Vol. 5, p. 2075. This case is also briefly reported in *Ch'ing Code*, Vol. 4, pp. 2529-2530, middle section.

117. *In Re Juan Kuo-cheng* (1793) and *In Re Wen Ho* (1796), *HAHL*, Vol. 5, p. 2076.
118. *Ibid., In Re Wen Ho*. The Commission admitted that the original record of this case was not available (*yüan-an wu-ts'ung chien-ch'a*).
119. *HAHL*, Vol. 5, pp. 2076-2078.
120. The available case record does not indicate the governor's opinion on the amount of money to be exacted from the offender. Since the accidental killing in this case involved two victims, the offender was required by law to pay 12.42 silver taels to the family for each victim. *Ch'ing Code*, Vol. 1, p. 466; Boulais, p. 84, section 154; under the Code section entitled "Liang-tsui chü-fa i chung lun" [Concurrence of offenses]. Cf. also Bodde and Morris, pp. 342-343.
121. In 1810 the governor of Kwangsi had apparently requested an advisory opinion from the Board of Punishments concerning the appropriate punishment for Mrs. Huang, née Wei. The Kwangsi Department held that she should not be sentenced to death; instead, she should be ordered to pay double the amount of "funeral money." *HAHL*, Vol. 5, p. 2077. Unfortunately, the record of the 1810 ruling is not available. The governor somehow ignored the opinion of the Department and the following year recommended that Mrs. Huang be punished for accidental killing. The recommendation was handled by the same Department that prepared the following memorandum for the directorate.
122. Notes 112 and 115 above.
123. *Ch'ing Code*, Vol. 3, p. 2453; Boulais, p. 552, section 1252; a substatute under the Code section entitled "Sha i-chia san-jen" [Killing three members of the same family]. According to this provision, one-half of the offender's property was given to the victims' family as compensation.
124. Note 113 above.
125. According to a statute of the Code section entitled "Kung yüeh-hu chi fu-jen fan-tsui" [Offenses committed by government artisans, musicians, or women] female offenders punishable by banishment or penal servitude were allowed to redeem that part of their sentence, but any prescribed beating with heavy bamboo was to be administered. *Ch'ing Code*, Vol. 1, p. 383; Staunton, pp. 22-23; Boulais, pp. 72-73, section 127. There were, however, several exceptions to the rule in which female offenders were denied the privilege of redemption and instead sent to the frontiers to serve as slaves to soldiers. For example, women who beat government runners and created

disturbances in the court were so sentenced. *Ch'ing Code*, Vol. 1, p. 387; Boulais, p. 73, section 128; a substatute under the same Code section.

126. *HAHL*, Vol. 3, pp. 1259-1260.
127. *Ch'ing Code*, Vol. 3, pp. 2116-2119; a substatute under the Code section entitled "Tao ma-niu ch'u-ch'an" [Stealing horses, cattle and other domestic animals].
128. *Ibid.*
129. *Ibid.* For the theft of six to nine head of cattle, the principal offender was deported to a malarial region in Yunnan, Kweichow, Kwangtung, or Kwangsi, and the accessories were sent to Hukwang or some other adjacent province.
130. *Ch'ing Code*, Vol. 3, pp. 2315-2316; Staunton, pp. 300-301; under a Code section entitled "Kung-ch'ü ch'ieh-ch'ü chieh-wei tao" [What constitutes a theft or robbery, and what constitutes only an attempt].
131. *HAHL*, Vol. 3, p. 1259. The quotation is identified as coming from Wan Wei-han's *Chyi-chu*, but an identical passage is found in *CC*, 18:27b.
132. *HAHL*, Vol. 7, p. 3127.
133. *CC*, 23:3; *HAHL*, Vol. 7, p. 3127; *Ch'ing Code*, Vol. 4, p. 3050, middle section.
134. *Ch'ing Code*, Vol. 4, pp. 3047-3054; Staunton, pp. 379-381; Boulais, pp. 654-656, section 1517-1520; under the Code section entitled "Kuan-li shou-ts'ai" [Officials and clerks accepting bribes].
135. *Ch'ing Code*, Vol. 4, p. 3050; Staunton, p. 380; Boulais, p. 655, section 1519; cf. especially the official interlinear commentary.
136. *Ch'ing Code*, Vol. 4, p. 3051; Staunton, p. 381; Boulais, p. 655, section 1519.
137. *Ch'ing Code*, Vol. 4, p. 3052; Staunton, p. 381; Boulais, p. 655, section 1519.
138. *Ch'ing Code*, Vol. 4, p. 3081; Philastre, Vol. 2, p. 477; a special provision under the Code section entitled "Yu-shih i-ts'ai ch'ing-ch'iu" [Offering a bribe].
139. *Ch'ing Code*, Vol. 3, p. 2197; Staunton, p. 289; Boulais, pp. 523-524, section 1171; a statute under the Code section entitled "Cha-ch'i kuan-ssu ch'ü-ts'ai" [Fraudulently obtaining public or private property].
140. Note 134 above.
141. *Ch'ing Code*, Vol. 3, p. 2069; Staunton, p. 284; Boulais, p. 503, section 1117; cf. especially the official interlinear commentary.
142. *CC*, 23:3; *Ch'ing Code*, Vol. 4, p. 3050, middle section.
143. Note 136 above.
144. *Ch'ing Code*, Vol. 4, p. 3047; Staunton, p. 379; Boulais, p. 654, section 1517.
145. *Ch'ing Code*, Vol. 3, p. 2201; Boulais, p. 524, section 1174.
146. The governor-general recommended punishing him with 100 blows of the heavy bamboo and three years of penal servitude on the theory that Ch'ien's punishment of military banishment to the near frontier should be reduced by one degree. The reason for the reduction was not mentioned in the record. The Board held that according to a substatute the person who offered a bribe was to be punished like the bribe taker, and if the bribe giver was not a salaried official, a one-degree reduction was granted. Since Ch'ien's (the bribe taker's) original punishment was 100 blows of the heavy bamboo and

banishment to 2,500 *li* for his accepting a bribe of 50 silver taels, and since Han was not a salaried official, the punishment for Han was thus reduced by one degree to 100 blows of the heavy bamboo and three years of penal servitude. *HAHL*, Vol. 7, p. 3127; note 138 above.

147. *In Re T'ien Ch'ing-chih* (1870), *HAHLHP*, 27:1-3. Cf. also *In Re Chang Ching-i* (1840), *ibid.*, 27:3-4b.

148. *HAHL*, Vol. 3, p. 955.

149. *Ch'ing Code*, Vol. 3, pp. 1933-1944; Staunton, pp. 277-278; Boulais, pp. 477-479, section 1051-1053; under the Code section entitled "Chien-shou tzu-tao ts'ang-k'u ch'ien-liang" [Embezzlement of public property]; *Ch'ing Code*, Vol. 3, pp. 1945-1952; Staunton, p. 279; Boulais, pp. 479-480, section 1054-1056; under the Code section entitled "Ch'ang-jen tao ts'ang'k'u ch'ien-liang" [Theft of public property]. Depending on the circumstances, a treasury janitor could be charged with either embezzlement or theft of public property. Cf. a 1823 Kweichow case *In Re Chang Chin, HAHL*, Vol. 3, p. 963.

150. *Ch'ing Code*, Vol. 3, pp. 1942-1943; Boulais, p. 478, section 1052. During the Yung-cheng reign, a new substatute was enacted to minimize the losses suffered by the government treasury. To encourage the return of embezzled property, the state promised to remit or reduce substantially the prescribed statutory penalty if the repayment was made within one year. Even the capital offense of embezzling over 1,000 silver taels was reduced by two degrees to become three years of penal servitude plus 100 blows of the heavy bamboo. Should the offender fail to meet the one-year deadline, he was allowed a two to three-year grace period with less favorable treatment upon repayment. This substatute was subsequently revised a few times, but the general tenor remained the same. Hsüeh, *Tu-lü ts'un-i*, 25:58b-61a.

This substatute's lenient treatment of embezzlement contrasts sharply with the severity of the statutes dealing with ordinary theft of government property.

151. The Department's decision is not clear from the available record of this case. However, since the directorate's comment on the ruling, found in the *Yü-chih hsing-lü shuo-t'ieh* (but not in the *Hsing-an hui-lan*) indicates that the directorate endorsed the decision of the lower court and asked the Statutes Commission to deliberate on the Department's decision, I think the Department must have overruled the governor's recommendation to exempt Liang from punishment. This work is not paginated; cf. the vol. dated 1806.

152. *CC*, 18:13b; *HAHL*, Vol. 3, p. 955.

153. *HAHLHP*, 12:84-87b.

154. *Ch'ing Code*, Vol. 3, pp. 2315-2316; Staunton, pp. 300-301.

155. See the text accompanying note 131, above; *CC*, 18:27b; *HAHLHP*, 12:84b-85.

156. *HAHLHP*, 12:84b-85.

157. *Ibid.*, 10:68-70b.

158. *Ch'ing Code*, Vol. 3, pp. 2088-2089; Boulais, p. 505, section 1122.

159. *Ch'ing Code*, Vol. 3, p. 2083; Boulais, p. 505, section 1124.

160. The offense of pickpocketing (*t'ao-mo*) is regulated in the Code section gov-

erning ordinary theft. *Ch'ing Code,* Vol. 3, p. 2069; Boulais, p. 503, section 1118.

161. The offenses of embezzlement and theft of public property have been discussed in note 149 above.
162. The term used for "unarmed robbery" is *ch'iang-tuo*. In general, cf. *Ch'ing Code*, Vol. 3, pp. 2027-2068; Staunton, pp. 283-284; Boulais, pp. 494-501, sections 1092-1108; under the Code section entitled "Pai-chou ch'iang-tuo" [Daytime unarmed robbery].
163. *CC*, 18:28; *HAHLHP*, 10:68b; *Ch'ing Code*, Vol. 3, p. 2070, middle section.
164. *HAHLHP*, 10:68b.
165. *Ch'ing Code*, Vol. 3, p. 2070; Staunton, p. 285; Boulais, p. 504, section 1119.
166. *Ch'ing Code*, Vol. 3, pp. 1945-1946; Staunton, p. 279; Boulais, p. 479, section 1054.
167. *Ch'ing Code*, Vol. 3, p. 2069; Boulais, p. 503, section 1117; cf. especially the official interlinear commentary.
168. *HAHLHP*, 10:69.
169. Note 159 above.
170. *HAHLHP*, 10:69a-b.
171. *Ch'ing Code*, Vol. 3, pp. 2027-2029; Staunton, p. 283; Boulais, p. 494, section 1093.
172. *Ch'ing Code*, Vol. 3, pp. 2032-2034; *Ta Ch'ing lü-li an-yü* (1847) 81:32a-34b.
173. *HAHLHP*, 10:70. The 1826 ruling is in *HAHL*, Vol. 3, pp. 1107-1108, a memorandum by the Statutes Commission.
174. *HAHLHP*, 10:70. However, Shen Chih-ch'i's opinion seems to differ from the Commission's view. *CC*, 18:25.
175. *HAHL*, Vol. 3, pp. 1406-1407.
176. *Ch'ing Code*, Vol. 2, p. 889; Staunton, p. 85; Boulais, p. 177, section 374; under the Code section entitled "Shou-liu mi-shih tzu-nü" [Receiving stray children and women].
177. *Ch'ing Code,* Vol. 3, pp. 2221-2222; a substatute under the Code section entitled "Lüeh-jen lüeh-mai jen" [Kidnapping and sale of human beings]. The Board's view is discussed in the text following.
178. *HAHL*, Vol. 3, p. 1407.
179. The quotation is identified as coming from Wan's *Chyi-chu*, but it is identical with Shen's version; cf. *CC*, 4:10b and *Ch'ing Code*, Vol. 2, pp. 890-891, middle section.
180. *Ch'ing Code*, Vol. 3, pp. 2221-2222.
181. *Ibid.*
182. *Ch'ing Code*, Vol. 1, p. 393; Staunton, pp. 22-23; Boulais, pp. 72-73, section 127.
183. *HAHL*, Vol. 3, p. 1401.
184. Note 180 above.
185. *Ch'ing Code*, Vol. 2, p. 1083; Staunton, p. 120; Boulais, p. 301, section 637; under the Code section entitled "Ch'u-ch'i" [Law of divorce].
186. *CC*, 6:20b; *HAHL*, Vol. 3, p. 1401.
187. Note 185 above.
188. The statement usually reads "*Yeh-i (ping-ku* or *tzu-chin*), *ying wu-yung-i*"

[Since the offender has already died (from sickness, or suicide), the matter need not be deliberated further]. For example, cf. *In Re Ch'ang Le-san* (1812) *HAHL*, Vol. 4, p. 1523; *In Re Mrs. Chu, née Li* (1796), *HAHL*, Vol. 3, p. 1401; and *In Re Ch'en Hsiang-li* (1763), *PAHP*, 4:39b. Cf. also Bodde and Morris, pp. 313-315.

189. *CC*, Vol. 1, Shen's preface; *Ch'ing Code*, Vol. 1, p. 65.
190. When a review memorandum (*shuo-t'ieh*) submitted to the directorate by members of the Board of Punishments was approved, the authors of the memorandum then prepared a second document called *kao-wei* to be issued to the province concerned. In this type of reply, all references to any private commentary were eliminated. For example, *In Re Mrs. Huang, née Wei* (1811), reported in *HAHL*, Vol. 5, pp. 2076-2078 and discussed in the text is also reported in the *Yü-chih hsing-lu shuo-t'ieh*. In the latter, the *shuo-t'ieh* contains a quotation from Shen's *Chi-chu*, but the *kao-wei* does not mention Shen's work at all. Cf. the volume dated 1811 (no pagination). Since these two separate documents, concerning the same case, are merged into one single document by the authors of the *Hsing-an hui-lan*, the distinctions drawn by the members of the Board can not be isolated. Cf. also Shen Chia-pen, *I-shu*, Vol. 2, p. 976.
191. The twelve cases are: *In Re Huang Yao* (1749), *HAHL*, Vol. 4, pp. 1732-1733; *In Re Chang Yung* (1789), *HAHL*, Vol. 6, pp. 2742-2743; *In Re T'ang Hua-ching* (1789), *HAHL*, Vol. 6, pp. 2505-2506; *In Re Mrs. Chao, née Ch'en* (1789), *HAHL*, Vol. 1, p. 455; *In Re Liu Erh* (1792), *HAHL*, Vol. 8, pp. 3356-3357; *In Re Mrs. Chao, née Chang* (1802), *HAHL*, Vol. 6, p. 2465; *In Re Liang Fen-yung* (1806), *HAHL*, Vol. 3, p. 955; *In Re Wang Shui* (1810), *HAHL*, Vol. 5, pp. 1925-1926; *In Re Li Wen* (1817), *HAHL*, Vol. 7, pp. 3040-3042; *In Re Wang Ch'i* (1826), *HAHL*, Vol. 6, p. 2741; *In Re Ch'ing-jui* (1862), *HAHLHP*, 26:6b-7b; and "On theft" (1865), *HAHLHP*, 12:84-87b. Cf. also Bodde and Morris, pp. 378-383 and 389-391.
192. Note 16 above.
193. *In Re Ying Liang* (1789) and *In Re Shih Ta-p'eng* (1792).
194. *HAHL*, Vol. 9, p. 3853. In yet another case dated 1829 (*In Re Wo-sheng-e*), the Board of Punishments criticized the government in Mukden, a special district, for its reliance on a private Code commentary entitled *T'ung-tsuan*. The Board pointed out that the said commentary was published by a private bookstore rather than by the Board; therefore the citation of that work in judicial decisions should be prohibited. *HAHL*, Vol. 9, p. 4036. For the Code commentary in question, see p. 83 of my doctoral dissertation, note 7 above.
195. John P. Dawson, *The Oracles of the Law* (Ann Arbor, Mich.; 1968), pp. 122-147.
196. *Ibid.*, pp. 127 and 139.

VII

CH'ING LEGAL JURISDICTION OVER FOREIGNERS

R. Randle Edwards

The ideal policy is to show concern and kindness to the outer barbarians, while not departing from the fundamental regulations of the Celestial Empire. *The Tao-kuang emperor, 1830*[1]

Although trade was the primary motive of most of the Europeans[2] who went to China in the seventeenth, eighteenth, and early nineteenth centuries, the chief concern of the Chinese government was to maintain order among the unruly "outer barbarians" (*wai-i*), so as to minimize the disruptive effect their presence might have upon the Chinese populace. The Ch'ing court sought to achieve this objective by applying to newcomers from the "western ocean" (*hsi-yang*), the principles and rules of the Chinese system of world order known as the "tribute system."[3]

The tribute system, consisting of elaborate ceremonies and detailed rules closely regulating behavior of foreigners coming to China to "bring tribute" (*ju-kung*), was founded upon an assumption of the superiority of Chinese culture and institutions. All foreigners, including Westerners, had to comply with the tribute system protocol if they wished to establish continuing commercial relations with China.

It proved difficult, however, for the Ch'ing government to compel the Europeans to comply with the rules of the tribute system, for they came to China with perceptions and expectations shaped by traditions and values quite alien to those of the Chinese. As John Fairbank has put it: "the arrival of the English by sea posed utterly novel problems, and at the same time inspired the court at Peking to act primarily with a view to preserving the political control over China which it had built up with such care."[4]

In this chapter I will discuss how over the years the Ch'ing government, working within the framework of the spirit and institutions of the traditional tribute system, developed special jurisdictional policies and trial procedures for handling alien offenses, in order to cope with the unique threat to stability and harmony created by the presence of the Europeans living and trading at Canton and Macao.[5] Contrary to the opinion expressed by many Europeans living in China prior to the imposition of the "unequal treaty" system in the mid-nineteenth century, during that period the disposition of serious criminal cases involving aliens was not arbitrarily dictated by the whim or prejudice of the Kwangtung local officials. Instead, the Ch'ien-lung emperor as early as 1744 enunciated a policy of "deferring to barbarian wishes" (*fu-shun i-ch'ing*) by asserting criminal jurisdiction over aliens only in cases involving the homicide of a Chinese subject.[6]

Yet, because certain principles of Chinese substantive criminal law and certain aspects of Chinese criminal procedure were repugnant to the English, after 1784 they refused to submit to Chinese criminal jurisdiction. The ensuing disputes between the Chinese and the English over the surrender of English sailors to Chinese justice left a legacy of misunderstanding, suspicion, and resentment which contributed greatly to the outbreak of armed conflict in 1839 and to the subsequent establishment of the unequal treaty system which is still regarded with bitterness by all Chinese.

Previous studies of the origin of legal extraterritoriality in China have relied almost exclusively upon Western sources.[7] Most of them have not referred either to the Ch'ing Penal Code or to Chinese documentary collections containing the memorials and edicts giving the official Ch'ing government view of the facts and disposition of alien criminal cases. Drawing upon these documents, this chapter will show how a clear and reasoned policy emerged for dealing with such cases prior to the treaty system. It should be pointed out, however, that the Western records remain valuable because they appear to contain a more reliable statement of the facts and of certain steps in the pretrial and trial procedure. Comparison of the Chinese and English records suggests that in many instances the governor-general's memorials concerning alien criminal cases stated what he thought the emperor would like to hear and not what had really transpired.[8]

Alien Jurisdiction Statutes

As with other aspects of administration, the early Ch'ing rulers had a rich background of theory and experience to draw upon in handling the challenge to law and order presented by the aggressive Western traders. Problems occasioned by the presence of foreign merchants in China and the existence of an alien community, with the resulting potential for violence and the spread of unorthodox and unsettling ideas, were not new phenomena in Chinese history.

Communities of Arab traders had existed at Canton from the early T'ang dynasty and at Zayton (Ch'üan-chou in Fukien Province), Hangchow and Yangchow during the Sung.[9] To regulate such communities, the T'ang Code, embodying the approach of allowing to foreign residents a limited degree of autonomy in the resolution of disputes, contained the following provision on legal jurisdiction over aliens:

1. With respect to offenses committed by aliens in China, if the offense involves only persons of the same nationality, the case shall be decided according to the laws of their own country;
2. Where the offense involves persons of different nationalities, the case shall be decided according to the T'ang Code.[10]

Although there is some difference of opinion about whether in a case involving aliens of the same nationality the law of that nation would be applied by Chinese judicial officials or by the foreign headman, the better view seems to be that in both the T'ang and Sung periods the matter was left to the foreign community. Indeed, Jitsuzō Kuwabara suggests that: "in the Sung era she went a step further, and when a foreigner committed an offense against a Chinese, the case, unless it be very serious, was left to the foreigners to decide according to their own law."[11]

The Ming alien jurisdiction statute appears to adopt the principle of unlimited territorial jurisdiction: "All aliens who commit offenses [on Chinese soil] shall be sentenced according to the Chinese Penal Code." (*Fan hua-wai-jen fan-tsui che ping i-lü ni-tuan.*)[12] However, Kuwabara states that in practice the Ming authorities generally refrained from exercising criminal jurisdiction over alien offenses. He even cites a case where a Japanese who killed a Chinese was sent back to Japan to be punished according to Japanese law.[13]

The Ch'ing Code of 1646 retained the Ming alien jurisdiction provision, adding only the modifying phrase "who come to submit" (*lai-hsiang*) after the term "alien" (*hua-wai*), so that the provision reads: "All aliens who come to submit themselves to the government of the empire shall, when they commit offenses [on Chinese soil] be sentenced according to the Chinese Penal Code." (*Fan hua-wai lai-hsiang-jen fan-tsui che ping i lü ni-tuan.*)[14] A final amendment was made in 1725 when there was added to the alien jurisdiction statute the stipulation that: "Cases which fall within the jurisdiction of the Mongolian Superintendency (*Li-fan-yüan*) shall still be decided according to the regulations earlier enacted for the government of the Mongol tribes." (*Li li-fan-yüan che jeng chao yüan-ting Meng-ku li.*)[15] The "general commentary" (*tsung-chu*) following the Ch'ing alien jurisdiction provision explains that, since aliens have attached themselves (*kuei-fu*) to the empire, when they commit offenses they should be punished just as ordinary Chinese subjects.[16]

In examining the Ch'ing exercise of criminal jurisdiction over Europeans at Canton and Macao, we should first study the above statute. Two important problems of interpretation immediately confront us: first, what is the meaning of the term *hua-wai-jen* (lit. "persons from beyond the pale of Chinese civilization"), rendered here as "alien"? Next, what actions are necessary or sufficient to establish that such persons have "come to submit" (*lai-hsiang*)?

Sir Ernest Alabaster, arguing that the term *hua-wai jen* referred only to Mongols, insisted that the jurisdiction statute was not intended to apply to persons such as the European merchants at Macao and Canton.[17] As for the significance of the modifying phrase *lai-hsiang*, the Chinese legal historian, Tai Yen-hui, has expressed the opinion that it imports into the jurisdiction statute a requirement that an alien had to become a naturalized Chinese (*kuei-hua*) and abandon his foreign nationality (*fei wai-kuo chi che*) before he would be made subject to the Ch'ing Penal Code.[18] Without further digression on this interesting subject, it is sufficient for our present purposes to state that the Ch'ing judicial authorities clearly considered the provision to be applicable to all aliens at Canton and Macao, including traders, their servants, and all personnel of any merchant ships or warships visiting China.

The conclusion that the alien jurisdiction statute did apply to European traders is based primarily on the explicit citation of the provision in memorials and edicts dealing with crimes committed by such persons. A most unambiguous statement of this applicability of Chinese law to Europeans is contained in a memorial submitted by Governor-general Juan Yuan of Liang-Kuang on his handling of an 1821 homicide case involving English sailors from the warship *Topaze*: "When a barbarian sailor commits an offense on Chinese soil, such act constitutes 'an offense by a person from beyond the pale of Chinese civilization' (*chi hsi hua-wai-jen yu-fan*). Thus, the case should be handled in accordance with Chinese law."[19]

Further support for the conclusion that extension of Chinese criminal jurisdiction to Europeans at Canton and Macao was based upon the *hua-wai-jen* statute is evidenced by the fact that an annotated edition of the Ch'ing Code, dated 1832, contains summaries of three cases involving Europeans; these cases are appended to, and illustrative of, the alien jurisdiction provision.[20] The fascinating question of the extent to which other aliens, such as Koreans, Japanese, Vietnamese, and Russians, were considered subject to the Ch'ing Penal Code with respect to criminal acts committed on Chinese soil is beyond the scope of the present chapter. However, it is a question that must be answered in the future if we are ever to understand fully Chinese traditional practice regarding the rights and responsibilities of aliens in China.[21]

Macao: Evolution of a Policy of Limited Jurisdiction and Modified Criminal Procedure for Alien Offenses

The story of the exercise of Chinese criminal jurisdiction over Europeans should begin with the Portuguese who, after establishing a colony at Goa in India in 1510, opened trade with China at several places, including St. John's Island, Lampaco, Ch'uan-chou, Foochow, and Ningpo. Because of their unruly behavior, however, they were driven from all of these places by the Ming emperor. In 1557 the Portuguese withdrew to the peninsula of Amakau, where they were permitted by the Chinese local authorities to establish a trade depot.[22]

This depot quickly grew into a mixed Chinese-Portuguese community of several thousand individuals; known to the Chinese as Ao-men, it has always been called Macao by Europeans. From the sixteenth century onward, the Portuguese inhabitants of Macao were governed by officials appointed from Goa or Portugal, including a governor, a chief judge, two lower judges, a military commander, and a bishop; in addition, an elected senate advised the governor on policy matters.[23] In criminal cases, appeals could be taken to the chief judge at Macao and to a higher court in Goa. The Portuguese courts in Macao never exercised jurisdiction over Chinese defendants and, as we shall see below, exercised jurisdiction over Portuguese defendants only intermittently and against strenuous Chinese objections if the complainant was a Chinese subject.

In spite of Portuguese claims to hold a Golden Charter from the Ming emperor granting sovereignty over Macao, the Chinese government in fact never ceased to regard Macao as Chinese territory.[24] From the very beginning, the Portuguese at Macao paid an annual ground rent to the Chinese government, as well as paying to the Chinese customs officials the prescribed tariff on all maritime trade. Moreover, in the late Ming, the Portuguese officials in Macao were required on more than one occasion to acknowledge Chinese sovereignty and to promise to adhere to Chinese law.

It appears, however, that during the first century of the Ch'ing dynasty, the Chinese local officials were not eager to assume the difficult task of directly governing such a complex community as Macao. They were especially reluctant to report to their superiors any offenses committed by the Portuguese, because the latter were adamant in refusing to submit to the Chinese criminal process. If the local official reported the case and did not subsequently apprehend the offender, he himself would be subjected to administrative discipline and would put his career in jeopardy. Consequently, the Chinese local officials were easy marks for the bribery which the Portuguese, and in later years other Europeans as well, employed to secure for themselves *de facto* legal extraterritoriality.[25]

In some cases involving homicide of a Chinese by a Portuguese resident of Macao, the Portuguese authorities would pay the family of the victim to keep silent; in such cases, the Portuguese would punish the offender lightly, if at all. However, where the victim's family insisted upon lodging an accusation with the Chinese local officials, the Portuguese would bribe the official not to report the case. While the victim's family could of course bypass the corrupt local official and appeal to higher authorities, the higher authorities would probably accept the local official's explanation that the appeal was instigated (*chiao-so*) by a "litigation trickster" (*sung-kun*) seeking to extort money from the foreigners. The relative making the appeal would be punished and a search would be instituted to find the pettifogger.

In spite of a consistent Portuguese practice thus to evade Chinese criminal law, it was not until 1743 that a reform-minded and vigorous Manchu governor-general, Ts'e-leng, decided to take steps to recover effective control of the fiscal and legal administration of Macao. He submitted a memorial to the emperor in which he stated that:

> Canton is an important city, so the approaches to it, including Macao, should be strengthened. An assistant district magistrate (*hsien-ch'eng*), as is now stationed at the Ch'ien-shan (Casa Blanca) fortress, is insufficient to restrain the barbarians. . . . It is appropriate to adopt the procedure employed for controlling the Yao tribesmen. . . . The Chao-ch'ing subprefect (*t'ung-chih*) should be transferred to the Ch'ien-shan fortress to assume responsibility for maritime defense and supervision of the Chinese and foreigners in Macao . . . the assistant district magistrate of Hsiang-shan district should be moved to Macao to take charge of investigating all litigation (*tz'u-sung*) between Chinese and foreigners, which he shall report to the subprefect for handling.[26]

The first test of the new resolve of the Chinese authorities to enforce Chinese law in Macao came in late 1743 when a drunken Chinese got into a quarrel with a Portuguese who pulled a knife and fatally stabbed him.[27] Apparently the victim's relatives could not be bought off, for the homicide was reported to the Hsiang-shan district magistrate who, after conducting an inquest and interrogation of the suspect, demanded that he be turned over to the Chinese for trial and punishment. The Portuguese governor refused the demand and himself took the offender into custody (*tzu-hsing shou-kuan*). The district magistrate thereupon submitted a confidential report (*mi-ping*) to his superiors, explaining that the Portuguese governor's intransigence was due to the fact that: "Portuguese barbarians who commit crimes in Macao have hitherto never been sent from Macao for trial in the provincial capital [Canton]."[28]

When the governor-general and governor strictly ordered the district magistrate to try the offender according to Chinese law and send him to Canton, the district magistrate submitted another report, enclosing a lengthy petition from the Portuguese governor of Macao, explaining the reasons for Portugal's refusal to submit to Chinese judicial process and begging that it be permitted to continue exercising autonomous jurisdiction over offenses committed by Portuguese in Macao. In memorializing the concluded case to the emperor, the Liang-Kuang governor-general, Ts'e-leng, took note of the special nature of the community of Macao and pointed out that the local officials had been in the habit of not reporting barbarian offenses so that for a hundred years no Macao barbarian had paid the death penalty for killing a Chinese. He stated that in handling this particular case he had felt that to insist upon surrender of the suspect might "cause the barbarians to become suspicious and frightened, thus giving rise to new incidents."[29] Thus, he had directed the Canton prefect and the Hsiang-shan district magistrate to go to Macao to witness the strangling of the offender by the Portuguese authorities.

Although he considered the present case to have been concluded satisfactorily, Ts'e-leng stated that the matter of exercising Chinese criminal jurisdiction over aliens was too important a subject to be left for ad hoc settlement. He thus stressed the necessity of punishing barbarians guilty of committing homicides against Chinese under circumstances calling for the statutory penalty of decapitation or strangulation. However, he expressed the opinion that, in view of the Portuguese refusal to surrender criminal suspects to the Chinese, it would be desirable for the emperor to establish special procedures for handling offenses by Macao barbarians.

He proposed that in cases of homicides against Chinese, the alien offender should be detained and interrogated at a spot in or near Macao under joint Chinese and Portuguese supervision. The coroner's report, defendant's statement, depositions of witnesses and the recommended sentence would all be forwarded to the governor-general. The latter official would review the above documents, make sure that the law was correctly applied, and order the district magistrate to go in conjunction with the Portuguese governor (*i-mu*, lit. "barbarian headman") to execute the offender in the presence of the victim's family and the entire foreign community. The governor-general would then report the case to the emperor and forward the case record to the Board of Punishments for filing. Ts'e-leng predicted that: "The effect of adopting and implementing these proposed procedures will be to extend the application of the laws of our country while at the same time deferring to barbarian wishes . . ."[30]

In recommending approval of the memorial, the Board of Punishments noted that the Ch'ing Code provided that Chinese law should be applied to alien offenders. The Board also stated that in handling alien cases:

> It is hoped that there will be no erroneous conviction of the innocent [*wu-wang*] nor erroneous acquittal of the guilty [*wu-tsung*] and that the facts will be found accurately and the recommended punishment will be fitting. As for the other procedural provisions of the Code, however, such as the rules concerning detention [*shou-chin*] and obtaining a confession [*ch'eng-chao*], it is not at all necessary completely to conform to the pattern followed in the interior. On the contrary, such strict conformity might even make it more difficult to decide the case."[31]

The emperor granted approval of the procedure proposed by Ts'e-leng and ordered that it be made an official rule of procedure (*ling*) to be followed by all judicial officials handling such cases. This approved memorial is the fundamental document in this study, for it established the guidelines followed by Chinese officials in handling later cases involving homicides of Chinese by aliens.

A notable feature of the procedure thus established is that alien offenders are deprived of the numerous automatic and appellate reviews, including the autumn assizes, which gave Chinese subjects sentenced to death real opportunities for reversal of conviction or mitigation of punishment.[32] Europeans arriving in China in the late eighteenth and early nineteenth centuries complained bitterly that they were subjected to discrimination and denial of justice by the abbreviated process[33] which, unknown to them, had originally been designed to "defer to barbarian wishes" and "avoid further incidents."

The Ts'e-leng memorial contains no explicit provision concerning the disposition of alien offenses other than the homicide of a Chinese. However, subsequent memorials and edicts in which lesser alien offenses are mentioned sometimes cite the pertinent provision in the Ch'ing Penal Code and then proceed to quote instructions to the foreign headman (*i-mu*) to subject the offender to the punishment prescribed by Chinese law.[34] In other cases, the foreign headman is merely ordered to investigate and punish the offender "according to the barbarian law" (*chao i-fa chiu-pan*),[35] and usually in such cases, the offender's deportation is also ordered (*ch'ien-hui pen-kuo*).

The distinction between the two types of phraseology used to instruct the foreign headman how to punish his nationals for committing lesser offenses is not very significant in fact, because the Chinese authorities lacked the power to enforce either type of instruction. From the general practice of not asserting formal Chinese criminal jurisdiction, except in homicides of Chinese where punishment had to be meted out to satisfy the bereaved Chinese family and the hostile Chinese masses, one may conclude that the foreign community was held responsible for maintaining order in its ranks and the Chinese government was not particular about how it was accomplished.

As an outpost of Europe, Macao as early as the seventeenth century served as a temporary haven for European ships and traders.[36] As the English trade at Canton increased during the mid-eighteenth century, Macao became the winter home for English merchants, who were not permitted to remain in Canton during the off-season. Also, since foreign women were never allowed in Canton, married European traders had to leave their families in Macao. Since there seems never to have been any intergovernmental agreement between Portugal and other Western states regarding protection of the rights of their nationals in Macao, the latter were totally dependent upon the goodwill of the government of Macao and upon any arrangements made by that government with the Chinese authorities concerning criminal jurisdiction, entry and exit permits, and other matters. Finally, since the Chinese government regarded all Westerners as basically the same, referring to them all as "outer barbarians" (*wai-i*), rules and procedures worked out to deal with the Portuguese at Macao were sometimes applied as well to other Europeans there connected with the Canton trade.[37]

Although later memorials and edicts dealing with homicides of Chinese committed outside of Macao by English or American sailors all cited the authority of the approved 1744 memorial of Ts'e-leng, it should be pointed out that the procedure applied to the Portuguese in Macao actually differed significantly from that applied to the English and Americans in Canton. In cases involving alien homicides of Chinese committed outside of Macao, the Chinese demanded that the foreign taipan or ship captain search out (*ch'a-ch'u*) and surrender (*chiao-ch'u*) the alien offender to the local authorities for trial and punishment in accordance with Chinese law and the modified criminal procedure established in 1744. In such cases, the Chinese authorities did not allow the foreign community to execute the punishment in company with the local Chinese magistrate, as had become the custom with homicides of Chinese by Portuguese in Macao.[38]

The Portuguese had a government and a court system in Macao with the authority to carry out capital punishment and they did comply essentially with the 1744 procedure in homicide cases occurring in 1783, 1805, and 1826.[39] However, in a case arising in 1748, where two Portuguese soldiers in Macao killed two Chinese and threw the bodies into the sea, the Kwangtung governor allowed the Portuguese to sentence the offenders to banishment to Timor in accordance with Portuguese law. The governor was severely reprimanded by the emperor, who stated: "From now on, the local magistrates must carefully study any such case, uphold our law, and punish the criminals. Never should they spare the foreigners lest their proud and loose habits be encouraged and cause more trouble."[40] The emperor apparently meant that the magistrate should punish the alien offender according to the modified procedure established in 1744; since the 1744 procedure was followed in subsequent cases, it obviously was not rescinded by the emperor in 1748.

When a case arose the next year involving Chinese Christian converts being harbored in a church in Macao, the emperor issued an edict to the governor-general and governor. It directed the Chinese local officials to negotiate an agreement with the Portuguese authorities, providing in detail for the future government of Macao.[41] Initial Portuguese resistance was overcome by the tactic of withdrawing from Macao all Chinese servants and shopkeepers and cutting off all supplies. Macao's governor had no choice but to comply, so in 1749 a document called the Conventional Pact[42] was drawn up and inscribed in Chinese and Portuguese on stone pillars placed prominently in public places in Macao. Among its provisions were two on legal matters: Article 4 basically declared that the Portuguese had no jurisdiction over any offenses committed in Macao by Chinese subjects. Article 5 stated that in the case of homicides of Chinese committed by Macao barbarians, a procedure similar to that unilaterally proclaimed by the Chinese in 1744 should be followed.

As has been suggested above, since the Portuguese were land-based and dependent upon Chinese supplies, they were quite vulnerable to Chinese pressure and thus acquiesced more readily to the Chinese demand for punishment of persons killing Chinese than did the British, who were ship-based and could easily escape Chinese jurisdiction.

The Portuguese essentially complied with the Chinese substantive law of homicide; on several occasions they tried and executed persons guilty of committing homicide in a fight without considering the degree of provocation or who struck the first blow, as they would have under their own law. However, the Portuguese judges reportedly were more careful than the Chinese judges in establishing that the accused was indeed the actual killer. Moreover, the Portuguese court in Macao adhered to rules of criminal procedure calculated to give the accused a chance to defend himself. In other words, a Portuguese subject accused of killing a Chinese was assured of a reasonably fair trial, but if found guilty he would be executed.

Other Europeans residing in Macao were not so fortunate as the Portuguese subjects, for the Portuguese local officials were loathe to jeopardize their relations with the Chinese government by resisting Chinese demands for surrender of non-Portuguese aliens. For example, in 1773, an Englishman named Francis Scott was tried and acquitted by the Portuguese court in Macao of a charge of killing a Chinese.[43] But when the

Chinese authorities threatened to take action against the entire community if the offender was not turned over to them, the Macao Senate voted to surrender Scott to the Chinese, who subsequently executed him. The vicar-general of Macao justified the surrender of Scott to Chinese justice with the following argument, which well illustrates the dependent status of Macao, the effectiveness of Chinese use of the principle of collective responsibility to enforce compliance with their demands, and the insecure status of non-Portuguese residents of Macao: "Moralists decide that when a tyrant demands even an innocent person, with menaces of ruin to the community if refused, the whole number may call on any individual to deliver himself up for the public good, which is of more worth than the life of an individual. Should he refuse to obey, he is not innocent, he is criminal."[44]

In answer to a protest delivered by the English East India Company's Canton representative to the effect that Scott was innocent and should be released, the Chinese governor-general replied: "Mr. Scott having been delivered by the Senate as the guilty person that therefore should he not be guilty it would be necessary before he could be released that the guilty person or persons should be discovered. . . ."[45] Or, as Morse says: "the Macao Senate, having handed Francis Scott to Chinese justice, must be assumed to have satisfied themselves of his guilt; whether guilty or not, his execution—a life for a life—would satisfy the relatives and neighbors of the murdered man . . ."[46] It is not surprising that many Europeans in China began to believe that to turn one of their number over to the Chinese for trial on a homicide charge was equivalent to convicting him without benefit of a fair trial.

Offenses by Europeans Outside of Macao: Cross-purposes, Clashing Values, and Conflict

The Early Period

Although the Portuguese at Macao resisted Chinese jurisdiction whenever possible, we have seen how they were eventually forced to comply with certain demands and procedures imposed upon them by the Chinese authorities. The English, however, from the moment of their first contact with China, proved to be most unruly and unwilling to observe the ceremonial forms and institutions established by the Chinese government to control the "outer barbarians."

The English vainly attempted to enter into the China trade in the late Ming period, but their overtures were rejected by the Chinese officials, who had been bribed by the Portuguese at Macao to turn away the ships of other foreign countries seeking to make inroads on the Portuguese monopoly of China's foreign trade.[47] At the end of the Ming dynasty, Captain John Weddell, who forced his way up the river to Canton in 1637 after silencing the guns of the Chinese battery at the Bogue, was allowed to trade only after promising that he and his men would "act in conformity with the laws of China" and that "should we act in any way contrary thereto, we will submit to any punishments the Mandarin and the City of Macao shall order."[48]

For the first forty years after the establishment of the Ch'ing dynasty in 1644, the southeastern coastal region was partly controlled by the rebellious Cheng family and their Ming loyalist adherents; it was not until 1683 that the Ch'ing forces finally captured the stronghold of Cheng Ch'eng-kung (Koxinga) on Taiwan and put an end to rebellious activities along the coast. Since the Ch'ing government had curtailed foreign trade while it was contending with Koxinga, European trade with China during this period was limited to intermittent Dutch trade, the Portuguese trade at Macao, and the English trade with the rebel regime of Koxinga.[49] After finally quelling internal rebellion and piracy along the coast, the K'ang-hsi emperor in 1685 declared all coastal ports open to foreign trade, and for the next seventy years traders from several Western countries traded at Ningpo, Chusan, and Amoy, as well as at Canton and Macao. This early period was characterized by struggle among the Chinese officials for shares of the illicit rake-off from the foreign trade and struggle between the officials and the foreign merchants over the terms and conditions of trade.[50]

Regarding crimes committed on Chinese soil by Westerners during the period from 1685 to 1744, the Chinese local officials do not appear to have followed any clear and uniform policy concerning the scope of jurisdiction to be exercised or to have adopted any special principles or procedures to be applied to the trial and disposition of alien offenders. The only references to the handling of violations of Ch'ing law and order by Westerners prior to 1743 are contained in Western records, chiefly in the records of the British East India Company, edited by Hosea Ballou Morse.[51] The absence of any mention of such cases in the Chinese records kept locally or in Peking suggests that the Chinese local officials were covering up their inability to enforce the law or their use of such occasions to extort illegal payments from the foreign merchants. Obviously, they would not be inclined to report such transactions to their superiors in Peking.

The earliest recorded serious case occurred in 1689 when officers and men from the East India Company's merchant ship, the *Defence*, opened fire on a Chinese military officer after an altercation over return of the company ship's mainmast, which had been removed by the Chinese in accordance with an established rule designed to control the behavior of foreign sailors and insure payment of customs fees.[52] One Chinese soldier was killed and eight Englishmen, including the ship's doctor, were detained in jail. The company record states that the English sent a supercargo (commercial agent aboard ship) named Watts ashore to offer 2,000 taels to settle the affair "but the Mandarins insisted on 5,000 Taels; which the supercargoes refusing, Watts was detained, and there being no prospect of the Mandarins lowering their demand, the Ship sailed. . . ."[53] There is no mention in the records of the subsequent fate of the nine Englishmen left behind. However, the incident obviously was not forgotten, for when several East India Company ships went to Canton to trade in 1715, they presented the following demand to the customs official known as the "Hoppo":[54] "that if their English servants should commit any disorder or fault deserving punishment, the Chinese should not take upon them to punish, but should complain to the supracargoes, and they would see them sufficiently punished according to the crime."[55]

Before jumping to the conclusion that Chinese acquiescence in this demand represents early and convincing proof of their official willingness to concede extraterritorial criminal jurisdiction to Westerners in China, let us look at the next serious case to disturb the Canton trade, a homicide which occurred at the Whampoa anchorage near Canton in 1721, when a Chinese subject was fatally shot by a seaman from the English ship *Bonitta*.[56] Although the record implies that the shooting was accidental, the entire body of English traders and sailors were apprehensive of being held criminally responsible for the unintentional act of an unidentified individual, for the supercargoes of another English ship, the *Cadogan*, state: "so arbitrary are the Laws, or the abuse of those Laws, in this Country, that our friends the China Merchants have advised us to keep within doors, and not stir out for some days, for fear of being mobbed or taken up by the Mandarins, contrary to all reason and justice."[57] Their fear proved well founded for, about two weeks later, an officer and four sailors from the *Cadogan* were seized and carried away by soldiers acting under the order of the provincial commander-in-chief of the Chinese Army of the Green Standard. The English supercargoes complained to the Hoppo, telling him that if the men were not released the English would cease trading at Canton and that English warships might be ordered from India if the Chinese authorities were to persist in denying justice to the English traders.[58] This dual threat was apparently successful in bringing about the release of the prisoners and the dismissal of the commander-in-chief.

Here again the records fail to tell us whether any formal investigation of the shooting ever took place or whether the English paid any compensation to the family of the deceased Chinese. This case is, nevertheless, quite significant for it illustrates some problems which remained central to the Sino-Western dispute over criminal jurisdiction for the remainder of the pretreaty period.

First we note, in the statement about "fear of being mobbed," that the English were already aware of xenophobia among the Chinese masses. This antiforeign feeling played a major role in the formulation of rules regulating foreign movement and life so as to minimize contact between the barbarians and the Chinese people. Intense local feeling also strongly influenced the handling of individual cases, forcing the Chinese authorities to take a hard line in punishing "vicious barbarian killers" (*hsiung-i*). Perhaps even more important in shaping the opinion of the foreign community about Chinese law and contributing ultimately to the English resolve not to submit to it was the principle of collective responsibility. For many serious crimes, the Ch'ing Criminal Code imposed harsh sanctions not only upon the offender himself but also upon his close relatives—and, sometimes, even upon his neighbors. The fact that these statutes had never been applied to Westerners did not lessen the Westerners' distaste for the principle and their fear that it might be applied to them in the future. Moreover, there were numerous instances when the Chinese authorities detained innocent foreigners as hostages to force surrender of the real suspect. Although the hostages were not subjected to any punishment beyond detention, they were deprived of their freedom—sometimes for several days—and were placed in considerable danger of bodily harm from the aroused local populace.

Another interesting aspect of the *Bonitta* case is the appearance of a tactic which in later years was employed by both the Chinese and English in disputes over trade or legal jurisdiction, namely, resort to the dual threat of cessation of trade and the use of armed force. The intervention of the commander-in-chief and his subsequent dismissal illustrate yet another feature of the early disputes over the proper disposition of cases involving disorderly acts by aliens—the confusion resulting from the failure of the Ch'ing government to make clear which local officials had authority to act in cases involving aliens. This confusion hampered the handling of trade disputes as well as the disposition of criminal cases.

In hopes of protecting themselves from extortion as well as from collective criminal responsibility, the company supercargoes in 1729 procured the Hoppo's assent to an extraterritoriality provision even broader than the ineffective agreement of 1715. The 1729 agreement states that: "if any of our people should be found to be the Aggressors in any broils . . . , we ourselves only shall inflict such punishments upon them as they shall deserve and according to the laws of our country."[59] It is clear from measures taken by the Chinese authorities in subsequent jurisdictional disputes that they did not consider themselves bound by either the 1715 or 1729 agreements made by the Hoppo with the company supercargoes; indeed, neither agreement is reported or even mentioned in the Chinese records. It seems probable that the Hoppo, whose function was to administer customs regulations, did not possess authority to make agreements relating to criminal jurisdiction. It is even more apparent, as we shall see below, that the supercargoes were making a promise that they had no legal authority to fulfill.[60]

The next recorded homicide involving a European occurred in 1736, when a Frenchman while hunting accidentally shot and killed a Chinese. The English company's record states that: "The Mandarins . . . insisted on their [the French] delivering up one of their people, which they did, and he has been in prison ever since, tho' noways concerned in the Affair."[61] Also, the chief of the French trading establishment, a man named Devulaer, was arrested and placed in close confinement and was threatened with torture if he would not confess. Although he was eventually released upon intercession of the governor-general, there is no record of what happened to the other detained Frenchman.

As for less serious offenses committed by Europeans in this early period, the practice of the Chinese authorities appears to have been to allow or even encourage settlement out of court. For example, in 1735 a British sailor on sentry duty wounded a Chinese woman; she was treated by the ship's doctor and the Chinese authorities refrained from intervening.[62] In 1739, there again occurred a similar case of wounding not followed by any official intervention by the Chinese; however, on this occasion the English merchants were unofficially required to pay the injured party a sizeable sum of money to avoid trouble.[63] It was not unusual for peaceful resolution of such matters to be facilitated by payment of monetary compensation, part of the sum often going to the officials and part to the injured party.

Establishment of the Restrictive Canton System

By the 1740s, the English merchants had already taken over the lion's share of the Canton trade and in addition had begun a vigorous effort to "open up China" to expanded foreign trade under conditions that would insure a steady and lucrative profit as well as security of the person and property of resident Europeans. The English became increasingly frustrated during the 1740s and early 1750s because of the numerous unofficial exactions levied on foreign trade by the various local officials, who regarded an assignment in Canton as their once-in-a-lifetime chance to amass a personal fortune.[64] The confusion of responsibilities due to the duplication of officials' functions connected with foreign trade in Canton, coupled with widespread corruption and the increasing difficulty of access to the higher officials, led the English merchants in the mid- and late 1750s to take the unprecedented (and illegal) step of attempting to present directly to the emperor a petition outlining their grievances and asking for punishment of the corrupt local officials and the establishment of a regular tariff and other rules for improving the trade and living conditions of the Europeans in Canton.[65] The effort partially succeeded since several local officials were dismissed. However, no greater freedom of trade or personal freedom of movement resulted. Instead, the British complaints about confusion and corruption led to a series of imperial edicts establishing strict rules for the conduct of trade with Europeans and even rules to regulate their style of living and manner of recreation.

Among the regulations comprising this so-called Canton System were the following: all Western trade was limited to the port of Canton; Westerners were forbidden to stay throughout the year in Canton—they had to return to Europe or else reside in Macao during the off-season; all Westerners trading at Canton had to live and transact their business in restricted "factory" areas leased from a Chinese merchant—they were not allowed to go into the city of Canton for any reason; Westerners were not allowed to bring foreign women with them to Canton; Westerners at Canton and Macao were prohibited from sending letters into the interior of China to obtain market information or to communicate with foreign missionaries; Westerners were required to conduct all communication with the Chinese authorities via the "hong merchants," a limited group of Chinese merchants licensed to conduct foreign trade; Chinese merchants could not borrow money from the foreign merchants; each foreign ship's payment of fees and compliance with port regulations was guaranteed by one of the hong merchants who was considered that ship's "security merchant"; finally, the security merchant (*pao-shang*), the linguist (*t'ung-shih*), and the comprador (a merchant responsible for supply and repair of foreign ships) were made responsible for compliance with all Chinese laws and regulations by the officers and men of the foreign ships with which they were doing business, and the foreign taipan and the supercargoes of the foreign ships were made responsible for "restraining" (*t'an-ya*) the boisterous crew and for surrendering any sailor guilty of killing a Chinese.[66]

Although many foreign traders, especially the English, were alarmed by this development and predicted that the result would be to place them so completely at the mercy of the Canton officials and hong merchants that they would go bankrupt, in fact trade continued to prosper and expand. No less an authority than Captain Charles Elliot, who held an appointment as His Majesty's Superintendent of Trade in China during the 1830s, summed up seventy years of Sino-British trade in a communiqué to the British foreign secretary, Lord Palmerston. Elliott stated that under the Canton System the Chinese government had in effect guaranteed the payment of the Chinese merchants' debts to the foreign trading community, as the *quid pro quo* for the privations the foreigners were forced to suffer in abiding by the restrictive rules promulgated in the mid-eighteenth century.[67]

Serious disturbances of the peace by foreign sailors in the first quarter of a century after the establishment of the Canton System appear to have been kept to a minimum by mutual efforts. The Chinese authorities posted soldiers near the foreign factories to keep away the hostile antiforeign Canton populace, and the foreign taipans urged ship captains to keep their "liberty men" under control.[68] After fighting between French and English sailors in 1754, which resulted in the death of an Englishman, the Chinese authorities had assigned what came to be known as "French Island" to the French for recreational purposes and "Dane Island" to the English and Danes.[69]

Small groups of foreign sailors were allowed to go to Canton to visit curio shops on the street in front of the foreign factories and, since sailors are always thirsty, drunkenness was the usual condition of the sailors on liberty at Canton. Thus, brawls with the Chinese were a frequent occurrence, but the Chinese soldiers assigned to the foreign detail usually put a quick stop to any such fights. If any Chinese were injured, a small cash payment would in most cases keep them from reporting the incident to the local authorities. In 1781, however, the European community at Canton was confronted with a potentially serious situation when a 12-year-old English cabin boy accidentally killed a Chinese man who was teasing him. Because the boy was a minor, the ship's Chinese security merchant was able to persuade the local officials not to suspend English trade or demand surrender of the boy for Chinese trial.[70]

The Lady Hughes *Case and the Subsequent British Resolve to Resist Chinese Criminal Jurisdiction*

The most serious threat to Sino-foreign relations at Canton in the latter half of the eighteenth century occurred in 1784 when a gunner from the *Lady Hughes*, a country ship[71] from Bombay lying at the Whampoa anchorage, fired a gun salute that happened to kill two minor Chinese officials.[72] When Chinese officials the next day paid a visit to Mr. Pigou, chairman of the East India Company's Council of Supercargoes[73] at Canton, and demanded that the gunner be surrendered to the Chinese authorities for investigation of the incident, Mr. Pigou replied that the gunner had absconded.[74] When the Chinese demand was repeated the following day, Mr. Pigou said that the council possessed no authority over private ships, adding that: "Mr. George Smith, Supra Cargo of the *Lady Hughes*, was better qualified to give them the satisfaction they required.

. . ."[75] Seeing that Mr. Pigou was unwilling to comply with their demand, the Chinese officials followed his advice and directed their attention to Mr. Smith. On November 27th, he was enticed out of his factory and was seized and carried into the city of Canton.

The Chinese authorities then barricaded the streets leading to the factories, stationed soldiers in the vicinity, ordered all Chinese to leave the factories and cut off communications between the Canton factories and the foreign ships at Whampoa.[76] All trade with the factories was stopped; for this reason, and because they were afraid for their own personal safety, the French, Dutch, Danes, and Americans all rallied behind the British. Each of them ordered armed boats up from Whampoa to Canton; the boats arrived in the evening of November 27th—although they were fired upon and two men wounded, the foreign boats complied with orders of the foreign supercargoes directing them not to return the Chinese fire.

On the same evening, the supercargoes were given the following mandate from Governor Sun Shih-i:

> A Native of this Country having been killed by a gun fired from the Ship of Captain Williams, whether by accident or design it is necessary that this Man should appear before me for examination that he may be tried conformably to our Laws; nevertheless Mr. Smith who is detained in the City is very prudent and discreet, he has consented to write to Whampoa to demand this Gunner that he may appear before our Tribunal & I can return Mr. Smith to you as soon as this Gunner shall arrive . . . if you dare in our country to disobey & infringe our Laws, consider well that you may not repent when it is too late.[77]

On the morning of the 28th, the councils of all the nations jointly protested Mr. Smith's detention and demanded his release, saying that Mr. Smith's presence at Canton on the 24th "withdraws from him all suspicion of his being anywise to blame."[78] Morse correctly points out that: "This was besides the mark. The Governor did not hold Mr. Smith responsible for the occurrence, but only for producing the gunner who was personally responsible; and he held the Chief of the English Company's Council responsible for Mr. Smith's compliance."[79]

The governor soon showed himself to be adept at applying the traditional tactic of divide and rule. On the afternoon of the 28th of November, a mandarin informed the representatives of all nations except the English that all who agreed to send their armed boats back to Whampoa could immediately resume trade; that evening, the governor invited the same representatives to his official residence, where he regally entertained them, gave them presents, and assured them that Smith would not be harmed and would be released as soon as the gunner was given up.[80]

All except the Americans thereupon deserted the English and the next day resumed trade with the Chinese. The English seem to have given up at that point for, on the 29th, they forwarded to the *Lady Hughes* a letter from Smith requesting that the gunner be given up; on the same day, Pigou himself ordered the captain of the *Lady Hughes* to surrender the gunner to the Chinese.[81]

On November 30th, the gunner was accordingly given up by Captain Williams and brought to the Canton factory; he was then turned over to a high-ranking Chinese official who said that he:

> desired the Gentlemen present not to be uneasy respecting his fate, that nothing should be done till the Emperor's pleasure shall be known, & care would be taken to represent his case in the most favourable light, & he had no doubt that in about 60 days[82] he would be sent back again. In about an
>
> Hour . . . Mr. Smith arrived at the factory & gave a very satisfactory account of the Treatment he met with & the Civilities received from the several Mandareens most of whom visited him and sent him presents.[83]

The embargo on trade with the English was removed on December 6, 1784, after having been in force for nine days, and the *Lady Hughes* sailed on the 7th, leaving the gunner in Chinese custody.

Meanwhile, the foreign community at Canton had returned to their preoccupation with commerce, congratulating themselves on what everyone felt was an honorable conclusion to a dangerous crisis. They were totally unprepared when, on January 8th, two representatives of each nation, together with all the hong merchants, were summoned before the provincial judicial commissioner, who told them that the emperor: "was displeased that the [English] had delayed for five days to deliver up the gunner who had killed his subjects . . . [and that] the Government had been extremely moderate in demanding one for the lives of two of its subjects. . . . We were afterwards informed that this unhappy Man had been strangled at about the time we were receiving the above recited admonition."[84]

This is the end of the factual account as contained in Western sources. Chinese sources, however, supply a document of critical importance which apparently was not available to any Westerners who have previously commented on the *Lady Hughes* case.[85] This document is the imperial edict directing Governor Sun Shih-i to execute the gunner.[86] It clearly reveals that Governor Sun had not been deceitful when he assured the foreigners that the case would be represented "in the most favourable light." In cases of homicides of Chinese by aliens, we have seen how in 1744 an abbreviated procedure was established, providing for a memorial to the emperor only *after* execution of the offender, following review and approval of the district magistrate's recommendation by the governor-general. The reason why the governor here first memorialized the emperor is that he proposed a finding of accidental homicide and release of the offender upon payment of the nominal statutory compensation of 12.2 taels to the victims' families. Obviously, the governor's proposed sentence was disapproved by the emperor.

To explain this reversal of Sun's recommendation, we must look beyond the usual procedure for handling alien homicides of Chinese and search for an explanation in the broader arena of the domestic political context. Of special significance is the antiforeign attitude that prevailed at the Ch'ing court in late 1784 and early 1785. This attitude reflected heightened concern in Peking over illegal penetration by European missionaries into the interior of China.[87] Fu-k'ang-an, a leading general and a henchman of the infamous minister Ho Shen, had just succeeded in putting down a serious Moslem revolt; apparently the emperor was afraid that similar unrest might result from the activities of the Western missionaries. Thus, the Chinese government had instituted a ruthless policy of suppression of all foreign missionaries in the provinces;[88] an important step in implementing this policy was prevention of the entry into China of additional missionaries.

Stern treatment of the *Lady Hughes* gunner was calculated to intimidate the foreign community and to deter them from again assisting missionaries to enter the interior. The handling of this case illustrates the principle that all infractions of Chinese law by aliens were considered not simply as violations of the law by an individual but as potentially explosive problems in foreign relations. Thus, the handling of alien cases was frequently influenced by political considerations, such as local feeling against foreigners or a general fear of missionary subversion. The influence of the latter factor is reflected in the Ch'ien-lung emperor's statement that: "at the present time, when we are in the midst of investigating and suppressing foreign missionary activity, it is all the more fitting that the law should be strictly enforced."[89]

After the 1785 execution of the *Lady Hughes'* gunner for what the British considered to be accidental homicide, the Council of Supercargoes wrote to the East India Company's Court of Directors in London, stating their resolve never again to submit to Chinese criminal jurisdiction and requesting the court's approval of a procedure whereby: "in case of murder, the perpetrator should be tried by us, in the presence of a Chinese magistrate; that if he be found guilty he should be delivered up; but, if innocent, then we should be allowed to protect him . . . in case the delinquents have really escaped, no substitute shall be demanded."[90] In its reply to the above letter, the Court of Directors: "censured the supercargoes for their conduct in the affair and told them that resistance to the Chinese government was useless, that they had absolute power to seize Private traders and jurisdiction over country ships . . . that in cases of murder they were to aid the Chinese officials in apprehending the criminal."[91] However, it is important to note that "measures were nevertheless set afoot in England to carry out the recommendations of the supercargoes."[92]

Although the general opinion prevailing in England during the period between the *Lady Hughes* case and the Opium War (1839-1842) appeared to be in sympathy with the plea for the immediate establishment of an English court in China, the consensus among government leaders and legal experts seemed to be that, under current international law, no competent court could be legally established unless China had signified its approval in a binding international agreement.[93] The securing of such approval was one of the chief goals of both the aborted Cathcart Embassy in 1788 and the Macartney Embassy in 1793. In the official instruction to Lt. Col. Cathcart, who was appointed a royal ambassador commissioned to adjust the difficulties affecting British trade in China, it is stated that:

> Our supercargoes are denied open access to the tribunals of the Country and the Fair Execution of its laws, and are kept altogether in a most arbitrary and cruel state of depression incompatible with the very important concerns which are intrusted to them and such as one hardly supposes could be exercised in any country that pretends to Civilization. . . . Whether these Evils have arisen from any settled Policy of the Imperial Government or . . . whether they are created merely by the corruption and Abuses of a distant Provincial Administration it be Your Business to ascertain.[94]

Lt. Col. Cathcart was also directed to negotiate for the cession of a depot for the storage of trade goods; he was to seek Chinese agreement that within the depot British subjects would be subject to British law and the English chief would be held responsible only for his own actions.[95] Lord Macartney in 1793 was also instructed to negotiate cession of a depot where the British would exercise: "[criminal] jurisdiction over our own dependents for which competent powers would be given so as effectively to prevent or punish the disorder of our own people which the Company's Supracargoes in their limited sphere of action must see committed with impunity."[96]

This passage reveals a British aim that was unrealized until the Treaty of Nanking was concluded in 1842—the aim of obtaining from the Chinese government formal agreement to British exercise of criminal jurisdiction over acts of British subjects connected with the China trade.

It also identifies the major cause of future controversy—while the British in China refused to submit to Chinese jurisdiction, no resident British representative possessed sufficient powers to exercise criminal jurisdiction over British subjects.[97] The result was a dangerous power vacuum—the British representatives on the scene frequently supported their refusal to surrender criminals to the Chinese with a promise to punish them in accordance with British law, either aboard an English vessel or upon return to England. This was a promise they were never legally competent to fulfill.[98] Thus, there is no record of a single instance of a British subject being punished in England for a crime committed against Chinese in China prior to 1842.[99]

The English refusal to surrender suspects to the Chinese for trial and their efforts at the intergovernmental level to secure formal concession of extraterritoriality were met on the Chinese side by continuing insistence on investigation and punishment of alien homicides of Chinese and by the evolution of a procedure for handling alien criminal cases which differed to some extent from the Macao procedure discussed above. The Liang-Kuang governor-general, Juan Yuan, in 1821 described the procedure for handling alien criminal cases outside of Macao as follows:

> We note that with barbarian ships anchored for long periods in Kwangtung waters, quarrels resulting in wounding and deaths are a frequent occurrence. Since the Chinese officials and clerks do not understand the barbarian tongue, the procedure hitherto in handling such cases had been to order [*tse-ling*] the taipan of the country involved to search out the actual offender [*cheng-hsiung*] and interrogate him carefully. The guilty barbarian is then surrendered to the Chinese authorities and brought to the provincial capital with a linguist for interrogation, recording of his testimony, adjudication, and handling of his case.[100]

Notice of Law and the Problem of Communication Generally

One of the most important elements in the Western concept of due process of law is the requirement of notice—the idea that a person must have actual or constructive notice before he is considered bound by a legal rule. It may come as a surprise to the reader to learn that in regard to acts committed by aliens on Chinese soil, the Ch'ing government also appears to have adhered to the principle of notice. The rule of giving notice to aliens was cited with approval in Wang K'en-tang's *Chien-shih* commentary to the Ch'ing Penal Code, where it is stated that: "It is proper to treat leniently [*k'uan-ch'u*] aliens who have newly settled [*hsin-fu*] in China and are not yet familiar with the laws [*wei-chih fa-tu*]."[101]

The emperor frequently issued instructions to the "outer barbarians" to obey Chinese law and refrain from committing violent and disorderly acts. Such instructions were communicated in writing to the foreign community via the local officials and the hong merchants. Furthermore, the regulations comprising the restrictive Canton System, discussed above, were reissued annually and were posted outside the foreign factories as a reminder.[102] Also mentioned above was the public posting of the Conventional Pact of 1749, which established rules for the administration of Macao.

In disposing of individual cases of alien violations of Chinese law, the emperor more than once exempted the offending alien from punishment and allowed retention of illegally acquired property because the alien had not received actual notice of the pertinent law.[103] Finally, in at least two cases, arising in 1800 and 1821 respectively, the Liang-Kuang governor-general ordered pertinent extracts from the Ch'ing Penal Code to be copied out and communicated to the English taipan.[104] In the latter case, the governor-general ordered the statutes on "Jurisdiction over aliens" (*hua-wai-jen*), "Homicide in a fight" (*tou-ou sha-jen*), and "Policemen killing in self-defense an offender resisting arrest" (*ko-sha*) to be translated and sent to the English taipan "for the instruction of the barbarians."[105]

Although a desire to smoothly control the barbarians and avoid disruptive incidents was probably the primary motive for the Ch'ing policy of transmitting to the foreign community "enlightening instructions" (*hsiao-yü*) advising them of the rules and sanctions applicable to them, the traditional Confucian preference for moral education and reform of the individual, instead of application of harsh punitive sanctions, is suggested by statements such as that made by Imperial Commissioner Lin Tse-hsü in his 1839 letter to Queen Victoria. In commenting on the law providing the death penalty for foreign opium smugglers, he said: "the emperor cannot bear to execute people without having first tried to reform them by instruction."[106]

The reader may also be surprised to learn that, at least by the mid-eighteenth century, the rules and other notices promulgated for the benefit of the Westerners in Canton were not simply pasted on the wall in the Chinese language but were delivered, translated, and fairly well understood by the European community. There were, however, still many edicts, such as the one approving the 1744 procedure, which were for official eyes only and were not transmitted to the foreigners. Nevertheless, the records of the East India Company, edited by Morse, contain numerous translations of imperial edicts, as well as translations of locally promulgated rules. Comparison of some of these translations with the original Chinese document reveals that most of the translations are faithful renderings of the original; some are superbly done.

The foreign community in Canton came to an early realization of the vital importance of training some of their own people in the Chinese language. In the first place, the Chinese who served as "linguists" were usually lacking in any real proficiency in any foreign language.[107] Second, they were afraid to translate literally anything that might offend the reader and bring loss of face or, worse, disaster to themselves. Consequently, the foreign community seems to have relied mostly on European translators and interpreters even before the time of such competent and well-known experts as Sir George T. Staunton and Robert Morrison.[108] One of the earliest Europeans to learn Chinese was James Flint who, after arriving in China in 1736, spent three years studying Mandarin. Thereupon, he served the East India Company in Canton as interpreter-translator until 1759, when the Chinese Government sentenced him to three years in jail for presenting a grievance petition directly to the emperor's representatives at Tientsin.[109]

Sino-British Struggle over Criminal Jurisdiction, 1785-1839

It is important for us to know how well informed the Western traders were about the rules promulgated to regulate their life and business, for the stubborn refusal—especially by England—to comply with Chinese laws cannot be attributed to ignorance but must rather be ascribed to a real aversion to certain principles and values embodied in the Chinese laws. Chief among the Chinese legal principles considered incompatible with English legal thought of the time was the principle of collective responsibility—the notion that various social groupings, rather than the individual alone, should be held accountable for the acts of an individual.[110] Thus, in regard to the European trade, the Chinese security merchant, the linguist, the foreign taipan, and occasionally the foreign ship's supercargo and captain were all deemed responsible for detecting and surrendering for Chinese trial offenders guilty of homicide against a Chinese subject. Moreover, the entire foreign community was besieged on one occasion (the *Lady Hughes* case) in order to compel surrender of a suspect, and on several occasions the Chinese authorities suspended trade to force the surrender of an alien offender.

Another factor that contributed substantially to the British resolve after 1784 never again to surrender an Englishman for unsupervised trial by the Chinese authorities was the broad variance between the Chinese and English substantive law of homicide.[111] English disenchantment is reflected in the following statement made by the East India Company's Canton Select Committee in 1806 when reporting a case to London: "the Chinese laws . . . are not only very arbitrary and corruptly administered, but founded on a system in many respects incompatible with European ideas of equity or justice."[112]

Furthermore, as the Select Committee stated in 1810, there were six kinds of homicide cases in which the Chinese authorities would demand surrender of an alien offender for almost certain execution:

> (1) In cases where a Chinese may be killed entirely accidentally as from a gun unintentionally going off or otherwise.
> (2) In cases where a Chinese is killed by an European who is acting in self defence or against an attack of robbery or a Chinese being killed on entering either a ship or house by night in order to steal.
> (3) Where a Chinese is killed by an European acting in the execution of his duty as centinal watchman or the like. A case similar to this occurred in 1800 when Capt. Dilkes was in China.
> (4) In cases of affray where from the numbers engaged it may be impossible to fix on the offender. Similar to this was the discussion in 1807 relative to the seamen of the *Neptune*.
> (5) In cases where there may be presumptive proof of guilt but such as would not be deemed sufficient to convict a man by the English law.
> (6) In cases where wilful murder is clearly proved. In these indeed our orders already direct explicitly the immediate delivery up of the offender.[113]

Since they were firm in refusing to surrender anyone but a known murderer (a possibility that remained hypothetical), members of the English trading community employed various stratagems to circumvent Chinese efforts to assert criminal jurisdiction. They frequently demonstrated their readiness to resort to any ruse or device, no matter how illegal or unethical, in order to avoid turning a British subject over to the Chinese judicial authorities. For example, in 1817, when advising English ship captains to resist a get-tough policy of the Chinese authorities who had ordered a search of all foreign ships at Whampoa (well inside Chinese internal waters) to detect illegally smuggled opium, the English Select Committee questioned the right of the Chinese government to enforce laws that had long gone unenforced. In support of its stand, the Select Committee used the following curious argument: "as in China custom alone is referred to by the government as their guide and rule, when the repeal of absurd and unjust restrictions is asked by foreigners, it is at least equitable that the reference to this standard be reciprocal, and that it is therefore our duty to oppose all innovations of a restrictive nature, upon a trade already too confined and oppressed."[114]

The English ingenuity, and purse, were constantly being taxed due to the fact that: "disorderly behavior of the seamen and especially their frequent ill-treatment of the Chinese has been such as to keep us in a constant state of alarm and apprehension . . ."[115] and due to the lack of adequate English police powers for preventing such irregularities. *Yamen* policemen were assigned by the Chinese to patrol the waters around the foreign ships to suppress (*t'an-ya*) the rowdy barbarian sailors, but obviously they were not very effective.

Two cases of British sailors wounding Chinese in 1787 and 1794 were concluded without serious repercussions because the English doctors nursed the victims out of danger and the English taipan paid them money to compensate them and to purchase their silence.[116] Homicides, however, were far more complex, in view of the official policy of insisting on jurisdiction, and because the relatives of the victim had a moral obligation to exact retribution from the offender.

The first homicide to disturb the English trading community at Canton after the *Lady Hughes* case was the H.M.S. *Providence* case in 1800.[117] A British sentry shot at a boat carrying two Chinese who apparently intended to cut the ship's cable while it was anchored at Whampoa. One of the Chinese was wounded and the other drowned trying to escape. A lengthy dispute over surrender of the British sailor finally ended with an inquiry presided over by the provincial judicial commissioner (*nieh-ssu*) and attended by several foreigners, including Captain Dilkes of the H.M.S. *Madras*, the English taipan, and Sir George Staunton. The *nieh-ssu* refused to allow Staunton to participate as interpreter, in spite of the obvious incompetence of the Chinese linguist. Nevertheless, the crisis was surmounted without capitulation or loss of trade, due to the survival of the wounded man beyond the statutory forty-day period of responsibility (*pao-ku hsien*). The governor-general ruled that the drowning was completely accidental, so the accused English sailor was deemed guilty only of the offense of wounding in a fight. Thus, he was ordered by the *nieh-ssu* to be deported from China for appropriate punishment in England.

Another interesting aspect of the *Providence* case was the eviction of Staunton and Captain Dilkes from the courtroom for attempting to introduce evidence tending to prove that the wounded man had been involved in a robbery attempt. The *nieh-ssu* was amazed at the gall of the English devils who attempted to take the initiative in a court proceeding.

In 1807 there occurred another difficult homicide case, when a gang of English sailors from the *Neptune* fought a mob of Chinese, killing two of them.[118] Trade was stopped by the Chinese authorities in an effort to compel surrender of the killers but the English taipan pleaded that in such a confused brawl it was impossible to determine who struck the fatal blows. Finally, after considerable pressure and lengthy negotiations, the English leader agreed to join with the Chinese local officials in conducting an investigation. Although the English observers, again including Staunton, reported that no conclusive evidence was introduced to prove that any of the sailors examined had struck a fatal blow, the Chinese officials finally selected one sailor as a scapegoat. However, they convicted him not of the capital offense of killing in a fight but of the redeemable offense of accidental homicide,[119] supporting their decision with a completely fictitious story for the benefit of the emperor. They thus cooled down the crisis with the English and reopened trade, also saving themselves from administrative sanctioning by "apprehending and punishing the offender." The story concocted by the local officials did not fool everyone. The local populace, already hostile toward Europeans for decades, was incensed at this lenient treatment of a barbarian killer, and numerous placards sprang up all over the city of Canton, accusing the officials of selling out to the foreign devils.[120]

The next homicide occurred in 1810, when a Chinese was fatally stabbed at Whampoa, apparently by an unidentified sailor from an English ship, the *Royal Charlotte.*[121] In response to the Chinese demand for surrender of the killer, which was backed up by an order suspending trade with the English, the captain of the *Royal Charlotte* simply sailed away without a port clearance, promising to have the offender punished in England in accordance with English law.[122] Trade was restored only after a long and costly interruption; as for the offender, there is no record that he was even brought to trial in England, much less convicted and punished.

In 1820, the Select Committee—through a stroke of luck—quickly ended a difficult impasse over surrender of a sailor who accidentally shot and killed a Chinese.[123] When the butcher on another ship committed suicide at about the same time, the English led the investigating Chinese officials to believe that he had killed himself out of remorse for causing the death of the Chinese. In his memorial to the emperor, the governor-general stated that for the offense of recklessly firing a gun and thereby causing the death of a Chinese subject the alien offender should be sentenced to decapitation after the assizes (*chan chien-hou*) under the provisions governing intentional homicide (*ku-sha*); however, since the offender became afraid of punishment (*wei-tsui*) and cut his own throat, his case should not be further considered (*ying wu-yung-i*).[124] As for the other English sailors present at the scene of the shooting, they should each be given 80 blows of the heavy bamboo for doing what ought not to be done (*pu-ying-wei*) in not reporting the offense immediately; but since they were barbarians, they should be turned over to the English barbarian headman for execution of the punishment (*fa-lo*).

The following year there occurred the case of Francis Terranova, an Italian sailor aboard an American ship, the *Emily*; he was accused of killing a Chinese woman who had come to the ship to sell fruit.[125] The Americans at first refused to surrender the accused but, after the Chinese authorities imprisoned the *Emily*'s security merchant, the Americans agreed to have the Chinese officials conduct a trial aboard ship. The

Chinese finally assented to this compromise procedure and the trial was held. However, according to the American reports, the accused was not given an opportunity to defend himself or to rebut any of the patently false testimony of the Chinese witnesses. For this reason, the American captain refused to turn over Terranova after the trial. Only after the Chinese authorities assured him that the accused would be given a fair trial in Canton did the ship captain acquiesce and surrender him.

According to the governor-general's memorial, which dutifully cites the Code provision on alien jurisdiction as well as the 1744 Macao procedure, Terranova's subsequent conviction under the statute governing homicide in a fight was based upon a confession.[126] But, judging by the poor quality of the Chinese linguists (no Europeans were allowed at Terranova's Canton trial), the unfortunate sailor probably did not realize what he had signed until he was led to the execution ground and strangled.

The English expressed horror at the weakness the Americans displayed in thus submitting to the Chinese. They also predicted that the American capitulation would cause the Chinese officials to take a hard line in dealing with the entire foreign community in Canton.[127] None of the English accounts, however, discuss what may have been the real reason why the Americans gave in: the *Emily* was unloading a cargo of illegal opium and she could ill afford to take a firm stand in demanding a just execution of the Chinese laws.[128]

The Terranova case was followed three months later by another homicide case, in which sailors from an English warship, H.M.S. *Topaze*, went ashore on Lintin Island for water and got into a brawl with villagers which resulted in the death of two Chinese.[129] Captain Richardson of the *Topaze* refused the Chinese demand for surrender of the responsible sailors and instead made a counter-accusation against the villagers for provoking a fight that led to the wounding of fourteen English sailors. The governor-general was adamant in his demand; he followed the customary steps of suspending English trade and putting pressure on the English taipan. The taipan disclaimed responsibility for actions of the crew of the "king's ships" but, fearing nevertheless that he might be seized as a hostage, withdrew himself and the entire English trading community aboard ship and threatened to leave China with empty holds if the governor-general did not retract his demand.

The crisis was finally resolved in the same way as the 1810 case; the warship just sailed away, promising to turn the offender over to the English authorities for trial and punishment. The governor-general reopened trade on the taipan's promise to see that the offenders were returned on the next ship from England to China for punishment. The fact that the offenders were never returned was frequently alluded to in private appeals lodged by the victim's relatives and in memorials submitted by advocates of a hard-line policy for controlling the Europeans at Canton.[130]

The problem of controlling English sailors became even more difficult in the late 1820s and early 1830s. The "free merchants," British nationals who challenged the East India Company's monopoly of the China trade, denied company police power over sailors on their ships, and the increasingly numerous opium ships defied anyone's control.[131] In addition to these two groups, we have already noted that sailors on "king's ships" were not subject to the restraining influence of the company taipan. The structure developed within the tributary framework for controlling the foreigners clearly was beginning to break down.

The Chinese authorities frequently expressed serious doubt about whether punishment would ever be meted out to offenders once they had absconded or had been permitted to leave China;[132] this suspicion contributed to their insistence upon the surrender of Europeans suspected of killing Chinese. However, if the English government had allowed a British representative in China to exercise *de facto* judicial powers over British subjects—rather than do nothing because of a belief that such a practice would violate English or international law—the Chinese would probably have been less adamant in demanding surrender of English sailors suspected of killing a Chinese. The 1744 and 1749 Macao arrangements and the subsequent practice there indicate that the Chinese government was willing to compromise on the jurisdiction issue, provided arrangements were made to satisfy the basic requirements of maintenance of order and retribution for homicides of Chinese.

British Attempt Unilaterally to Establish an English Court in China

Actually, the British government in the 1830s did recognize the danger inherent in a situation where British subjects in China were beyond the control of any law; it realized that the termination of the East India Company's China trade monopoly in April 1834 would remove even the limited restraint that had been exercised by the company's Canton supercargoes. Thus, legislation was enacted in 1833 providing for the establishment of a British court in China with admiralty and criminal jurisdiction, to be presided over by the superintendent of trade in accordance with English law and procedure.[133]

The British government appreciated the questionable status of the court, which it had established without the consent of the Chinese government. Therefore, the first superintendent of trade, Lord Napier, was instructed to exercise his judicial powers with the greatest restraint. He also received the rather anomalous instruction that:

> we do require you constantly to bear in mind, and to impress, as occasion may offer, upon Our subjects resident in, or resorting to China,

the duty of conforming to the laws and usages of the Chinese Empire, so long as such laws shall be administered towards you and them with justice and good faith; and in the same manner in which the same are or shall be administered towards the subjects of China, or towards the subjects or citizens of other foreign nations resident in, or resorting to China.[134]

Neither Lord Napier nor the two succeeding superintendents, who served from 1834 to 1836, attempted to exercise the judicial powers conferred upon them by the 1833 legislation. However, the fourth superintendent, Captain Charles Elliot, being convinced that the Chinese authorities would welcome any arrangements for the maintenance of order among the British sailors, in 1837 formulated and promulgated a set of regulations for the preservation of order on the British ships at Whampoa.[135] These regulations were very short-lived, however, for the foreign secretary, Lord Palmerston, informed Elliot that the government's legal advisers were of the opinion that: "[such] regulations, within the dominions of the Emperor of China, would be an interference with the absolute right of sovereignty enjoyed by independent states, which can only be justified by positive treaty, or implied permission from usage."[136] Prior to receiving this instruction, Elliot had tried and sentenced to imprisonment several British sailors who had assaulted Chinese. These convictions were overturned by courts in England on the ground that Elliot's actions were inconsistent with China's sovereignty.[137]

The British government again in 1838 introduced legislation to establish a court in China with civil as well as admiralty and criminal jurisdiction. It was forced to withdraw the bill when the opposition demanded that the government first secure the agreement of the Chinese government.[138]

Sino-British relations in the late 1830s became increasingly bitter when the British government refused to cooperate with the efforts of the Chinese government to enforce its laws prohibiting the importation of opium,[139] which had assumed chief importance in Britain's China trade. It was now too late to reach a compromise solution of the jurisdiction question. Emotions had become inflamed, and both governments were forced into rigid positions.

The last act in the protracted Sino-British dispute over criminal jurisdiction took place in July 1839, when some drunken British sailors killed a Chinese named Lin Wei-hsi at Kowloon.[140] In response to Commissioner Lin Tse-hsü's repeated demands for surrender of the killer, Captain Elliot replied that it was against British policy and practice to comply with such a demand. However, he did conduct an investigation aboard an English ship; an indictment for murder was rejected, but several of the seamen were sentenced to imprisonment and fines for rioting.

When the sailors were returned to England, however, they were set free by the government on the ground that Captain Elliot had no judicial authority over English subjects in China.[141] Thus, the problem of control over criminal acts of British sailors in China was left unresolved until after the Opium War and the conclusion of the "extraterritorial treaties."

Cases Involving Aliens Only

The Ch'ing government's general policy of nonintervention in criminal cases not involving Chinese subjects has been mentioned already at the beginning of this chapter. An early application of this policy occurred in 1735, when six sailors from a Dutch ship wrecked on China's shore mutinied against their captain. The Chinese authorities requested the English to take custody of the six Dutch mutineers and detain them aboard an English ship pending the arrival of a Dutch ship to take them back to Holland for punishment.[142]

The real test of the policy of nonintervention, however, came in 1754 with the murder of an English sailor, Charles Brown, by a French officer.[143] Although the French urged the English to allow them to send the offender to France for trial, the English supercargoes had reason to believe that if they complied with the French request the aroused English sailors would mutiny and take the law into their own hands. Thus, they formally requested the Chinese authorities to investigate the case and punish the French officer. The Chinese governor-general reluctantly assumed jurisdiction only after vainly trying to persuade the English to withdraw their complaint. Shortly thereafter, a Frenchman—said by the English to be a scapegoat for the guilty officer—was surrendered to the Chinese, tried, and sentenced to death, but was detained in jail in Canton pending imperial approval of the sentence.

The Ch'ien-lung emperor, however, did not approve assertion of Chinese jurisdiction over the case, since it involved aliens only. Instead, he took advantage of the opportunity to reiterate the rule of nonintervention in clear and unmistakable terms:

> In the event that barbarians from the outer oceans fight and kill each other, we should not apply the law of our interior.
>
> We order that all affairs concerning this criminal, Shih-lei-shih, be handled by the ship of the French barbarians. Let the captain take him back to France. We shall write a letter to the chief of that barbarian country saying that according to our law, their criminal deserves to be strangled, but we will let him punish this criminal himself. The viceroy and governor of the province should firmly proclaim to all barbarians of the several countries represented at Canton, saying that hereaf-

> ter they should not commit crimes and cause incidents, that they should also appoint officers to suppress such criminals in order to teach them to fear our law and learn to maintain our peace while trading with us.[144]

When the above edict arrived at Canton, the French ship had already sailed, so the embarrassed governor-general had to keep the man in detention until the French trading ships returned the following year; he was then able to use the pretext of a general amnesty, fortuitously declared at that time, to announce that the prisoner was being released as a demonstration of the boundless grace and kindness of the emperor.[145] This chance development enabled the Chinese officials to avoid a public admission that they had mistakenly assumed jurisdiction over this case; however, it left a false impression with the foreign community that this case marked the beginning of a new Chinese policy of extending criminal jurisdiction over offenses involving only aliens.

This misunderstanding was further compounded in 1780 when the Chinese seized and executed a French sailor for the homicide of a Portuguese sailor at Canton.[146] The governor of Kwangtung issued a statement "justifying his action on the ground that he was responsible for the maintenance of good order and that he could have no assurance that the accused would be duly punished if he were sent to his own country for trial, as had been proposed."[147] Moreover, a brief summary of this case, contained in a private edition of the Ch'ing Penal Code, states that the killer was executed according to barbarian law (*chao i-fa ch'u-ssu*) at the place where the crime was committed.[148]

In keeping with the basic policy of nonintervention in cases involving aliens only, the Chinese officials had declined to get involved in a 1778 case involving a brawl between the British and the Dutch;[149] they similarly refused to take cognizance of a 1780 dispute between the British and the Danes.[150]

Nor did the Chinese authorities intervene in homicide cases arising in 1806, 1813, and 1814. In the first of these, a Spaniard serving aboard an English ship killed an English sailor while the two were in Canton on leave.[151] The killer was returned to England where he was tried and released after the court ruled it had no jurisdiction over the offense since it was committed neither on English soil nor on an English vessel on the high seas. The killer in the second case was likewise returned to England but the records do not indicate how his case was finally handled.[152] The 1814 case involved the murder of an English sailor at Macao by two Portuguese soldiers; the murderers gave themselves up to the Portuguese authorities, who put them in irons and sent them to Goa to stand trial.[153] Again, the result of the trial is not recorded.

Indeed, during the sixty-year period following the 1780 French-Portuguese homicide case, which the European community in China termed a "dire precedent," I have discovered only three recorded attempts by the Chinese to assume jurisdiction over a crime or dispute involving aliens only. The first case was the suicide of a Swiss mechanic in 1797; the Chinese district magistrate examined the corpse and, after verifying the fact that it was indeed a suicide, permitted the corpse to be buried.[154]

The second case occurred in 1814 when a Chinese military official ordered the chief of the East India Company's Select Committee to direct the captain of the British cruiser, H.M.S. *Doris*, to release an American prize ship which it had seized in violation of Chinese law.[155] The committee replied that, since the capture had taken place on the high seas southwest of the Grand Ladrone island, the matter was outside Chinese jurisdiction; America and Britain then being in a state of war, "by the law of nations, the capture was fully justified."[156] The American ship was then taken to the admiralty court in India for disposition, in defiance of the orders of the Chinese government. There is no record of any Chinese official reference to the English citation of international law on this occasion; nor did they expressly accept the British argument that the seizure took place outside Chinese jurisdiction. However, the Chinese were powerless to enforce compliance with their demand once the American ship had been taken to India.

Later, the *Doris* entered Chinese waters (*nei-yang*, lit. "inner sea") in pursuit of another American merchant vessel, following it as far as Whampoa.[157] Since this constituted a violation of the long-standing prohibition against foreign warships entering the *nei-yang*, the governor-general threatened to suspend the English trade unless the *Doris* withdrew to the outer sea (*wai-yang*).[158] The ranking British admiral subsequently ordered all English "king's ships" to "cause the same respect to be paid to the Neutrality of the Chinese Empire as is agreeable to the Laws of Nations and conformable to the Rulers of other Neutral States under similar circumstances."[159]

The last recorded case of an attempt by the Chinese to assert formal criminal jurisdiction over a crime between aliens was three Parsees' 1830 homicide of a British subject named Mackenzie.[160] According to the Western account of the case, the Chinese demand for surrender of the suspects was refused by Britain; they were sent to India for trial but were there released because the court ruled that British courts in India had no jurisdiction over crimes committed on Chinese soil.[161]

In the account of the Mackenzie case given in the governor-general's memorial to the emperor, however, it is stated that the barbarians hushed the matter up, buried the corpse, and sent the offenders to *Meng-mai-fu*

(Bombay) before the Chinese authorities learned of the homicide.[162] The governor-general reviewed past practice in handling homicides involving aliens only; noting that the previous cases had not been handled uniformly (*pan-li pu-i*), the governor-general declared in favor of asserting Chinese jurisdiction in the present case. Consequently, he launched an investigation and obtained from the Dutch taipan[163] the depositions made by the offenders. On the basis of the written record, he conducted a trial *in absentia*, convicting the person who struck the first blow of being the principal in the crime of homicide in a fight and convicting the other two of being accessories. He sentenced the principal to strangulation after the assizes according to Chinese law and sentenced the accessories to banishment and 100 blows of the heavy bamboo.

Finally, the governor-general instructed his subordinates to order the English taipan to "send a letter to England directing that the above recommended punishments be imposed on the offenders in England."[164] In support of his decision to order punishment to be carried out in the offenders' home country, the governor-general invoked the precedent of the 1754 Charles Brown case.

The discrepancies between the Chinese and the English account of this case illustrate a point made in the introduction—the Chinese officials in the provinces were under great pressure, when memorializing to the emperor their handling of a case involving European barbarians, to alter the facts to conform with an ideal model that would please him.

Offenses by Chinese Against Aliens

Even severe critics of early Ch'ing legal treatment of Europeans concede that when the latter were the victims of crimes committed by Chinese subjects the Chinese authorities moved swiftly and sternly to punish the offenders and compensate the victims.[165] This was especially true after the establishment of the Canton System. The reader will recall from an earlier section that after the 1750s Europeans were not allowed to trade anywhere other than Canton; nor were they permitted to submit statements of grievances or petitions to any persons but the licensed Canton hong merchants. To protect the European merchants from being victimized by petty local officials and corrupt merchants, who were ready to take advantage of the foreigners, the emperor in 1777 issued an edict to all military commanders, governors-general, and governors that:

> The Middle Kingdom's reign and pacification of the foreigners depend entirely upon justice and fairness so that they may be grateful and respect us . . . if when they have grievances and appeal to our government, we show partiality to our peoples and fail to alleviate the

> foreigner's difficulties, then, since they cannot go to Peking to present further accusations, they have no recourse, but to store up and suppress hatred for us in their hearts. . . . Moreover . . . they all will hesitate to come here in the future. Foreign ships visiting our shores will be reduced to a mere handful. . . . Whenever there is a foreign negotiation or a lawsuit they should never support only our people to the injury of the foreign barbarians.[166]

Although this edict concerns a case of debt owed by the Chinese merchants to European merchants, the record of Chinese officials' disposition of cases involving Chinese crimes against Europeans also reflects the policy of granting redress for foreign grievances, which is here endorsed by the emperor. In the English-language records alone, we have references to assaults upon Europeans by Chinese in 1813, 1814, 1819, 1821, and 1826 respectively, the Chinese offender in each case being arrested and punished according to Chinese law.[167]

In cases of theft of the property of Europeans, however, the Chinese authorities do not seem to have been as successful in apprehending the offenders. In cases occurring in 1778 and 1779, respectively, the thieves apparently were not caught; however, it is significant that, at least in the latter case, the security merchant compensated the foreign ship to the full amount of its loss.[168]

As for homicides of Europeans by Chinese, in six cases, occurring in 1781, 1785, 1787, 1796, 1817, and 1828, the offenders were apprehended, tried, sentenced according to Chinese law, and executed in the presence of fellow nationals of the homicide victim.[169] Most of the homicide cases were initiated by a complaint from the foreign community, which usually communicated to the Chinese officials a demand that the death penalty be imposed. For example, in connection with the 1785 case in which an English seaman was killed fighting with Chinese, the East India Company's Council of Supercargoes—which, after execution of the *Lady Hughes* gunner the year before, had condemned the Chinese homicide laws for being too severe and had resolved never again to surrender a British subject to Chinese criminal jurisdiction—now sent to the Chinese authorities a communication stating that: "we expect capital punishment to be inflicted on the offender agreeable to the laws of the country."[170] In at least one of the cases, the trial magistrate asked the supercargo from the victim's ship to sign a statement indicating "willingness that Justice should take its course according to the Chinese Laws."[171]

The two bloodiest cases occurred in the latter part of the period under study. The first took place in 1817 and involved the murder of an officer and six seamen aboard the American opium ship, *Wabash*, which was anchored in the outer sea (*wai-yang*) at Macao Roads.[172] The American consul wrote to the Chinese authorities, reporting the murders and the robbery of all the silver on board, for which he demanded reparation; for reasons discussed below, he made no mention of the fact that the ship's principal cargo—opium—had also been stolen. In response to the communication from the American consul and a supporting letter from the English committee, the governor-general offered a $3,000 reward for the arrest of the murderers. Eleven men were apprehended and the Kwangchow prefect conducted a trial to which he invited the American captain of the *Wabash*. Five of the defendants were convicted of murder during a robbery (*ch'iang-to sha-jen*) and were sentenced to immediate decapitation and exposure of the head (*chan li-chüeh hsiao-shih*).[173] All the American merchants in Canton were asked to witness the execution.

In his memorial to the emperor concerning the *Wabash* case, the governor-general emphasized the fact that the American ship, though loaded with prohibited cargo (*chin-wu*), had not entered the river, but instead had remained in the "outer sea." Thus, technically, the ship had not violated the law against importing opium into China; had it done so, the implication is that it would have waived any rights to protection against, or compensation from, Chinese robbers. The governor-general relied on this narrow distinction in deciding to enforce strictly the Chinese law against the murderers and to justify the compensation that he ordered to be paid to replace the stolen silver.[174] He refused, however, to authorize compensation for the stolen opium; moreover, he ordered the *Wabash* to leave China forever.

The other case involved the murder of thirteen French sailors by Chinese merchant seamen from Fukien Province.[175] The Frenchmen, sailors from the merchant ship *Navigateur* wrecked on the coast of Cochin-China in the summer of 1828, hired a Fukien junk to take them and their $60,000 cargo to Macao. The Frenchmen and the Chinese apparently did not enjoy their voyage together, as it is reported that the French leader frequently cursed the Chinese captain for making slow progress. This bad relationship, plus the temptation of so much silver, proved too much for the Chinese; one night, as the junk was approaching the Grand Ladrone island not far from Macao, they attacked the French sailors and killed thirteen of them. Unfortunately for the Chinese, however, one Frenchman escaped and made his way to Macao, where he reported the murders to the Chinese authorities.

The case attracted immense attention in the European community, and the Chinese officials were determined to give the impression that the Chinese government would deal severely with any Chinese subject who dared to injure foreign visitors. The governor-general of Liang-Kuang assumed jurisdiction over the case, even though in his memorial to the emperor he states that the crime occurred on the deep foreign sea (*hei-shui i-yang*, lit. "black water barbarian ocean"). The Liang-Kuang governor-general sent express messages to the governors of Chekiang and Fukien, as well as to all military commanders and district magistrates along the Kwangtung coast, directing that a thorough search be made for the offenders.

After most of the offenders had been apprehended, the emperor directed that all be sent to Kwangtung Province for trial. The surviving Frenchman was brought from Macao to Canton, together with an interpreter and several Chinese witnesses who had been detained awaiting the trial; the Canton prefect was then ordered by the provincial judicial commissioner to interrogate the defendants in the presence of the surviving Frenchman and the Chinese witnesses. The written record of this testimony was next reviewed by the judicial commissioner. Finally, the governor-general, sitting together with the judicial commissioner and the taotai, personally conducted another interrogation of the defendants.

Seventeen of the defendants were convicted of the crime of premeditated murder for profit (*t'u-ts'ai mou-sha*); sixteen of them were sentenced to immediate decapitation and exposure of the head. The principal offender, however, was sentenced to death by slicing (*ling-ch'ih*), since the Ch'ing Penal Code provides that penalty for the offense of killing more than three or four persons from one family;[176] the French sailors were deemed to be the same as a single family (*yü i-chia wu-i*) since they had served aboard the same ship (*t'ung-tso i-ch'uan*).

The trial had taken place on January 23, 1829, and the seventeen defendants sentenced to death were executed on January 30 in the presence of several invited foreigners.[177] Apparently it was unnecessary to receive imperial approval of the death sentences because capital punishment could be carried out against pirates and bandits without prior imperial endorsement of the sentences. As for the Western view of the trial, the East India Company's diary records that:

> The activity and energy which have been evinced by the Chinese government in bringing these offenders to punishment have excited great astonishment and are deserving of the highest commendation. Their desire to give the most ample satisfaction to foreigners has been strongly marked in every stage of the proceeding and we understand is the effect of the emperor's most positive orders. . . . The free access to the court of justice held there [in the Consoo Hall belonging to the hong merchant guild] is a proof that the government are desirous to give the utmost publicity to their proceedings on this occasion, and it must be admitted that if they are tenacious of requiring the sanguinary atonement of life for life from foreigners they have shown in the present instance that however insurmountable the difficulties may at first

sight appear they will execute a reciprocal justice upon their own countrymen where they are the offenders."[178]

Conclusion

From the above discussion of the Chinese government's handling of legal questions relating to the alien trading community at Canton and Macao in the eighteenth and nineteenth centuries, we can draw certain conclusions concerning the traditional Chinese mode of conducting foreign relations, as well as the more narrow question of Ch'ing doctrine and practice with regard to the exercise of criminal jurisdiction over aliens. The materials surveyed in this paper generally support the view that the Ch'ing government attempted to regulate relations with the European traders by resort to the traditional principles and institutions known as the tributary system.

In cases involving violations of the law by Westerners, the Ch'ing government adopted the traditional policy of allowing the foreign community a certain degree of autonomy in the resolution of disputes and the punishment of minor offenders. By the middle of the eighteenth century, the Ch'ing government had laid down a rule that Europeans were to be tried and punished in China according to Chinese law only in cases involving the homicide of a Chinese subject. In all other cases, the foreign community would be instructed to impose an appropriate punishment upon the offender.

The eventual failure of this technique to provide the harmony and stability desired by the Chinese government was not due to a change of Ch'ing policy but instead stemmed from England's unwillingness to subject its nationals to laws and procedures considered excessively severe and lacking in adequate safeguards for the liberty and rights of the individual.

In several respects, the legal treatment of Westerners by the Chinese government was more lenient or in other ways more favorable than the treatment given to the Chinese themselves. First, as we have just noted, formal criminal jurisdiction was rarely asserted over Westerners. Second, it was an official policy, generally observed in practice, not to intervene in disputes or criminal cases not involving Chinese subjects. Third, where Chinese subjects committed offenses against Westerners, the government moved promptly and sternly to punish the offenders, to show consideration to the visitors from afar and to deter vicious elements among the people.

The Westerners, however, were not appreciative of the consideration shown to them by this special treatment. One reason for their ungrateful attitude is that the Chinese government policy for controlling the foreign community, and the particular rules implementing this policy, were dictated by the emperor in response to recommendations from the local officials. Since the foreign merchant community after 1760 was forbidden to communicate directly with the Chinese officials and was thus unable to protest effectively against unfairly restrictive rules, the foreigners eventually resorted to evasion of the rules, by bribing the local officials, by lying and deception, or by outright defiance and refusal to comply.

The English were especially unruly and recalcitrant. From the moment of their first arrival in China, they had given the Chinese officials trouble because of their unwillingness to comply with the ceremonial forms of the tribute system; as English colonial and naval power grew, the English who ventured to China became increasingly irritated by the tributary system and the Chinese attitude of superiority. Although the East India Company's representatives in China, motivated more by profit than by national chauvinism or concern for the rights of individual Englishmen, were willing and able to keep order within the English community at Canton until the late eighteenth century, they gradually lost this ability after the number of free traders, "king's ships," and opium smugglers in Chinese waters multiplied.

After the *Lady Hughes* case in 1784, the English resolved never again to submit to Chinese criminal jurisdiction. Although the British government made several attempts over the next half-century to get the Chinese government to agree to let British officials exercise criminal jurisdiction over British subjects in China, the Chinese consistently refused to grant such a request.

This impasse left Englishmen in China beyond the control of any law, and the hostility resulting from the ensuing Sino-British struggle over the surrender of English offenders was a major factor in shaping the increasingly rigid policies of both the Chinese and English governments, which resulted in a nonnegotiable confrontation and armed conflict. Perhaps even more significant is the fact that the violence of European sailors and their frequent escape from any punishment helped to make the Canton populace rabidly antiforeigner. This animosity on the part of the people was to prove an enduring and troublesome obstacle to later efforts at establishing amicable Sino-Western relations.

NOTES

1. Edict ordering the Liang-Kuang governor-general to instruct the British taipan (senior Canton merchant) to send his wife back to Macao and abide by all of the established regulations. *Ch'ing-tai wai-chiao shih-liao* [Historical Materials Concerning Foreign Relations in the Ch'ing Period], 6 *ts'e* for the Chia-ch'ing period, 1796–1820, 4 *ts'e* for the Tao-kuang period to 1831

(Peiping, 1931-1933), (hereinafter cited as *CTWCSL:CC* or *CTWCSL:TK*) *TK*, 3:50b-51, at p. 51 (1968 Taiwan reprint, 2 vols., Ch'eng-wen ch'u-pan she, Vol. 2, pp. 334-335, at p. 335).

2. Prior to the American entry into the China trade in 1784, all Westerners in China were Europeans. To avoid the cumbersome "Europeans and Americans," the term "Westerner" has been used in all cases.
3. Cf. generally Fairbank, "On the Ch'ing Tributary System," in S. Y. Teng and J. K. Fairbank, *Ch'ing Administration: Three Studies* (Cambridge, Mass., 1961).
4. J. K. Fairbank, *Trade and Diplomacy on the China Coast* (Cambridge, Mass., 1953).
5. For example, cf. Peter Auber, *China: An Outline of Its Government, Laws, and Policy* (London, 1834), p. 38.
6. Imperially approved memorial submitted by the Liang-Kuang governor-general in 1744. *Ao-men chi-lüeh* [Topography and History of Macao], comp., Yin Kuang-jen and Chang Ju-lin, 4 *ts'e* (1743-1751), "shang-chüan," "kuan-shou pien," 38b-40b (hereafter cited as *AMCL*).
7. George W. Keeton, *The Development of Extraterritoriality in China*, 2 vols. (London, 1928); V. K. Wellington Koo, *The Status of Aliens in China*, Columbia Studies in History, Economics, and Public Law, Vol. 50, No. 2, Whole No. 126 (New York, 1912); and Yu-hao Tseng, *The Termination of Unequal Treaties* (Shanghai, 1933), pp. 249-270. The first two cite no Chinese materials and the third cites the Ch'ing Code but none of the cases which illustrate how the practice departed from the broad jurisdictional claim of the Code's alien jurisdiction provision.
8. Compare, for example, Sir George T. Staunton's eyewitness account of an 1807 alien case, quoted in Keeton, Vol. 2, pp. 175-183, with the account of the same case given in a memorial submitted to the emperor by the Liang-Kuang governor-general; English tr. by Staunton, in his *Ta Tsing Leu Lee* (London, 1810), pp. 521-524.
9. Kuwabara Jitsuzō, "On P'u Shou-keng," *Memoirs of the Research Department of the Tōyō Bunko*, No. 2 (1928), pp. 1-79, at pp. 2-3, 21, and 34-35.
10. *T'ang-lü shu-i* [Official Commentary to the T'ang Penal Code], 6:9; for a similar provision in the Sung dynasty, cf. *Sung hsing-t'ung* [Compendium of the Penal Laws of the Sung Dynasty], 6:9b.
11. Kuwabara Jitsuzō, p. 34.
12. *Ming-lü chi-chieh fu-li* [Annotated Ming Penal Code with Supplemental Statutes], 1:84b.
13. Kuwabara Jitsuzō, p. 46.
14. *Kuang-hsü hui-tien shih-li* [Collected Statutes of the Ch'ing Dynasty, with Precedents] (1899), 739:1; *TCLL* (1964 Taiwan reprint), 1:527; Staunton, *Ta Tsing Leu Lee*, pp. 36-37.
15. *Idem.*
16. *Idem.*
17. Sir Ernest Alabaster, "Notes on Chinese Law and Practice," *Journal of the North China Branch of the Royal Asiatic Society*, Vol. 38 (1906), pp. 83-100, at p. 94.

18. Tai Yen-hui, *Chung-kuo fa-chih shih kai-yao* [A Concise History of the Chinese Legal System] (4th printing, Taipei, 1966), p. 168.
19. *CTWCSL:TK*, 1:11b-13b, at 13a (1968 Taiwan reprint, Vol. 2, pp. 30-34, at p. 33).
20. *Ta Ch'ing lü-li ch'ung-ting hui-t'ung hsin-tsuan* [New Complete Revised and Annotated Ch'ing Penal Code] 36 *chüan* (Peking, 1832), 4:63; *Ta Ch'ing lü-li hui-t'ung hsin-tsuan* [Comprehensive New Edition of the Great Ch'ing Code], 1873 private ed. (1964 Taiwan reprint by Wen-hai ch'u-pan-she, with continuous pagination in 5 vols.) (hereafter cited as *TCLL*), 1:528-530, upper commentary. Moreover, in 1810 Staunton stated that: "This section of the code has been expressly quoted by the provincial government of Canton, and applied to the case of foreigners residing there and at Macao for the purposes of trade. The laws of China have never, however, been attempted to be enforced against those foreigners, except with considerable allowances in their favor . . .," *Ta Tsing Leu Lee*, p. 36n.
21. There is a difference of opinion on the issue of whether or not the Sino-Russian treaties of 1689 and 1727 provided for reciprocal extraterritorial criminal jurisdiction. Morse states that they do so provide. Cf. Morse, *International Relations of the Chinese Empire*, 3 vols. (Shanghai and London, 1910-1918), Vol. 1, p. 60. Keeton agrees, Vol. 1, pp. 72 and 90-91. Koo, however, points out that ". . . the Chinese text appears to confirm rather than impair the principles of territorial jurisdiction." *Status of Aliens*, p. 52. Art. 4 of the Chinese text of the 1689 Treaty of Nerchinsk states that where nationals of either party go without authority into the territory of the other party to hunt, steal, or rob, "they should be immediately arrested and sent to the local authorities to be punished according to the gravity of their offense" (*chi-hsing ch'in-na sung so-tsai kuan-ssu chün so-fan ch'ing-chung ch'eng-ch'u*). *Treaties, Conventions, etc. between China and Foreign States*, Chinese Maritime Customs, 2nd ed., 2 vols. (Shanghai, 1917), Vol. 1, p. 6. Also, art. 10 of the Chinese text of the 1727 Treaty of Kiakhta provides that nationals of either contracting party committing offenses in the territory of the other party shall be punished at the place where the offense is committed. *Treaties, Conventions, etc.*, Vol. 1, p. 15. Further support is given to Koo's view by the fact that in 1773 several Russian criminals were serving life sentences in Fukien Province. Cf. English tr. of imperial edict in Fu Lo-shu, *A Documentary Chronicle of Sino-Western Relations (1644-1820)*, 2 vols. (Tucson, 1966), Vol. 1, p. 271.
22. Morse, *International Relations*, Vol. 1, pp. 42-43.
23. Chang T'ien-tse, *Sino-Portuguese Trade 1514-1644* (Leiden, 1934), p. 96.
24. Cf. Appendix entitled "International Status of Macao Before 1887," in Keeton, Vol. 2, pp. 287-295.
25. Kuo T'ing-i, *Chin-tai Chung-kuo shih* [A History of Modern China] 2 vols. (Changsha, 1940), Vol. 1, p. 524.
26. *Hsiang-shan hsien-chih* [Hsiang-shan District Gazetteer] (1827 ed.), 4:94. Cf. English tr. of approved memorial in Fu Lo-shu, Vol. 1, p. 176.
27. The following discussion of the facts of this case and the procedures that emerged from it is based upon memorials quoted in *AMCL*, 38b-40b; the

same documents are also quoted in Kuo T'ing-i, Vol. 1, pp. 524-527. A brief summary of the case appears in the *TCLL* (1964 Taiwan reprint), 1:528-529, upper commentary. The procedure laid down here in the approved memorial from Governor-general Ts'e-leng is cited as authoritative in memorials dealing with later alien homicide cases. For example, cf. English translations of memorials concerning cases arising in 1807 and 1821, respectively reported in Staunton, *Ta Tsing Leu Lee*, pp. 521-524, at p. 523, and Keeton, Vol. 2, pp. 197-198; both memorials contain lengthy quotations from the 1744 Ts'e-leng memorial.

28. *AMCL*, 39.
29. *AMCL*, 39b.
30. *AMCL*, 40.
31. *Idem*.
32. Sir Ernest Alabaster, *Notes and Commentaries on Chinese Criminal Law*. (London, 1899), pp. 21-29, or Shiga Shūzo, "Criminal Procedure in the Ching Dynasty," *Memoirs of the Research Department of the Tōyō Bunko* (Tokyo), No. 32 (1974) and No. 33 (1975).
33. For example, cf. H. B. Morse, *Chronicles of the East India Company to China, 1635-1834* (Oxford, 1926), II, 59-60. See Vol. 5 for 1742-1774 (Oxford, 1929).
34. For an illustration of this approach, see the Liang-Kuang governor-general's memorial concerning a case arising in 1820 involving English sailors. *CTWCSL:CC* 6:57-58b, at 58a (1968 Taiwan reprint Vol. 1, pp. 707-710, at p. 709).
35. Staunton, *Ta Tsing Leu Lee*, p. 523.
36. Morse, *International Relations*, Vol. 1, p. 46.
37. Keeton, Vol. 2, pp. 288-289.
38. *Idem*.
39. Cf. respectively Morse, *Chronicles*, Vol. 2, p. 36; Vol. 3, p. 15; and Vol. 4, pp. 136-138.
40. *Ch'ing shih-lu: Ch'ien-lung ch'ao* [Veritable Records of the Emperor: Ch'ien-lung Period], 340:23b-24b. English tr. in Fu Lo-shu, Vol. 1, pp. 187-188; cf. also two earlier edicts concerning the same case, Fu Lo-shu, Vol. 1, p. 186.
41. Morse, *International Relations*, Vol. 1, p. 45; Fu Lo-shu, Vol. 2, p. 531 (note 69).
42. *Idem*; cf. also Chinese text of the Convention in *AMCL*, 40b-41b.
43. Morse, *Chronicles*, Vol. 5, pp. 182-185.
44. Morse, *Chronicles*, Vol. 5, p. 183.
45. Morse, *Chronicles*, Vol. 5, p. 183.
46. Morse, *Chronicles*, Vol. 5, p. 185. This view of the fatal significance of surrendering a "suspect" to the Chinese is reflected in the following statement in the East India Company's Canton Select Committee journal for 1811: ". . . whenever a murderer is demanded by the Chinese Government, our consequent selection and surrender of any individual into their hands is completely equivalent in effect to a provisional sentence of death." Morse, *Chronicles*, Vol. 3, p. 172.
47. Morse, *International Relations*, Vol. 1, pp. 51-53; *Chronicles*, Vol. 1, pp. 17-30.

48. Morse, *Chronicles*, Vol. 1, pp. 25-26.
49. John E. Wills, Jr., "Ch'ing Relations with the Dutch 1662-1690," J. K. Fairbank, ed., *The Chinese World Order* (Cambridge, Mass., 1968), pp. 225-256; Fairbank, *Trade and Diplomacy*, p. 48; Morse, *International Relations*, Vol. 1, p. 52; *Chronicles*, Vol. 1, pp. 41-49.
50. Fairbank, *Trade and Diplomacy*, p. 49; Morse, *Chronicles*, Vol. 2, pp. 78-294, especially pp. 99-108 on "The Conditions of Chinese Trade."
51. Morse, *Chronicles*, Vol. 1, covering the years 1635-1753.
52. Morse, *Chronicles*, Vol. 1, pp. 82-84; Keeton, Vol. 1, p. 29.
53. Morse, *Chronicles*, Vol. 1, p. 83.
54. This official's formal title was *Yüeh hai-kuan chien-tu* [Imperial commissioner of Kwangtung maritime customs] but he was called the "Hoppo" by the European community at Canton. His role and the derivation of the nickname are discussed in Fairbank, *Trade and Diplomacy*, p. 49 and p. 490, n. 15.
55. Auber, pp. 153-154.
56. Morse, *Chronicles*, Vol. 1, pp. 168-169; Keeton, Vol. 1, p. 30.
57. Morse, *Chronicles*, Vol. 1, p. 168.
58. Morse, *Chronicles*, Vol. 1, p. 169.
59. Morse, *Chronicles*, Vol. 1 p. 193; Keeton, Vol. 1, p. 31.
60. See subsection entitled "The *Lady Hughes* Case and the Subsequent British Resolve to Resist Chinese Criminal Jurisdiction."
61. Morse, *Chronicles*, Vol. 1, p. 254.
62. Morse, *Chronicles*, Vol. 1, p. 236.
63. Morse, *Chronicles*, Vol. 1, p. 270.
64. Cf. generally Edward L. Farmer, "James Flint Versus the Canton Interest (1755-1760)," *Papers on China*, Vol. 17 (Harvard University, East Asian Research Center, 1963), pp. 38-66.
65. *Idem*.
66. Farmer, "James Flint"; cf. also Morse, *Chronicles*, Vol. 5, pp. 36-44 for English tr. of imperial edicts issued in 1755, and Morse, *Chronicles*, Vol. 5, pp. 94-98, for the culminating edict of 1760, promulgating the "Regulations for the Control of Trade at Canton." The 1760 edict is also tr. in Fu Lo-shu, Vol. 1, pp. 224-226. The rules summarized below are set forth either in one of the 1755 edicts or in the 1760 edict, so they will not be cited individually, except for the provision making the Chinese security merchants, linguists, and compradors, and the foreign taipans and supercargoes, collectively responsible for maintaining order and securing the surrender of alien criminal suspects, which can be found in Morse, *Chronicles*, Vol. 5, p. 40.
67. Communication dated February 19, 1838, in *China Correspondence 1838-1840* (London, 1840), pp. 276-291, at p. 283.
68. For example, the following instructions were issued by the East India Company's Council of Supercargoes in 1779 to each English ship upon its arrival: ". . . that neither you nor your Officers are to go ashooting on any pretence whatsoever, and that you give positive Orders to your Officers to keep your Ship's Company within the bounds of Sobriety and Decency so as not to give offence to the Chinese Government." Morse, *Chronicles*, Vol. 2, p. 37.

69. Morse, *Chronicles*, Vol. 5, p. 19; and Vol. 2, p. 37 and p. 108.
70. Morse, *Chronicles*, Vol. 2, p. 72. An English ship licensed and controlled, but not owned, by the British East India Company, and engaged in the trade between India and China. Morse, *International Relations*, Vol. 1, p. 102n.
72. The most complete account of the *Lady Hughes* case is contained in Morse, *Chronicles*, Vol. 2, pp. 98-107; see also Keeton, Vol. 1, pp. 40-42, and Vol. 2, pp. 174-175.
73. Starting in 1715, the supercargoes (commercial agents) on the British East India Company's ships in Canton formed a single council to formulate trading policy for each season, one person being designated chief of the council. Morse, *Chronicles*, Vol. 1, p. 75. From 1786 until dissolution of the East India Company's monopoly in 1834, its commercial interests in China were under the management of a Select Committee of supercargoes, which took the place of the Council of Supercargoes. Morse, *Chronicles*, Vol. 2, p. 118.
74. Morse, *Chronicles*, Vol. 2, p. 99.
75. Morse, *Chronicles*, Vol. 2, pp. 99-100.
76. Morse, *Chronicles*, Vol. 2, p. 101.
77. Morse, *Chronicles*, Vol. 2, p. 102.
78. *Idem*.
79. Morse, *Chronicles*, Vol. 2, p. 103.
80. Josiah Quincy, ed., *The Journals of Major Samuel Shaw* (Boston, 1847), pp. 186-195, at p. 189.
81. Morse, *Chronicles*, Vol. 2, p. 103.
82. This was an estimate of the time it would take to have an exchange of communications with Peking on the matter, if the communications had been sent both ways by ordinary horse post. Cf. J. K. Fairbank and S. Y. Teng, "On the Transmission of Ch'ing Documents," *Ch'ing Administration: Three Studies*, pp. 13 and 33. However, since the edict in reply to the governor's memorial was transmitted at the express rate of 600 *li* per day (200 miles), only 39 days elapsed between the date of the gunner's arrest and the date of his execution pursuant to the imperial edict.
83. Morse, *Chronicles*, Vol. 2, p. 104.
84. Morse, *Chronicles*, Vol. 2, p. 105.
85. For example, Morse, *International Relations*, Vol. 1, p. 102.
86. *Ch'ing shih-lu: Ch'ien-lung*, 1218:18b-20 (partial English tr. in Fu Lo-shu, Vol. 1, pp. 297-298).
87. Cf. Kenneth Scott Latourette, *A History of Christian Missions in China* (New York, 1929), pp. 172-173.
88. Cf. edicts to the Grand Council in late 1784. *Ch'ing shih-lu: Ch'ien-lung*, 1214:11b-13, 17-18; 1216:4b; 1218:5; 1219:5-6; and cf. also Latourette, pp. 172-173.
89. *Ch'ing shih-lu: Ch'ien-lung*, 1218:18b-20; cf. Fu Lo-shu for a slightly different tr. of this passage, Vol. 1, pp. 297-298.
90. Quoted in Earl H. Pritchard, *The Crucial Years of Anglo-Chinese Relations 1750-1800* (Pullman, Washington, 1936), p. 229.
91. Pritchard, p. 230.
92. *Idem*.
93. Koo, pp. 109-111.

94. Morse, *Chronicles*, Vol. 2, p. 160.
95. Morse, *Chronicles*, Vol. 2, p. 156.
96. Morse, *Chronicles*, Vol. 2, p. 218.
97. Keeton, Vol. 1, p. 70. Ship captains did occasionally punish sailors for minor breaches of the peace committed on Chinese soil, but they were powerless to handle serious offenses. Morse, *Chronicles*, Vol. 2, pp. 147-148.
98. Keeton, Vol. 1, p. 53 (note 1), pp. 64-65 and 71.
99. Keeton, Vol. 1, p. 71.
100. *Shih-liao hsün-k'an* [Historical Materials Published Every Ten Days], 40 vols. (Palace Museum, Peiping, 1930-1931), 210b; (1963 Taiwan reprint, Kuo-feng ch'u-pan she, p. 113). Cf. somewhat different English tr., done by Robert Morrison in 1821, quoted in Keeton, Vol. 2, p. 195.
101. *Wang K'en-t'ang Chien-shih* (1689), Vol. 1, "ming-li," 71.
102. W. C. Hunter, *The 'Fan Kwae' at Canton Before Treaty Days* (London, 1882) p. 28.
103. One such case occurred in 1780 when the emperor ordered Chinese merchants to repay foreign merchants for loans made in violation of the imperial edict of 1760 which prohibited such loans. The emperor allowed the foreigners to collect on the illegal loan because they claimed to be ignorant of the prohibition. Morse, *Chronicles*, Vol. 2, p. 57.
104. Morse, *Chronicles*, Vol. 2, p. 343 (the 1800 case); and *CTWCSL:TK*, 1:13 (1968 Taiwan reprint, Vol. 2, p. 33) (the 1821 case).
105. *CTWCSL:TK* 1:13 (1968 Taiwan reprint, Vol. 2, p. 33).
106. W. T. DeBary, ed., *Sources of Chinese Tradition*, Vol. 2, p. 9.
107. Morse, *Chronicles*, Vol. 3, p. 7.
108. Cf. mention of the important role played by Staunton and Morrison in interpreting and translating for the British East India Company at Canton. Morse, *Chronicles*, Vol. 2, p. 327; Vol. 3, pp. 7, 31, 72, 134, and 165.
109. Morse, *Chronicles*, Vol. 1, p. 277.
110. Cf. discussion in Morse, *International Relations*, Vol. 1, pp. 114-117; Keeton, Vol. 1, pp. 119-121; also see note 67 above for citation of imperial edict on collective responsibility for alien crimes.
111. Cf. Keeton, Vol. 1, pp. 109-119, especially p. 118, where he states that Chinese law ". . . failed to recognize the validity of a plea of self-defense, and purely accidental homicide involved criminal liability . . ."
112. Morse, *Chronicles*, Vol. 3, p. 40.
113. Morse, *Chronicles*, Vol. 3, pp. 155-156. It should be pointed out that the Select Committee is not entirely accurate in its appraisal of the Chinese practice, for there were instances, to be further discussed below, where aliens were exonerated or only lightly fined for accidentally killing a Chinese subject. Also, cases 2 and 3 are subject to some question since the Chinese authorities do not appear to have succeeded in gaining jurisdiction over any such case so it is impossible to say how they would have decided it.
114. Morse, *Chronicles*, Vol. 3, p. 321.
115. Morse, *Chronicles*, Vol. 2, p. 260.
116. Morse, *Chronicles*, Vol. 2, pp. 148 and 260, respectively.

117. Morse, *Chronicles*, Vol. 2, pp. 337-339, 429; Keeton, Vol. 1, pp. 45-46.
118. Morse, *Chronicles*, Vol. 3, pp. 40-49, 70; Staunton, *Ta Tsing Leu Lee*, pp. 521-524; Keeton, Vol. 2, pp. 175-183.
119. Morse, *Chronicles*, Vol. 3, p. 46; Keeton, Vol. 2, p. 183; also recall the discussion of monetary redemption of the punishment for accidental homicide, in note 68 above. In a later case, occurring in 1827 when the anchor cable of the English ship, *Golconda*, parted and killed a Chinese, the district magistrate investigated and ruled that the death was completely accidental; thus, there was not even a demand for surrender of a suspect for a show trial such as the one which led to the conviction of Edward Sheen in the *Neptune* case in 1807. Morse, *Chronicles*, Vol. 4, pp. 154-155.
120. Keeton, Vol. 2, p. 192.
121. Morse, *Chronicles*, Vol. 3, pp. 123-125.
122. Morse, *Chronicles*, Vol. 3, p. 125.
123. Morse, *Chronicles*, Vol. 3, pp. 377-382; Keeton, Vol. 1, pp. 56-57.
124. *CTWCSL:CC*, 6:57-58b (1968 Taiwan reprint, Vol. 1, pp. 707-710, at p. 709).
125. Morse, *Chronicles*, Vol. 4, pp. 11-13, 23-27; Keeton, Vol. 1, pp. 58-59; Vol. 2, pp. 183-201. For the memorial of the governor-general, reporting the handling of this case, cf. *CTWCSL:TK*, 1:7b-9b (1968 Taiwan reprint, Vol. 2, pp. 22-26).
126. *CTWCSL:TK*, 1:9 (1968 Taiwan reprint, Vol. 2, p. 25).
127. Morse, *Chronicles*, Vol. 5, pp. 26-27.
128. Cf. Jacques M. Downs, "American Merchants and the China Opium Trade, 1800-1840," *Business History Review* (Harvard Business School, Winter 1968), pp. 418-442.
129. Morse, *Chronicles*, Vol. 4, pp. 18-19 and 27-41; Keeton, Vol. 1, pp. 59-61.
130. Morse, *Chronicles*, Vol. 2, pp. 131 and 176. *CTWCSL: TK*, 1:23a-b (1968) Taiwan reprint, Vol. 2, pp. 53-54); *CTWCSL:TK*, 1:45b-46; in 1830, the *Topaze* case is still referred to in Chinese documents as "not yet concluded," *CTWCSL:TK*, 4:46.
131. Morse, *Chronicles*, Vol. 4, pp. 245-246.
132. Cf. for example, Fu Lo-shu, Vol. 1, p. 186.
133. Auber, pp. 409-412; Morse, *International Relations*, Vol. 1, p. 118; Koo, pp. 95-112.
134. Instructions of Dec. 31, 1833, in *China Correspondence, 1838-1840* (London, 1840), p. 3.
135. *China Correspondence, 1838-1840*, p. 296.
136. *China Correspondence, 1838-1840*, pp. 317-318.
137. Arthur Waley, *The Opium War Through Chinese Eyes* (London, 1958), p. 55; Hsin-pao Chang, *Commissioner Lin and the Opium War* (Cambridge, Mass., 1964), p. 197.
138. Koo, pp. 112-121.
139. Keeton, Vol. 1, pp. 170-174; Hsin-pao Chang, pp. 96-98.
140. Keeton, Vol. 1, pp. 143-170; Hsin-pao Chang, pp. 196-200.
141. Hsin-pao Chang, p. 197.
142. Morse, *Chronicles*, Vol. 1, p. 236.

143. Morse, *Chronicles*, Vol. 2, pp. 15-19; Keeton, Vol. 1, p. 32.
144. *CSL:CL*, 476:16 (English tr. in Fu Lo-shu, Vol. 1, pp. 193-194).
145. *SLHK*, 12:425-426 (partial English tr. in Fu Lo-shu, Vol. 1, p. 196).
146. Morse, *Chronicles*, Vol. 2, pp. 59-60 and 99; Keeton, Vol. 1, pp. 39-40; Kuo T'ing-i, Vol. 1, pp. 560-561.
147. Morse, *Chronicles*, Vol. 2, p. 60.
148. *TCLL*, 4:64; *TCLL* (1964 Taiwan reprint), 1:529.
149. Morse, *Chronicles*, Vol. 2, p. 34; Keeton, Vol. 1, p. 37.
150. Morse, *Chronicles*, Vol. 1, p. 59; Keeton, Vol. 1, p. 39.
151. Morse, *Chronicles*, Vol. 3, p. 40; Keeton, Vol. 1, pp. 49-50.
152. Morse, *Chronicles*, Vol. 3, p. 203.
153. Morse, *Chronicles*, Vol. 3, pp. 212-213.
154. Morse, *Chronicles*, Vol. 2, p. 389.
155. Morse, *Chronicles*, Vol. 3, p. 215.
156. Morse, *Chronicles*, Vol. 3, p. 216.
157. Morse, *Chronicles*, Vol. 3, p. 217. Ch'ing laws, regulations, and administrative records make clear that the locus of activity in the "inner sea" (*nei-yang*), as opposed to the "outer sea" (*wai-yang*), brings it directly within the ambit of Chinese territorial legal jurisdiction; however, the exact scope of these areas is unclear.
158. Cf. the memorial concerning this matter submitted to the emperor by the Liang-Kuang governor-general and other provincial officials. *CTWCSL:CC*, 4:21b-23b, at 22b (1968 Taiwan reprint, Vol. 1, pp. 400-401, at p. 402); (partial English tr. in Fu Lo-shu, Vol. 1, pp. 393-394).
159. Morse, *Chronicles*, Vol. 3, p. 219.
160. Morse, *Chronicles*, Vol. 4, pp. 232-234.
161. Keeton, Vol. 1, pp. 64-65.
162. *CTWCSL:TK*, 3:40-41, at 40 (1968 Taiwan reprint, Vol. 2, pp. 313-315, at p. 313).
163. Mackenzie was captain of a Dutch ship so the Dutch taipan conducted the inquest.
164. *CTWCSL:TK*, 3:41 (1968 Taiwan reprint, Vol. 2, p. 315).
165. For example, cf. Keeton, Vol. 1, p. 47.
166. *CSL:CL*, 1021:11b-15 (English tr. in Fu Lo-shu, Vol. 1, pp. 277-280).
167. Cf. Keeton, Vol. 1, pp. 54, 55, 56, 57, and 62 respectively.
168. Cf. respectively Morse, *Chronicles*, Vol. 2, p. 34, and Keeton, Vol. 1, p. 38.
169. Reported respectively in Morse, *Chronicles*, Vol. 2, pp. 72, 108-109, 148 and 289; Vol. 3, pp. 318-320; and Vol. 4, pp. 176-177.
170. Morse, *Chronicles*, Vol. 2, p. 109.
171. Morse, *Chronicles*, Vol. 2, p. 289; Keeton, Vol. 1, p. 44.
172. Morse, *Chronicles*, Vol. 3, pp. 318-320.
173. Cf. the memorial concerning this case submitted to the emperor by the Liang-Kuang governor-general. *CTWCSL:CC*, 6:43-45b, at 44b (1968 Taiwan reprint, Vol. 1, pp. 679-684, at p. 682).
174. *CTWCSL:CC*, Vol. 1, p. 682.
175. Information used in the following discussion of this case is primarily derived from a memorial concerning the measures taken by the provincial

officials; the memorial was submitted to the emperor on February 19, 1829, by the governor-general of Liang-Kuang and the governor of Kuangtung. *CTWCSL:TK*, 3:1-4 (1968 Taiwan reprint, Vol. 2, pp. 235-241). This case is rather unique in that the Chinese report of the facts and handling are very close to the version contained in the Western records. See Morse, *Chronicles*, Vol. 4, pp. 176-177; Keeton, vol. 1, p. 63. Also cf. an eyewitness account of the trial by a European observer, reported in the *Canton Register* of February 2, 1829, and a sequel containing the deposition of the lone survivor of the massacre, reported in the *Canton Register* of April 18, 1829; both documents are quoted in Keeton, Vol. 2, pp. 201-212.

176. *TCLL* (1964 Taiwan reprint), 3:2460.
177. Morse, *Chronicles*, Vol. 4, p. 177.
178. *Idem*.

VIII

CHINESE INFLUENCES ON EIGHTEENTH-CENTURY TOKUGAWA CODES

Dan Fenno Henderson

Chinese legal studies influenced Tokugawa codifiers in eighteenth-century Japan. This influence was felt in the major areas of jurisprudence and codification. Originally sponsored by the eighth Shogun Yoshimune, the Chinese influence nurtured a new Japanese jurisprudence and a group of "jurists" able to use concepts, classifications, and codification methods previously little known in the Tokugawa era (1603-1868).[1] Chinese influence on codification—the subject of this chapter—was in the more concrete field of code adaptation. It comprised specific legal borrowings, some found in the Shogunal law itself, but most found in penal codes of certain leading daimyo domains (*han*).[2]

To begin with, a balanced perspective is essential to a discussion of Chinese influences on Tokugawa law. For Tokugawa law, coming as it does at the end of a millennium of indigenous legal evolution, is ordinarily seen as the apogee of Japan's purely native legal attainment between two foreign law receptions—the importation of the law of China's T'ang dynasty during the eighth century and the introduction of Western law during the last decades of the nineteenth century. It is not my intention to disturb that image much. But the intrinsically interesting borrowing of Chinese legal ideas, which did indeed occur in eighteenth-century Japan, can be appreciated without exaggerating its importance if we keep several basic premises in mind.

First, we must remember that the Tokugawa borrowing was eclectic and subject to Japanese adaptation, which after all produced a distinctive, emphatically Japanese, legal system of merit in its own peculiar context. Second, we must remember that the borrowing of specific Chinese laws, as opposed to borrowing of the general juristic methods, was geographically scattered and generally confined to a rather narrow range of subject matter. It was scattered because only a few outlying daimyo consciously borrowed from the Chinese codes; most daimyo codifiers in fact followed local custom exclusively, or followed Shogunal law, which had only slight traces of Chinese law. The influences were narrow in that they were almost entirely from the penal law found in the Ming and Ch'ing Codes.

As a final point, we need to bear in mind that since Japan's massive reception of T'ang law beginning before A.D. 700, continuing Chinese legal influences had long been felt in Japan, and it is therefore frequently difficult to date the source of Chinese elements in Tokugawa law. For example, several Tokugawa institutions that are clearly Chinese-based are not so clearly identifiable as being specifically of T'ang or Ming or Ch'ing derivation. These dynasties had a common core of analogous institutions and overlapping legal provisions in their penal codes, so that to trace the source of Tokugawa practice, we need to know which legal texts the Japanese were studying. By Tokugawa times, T'ang law was dead law in China, and in Japan most of the T'ang-styled Japanese Penal Code (*ritsu*) of 702 and 718 A.D. had long been lost. Tokugawa legal scholarship was confined to an elite group of rulers (for example, Yoshimune, Maeda Tsunanori, and Hosokawa Shigekane) and their top Confucian advisers (*jukan*) (for example, Sakakibara Kōshū, Takase Kiboku, Arai Hakuseki, Muro Kyūsō, Fukami Yurin, Ogyū Sorai, and Ogyū Hokkei [Kan]). These men concentrated on the Ming law and the Ch'ing Code, which until 1725 was largely a republication of the Ming statutes. Ogyū Kan completed a punctuated edition of the Ming Penal Code for Yoshimune in 1723. In 1725 his elder brother Ogyū Sorai did a comprehensive Japanese commentary for the Ming Code using relatively simple language.[3] Both of these works were soon printed, and their availability made the Ming Penal Code an important model from Chinese law until the end of the Tokugawa period. In contrast, the T'ang Code "Commentary" (*T'ang-lü shu-i*), though existent in manuscript in Edo, was not printed until after 1800.

As for the Ch'ing Code, it was translated into Japanese, over a five-year period (1721-1727) in Nagasaki, by Fukami Yūrin (whose great grandfather was a Chinese named Kao Shou-chüeh). Fukami was aided by Sun Fu-chai, a Chinese merchant at Nagasaki. Unfortunately, they translated the older version of 1690—only a slight revision of the original Ch'ing Code of 1646, which in turn was very similar to the late Ming Code. During the same period (1723-1727), ironically, the Chinese were revising the Ch'ing Code, which when published in 1727 remained (with slight changes in 1740) the definitive version of the Code statutes, though new substatutes and precedents continued to accumulate. Because of Fukami's position as adviser to Yoshimune, we may assume that the older version of the Ch'ing Code as filtered through Fukami and his Chinese advisers served to answer many questions about Chinese law raised by Yoshimune, but the Fukami translation was apparently never published and only a small portion of the manuscript remains today.[4]

The uses to which the new versions of the Ch'ing Code (1727 and 1740) were put in Tokugawa Japan is a subject ripe for research.

With these perspectives, we can enumerate the major instances of the influence of Chinese law during the Tokugawa period, both in the Shogunate itself and in the daimyo domains.

The eighth Shogun Yoshimune's original domain (when he was a daimyo) was Wakayama *han*, the earliest center of Ming Code studies that began well before 1700. Sakakibara Kōshū and Takase Kiboku, two of the most eminent students of Ming law, both served Yoshimune when he was at Wakayama (1705-1716). Yoshimune, as Shogun (1716-1745), then spent nearly thirty years systematizing the Shogunal law in Edo, and finally completed in 1742 the major Tokugawa compilation, the *Kujikata Osadamegaki*, which with some additions remained the chief guidebook for Shogunal adjudication until the Meiji Restoration (1868). Yoshimune's attitude toward Chinese law was ambivalent. On the one hand, he was the leading sponsor of the revival of Chinese legal studies in the early 1700s and he learned much from his studies. On the other hand, he borrowed little from China in drafting the specifics of the *Osadamegaki*, which emerged as a largely native Japanese product.

Though there were some 265 daimyo, we now know of less than a dozen that systematized their *han* law in a form that could be called a code. Also, the daimyo had a duty, as stipulated in the *Buke Shohatto* (the *Various Laws for Warrior Houses*, a basic law fixing relations between daimyo and the Shogunate), to follow the law of the Shogunate; so most of those few daimyo who issued codes modeled them after the *Osadamegaki* (for example, Fukui, Morioka, Kameyama, and Matsushiro). As noted, however, others borrowed from the Ming Code (for example, Wakayama, Kumamoto, Hirosaki, Aizu, and Shibata) and to lesser extent from the Ch'ing Code. We can roughly classify the *han* codes into two types after 1742: those following the Chinese, and those patterned after the *Osadamegaki*. However, several of the codes actually showed both Shogunal and Chinese influences (for example, Shibata, Aizu, and Wakayama);[5] indeed, even those revealing the greatest Chinese influence had traces of Shogunal law in them. In addition, many *han* followed their own peculiar customary law. Thus, much diversity of legal practice in fact existed until the end.[6] We will generally survey *han* codes of the Chinese type, after first considering the lesser Chinese influences discernible even in the law of the Shogunate.[7]

Chinese Influences on the Law of the Shogunate

General Institutional Influences

The New Jurisprudence. Before explaining specific influences from China in the *Osadamegaki*, perhaps we should note again that the Chinese legal literature imported in the early eighteenth century, especially the Ming Code commentaries, had a pervasive influence on the major jurists and jurisprudence of the Shogunate, and seems to have sparked several institutional changes as well. The Chinese sources taught the Edo jurists the value and technique of codification and were highly esteemed as reference materials.[8] Illustrative of such influence on the new Edo jurisprudence is the preface of compilation of Edo law just prior to the *Osadamegaki*, which includes remarks on the Ming Code showing the authority it had among the Tokugawa elite: "The Broad Meaning of the Code of the Great Ming (*Ta Ming lü ta-i*; *Dai Min ritsu no taii*) says that the codes are the law for governing All-under-Heaven . . . the above-mentioned compilation is not the work of private imaginations. Rather, the preface of the Code of the Great Ming is nothing other than a record in brief of the August thoughts of the Sage Kings of yore."[9]

Remarks by daimyo Maeda Tsunanori, by the Confucian scholar, Hayashi Nobuatsu, and also by several *han* jurists imply a similar respect for the Ming Code. But there was also an overriding Japanese independence of judgment easily detectable in potentates such as Yoshimune and Tsunanori, and in advisers such as Muro Kyūsō and Arai Hakuseki; even though they valued Chinese legal references, they would use them to support Japanese ideas. Besides the reservations that Maeda Tsunanori had about the Ming Code, which we will discuss below, we have Arai's discussion—typical of the more independent jurists—of a major criminal case that arose under the sixth Shogun Ienobu (1709-1712).[10]

The case turned on the issue of whether it was criminal for a wife to report to the authorities that her father had murdered her husband. Of course the father's act was criminal, but the rule, peculiar by Western standards, was that a child committed a public crime by reporting to authorities crimes of its father (or other family superiors).[11] The question here was whether the usual rule was inapplicable because the daughter's husband was the victim. Did the duty of wife to husband override the duty of child to father, or, stated in public terms, did the duty to the government to report the murderer of one's husband override the duty to the government not to report the father as a murderer? Though Hakuseki's statement of the case can be read in different ways,[12] it seems to frame the question in terms of whether duties of filial piety (*kō*) supersede duties of loyalty (*chū*). By accepted theory the Japanese would answer negatively: the proper relationship is loyalty over filial piety (*chū-kō*).

Quite apart from what the actual answer might be in a positive-law approach, it is fascinating for a sure-footed case lawyer to see Arai Hakuseki argue, when asked to advise Ienobu, first that the husband-wife relationship is analogous to the duty of loyalty (*chū*), and then that the wife was not guilty for reporting her father. In so arguing, Hakuseki cited the "Code" and several Chinese examples. Opinions were also expressed by two other leading Shogunal Confucianists (*jukan*): Muro Kyūsō and Hayashi Nobuatsu. Hayashi argued, also citing Chinese texts, that many men could be a husband, but that there is only one father. Muro Kyūsō took a position rather similar to that of Hakuseki, exonerating the wife. We can omit the niceties and simply point out the stress on Chinese law. All three men, in the account given by Arai Hakuseki, referred to the Code and cited classical Chinese rules and cases to assist in solving this problem.[13] But the result was more Japanese than Chinese; the wife was allowed to enter a Buddhist "convent" at her own suggestion. Actually, under the Ming Code also it seems clear that the wife would have been found guiltless. Perhaps more important than the resolution of this substantive issue is the fact that Confucianists by this time were being asked for advice in such cases, and therefore Chinese legal sources were regarded as naturally proper in the rhetoric of adjudication, at least when a case merited the Shogun's attention. We hasten to add that one reason that the Shogun Ienobu was involved in this case was because the Conference Chamber (*hyōjōsho*) was having difficulty in deciding the case, but seemed to favor conviction of the wife based on an inapposite precedent of its own.

This case is an example of what is often called the Confucianization and bureaucratization of the Shogunate during this period. Overall, the criminal law was moving from a harsh military to a softened civilian system of penalties. Chinese legal studies were useful in supplying the modes for expressing these new principles as the above arguments of Arai Hakuseki, Muro Kyūsō, and Hayashi Nobuatsu show.

Six Admonitions. To further the new jurisprudence, Yoshimune conceived the idea of distributing the *Amplification of the Six Admonitions* (*Rikuyu engi; Liu-yü yen-i*) from China. In 1397, on the order of Emperor T'ai-tsu of the Ming dynasty, the Board of Revenue had circulated a simple version to the people of China on wooden plaques:[14]

> His Majesty commanded the Board of Revenue to hand down an order to the people of All-under-Heaven, that each village was to equip itself with one wooden bell, and that it was to select from among its own people an aged or a blind person, who six times every month was to go through the streets, bell in hand, proclaiming:
> (1) Be respectful and obedient to your fathers and mothers!
> (2) Revere and honor your elders and superiors!
> (3) Keep peace and harmony in the village!
> (4) Instruct your children and grandchildren!
> (5) Be content each with his own livelihood!
> (6) And commit no wrong!!

Then in Ch'ing times we are told that the Shun-chih emperor issued his *Liu-yü* in 1652, and that a longer version (sixteen articles) entitled *Sheng-yü* (*Holy Admonitions*), was distributed in 1670.[15] A copy of the *Liu-yü* issued by the Shun-chih emperor in 1652, with a commentary in colloquial Chinese by Fan Hung, was printed as the *Amplification of the Six Admonitions* and taken to the Ryukyus by Tei Junsoku (Ch'eng Shun-tse). Thence a copy came to Shimazu Yoshitaka, daimyo of Satsuma at the southern tip of Kyushu island; he in turn presented a copy to Yoshimune in 1721.[16] Yoshimune had Ogyū Sorai supply it with diacritical markings (*kunten*), so that the colloquial Chinese could be more easily understood by Japanese readers, and had Muro Kyūsō[17] do a simple Japanese translation (*wakun*) and commentary. The resultant Japanese version of the *Amplification of the Six Admonitions* was then distributed for use as a model for calligraphy practice in the temple schools (*terakoya*)[18] maintained for the education of commoners. Law and morality are quite mixed in an official measure of this sort, but such mixture itself is characteristic of jural life of the times, and it illustrates as well the interest of the Shogun in influencing behavior by widely communicating standard sets of Confucianistic norms throughout the populace.[19]

Complaint Box. The complaint box (*sojo bako*) was one of Yoshimune's much debated innovations. If the idea came from Chinese practice ("complaint drum": *teng-wen ku*), it must have come to Yoshimune's attention early during his Chinese law studies in Wakayama, for he installed his first complaint box there while he was still a daimyo (1705-1716). At about the same time, Ienobu (sixth Shogun) was being flooded with anonymous complaints and "dropped" letters (*sute-bumi*) in the wake of the prior excesses of Tsunayoshi, the "Dog Shogun." Muro Kyūsō (favoring) and Arai Hakuseki (opposing) debated the advisability of Ienobu's accepting such petitions in some routine fashion.[20] Hakuseki, because of his persuasive, advantageous position near the seat of power, prevailed temporarily, and so petitions were largely suppressed under Ienobu and Ietsugu.

Hakuseki argued that the petitions, if accepted and routinely processed by whatever procedure, would have little value; whereas Muro Kyūsō argued that some might contain useful ideas and that, in any event, granting petitioners direct access to the Shogun would stimulate to a better performance all officials who might be thus subject to criticism. In 1721 Yoshimune, agreeing with Muro Kyūsō's reasons, installed a complaint box in front of the Conference Chamber (*hyōjōsho*), the highest "court" in Edo, with a bulletin board (*kōsatsu*) alongside providing instructions for its use.[21] Yoshimune himself kept the only key to the box, and several useful and well-publicized complaints were received.

The Ming Code, consistent with a long tradition, had provided that honest, direct complaints to the emperor could be made with impunity:[22] "If anyone shall appear as a suppliant before the Imperial carriage, or beat the complaint drum (*teng-wen ku*), then present a petition not supported by fact, he shall be punished with 100 blows of the heavy bamboo. If the offense is a grave one, the punishment shall be determined in accord with its gravity. If the petition proves to be factual the petitioner shall be considered guiltless.[23]

These Chinese and Tokugawa practices had a similar purpose,[24] but they differed in some details. One should probably not press the analogy beyond indicating the possibility that Yoshimune's innovation was suggested by his knowledge of the Chinese tradition, which predates the Ming,[25] of maintaining a "complaint drum" to give people direct access to the emperor. However, we find no references to Chinese practice in Yoshimune's records as direct proof of borrowing in this instance.

Specific Shogunal Borrowings in the Osadamegaki Hyakkajo[26]

Fines. In 1718 Yoshimune instituted fines for the first time in the Tokugawa penal system. The provision for execution of fines is found in the *Osadamegaki*, Book II, Article 103:[27]

> [Article 103] (Of the Modes of Punishment)
> FINES.
> To be of three *kwammon* and of five *kwammon*
>
> However, in the more serious cases, ten *ryō* and even twenty or thirty *ryō* may be imposed according to the offender's means, or in case of villages in proportion to their tax assessment, the amount of the fine to be fixed by the court, the payment to be made within three days from the date of judgment. In cases where the offender's means are very small and he is unable to pay a fine, hand-cuffing to be imposed instead. (1718)

Apparently the T'ang-influenced Japanese *Yōrō-ritsu* of 718 contained a system of fines called "restitutive copper" (*shokudō*),[28] and though the term used in the *Osadamegaki* is *karyō*, Yoshimune seems to have used the term *shokudō*[29] in considering the adoption of the new system of fines, thus suggesting that he was aware of the precedent in the Japanese T'ang-styled Code. Before Yoshimune, the last use of fines in Japanese legal experience seems to have been in some of the pre-Tokugawa provincial codes of the so-called era of warring provinces (*Sengoku jidai*), 1467-1567.[30] Yoshimune's revival of fines thus occurred a century after the last known Japanese use, at least by the central authority. It would seem rather likely, though direct evidence is again lacking, that Yoshimune was at least in part influenced by the Ming use of a restitutive copper system (*shu-t'ung chih*) or by the Chinese precedents in general, though his use of fines was more limited and not a general system of redemption.[31] Some opposition arose to the adoption of fines, which Yoshimune is said to have answered by citing ancient Chinese precedent:[32]

> Now, although fines had not existed down through the incumbency of his predecessor, he [Yoshimune] commanded the levying of respective fines, on the grounds that they had been in practice in the government of King Wen of Chou. Though there were many who said, "What does this mean? What is one to think of the act of buying off one's guilt by paying gold and silver into the public exchequer?," they proved by this not only that they failed to understand the distinguished thinking of an enlightened lord, but also that they were themselves without learning.

Collateral evidence of Ming influence on the fines in the *Osadamegaki* may be found in the *Provincial Penal Code* (*Kokuritsu*) of Wakayama *han*. The compilers of that Code felt that the fines imposed by the *Osadamegaki* were based on analogies to Ming practice.[33] But of more interest is Yoshimune's inquiry of Maeda Tsunanori about the latter's use of fines in Kanazawa. The interview took place, with Hayashi Nobuatsu mediating as spokesman for Yoshimune, a year after he had adopted the fines (1719) and after some opposition had arisen:[34]

> [Hayashi]: "Now in your province how is the *kasen* fine imposed? Does it depend on the social status of the person concerned? Also, what are the purposes to which revenues from the fine are applied?"
>
> To these august questions, the reply was as follows:
>
> [Tsunanori]: "The *kasen* fine, to be sure, does exist. Without change since my predecessor's time, it has been imposed on persons of low status such as townsmen and peasants. On persons of consequence, however, be they even persons of only petty dignity, *kasen* is not imposed. Nor do the details of the levy vary with the person on whom the levy is made, for the sum is fixed beforehand. The sum levied is determined by the gravity of the offense. When it is a matter of mere restitution through payment, depending on the sum of the fine, those with wealth actually go off free. *Kasen* revenue is used throughout the province for highways, excavations, bridges, and the like, and is never applied to our own private purposes. . . ." Since his Lordship had examined the Code of the Great Ming beforehand, he was at no loss for

an answer. Such, at any rate, is the somewhat boastful tone in which the story is told . . .

Yoshimune had considerable respect for Tsunanori as an elder, a legal scholar, and major daimyo, and we may suppose that Tsunanori's answer, based allegedly on his reference to the Ming Code, influenced Yoshimune to retain the fines. Tsunanori's proud reliance on the Ming Code itself tells us something of the Code's role in Tokugawa jurisprudence, even if we discount the official records for the usual pedantic Chinese bias of their Confucian authors.

Beating. Similarly, Yoshimune's adoption of the penalty of beating (*kōkei*) in 1720 for the first time in Tokugawa practice may have been suggested to him by his Ming studies. Execution of the penalty was specified in the *Osadamegaki*, Book II, Article 103:[35]

> [Article 103:]
> BASTINADO [beating].
>
> Fifty blows to be the normal number; severe flogging, one hundred blows.
>
> To be inflicted publicly before the prison gate, along the culprit's shoulders, back and buttocks, avoiding the spine, so that he may not faint. [Two] coroners are to be sent [from the court] and the flogging is to be administered by the prison wardens [*dōshin*].
>
> If the culprit be a townsman, his landlord and the headman of his street, if a countryman, his village mayor and the headman of the punchayets [five-man group; *goningumi*] are to be summoned to witness the flogging and to take charge of him afterwards. If he has no home, he is to be discharged to go his way in front of the prison gate. (1720)

Because of its novelty in Tokugawa Japan, beating also encountered some opposition in Edo circles. This time Yoshimune got no support from Tsunanori, who apparently opposed beating on humanitarian grounds, despite its use in China.[36] Nevertheless, Yoshimune enforced this innovation in order to have a broader range of penalties especially appropriate to lighter offenses. Very probably he took his cue from the Ming practice. In any event, beating was practiced until the end of the era, except for a two-year period (1747-1749) when it was abolished temporarily.[37]

Abolition of the Penalty of Severing Ears and Noses. Severing ears and noses, or fingers, was an ancient Japanese penalty widely practiced in early Tokugawa Japan. In 1709 Ienobu abolished these cruel penalties, but in 1718 Yoshimune reinstituted them. Then in 1720, when tattooing was adopted as a lighter penalty, severing of ears and noses was discontinued forever by the Shogunate. Again, the abolition of these penalties may have been determined ultimately by their absence in the Ming Code, a fact that Tsunanori made known in another amusing dialogue held with Hayashi at Yoshimune's request:[38]

> [Hayashi]: "The Shogun [in 1718] is also of the opinion that flesh punishment [*nikkei*] should be introduced. How should this be gone about? Does flesh punishment obtain in your province as well?"
>
> [Tsunanori]: "This, I believe, would be all the better. To be sure, it had been in practice in my province as well since previous generations, but since the time of Joken'in [Ienobu], there appears to be no use of flesh punishment, no matter where one inquires. This means that in recent years it has been discontinued. In my view, it would be well to reinstitute it."
>
> When he had said this, Hayashi added: "To be sure, since it is found in the Great Ming Code as well, I believe it would be well to institute it."
>
> [Tsunanori]: "It has never been in the Great Ming Code! Even if it were, the penalties of the Great Ming Code are inadequate for use of the Shogunate!"
>
> [Hayashi]: "Why do you say that? If it is in the Great Ming Code, it is appropriate as penal law."
>
> To that, in turn, [Tsunanori's] retort was: "That is not so! The Ming Court did not have a single sage-prince or wise minister in several generations! Such being the case, it is inadequate. Besides, there is the law that has come down from sages since the time of Yao and Shun, which is the law of the Five Punishments. How can one set it aside and adopt the Great Ming Code instead? Flesh punishment such as the severance of ears and noses, being the law of the Sages, is, in my view, proper."

Thus, for his short-lived use of these harsh penalties (1718-1720), Yoshimune had the full support of Tsunanori, who, as in his opposition to beating, was disposed to stick closely to Japanese precedent. Conservative though he was, Yoshimune was willing to innovate, and after a brief two years he gave up the severance of ears and noses, even though such practices were approved in the Japanese tradition.

Summary of Chinese Influence in Shogunal Law

In considering Chinese legal influences on the Edo Shogunate, I have emphasized above only the innovations that were made by Yoshimune during his institutional reforms or were included in his compilation of the *Osadamegaki* (1742). My discussion did not attempt to deal with the other pervading similarities (and differences) of family and social philosophy arising from a long history of Japanese adaptations from Chinese law. To recapitulate, I have theorized that the popular rules in the *Six Admonitions*, and perhaps the institution of the complaint box as well, came from China. Also, I suggested that Yoshimune and his colleagues had the Ming (or T'ang) Codes in mind when they adopted fines and beating, and when they abandoned the "flesh penalties."

On the other hand, the vast differences between the *Osadamegaki* and the Ming Code need little emphasis. In a rough way the drafters of the *Osadamegaki* tried to follow the T'ang *ritsuryō* format containing two parts: administrative decrees (Book I), and penal provisions (Book II), the latter popularly known as the *Hyakkajō* (100 articles). But the *Osadamegaki* was simple, short (81 articles in Book I; 103 in Book II) and not very systematic; it lacked the analytically sophisticated definitions and general principles of the Ming Code. The *Osadamegaki* was new and direct, even rough, whereas the Ming Code was heir to a tradition of code making, awesome in all history for its continuity and refinement. Actually, the Tokugawa penal *Hyakkajō* (Book II) was largely made up of redactions of prior Tokugawa case precedents, much like the substatutes (*t'iao-li*) of later Ming practice, but without the analytic code organization or abstract structuring of the *lü*. To the extent that the substatutes later became, in fact, the bulk of the "law" in Ch'ing times, the Chinese sources of law and the ever-accumulating Tokugawa case law may have been becoming more similar in juristic method toward the end of their respective eras.

But a much more basic difference lies in their functions. The *Osadamegaki* was to be kept secret from the populace and was compiled for the convenience of judicial officers only; hence the formal name *Kujikata Osadamegaki*—*Kujikata* meaning judicial affairs. The *Osadamegaki* was intended as a guide for internal distribution. In contrast, the Ming law was not so limited; to encourage popular awareness, the early Ming emperors had mitigated penalties for those defendants who possessed a copy of the early law (*Ta-kao*).

Ideally, Tokugawa jurisprudence was conceived as a kind of equity uninhibited by legal rules. The Solomon-like judge rendered justice based on the consideration of the whole man and all of the circumstances. This simplistic and synoptic model of adjudication failed in practice because the "judges" (*bugyō*), who were primarily administrative officers, soon became too busy to learn all of the circumstances in each case. They began to render perfunctory decisions based on the records prepared by clerks, who in turn followed the rules of unpublished precedents. The

Osadamegaki was actually compiled to replace the assorted private compilations by providing an official guide. Even so, the theory of the *Osadamegaki* was ambivalent in purpose. It seemed to envisage the judge as reaching decisions according to his own conscience, with such reference to the *Osadamegaki* as he might find convenient.

This is a far cry from the legalistic structures of the Ming Code, particularly as found in the substatutes and cases. These seemed to bind judges and thereby to protect the absolute authority of the emperor to legislate and to ultimately decide all major cases on appeal. In contrast, the Tokugawa legal system (*bakuhan*) was the epitome of delegated judicial decision making: the "judge" in each tiny domain was the court of first and last instances for most cases (excluding diversity cases). The Shoguns themselves by the eighteenth century had no active role in adjudication. However, we should note that within the Shogunal domain (about one-eighth of Japan), there was a system of "appeal" that required lower officials to ask instructions from Edo superiors before the graver penalties could be ordered and executed. Also, as was seen above, even some of the smaller daimyo *han* did in fact request Shogunal instructions before executing graver penalties—even though such deference to Edo was not required by law.[39] With these basic differences, we would not expect the Ming or Ch'ing influence on the *Osadamegaki* to be very extensive, and it was not. Several of the daimyo codes compiled later show much more direct influence.

Chinese Influences on Several Daimyo Codes

Throughout over 260 years of feudal Tokugawa hegemony, only a rather small number of the approximately 265 daimyo, who quite autonomously governed fiefs comprising about three-fourths of the rice yield, compiled their penal laws in any form resembling a code. As noted, the *Buke Shohatto* required the daimyo to conform to Edo law, and most of the small ones seem to have done so in a general way, or managed with their own customs without a comprehensive code of their own. Those of the larger *han* that did in fact compile their own codes usually followed the *Osadamegaki* rather closely, but a few larger *han* compiled codes that were partially modeled on the Ming Code, especially that code's penal part (*hsing-lü*). The chief examples are:

(1) The *Draft Penal Law* (*Keihō sōsho*; 1754) of Kumamoto *han*.[40]
(2) The *Provincial Penal Code* (*Kokuritsu*; 1801-1804) of Wakayama *han*.
(3) The *Catalogue of Penal Law* (*Go-keihō-chō*; 1797) of Hirosaki *han*.
(4) The *Criminal Rules* (*Keisoku*; 1790) of the Aizu *han* in the northern province, Mutsu.

(5) The *New Penal Code* (*Shinritsu*; 1793) of the Shibata *han* in Echigo province.

Late in the period (1862), Kochi *han* in Tosa compiled a most unusual and interesting Code, which revealed considerable Chinese legal influence.[41] It consisted of two parts—the *Kainan seiten* and the *Kainan ritsurei*—and was written in Japanized Chinese (*kambun*).[42] It followed the overall format, but not necessarily the content, of the T'ang Code (i.e., *seiten* was administrative and *ritsurei*, penal).

Even those compiling the *han* codes on the basis of Ming and Ch'ing law often did so in conjunction with study of the *Osadamegaki* and, as might be expected, even those *han* codes which borrowed most from the Ming or Ch'ing Codes made drastic changes in the Chinese law to adapt it to Japanese conditions. The tiny Japanese domains were hardly comparable to the vast Chinese empire. In their practice of adaptation, the compilers echoed the Confucianist Ogyū Sorai when he argued for rejection of the orthodox Tokugawa *Shushigaku* (neo-Confucian Chu Hsi Learning) and for adoption of the more ancient texts,[43] with their smaller models more suitable for Japan. The compilers felt that the smaller Japanese context required a more personalized and more direct approach to Japanese social problems. Thus, with the exception of some of the titles of the Wakayama Code, all portions of the Ming Code dealing with crimes of officials and the hierarchical Chinese administrative and military practices were largely ignored. Only the provisions for ordinary crimes were used as models. Although after further study other *han* codes may be found to have Chinese influence,[44] I will here comment briefly on the five best known of the Chinese-styled, *han* penal codes, in order to indicate some of the uses made of Chinese law in the latter half of the eighteenth century.

The Kumamoto Code

Best known of all the *han* codes for its early and extensive borrowing from Ming law is the *Draft Penal Law*[45] (*Keihō sōsho*; 1754) of Kumamoto *han* (540,000 *koku*; 1 *koku* = 4.96 bushels) in Kyushu. Kumamoto was governed by the important outside (*tozama*) daimyo family named Hosokawa, and the *Draft Penal Law* was one part of much broader reforms[46] effected by a famous incumbent, Hosokawa Shigekane (tenure 1747-1785). The Great Commissioner (*dai-bugyō*) Hori Heitazaemon Katsura supervised the reforms and Shimizu Saisuke and others assisted with the legal drafting. Hori is said to have had himself beaten with the "light bamboo" in order to understand its effectiveness and the danger of overuse.[47] A major reason for the new code was to adopt a new system of more varied and more humane penalties to replace the harsh penalties imposed during the political and social chaos of the sixteenth century.

As the name *Draft Penal Law* implies, the Kumamoto Code was to be perfected later, apparently through use and experiment. Indeed, this cumulative process is clearly shown in the particular version published by Kyoto University in 1943. Comments and new precedents were added from time to time in the blank spaces left for such additions after each provision. However, the original provisions remained in effect and unchanged for 116 years until 1871, when all daimyo in Japan relinquished their fiefs to the newly restored imperial government in Tokyo. This Code was thus the oldest, and its materials the most complete, of all the daimyo codes that manifested extensive Chinese influences. The Kumamoto records (showing the Code's growth and application [1754-1871], as well as its sources and genesis during the pre-1754 drafting process) deserve a full-scale comparative study.

The 94 articles of the Code are organized into eight chapters (*hen*). The chapter titles are drawn with only slight changes from the penal law part that is one of seven major parts in the Ming Code. In addition, the important initial part of the Ming Code, "Terms and General Principles" (*Ming-li lü, Myorei ritsu*) was included. It was first appended to the end of the Kumamoto *Draft Penal Law* of 1754, but was later slightly revised and brought to the front, as in the Ming Code. The other five principal parts of the Ming Code (Administrative, Civil, Ritual, Military, and Public Works) were relevant mainly to the huge hierarchy of administrative units in China. The *han* code adapted these provisions only if they seemed functional in the context of a penal code of a tiny, semi autonomous, Japanese fief. Other provisions, not found in the Ming Code, but necessary in the Japanese context, were written in. Minor references to the Ch'ing Code are also found. (For example, see the chapter on assault and battery.)[48]

A distinctive Ming feature was the insertion of Kumamoto case derived substatutes (*li*; *rei*) at the end of each main statute (with room for such additions as might accrue with use). Probably the model was the compilation of substatutes, *Monkei jōrei* (*Wen-hsing t'iao-li*), as found in Ogyū's *Ming Code and Commentary*. The format on each page of the Kumamoto draft was similar to that of a Chinese printed code, perhaps suggesting reference to Ch'ing materials in later years. Approximately the lower 60 percent of each horizontally divided page was taken up with the main statutes (*lü*), followed by any substatutes. The upper 40 percent was reserved for pertinent comments and precedents in chronological order. Fortunately, the printed version[49] available to scholars today is based on a late copy apparently used by a Kumamoto *han* "judicial" official until 1872. Thus, it has many valuable comments, substatutes, and precedents. The substatutes were first compiled in 1839, but others were added regularly thereafter. The earliest substatute appearing in the printed version of the Code is 1754, the latest, 1871.

As noted, a striking Ming import was the introductory chapter of "Terms and General Principles." However, the content of the *Draft Penal Law* generally reflected its purpose to reform and ameliorate the outmoded system of penalties. Before the 1754 codification Kumamoto had had two main types of penalties: death (*shikei*) and banishment (*tsuiho*).[50] There were also some special penalties—such as the one for nonpayment of rice taxes: the delinquent farmer was placed in the "water prison" (*mizurō*) (i.e., tied to a stake and submerged). This unusual penalty was later abolished and two new penalties—beating and penal servitude (*t'u; to-kei*)—were borrowed from Ming practice. Penal servitude (always accompanied by beating in Kumamoto) was a complete novelty in Tokugawa practice[51] at this time, though Hirosaki and other *han* used it later. In addition, the almost complete abolition of banishment in Kumamoto was unusual in Tokugawa Japan; this practice was followed only by Aizu and not by Hirosaki or Wakayama when those *han* eventually adopted penal servitude.[52]

Although, in general, the *Draft Penal Law*'s penalties were lighter than either those of the Ming or the customary penalties of Kumamoto law, there were exceptions. For example, whereas under the Ming Code a person convicted of intentionally killing a parent or grandparent would be punished with immediate execution of the sentence of death by slicing, the Kumamoto Code provided for immediate crucifixion plus delivery of the criminal's wife and children to slavery. Even this harsh penalty was increased by an 1822 substatute: the murderer's house was destroyed and the house lot left permanently vacant after digging off the top soil.[53]

Despite the influence of Ming law, the effect of the *Osadamegaki* on the Kumamoto Code was still evident—as was required by the *Various Laws for Warrior Houses* (*Buke Shohatto*). For example, concerning counterfeiting, falsifying weights or measures, and sale of humans, the Kumamoto Code compilers first wrote down only the titles of the crimes with a note to check Edo practice and fill in the penalties. Then, in 1814 there is a note that these provisions had been filled in by reference in Shogunal law.[54]

The Wakayama Code

The *Provincial Penal Code* (*Kokuritsu*)[55] was compiled *c.* 1801-1804 (precise date unknown) under Tokugawa Iehiro, apparently by his Confucianist adviser, Yamamoto Tamenoshin (d. 1806).[56] Wakayama, fief of Yoshimune before he became the eighth Shogun (1716), was one of the largest *han* (555,000 *koku*). It was presided over by one of the most important daimyo, a member of one of the Three Branch Houses (*gosanke*) of the Tokugawa family with holdings including the whole province of Kii. The territorial extent and political prestige of the Wakayama *han* is reflected in the title of the *han* Code, *Provincial Penal Code*, and in its independence of content, which drew heavily on the Ming Code. Some influence of the *Osadamegaki* is discernible, however. The Ming influence is not surprising, since a tradition of Ming Code studies had started more than a century before this *Provincial Penal Code* emerged, with the Wakayama Confucianist Sakakibara Kōshū (d. 1706) followed by Takase Kiboku, and then by Yoshimune himself as daimyo (1705-1716).

Fortunately, in addition to the printed copy (*Murata-bon*) of this Code, another manuscript copy exists at Kyoto University in two major volumes with the important later supplement (*Kokuritsu hojo*), dating sometime after 1844, printed separately.[57] Both the Code and the supplement have eighteen divisions (or *lü; ritsu*). The Code has fifty-six subdivisions (*hen*), the supplement, sixty-five. Figure 8.1[58] shows the correspondence of the eighteen divisions (*ritsu*) of the *Provincial Penal Code* with subdivisions of the seven divisions (*lü*) of the Ming Code.

FIGURE 8.1

Comparison of Format of Ming and Wakayama Codes

Ming Code	*Provincial Penal Code and Supplement*
	Terms (Ming-li lü)
Terms and general principles (*Ming-li-lü*)	Terms and general principles (*Myōrei ritsu*) (1)
	Administrative Law (Li lü)
Administrative regulations (*Chih-chih*)	
Standards of official behavior (*Kung-shih*)	Standards of official behavior (*Kōshiki ritsu*) (2)
	Civil Law (Hu lü)
Family and corvee (*Hu-i*)	
Land and fields (*T' ien-chai*)	
Marriage (*Hun-yin*)	
Government granaries and treasuries (*Ts'ang-k'u*)	Government granaries and treasuries (*Sōko ritsu*) (5)
Taxes and tariffs (*K'o-ch'eng*)	

Ming Code	*Provincial Penal Code and Supplement*
Moneylending (*Ch'ien-chai*)	
Public markets (*Shih-ch'an*)	

Ritual Law (Li lü)

Ming Code	*Provincial Penal Code and Supplement*
State sacrifices (*Chi-ssu*)	State sacrifices (*Saishi ritsu*) (6)
Ceremonial regulations (*I-chih*)	Ceremonial regulations (*Gisei ritsu*) (4)

Military Law (Ping lü)

Ming Code	*Provincial Penal Code and Supplement*
Imperial palaces and guards (*Kung-wei*)	Defense of forbidden area (*Eikin ritsu*) (3)
Administration of the armed forces (*Chün-cheng*)	
Frontier guard posts (*Kuan-ching*)	Barriers and fords (*Kanshin ritsu*) (7)
Horses and cattle (*Chiu-mu*)	
Postal services and transport (*Yu-i*)	

Penal Law (Hsing lü)

Ming Code	*Provincial Penal Code and Supplement*
Violence and theft (*Tsei-tao*)	Theft and violence (*Tōzoku ritsu*) (8)
Homicide (*Jen-ming*)	Homicide (*Jimmei ritsu*) (9)
Affrays and blows (*Tou-ou*)	Affrays and blows (*Tōō ritsu*) (10)
Abusive language (*Ma-li*)	
Accusations and suits (*Su-sung*)	Accusations and suits (*Soshō ritsu*) (11)
Bribery and squeeze (*Shou-tsang*)	
Deception and fraud (*Cha-wei*)	Deception and fraud (*Sagi ritsu*) (12)
Sexual violations (*Fan-chien*)	Sexual violations (*Hankan ritsu*) (13)
Miscellaneous offenses (*Tsa-fan*)	Miscellaneous offenses (*Zappan ritsu*) (14)
Arrests and escapes (*Pu-wang*)	Arrests and escapes (*Hobō ritsu*) (15)
Trial and imprisonment (*Tuan-yü*)	Trial and imprisonment (*Dangoku ritsu*) (16)

Ming Code	Provincial Penal Code and Supplement
Public Works Law (Kung lü)	
Public construction (*Ying-tsao*)	
River conservancy (*Ho-fang*)	

NOTE: The number enclosed in parentheses is the number of the particular "law" (*lü*) within the *Provincial Penal Law* and its *Supplement*.

Of the seven major parts of the Ming Code, the seventh, "Public Works Law" (*Kung-lü*), is left out entirely in the *Provincial Penal Code*'s titles, and two parts not found in the Ming Code are added for special Japanese reasons: the "Temple and Shrine Law" (*Jisha ritsu*) and the "Related Guilt Law" (*Renkyū ritsu*). However, the chief emphasis is on the ordinary crimes, and some provisions of all major subdivisions of the penal part of the Ming Code are included, except the one on "Abusive Language" and the one on "Bribery."

Several distinctive features of this particular Code are notable. First, unlike most of the other daimyo codes, it includes titles and borrowing from parts other than the penal law. Second, the *Provincial Penal Code* includes the important "Terms and General Principles" (*Ming-li lü*) at the beginning, as in the Ming Code. Third, the "Ten Abominations" (*shih-o, juaku*) and "Eight Considerations" (*pa-i; hachigi*) are included. Last, the non-Ming "Related Guilt Law" is novel in this kind of Tokugawa Code.

In addition, the comments in the Kyoto University copy of the Code (red notations on the manuscript)[59] refer three times specifically to the Ming Code, and nineteen times to the "Law" (*lü*)—unmistakably the Ming Code, as its language is quoted rather directly in most instances. Although the practice of adding these red comments was more indicative of the application of the Code than of its drafting process, in an examination of the corresponding provisions in the *Provincial Penal Code*, Kobayakawa found that their language conforms to that of the Ming Code in substance with only minor adaptation to *han* conditions.

Occasional adjustment in the Ming Code was made. For example, in one place the *Provincial Penal Code* comments (in red):

> Whereas the *Kōsai* [*Osadamegaki*] says that one who kills his master shall be crucified, the [Ming] Code says that one who kills the head of his former household shall be treated like an ordinary criminal; there is a great deal of difference in degree of gravity between the two. Such being the case, the penalty shall be decapitation with exposure of the severed head, which is more appropriate.[60]

Our comparisons above show clearly enough that the *Provincial Penal Code* of Wakayama was drawn up about 1800 and was based largely on the Ming Code format. For content, it drew to a considerable extent upon the *Osadamegaki* as well,[61] though detailed qualitative comparison must await other analysis.

Hirosaki Han

The Ming Code was most influential in northern Japan through the codification projects in Hirosaki *han* (100,000 *koku*) in Mutsu province. Major reforms were undertaken under Tsugaru Nobuaki (1784–1791), eighth daimyo of the Tsugaru, a distinguished feudal family with Outside Lord (*Tozama*) status. These reforms were continued by his successor, Tsugaru Yasuchika (ninth), who established a *han* school (*Keikokan*) in 1796 where the Ming Code was used as a textbook for study.

Codification by reference to the Ming Penal Code, as well as the Shogunal law and local precedents, was also begun under Nobuaki and completed under Yasuchika. Makino Sajirō, a chamberlain (*goyōnin*), was first in charge of the actual research and drafting, but he was succeeded by a Ban Saisuke who completed a shorter version of the Code called *The Catalogue of Penal Law* (*Go-keihō-chō*) in 1794 (effective in 1797). Extensive revisions were completed in 1810,[62] and a printed copy of this document is available.[63]

The Catalogue of Penal Law has seven chapters (*hen*) resembling Ming nomenclature:

(1) Terms and General Principles (*Myōrei; Ming-li*)
(2) Homicide (*Jimmei; Jen-ming*)
(3) Violence and Theft (*Tōzoku; Tsei-tao*)
(4) Bribery (*Wairo; Shou-tsang*)
(5) Land and Fields (*Dentaku; T'ien-chai*)
(6) Storehouses (*Sōko; Ts'ang-k'u*)
(7) Complaints (*Soshō; Su-sung*)

Two *han* officials (Hasegawa Kenkichi and Kurotaki Tōta) were sent to Edo to discuss the draft with Shogunal jurists (*hōritsuka*). This consultation is said to have produced some changes; for example, the penalty of burning at the stake (*kakei*) followed the *Osadamegaki*.[64] As noted, the Code was then enforced in 1797, but revised in 1810 in a version called the Bunka Code (1804–1817). The earlier version had only 98 articles, but the revision contained 175. The initial chapter entitled *Go-keihō meimōku* ("List of names for the penal law"), is somewhat similar to the Ming Code's "Terms and General Principles."[65]

Some of the provisions of this Code are very similar in their language to Ming provisions, and the Code contains Ming penalties such as beating and penal servitude as well as fines (though by this time, 1797, Edo practice also included beating and fines). Moreover, a memorializing preface[66] to the *Catalogue* helps us to clearly understand the use made of the Ming Code in drafting this work:

> Having been commanded on this occasion to reform the penal law, we have conducted an examination, whereupon we have found that the Ming Code, having been fixed by adding to and detracting from the penal law codes of previous ages, takes a position correct in both theory and practice on the relative gravity of offenses. Yet, upon comparison with our own times, the Code as a whole is too severe. Therefore, where the Ming Code prescribes beating with the light bamboo, we make do, in general, with mere barred-door [*tojime*] confinement. Since there are differences in the penal codes quite apart from this, these days, when it is difficult to apply [the Ming Code], we have attached the names of penalties currently in use among us to the categories of the Ming Code, making allowances for differences, and have determined the relative gravity of the respective penalties in accord with the above principles. Of course, within this framework, when guided by the decisions of the Shogunate [*kōgi onsadame*] and governed by our prior laws, there are areas in which the gravity is hard to determine. In these cases we have given and gained [*yotoku*], sifted and strained [*sata*], spooned and ladled [*shin-shaku*], added and subtracted [*kagen*]. As a result, even if upon examination of the penalties prescribed there should prove to be inadvertent omissions among the articles fixed by us on this occasion, we humbly believe that anyone who consults the Ming Code in the spirit just described will readily agree that there is no difference between the two codes where gravity of offenses is concerned. The correspondences, then, with their respective differences, between the titles of the penal laws fixed by us on this occasion and the names of the penalties in the Ming Code are as follows: . . .

Thus, one of the fascinating features of the Hirosaki Code is a list showing *han* penalties and the corresponding harsher Ming penalties.[67] For now, we will pass over the lingual comparison of provisions which can be readily identified as Ming.[68]

The Aizu Han *Code*

In 1790 the Aizu *han* instituted its *Penal Rules* (*Keisoku*).[69] Established in 1643 by the second Shogun Hidetada for his fourth son, Hoshina Masayuki, and his heirs (later given the Tokugawa kinship name of

Matsudaira), Aizu *han* (230,000 *koku*) had a distinguished lineage. Its daimyo was accorded Tokugawa House Family rank (*kamon*). Aizu was located in a part of Mutsu province, now in Fukushima prefecture. In addition to his own land with a putative yield of 230,000 *koku*, the Aizu daimyo managed large lands (50,000 *koku*) entrusted to him by the Shogunate (*azukarisho*).

The *Penal Rules* deserve mention here for their Chinese features, even though the compilers demonstrated both high selectivity and legislative independence. In fact, it seems quite possible that after a new, more extensive *han* Code, the *Collected and Classified Punishments* (*Shioki ruiki*), was compiled during 1802-1814, the Aizu law came to rely more heavily on the *Osadamegaki* than on the Chinese Code. There is evidence of consultations between Hitotsuyanagi Shinzaburō, compiler of the *Shioki ruiki*, and certain Edo officials including Hayashi Daigaku-no-kami,[70] but we know little about the post-1814 Code, because it was never printed and the original has been lost, even in Japan. We only know that it was compiled in 1814 to supersede the *Penal Rules* and to serve as the new Penal Code for Aizu *han*.

The *Penal Rules* of 1790 were compiled under the supervision of an Aizu House Elder (*karō*) named Tanaka Saburōbē in connection with broader reforms of the entire administration. At an early date, Tanaka was on intimate terms with Hori Heitazaemon, who had been a leading figure in the compilation of the *Draft Penal Law* (1754) for Kumamoto *han*. It is said that Tanaka used the Kumamoto reforms as a model, including some of the *Draft Penal Law*'s provisions that had been influenced by Ming law.[71]

Substantively, the *Penal Rules* dealt mainly with penalties. They were intended to ameliorate the harsh methods of punishment previously prevailing in the Aizu administration of criminal justice. Notable was the abolition of the penalty of banishment, and adoption of beating and imprisonment instead.[72] In order to avoid use of the death penalty, the Japanese penalty of severing noses and ears was retained and, together with imprisonment, replaced severer penalties in some instances. Legislative independence is evident, also, in the age range provided for criminal capacity (i.e., over 10, under 80), which was broader than the *Osadamegaki* or the Ming Penal Code.[73] However, Shogunal law continued to require inquiries (*ukagai*) to Edo before penalties could be imposed on criminals from the Shogun's land that had been entrusted to Aizu management (*azukarisho*).

In summary then, the Aizu *Penal Rules* was short-lived (1790-1814), eclectic, and of narrow scope, evidencing independence in several important respects. It contained several identifiable Ming influences, which may have been replaced in part or altered by the new Aizu Code, *Collected and Classified Punishments*, about which we know virtually nothing, as it has apparently been lost to history. The inclusion in the *Penal Rules* of identifiable Chinese legal influences, whether borrowed directly from the Ming Code, or indirectly through the Kumamoto model, is, however, of interest to our subject.

Shibata Code

This Code, called the *New Penal Code*, was completed about 1784 under the supervision of outside (*tozama*) diamyo, Mizoguchi Naoyasu, with the aid of Sato Shōshi and Itakura Kōki.[74] The castletown was Shibata in Echigo province, and the Mizoguchi fief had a putative rice rating of 50,000 koku until it was raised by the Shogunate to 100,000 in 1860.[75]

Naoyasu was devoted to the philosophy of Yamazaki Anzai, and there is considerable evidence in both the arrangement and content of the *New Penal Code* to show that its compiler used both T'ang and Ming sources. In particular, it is also clear that in several sections they adapted the phraseology specifically from Ogyu's *Ming Code and Commentary*.[76] They compiled both the *New Penal Code* and the *Administrative Code* (*Shinryō*) together, suggesting the T'ang format. Influences from the *Osadamegaki* (Book II) are also apparent.

Apart from numerous Ming borrowings traceable in individual provisions, the Ming influence is especially important in two features of the *New Penal Code* affecting its overall conception and arrangement. The first is the order and titles of its ten subdivisions. Like other *han* codes, it was narrowly penal; so it drew seven of its titles from the subdivisions of the Penal Law (*Hsing lü*), but interestingly enough it took for the first three titles the titles of the first three subdivisions of the Ming division entitled, Civil Law (*Hu lü*). All the *New Penal Code* titles are listed below:

(1) Family and Corvée	(*Koyaku; Hu-i*)
(2) Landed Property	(*Dentaku; T'ien-chai*)
(3) Marriage	(*Kon'in; Hun-yin*)
(4) Deceptions and Frauds	(*Sagi; Cha-wei*)
(5) Sexual Violations	(*Hankan; Fan-chien*)
(6) Accusations and Suits	(*Soshō; Su-sung*)
(7) Theft and Violence	(*Tozoku; Tao-tsei*)
(8) Affrays and Blows	(*Tō-ō; Tou-ou*)
(9) Homicide	(*Jimmei; Jen-ming*)
(10) Miscellaneous Offenses	(*Zatshuhan; Tsa-fan*)

The second feature is found in a memorandum appended at the end of the Code entitled *Memorandum on Applying the New Penal Code* (*Shinritsu toriatsukai no oboe*). This memorandum has several provisions reminiscent of the Ming Code. For example, the provision on "toleration of concealment" (*yoin; jung-yin*) reads as follows:[77]

> Item. A person who has seen or heard of another perpetrating an evil deed in violation of the law must immediately report that person. Yet even if a person has plainly seen an evil deed of his grandfather or grandmother, father, mother, uncle (father's brother, whether elder or younger) or aunt (the uncle's wife or the father's sister), elder or younger brother or sister, cousin (son or daughter of one's father's brother whether older or younger than oneself), son of an elder or younger brother, son of an elder or younger sister, son or grandson, son's or grandson's wife, [in the case of a woman], her husband, or husband's mother or father, or husband's elder or younger brother, or a maternal grandfather or grandmother, or one's daughter's son, or the wife of a daughter's son, or a maternal uncle or aunt (mother's brother or sister), is not to report the crime, since such persons are not to inform on one another. This is called leniency [by the authorities] toward toleration and concealment [of relatives' offenses]. Addendum. Concealment by a servant of an evil deed of his master is the same sort of thing.

This corresponds closely to one of the statutes (section 31, *ch'in-shu hsiang wei jung-yin*) of the "Terms and General Principles" of the Ming Code.[78] There are other provisions resembling Ming law in the memorandum, but the foregoing will be sufficient to indicate the nature of the Chinese influence on the *New Penal Code*.

Conclusion

Thus, in addition to the impact of the new Chinese-based jurisprudence and the new "jurists" in the Edo Shogunate, an investigation of several daimyo codes of the late Tokugawa period shows that the Ming Code influenced legal compilations of that time. The influences are especially evident in the large Wakayama, Kumamoto, and Hirosaki domains, with lesser impact on the Aizu and Shibata codes, and perhaps on others yet to be discovered.

The adoption in Wakayama of several subtitles drawn widely from all of the seven "law" titles (except "Public Works"), not just the penal law, shows the heavy influence of the Ming Code in the fief where Ming Code studies seem to have begun in Tokugawa Japan. The introductory "Terms and General Principles," the analytical symbol of the Ming Code, as well as the "Ten Abominations" and the "Eight Considerations" were all adapted to Wakayama needs. These features all create a pronounced Chinese flavor. It was Kumamoto *han*, however, which left the most interesting materials available to show the codification process and the growth thereafter of the Chinese-styled Code during more than a century of application. Here the use of the substatute technique (*t'iao-li*) and the accumulation, as decrees and precedents were added, of an upper commentary show the profound impact of sophisticated Chinese juristic methods on Kumamoto law experts, even though the Code itself was confined almost entirely to the common crimes of ordinary people—a subject covered in a single division of the Ming Code.

Doubtless it was their experience in utilizing China's legal tradition that made the Kumamoto *han* officials Hosokawa Gōkyō (heir apparent), Mizoguchi Kōun (house elder), and Komura Tokutarō prominent during the Meiji Restoration's brief nineteenth-century reception of Chinese penal law.[79] A Chinese-styled criminal code was desired just after the Restoration, because the new imperial Japanese government initially structured itself on ancient Japan's T'ang-styled *ritsuryō* pattern. Though the resulting Code, *Kari keiritsu*, was not promulgated and was effective only for a couple of years (1868–1870) as a guide to officials, the Kumamoto jurists were useful during this interesting episode. The next codes (*Shinritsu kōryo*, 1870; and *Kaitei ritsurei*, 1873) also had Chinese features (mostly Ch'ing), but their passing (1882) virtually ended over a millennium of Chinese influence upon Japan's formal law.

NOTES

1. See Dan F. Henderson, "Chinese Legal Studies in Early 18th Century Japan: Scholars and Sources," *Journal of Asian Studies*, Vol. 30 (1970), pp. 21-56. For Ming Penal Code materials, cf. also Wolfgang Franke, *An Introduction to the Sources of Ming History* (Kuala Lumpur, 1968), p. 184.
2. A word of explanation may be helpful to nonspecialists. The Tokugawa feudal regime was comprised of the Tokugawa Shogun's central domain, which provided about one-quarter of the Japanese rice production. This huge domain was managed by a government called the Shogunate (*bakufu*) in Edo (now Tokyo). The *bakufu* also enforced certain policies, such as isolation, uniform currency, and weights and measures throughout the whole country. The rest of Japan was broken up into some 265 daimyo domains (*han*), and the daimyo acknowledged feudal subordination to the Tokugawa Shogun, but within their *han* (one might say "fief") they had full governing powers to make and enforce law and hold court with only minimal restrictions from Edo. This whole legally decentralized system is called the *bakuhan taisei* by modern historians, and it is necessary to note the daimyo's legal autonomy described above in order to understand his use of Chinese law in code-making activities dealt with hereafter. The daimyo autonomy in criminal law matters is explained well in Hiramatsu Yoshirō, *Kinsei keiji soshōhō no kenkyū* [Study of the Law of Criminal Procedure in the Pre-Modern Period], (To-

kyo, 1960), pp. 3-245. Particularly cf. p. 195 where Hiramatsu explains the tendency of the vast majority of daimyo (the many lesser ones with lands of 50,000 *koku* or less) to rely on instructions of the Shogunate, instead of exercising the full autonomy which the Shogunate itself recognized they had. This voluntary deference to Shogunal practice and instructions doubtless explains in part the fact that, by present count, only ten or twelve of the domains ever issued its own law in a form extensive and sophisticated enough to call a Penal Code.

3. Both Kan's Code and Sorai's commentary were handsomely printed in 1966: Uchida Tomoo and Hihara Toshikuni, eds. [*Ogyū Sorai Butsu Shigekimi*] *Ritsurei taishō teihon, Min ritsu kokujikai* [Standard Text of the Ming Penal Code with Comments in Our Script; with Laws and Substatutes Cross-Referenced] (Tokyo, 1966 printing of the 1723-1725 work), hereafter, Ogyū's *Ming Code and Commentary*.
4. For Fukami's tr., and the importation and Tokugawa use of the Ch'ing Code in general, cf. Ōba Osamu, "Tokugawa Yoshimune to *Ta Ch'ing hui-tien*—Kyōhō jidai ni okeru Nisshin kōshō no ippan" [Tokugawa Yoshimune and the Ch'ing Code—an aspect of Sino-Japanese relations in the Kyōhō period (1716-1735)], *Hōseishi kenkyū*, Vol. 21 (1971), pp. 61-95.

   The 1874 printing of the Ch'ing Code is the earliest Japanese printing I have: Mizumoto Narumi, ed., *Zōshū kunten Shin-ritsu isan* [Enlarged Compendium of the Ch'ing Penal Code with Diacritical Markings Added], 12 vols. (*kan*) (Tokyo, 1874). Oba says parts of Fukami's translation still exist. Cf. Ōba, p. 72.
5. Cf. Tezuka Yutaka, "Aizu han 'Keisoku' kō" [Thoughts on the "Criminal Rules" of the Aizu Domain], *Keiō Gijuku sōritsu hyakunen kinen rombunshū—hōgakubu* [Commemorative Collection of Articles on the Centennial of Keio Gijuku, Law Faculty] (Tokyo, 1958), p. 81. He mentioned three types of influence: Osadamegaki, Ming, and mixed (e.g., Shibata).
6. For some of the diversity, cf. Hiramatsu. Cf. also Inoue Kazuo "Nihon kinsei hampō no seiritsu" [Establishment of Han Law of Pre-modern Japan], *Shihō kenshujo-hō* [Reports of the Legal Training and Research Institute], No. 14 (1955), pp. 88-153; and idem, *Hampō bakufu-hō to ishin-hō* [Domain Law, Shogunate Law and Restoration Law], 3 vols. (Tokyo, 1965 reprint; 1st printed 1940). For a voluminous, reliable and modern source of *han* law cf. Hampō Kenkyūkai, compiler, *Hampōshū* [Collection of Domain Law], (Tokyo, 1961-1975). 12 vols. have appeared covering Okayama (2 vols.), Tottori (2 vols.), Tokushima, Kanazawa (2 vols.), Kumamoto, Kagoshima (2 vols.), Morioka (2 vols.) and Kurume, plus two vols. entitled *Shohan* meaning "various domains." In all there are fifteen large vols. because some are numbered, e.g., 6A and 6B.
7. Besides the various codes themselves and the chronicles and the diaries cited hereafter, this chapter owes much to the pioneering work of the following Japanese scholars: Kobayakawa Kingo, "Min-ritsuryō no waga kinsei-hō ni oyobaseru eikyō" [Ming Code Influences Extending into our Law of the Pre-Modern Era (Tokugawa period)], *Tōa jimbun gakuhō* [Report of Studies in East Asian Culture], Vol. 4 (1945), pp. 197-257; Maki Kenji, "Higo-han

'Keihō sōsho' no seiritsu; toku ni sono Minritsu sanshaku ni tsuite" [The Establishment of the 'Draft Penal Law' of the Higo Domain, Especially Concerning its Reference to the Ming Penal Code], *Hōgaku ronsō* [Kyoto Law Review], Vol. 48 (1943), pp. 701-745; Kaneda Heiichirō, "Kumamoto-han 'Keihō sōsho' kō" [Thoughts on the "Draft Penal Law" of the Kumamoto Domain], *Hōsei kenkyū* [Studies of Law and Politics], Vol. 12 (1942), pp. 135-205; Matsushita Chū, "Dai-Minritsu kenkyū ni okeru Kishū-han to Ken'engaku-ha" [Studies of the *Great Ming Penal Code* of the Kii Domain and the Ken'en Scholarly Group (Ogyū Sorai's)], *Wakayama daigaku gakugei gakubu kiyō, jimbun kagaku* [Reports of the Department of Arts and Cultural Sciences, Wakayama University], Vol. 3 (1953), pp. 68-85; Yaezu Yōhei, " 'Keihō sōsho'wo chūshin to shita Kumamoto-han no keibatsu taikei ni tsuite" [Concerning the System of Penalties of the Kumamoto Domain Centering on the "Draft Penal Code"], *Hō to seiji* [Law and Politics], Vol. 8 (1957), pp. 451-481; Ebina Yōichi, "An'ei-ki no Hirosaki-han keihō—'Kansei-Ritsu' to no hikaku" [Comparison of the Criminal Law of the Hirosaki Domain in the An'ei Period (1772-1780) with its "Kansei (1789-1800) Code"], *Hirosaki daigaku kokushi kenkyū* [Studies in National History, Hirosaki University], Vols. 19-20 (1959), pp. 29-45 (mimeo.); Ebina, "Hirosaki han 'Go-keihō-chō' (Kansei [1789-1800] ritsu)" ["The Catalogue of Penal Law" (Kansei Code) of the Hirosaki Domain], *Hirosaki daigaku kokushi kenkyū*, Nos. 15 and 16 (1959), pp. 11-45 (mimeo.); Fuse Yaheiji, "Tsugaru-han no 'Keihō-chō' ni tsuite," [Concerning "The Catalogue of Penal Law" of the Tsugaru Domain], *Nihon hōgaku* [Japanese Jurisprudence], Vol. 21 (1955), pp. 144-172; Tezuka Yutaka, "Aizu han 'Keisoku' kō" [Thoughts on the "Criminal Rules" of the Aizu Domain], *Keiō Gijuku soritsu hyakunen kinen rombunshū—hōgakubu*, pp. 81-130; Tezuka Yutaka, "Wakayama-han 'Kokuritsu' " ["The Provincial Penal Law" of the Wakayama Domain], *Hōgaku kenkyū* [Studies in Jurisprudence], Vol. 26 (1953), p. 425; Tabe Hō, "Kyū Tsugaru-han hōritsu ippan" [An Aspect of the Law of the Old Tsugaru Domain], *Hōgaku kyōkai zasshi* [The Journal of the Jurisprudence Association], Vol. 10 (1892), pp. 144-177, 265-71, 387-90, 477-80, 573-78, 668-77, 745-48, 825-29; and, generally, Inoue Kazuo, *Shohan no keibatsu* [Penalties of the various domains], 458 pp. (Tokyo, 1965). See also recent works: Ōba Osamu, note 4 above, and Matsushita Chū, *Kishu no hangaku* (Domain Scholarship in Kii Province), (Tokyo, 1974); Kamata Hiroshi, "Kumamoto-han ni okeru keisei no tenkai" [Development of Penal Administration in the Kumamoto Domain], in Harafuji Hiroshi and Koyama Sadao, eds., *Hō to kenryoku no shiteki kōsatsu—Sera kyōju kanreki kinen* [Historical Considerations of Law and Authority—Commemoration of Professor Sera's 60th Birthday], (1977), pp. 606-639; Hiramatsu Yoshirō, "Ishin-ki Nagoya-han no tokei shiryō—Muratabon 'Kyū-Nagoya-han Sadamegaki' " [Materials on imprisonment in the Nagoya Domain at the Restoration Period—the Murata book entitled, "Old Nagoya Domain Provisions"] in *Meiji hōseishi-seijishi no sho-mondai—Tezuka Yutaka Kyōju taishoku kinen rombunshū* [Various Problems in Meiji Legal and Political History—A Collection of Articles in Commemoration of Professor Tezuka

Yutaka's Retirement] (1977), pp. 581-605. Each of the above works will be cited hereinafter only by the author's name and the pertinent pages.

8. See Henderson, note 1 above. Whether the Tokugawa jurists correctly understood the specifics of the Ming Code is a separate comparative study itself, indeed several studies, which cannot be undertaken in a survey of this sort. Rather, we are only attempting a preliminary outline of the places and ways in which the Ming Code was used in early eighteenth-century Japan.
9. Ujinaga, "Ritsuryō yōryaku" [Essentials of Penal Laws and Regulations], Ishii Ryōsuke, ed., *Kinsei hōsei shiryō sōsho* [Compilation of Writings on Legal History of the Premodern period] (Tokyo, reprinted 1959; 1st printed 1941), p. 297.
10. "Ketsugokkō," *Arai Hakuseki zenshū* [Complete Works of Arai Hakuseki], Vol. 5 (Tokyo, 1907), pp. 272-275.
    I am grateful to Kate Nakai (Oregon) for reference to Hakuseki's version of this case.
11. *Ta Ming hui-tien* [Collected Institutes of the Great Ming] (1587 ed., reprinted Taipei, 1963), 355:31 (hereafter *TMHT*); and Ogyū, *Ming Code and Commentary* (1966), p. 100.
12. Miyazaki Michio, ed., *Teibon Oritaku shiba no ki* [Autobiographical Notes of Arai Hakuseki] (Tokyo, 1964), p. 439.
13. Miyazaki, *Oritaku shiba no ki*, pp. 433–436.
14. *Huang-Ming T'ai-tsu shih-lu* [Veritable Records of the Ming Emperor T'ai-tsu] 255th fascicle (Taipei reprint, 1966), p 3677.
    The quotations in the text at footnote numbers 14, 32, 34, 38, 60, 66, and 76 were tr. Leon Hurvitz, Department of Asian Languages and Literature, University of Washington, with the kind advice of Tai Yen-hui on several Chinese terms.
15. *Huang-ch'ao wen-hsien t'ung-k'ao* [Compendium of Historical Records of the Ching Dynasty], 21st fascicle, official positions (*chih-i*), section 1 (Shanghai, 1936), p. 5047. *Sheng-tsu Shih-lu* [The Veritable Records of the K'ang-hsi Emperor], 34th fascicle. Cf. also Hsiao Kung-ch'üan, p. 185.
16. "Yūtokuin dono go-jikki" [Chronicles of Lord Yūtokuin (Yoshimune)], Kuroita Katsumi, ed., *Shintei zoho kokushi taikei* [Revised and Supplemented Compendium of Japanese History] (Tokyo, 1934), Vol. 46, p. 245 (top) (hereinafter cited as "Jikki," *Kokushi taikei*, Vol. 46).
17. "Kenzan reitaku hisaku" [A Secret Policy of Kenzan] in *Nihon keizai taiten* [Compilation on the Japanese Economy], Vol. 4 (1928), p. 530. Kyūsō's tr. was entitled "Rikuyu engi taii" [The Broad Significance of the Amplification of the Six Admonitions], printed in *Nihon kyōiku bunko* [Library on Japanese Education], Vol. 2 (1910).
18. For the *terakoya*, cf. Ronald Dore, *Education in Tokugawa Japan* (Berkeley, 1965), p. 252.
19. See, generally, Henderson, "Promulgation of Tokugawa Statutes," *Journal of Asian and African Studies*, Vol. 1 (Leiden, 1967), p. 9.
20. Tsuji Tatsuya, *Kyōhō kaikaku no kenkyū* [Study of the Kyōhō (1716-35) Reforms] (Tokyo, 1963), p. 119. The essentials of this whole problem are discussed also in Tsuji Tatsuya, *Tokugawa Yoshimune-kō den* [Biography of Tokugawa Yoshimune] (1962), p. 237.

21. Ishii Ryōsuke, ed., *Tokugawa kinreikō, bekkan* [Notes on Tokugawa Regulations, Supplementary Volume] (Tokyo, 1961), p. 18, for the *Kujikata Osadamegaki, jōkan*, art. 9 (hereafter, *Kinreikō, bekkan*).
22. *TMHT*, 355 (1587 ed., reprinted Taipei, 1963). Also Ogyū, *Ming Code and Commentary*, (Tokyo reprint, 1966), p. 432.
23. Cf. George Thomas Staunton, *Ta Tsing Leu Lee*, (1810 ed., reprinted Taipei, 1966) p. 359, art. ccxxii, for another English tr. of a similar provision, but from the later Ch'ing Code, where the phrasing has been slightly supplemented.
24. Cf. Charles Hucker, *The Censorial System of Ming China* (Stanford, 1966), p. 98; cf. also Hucker, p. 100, for an interesting Ming case.
25. Cf. Derk Bodde and Clarence Morris, *Law in Imperial* China (Cambridge, Mass., 1967), pp. 352, 426, and 461, for interesting Ch'ing cases; cf. also p. 465 for a useful comment by the author on the history and use of the drum.
26. For Shogunal penalties generally, see Ishii Ryōsuke, *Edo no keibatsu* [Penalties of Edo], (Chūō Kōronsha, Tokyo, 1965) 202 pp.; and for interesting descriptions of the execution of penalties cf. Hiramatsu, *Kinsei keiji soshōhō no kenkyū*, p. 912.
27. John Carey Hall, "Tokugawa Legislation IV," *Transactions of the Asiatic Society of Japan* (hereafter Hall, *TASJ*), Vol. 41 (1913), p. 800; cf. also *Kinreikō, bekkan*, p. 134.
28. Ishii Ryōsuke, *Nihon hōseishi gaisetsu* [General Survey of Japanese Legal History] (Tokyo, 1960), pp. 144-146, 174.
29. "Jikki," *Kokushi taikei*, Vol. 46, p. 157 (bottom). Query whether this term was introduced by a later historian in writing up the "Jikki"?
30. Marius Jansen, "Tosa in the Sixteenth Century: the 100-Article Code of Chōsokabe Motochika," John Hall and Marius Jansen, eds., *Studies in the Institutional History of Early Modern Japan* (Princeton, 1968), pp. 89, 101 (cf. arts. 34, 72, and 74).
31. Cf. Hall, *TASJ*, Vol. 41, arts. 22, 23, 25, 26, 28, and 30, and other instances of later uses of fines as penalties, but not as redemption.
32. *Meikun Kyōhō-roku* [Kyōhō (1716-1735) Records of an Enlightened Lord], 8 fascicles.
33. Kobayakawa, p. 228.
34. The notes were taken by Tsunanori's attendant, Tominaga Kazuma, at the interview. Quoted in Kondō Iwao, *Kaga Shōun-kō* [Lord Shōun (Tsunanori) of Kaga Province], Vol. 2, p. 705. Similar notes were also taken by another attendant, Nakamura Kosho. Cf. "Shōun-kō go-yawa" in Kondō, *Kaga Shōun-kō*, p. 703.
35. *Kinreikō, bekkan*, p. 133. For an English tr. of this article, see Hall, *TASJ*, p. 799.
36. Kondō, *Kaga Shōun-kō*, Vol. 2, p. 702.
37. "Jikki," Kokushi taikei, Vol. 46, p. 157.
38. Kondō, *Kaga Shōun-kō*, Vol. 2, p. 703. Again, this is the record of Tominaga Kazuma.
39. Within the hundreds of tiny "jurisdictions" in Tokugawa Japan there was, therefore, an analogy to the Chinese practice of requiring imperial decisions on death penalties, but the Shogun's authority was permanently delegated to

the Senior Council (*rojū*). Cf. Hiramatsu, *Kinsei keiji soshōhō no kenkyū*, pp. 3, 458, and 844.

40. Note that I have consistently designated each *han* by the name of the castle town rather than by the daimyo or province name; thus Kumamoto is the castle town of "Kumamoto *han*" in Higo province in Kyushu; the family name of the daimyo was Hosokawa.
41. Ishio, Yoshihisa, "Kainan seiten, Kainan ritsurei no kenkyū" [Studies on the *Kainan seiten* and *Kainan ritsurei* Codes], *Kansai daigaku hōgaku-ronshū*, Vol. 16 (1966), pp. 263, 318.
42. Text printed in Ishio, Y., *Kainan seiten no kenkyū* [Study of the *Kainan Seiten*] (Osaka, 1969), p. 281. Cf. also his discussion of textual variations and other copies.
43. Cf. J. R. McEwan, *The Political Writings of Ogyū Sorai* (Cambridge, 1962), p. 4. McEwan believes that Sorai was influenced by Hsün Tzu, but did not accept his view that human nature is evil.
44. As noted in the text, for example, in 1861 Tosa *han* compiled a Code, *Kainan ritsurei*, with several Chinese features. For Ming influences cf. Ishio, "Kainan seiten, Kainan ritsurei no kenkyū," *Kansai daigaku hōgaku ronshū*, Vol. 15 (1965), pp. 57, 101, and 195; Vol. 16 (1966), pp. 28, 156, and 263. This Tosa Code followed the *ritsuryō* format (*seiten* corresponding to the *ryō*, and the *ritsurei* to the *ritsu*). There is a controversy over the extent to which the Code was fully implemented, because its compiler and sponsor, Yoshida Tōyō, was assassinated just after the Code was completed. Also, Uwajima *han* referred to the Ming Code in case of gaps. Cf. Inoue Kazuo, *Shohan no keibatsu*, pp. 21-23.
45. "Kumamoto han go-keihō sōsho furei" [The Draft Penal Law of Kumamoto Han with Substatutes Appended], in Kyoto Teikoku Daigaku Hōgakubu, ed., *Kinsei hampō shiryō shūsei* [Collection of Historical Materials on Han Law of the Pre-Modern Period], Vol. 2 (Kyoto, 1943).
46. Cf. generally, Maki, *Hōgaku ronsō*, Vol. 48 (1943), pp. 701-747; Kaneda, *Hōsei kenkyū*, Vol. 12 (1942), pp. 135-205; Yaezu Yōhei, *Hō to seiji*, Vol. 8 (1953), pp. 451-481; Kamata, pp. 606-639.
47. Maki, p. 714.
48. Maki, p. 710.
49. See note 38.
50. Yaezu, p. 453.
51. Yaezu, p. 461. Cf. also Niida Noboru, "Shina ni okeru keibatsu taikei no henkan—toku ni jiyukei no hattatsu" [Changes in the System of Penalties in China—Especially the Development of the Penalty (Against) Freedom], *Hōgaku kyōkai zasshi*, Vol. 57 (1939), p. 405. Cf. also Tezuka Yutaka, "Nagaoka han no yoseba to Matsuyama [Takahashi] han no tokeisho" [Prisons of the Nagaoka and Matsuyama Domains], *Hōgaku kenkyū*, Vol. 31 (1953), p. 311, for the thesis that penal servitude in Nagaoka was modeled after Western practice.
52. By the mid-eighteenth century the problems caused by the continued use of banishment (*tsuihō*) by all the daimyo as well as the Shogunate were serious. Banishment served fifteenth- and sixteenth-century needs when banished

criminals could take up military service in another warlord's realm, but after the Tokugawa peace they caused social problems in the other areas to which they were sent. Cf. Hiramatsu Yoshirō, "Nagoya-han no tsuihō-kei" [The Penalty of Banishment in the Nagoya Domain], *Nagoya daigaku hōsei ronshū* [Collection of Essays on Law and Politics, Nagoya University], Vol. 4, No. 1 (1952), pp. 1-53.

53. Kobayakawa, p. 242.
54. *Kinsei hampō shiryō shūsei*, Vol. 2, p. 3.
55. One copy of the *Kokuritsu* was published without the supplement (*Kokuritsu hojo*). Cf. Tezuka Yutaka, "Wakayama-han Kokuritsu, Murata-hon" [The Provincial Penal Law of Wakayama Domain, the Murata Copy], *Hōgaku kenkyū*, Vol. 26 (1953), pp. 426, 427-451. For *Kokuritsu hojo*, see note 57 below.

   For other aspects of Wakayama legal development, cf. Hirayama Kōzō, "Hōreki sannen no Kishū hampō" [Kii Domain Law of the Third Year of Hōreki], *Wakayama daigaku gakugei gakubu kiyō, jimbun kagaku, shiryō-hen*, No. 11 (1962), pp. 41-61; *Kenkyū-hen*, No. 11 (1962), pp. 41-61; *Kenkyū-hen*, No. 12 (1962), pp. 73-88. Cf. also Hirayama, "Kishū han hampō shūi" [Gleanings from the Kii Domain Law], *Wakayama daigaku gakugei gakubu kiyō—jimbun kagaku*, No. 14 (1964), pp. 25-35; Hirayama, "Bunsei yonen no Kishū hampō" [Domain Law of Kii of the Fourth Year of Bunsei], *Wakayama daigaku gakugei gakubu kiyō, jimbun kagaku*, No. 15 (1965), pp. 29-44.

56. Kobayakawa, pp. 235-249. Cf. also Tezuka, *Hōgaku kenkyū*, Vol. 26 (1953), p. 426.
57. *Nanki Tokugawa-shi* [History of the Tokugawa of Southern Kii], Vol. 17 (1910), pp. 1050-1084 for the *Kokuritsu hojo*.
58. Adapted from Kobayakawa, p. 239.
59. Tezuka, p. 426, says there are no such "red comments" in the Murata copy.
60. Kobayakawa, p. 201.
61. Tezuka, p. 426. Also Tezuka, "Aizu han 'Keisoku' kō," *Keio Gijuku Sōritsu hyakunen kinen rombunshū, hōgakubu*, p. 130, n. 5.
62. Cf. Ebina Yōichi, "Hirosaki han 'Go-keihō-chō'," *Hirosaki daigaku kokushi kenkyū*, Nos. 15 and 16 (1959), p. 11, where the date of the perfected Code is given as 1810; but Fuse, *Nihon hōgaku*, Vol. 21 (1955), p. 144, says 1794. Hirosaki-shi, ed., *Hirosaki shishi, hansei-hen* [History of Hirosaki City: Part on the Domain System] (Hirosaki, 1963); Ebina Yōichi, *Hirosaki daigaku kokushi kenkyū*, Nos. 19-20.
63. Tabe, *Hōgaku kyōkai zasshi*, Vol. 10 (1892), p. 265; also Fuse worked with a manuscript copy, see Fuse, p. 172; and a mimeographed copy of the original *Kansei ritsu* (before revision) in 99 arts. is published by Ebina, pp. 13-37 (1959).
64. Tabe, p. 267.
65. Ebina, *Hirosaki daigaku kokushi kenkyū*, Nos. 19-20.
66. Tabe, p. 265 (1892); also Ebina, Nos. 15 and 16 (1959), p. 13.
67. Tabe, p. 266.
68. There are several listed by Kobayakawa, p. 250.

69. Yutaka Tezuka, "Aizu han 'Keisoku' ko," (1958) p. 121, n. 1, supra, note 5. Information for the text relating to the Aizu *Penal Rules* is drawn from Tezuka unless otherwise noted.
70. Tezuka, (1958), p. 128; for references to other works of Tanaka Saburōbē and Hitotsuyanagi Shinzaburō, see Kasai Sukeharu, *Kinsei hanko ni okeru shuppansho no kenkyū* [Study of Books Published in the Han Schools of the Recent Era], (Tokyo, 1962), p. 606.
71. Tezuka, (1958), p. 88.
72. Tezuka, (1958), p. 102.
73. Tezuka, (1958), p. 116.
74. The *New Penal Code* and the *Administrative Code* (*Shinryō*) have been printed in Shibata-shi shiryō hensan iinkai, ed., *Shibata-han shiryō* [Historical Materials on Shibata Domain], *Shibata-shi shi shiryō dai-3-kan* [Materials on the History of Shibata City, Vol. 3], but this volume is not readily accessible now. Much more adequate material for study of the Shibata-han will be available when the *Shibata-shi shi* (History of Shibata City) is published in two volumes, projected beginning in 1980. I am indebted to Fujii Shigeo and Takahashi Reiya (editor in Shibata) for the advanced copies, which they kindly provided for use here.
75. For general information on Shibata-han, see Otaki Toshiko, "Shibata-han ni okeru kashin kōsei ni tsuite" [Concerning the Composition of the Retainers in the Shibata Domain], *Shigaku ronkō* [Consideration of History], No. 4 (1957), p. 2; Niida Gendō, "Shibata-han kenkyū" [Study of the Shibata Domain], *Shigaku ronkō*, No. 4 (1957), p. 7; and Niida Gendō, "Shibata-han ni okeru chigyō-sei yori hōrokusei e no suii ni tsuite" [Concerning the Transition from a Fief System to a Stipend System in the Shibata Domain], *Essa*, No. 14 (1958), p. 1-9. The *Shinryō*, article 1, supra, note 74, p. 331, specifically requires exclusive study of the orthodox (*teishūgaku*) philosophy of Anzai. Fujii Shigeo, "Igaku no kin ni tsuite" [Concerning the Prohibition of Unorthodoxies], *Niigata daigaku kyōikugaku-bu kiyō* [Bulletin of the Education Department, Niigata University] No. 5 (1964), pp. 115-130, and No. 6 (1964), pp. 112-119
76. Fujii Shigeo, "Tō Min ritsu to hanpō to no kankei ni tsuite [Concerning the Relationship between the Domain Law and the T'ang and Ming Codes], *Niigata daigaku kyōikugaku-bu kiyō*, Vol. 9 (1975), p. 61. He gives extensive lists of provisions throughout the *New Penal Code* which may be traced to Ming borrowings at p. 66 and 67.
77. "Memorandum on Applying the New Penal Code," *Shibata-han shiryō*, Vol. 3 (1966), p. 359, supra. note 74. Fujii Shigeo, supra, note 76, lists (p. 65) about a dozen provisions from the *Memorandum on Applying the New Penal Code*, which are traceable to the "Terms and General Principles" (*Ming-li-lü*), only one of which we deal with in the text here. Kobayakawa, p. 25, also has such a list. For the similar Ming Code provision, *TMHT*, Vol. 1 (Taipei, 1965); Ogyū, *Ming Code and Commentary*, p.100.
78. *TMHT*, Vol. 1 (Taipei, 1965), Ogyū, *Ming Code and Commentary*, p. 100.
79. Tezuka yutaka, *Meiji shoki keihō-shi no kenkyū* [Study of the History of Early

Meiji Criminal Law] (Tokyo, 1956), pp. 7-8; Kobayakawa Kingo, *Meiji hōseishi-ron* [Treatise on Meiji Legal History], Vol. 2 [*gekan*], (Tokyo, 1940), p. 978; and Rikō Mitsuo and Kasumi Nobuhiko, "Hachigyaku rokugi wo meguru sho-mondai" [Various Problems Revolving Around the Eight Abominations and the Six Considerations] in *Meiji hōseishi-seijishi no sho-mondai–Tezuka Yutaka Kyōju taishoku kinen Rombunshū* [Various Problems in Meiji Legal and Political History—A Collection of Articles in Commemoration of Professor Tezuka Yutaka's Retirement] (1977), pp. 1081-1127.

IX

TRADITIONAL KOREAN LAW AND ITS RELATION TO CHINA

William Shaw

The study of Korean legal history is still awaiting its Maitland. Even in Korea, no more than two or three scholars are actively interested, and probably not more than two or three books and a half-dozen articles have appeared on the subject in the past decade, despite a general publishing boom in Korean history.[1] In the West there seems to be even less activity, and the departure of Hahm Pyong-choon from the academic world has all but dried up writing on Korean law and legal history in English.[2]

One result is that while Chinese legal studies have, with this volume if not before, reached what might be termed a second-generation stage of inquiry, Korean legal history appears to lag somewhat behind. Although this relative neglect is perhaps understandable, it is unfortunate. Study of traditional Korean law should be able to inform our study of Chinese legal history in a unique way, for both involved the operation of highly developed systems of legal norms in "Confucian" states. And there may still be much of interest that legal history will be able to tell us of the varying responses of China, Japan, Korea and Vietnam to the reforms and revolutions of the nineteenth and twentieth centuries, to say nothing of how these various but historically related traditions are functioning today. By way of a modest preface to further research on these "second-generation" concerns, this chapter will address several topics of a general nature selected for their value as background and for their interest to students of Korean and Chinese legal history.

The most extensive sources of the principles and operation of the traditional Korean legal system are legislative and case records from the seventeenth and eighteenth centuries.[3] Most of these are records produced by the central government and thus to a certain extent are focused upon problematic aspects of government as seen from Hansŏng (modern Seoul) rather than routine judicial administration at the provincial or magistral level. These are precisely the cases in which local or provincial governments failed in the administration of justice, or in which conflicting norms and contending forces are laid bare, and it is through them that we can gain the clearest idea of what it was that the Yi dynasty (1392-1910) rulers were trying to accomplish and what some of their problems were. The fact that most of these cases are up for review also gives us a unique opportunity to examine the kinds of arguments and reasoning employed in the decision of difficult cases and to examine the procedures by which cases moved from the various local or central bureaucratic jurisdictions into the spotlight of court attention and activity.

Yi Dynasty Law

Chinese criminal law was of major, perhaps even overwhelming importance in the administration of traditional Korean justice. The first article of the criminal provisions of the early Yi dynasty Code, the *Kyŏngguk taejŏn*,[4] by no means the first mention of the matter in the Yi period, stated unequivocally that the Ming Criminal Code, the *Ta Ming lü*,[5] was to be used, and it was not until the middle of the eighteenth century that preference for Korean statutes, in case of conflict, was formally enshrined in a Korean codification, though this may have been somewhat after the fact.[6]

In this fashion, basic principles of Chinese law were imported along with specific Code provisions.[7] Chinese law can be characterized as universalistic, comprehensive, and sophisticated. Its universalism[8] lay in its insistence that in principle all power be derived from the central government and in its general character as a system of norms to which, no less than those of Confucian orthodoxy, all men were subject in some measure. Chinese law sought to encompass all possible cases and circumstances of violation in a comprehensive, "gapless" system of rules, and provided for the orderly creation of new law to incorporate exceptional cases.[9]

In application, Chinese law—by T'ang times, if not before—was complex, precise, and internally consistent, if occasionally subverted by corruption and the problems of maintaining rule over so many diverse regions and peoples.[10] The central concept was that the punishment, fixed beforehand in the Code, should fit the crime; consideration was given (in the codes, that is, and not by some sort of Confucian or Khadi-like discretion) to such matters as whether capacity to commit crime existed on the part of the defendant, whether the act was intentional or accidental, planned or actually carried out, or committed in the capacity of principal offender or simply that of an accomplice, and punishments were carefully scaled to take such differences into account.[11]

Beyond these purely criminal law considerations, other broad contributions of the law-oriented frame of mind to the structure and functioning of Chinese and Korean institutions might be pointed out.[12] Law was a standard not merely for punishment, but in principle for all areas of government activity including the land and tax systems, household registration, census systems, and weights and measures; these and a thousand other aspects of administration were all subject to written formal rules. The concept of the single standard also underlay the examination system and the censorial system of regular performance evaluation and surveillance of bureaucrats.[13]

There is one further contribution of the law which might be mentioned; this is that the legal codes, and the criminal statutes in particular, embodied certain Confucian ethical concepts and aided in their diffusion, ensuring their survival and strong position *vis-à-vis* local social and geographical factors which might have caused much more erosion of those conceptions, especially in China but in Korea as well. This did not mean a "Confucianization of Law," but rather the reverse.[14]

An example taken from the records of the Board of Punishments as compiled in the *Ch'ugwanji* might illustrate how this worked.[15] In 1734 the governor of Hwanghae province memorialized concerning a case in which a man had cremated his brother's corpse; the governor requested that the king ask the government ministers to give an opinion on the matter. A possible legal penalty was 70 blows of the rod and one and a half years of penal servitude.[16] One minister noted that this seemed too lenient but that the death penalty seemed excessive. The king asked for an explanation of the "[foul] Buddhist practice" of cremation. The minister replied with what today we would call a sociological explanation: "In the remote countryside," he pointed out, "the ignorant [sic!] people sometimes burn a corpse to prevent the spread of disease." The minister hastened to add that it was indeed a "thoroughly abhorrent practice."

Another official argued for the death penalty: "Even taking into account the poor ignorance of a man which would allow him to do such a thing, this is truly an unprecedented monstrosity. In governing a country, nothing can be too great or too minor to escape the ruler's attention. The ruler should exercise preventive measures against such degenerate practices, applying the heaviest of penalties." The king accepted his reasoning but agreed with the first minister that the death penalty was too harsh.

The term translated here as "degenerate practices" (*yup'ye*) is an interesting one. It can mean either simply the traditional customs of a region, as contrasted with the mainstream practices of state Confucianism, or it can be understood as a shorter form of the phrase, "the corrupt practices of a degenerate age" (*mallyujip'ye*). In this sense it would be used in a Confucian critique of a ruler's mandate, in an implicit challenge to his moral capacity and right to rule. To those familiar with the unhappy history of the censorate in Ming China, it might seem extraordinary that such a phrase, with its ambiguous character, would not result in the immediate dismissal, or worse, of the official who addressed it to the sovereign.[17] Certainly there were from time to time Korean kings with equal sensitivity to such implications. But in general the Korean tradition of remonstrance was so well established that this sort of remark was practically commonplace.[18]

Whichever connotation we adopt, however, the remark is clearly a form of ideological pressure, directed to uphold Confucian social practices against contrary trends, even at the cost of imposing a higher penalty, and to harness law to this purpose. Here we clearly see that law—not "moral suasion"—is being treated as a device to bring deviant customs into line with centrally imposed norms of a moral rather than a purely legal nature.[19]

In Korea, the Ming Criminal Code was known in the late Koryŏ period and accepted, as a possible model at least, from the earliest days of the Yi dynasty, being prescribed in the enthronement edict of T'aejo (r. 1392-1398), the founder.[20] An *idu* version was available by 1395.[21] Supplementary codification was also undertaken at an early date, both to provide a form for new policies and to account for new cases or circumstances not provided for in Ming law. Such codification was early recognized as a major task of government, and scholars and officials of the most respected reputation and qualifications were placed in charge. For example, Cho Chun (1346-1405), who worked on an *idu* version of an early Yi Code,[22] is usually remembered most for being a principle architect of Yi Sŏng-gye's land reforms. He held a number of important posts under both the Koryŏ and Yi governments.[23]

Ha Yun (1347-1416) was another important contributor to codification during the early years of the dynasty. Ha was a man of many talents; as an expert in geomancy he was said to have played an important role in the selection of the site of the new capital in Hansŏng, and later served as chief magistrate of the city. He also participated in an embassy to China and was a compiler of a history of Korea, the *Tongguk saryak*, which was widely respected and read throughout the Yi period.[24]

Another scholar and major political figure in the early years of the new dynasty, Chŏng To-jŏn (d. 1398),[25] served at the state Confucian College at Sŏnggyun-gwan under both the Koryŏ and Yi dynasties, and also participated in an early draft of what was to become the official history of the Koryŏ period, the *Koryŏsa*.[26] His "Model Code," the *Chosŏn kyŏnggukchŏn*,[27] was never put into practice, but won high praise from T'aejo; Chŏng's work and high reputation as a scholar undoubtedly stimulated later efforts at code compilation.

In the middle of the fifteenth century, Sin Suk-chu (1417-1475) was entrusted with work on what was eventually to become the dynastic Code, the *Kyŏngguk taejŏn*.[28] He was no narrow legalist, no technocrat, but a widely competent scholar who had served with King Sejong's prestigious Academy of Worthies (Chiphyŏnjŏn) and participated in embassies to Japan and China. His compilation experience included work on books of ritual, such as the *Kukcho oryeŭi*, history (the *Kukcho pogam*), and phonology (the *Tongguk chŏng-un*).[29]

Ch'oe Hang was another mid-century scholar who had served on compilation committees for the new alphabet (*Hunmin chŏngŭm*), the royal praise poem *Yongbi ŏch'ŏn'ga*,[30] and the official annals of King Sejong's reign. He was also noted for adding Korean grammatical forms written in the new alphabet to the Confucian four books and five classics to make them more easily used by students. Remembered today for such orthodox literary and historical activities, in the 1460s he, too, was applying his talents and experience to the writing of the new dynastic Code.[31]

In the later Yi period the tradition of careful compilation continued, and in the eighteenth century both Yŏngjo and Chŏngjo took a personal interest in problems of compiling major Code revisions during their reigns.[32] It is something of a commentary on the important place that law generally held among the priorities of Yi dynasty sovereigns that the longest period of time without some attempt to update the published laws and edicts was the century and a half preceding Sukchong's late seventeenth-century publication of the *Sugyo chimnok* (*Collected Edicts*). Even this period should be put into perspective; it spanned both the Japanese and Manchu invasions, with their accompanying dislocations of rural agriculture and administration alike.

To suggest, as some have, that law got short shrift in the Yi period, is simply to ignore the evidence that leads us to our conclusions; there was law in traditional Korea, very sophisticated law running into thousands of generally consistent provisions, and its compilation and amendation were given high priority, in terms of royal interest, publication, and personnel, throughout the period.

Law and Confucianism

There is a view, apparently taken over intact from earlier studies of Chinese law, which acknowledges the use of law in traditional Korean government but stresses the prior importance of Confucian principles and rule by moral example. Law, it is said, was simply beneath the consideration of the Confucian scholar, not a fit subject for a gentleman's discussion, and the last resort of a clumsy and morally defunct ruler.[33] One who wished to take this view might point to the fact that neither

China nor Korea produced much systematic legal literature or legal thought.[34] An examination of the catalogues of such private Confucian academy libraries as remain today might also lead to the conclusion that legal codes and case books were not high on the acquisition list for Yi dynasty scholars and did not receive much attention in even relatively advanced education.[35]

The Yi dynasty bureaucrat, like his contemporary in China, is commonly supposed to have resembled the old-fashioned American conception of a foreign service officer: talented, sensitive, with a well-rounded education and proper social credentials, but without any special area of competence. He was supposed to learn on the job. Legal training or even exposure to legal problems was not normally a part of the fledgling official's mental makeup (although it could be argued that historical studies, with their emphasis on analogical reasoning, provided good general training in the kind of reasoning used in deciding criminal cases).[36] Nor were the traditional state or private schools likely to prepare the future upper-level bureaucrat in any of the specific disciplines necessary for government administration.

Once on the job, however, practical problems impinged upon his awareness and his time. Poetry often had to wait until taxes had been collected, or until that troublesome irrigation problem had been solved, or until farmer Pak's claim against farmer Kim's wayward cow had been heard. There were several sources of expertise to which the new man had access. The local clerks had some of the specialized information he needed and an even greater wealth of knowledge about local conditions. His legal secretary would remind him that failure to file records in many kinds of criminal cases could bring an investigation and charges against him. A magistrates' handbook—and there were many produced throughout the period—might provide him with important insights and texts of appropriate laws and bureaucratic forms.[37]

If his first assignment placed him in one of the agencies of the central bureaucracy in the capital, the young bureaucrat would perhaps find himself researching an administrative problem in the agency files to provide information for his superior's next memorial. One way or another, an aspirant to higher position (and especially to one of those positions permitting and requiring direct participation in legal decisions) virtually had to acquire in the course of his early career a more or less intimate knowledge of the law, and not just its criminal provisions, but the numerous edicts, policy statements, administrative rules, and decisions in important or controversial cases.

Judging by the frequency with which statutes and other pertinent rules were referred to or quoted in debates over policy questions and case decisions alike,[38] it seems clear that many of the Yi dynasty higher officials possessed, or at least possessed access to, precisely this kind of knowledge. And, as we have already seen in our discussion of codification, such legal knowledge was not at all regarded as incompatible with outstanding literary and political attainments. On the contrary, barring those instances in which the rule of force obviated any consideration save that of the sword and the poisoned cup, knowledge of the text of the laws was probably as important an element of continued success in Korean government as the ability to quote from the histories and classics.

This does not mean that ignorance of the law did not exist among a segment, perhaps a sizable segment, of Korean officialdom. What must be remembered is that this was not at all the simple consequence of presumed Confucian prejudice against legal norms or legal knowledge, but was due rather to corruption, inexperience, or any of a number of other purely fortuitous factors, and that there were at nearly all times strong pressures tending toward the correction of such ignorance when it became evident. Indeed, review procedures for serious cases were designed to ferret out and correct errors of just this nature.[39]

What of the notion, then, that reliance on the use of punishments in government somehow indicated a moral failure on the part of the official or ruler? It will be seen at once that this view is in difficulty with respect to the cremation case which was discussed earlier, for it was the Confucian "purist" who, while lecturing the king on moral grounds, was in fact arguing strongly for the deterrent use of harsh penalties rather than moral suasion to prevent future occurrences.

This view would also be difficult to fit into the traditional concept of the Chinese dynastic cycle, because it was after all at the beginning of a new dynasty, at precisely the moment when the "Mandate of Heaven" was clearest and the presumed *virtu* (Ch. *te*) of the new regime the greatest, that we find the heaviest reliance on legal mechanisms in the process of establishing the new order. And at the end of the cycle, when a dynasty was in difficulty and rebellion was sweeping the land, it was precisely those legally instituted systems of tax collection, flood control, and administration of justice which had broken down and given rise to the people's discontent. Moral and institutional degeneration are not opposed in this model, but seem rather to occur together.

In the treatise on punishments of the officially sponsored history of the Koryŏ period, for example, the fall of the preceding dynasty is linked to a radical deterioration of institutional élan: "Prohibitions and laws became lax and penalties mild; irregular amnesties multiplied and lawless bands arose at will, unrestrained. In the final period of the dynasty the problem became acute." Constructive proposals and code-drafting attempts failed to stem the lawless tide, as "the institutional-moral fibre (*taegang*) had collapsed and the power of the state began to decline; there was nothing to be done."[40]

The most important source of tension in Yi government was not between legal norms and Confucian moral conceptions,[41] but rather was to be found in the endless struggle between the center and the periphery, between rival demands upon the grain and human resources of the countryside. This was the struggle between central law and no law; between the combination of law and morality together embodied in the codes, and local interests; and between the civil morality of the state and the personal moral insight of Confucian scholars and high officials alike. At times the priority of the state in this conflict was subject to challenge, but often statist values were internalized by the "Confucian" officials themselves, as can be seen in the following case from the late seventeenth century.[42]

In 1674 the Kyŏnggi governor memorialized concerning an incident in which a man had accidentally killed his mother while practicing archery. He had tried to commit suicide, but his father had intervened and sent him to the magistrate for punishment. The case was referred to the Board of Punishments and to high officials for deliberation. One official stated:

> The man, being directly responsible for his mother's death, should have done away with himself without delay; when he tried to strangle himself, however, he bungled that too and was saved by his father. In the fact that he is still alive we can see his perversely stubborn character and wormlike clumsiness. However, the law provides 100 blows of the rod and banishment to 3,000 *li* for one who accidentally kills his mother or father.[43] Since the statute covers the matter, there can be no grounds for judgment by analogy which would enable the penalty to be raised. In our use of the law, we cannot simply disregard a statute and increase the penalty provided by law.

The king accepted this opinion, and the case was concluded. This decision was later incorporated into a collection of royal edicts prepared for the reference of judicial and other officials.[44] Thus, even a high minister, torn as a Confucian between his strong emotional reaction to this crime and his commitment to the supremacy of law—that is, his confidence in the moral propriety of the penalty in the Code—supported the formal written law in spite of his personal feelings.

In the conflict between the central government and local interests, the magistrate was often enough caught in the middle: appointed and evaluated by the central government, yet dependent for many forms of assistance upon local clerks and unemployed literati. From the point of view of those in government, there could be no question whenever this conflict surfaced in the form of a legal problem. The magistrate was expected to uphold the laws, both in the performance of his administrative duties and in the judging of criminal cases and lawsuits, and the records show that he was frequently punished for his failure to do so.[45]

The concept of responsibility to the law can be amply illustrated from the writings of Yi dynasty thinkers. An Chŏng-bok (1712-1791) quoted with approval the remark of Liu Yüan-ch'eng, a student of Ssu-ma Kuang: "The *Han Shu* says 'the official regards the laws (*fa-ling*) as his master (*shih*)'; one must indeed peruse the statutes at every opportunity. When one does this then he will be able not only to govern men, but to preserve himself as well."[46] Chŏng Yag-yong (1762-1836), in his magistrates' handbook *Mongmin simsŏ*, advised magistrates to lay down the open code books in front of them while judging a case, and had no use whatsoever for "discretionary" or fence-sitting kinds of decision making: "Laws are the commands of the sovereign. To fail to respect them is to be disrespectful of the sovereign's commands. How could a subject dare to do this?"[47] Thus, the law spread Confucian norms and in turn Confucian concepts—such as the obedience inherent in the sovereign-minister relationship—could be used to buttress the authority of the codes.

This civil morality embodied in the codes was of a rather elementary sort, but it effectively subsumed virtually all the possible daily-life activities of the people and a major portion of official administrative performance as well. It is by no means certain that a less mundane, more philosophical, or more humane form of Confucianism replaced the state morality in those areas of political and administrative life where the codes did not reach. To consider this more fully, it will be useful to look at another conventional criticism of Korean and Chinese law.

Social Elites and the Law

It has become a commonplace that the law in China embodied certain class characteristics; its universalism was blunted if not undermined by the privileged treatment accorded to offenders of higher social or political status.[48] The concept of relative status was in fact an important if not the only organizing principle of the graduated scale of punishments contained within the codes.

Class elements within the Korean criminal codes may be placed within one of four categories. The first of these, differential punishments, has already been mentioned. There were also procedural differences, perhaps the most important being the requirement in a murder trial that, for suspects from certain social strata, higher authorities be notified and heard from before interrogation could be begun.[49]

Another group of provisions clearly oriented toward the maintenance of social distinctions was the group of sumptuary rules governing the use of certain luxury goods. In the *Kyŏngguk taejŏn* (final publication 1485), for example, red lacquer implements, gold and silver paper, folding flowers, and embroidered flowers and birds on clothing were prohibited to all but the wives and daughters of royal relatives and higher officials, and commoners were forbidden to use red clothing, cotton belts, gold, silver, or painted drinking utensils, silks of two colors, and a number of other items.[50]

A fourth category of class-related rules was that governing the commutation of certain penalties for officials or *yangban* to the payment of a monetary fine. This was clearly influenced by the Chinese model in the early part of the dynasty, but later changes, especially those after the devastations of the Hideyoshi and Manchu invasions, may have reflected financial need as well.

As important as these class-related features of the law were, however, there were certain features of the legal system that tended to operate in a contrary fashion. The first of these was that the laws in principle tended to regulate and limit the degree to which class considerations could affect the outcome of a criminal trial or lawsuit. Where before the class system had been able to dominate and totally influence an informal or unwritten legal process, class relationships themselves were now to some extent the subject of legal norms.

This trend can be clearly seen in a case which came up for review in 1779 in which a man had struck and killed a former slave of his brother. Here the difference between the traditional status-oriented view of the local governor and the law orientation of the king and Board officials is evident; the governor memorialized that putting the man on trial for his life is injurious to the distinction between slave and master. It is true that the law did not require the death penalty when a master killed a slave. But the legal officials answered that the issue was whether the victim was a slave at the time of the incident. They decided that, since the commutation papers were in order, the master-slave relationship had been legally dissolved and the defendant had to be tried as he would be in a straightforward murder case. As the king commented: "If even for the space of one day the master-slave relationship does not exist, the former master must provide requital for a [murdered] life . . . one cannot arbitrarily change the [commutation] rule."[51]

Moreover, there is considerable evidence, at least from the seventeenth and eighteenth centuries, that the laws were often enforced to the disadvantage of purely class considerations. A number of cases can be found, for example, in which commoners were upheld against a magistrate or other local official who had improperly or dishonestly handled a criminal case, or in other ways abused his authority. Nor was class alone a barrier to lawsuits over property. Anyone, of whatever social status, could file a lawsuit or be the object of a suit over property rights.[52]

We have noted that there existed a tension in the Yi period between the needs, goals, and policies of the central government and the interests and responses of the official and semiofficial bureaucrats in the local governments. This resulted in certain other societal pressures against the central legal system, at least two of which deserve mention here.

The first of these was the dependence of the magistrate upon the counsel and goodwill of his local assistants, both those among the hereditary clerks in the magistrate's office and among the local literati. This certainly led in some cases to corruption and the vitiation of the magistrate's capacity to carry out his centralizing function without compromise. There were many reasons why the magistrate was placed in this uncomfortable position, but an important one was the economy of utilizing unsalaried local leadership; the central government was probably never capable of providing paid employment to all of the graduates of the literary examination, or to all of the underlings necessary in both the central and local bureaucracies.[53] Of course, resulting administrative difficulties compounded the government's fiscal problems, and the effects were certainly felt in the area of legal administration as well.

A second and more important feature of the society, which tended to resist the extension of the rule of law, was the existence of considerable areas that were either totally or partially outside of legal jurisdiction. The chief entities virtually beyond the reach of law were the large estates under the control of, and providing income for, various segments of the royal family and some official families. These are best thought of as economic rather than geographic units, but those who lived and worked within their jurisdiction were rarely, if ever, exposed to the operation of the normal mechanisms by which the central government attempted to extend its control and legal jurisdiction over the countryside.[54]

In summary, we might suspect that the law, in spite of its class content, was something of a leveling influence, in the sense that the effects of class differences upon the legal system were probably far greater and more significant in areas which, whether for historical or economic reasons, were only partially within the reach of law. And from a humanitarian point of view, the law was probably much superior to what it replaced in terms of severity of class distinctions. Whenever a case appears that is particularly offensive not only to our modern sensibilities but also in terms of abuse of privilege and status in Yi dynasty terms as well, it is almost always a case of not enough law, rather than too much. The comprehensiveness of the Yi legal system and the law-oriented perspective were the strongest factors in challenging regional and other class and religious elites which had been active during the late Koryŏ period, and paved the way for a social and administrative change of great proportions during the first century of Yi rule. There are some indications that the challenge was never completely successful, but this was clearly the thrust and significance of the early Yi reforms in economy and government, reforms which in many instances proceeded on the back of the law.

The Sovereign and the Law

Such writing as we have from the Yi period illuminates a serious problem in the relationship of the sovereign to the law. Some Yi dynasty writers stressed the concept that the law was the will of the king. Yet this did not mean, either in theory or practice, that he could do as he liked. It was rather a device (not the only one) by which the law was formally legitimized. Another legitimizing device was the conception that the law embodied certain immutable principles, intimately involved with the nature of the universe itself. According to this notion, improper punishment of a crime by the authorities implied a breach of the natural order and had to be requited, generally in the form of some natural disaster. This is one source of the Yi court's interest in astronomy and unusual occurrences in the weather and is clearly related to the periodic issuance of large-scale pardons.[55] A separate study would be required to develop the full implications of this for Yi Korea and the contemporaneous Ming and Ch'ing dynasties. There are indications, however, that whether this doctrine was already "archaic" by Han times or not, it was very much alive well over ten centuries later in both China and Korea.[56] A third conception, that changing circumstances might necessitate changes in the law, was recognized at an especially early point in the Yi dynasty, as it became necessary to reconcile the first and second of the above doctrines with the obvious need to formulate and construct a new economic and administrative system.

In practice in the Yi dynasty, no one of these conceptions could operate for any length of time without restraint from the other two. The key to understanding the way in which these balanced each other lies in an examination of Yi dynasty legislative practice. How was new law created? How free was the king to modify the laws he had received from his predecessors? How free was he to modify his own laws?

Space does not permit full discussion of these questions, but we might note four types of restraint which operated on the king in the legislative process. Two of these are at least semilegal in origin. One is that the received law was considered to have been handed down from (and was in fact derived from) the legislative enactments of former kings, or in the quasireligious language used, the "royal predecessors." Whenever a new Code was compiled, reference to the need to respect these was coupled with apologetic mention of the forces of circumstances which made new enactments necessary.[57]

The other legal restraint was the detailed content of existing law. Time and again, in debates over creating new rules or settling difficult cases, reference was made to a point of law or to the fact that a proposed course of action is not provided for in the statutes. Sometimes these two were combined when an official would point out that a proposal "has no precedent in the laws of the royal predecessors." In many cases the king was very responsive to this line of argument.

Other restraints upon the king's freedom to make law were the ideological and institutional forces which made the king the focus of a wide circle of ministers, councillors, tutors, royal lecturers, and official court historians, all of whom were entitled *ex officio* to cast a hard Confucian eye upon royal activities.[58] For all but the strongest and most ruthless kings, the Korean decision-making process amounted to a royal ratification of the group consensus.[59] This process had deep roots in Korean political history and ideological justification in the Confucian conception of the minister as councillor and critic of his sovereign.

Thus, a variety of restraints, some intrinsically deriving from the legal order itself and others from intellectual or historical patterns, were at work in determining the latitude a king might have in revising the laws. While it could be said by some that law was the will of the sovereign, few apparently believed that the sovereign's will, that is to say his uncounselled first opinion, should always be law. Although until the eighteenth century these patterns acted to restrict fully rational and systematic codification, they also limited royal arbitrariness.

Popular Attitudes toward the Law

In discussing the attitudes of ordinary people to the law and its operation in the Yi dynasty, efforts must be made to distinguish very carefully between the different types of research sources that may be used. The Yi rulers were at pains throughout the dynasty to ensure as wide an acceptance of certain values and attitudes as possible, and it is often difficult to be certain of their success, of the exact degree of absorption of these attitudes among the people. Written history has left us a very heavy burden of documentation pertaining to the upper classes and the literate life and very little that is authentically about the people beneath this small fraction. In general, three types of sources can be distinguished, although the boundaries between each category may be slightly blurred.

Books for the Educated

The first category would include the deliberately created images of what a good subject should be like in his attitudes toward the various segments of society. Books such as the *Oryun haengsilto* (Illustrated five virtues in practice) with its *han'gŭl* rendition of each exemplary tale were obviously intended to be useful for popular education, yet with their costly printing and fine woodcut illustrations it is unlikely that they could have had too much influence on peasant attitudes.[60] In this book and others of its type, there is a highly idealized supremacy of Confucian virtues. Cosmological sanctions are evident in the tendency in some of the stories to shade almost imperceptibly into the realm of the fabulous, as in the tale of the filial son whose faithfulness causes the bamboo shoots to sprout through the river ice so that he can feed his ailing mother a favorite dish.

More straightforward, and possibly more widely read—were books like the sixteenth-century *Kyŏngminp'yŏn*, the "book to warn the people," which appended short Confucian injunctions to quite explicit and direct discussions of the statutory penalties for major crimes. This statement from the preface is illustrative of the compiler's motivation:

> In editing this I have placed the fundamentals first and included the discussions of ethical principles so that there might be an awakening and an arising of awareness. I have then quoted from the laws and set law with principle side by side, so that the people might be made circumspect, and learn how to avoid difficulties. I have used plain speech and common language so that the ill-educated might become easily enlightened.

But he also hoped that fellow officials would make use of the book:

> If, failing fully to devote his mind and heart to the task of educating the people and rectifying their behavior, my reader were instead to make exercise paper of this book and then relegate it to some dim and distant corner, and just sit back and eat up his government salary, passing his time in enjoyment, then I will have failed in my purpose. All of us who shepherd the people [i.e., govern them as magistrates] really ought to give this more of our concern.[61]

Books of this sort are often as important for what they tell us about the compilers as for what they tell us of the reading tastes and mores of their intended audience.

Semipopular literature

In sources of a semipopular nature, Confucian elements mix more freely with folklore and material of popular dramatic interest, not to say prurient appeal. Often the stories mix in an oral tradition with written versions existing at the same time. The tale of Ch'unhyang is interesting in this respect, because of its legal content and great popular appeal during the last part of the Yi period.[62] Although the dramatic confrontation between the secret royal censor and the corrupt local official may represent a romantic exaggeration, it is not unfair to say that the story upholds the notion of legal mechanisms, albeit extraordinary ones, as rectifying injustice.

Another category of writings that were even more loosely related to the actual functioning of the legal process but seem to have had some history of popularity in Korea was the stories of the clever magistrate or secret censor—the name Pak Mun-su comes most readily to mind—who rendered judgment in impossibly difficult cases with both caginess and justice. The diffusion of these is difficult to trace, but it is of interest that a major collection of such stories from thirteenth-century China, the *T'ang-yin-pi-shih*, was reprinted in Korea during the Koryŏ period.[63] Although such stories do not seem to have been as popular in Korea as in China—a *kung-an* (Chinese detective story) genre as such is scarcely to be found—they did exist and would seem to reflect a measure of cynicism toward the judicial process.

Popular Sources

As one enters the world of literary materials whose popular origin is so undeniably authentic that the chief sources are oral and not written, the degree of cynicism increases, although solid references to the legal system as a distinct aspect of government are increasingly rare. Some tracings can be found in the satiric mask dramas, and a small repository of folk sayings have to do with legal matters, but it is not at present a fertile area for exploration, as important as such research would be if the material were more ample.

One possible explanation for this lack of references to law might be that legal consciousness among the common people was quite low. Litigation experts, people who prepared the necessary documents for suits and trials, did exist in the early years of the Yi dynasty, but by the last quarter of the fifteenth century their activities were proscribed.[64] Korean historians are divided over the question whether conceptions of property rights were highly developed, economic historians tending toward skepticism and legal historians toward the view that property concepts were developed and widespread.[65] In retrospect it seems clear that these conceptions, however widely diffused, were insufficiently universalized and modern to provide a basis for resistance to colonial Japanese land policies in the early twentieth century.

Suits over gravesites were very popular in the eighteenth century, though lawsuits were perhaps not as widely resorted to as "out-of-court" settlements, sometimes involving substantial skirmishes between large armed groups. Hulbert found that a popular saying in the early 1900s was "*Chaep'an hapsida*" ("Let's take it to court") although his point was a different one, namely that the threat of a lawsuit was a means of intimidation and blackmail.[66]

The Growth of Korean Law

Some summary observations might be made about the growth of law in Korea and what it signified. First, we would have to say that the growth of law acted to weaken conflicting bases of power and authority, such as local interests and nongovernmental jurisdictions. Of course, law was not the only instrument of this change, especially in the early years of the dynasty, and new interests were continually rising to challenge the rule of law throughout the period, but law was a major element of the conflict, and its growth and increasing rationalism always acted to reinforce the central government in its power position. The situation within the central bureaucracy was much more complex, and further study of the relationship between legal cases and political strife will have to be made before any firm conclusions can be drawn.

Secondly, it may have been that the use of a written, uniform and widely diffused law and legal system weakened the potential of Confucianism for independent, varied development at the same time that it universalized certain Confucian conceptions through the codes. It was this centralizing effect of the codes, surely, and not "neo-Confucianism" *per se* which led to rigidity. Neo-Confucianism was also orthodox in Japan. Yet much more variety in political thought was made possible there by the existence of more than two hundred individual local governments, each with its separate financial, political, and educational administration. The codes in Korea have to be given some of the credit (or blame) for the fact that the great achievements of Yi Confucian thought, with some exceptions, were principally in metaphysics and not government theory.

A third observation would be that the victory of law in Korea was never complete. As important as they were to the functioning of the Korean government, for example, legal specialists were never large enough in number, nor sufficiently highly placed in government, for them to exercise a consistent, rationalizing influence in the judicial decision-making process that might have spread to other areas of admininstration as well. As it was, judicial decision making may have been one of the more rationalized areas of government decision making.

Economic problems were also a continuing barrier to the growth of law. Even if legal mechanisms had been more thoroughly entrenched, economic theory was inadequate to the task of providing necessary financial leeway in the administration to make a serious attempt at eliminating corruption. The problem was exacerbated by the continued existence and slow growth of economic areas—the great estates we have mentioned—outside the taxation and legal systems.

The high point of legalization of the Korean government structure may have been 1800, after which, as one writer has suggested, the association in people's minds of many economic and administrative reformers with Catholic thought severely reduced their long-term effectiveness and credibility in the government, implicating some of Korea's most creative thinkers on the eve of the Western impact.[67] From the legal point of view, it also seems possible that the late eighteenth-century Catholic crisis contributed to a resurgence of Confucianism as a political force, dispelling the atmosphere created by the political stabilization policies of Yŏngjo and Chŏngjo, reintroducing a heavy ideological flavor to criminal hearings and the court atmosphere, and helping to shatter, perhaps irreparably, the nascent supremacy of legal norms.

Korean Law and the Modernization of Asian Law

One question of great interest to students of modern Asian history and the history of recent contacts between East and West is how the indigenous legal systems of China, Japan, and Korea met the challenge of ridding themselves of the "unequal treaties" that had been forced upon them during the nineteenth century. Legal change under such circumstances was far from an academic question, as it was directly related to the question of eliminating extraterritorial jurisdiction and to treaty revision in general. (Those who remember the signing of the Status of Forces Agreement between the United States and the Republic of Korea in 1966 will recognize that the question is not altogether dead even to this day.)

While scholars have paid much attention to the processes of political, economic, and even cultural modernization in China and Japan, and to a lesser extent in Korea, work is just now beginning on the study of how the traditional Asian legal systems met and often persisted under the "Westernizing" reforms demanded by the treaty powers. Could a modern legal system, acceptable to the treaty powers and yet meaningful within the domestic tradition as well, have been fashioned from the raw materials in existence in the middle and late nineteenth century? Though rendered moot by the course of history, some retrospective examination of this question might be illuminating for our discussion.

To get some idea of what a possible answer might have been had other conditions been more favorable during those critical years, let us look at some of the proposals submitted to King Kojong in 1888 by a Korean reformer and leader of the "enlightenment party," Pak Yŏng-hyo. Pak was a leader in the unsuccessful *kapsin* coup attempt of 1884 and was a member of the Korean government again at the time of the *kabo* reforms of 1894. In 1888, however, he was in Japan, from where he sent a lengthy "reform memorial" with proposals touching on many areas of Korean society and government.

It is interesting to compare the language of this memorial with that of earlier Yi dynasty works. For example, the preface to the sixteenth century *Kyŏngminp'yŏn* mentioned above contains the following passage:

> The making of punishments and laws stems from the compassionate and loving concern of the ancient kings for their people. Simply to take the laws and decide punishments without first instructing and leading [the people] would be almost like deceiving them. . . . Unaware as the dull and witless are of the cardinal importance of even the five human relationships, how can they be expected to be cognizant of the details of the law? In their innocence they are like the blind or deaf; they just ignorantly grasp at [the simple necessities of] food and clothing, completely unaware that they may be breaking a law. Then once they are apprehended in a crime, for the authorities to rule on the matter with the law [as they do] is like catching a bird in a snare or an animal in a trap. How does this help the people move toward the good and put the bad from them?[68]

Pak Yŏng-hyo's reform memorial of 1888 states:

> Laws and statutes constitute standards for the lives of the common people. They encourage that which is right and prohibit that which is evil, and should be applied without partiality or favor, taking into account the right and wrong, the true and false. The basic purpose of laws and statutes does not lie in just rigidly enforcing the literal meaning, but in bringing human-heartedness into it as well, and thus [eventually] doing away with violations. Thus one comforts the people with humane benevolence, governs them with right conduct, comforts them with good faith and sincerity, all the while using both the sparing grace and awesome dignity [of the sovereign], and preserving the law intact and fostering government. Difficult as it is to change ancient institutions on short notice, one may bring about a firm and

just order gradually, even in the face of opposition, if one just places good faith and sincerity foremost in setting up and putting into force the laws.[69]

It would be tempting to use the Confucian-tinged rhetoric of these two passages to show that Pak was hopelessly old-fashioned and tradition bound, tied to the futile and empty language of a Confucian past that was clearly inadequate to serving the needs of his time. Yet a closer examination could well lead to the opposite conclusion—that traditional Korean legal values contained the necessary elements for success in the modern world, even if late nineteenth-century legal behavior was badly in need of reform. In both passages there can be found confirmation of the proposition that law is a necessary aspect of government, and that its purpose of providing standards for society must not be lost. The "modernity" in this sense of traditional Korean legal ideals can be seen even more clearly in Pak's specific suggestions for the reform of the legal system:

(1) Suits and criminal cases should be handled exclusively by the courts, with no interference from the king.
(2) Cruel penalties should be abolished.
(3) Collective family punishment should be eliminated.
(4) The practice of torturing suspects, with the resulting false confessions, should be ended.
(5) Circumstances and evidence should be investigated carefully, with conviction only after a voluntary confession.
(6) Written documents should be required in loan and sale transactions so that these can be used in settling later suits. No suits should be permitted without such documentation.
(7) Gravesite disputes should be eliminated by establishing graveyards on a public basis for all citizens regardless of status.[70]

These were not the proposals of a hide-bound traditionalist, but rather of a sophisticated, gifted reformer, made on the basis of his travels abroad and extensive experience with foreign leaders. Yet clear precedent for all of these proposals but the first—that the king's role in judgment be eliminated—can be found in Yi dyansty reform writings and practices and in government debates from the mid-eighteenth century and before. Even the last proposal, concerning gravesites, was foreshadowed in Pak Che-ga's harsh criticism, in *Pukhag-ŭi*, of Korean burial practices and the resulting disputes.[71]

In the language of the day, these were "enlightened" proposals, in the sense that they would have made the Korean system more compatible with those of the great powers in the late nineteenth century. But there is little in them that does not derive in significant measure from Korea's own legal traditions and conceptions. After further examination and analysis of the principal source materials, we may well conclude that traditional Korean law, at least as late as 1800, and possibly for some time later, may well have contained within itself the necessary elements for successful accommodation to the challenges of the late nineteenth and early twentieth centuries.

NOTES

1. Cf., for example, Sŏ Il-gyo, *Chosŏn wangjo hyŏngsa chedo ŭi yŏn'gu* [A Study on the Criminal Law and Procedure of the Chosun (Yi) Dynasty 1392-1910] (Seoul, 1968); Chŏn Pong-dŏk, *Han'guk pŏpchesa yŏn'gu* [Researches in Korean Legal History] (Seoul, 1968); a collection of arts. including a revised version of Chŏn's doctoral dissertation on the *amhaeng ŏsa* ("secret censor") system; and Pak Pyŏng-ho, *Han'guk pŏpchesago* [Studies in Korean Legal History] (Seoul, 1974), which contains nearly all of the articles Professor Pak (Seoul National University College of Law) has published over the past decade and a half.
2. Hahm Pyong-choon, *The Korean Political Tradition and Law* (Seoul, 1967). This is a collection of articulate essays in Korean legal history. The title essay differs diametrically from the interpretation here. Cf. also Hahm's "Korea's Initial Encounter with the Western Law: 1866-1910 A.D.," *Korea Observer* Vol. 1, No. 2 (1969), pp. 80-93.
3. *Simnirok* [Records of Review Hearings] (hereinafter *SR*). Typeset from the 16 *kwŏn* ed. of 1801 in 2 vols. (Seoul, 1968). This contains accounts of nearly 1,000 cases for the reign of King Chŏngjo (r. 1776-1800). Several official copies are still extant. Another important source is the *Ch'ugwanji* [Records of the Board of Punishments] Chōsen sōtokufu cūsūin ed. (hereinafter cited as *CKJ*) (Keijō [Seoul], 1939). This is an early nineteenth-century compendium based on Board of Punishments files. Some 200 criminal case records of the *simni* type are included, as well as numerous internal regulations and accounts of the internal administration and evolution of the Board. A late seventeenth-century collection of royal edicts having legal force as precedents is the *Sugyo chimnok* [Collected Edicts] of 1698. A supplement, the *Sinbo sugyo chimnok*, was issued in 1711.
4. The best modern ed. of the *Kyŏngguk taejŏn* (hereinafter cited as *KT*) is that collated and reprinted by the Chōsen sōtokufu chūsūin (Keijō [Seoul], 1934).
5. The 1395 Korean text of the Ming Code, titled *Taemyŏngnyul chikhae* [The Directly Translated Great Ming Code] (hereinafter cited as *TMC*), is the earliest extant ed. A Korean tr. has been published (Seoul, 1964).
6. *Soktaejŏn* [hereinafter cited as *ST*], Chōsen sōtokufu chūsūin ed. (Keijō [Seoul], 1938), p. 395.
7. Inquiry into the specific processes by which principles of interpretation and specific articles were adopted in Korea is still pending. It is safe to suppose

that the reception of Ming law was substantially complete by the late fifteenth century.

8. Chinese law was not without its "particularistic" features, its tendencies to reflect social or familial distinctions found in Chinese society. Indeed, many students of the matter, content to compare Chinese *practice* with Western democratic *ideals*, have made of particularism a major key for the interpretation of the Chinese tradition. Yet the all-encompassing and centralized nature of the Chinese political and institutional traditions is of much greater antiquity than most scholars have (until recently) suspected, and worthy of equal attention. Cf. Herrlee G. Creel, *The Origins of Statecraft in China*, Vol. 1, *The Western Chou Empire* (Chicago, 1970), chaps. 1 and 8.
9. Derk Bodde and Clarence Morris, *Law in Imperial China* (Cambridge, Mass., 1967), pp. 64-67.
10. Cf. Ch'ü T'ung-tsu, *Local Government in China under the Ch'ing* (Cambridge, Mass., 1962), pp. 180-192, for discussion of some of the problems of Chinese magistrates who, because of the rule of avoidance, had been assigned to posts outside their native province, where they often did not speak the local dialect.
11. Bodde and Morris, pp. 505-517. Professor Morris's critique of Chinese legal reasoning as too narrowly confined to the precise letter of the law reflects the common lawyer's preference for a relatively loosely woven legal fabric that permits judicial flexibility, plea bargaining, considerations of equity, "common sense," and room for sociological or policy considerations. These qualities, however well suited to the Anglo-American legal tradition, are not as sympathetically viewed from the Continent. Had Weber had access to the cases in *Law in Imperial China*, he would probably have felt Chinese legal reasoning to be more "formally rational" than that of England and the United States.
12. I have here chosen the phrase "law-oriented" in preference to the more traditional "legalist." A good case can be made for the argument that it is in the noncriminal aspects of government that the administrative insights of Shen Pu-hai and Han Fei-tzu are most closely in harmony with what were later to be termed the "statecraft" concerns of Confucian thinkers. Cf. Creel, "The Fa-Chia: 'Legalists' or 'Administrators'?" *The Bulletin of the Institute of History and Philology, Academia Sinica*, extra Vol. 4 (Taipei, 1961).
13. Creel, "The Fa-Chia," pp. 632-634.
14. The term "Confucianization of Law" is Ch'ü T'ung-tsu's. Precise study of the influence of neo-Confucian social thought on the criminal codes of the Sung and later periods is necessary before we will be able to sort out the exact nature of the relationship between law and Confucian thinking as it developed over centuries of history. The contention here that the Code in Korea may have had an influence on the percolating-down of Confucian social perceptions and values is meant to provoke further study rather than to provide a definitive answer.
15. *CKJ*, pp. 186-187.
16. *TMC*, p. 397; *Chŭngbo munhŏn pigo*, Kojŏn kanhaenghoe ed., 3 Vols. (Seoul, 1957), *kwŏn*, 137:2b-3a.

17. Charles O. Hucker, *The Censorial System of Ming China* (Stanford, 1966).
18. Cf. Sohn Pow-key, "Social History of the Early Yi Dynasty 1392-1592: with an Emphasis on the Functional Aspects of Government Structure" (unpubl. Ph.D. Thesis, Berkeley, 1963), chap. 4. Cf. also Edward Willett Wagner, *The Literati Purges: Political Conflict in Early Yi Korea* (Cambridge, Mass., 1974).
19. The "intrusion" of an extrinsic system of moral norms into legal decision making is an example of what Weber referred to as "substantive rationality." Cf. Max Rheinstein, ed., *Max Weber on Law in Economy and Society*, Edward Shils and Max Rheinstein, trs. (Cambridge, Mass., 1954), p. 225. The inability to conceptualize moral and legal values as aspects of a unified whole rather than as conflicting and potentially exclusive categories is typical of modern Western thought and has its origin in late medieval times. Cf. Francis A. Schaffer, *Escape From Reason* (Downers Grove, Illinois, 1974), pp. 9-18.
20. *T'aejo sillok, kwŏn*, 1:44. There is some ambiguity concerning T'aejo's mention of the Ming Code. Korean and Japanese scholars generally assert that the Ming Code was prescribed as a whole at this time. The passage cited, however, seems to make operative only those provisions dealing with the handling of crimes committed by officials.
21. *TMC*, pp. 557-558. *Idu* were selected Chinese characters used in a proto-syllabary to append Korean inflections to Chinese sentences, or sometimes even in a kind of mixed script in which a Chinese text was recast in Korean word order. The resulting text was more easily read by those officials whose ability to read unmodified Chinese was weak or questionable. When read aloud, the Korean *idu* version of the Ming Code would have been intelligible to any fifteenth-century Korean who had a grasp of the requisite vocabulary, whether he could read Chinese or not. It is not surprising that such a translation was used in Korea. Chu Yüan-chang had, as early as 1366, found it necessary to prepare a similar "direct interpretation" of an earlier version of his Code for the benefit of Chinese readers, but the motive, to make the laws accessible to ordinary people, was different from that of T'aejo, who simply wanted his officials to be able to use the Code, *(Ming) T'ai-tsu Shih-lu*, Vol. 2, (Taipei, n.d.), p. 487. Requests from Korean officials for translations of the Ming Code can be found as early as 1388, the year the Code was brought to Korea, and as late as 1404. *Koryŏsa*, 84:34b-35a; *T'aejong sillok*, 8:26.
22. *T'aejong sillok*, 9:26b-27a.
23. An Chong-hwa, *Kukcho immulchi* (hereinafter cited as *KI*), (Seoul, 1909), Vol. 1, p. 2.
24. *KI*, Vol. 1, pp. 30-31. *T'aejong sillok*, 32:25b-27a; Maema Kyōsaku, *Kosen sappu* (Tokyo, Vol. 1 [1934], Vol. 2 [1956], Vol. 3 [1957]), p. 1460; Yi Hŭi-sŭng *et al.*, eds., *Han'guk immyŏng taesajŏn* (hereinafter cited as *HITS*) (Seoul, 1967), pp. 982ff.
25. *HITS*, pp. 321f.; *KI*, Vol. 1, pp. 2-4.
26. *T'aejong sillok*, 7:2b-3b.
27. *KI*, Vol. 1, p. 204. The text of this interesting work may be found in Chŏng's collected writings, the *Sambongjip*, Kuksa p'yŏnch'an wiwŏnhoe ed. (Seoul, 1961), pp. 204-253.

28. Ushijima Shōzō, *Richō hōtenkō* [Studies in Yi Dynasty Legal Codes] (Keijō [Seoul], 1936), p. 50.
29. *HITS*, p. 404. Information about these various works may found in Maema, *Kosen sappu*.
30. Peter H. Lee, *Songs of Flying Dragons: A Critical Reading* (Cambridge, Mass., 1975). This is the latest and most thorough work on *Yongbi ŏch'ŏn'ga* in English.
31. *HITS*, pp. 967ff.
32. Discussions between Yŏngjo and his officials concerning the content of the *Soktaejŏn* (published 1746) are quoted from court records in Ushijima, *Richō hōtenkō*, pp. 149-159.
33. Hahm, *Korean Political Tradition*, pp. 29-30. For a corrective to this overly simplistic view of Confucian thought, cf. Benjamin Schwartz, "Some Polarities in Confucian Thought," David S. Nivison and Arthur F. Wright, eds., *Confucianism in Action* (Stanford, 1969), pp. 50-62.
34. While systematic Korean legal treatises were rare, Korean writers, like their Chinese counterparts, often referred to legal matters in discussions of government problems. By the late Ming period there was a well-developed Chinese tradition of private commentaries upon the codes which continued unabated into the Ch'ing period. Cf. Fu-mei Chang Ch'en, "Private Code Commentaries in the Development of Ch'ing Law (1644-1911)" (unpubl. Ph.D. Thesis, Cambridge, Mass., 1970). Cf. also Ch'en's chapter in the present volume, "The influence of Shen Chih-ch'i's *Chi-chu Commentary* upon Ch'ing Judicial Decisions."
35. Yi Ch'un-hui, *Yijo sŏwŏn mun'gogo* [A Study of Confucian Academy Libraries] (Seoul, 1969). However, no less a Confucian luminary than Song Si-yŏl (1607-1689) apparently owned a copy of the *Kyŏngguk taejŏn*. Cf. the introduction to the Chōsen sōtokufu chūsūin ed. cited above, note 4. Legal knowledge was required for the magistrates' examination. *KT*, p. 152.
36. Chŏng Yag-yong, *Hŭmhŭm sinsŏ* (early nineteenth century), *kwŏn* 1, p. 1. Chŏng suggested that historical examples could be useful in deciding cases when no appropriate statute could be found.
37. Cf., for example, Kim Paek-kan, *Sasong yuch'wi* (sixteenth century). A modern Korean tr. was published by the pŏpchech'ŏ (legal material series, No. 16, Seoul, 1964).
38. For the first two decades of the Yi period alone, perhaps 200 references to the Ming Code or to Korean laws can be located in the *sillok*, despite the apparent fact that the Code was only gradually coming into use. For later periods, it is rare indeed that three or four pages of the *sillok* will not contain at least one reference to written law of either Chinese or Korean origin. When one considers that the *sillok* is a highly formalized record abstracted from far more detailed court and other official records and that specific statutes only appear insofar as they are linked to events making up the official historiographic inventory, the importance of law to Yi dynasty governmental operations becomes much clearer.
39. Thus, a number of review cases in the *Simnirok* involve error at the magistral level or even higher. In serious cases involving the death penalty, such error

might be discovered after petition (*kyŏkko*, "striking the drum"; *sang'ŏn*, "petitioning," etc.) by a relative of the accused or through review investigations into the facts of the case conducted by the provincial governor or the Board of Punishments. In general, the less serious the case, the less likely were such procedures to be effective at rooting out official incompetence or corruption. There were "secret censors" (*amhaeng ŏsa*), however, who were often dispatched in the late Yi period to conduct surveillance of various aspects of administration throughout one or more provinces. For a study of this system, cf. the volume by Chŏn Pong-dŏk cited above, note 1.

40. *Koryŏsa*, 84:1a-2b.
41. Thomas A. Metzger, *The Internal Organization of the Ch'ing Bureaucracy; Legal, Normative and Communication Aspects* (Cambridge, Mass., 1973), pp. 28-91, provides a well-documented enumeration of areas of values shared by the Confucianist and "legalist" positions in Chinese political thought.
42. *CKJ*, p. 129.
43. *TMC*, p. 433.
44. *Sinbo sugyo chimnok* (Seoul, 1964), p. 363.
45. *SR*, Vol. 1, p. 72. In this case the governor of Kyongsang province was punished for improper investigative procedures.
46. An Chŏng-bok, *Imgwan chŏngyo* [Essentials of Government for Those in Office], collated with Korean tr. by Kim Tong-ju, *ŭryu mun'go* series, Vol. 133 (Seoul, 1974), pp. 180 and 350.
47. *Mongmin simsŏ* (early nineteenth century), 3:5a in Munhŏn p'yŏnch'an wiwŏnhoe, compiler, *Chŏng Ta-san chŏnsŏ* (Seoul, 1961), Vol. 3, p. 337.
48. Ch'ü T'ung-tsu, *Law and Society in Traditional China* (Paris and the Hague, 1961), chaps. 3 and 4.
49. *KT*, p. 470.
50. *KT*, pp. 482-483.
51. *SR*, Vol. 1, pp. 51, 173, and 352-353. Quotation is at p. 353.
52. Pak Pyŏng-ho, *Han'guk pŏpchesago*, p. 256. Professor Pak's study on rights consciousness in the Yi period is a useful corrective to the commonly accepted view.
53. An Chŏng-bok, *Imgwan chŏngyo*, pp. 58-64 (291-293) has a section on selecting a *hyangso*, or a magistrate's advisory council, from among local worthies.
54. Kim Yongsŏp, *Chosŏn hugi nongŏpsa yŏn'gu: nongch'on kyŏngje; sahoe pyŏndong* [Studies in the Agrarian History of the Late Yi Dynasty, with Emphasis on the Peasant Economy in the Changing Phase of Social Structure] (Seoul, 1970), pp. 295-393.
55. Ch'ü T'ung-tsu, *Law and Society in Traditional China*, pp. 213-218; Bodde and Morris, *Law in Imperial China*, pp. 43-48 and 561-562, for general discussions.
56. The word "archaic" is from Hulsewé, *Remnants of Han Law*, Vol. 2 (Leiden, 1955), p. 5. The records of the *Koryŏsa* for the last few Koryŏ rulers are replete with unnatural occurrences, unseasonable weather, and strange meteorological phenomena, and the treatise on the five elements (*Ohaengji*) explicitly links some types of these to faulty administration of justice.
57. Yŏngjo's preface to the *Soktaejŏn* is a good example of this genre. References

to received law used a variety of value-laden terms, ranging from the purposefully ambiguous *sŏnwang* ("former kings"), to *chojong* ("the royal ancestors") and *yŏlsŏng* ("the successive sage rulers").

58. Sohn Pow-key, "Social History," chap. 4.
59. For an example of this, cf. the Code provision on the ratification (*ŭich'ŏp*) of new laws, *KT*, p. 284. The "clearance" (*sŏgyŏng*) procedure referred to was also used to check royal discretion in making bureaucratic appointments.
60. *Oryun haengsilto*, photo-lithograph of 1797 ed., tr. Yi Min-su (Seoul, 1972). The story cited may be found at pp. 51-52 (*kwŏn* 1:23a).
61. Kim Chŏng-guk, *Kyŏngminp'yŏn* [A Compendium to Warn the People], photolithograph of 1658 woodblock ed., published as part of Vol. 1 in the *Taehak kugŏ kojŏn ch'ongsŏ* series of the Sangmun'gak Press (Seoul, n.d.), pp. 1-2.
62. Richard Rutt and Kim Chong-un, trs., *Virtuous Women: Three Masterpieces of Korean Fiction* (Seoul, 1974), pp. 237-333.
63. R. H. van Gulik, tr., *T'ang-yin pi-shih, "Parallel Cases from Under the Pear Tree," a thirteenth-century manual of jurisprudence and detection* (Leiden, 1956), pp. 12ff.
64. Pak Pyŏng-ho, p. 316.
65. Chŏng Ch'ang-yŏl, review of Pak Pyŏng-ho's *Chŏnt'ongjŏk pŏpch'egye wa pŏbŭisik* [The Korean Traditional Legal System and Legal Consciousness] (Seoul, 1972), in *Sintonga* (June 1973), pp. 346-349.
66. Homer B. Hulbert, *The Passing of Korea* (Seoul, 1969).
67. Gari Ledyard, *The Dutch Come to Korea* (Seoul, 1971).
68. Kim Chŏng-guk, *Kyŏngminp'yŏn*, pp. 1-2.
69. *Toksŏ Sinmun*, No. 123 (April 15, 1973), p. 12.
70. *Ibid.*
71. Pak Che-ga, *Pukhagŭi* [Essays on Northern (Ch'ing) Studies], with Korean tr. by Yi Ik-sŏng, *Ŭryu mun'go* series (Seoul, 1971), pp. 214-218 and 369-371.

X

SLAVERY AT THE END OF THE CH'ING DYNASTY

Marinus J. Meijer

"Of all things brought forth by Heaven, man is the most precious." This resounding phrase, quoted from the *History of the Later Han Dynasty*,[1] formed the introduction to a memorial submitted to the emperor by the acting governor-general of Liang-chiang, Chou Fu,[2] on March 25, 1906.[3]

According to Chou, slavery had not existed in the glorious past of the legendary kings, who had considered the safeguarding of the people's livelihood as the purpose of their reign and had held that "all people with hair on their heads and teeth in their mouths" could be equally educated to a perfect life. It was therefore inconsistent with a prosperous age and good government for there to be helpless citizens of inferior status who could not raise themselves to a position of equality with other human beings. The Ch'ing dynasty had endeavored to improve the condition of slaves and had made several attempts to regulate their manumission. The evil institution of slavery, however, had not been abolished.

The Western countries, Chou Fu continued, had progressed much further in this direction and had finally abolished slavery altogether. "At present our Dynasty, with a view to bringing prosperity to the country, is thoroughly revising its laws, but trade in human beings, which has roots in antiquity and is condemned all over the world, is still being practiced and has never been prohibited. This is not a point in favor of Your Majesty's reign and makes a bad impression on other states."

Chou Fu's comments offer intriguing theories on the history of slavery in China. We are not , however, directly concerned with the question of whether this presentation of the development of slavery is based on historical truth;[4] what interests us is its development under the Ch'ing and, finally, the abolition of slavery as an institution.

Nieboer considered slavery to be "the fact that one person is the property of another."[5] According to him, slavery was likely to develop in countries where land was freely available and where there were tribes of a lower cultural level to furnish the slaves.[6] In countries where there were

0-691-09238-9/80/000327-32$01.60/1 For copying information, see copyright page

no such conditions there could be only "intratribal" slavery.[7] Debt slavery or slavery by way of punishment—a form of public slavery—is included in this category. Nieboer draws a sharp line between real slavery and other phenomena that resemble it superficially, as for instance the abject condition of wives and children, whose relationship to the husband and father is very different from that between masters and slaves.[8] Even though the wife may be obliged to perform heavy labor for the husband, her essential function is still that of a wife and bearer of children, and even when children are completely under the domination of the father they are nevertheless brought up to freedom and not to servility. "They are never a subject class."[9]

Turning to China, we find a country where land was scarce and where tribes of a lower cultural level were far away. The tribes in the southern and southwestern parts of the country, now known as "minorities," were occasionally raided by hooligans who abducted children as slaves, but such practices were forbidden[10] and did not assume major proportions.

Accordingly, the types of slavery found in China under the Ch'ing dynasty were of the intratribal kind, which may be classified under two categories: private and public slavery.

Public Slavery

Enslavement by the state was inflicted as an aggravated form of punishment for heinous offenses. In exceptionally serious cases, it was imposed not only on the offender but also on his relatives. The Ch'ing Code prescribes enslavement as the only punishment for women and children below the age of 16 who, at the time of the crime, were living under the same roof with criminals guilty of high treason (*mou-fan ta-ni*) and a few other serious offenses.[11] In such cases the magistrate invoked the doctrine of vicarious responsibility (*yüan-tso*), which in the pre-T'ang era had a much wider sphere of application. The provisions of the Ch'ing, however, adopted the restricted rule first enacted in the T'ang Code.[12] The offender's female relations and children who fell within the ambit of this rule were presented to "meritorious officials," usually at a great distance from the capital; after 1834 they were given as slaves to the garrison troops.[13] They could not be sold, pawned, or manumitted, nor were they allowed to redeem themselves or to profit from ordinary acts of grace.[14] Whether or not this was a hereditary kind of slavery is not clear; in some cases the question did not arise because the male descendants of the main offenders were castrated.[15]

Aside from this practice, enslavement was an aggravation of the principal offender's punishment of banishment or military banishment. A person could, for instance, originally be sentenced to banishment at 2,000 *li* (Chinese miles) and the punishment then be increased to becoming a slave of the garrison soliders, usually stationed on the Amur River, in Sinkiang, or at other places on the border. At the place of destination he would be sold to an officer or bannerman; the purchaser was forbidden to resell, pawn, or manumit him. Only when for some cogent reason the master wanted to sell the slave he could, with the permission of his superior officer, transfer him in pawn or sell him to another bannerman or soldier in the same region.[16] In general this kind of slave could be set free as a result of an imperial amnesty proclamation; however, slaves were not allowed to purchase their own freedom.

This type of slavery was of a personal nature, that is to say, only the offender himself became a slave. If his wife and children voluntarily followed him into banishment, they were listed as free persons in the population registers at the place of banishment.[17] If the offender died on the way or during his period of banishment, his wife and children could either return to their place of origin or settle at the place of banishment.[18] The master of the deceased slave could not prevent the latter's dependents from returning to their original home.[19] The noncriminal status of the relatives who voluntarily accompanied criminal offenders to their place of banishment is frequently noted in official Ch'ing administrative compendia.[20]

Banishment and settlement in the border regions had long been a well-known means of colonizing sparsely inhabited areas, but in the last decades of the Ch'ing dynasty its value for such a purpose had diminished greatly.[21] Unrest and maladministration were among the reasons for this development, but a still more important reason was that the continuation of banishment as a punishment itself became the subject of searching scrutiny during the legal reform that took place in the last decade of the dynasty. The utter inefficiency of the institution of banishment was criticized by the acting governor of Shantung, Chao Erh-hsün, in 1902, with the result that in 1903 banishment was replaced with the sanction of imprisonment or with a combination of banishment and imprisonment at the place of destination, with eventual settlement in that region as a "good" citizen.[22] This measure virtually put an end to public slavery as well.

Private Slavery

Private slavery existed in several forms. A private slave was either born into slavery or sold into it. In the latter case, the form of the contract of sale was of critical importance. The form could be either a "red" or a "white" contract.

The red contract was marked by the personal seals of the buyer, the seller, and the middleman, and then stamped by the magistrate with his official red seal.[23] If the slave had previously been a freeman, the magistrate would remove his name from the population register and record his name under the household of his master. The red contract confirmed the status of the slave so that all regulations on slaves in the code would be applicable to him. If the slave later was manumitted or allowed to buy his freedom, the magistrate had to be notified and the population register amended.[24]

The red contract was not required by law. The sale of a human being could be validly effected by an official instrument called a "white contract," or even without any contract at all.[25] In cases where there was no contract, slave status could be inferred from the factual circumstances. Since in a sale by white contract the cooperation of the magistrate was not required, the population registers may have failed to show the change of status of the person so sold.

A white contract slave who had served the same master for over three years, or who had received a spouse from the master, was regarded in the eyes of the law as a red contract slave. A white contract slave who had not met these conditions, however, was in at least one respect considered by the law to have a higher status than a slave. Namely, a master who killed such a slave would be more severely punished under the laws governing killing a hired laborer; in the reverse situation, however, the white contract slave would be punished as any other slave killing his master.[26]

Up to the time when the famous scholar, Chang Chao, served as vice-president of the Board of Punishment during the 1730s, slave girls were always considered to have been bought on a red contract. Owing to the efforts of this eminent scholar, however, they were thereafter treated as white contract slaves, unless a red contract could be produced or they had been married to a red contract slave (see Appendix 10.1).

In Ming times the Code had contained the provision: "When households of the common people keep and raise slaves, they shall be punished with 100 strokes of the heavy bamboo." From the commentary it appears that only *kung-ch'en*, meritorious officials, were legally allowed to keep slaves. In practice, however, it appears that many commoners owned slaves.[27] The Ch'ing Code of 1646 retained the Ming provision prohibiting commoners from owning slaves. But it added an interlinear official commentary, which inserted after the words "keep and raise" five characters in small print saying "male and female persons of good families"; from this it may be concluded that common people also could legally keep slaves under the Ch'ing provided they had not forced a "good" person into slavery, a prohibition which of course also extended to meritorious officials. This addition in fact tended to render the provision a dead letter.[28]

The only sales of human beings authorized in the Ch'ing Code were the sale of a slave born in slavery and that of a "good" person who sold himself. As a rule all other kinds of sales of human beings were forbidden.[29] For example, parents who sold their children into slavery were to be punished with 40 blows of the heavy bamboo.[30] They were only allowed to sell their sons to be adopted sons (*i-tzu*) in another family, because this did not involve the *capitis diminutio* of slavery. Men who sold their wives into slavery without their consent were punished with 100 strokes of the heavy bamboo and banishment at 3,000 *li*; if the wife had consented to the sale the punishment was an equal number of strokes and penal servitude for three years.[31] The punishment for selling a concubine was considerably less.[32] The Code allowed husbands to sell their adulterous wives or concubines, but it did not explicitly permit their sale as slaves.[33]

The punishments prescribed by statute for the illegal sale of human beings were not severe when, from the circumstances surrounding the sale, it could be inferred that the offender was driven to the act by financial necessity. For example, in the official interlinear commentary to the provision forbidding the sale of children it is stated that, where such illegal sales do take place, the parents are punished lightly because it is assumed that they "could not act otherwise" (*pi-yu pu-te-i chih ch'ing*).[34] Moreover, in practice even the mild statutory punishment was seldom imposed, so that poor people who had no other means of keeping their children alive sold them with impunity.

Even the law against selling one's wife, which prescribed the relatively severe punishments of 100 strokes of the heavy bamboo and three years of penal servitude, could hardly be applied to poor peasants, who were frequently forced to resort to this practice. In fact, these nominally illegal sales were even legally enforceable in a way—persons who had sold their wives or children and later induced them to run away from the purchaser were severely punished.[35] In contrast to the laws against parents selling their own children, the law prohibiting the kidnapping and sale of children by persons other than their parents was strictly enforced; furthermore, a purchaser of kidnapped children who was aware of the criminal nature of the transaction was also subject to criminal prosecution.[36]

In cases of self-enslavement it would seem to have been possible to sell only oneself and leave one's family free. Such a situation would have been similar to that of a person who had been banished as a slave to a garrison and was accompanied by his family.[37] If, however, the family had been included in the contract or if the slave had received a spouse from his master, the offspring would be slaves for life unless they were manumitted or allowed to buy themselves free.[38] Such unfortunate people were called *shih-p'u*, hereditary slaves.[39]

The relationship between a master and his slave might be classified as a quasi-kinship relation. Chang Chao, mentioned above, described it as follows: "The distinction between master and slave is of a lower order than that between sovereign and subject. Though when a slave commits an offense against his master it is not so grave a matter as when a subject does not obey his sovereign, it still comes within the category of sons and grandsons (who disobey their fathers and grandfathers)."[40] Chang's intention was not to equate the status of children with that of slaves in all respects. He merely meant to say that there was a similarity between the punishments meted out to children who committed offenses against their parents and those meted out to slaves who offended in the same way against their masters.

The relationship of the slave with the master was primarily a power relationship qualified by the concept *i*, which ideally implied righteousness from the master's side, and consciousness of his inferior status with faithful fulfillment of the duties pertaining thereto on the slave's part. The dutiful, devoted slave was known as an *i-nu*, the trusted servant of the family whom we meet in popular novels. He often assumed the master's family name, administered his property, or accompanied his son when he went to study in the capital. The master was supposed to treat the slave correctly, as a human being, albeit one of a lower order. We are reminded of Max Weber's qualification of slavery in the East: "the nature of oriental theocratic or patrimonial authority and the tendency to express all relationships of dependence in terms of patriarchal authority have created such a conventional security for the slave with respect to the master that his exploitation in the sense of late Roman slavery is practically excluded."[41]

The slave was nevertheless a very inferior member of the household. He did not eat at the same table with the family, and he never used the personal pronouns "you" or "I" in addressing the master.[42] He owed the master gratitude for receiving the favors (*en*) of being supported and provided with a spouse. The highest favor was his manumission or permission to buy himself free.

As the slave's owner, the master had the right to sell him. The question whether the master could sell the slave and keep his family, thus disrupting the family ties ("separating flesh and bones"), needs further study. Considering the great importance attached to matrimony in China, it would seem doubtful that the master was entitled to separate a slave couple, but selling a slave's children was another matter.

A master had certain responsibilities toward the family needs of his slaves. According to the Code, he had to provide his female slaves with a husband; failure to do so would cost him 80 strokes of the heavy bamboo.[43] It would seem logical that he also had to find a spouse for his male slaves, though the Code (perhaps because female slaves were so much in the majority?) did not so provide. At any rate it would have been in the master's own interest to find a marriage partner for his male slaves, if only to settle them down quietly.

Once the slave's family was established, the master's role was clearly defined. His relationship with his slave's wife was different from his relationship with his slave's unmarried daughters. If the slave had been provided with a wife, the master was not allowed to fornicate with her. Though the punishment was light, only 40 strokes of the light bamboo, and commutable to a fine,[44] it meant nevertheless that such acts were considered improper.[45] Fornication with the slave's unmarried daughters, on the contrary, was not considered wrong. The offspring would be legitimate, and sons produced by a union between the master and any female slave would participate in the division of family property on the same footing as sons of the main wife or concubines.[46] The master was also entitled to give his slave's daughters in marriage. In fact, a slave who gave his own daughter in marriage was considered to have cheated his master of his rights.[47] The latter fact has led to the conclusion that the master had the right to sell the slave's daughters and sons. It does not follow, however, that he could sell the slave's wife.

An important aspect of the master's authority was his right to punish a slave for disobedience or neglect of duty. A disobedient slave could be administered a beating on the buttocks, and if he died unexpectedly under the beating the master would not be prosecuted.[48] Even if the punishment had been administered in an unauthorized way and the slave was seriously hurt, the master would not be punished. This did not mean, however, that the master had the right of life and death over the slave. If the master or one of the master's relations within the second degree of mourning killed a red contract slave intentionally, he was liable to 60 blows of the heavy bamboo and one year's penal servitude; for the intentional killing of a white contract slave the punishment was strangulation after the assizes.[49]

If a slave committed an offense (theft or fornication), the master had to report the matter to the magistrate and was not permitted to punish the slave himself. If he did, and the slave died, his punishment would be 100 strokes of the heavy bamboo, provided the slave was guilty.[50] If a master went so far as to kill three of his slaves without their being guilty of a capital crime, he would be exiled and put to hard labor in the region of the Amur River if he was an official or a bannerman; he would be exiled and himself made a soldier's slave if he was a commoner.[51] In all these cases the slave's wife, parents, and children would be set free, as they could not be expected to remain loyal to the man who had killed their husband, son, or father.[52]

The authority of the master over the family of a slave who had sold only himself was naturally more restricted. As all relationships of dependence were subsumed under kinship relations, the master was then considered a senior relative of the slave's family members. A master who sold the free daughter-in-law of his slave, or abducted her after the slave had given her as a concubine to someone of his choice, was punished as a senior relative who in order to make profit sold by force a junior relative (see Appendix 10.2).

The master's parents and grandparents enjoyed the same authority over the slave as the master himself.[53] The authority of senior relatives of lower rank (calculated according to the degree of mourning to be worn for them) was more limited. Special rules applied in the case of mistreatment of slaves by wives, daughters, and concubines.[54] They might also, however, be considered to be acting as the master's agent, in which case they would either enjoy his privilege and immunity or be held to have assumed his responsibilities. The *Hsing-an hui-lan* gives an instance of a daughter of the house who killed her personal slave girl out of fear that the girl might betray an illicit relationship which the daughter entertained with her neighbor. The Board of Punishments seems to have made no distinction between her authority and her father's, since she was considered to be the mistress of the girl and was punished for the crime.[55] Cruel treatment of slave girls by the lady of the house seems to have been more frequent among officials than among slave-owning commoners. These titled ladies would invoke their status in order to escape punishment. Once during the reign of the T'ung-chih emperor (1861-1875) a censor, enraged at the impunity with which such women could vent their sadistic inclinations on their slave girls, wanted to hold the official himself responsible. The Board of Punishments sympathized with the censor's intentions (respect for human life), but at the same time wished to maintain the social distinction and proposed a compromise (see Appendix 10.3).

One of the censor's arguments was that officials could entrust the commission of such crimes to their wives and so circumvent the law. This leads us to the question of how far a master could employ a slave to do his dirty work for him. The Code provided for such circumstances: for instance, if a master employed his slave to beat up or kill an enemy, he could be punished as if he had committed the crime himself, though the slave would not not be exempted from punishment but would be dealt with as an accomplice.[56]

The master was supposed to rule his household in such a way that its members did not contravene the law. If his sons became thieves, he was punished;[57] bad behavior on the part of his slaves likewise reflected upon him. If a slave beat or offended an official, the master received 50 strokes of the heavy bamboo.[58] If a slave kidnapped a woman, and the master, knowing the facts, did not report him to the magistrate, he would be considered the buyer of abducted women and be punished accordingly.[59] Thus, authority over a slave was to some extent counterbalanced by responsibility for the slave's acts, or even the assumption of complicity.

The Legal Status of Slaves

In addition to his being subject to the master's authority within the household, a slave's behavior was further regulated by the law. A slave who killed his master was punished by death by slicing; if he killed him accidentally the penalty was immediate strangulation.[60] The slave was subject to immediate decapitation for beating his master.[61] If he used abusive language against his master, the sentence was strangulation after the assizes.[62] Fornication with the master's main wife or his daughter entailed immediate decapitation for the slave;[63] if the offense was with the master's concubine, however, the punishment was strangulation after the assizes.[64] Alabaster and others[65] give further details concerning official legal discrimination against slaves who committed offenses within the household. The fact that offenses committed by a slave against the master or his superior relatives entailed such heavy penalties was not merely a consequence of his being a slave, for relatives of inferior rank were similarly discriminated against. Likewise, the fact that he could not legally leave his master was not necessarily because he was regarded as a human chattel. Sons were also denied the right to leave the parental home without the permission of their parents.[66]

An extension of the *capitis diminutio* was the legal discrimination against a slave who committed offenses outside the household. In general, slaves who offended against freemen were punished one degree more severely than ordinary citizens. Conversely, freemen found guilty of an offense against slaves were punished one degree less severely than they would have been had they committed the same offense against another freeman.

Within the general status grouping of slaves there were some accorded special position. One such special group was the *pao-i*, hereditary slaves of the Manchu princes, who occupied a position of trust on their estates. They were persons of importance and were allowed to obtain official degrees.[67]

The relationship between a slave and his master could, of course, be altered by circumstances. However, slaves who had been manumitted, and their children, remained in a position of obligation toward their former masters. One of the legal manifestations of this continuing subordinate relationship was that, with respect to offenses committed against a former master, a freed slave was still subject to the aggravated punishment given to slaves offending against their masters. In contrast, slaves who had been sold no longer owed any special respect toward their former masters; the act of sale extinguished the obligation (*chüeh-i*).[68] This principle is illustrated by a decision of the Board of Punishments in a case involving a slave girl who had fornicated with her mistress's tenant. The tenant had been dismissed and the girl exchanged for the slave girl of another lady. The tenant out of revenge then murdered his former landlady, after having informed the girl in question of his intention. The girl had not divulged this knowledge to her former mistress, but the Board considered that as her relations with the former mistress had been terminated, she could only be punished as an accessory, not as her slave.[69]

Some scholars have denied that slaves during the Ch'ing had the right to possess property. Though the law contains no specific provisions on this matter, it tells us enough to question the validity of this view. The view we are challenging is strongly stated by Boulais, who categorically denies that a slave could possess anything of his own.[70] He says the slave could buy himself free only with the small sums which the master might occasionally bestow on him. Toni Pippon and Wang Shih-chieh are of the same opinion.[71] This may seem logical since, in the words of a Yung-cheng edict, a slave was "to look up to the master for everything."[72] He could not even call his children his own. On the other hand, we read in the Code of slaves whose property had been encroached upon by freemen and who had the right to defend it.[73] Even concubines of slaves are mentioned.[74] Hoang states: "Slaves have no salary, but they may receive gratifications from their master, his parents or friends, and some of them succeeded in amassing considerable wealth in silver or immovable goods."[75] Niida quotes sources from Mongol times to the effect that slaves in that period could be rich and could even possess slaves of their own.[76] Pippon, however, explains the slave's right to defend his property against a freeman by saying that in that case he was defending his master's property,[77] but there is nothing either in the text of the law or in the commentaries on which such an assumption can be based.

Termination of Slave Status

Public slavery could be terminated only by an imperial act of grace. This happened fairly frequently on auspicious occasions. The Board of Revenue (*Hu pu*) was charged with the correction of the population records. Those who had committed very serious offenses were excluded from ordinary acts of grace.

Private slavery ended by manumission or redemption. Neither was a right of the slave; redemption, like manumission, was a favor.[78] Although the purchase of a slave by white contract did not involve the intervention of the magistrate, redemption required official cooperation. The elevation of a slave of a bannerman to status of a free or a "good" person had to be confirmed by the authorities and recorded in the population registers.[79] Such confirmation precluded claims by the master himself or by his heirs, in the event of his changing his mind.[80] It also served to prevent slaves from running away, since they could not legally settle anywhere else without producing documents relating to their former domicile.

The government therefore issued regulations on manumission and redemption and specified the conditions under which they were allowed. The considerable number of such regulations promulgated in the first century of the Ch'ing dynasty go into minute detail and many of them deal with slaves of the Manchus.

The general rule for slaves of the Manchus was that those bought on a white contract after 1722 could buy themselves free, provided that they had not been granted a wife by the master. Those bought before that time were considered red contract slaves. The determining year was later changed to 1735.[81] It is to be noted, however, that after 1760 the redemption of white contract slaves of bannermen was conditioned solely on the consent of the master.[82]

Red contract slaves could buy their freedom if they (or their forefathers) had been chosen by their Manchu masters for three generations to serve as infantry soldiers to fill vacancies under the banners, or if they had served diligently for several generations and their master was willing to grant them the favor.[83] In the latter case, their origin as freemen had to be traceable through the enslavement contract and the population registers, and the proper procedure, through the banner administration and the Board of Revenue, had to be followed. When a bannerman could not support his white contract slaves he could also allow them redemption.[84] This general rule also applied to the slaves of the Chinese, and a Chinese master could set his slaves free when they had served him for several generations.[85]

Although the legislation on redemption of the Manchu slaves is rather extensive and too intricate to allow for thorough analysis here, we will take up a few of the substatutes, as they throw some light on the situation of slavery in general. For example, one such provision refers to slaves who obtained their own or their child's freedom in various devious ways: some made agreements with their masters to report their redemption as having taken place at a date within the statutory limitation period or not to report it at all;[86] others had their children entered into the population registers as children of friends who were freemen;[87] still others ran away and had themselves registered under false names;[88] and some even intimidated their masters into setting them free.[89]

Because the practices described in the foregoing paragraph occurred so frequently that legislation was necessary to curb them, it is quite clear that discipline among slaves, and especially among male slaves, at least at the end of the eighteenth century, was generally poor. The amount of legislation seems to be commensurate to the concern with which the Manchu government considered deterioration of male slavery and tried, though with little success, to stem the tide. Niida, Hsüeh Yün-sheng and others point out that male slavery at the end of the Ch'ing was a rare phenomenon.[90] I do not think that the large amount of legislation, especially on male slavery in the first half of the dynasty, indicates that it was a feature of great importance in China's economic life during that period. The apparent contradiction could probably be explained in the light of the contrast between Manchu and Chinese societies, the Manchus being a militarily organized people. The warning of the Yung-cheng emperor to the Manchus to maintain strict discipline among their slaves, and not to indulge in the laxity displayed by the Chinese, could be revealing in that sense.[91] On the other hand, the same emperor's concern with the arbitrary ways the Manchus sometimes treated their slaves, and his efforts to punish unnecessary violence by the slaveholders, might show a certain sensitivity to Chinese public opinion, as does his expression: "Though slaves are of low condition, yet they are people."[92] His efforts to regulate precisely the condition of slaves, the distinction between red and white contract slaves, and the minute rules on their manumission are probably due to the disciplinarian streak in his character.

Such reflections on possible motives on the part of the Manchu emperors may help to explain the complexity of the legislation, but not the decline of male slavery itself. For the explanation of this phenomenon the study of the law will never be sufficient, but it can provide some sidelights on the problem that may be helpful for other scholars who are interested in the structure of Ch'ing society.

Abolition of Slavery

When we consider the conditions of slavery as described above, Chou Fu's memorial mentioned at the beginning of this chapter—advocating total abolition of slavery—probably was not a very revolutionary step, especially as by that time many of the old distinctions in society had either fallen completely into disuse or had become greatly diminished in practice. The official examinations had been abolished in 1905, the laws on public slavery as a consequence of collective responsibility for the most serious crimes had been abrogated in the same year, and the disorder in the empire was such that it was no longer feasible to banish people to the outer frontiers to act as slaves for soldiers whose own loyalty was perhaps questionable. In the field of private slavery, the reformers expected some resistance from the pillars of the throne, the Manchu princes, and some high officials, but apparently they were willing to risk such opposition in their quest for China's rehabilitation.

Chou Fu's proposals extended beyond slavery to all transactions involving the buying and selling of human beings, whether as slaves or not. They were contained in a list of six items:

(1) The substatutes permitting people to buy and sell slaves on a red or white contract would be repealed, regardless of whether the buyer was a Manchu, a Chinese military or civil official, or an ordinary civilian. These laws would be replaced by a prohibition of such activity. The punishment for infraction of this rule was to be confiscation of the money, while the person concerned would be returned to his family.

(2) When local calamities occurred, people would no longer be permitted to sell their children. Instead, poor people who could not raise them would be permitted to hire them out for an agreed number of years. Such an agreement would record the sum received and the period of service, which was to expire when the person so hired became 25 years of age. If the child was 9, for instance, the maximum period would be 16 years, after which he or she would be free to go home. If the master moved to a distant place during that time he was to notify the child's family. If they agreed, he could take the child along; if not, they were obliged to pay to the master the amount of wages not yet earned and the child could then return home. After having fulfilled the contract the male laborer could establish himself, set up a family, and either continue working for the same master under a new contract or seek another job. If the laborer was a woman and had no parents, she would be sent to her nearest relative, who was to find her a husband. The provisions of the law on hired laborers were to be observed by both parties during the contractual period. If the child was cruelly treated, the family could take him back and pay the master the wages not yet earned.

(3) Existing slaves would become laborers considered to have been hired on a contract expiring on their 25th birthday. On the expiration of this imaginary contract the rules referred to under item 2 would become applicable. In the case of a woman who had no relatives or whose relatives could not be traced, the master's family would find her a husband. No pressure was to be brought to bear on laborers to continue in the master's service.

(4) The purchase of concubines would no longer be permitted. The free consent of both parties (i.e. the husband-to-be and the parents of the girl) would be required. The woman's mother would have the right to

come and see that her daughter was treated in a way consistent with her status as a concubine. "She should not be hidden away."

(5) Although under the old law it was in fact forbidden for parents and senior members of a family to sell their children or junior family members, "everyone thought that it would be right in his position" to do so. This had to be stopped, as had also the profitable trade in children for prostitution. The officials were to be encouraged to implement the new laws with the utmost severity.

(6) The above-mentioned five proposals, if accepted by the emperor, were to be made known publicly.

In this way Chou Fu tried to protect the rights of the slave owners for the immediate future. Their slaves became hired laborers whose wages were prepaid up to the age of 25, and there was no danger that a number of individuals "who did not belong anywhere" would suddenly be turned loose on society.

The memorial was sent by the emperor to the superintendency of political affairs (*tu-pan cheng-wu ch'u*)[93] with a brief rescript instructing the Superintendency of Political Affairs to deliberate this matter with the related boards. The superintendency passed it on to the Board of Punishments, apparently not at all happy about the proposed legislation. The Board in its turn ordered Shen Chia-pen, the commissioner for the revision of laws, to give his opinion: "[The Superintendency of Political Affairs informs us by communication that] the provisions of the statutes and the substatutes are so intricate that their revision would affect the whole legal structure (*ch'üan-t'i*). Therefore this Board should lay the matter before the commissioner for the revision of laws for comparison with Western and Chinese material on this subject and for drawing up a proposal to deal with the matter."[94]

Shen Chia-pen replied to the Board on June 12, 1906.[95] Shen's approach was somewhat different from Chou Fu's. After giving a summary of the latter's memorial, he stated that the seizure and sale of free persons as slaves was severely punished by law even if done with the consent of the victim, and that the sale of junior members of a family as slaves by senior members was also forbidden. Strictly speaking, it was still prohibited for commoners to buy and sell slaves.[96] One by one he examined the statutes and the substatutes forbidding the sale of free people as slaves, giving the historical background of each. This was intended to show that by abolishing slavery the emperor would simply be taking the final step on the road already followed by his illustrious predecessors. In China, Shen said, in years of famine poor people lacking all means of subsistence sold their children in order to keep them alive. Initially only bannermen and gentry were allowed to keep slaves, but in the course of time common people had also often come to possess them, thereby "exceeding the pattern." Bad people conducted a profitable trade in slaves and publicly pursued their business "as if they did not know they were committing a serious breach of the law." "They ill-treat and oppress those girls and the evil occurs everywhere." "The statutes forbid the slave trade, but the substatutes again allow people to draw up contracts and to buy slaves at a price. There are too many discrepancies in the law." "If an official beats a slave to death in an affray he is only punished with a fine, and a bannerman with the cangue. Compared with the slaughter of a horse or a cow this is punished lightly, and almost shows contempt for human life."

Shen studied Western legislation to compare it with Chinese practice, and finally summed up his ideas in eleven recommendations.

(1) All substatutes regulating the purchase of human beings should be repealed, and the purchase and sale of human beings should be strictly forbidden for whatever purpose, whether as slaves, as concubines, or as adoptive children.

(2) All Code provisions that exempted from punishment those persons who bought people without knowing whether they had been abducted by force or sold with their consent should be abrogated. Sellers of human beings, even those selling their own children for reasons of poverty, should be fined 15 taels of silver and the money they had received should be confiscated.

(3) The designation "slave" should disappear from the law altogether. The punishments for slaves committing offenses against their masters were too severe. Henceforth the term "slave" should be changed into "hired laborer" and the punishments assimilated to those imposed on hired laborers. Children sold or hired out by their parents because of poverty should be similarly treated. The punishments for laborers committing offenses against relatives of the master should also be mitigated.

(4) Poor people who could not raise their children should only be allowed to hire them out as laborers at a fixed price and for a period not exceeding the child's 25th year. On the expiration of the contract the laborer should be allowed to rejoin his family or settle down independently. The master should seek a husband for his female laborers.

(5) Slaves of bannermen formed a special category. They had acquired that status in one of three ways: they had been conferred on a bannerman as reward for merit; they had voluntarily entrusted themselves to the protection of bannermen; or they had been bought. There were substatutes on their manumission and redemption so that they would not remain slaves for generations to come, but in recent times the conferment of slaves had been discontinued and the voluntary sale of Chinese to bannermen rarely occurred. Only those who had not redeemed themselves and those who guarded the tombs on the estates were still slaves. These

people had been there for generations. If the masters so wished they could now allow them to redeem themselves according to the existing substatutes; if not, the slaves would be able to redeem themselves on reaching the age of 25, as proposed by this memorandum. However, these people were generally rather well provided for and perhaps they did not even want to leave their masters. In such cases the laws relating to hired laborers should generally apply, and they could continue to perform their former services without restrictions as to age. Only when they obviously abused their position, oppressing the orphans left by their masters, stealing land and property, or behaving badly in other respects, should the old laws relating to slaves under the banners still be applicable, though with some modifications.

(6) Hereditary slaves owned by Chinese should be released if they had served for three generations in their present employment. If they did not fulfill this condition, they should henceforth be considered hired laborers (up to their 25th year).

(7) Slave girls posed a special problem. They had usually been procured through a middleman and their families were hard to trace or were living far away. They should be married off by their masters after their 25th year. It was not recommended that they be given the status of hired laborers, probably because the commissioner did not see any advantage in that and he was not in favor of single women living independently in a society not prepared to receive them.

(8) For the acquisition of concubines a contract should be drawn up between the woman's mother and the intended husband expressly providing for concubine status. A go-between was needed. The right of the mother to visit her daughter and convince herself that such a status was indeed observed was to be recognized. The Western prohibition of concubinage was not suitable for China.

(9) The substatutes on banishment and enslavement should be changed. Over 120 sections of the Code dealt with banishment combined with enslavement. Shen made some sharply critical remarks about the Ch'ing system of banishment. He also proposed that henceforth all substatutes prescribing banishment and slavery be changed into perpetual banishment at 4,000 *li* and settlement in those regions, not as slaves but under the supervision of the local military commander. In practice, according to the revised penal law of 1903, this meant transportation and incarceration for ten years, after which the convicts were to settle in their place of banishment as free persons under military supervision.[97]

(10) Shen Chia-pen also took the even more radical step of proposing the abolition of all statutes recognizing the categories of "mean" and "good" people. In other words, he wished to abolish the entire category of mean people, such as prostitutes, actors, and some kinds of *yamen*

runners,[98] by revoking the prohibition of marriage between them and good people. The question of the prohibition against taking the official examinations was no longer an issue because the examinations had been abolished in 1905. Since slaves at any rate would become hired laborers and thus good people, who could marry anybody they wished, there was no reason to retain a ban on their marriage.

(11) Shen was particularly insistent on inflicting heavy punishment on those who seized girls and boys and sold them as singing girls (prostitutes) and male actors. Though the term "slave" was not actually attached to them, there was in fact no difference in their status. Of course the statutes forbade this practice, as well as the selling of "good" girls as prostitutes, but the officials had been so lax in enforcing the law that it had become a dead letter. Without rigorous application of these provisions the abolition of slavery would be of no avail. The officials should be sternly ordered to put an end to this evil.

In his memorial Shen had stated that he was waiting for an imperial rescript authorizing him to submit a list of statutes and substatutes concerning slavery which were to be abrogated, revised, or retained.[99] After that the matter seems to have rested there until the beginning of 1909 when the censor Wu Wei-ping submitted another memorial advocating the abolition of slavery, on the ground that it was inconsistent with the principles of constitutional government to which the emperor professed to adhere.[100]

The memorial was sent by a note of February 1909 from the Grand Council (*Chün-chi-ch'u*) to the Committee for the Compilation of Rules of Constitutional Government,[101] usually referred to as the Constitution Committee. The note embodied a rescript to the effect that the Constitution Committee and the commissioner for the Revision of Laws were to give their opinions, as was requested in the original memorial.

From all this delay we may conclude that Chou's and Shen's proposals had met with considerable opposition, though the abolition of slavery itself was probably not the main reason. The whole work on the revision of laws had been retarded in the years 1907 and 1908 for political reasons outside the scope of this article. Shen writes in his reply: "The prohibition and abolition of trade in human beings is deemed not to be a convenient matter in the opinion of the many people who have taken part in the discussion. The measures that have been proposed since 1906 have long been shelved." The date of Shen's reply is difficult to trace because it is not mentioned in the *Collectanea*.[102] The reply took the form of a memorandum (*i*) in which Shen attacked the three principal arguments against abolition. His main concession was to the Manchu princes.[103]

First of all, Shen dealt with the category of bondservant of the Manchu princes, called *pao-i*. They occupied a special position, and the ordinary rules for slaves did not apply to them. They were allowed to take the official examinations, and many titled officials could be counted among them. They had lived for many generations in the palaces of the princes and administered their estates. It is apparent from Shen's reply that he realized it would be embarrassing for the princes as well as for the *pao-i* themselves if they were suddenly to become hired laborers. They occupied a middle position, similar to that of the *pu-ch'ü* of the T'ang dynasty.[104] The term "slave," consequently, should not be applied to them.

A second category of slaves against whose liberation the owners made objections was that of the slaves of Manchu and Chinese officials. Shen simply repeated what he had said before, elaborating on some points. Male slaves frequently ran away and were difficult to control. They were infrequently used as guardians of the family tombs, but most bannermen currently employed local farmers to perform that task. The only ones who had remained were those whose ancestors had not been manumitted. It would be "blind obstinacy" to keep them in their present position.

The third category whose manumission would be "inconvenient" was that of slave girls. "Nowadays," Shen wrote:

> the custom of buying male slaves has ceased to exist, but the households which buy slave girls are not only those of Manchu and Chinese officials, but an abundance of ordinary wealthy Chinese as well, because it is cheaper to buy a maid than to hire one. This custom is difficult to stop. If we should change purchase and sale into "hire for wages," it is to be feared that these women would, relying on the fact that they were hired, refuse to accept orders or to keep the rules of the house, and their relatives might conspire with them to run away [so as to sell them again or to marry them off] or to engage in theft. Such matters cannot be overlooked.

Shen then stipulated that it should be made clear in the contract that the woman must respectfully observe all rules and commands, that her relatives have the right to visit her once a year, that her wages should be paid annually, and that the parents should not obstruct the execution of the contract. Shen ended by stating in strong terms that the abolition of slavery was an absolute necessity from the humanitarian as well as from the constitutional point of view.

It may seem strange that Shen proposed that instead of being sold as slave girls young women could henceforth be hired out on long-term contracts as "hired laborers." Such women could be subjected for many years to miserable treatment, though perhaps not to physical violence. Shen tried to preclude this abuse by advocating a statutory provision requiring the master to allow visits by relatives, even though all the relatives could do for the girl would be to buy her back if they had the money. Apparently he preferred the risk of a bad master or mistress to that of the craftiness of the relatives who had sold her in the first place and might well sell her again.

The Constitution Committee supported Shen's stand in a memorial which was approved by the throne on January 31, 1910. The *pao-i* were exempted from the measures, trade in human beings was to be strictly prohibited, concubines were not to be bought, all sections of the Code containing the term "slaves" were to be repealed, and existing slaves were to become hired laborers on a contract that expired when they reached the age of 25.[105] Thus, one of the last acts performed by Shen before he resigned as commissioner for the revision of laws proved to be successful, but only when the empire he had so loyally served was on the verge of collapse.

Appendix 10.1
Purchase of Slave Girls (abridged).[106]

Vice-minister Chang of the Board of Punishments memorialized:[107]

> . . . the Yung-cheng emperor, with a deep insight into our evil customs which stress the distinction between master and servant and cause human life [i.e., the servant's] to be regarded as of no importance, established the distinction between red and white contracts. A slave bought on a white contract was to be regarded as a hired laborer; when he was intentionally killed [the master] was sentenced to strangulation. The judicial officers in and outside the capital, however, have traditionally considered a female slave bought on a white contract as if she had been bought on a red contract, and have sentenced the master accordingly. For instance, in the case of the woman An, who had bought a slave girl on a white contract and had owned her only half a year, the department [of the Board which had reviewed the case] said that "such cases have always been handled that way."[108] I have examined old cases and found this to be true. I therefore feel it my duty to offer this memorial in order to clarify my point of view.
>
> The Board of Punishments is of the following opinion:
>
> In the established *li* it is provided that a bannerman who intentionally kills a slave bought on a white contract or a person whom he had received in pawn, shall be punished according to the *lü* on intentional homicide of a hired laborer and sentenced to strangulation after the autumn assizes. If he kills him in an affray he shall be sentenced according to the *lü*. Thus people bought on a red contract are domestic slaves

[*chia-nu*], while people bought on a white contract are identified with hired laborers. The provisions for killing them either intentionally or during an affray prescribe different punishment for the two categories. However, in the well-established precedents, masters who cause the death of a white contract male slave [*chia-jen*] have been punished as if they had killed a hired laborer, but in the case of a slave girl who had been bought on a white contract, they were sentenced as if she had been bought on a red contract. The reasons for this are that in the first place when bannermen or civilians buy slave girls it is always clearly stated in the contract either that the master has the right to find her a husband or that the master may assign her freely for domestic service. Thus, the contract could not be mistaken for a contract for provisional sale or pawn. Second, the *li* only mentions "persons bought on a white contract" or "male slaves bought on a white contract," and as far as homicide of slave girls bought on a white contract is concerned, there is no clear provision in the *li* prescribing what sentence is passed. Thirdly, bannermen never used a stamped contract to buy slave girls; the common people did not use it either. Therefore, when judicial officers had to pronounce judgment in cases involving the homicide of a slave girl, they always sentenced the killer as if a red contract had been used; but this was never done with the intention of acquitting the offenders or of reducing their punishment. However, in legislation we must strive for impartiality and our regulations must be rendered uniform. Since there is the distinction among male slaves between red and white contracts, such distinction should equally apply to female slaves, and this should be analyzed and clearly explained in order that the law be observed.

We should therefore request that it be decreed that henceforth when bannermen or civilians draw up contracts for the sale of female slaves, they shall all, in accordance with the *li* on buying domestic slaves, submit their documents to the magistrate in order to be stamped. In the case of bannermen, the buyer is ordered to go, together with the seller and the guarantor, to his commanding colonel and make a clear statement. The colonel examines the parties and registers the slave in the records of the banner. The seller's original stamped deed to the slave is handed to the buyer who personally takes it to the tax office where the stamp is verified. Since there is a guarantor supervising the sale, we can dispense with taking the woman to the official, so as to avoid disturbing the people. According to the *li* on buying house slaves, civilians shall draw up a contract and inform the local official, who shall affix his stamp. Bannermen living in Peking who buy a female slave from among the people shall inform the magistrate of the two prefectures Wu-ch'eng and Ta-wan. When they live in the provinces they shall inform the local official to make a sealed entry in the registers. If bannermen and civilians prefer a white contract, they may, but when there is a case of homicide with intent or during an affray, the judicial officer shall examine whether the contract is red or white and pronounce sentence accordingly.

Furthermore, it is our opinion that when a female slave has been bought on a white contract by bannermen or by civilians and is subsequently married to a red contract male slave, the law on red contract slaves shall be applied to her. In all other cases judicial officials may not arbitrarily apply to slave girls the law on red contract slaves in contravention of the established *li*.

Memorial received.
Circulated and incorporated into the *li*.

Appendix 10.2
A Master Kidnaps the Daughter-in-Law of a Slave in Order to Sell Her as Concubine.[109]

The governor of Kweichow submitted a case in which Wei A-i stabbed and wounded Wei A-ying, who subsequently died.

Wei A-k'ang had entered the service of Wei Shih-jung as a slave and though no contract had been drawn up mentioning the price paid for him, the status relationship between them was in fact one of master and slave.

Wei A-k'ang had a widowed daughter-in-law, the woman Wei, who did not live together with him. Nor had she become a slave. After some time Wei Shih-jung privately sold her to Wei A-k'uei as a concubine. However as the woman Wei's period of mourning was not yet over and Wei A-k'uei was away from home on business [the delivery did not take place]. When Wei A-k'ang wanted his daughter-in-law to remarry, Wei Shih-jung informed him that he had already sold her as a concubine to Wei A-k'uei and ordered him to wait for his return. However, since Wei A-k'uei took a long time returning, Wei A-k'ang sold the woman as a concubine to one Wei A-t'u. When Wei A-k'uei returned and heard that the woman Wei had already been sold to someone else, he went to Wei Shih-jung and demanded his money back. Wei Shih-jung then seized the woman by force, detained her in his house, and sent her to Wei A-k'uei to consummate the marriage. When Wei A-t'u engaged Wei A-ying and tried to kidnap the woman, Wei A-k'uei called to his aid Wei Shih-jung and one Wei A-i to stop them. [In the affray which ensued] Wei A-ying was stabbed with a knife by Wei A-i and died.

We [the Board] are of the following opinion: Wei A-k'ang had sold himself to Wei Shih-jung as a slave and, though there was no contract drawn up fixing the price, the relationship of master and slave existed between them. Wei Shih-jung had privately sold the woman Wei, daughter-in-law of Wei A-k'ang, to Wei A-k'uei as a concubine and had informed Wei A-k'ang; there was no question of kidnapping her by force. But then, Wei Shih-jung seized the woman by force and sent her to Wei A-k'uei to marry him. Although there is no *li* in the Code providing punishment for such act, yet when a slave or hired laborer seizes and sells his master's wife or daughter, he will be sentenced according to the *li* on junior members of a family who sell into marriage a senior relative of the second degree of mourning.[110] Therefore a master who takes by force his slave's daughter-in-law and sells her as a concubine should be sentenced by analogy to the *li* on senior relatives of the second, third, and fourth degree of mourning who, with a view to profit, sell by force a junior relative.[111]

The governor, according to the [above noted *li*], sentenced Wei Shih-jung to 100 blows of the heavy bamboo and banishment to 3,000 *li*. His sentence seems satisfactory to us and should be confirmed.

Department memorandum (1814).

Appendix 10.3
Titled Ladies Ill-Treating Their Slave Girls (abridged)[112]

The 10th year of T'ung-chih (1871)
The Department for Kwangsi [of the Board of Punishments] reports:

We have received the memorial from the censor concerned[113] to the effect that in recent years there have been many cases in which slave girls have been cruelly beaten to death. Looking into the causes of this phenomenon he finds that in all these cases the head of household was not stern enough in ruling his family and had allowed his wife to punish a slave girl for being slightly negligent. The wife [in each case] had in a perverted way subjected the girl to cruel treatment by means of scalding water and fire, burning her skin and flesh and scorching her all over the body, thus causing her death.

When such cases reached court, the head of household usually attributed the offense to his wife, who by virtue of the *li* could redeem the punishment.[114] This provision allowing female offenders to buy themselves free was originally meant as a token of benevolence bestowed beyond the strict rules of the law, but now it had suddenly become the road to avoid punishment altogether so that there was only an offense in name but no punishment in fact. No wonder they were so daring and unafraid of the law. How can we condone such people's indulging without fear in criminal conduct and not impose severe restrictions? Noting that in handling cases where women had committed criminal offenses under comparatively grave circumstances the Board at times had denied them the privilege of redeeming their punishment, the censor requests in his memorial that the Board be ordered to prepare regulations which would lead either to classifying such cases under *li* where redemption is not permitted or holding the head of household liable.

On this memorial a rescript was received enjoining the Board to give its opinion by memorial.

The Board's opinion is as follows:

When a head of household or his senior relative of the second degree of mourning has killed a slave either in an affray or intentionally, a distinction must be made according to the *lü* between slaves who were guilty of some offense and those who were not, before pronouncing sentence of bambooing or penal servitude. The difference in status between master and slave entails indebtedness on the part of the slave for being supported by the master and the duty of control on the part of the master. When the slave has been supported for a long time and the master [when exercising this control] inadvertently kills or injures the slave, he is punished by the *lü* as if he had killed or wounded a son or grandson. If he caused the slave's death intentionally, his punishment still does not exceed one year of penal servitude.

In the *li* for the first time the distinction was made between slaves bought on a red and those bought on a white contract, and among those bought on a white contract a further distinction was that, depending on the length of time the slave had been supported by the master, the master was convicted either under the *lü* on homicide of a slave or the *lü* on homicide of a hired laborer. The *li* and the *lü* are very explicit and there is no need to fear that undue lenience in judgment may occur. As regards offenses committed by women, apart from offenses involving sex, for which there are special provisions in the *li* prescribing that they actually shall be sent into banishment for offenses not involving sex, banishment is carried out only in cases where deportation is prescribed for female offenders found guilty of habitual banditry, harboring thieves and robbers, repeatedly committing vicious acts and deceit. For other offenses punishable with military banishment, banishment, or less, they are still permitted to redeem the punishment.[115] This stems from the idea of respect for a woman's moral integrity. Unless they have openly manifested a wicked and depraved character, it is impermissible actually to subject women to banishment since this would lead to the complete loss of their moral qualities.

Now this censor asks that when a woman kills a slave out of cruelty she shall, regardless of the seriousness of the crime, never be allowed to redeem the punishment, or that the head of household shall be held liable. Although in proposing these severe countermeasures against killing out of cruelty the censor is motivated by respect for human life, the status relationship between master and slave is in our opinion also extremely important and cannot be equated with ordinary relationships. The offense of killing a slave is equivalent to that of killing a son or grandson. If there is no provision imposing the punishment of actual banishment on a woman who intentionally kills her son or grandson, how could we then punish her more severely when she kills a slave? Moreover, in cases where a woman has caused the death of an ordinary person, no matter whether her punishment is reduced to military banishment or banishment, she is always allowed to redeem the punishment. How could we then, when there is a case of a woman killing a slave, an offense which is only punishable with penal servitude, condemn her to actual banishment? This would not seem to be compatible with the equity of a benevolent law.

The *lü* which provides that the husband is responsible for the offenses of his wife refers to the case when husband and wife commit an offense together and no damage or injury is inflicted on a third person.[116] If such damage or injury has been caused, then the distinction between principal offenders and accessories applies and only the woman is held responsible if the husband did not know the circumstances. There are certainly no cases where the husband is held responsible for death or injury caused by his wife.

The censor's memorial points out that redemption becomes a means for the woman to avoid punishment, and he therefore proposes to hold only the head of household responsible. This would mean, however, to forcibly apply the law on homicide to an innocent man simply because he failed to rule his household with the required severity, while the woman who should have been sentenced and then allowed to redeem herself according to the *li*, would be free from any punishment. This is manifestly at variance with the spirit of the law. Imagine that the woman had no husband, or that he could redeem the punishment on account of old age or infirmity, who would then be responsible? The question would be insoluble. Furthermore, when a woman has killed a slave for which she should be sentenced to strangulation after the assizes, we cannot leave the woman undisturbed instead and condemn the husband to strangulation in retaliation. This is unjust! We recommend that the censor's proposal of disallowing redemption to a woman who has killed a slave or holding the head of the household responsible should not be considered further, as it is not in conformity with the established *li*.

We note that in recent years cases where the death of a slave has been caused by a woman have occurred rarely among common people but mostly in families of officials. According to this censor, who holds the position of superintendent of police of the northern division of the capital, in the present case the wife of a second secretary of the Board of Revenue, Yang T'ing-fu, née Liang, beat with a stick and burnt a young slave girl, called Lai-hsi, of barely 13 years of age so cruelly that she died, and this solely because the girl did not obey the rules of the house. The case had been forwarded to the Board for review, but as the contract has not yet been received, the investigation is still in progress. Such women with a cruel streak in their characters rely on their status as principal wives of officials so that the penal law cannot be applied to them. Whenever a slave happens to commit a mistake or offense, they at once resort to all sorts of cruelty and with impunity cause the death of the slave. When the woman is prosecuted and comes before the magistrate, he can only charge her pro forma under a penal provision and then allow her to redeem the punishment according to the *li*. As was pointed out by the censor, if we do not duly punish such women to warn others, cruelty will increase and they will flout the law.

In the Code we find a *li* providing that when officials cause the death of a slave, the distinction is made between homicide during an affray and intentional homicide. The punishment accordingly can be forfeiture of salary, demotion, or dismissal.[117] Unlike common people, they are not sentenced to actual penal servitude. There is no express provision in the Code stipulating that wives of officials who commit this offense shall be given the same treatment as officials. When an official in his exalted position fails to control his wife and other female relations and when as a result of the wife's cruel treatment the death of a slave girl ensues, or when the official knowingly condones his wife's abuse of slave girls, then we may inflict punishment on him and he cannot avoid his responsibility. However, since the offenses have not been committed by the officials themselves, we would be ignoring the distinctions in legal responsibility if we punished them all equally with demotion or dismissal. Therefore, in our opinion an old *li* from the K'ang-hsi period [may provide the solution]. This *li* provided that when the grandmother, the mother, or the main wife of an official beat a slave [to death] she would be punished with a fine of one year's salary, using her husband's, son's or grandson's official rank as an indicator; if the killing was intentional, the punishment was a fine of one year's salary and confiscation of one slave by the government. If the husband, son, or grandson [of the woman offender] originally had held an official position, but had since died, a fine of one year's salary according to his last official rank should nevertheless be imposed. Later, when in 1740 the Code was revised, this provision was abrogated. Now that we want to give a warning, it seems best to return to the old *li* with some modifications.

We request that henceforth women of official families who beat to death or kill intentionally slaves and hired laborers shall be punished with a fine according to the following criteria. Aside from offenses for which the Code prescribes the penalty of death or bambooing and in which case the pertinent *lü* or *li* shall be applied, in other cases the criteria for punishment shall be: one year's salary of the husband or head of household when the prescribed punishment is one year of penal servitude; two years' salary when the offense is punishable by banishment. When the husband or the head of household is dead, the fine shall be calculated according to the rank he last possessed. The woman's privileged status shall be withdrawn and she shall no longer be able to claim official status, so that persons who commit cruelty shall control themselves. The possible contravention of several *lü* and *li* provisions [that may occur if the censor's original proposal were adopted] can thus be averted.

NOTES

1. *Hou Han Shu* [History of the Later Han Dyansty] edict of Kuang Wu Ti, annals, Chien-wu, 11th year. Also quoted by Shen Chia-pen, Commissioner for the Revision of the Laws, 1902-1910, in his *Hsing-fa fen-k'ao* [Detailed examination of the Criminal Law], in *Shen Chi-i hsien-sheng i-shu* [Bequeathed Writings of Shen Chi-i], reprinted in Taipei, 1964, p. 173. Hereinafter cited as *Shen Chia-pen*.
2. Chou Fu, 1837-1921; cf. Arthur W. Hummel, *Eminent Chinese of the Ch'ing Period* (U.S. Government Printing Office, Washington, 1943-1944. Reprinted Taipei, 1964), p. 471.
3. *Ch'ing-ch'ao hsü wen-hsien t'ung-k'ao* [Compendium of Historical Records of the Ch'ing Dynasty, Supplement] (Wan-yu wen-k'u ed.), p. 7782.
4. For material on this matter cf. E. G. Pulleyblank, "The Origins and Nature of Chattel Slavery in China," *Journal of Economic and Social History of the Orient* (1958), pp. 184-220. This article gives a survey of the literature up to 1958 and of the controversies on the subject. Cf. also Martin Wilbur, *Slavery in China during the Former Han Dynasty* (Field Museum Press, 1943).
5. H. J. Nieboer, *Slavery as an Industrial System* (The Hague, 1912), p. 9.
6. *Ibid*., p. 10.

7. *Ibid.*
8. *Ibid.*, p. 29.
9. *Ibid.*, p. 30.
10. *Ta Ch'ing lü-li hui-t'ung hsin-tsuan* [Comprehensive New Edition of the Great Ch'ing Code] (Taiwan ed., 1964), Vol. 4, pp. 2224-2226 and 2228-2231. (Hereinafter cited as *Code*.) The text of these provisions, together with very useful commentary, is found in Hsüeh Yün-sheng's *Tu-li ts'un-i* [Concentration on Doubtful Matters while Perusing the Substatutes] (Peking, 1905), sections 275:5-275:9. A new ed. of this valuable book appeared in 1970 in Taiwan, punctuated and ed. Huang Ching-chia. Both the pages and the statutes have been numbered consecutively and the substatutes have been subnumbered under the statutes. Henceforth referred to as *TLTI*. For the tr. of the terms *lü* ("statute") and *li* ("substatute"), I have followed Derk Bodde and Clarence Morris, *Law in Imperial China* (Cambridge, Mass., 1967). In the appendixes I have left these terms untranslated.
11. *Code*, Vol. 3, p. 1867; cf. also Guy Boulais, *Manuel du code chinois* (Shanghai, 1924), p. 1024; cf. also Bodde and Morris, pp. 286-287. The punishment was increased in 1791, when it was decreed that male children were to be castrated, cf. P.L.F. Philastre, *Le Code annamite* (Paris, 1909), Vol. 2, pp. 13-14 and *Code*, Vol. 3, p. 1872. Some other offenses involving vicarious responsibility were: disloyal activities (*mou-p'an*), *Code*, Vol. 3, p. 1877; murder with intent to mangle and divide the body of the deceased for magical purposes (*ts'ai-sheng che-ke jen*), *Code*, Vol. 4, p. 2479; rearing venomous animals and preparing poisons (*tsao hsü ku-tu sha-jen*), *Code*, Vol. 4, p. 2489; cabals and state intrigues (*chien-tang*), *Code*, Vol. 1, p. 747.
12. *T'ang-lü shu-i* [T'ang Code with Commentary] (Kuang-hsü ed., 1890), chap. 17.
13. *TLTI*, section 254:3.
14. *Ta Ch'ing hui-tien shih-li* [Collected Statutes of the Ch'ing Dynasty with Precedents] (Kuang-hsü ed., reprinted in Taiwan, 1963), chap. 728, p. 1448 (hereinafter cited as *HTSL*); *T'ung-k'ao* (Wan-yu wen-k'u ed.), p. 6678; *Code*, Vol. 1, p. 295 and 304; *TLTI*, sections 15 and 15:1.
15. See note 11 above.
16. *Code*, Vol. 2, pp. 850-851; *TLTI*, section 76:25; Boulais, section 358.
17. *Code*, Vol. 1, p. 297; *TLTI*, section 15:4; Boulais, section 83.
18. When the principal offender had been convicted of high treason, disloyal activities, and some other offenses excluded from ordinary acts of grace or general pardon, the descendants were not allowed to return. *Code*, Vol. 1, p. 295; Boulais, section 79.
19. *Code*, Vol. 1, p. 301; *TLTI*, section 15:7.
20. For example, cf. *HTSL*, pp. 14479, 14480 and 14488.
21. *Ta Ch'ing Kuang-hsü hsin fa-ling*, Vol. 15, pp. 1-6.
22. *Ibid.*
23. *TLTI*, section 314:3. Philastre is of the opinion that red contracts were only used for the sale of government slaves (*Le Code annamite*, Vol. 2, p. 325). From the text quoted and from Appendix 10.1 it appears that in China they could be used for the sale of private slaves as well. Cf. also Pierre Hoang, *Mélanges sur l'administration* (Shanghai, 1902), p. 116.

24. *Code*, Vol. 2, p. 847 and Vol. 4, p. 2735.
25. *Code*, Vol. 4, p. 2735. Cf. Appendix 10.2; Niida Noboru, *Chūgoku Hōseishi Kenkyū; Tochihō, Torihikihō* [A Study of Chinese Legal History — Law of Land and Law of Transactions] (Tokyo, 1960), p. 379.
26. *Code*, Vol. 4, pp. 2737-2739; *TLTI*, section 314:4. The status of a hired laborer was much higher than that of a slave; he was not a "base" (*chien*) person. His position, however, was influenced by the fact that he was living within the master's household, for which reason the master had some disciplinary rights. Thus, some offenses toward the master or his household were punished more severely for them than for ordinary persons (e.g., fornication with the master's wife, concubines, or daughters). For beating to death a slave who was guilty of some offenses, the master, who should have brought him to the magistrate, suffered 100 blows of the heavy bamboo (commutable into a fine); if the slave was innocent the punishment was 60 blows of the heavy bamboo and one year of penal servitude. For beating to death a hired laborer the master would be punished with 100 blows.
27. This fact was noted in an approved memorial from a censor, submitted to the Wan-li emperor; the rule was also there laid down that slaves of commoners were to be considered commoners or hired laborers. Chiu Han-p'ing, *Li-tai hsing-fa chih* [Legal Treatises of the Various Dynasties] (2nd ed., Taipei, 1965), p. 577.
28. Cf. *Ming-lü chi-chieh fu-li* (Taiwan reprint of 1908) pp. 554 and 557 as compared with *Code*, Vol. 2, p. 876.
29. *Code*, Vol. 3, p. 2213 and 2231; Boulais, sections 1178 and 1186.
30. *Code*, Vol. 3, p. 2214; Boulais, section 1182.
31. *Code*, Vol. 3, pp. 2214-2215; Boulais, section 1183.
32. *Code*, Vol. 1, p. 221; Boulais, section 1182: namely, for sale without consent, 80 blows of the heavy bamboo and two years of penal servitude; and with consent, one degree less.
33. *Code*, Vol. 4, p. 3198; Boulais, section 1584.
34. *Code*, Vol. 3, p. 2219; Philastre, Vol. 2, p. 115.
35. Poverty was no excuse for selling one's wife, but the punishment was only 80 blows of the heavy bamboo, *Code*, Vol. 2, p. 1021; Boulais, section 561. The Code had a special article imposing severe punishment on husbands who sold their wives in marriage to others, pretending that they were their sisters, and who after payment of the price claimed the women back. *Code*, Vol. 2, pp. 1023-1024; Boulais, sections 559-561.
36. *Code*, Vol. 3, p. 2313; *TLTI*, section 314:6; Boulais, section 1178.
37. The Code mentions slaves who had sold only themselves (*tan-shen*) in contrast to those who came with their wives and children (*Code*, Vol. 2, p. 845; *TLTI*, section 76:2). In Appendix 10.2 we find a slave who had a daughter-in-law who was not a slave, but it is not explained how this had come about; it is simply mentioned as if it were an ordinary situation. The woman was a widow, so we do not know if the slave's deceased son had been a "good" person as well. Marriages between slaves and "good" persons were forbidden (*Code*, Vol. 2, p. 1081).
38. *Code*, Vol. 4, p. 2736.

39. *Code*, Vol. 2, p. 858; cf. also Ch'ü T'ung-tsu, *Law and Society in Traditional China* (Paris and The Hague, 1961), pp. 131-132n.
40. *Hsing-an hui-lan* [Conspectus of Penal Cases], (T'u-shu chi-ch'eng chü, Shanghai, 1886; reprinted Taipei, 1968), Vol. 6, p. 2457 (hereinafter cited as *HAHL*).
41. Max Weber, *Wirtschaft und Gesellschaft*, p. 431, my own translation. Cf. also E. H. Parker, *China* (New York, 1901), p. 286.
42. *Code*, Vol. 4, p. 2738; Philastre, Vol. 2, p. 319.
43. *Code*, Vol. 2, p. 1095; Boulais, section 622.
44. *Code*, Vol. 4, p. 3251; Boulais, section 1611.
45. For example, Hsüeh Yün-sheng noted "even though a slave's wife is a low person, she nevertheless has a reputation to lose" (*TLTI*, section 370:1). When a master killed his slave in order to fornicate with the slave's wife, the master's punishment would vary between banishment and strangulation after the assizes, depending on the form of contract (red or white) by which the slave had been bought and the time he had stayed in the master's house (*Code*, Vol. 4, p. 2739).
46. *Code*, Vol. 2, p. 922; Boulais, section 415.
47. *Code*, Vol. 4, p. 2746.
48. *Code*, Vol. 4, p. 730.
49. *Code*, Vol. 4, pp. 2729-2730; Boulais, sections 1390 and 1391. Note the discussion in the section on private slavery earlier in this chapter.
50. *Code*, Vol. 4, p. 2279; Philastre, Vol. 2, p. 315.
51. *Code*, Vol. 3, p. 2451; Boulais, section 1251.
52. *Code*, Vol. 4, p. 2742.
53. In fact the group enjoying this authority included all persons for whom the master had to observe mourning of the first and second degrees (*Code*, Vol. 4, p. 2727 and *passim* through the section on "Slaves beating their Masters").
54. Concubines who had borne children received a lighter punishment than those who had not. *Code*, Vol. 4, p. 2747; *HTSL*, p. 15274.
55. *In Re* Hsü Erh-chieh, *HAHL*, Vol. 6, pp. 2459-2460 (chap. 39, p. 7a-7b). The woman was sentenced to immediate strangulation.
56. E. Alabaster, *Notes and Commentaries on Chinese Criminal Law* (London, 1899), p. 33; *Code*, Vol. 4, p. 2709; Boulais, section 1380.
57. *Code*, Vol. 3, p. 2092; Boulais, section 1130.
58. *Code*, Vol. 4, p. 2723; Boulais, section 1384.
59. *Code*, Vol. 2, p. 1067; Boulais, section 611.
60. *Code*, Vol. 3, p. 2372, and Vol. 4, p. 2727; Boulais, sections 1226 and 1387. Killing the master with premeditation (*mou-sha*), with intent (*ku-sha*), or in a fight (*tou-sha*) constituted three such heinous crimes that the gamut of distinctive punishments was exhausted and they all had to be punished by slicing. Only when the master had been killed by accident (*kuo-shih sha*) would the punishment drop to immediate strangulation with the possibility of commuting the punishment to strangulation after the assizes. *Code*, Vol. 4, pp. 2735 and 2539; Boulais, sections 1394 and 1291.
61. *Code*, Vol. 4, p. 2727; Boulais, section 1387.

62. *Code*, Vol. 4, p. 2881; Boulais, section 1451.
63. *Code*, Vol. 4, p. 3249; Boulais, section 1608.
64. *Code*, Vol. 4, p. 3251; Boulais, section 1611.
65. Alabaster, *Notes and Commentaries*, pp. 207-215; Ch'ü T'ung-tsu, *Law and Society*, pp. 188 ff; Toni Pippon, *Beitrag zum Chinesischen Sklavensystem* (Tokyo, 1936), pp. 52 ff.
66. *Code*, Vol. 2, p. 921; Boulais, section 410.
67. Cf. below, the eleventh recommendation of Shen Chia-pen.
68. *Code*, Vol. 4, p. 2743; Boulais, section 1395.
69. *HAHL*, Vol. 6, pp. 2478-2479.
70. Boulais, section 362.
71. Pippon, *Beitrag*, p. 75. Pippon's work is based on Wang Shih-chieh, "Chung-kuo nu-pi chih-tu" [The Legal Existence of Slavery in the History of China], *She-hui k'o-hsüeh chi-k'an*, Vol. 3 (1925), pp. 303-328.
72. *Ta Ch'ing Shih-tsung huang-ti shih-lu* [Veritable Records of the Emperor Shih-tsung of the Great Ch'ing dynasty], Vol. 2, pp. 768-769. (Collected in the *Ta Ch'ing li-ch'ao shih-lu* [Veritable Records of Successive Reigns of the Great Ch'ing Dynasty], reprinted Taipei, 1964.)
73. *Code*, Vol. 4, p. 2719, especially the general commentary on p. 2721; *TLTI*, section 313.
74. *Code*, Vol. 4, p. 2881, upper commentary; Philastre, Vol. 2, p. 382.
75. Pierre Hoang, p. 116.
76. Niida Noboru, *Shina Mibunhōshi* [History of the Law of Status in China] (Tokyo, 1943), p. 919.
77. Pippon, p. 75.
78. *Code*, Vol. 2, p. 854; *TLTI*, section 76:16, a *li* from 1760. This *li* refers to slaves under the banners but there was no difference in this respect with slaves belonging to Chinese civilians. See *ibid.*, sections 76:2 and 76:5.
79. *Code*, Vol. 2, pp. 844-845.
80. *Code*, Vol. 2, pp. 845-846; *TLTI*, section 76:3.
81. *Code*, Vol. 2, pp. 844-845; *HTSL*, chap. 752, p. 14720.
82. *Code*, Vol. 2, pp. 854-855; *TLTI*, sections 76:2 and 76:16.
83. *Code*, Vol. 2, pp. 847, 845.
84. *Code*, Vol. 2, p. 854.
85. Edict of 1783, mentioned by Hsüeh Yün-sheng in comment to *TLTI*, section 76:5.
86. *Code*, Vol. 2, p. 846.
87. *Ibid.*
88. *Code*, Vol. 2, p. 853.
89. *Ibid.*
90. Niida, *Mibunhōshi*, p. 893; cf. also *TLTI* section 76:15, where Hsüeh Yün-sheng says: "Formerly, male slaves under the banners were very numerous. Whether they were hereditary slaves or bought by contract, cases in which people were falsely accused of being slaves also frequently occurred but nowadays they are rare. The great families also do not buy male slaves by contract any longer. The Way of Heaven has completely changed in

several decades, and circumstances in modern and olden times are not the same. . . ."

91. See note 72 above.
92. *HTSL*, 810:15.
93. This institution was established in 1901; cf. Immanuel Hsu, *The Rise of Modern China* (Oxford, 1970), p. 489; also Brunnert and Hagelstrom, *Present Day Political Organization in China* (Shanghai, 1912), p. 140.
94. Shen Chia-pen, p. 887.
95. *Ibid.*, pp. 887-889.
96. See note 26 above.
97. M. J. Meijer, *The Introduction of Modern Criminal Law in China* (Batavia, 1949), pp. 22-24.
98. For a list of "mean" people cf. Hoang, pp. 120-124.
99. Shen Chia-pen, p. 890.
100. All that is known about the censor is that he was a *chin-shih* of 1894. The date of his memorial is February 6, 1909. Cf. *Ta Ch'ing Hsüan-t'ung hsin-fa-ling* [New Laws and Ordinances of the Hsüan-t'ung Period of the Great Ch'ing Dynasty], 12:22a.
101. Established in 1907, cf. Brunnert and Hagelstrom, p. 47.
102. An approximation may be made for early January 1910, when the Constitution Committee said it had already discussed it. See *Ta Ch'ing hsien-hsing hsing lü* [The Criminal Law of the Great Ch'ing Dynasty Currently in Force] (Fang chu chen Co., 1910), n.p., chap. *tsou-shu* memorials, p. 13a.
103. Shen Chia-pen, pp. 890-891.
104. For the origin and development of the *pao-i*, cf. Jonathan Spence, *Ts'ao Yin and the K'ang-hsi Emperor, Bondservant and Master* (New Haven, 1966), pp. 2-18. For the *pu-ch'ü* cf. Wang Yi-t'ung, "Slaves and other Comparable Social Groups in the Northern Dynasties (386-618)," *HJAS*, Vol. 16 (1953), pp. 314f.; Niida, *Mibunhōshi*, pp. 859ff.
105. *Ta Ch'ing Hsüan-t'ung hsin fa-ling*, 12:22a-24a.
106. *HAHL*, Vol. 6, pp. 2457-2459 (39:6a-7a).
107. The first part in which the vice-president dwells on the philosophical aspects of the relationship between emperor and subject has been omitted. Reference has been made to it on page 9 of the text. The vice-president is Chang Chao (1691-1745), the famous scholar, poet, and calligrapher; cf. Arthur W. Hummel, p. 24.
108. 100 blows of the heavy bamboo and three years of penal servitude, *Code*, Vol. 4, p. 2730.
109. *HAHL*, Vol. 2, pp. 745-746 (9:17a-b).
110. *Code*, Vol. 2, pp. 1064-1065; Boulais, p. 610.
111. *Ibid.*
112. *Hsing-pu tsou-ting chang-ch'eng* [Regulations Established Through Memorials of the Board of Punishments], Kwangsi, section 1:76a-80b.
113. The Department first cites 7 provisions from the *lü* and the *li* which have a bearing on the case. They have been omitted in the translation. The censor, not mentioned by name, was concurrently superintendent of police in the

capital and had memorialized to the emperor about this matter. His memorial, together with an imperial rescript enjoining the Board to discuss the matter, is here introduced by one of the Board's departments. The Board then discusses it and requests permission to circulate the case to the various judicial authorities in the province pending its preparing a new set of rules which will be offered to the emperor for approval.

114. *Code*, Vol. 1, p. 277; Boulais, section 40.
115. *Code*, Vol. 1, p. 389.
116. *Code*, Vol. 1, p. 483; Boulais, section 112.
117. *Code*, Vol. 4, p. 2740; *TLTI*, section 314:7.

WORKS IN WESTERN LANGUAGES

Alabaster, E. *Notes and Commentaries on Chinese Criminal Law*. London: Luzac, 1899.

——— "Notes on Chinese Law and Practice." *Journal of the North China Branch of the Royal Asiatic Society*, Vol. 38 (1906), pp. 83-100.

American Law Institute. *Uniform Commercial Code* (Official Text with Comments). Philadelphia: A.L.I. National Conference of Commissioners on Uniform State Laws, 1962.

Auber, Peter. *China: An Outline of Its Government, Laws and Policy*. London: Parbury, Allen and Co., 1834.

Balazs, Etienne, tr. *Le Traité juridique du "Souei-chou."* Leiden: E. J. Brill, 1954.

Barclay, George W. *Colonial Development and Population in Taiwan*. Princeton University Press, 1954.

Blaustein, A. P. *Fundamental Legal Documents of Communist China*. South Hackensack, N.J.: Fred B. Rothman and Co., 1962.

Bloch, Marc. *Feudal Society*, tr. L. A. Manyon. University of Chicago Press, 1961.

Blume, W. W. "Legal Education in China." *The China Law Review*, Vol. 1 (1922-1924), pp. 305, 308-310.

Bodde, Derk and Clarence Morris, *Law in Imperial China*. Cambridge, Mass.: Harvard University Press, 1967.

Bohannan, Paul. "Law and Legal Institutions." In *International Encyclopedia of the Social Sciences*, Vol. 9. New York: Macmillan, 1968, pp. 43-78.

Boulais, Guy, tr. *Manuel du code chinois*. (Variétés Sinologiques Series, no. 55). Shanghai: Imprimerie de la Mission Catholique, 1924. Reprinted Taipei: Ch'eng-wen Publishing Co., 1966.

Brockman, Rosser H. "Customary Contract Law in Late Traditional Taiwan" (unpublished Ph.D. Thesis). Cambridge, Mass.: Harvard University, 1973.

Brown, Gertrude R., tr. Escarra, *Le Droit chinois*, in Brown, tr., *Chinese Law* (Works Progress Administration, W.P. 2799) Seattle: University of Washington Press, 1936. Reprinted (xerox) Cambridge, Mass.: Harvard University Law School and East Asian Research Center, 1961.

Brunnert, H. S. and Hagelstrom, V. V. *Present Day Political Organization in China*. Shanghai: Kelly and Walsh, 1912.

Bryon, Robert T., Jr. *An Outline of Chinese Law*. Shanghai: Commercial Press, 1925.

Bünger, Karl. *Quellen zur Rechtsgeschichte der T'ang-Zeit*. Monumenta Serica Monograph 9. Peiping: Monumenta Serica, 1946.

——— "The Punishment of Lunatics and Negligents According to Classical Chinese Law." *Studia Serica*, Vol. 9 (1950), pp. 1-16.

——— "Die Rechtsidee in der chinesichen Geschichte." *Saeculum*, Vol. 3 (1952), pp. 211, 212.

Buxbaum, David C. "Some Aspects of Civil Procedure and Practice at the Trial Level in Tanshui and Hsinchu from 1789 to 1895." *Journal of Asian Studies*, Vol. 30, No. 2 (Feb. 1971), pp. 255-279.

Chang, Hsin-pao. *Commissioner Lin and the Opium War*. Cambridge, Mass.: Harvard University Press, 1964.

Chang T'ien-tse. *Sino-Portuguese Trade, 1514-1644*. Leiden: E. J. Brill, 1934.

Chang Yü-chüan. "The Legal Practitioner in China." *The Chinese Social and Political Science Review*, Vol. 22 (1938-1939), pp. 146-184.

Ch'en, Fu-mei Chang. "The Emergence of the *Li* in the Ming Code" (unpublished seminar paper). Cambridge, Mass.: Harvard University, May 1965.

——— "Private Code Commentaries in the Development of Ch'ing Law (1644-1911)" (unpublished Ph.D. Thesis). Cambridge, Mass.: Harvard University, 1970.

——— "Review of Bodde and Morris, Law in Imperial China." *Harvard Journal of Asiatic Studies*, Vol. 29 (1969), p. 276.

Chinese Maritime Customs. *Treaties, Conventions, etc. between China and Foreign States*. 2nd ed., 2 vols. Shanghai: Statistical Department of the Inspector-General of Customs, 1917.

Ch'ü T'ung-tsu. *Law and Society in Traditional China*. Paris and The Hague: Mouton and Co., 1961.

——— *Local Government in China under the Ch'ing*. Cambridge, Mass.: Harvard University Press, 1962.

Cohen, Jerome Alan. "Chinese Mediation on the Eve of Modernization." *California Law Review*, Vol. 54, No. 2 (Aug. 1966), p. 1201.

——— *The Criminal Process in the People's Republic of China, 1949-1963: An Introduction*. Cambridge, Mass.: Harvard University Press, 1968.

——— "The Chinese Communist Party and 'Judicial Independence': 1949-1959." *Harvard Law Review*, Vol. 82, No. 5 (March 1969), pp. 967, 984ff.

——— "Continuity and Change in China: Some 'Law Day' Thoughts." *South Carolina Law Review*, Vol. 24, No. 1 (1972), pp. 3-18.

——— "Notes on Legal Education in China." *Harvard Law School Bulletin* (Feb. 1973), p. 18.

Cohen, Jerome Alan, ed. *Contemporary Chinese Law: Research Problems and Perspectives*. Cambridge, Mass.: Harvard University Press, 1970.

Cohen, Jerome Alan and Hungdah Chiu. *People's China and International Law*. Princeton University Press, 1974.

The Constitution of the People's Republic of China. Peking: Foreign Languages Press, 1975.

Creel, H. G. *Confucius, the Man and the Myth*. New York: J. Day and Co., 1949.

——— "The Fa-Chia: 'Legalists' or 'Administrators'?" *Bulletin of the Institute of History and Philology, Academia Sinica*, extra Vol. 4 (Taipei, 1961), pp. 607-636.

——— *The Origins of Statecraft in China*, Vol. 1, *The Western Chou Empire*. University of Chicago Press, 1970.

——— *Shen Pu-hai, A Chinese Political Philosopher of the Fourth Century B.C.* University of Chicago Press, 1974.

Davidson, James W. *The Island of Formosa*. London and New York: Macmillan, 1903.

Dawson, John P. *The Oracles of the Law*. Ann Arbor, Michigan: Michigan Legal Publications, The University of Michigan Law School, 1968.

DeBary, W. T., ed. *Sources of Chinese Tradition*. 2 vols. New York: Columbia University Press, 1960.

Dewall, Magdalene von. *Pferd und Wagen im frühen China*. Bonn: Habelt, 1964.

Dore, Ronald. *Education in Tokugawa Japan*. Berkeley: University of California Press, 1965.

Downs, Jacques M. "American Merchants and the China Opium Trade, 1800-1840." *Business History Review* (Harvard Business School), (Winter 1968), pp. 418-442.

Dubs, Homer, tr. *The History of the Former Han Dynasty* by Pan Ku. 3 vols. Baltimore: Waverly Press, 1938-1955.

Duyvendak, J.J.L., tr. *The Book of Lord Shang*. London: Arthur Probsthain, 1928.

Elliott, Charles. *China Correspondence 1838-1840*. (British Government Parliamentary Bluebook). London: 1840.

Escarra, Jean. *Le Droit chinois*. Peking: Henri Vetch, 1936.

——— "Law, Chinese." In *Encyclopaedia of the Social Sciences*. New York: Macmillan, 1933.

Fairbank, John K. *Trade and Diplomacy on the China Coast*. Cambridge, Mass.: Harvard University Press, 1953.

——— *The United States and China* (rev. ed.) Cambridge, Mass.: Harvard University Press, 1958.

——— "On the Ch'ing Tributory System." In S. Y. Teng and J. K. Fairbank, *Ch'ing Administration: Three Studies*. Cambridge, Mass.: Harvard University Press, 1961.

——— Edwin O. Reischauer and Albert M. Craig. *East Asia: The Modern Transformation*. Boston: Houghton Mifflin, 1965.

——— and S. Y. Teng, "On the Transmission of Ch'ing Documents." In *Ch'ing Administration: Three Studies*. Cambridge, Mass.: Harvard University Press, 1961.

Farmer, Edward L. "James Flint Versus the Canton Interest (1755-1760)." *Papers on China*, Vol. 17. Cambridge, Mass.: Harvard University, East Asian Research Center, 1963.

Franke, Wolfgang. *An Introduction to the Sources of Ming History*. Kuala Lumpur: University of Malaya Press, 1968.

Friedman, Lawrence and Stewart Macauley. "Contract Law and Contract Teaching: Past, Present, and Future." *Wisconsin Law Review*, Vol. 1967, No. 4 (Fall), pp. 805-821.

Fu Lo-shu. *A Documentary Chronicle of Sino-Western Relations (1644-1820)*. 2 vols. Tucson: Universtiy of Arizona Press, 1966.

Fuller, Lon L. "The Forms and Limits of Adjudication" (unpublished paper). Cambridge, Mass.: Harvard University, 1970.

Fuller, Lon L. and Robert Braucher. *Basic Contract Law*. St. Paul: West Publishing Co., 1964.

Gale, Esson M., tr. *Discourses on Salt and Iron* by Huan K'uan. Leiden: E. J. Brill, 1931.

Gilmore, Grant and Charles Black. *The Law of Admiralty*. New York: Foundation Press, 1957.

Gluckman, Max. *Ideas in Barotse Jurisprudence*. New Haven: Yale University Press, 1965.

Gulik, R. H. van, tr. *T'ang-yin pi-shih, "Parallel Cases from Under the Pear-Tree," a thirteenth-century manual of jurisprudence and detection*. Leiden: E. J. Brill, 1956.

Hahm Pyong-choon. *The Korean Political Tradition and Law*. Royal Asiatic Society Korea Branch Monograph Series, No. 1. Seoul: Hollym Corporation, 1967.

——— "Korea's Initial Encounter with the Western Law: 1866-1910 A.D." *Korea Observer*, Vol. 1, No. 2 (1969), pp. 80-93.

Hall, John Carey, tr. "Tokugawa Legislation IV." *Transactions of the Asiatic Society of Japan*, Vol. 41 (Part V) (1913), pp. 683-804.

Hamilton, Walton. "The Ancient Maxim Caveat Emptor." *Yale Law Journal*. Vol. 40, No. 8 (June 1931), pp. 1133-1187.

Han Fei Tzŭ, see Liao, W. K.

Hattori, Takaaki, assisted by Richard W. Rabinowitz. "The Legal Profession in Japan: Its Historical Development and Present State." In Arthur Taylor von Mehren, ed., *Law in Japan*. Cambridge, Mass.: Harvard University Press, 1963.

Henderson, Dan Fenno. *Conciliation and Japanese Law*. Seattle and Tokyo: University of Washington Press and University of Tokyo Press, 1964.

——— "Promulgation of Tokugawa Statutes." *Journal of Asian and African Studies*, Vol. 1 (Leiden, 1967), p. 9.

——— "Chinese Legal Studies in Early 18th Century Japan: Scholars and Sources." *Journal of Asian Studies*, Vol. 30, No. 1 (Nov. 1970), pp. 21-56.

Hoang, Pierre. *Mélanges sur l'administration*. Variétés Sinologiques, No. 21. Shanghai: Imprimerie de la Mission Catholique, 1902.

Holmes, Oliver Wendell. *The Common Law*. Mark DeWolfe Howe, ed., Cambridge, Mass.: Belknap Press, 1963.

Hsia, Tao-tai. *Guide to Selected Legal Sources of Mainland China*. Washington, D.C.: Library of Congress, 1967.

Hsiao Kung-ch'üan. *Rural China, Imperial Control in the Nineteenth Century*. Seattle: University of Washington Press, 1960.

Hsü, Immanuel. *The Rise of Modern China*. London: Oxford University Press, 1970.

Hucker, Charles. *The Censorial System of Ming China*. Stanford: Stanford University Press, 1966.

Hulbert, Homer B. *The Passing of Korea*. Seoul: Yonsei University Press, 1969.

Hulsewé, A.F.P. *Remnants of Han Law*, Vol. 1. Leiden: E. J. Brill, 1955.

Hummel, Arthur W. *Eminent Chinese of the Ch'ing Period*. Washington: U.S. Government Printing Office, 1943-1944. Reprinted Taipei: Ch'eng Wen Publishing Co., 1964.

Hunter, W. C. *The "Fan Kwae" at Canton Before Treaty Days*. London: Kegan Paul, 1882.

Jamieson, George. *Chinese Family and Commercial Law*. Shanghai: Kelley and Walsh, 1921.

Jansen, Marius. "Tosa in the Sixteenth Century: the 100-Article Code of Chōsokabe Motochika." In John Hall and Marius Jansen, *Studies in the Institutional History of Early Modern Japan*. Princeton University Press, 1968.

Jernigan, T. R. *China in Law and Commerce*. New York: Macmillan, 1905.

Jitsuzo Kuwabara. "On P'u Shou-keng." *Memoirs of the Research Department of the Tōyō Bunko*, No. 2 (1928), pp. 1-79.

Jones, William C. "Studying the Ch'ing Code—The Ta Ch'ing Lü Li." *American Journal of Comparative Law*, Vol. 22 (1974), pp. 330-359.

Karlgren, Bernhard. "Glosses on the Book of Documents (1)." *Bulletin of the Museum of Far Eastern Antiquities*, Vol. 20 (1948), p. 290.

——— "Glosses on the Book of Documents (2)." *Bulletin of the Museum of Far Eastern Antiquities*, Vol. 21 (1949), p. 142.

——— tr., "The Book of Documents." *Bulletin of the Museum of Far Eastern Antiquities*, Vol. 22 (1950), p. 40.

——— tr. *The Book of Odes* [Shih Ching]. Stockholm: Museum of Far Eastern Antiquities, 1950.

Keeton, George W. *The Development of Extraterritoriality in China*. 2 vols. London: Longmans Green, 1928.

Koo, V. K. Wellington. *The Status of Aliens in China*. Columbia Studies in History, Economics and Public Law, Vol. 50, No. 2, whole No. 126. New York: Columbia University Press, 1912.

Kroker, Edward. *Die amtliche Sammlung Chinesischer Rechtsgewohnheiten*. [The Official Collection of Chinese Customary Law.] Frankfurt am Main: Gerhard Kaffke, 1965.

——— "The Concept of Property in Chinese Customary Law." *Transactions of the Asiatic Society of Japan, 3rd Series*, Vol. 7 (1959).

Kuan-tzu. Tr. W. Allyn Rickett. Hong Kong University Press, 1965.

Lamley, Harry J. "The Taiwan Literati and Early Japanese Rule, 1895-1915" (unpublished Ph.D. Thesis). Seattle: University of Washington, 1964.

Latourette, Kenneth Scott. *A History of Christian Missions in China*. New York: Macmillan, 1929.

Ledyard, Gari. *The Dutch Come to Korea*. Royal Asiatic Society, Korea Branch, Monograph Series, No. 3. Seoul, Korea: Taewan Publishing Co., 1971.

Lee, Peter H. *Songs of Flying Dragons: A Critical Reading*. Cambridge, Mass.: Harvard University Press, 1975.

Leff, Arthur Allen. "Injury, Ignorance and Spite—The Dynamics of Coercive Collection." *Yale Law Journal*, Vol. 80, No. 1 (Nov. 1970), pp. 1-46.

Legge, James, tr. *The Chinese Classics*. 2nd ed. rev. London and Oxford: Clarendon Press, 7 vols., 1893-1895. Reprinted Hong Kong University Press, 5 vols., 1960.

——— tr. *Lî Kî* [Book of Rites] in *Sacred Books of the East*, ed. F. Max Mueller. Vols. 27-28. Oxford: Clarendon Press, 1885.

——— tr. *The Writings of Kwang-zze* (Chuang-tzu), in *Sacred Book of the East*, ed. F. Max Mueller. Vols. 39-40. Oxford: Clarendon Press, 1891.

Levenson, Joseph R. "The Place of Confucius in Communist China." *China Quarterly*, No. 12 (Oct.-Dec. 1962), pp. 1-18.

Liao, W. K., tr. *The Complete Works of Han Fei Tzŭ*. 2 vols. London: Arthur Probsthain, Vol. 1, 1939; Vol. 2, 1959.

Llewellyn, K. "What Price Contract?" *Yale Law Journal*, Vol. 40, No. 5 (March 1931), pp. 704-751.

Lo Ssu-ting. "Struggle Between Restoration and Counter-Restoration in the

Course of Founding the Chin Dynasty." *Peking Review*, Vol. 17, No. 17 (Apr. 26, 1974), pp. 7-10.

Lubman, Stanley. "Mao and Mediation." *California Law Review*, Vol. 55, No. 5 (Nov. 1967), pp. 1284-1359.

McAleavy, Henry. "Dien in China and Vietnam." *Journal of Asian Studies*, Vol. 17, No. 3 (May 1958), pp. 403-415.

Macauley, Stewart. "Non-Contractual Relations in Business." *American Sociological Review*, Vol. 28 (1968), pp. 55-67.

McEwan, J. R. *The Political Writings of Ogyū Sorai*. Cambridge University Press, 1962.

MacGowan, D. J. "Chinese Guilds or Chambers of Commerce and Trade Unions." *Journal of the China Branch, Royal Asiatic Society*, Vol. 21 (Shanghai, 1886), pp. 133-192.

Maitland, F. W. *Equity; also the Forms of Action at Common Law*. Cambridge University Press, 1913.

Maspero, Henri. "Contribution à l'étude de la société chinoise à la fin des Chang et au début des Tcheou." *Bulletin de l'École Française d'Extrême-Orient*, Vol. 46 (1954), p. 335.

——— "Le Serment dans la procédure judiciare de la Chine antique." *Mélanges chinois et bouddhiques*, Vol. 3 (1934-1935), pp. 257-317.

——— *Mélanges posthumes sur les religions et l'histoire de la Chine*. 3 vols. Paris: Civilisations de Sud, 1950.

Mehren, Arthur T., von. "The Creation, Modification and Discharge of Contractual Obligation" (unpublished paper). Cambridge, Mass.: Harvard University, 1971.

Mei, Yi-pao. *Ethical and Political Works of Motse*. London: Arthur Probsthain, 1929.

Meijer, Marinus J. *The Introduction of Modern Criminal Law in China*. Batavia: De Unie, 1949.

——— *Marriage Law and Policy in the Chinese People's Republic*. Hong Kong University Press, 1971.

Metzger, Thomas A. *The Internal Organization of the Ch'ing Bureaucracy: Legal, Normative and Communication Aspects*. Cambridge, Mass.: Harvard University Press, 1973.

Morse, Hosea Ballou. *Chronicles of the East India Company to China, 1635-1834*. 4 vols. Oxford: Clarendon Press, 1926. Vol. 5 for 1742-1774, Oxford: Clarendon Press, 1929.

——— *International Relations of the Chinese Empire*. 3 vols. Shanghai and London: Longmans Green, 1910-1918.

Münzel, Frank. "Some Remarks on Ming T'ai-tsu." *Archiv Orientalni*, Vol. 37 (1969), pp. 377-399.

Myers, Ramon H. *The Chinese Peasant Economy*. Cambridge, Mass.: Harvard University Press, 1970.

Nieboer, H. J. *Slavery as an Industrial System*. The Hague: M. Nijhoff, 1912.

Parker, E. H. *China*. New York: Dutton, 1901.

Peters, Ellen A. "Remedies for Breach of Contracts Relating to the Sale of Goods Under the Uniform Commercial Code: A Roadmap for Article Two." *Yale Law Journal*, Vol. 73, No. 2 (Dec. 1973), pp. 199-287.

——— *Commercial Transactions: Cases, Text, and Problems on Contracts Dealing with Personalty, Realty, and Services*. Indianapolis: Bobbs-Merrill, 1971.

Pfeffer, Richard. *Understanding Business Contracts in China, 1949-1963*. Cambridge, Mass.: Harvard University Press, 1973.

Philastre, P.L.F., tr. *Le Code annamite, nouvelle traduction complète*. 2 vols. Paris: C. Leroux, 1876 and 1909. Reprint of 1909 edition, Taipei: Ch'eng-wen Publishing Co., 1967.

Pippon, Toni. *Beitrag zum Chinesichen Sklavensystem*. Tokyo: Deutsche Gesellschaft fur Natur-und Völherkunde Ostasiens, 1936.

Pokora, Timoteus. "The Canon of Laws of Li K'uei—A Double Falsification?" *Archiv Orientalni*, Vol. 27 (1959), pp. 96-121.

Pritchard, Earl H. *The Crucial Years of Anglo-Chinese Relations 1750-1800*. Pullman, Washington: Research Studies of the State College of Washington, 1936.

Pulleyblank, E. G. "The Origins and Nature of Chattle Slavery in China." *Journal of the Economic and Social History of the Orient*, Vol. 1 (1958), pp. 184-220.

Quincy, Josiah, ed. *The Journals of Major Samuel Shaw, The First American Consul at Canton*. Boston: William Crosby and H. P. Nichols, 1847.

Rutt, Richard and Kim Chong-un, trs. *Virtuous Women: Three Masterpieces of Korean Fiction*. Seoul: Korean National Commission for UNESCO, 1974.

Sanborne, Frederick Rockwell, "Law Merchant." In *Encyclopaedia of the Social Sciences*, Vol. 9. New York: Macmillan, 1933, pp. 270-274.

Schaffer, Francis A. *Escape From Reason*. Downers Grove, Illinois: Inter-University Press, 1974.

Schram, Stuart. *Mao Tse-tung*. New York: Simon and Schuster, 1967.

Schwartz, Benjamin. "Some Polarities in Confucian Thought." In David S. Nivison and Arthur F. Wright, eds., *Confucianism in Action*. Stanford University Press, 1969.

Schwartz, R. "Social Factors in the Development of Legal Control: A Case Study of Two Israeli Settlements." *Yale Law Journal*, Vol. 63 (1954), p. 470.

Shiga Shuzo. "Criminal Procedure in the Ch'ing Dynasty." *Memoirs of the Research Department of the Tōyō Bunko*. Tokyo, No. 32 (1974) and No. 33 (1975).

Shih Ting. "Clarifying 'Burning Books and Burying Confucian Scholars Alive'," *Peking Review*, Vol. 17, No. 19 (May 10, 1974), pp. 25-28.

Skinner, G. William. "Marketing and Social Structure in Rural China, Part I," *Journal of Asian Studies*, Vol. 24, No. 1 (Nov. 1969), pp. 3-43.

Sohn Pow-key. "Social History of the Early Yi Dynasty 1392-1592: with an Emphasis on the Functional Aspects of Government Structure" (unpublished Ph.D. Thesis). University of California, 1963.

Speidel, William. "Liu Ming-ch'uan in Taiwan, 1884-1891" (unpublished Ph.D. Thesis). New Haven: Yale University, 1967.

Spence, Jonathan. *Ts'ao Yin and the K'ang-hsi Emperor, Bondservant and Master*. New Haven: Yale University Press, 1966.

Sprenkel, Sybille van der. *Legal Institutions in Manchu China*. London: Athlone Press for the University of London, 1972.

Staunton, George Thomas, tr. *Ta Tsing Leu Lee; Being the Fundamental Laws, and a Selection from the Supplementary Statutes, of the Penal Code of China*. London: Cadell and Davies, 1810.

Tawney, R. H. *Land and Labor in China*. London and New York: Harcourt, Brace, 1932.

Treadgold, Donald W., ed. *Soviet and Chinese Communism: Similarities and Differences*. Seattle: University of Washington Press, 1967.

Tseng Yu-hao. *The Termination of Unequal Treaties*. Shanghai: Commercial Press, 1933.

Tsurumi, Pat. "Taiwan under Kodama Gentaro and Gotō Shimpei." *Papers on Japan*, Vol. 4 (1967), pp. 95-149.

Wagner, Edward Willett. *The Literati Purges: Political Conflict in Early Yi Korea*. Cambridge, Mass.: Harvard University Press, 1974.

Waley, Arthur. *The Opium War Through Chinese Eyes*. London: Allen and Unwin, 1958.

——— *The Way and Its Power*. London: Allen and Unwin, 1934.

Watt, John R. *The District Magistrate in Late Imperial China*. New York and London: Columbia University Press, 1972.

Weber, Max. *Law in Economy and Society*, trs. and eds. Edward Shils and Max Rheinstein. Cambridge, Mass.: Harvard University Press, 1954.

——— *Wirtschaft und Gesellschaft*. 2nd ed., 2 vols. Tübingen: J.C.B. Mohr, 1925.

Wigmore, John Henry, ed. "Materials for the Study of Private Law in Old Japan." *Transactions of the Asiatic Society of Japan, Supplement 1*, Vol. 20 (1892).

Wilbur, Martin. *Slavery in China During the Former Han Dynasty*. Field Museum Press, 1943.

Wills, John E., Jr. "Ch'ing Relations with the Dutch 1662-1690." In John K. Fairbank, ed., *The Chinese World Order*. Cambridge, Mass.: Harvard University Press, 1968.

Works in East Asian Languages

AMCL, see Ao-men chih-lüeh.

An Chŏng-bok 安鼎福. Imgwan chŏngyo 臨官政要 (Essentials of Government for Those in Office). Collated with Korean tr. by Kim Tong-ju 金東柱. Ŭryu mun'go 乙酉文庫 series, Vol. 133. Seoul: Ŭryu munhwasa, 1974 乙酉文化社.

An Chong-hwa 安鍾和. Kukcho immulchi 國朝人物志. (Biographical Sketches of Prominent Figures in our Dynasty). Seoul, 1909.

Ao-men chi-lüeh 澳門紀略 (Topography and History of Macao). Compiled by Yin Kuang-jen 印光任 and Chang Ju-lin 張汝霖, 4 ts'e. 1743-1751.

CC., see Chi-chu, under Shen Chih-ch'i.

Chai-yao, see Shuo-t'ieh chai-yao ch'ao-ts'un.

Chan-kuo ts'e 戰國策 (Stratagems of the Warring States). Notes by Kao Yu 高誘 and Yao Hung 姚宏. Ssu-pu pei-yao 四部備要. Shanghai: Chung-hua shu-chü 中華書局, 1927.

Ch'eng-an so-chien chi 成案所見集 (Collection of Seen Leading Cases). Compiled by Ma Shih-lin 馬世璘. Four successive collections, covering 1736-1805.

Chi-chu, see Shen Chih-ch'i.

Ch'i Ssu-ho 齊思和. "Hsi-Chou shih-tai chih cheng-chih ssu-hsiang" 西周時代之政治思想 (Political Thought of the Western Chou). Yen-ching she-hui k'e-hsüeh 燕京社會科學 (Yenching Journal of Social Sciences), Vol. 1 (1948), p. 32.

Chiang-su chin-shih chih 江蘇金石志 (Stone Inscriptions of Kiangsu Province). Shih-k'o shih-liao ts'ung-shu 石刻史料叢書 series No. 19. Kiangsu: Chiang-su t'ung-chih chü 通志局 1927.

Chien-shih Commentary, see Wang K'en-t'ang chien-shih.

Chien-yen i-lai hsi-nien yao-lu 建炎以來繫年要録 (Brief Chronological Record of Events Dating from the Chien-yen Reign). By Li Hsin-ch'uan 李心傳. Ts'e 481-526, Kuang-ya ts'ung-shu 廣雅叢書 ed. Compiled by Hsü Shao-ch'i 徐紹棨, Canton, 1920.

Ch'ing-ch'ao hsü wen-hsien t'ung-k'ao 清朝續文獻通考 see Huang-ch'ao hsü wen-hsien t'ung-k'ao. 皇朝續文獻通考

Ch'ing-ch'ao wen-hsien t'ung-k'ao 清朝文獻通考, see Huang-ch'ao wen-hsien t'ung-k'ao. 皇朝文獻通考.

Ch'ing Code, Ch'ing Penal Code, see Ta Ch'ing-lü-li hui-t'ung hsin-tsuan. For Japanese printings, see Mizumoto Narumi (1874).

Ch'ing-ming chi 清明集 (Pure Clear Collection). Originally published 1203. 1261 ed. manuscript preserved in Seikado Library, Tokyo. Reprinted Tokyo, 1954.

Ch'ing-nien, see Shuo-t'ieh chai-yao ch'ao-ts'un.

Ch'ing-shih-kao hsing-fa-chih chu-chieh 清史稿刑法志註解 ("Legal Treatise" from the Ch'ing Draft History with Annotations). Compiled by Kuo-wu-yuan fa-chih-chü fa-chih-shih yen-chiu shih 國務院法制局法制史研究室 (Legal History Research Office, Bureau of Legal Affairs, Council of State). Peking: Fa-lü ch'u-pan-she 法律出版社, 1957.

Ch'ing-shih-lu, see Ta-Ch'ing li-ch'ao shih-lu.

Ch'ing-tai wai-chiao shih-liao 清代外交史料 (Historical Materials Concerning Foreign Relations in the Ch'ing Period). 6 *ts'e* for the Chia-ch'ing period, 1796-1820 (*CTWCSL:CC*), 4 *ts'e* for the Tao-kuang period to 1831 (*CTWCSL.TK*). Peiping: Palace, 1931-1933. Taiwan reprint, 2 vols. Taipei. Ch'eng-wen ch'u-pan-she 成文出版社, 1968.

Ch'ing-yüan t'iao-fa shih-lei 慶元條法事類 (Classified Laws of the Ch'ing-yüan Period [1194-1200]). Manuscript preserved in the Seikado 靜嘉堂 Library, Tokyo. Photolithograph of the original ed. in 80 *chüan*. Tokyo: Koten kenkyū kai 古典研究會, 1968. A new ed. has also been published by Shin-wen-feng ch'u-pan kung-ssu 新文豐出版公司 in Taipei, 1976.

Ch'iu Han-p'ing, see *Li-tai hsing-fa chih*.

Chŏn Pong-dŏk 田鳳德. *Han'guk pŏpchesa yŏn'gu* 韓國法制史研究 (Researches in Korean Legal History). Seoul National University Press, 1968.

Chŏng To-jŏn 鄭道傳. Sambongjip 三峯集 (Collected writings of Chŏng To-jŏn). Kuksa p'yŏnch'an wiwŏnhoe 國史編纂委員會 ed. Seoul: Kuksa p'yŏnch'an wiwŏnhoe, 1961.

Chŏng Ch'ang-yŏl 鄭昌烈. Review of Pak Pyŏng-ho's 朴秉濠 *Chŏnt'ongjŏk pŏpch'egye wa pŏbŭisik* 傳統的法治係와法意識 (The Korean Traditional Legal System and Legal Consciousness) (Seoul, 1972), in *Sintonga* 新東亞 (June 1973), pp. 346-349.

Chŏng Yag-yong 丁若鏞. Chŏng Ta-san chŏnsŏ 丁茶山全書 (Complete Writings of Chŏng Ta-san). 3 vols. Seoul: Munhŏn p'yŏnch'an wiwŏnhoe 文獻編纂委員會, 1961.

_____ Hŭmhŭm sinsŏ 欽欽新書 (New Writings on Circumspection in Judicial Decisions). 4 kwon. Seoul: Kwangmunsa 廣文社 , 1901.

Chosŏn wangjo sillok 朝鮮王朝實錄 . (Veritable Records of the Chosŏn dynasty). Photolithograph ed., 48 vols. Seoul: T'amgudang, 1968-71.

T'aejo kanghŏn taewang sillok 太祖康獻大王實錄 (Veritable Records of King T'aejo) 15 kwŏn.

T'aeping taewang sillok 太宗大王實錄 (Veritable Records of King T'aejong) 36 kwŏn.

Chou Fa-kao 周法高 . Chin-wen ling-shih 金文零拾 (Miscellaneous Comments on Bronze Inscriptions). Taipei: Institute of History and Philology, Academia Sinica, 1951.

Chu Hsi 朱熹 . Chu-tzu yü-lei 朱子語類 (The Classified Analects of Master Chu). Kyoto: Chu-bun shuppan-sha 中文出版社 ed., 1970.

Ch'üan Shih-ch'ao, see Po-an hsin-pien.

Ch'ugwanji 秋官志 (Records of the Board of Punishments; CKJ). Keijo [Seoul]: Chōsen sōtokufu chūsūin 朝鮮總督府中樞院 ed., 1939.

Chŭngbo munhŏn pigo 增補文獻備考 . 3 vols. Seoul: Kojŏn kanhaenghoe 古典刊行會 ed., 1957.

Chyi-chu, Ta Ch'ing lü-li chi-chu ("chyi-chu"), see Wan Wei-han.

CKJ, see Ch'ugwanji.

Collectanea, see Shen Chia-pen.

Conspectus of Penal Cases, see Hsing-an hui-lan.

CTWCSL:CC; CTWCSL:TK, see Ch'ing-tai wai-chiao shih-liao.

Documents, Document Classic, see Karlgren, tr. "The Book of Documents."

Ebina Yōichi 蝦名庸一 . "An'ei-ki no Hirosaki-han keihō--'Kansei Ritsu' to no hikaku," 安永期の弘前藩刑法一寛政律との比較 (Comparison of the Criminal Law of the Hirosaki Domain in the An'ei Period (1772-1880) with its 'Kansei [1789-1800] Code'), in Hirosaki daigaku kokushi kenkyū 弘前大學國史研究 (Studies in National History, Hirosaki University), Vols. 19-20 (1959), pp. 29-45.

______ "Hirosaki han 'Go-keihō-chō' (Kansei [1789-1800] ritsu)" 弘前藩御刑法牒(寛政律) ("The Catalogue of Penal Law" [Kansei Code] of the Hirosaki Domain). Hirosaki daigaku kokushi kenkyū, Nos. 15 and 16 (1959), pp. 11-45 (mimeo).

Fuse Yaheiji 布施彌平次 . "Tsugaru-han no 'Keihō-chō' ni tsuite" 津軽藩の「刑法牒」について (Concerning the "Catalogue of Penal Law" of the Tsugaru Domain). Nihon hōgaku 日本法學 (Japanese Jurisprudence), Vol. 21, No. 2 (1955), pp. 144-172.

HAHL, see Hsing-an hui-lan.

HAHLHP, see Hsing-an hui-lan hsü-pien (Third Supplement).

Hampō Kenkyūkai 藩法研究會 , ed. Hampōshū 藩法集 (Collection of Domain Law). 12 vols. Tokyo: Sōbunsha 創文社 , 1961-1975.

Han-fei-tzu 韓非子 . Ssu-pu pei-yao ed. Shanghai: Chung-hua shu-chü, 1927.

Han'guk immyŏng taesajŏn, see Yi Hŭi-sŭng.

Harafuji Hiroshi 服藤弘司 . "Go-keihō-chō" 御刑法牒 (The Catalogue of Penal Law). Kanazawa hōgaku 金沢法学 (Kanazawa Jurisprudence), Vol. 10, No. 2 (1964), pp. 85-132.

Hiramatsu Yoshirō 平松義郎. "Ishin-ki Nagoya-han no tokei shiryō--Murata-bon 'Kyū-Nagoya-han Sadamegaki'" 維新期名古屋藩の徒刑史料 一 村田本「旧名古屋藩定書」 (Materials on Imprisonment in the Nagoya Domain at the Restoration Period--the Murata book entitled "Old Nagoya Domain Written Regulations") in Tezuka Yutaka kyōju Taishoku kinen Rombunshu Henshu Iinkai ed. <u>Meiji hōseishi-seijishi no sho-mondai--Tezuka Yutaka kyōju taishoku kinen rombunshū</u> 明治法制史·政治史の諸問題 一 手塚豊教授退職紀念論文集(Various Problems in the Meiji Legal and Political History--A Collection of Articles in Commemoration of Professor Tezuka Yutaka's Retirement)(1977), pp. 581-605.

______ "Nagoya-han no tsuihō-kei" 名古屋藩の追放刑 (The Penalty of Banishment in the Nagoya Domain). <u>Nagoya daikaku hōsei ronshū</u> 名古屋大學法治論集 (Collection of Essays on Law and Politics, Nagoya University), Vol. 4, No. 1 (1952), pp. 1-53.

______ <u>Kinsei keiji soshōhō no kenkyū</u> 近世刑事訴訟法の研究 (Study of the Law of Criminal Procedure in the Premodern Period). Tokyo: Sōbunsha, 1960.

Hirayama Kōzō 平山行三. "Bunsei yonen no Kishū hampō" 文政四年の紀州藩法 (Domain Law of Kii of the Fourth Year of Bunsei). <u>Wakayama daigaku gakugei gakubu kiyō, jimbun kagaku</u> 和歌山大學學藝部紀要, 人文科學 (Wakayama University Reports of the Faculty of Education and Liberal Arts, Wakayama University, Arts and Cultural Sciences), No. 15 (1965), pp. 29-44.

______ "Hōreki sannen no Kishū hampō" 寶曆三年の紀州藩法 (Kii Domain Law of the Third Year of Hōreki). Wakayama daigaku gakugei gakubu kiyō, jimbun kagaku shiryō-hen 資料篇 No. 11 (1962), pp. 41-61; Kenkyū-hen 研究編 , No. 12 (1962), pp. 73-88.

______ "Kishū han hampō shūi" 紀州藩藩法拾遺 (Gleanings from Kii Domain Law). Wakayama daigaku gakugei gakubu kiyō, jimbun kagaku. No. 14 (1964), pp. 25-35.

Hirosaki-shi 弘前市 ed. Hirosaki shishi, hansei-hen 弘前市史. 藩制篇 (History of Hirosaki City; Part on the Domain System). Hirosaki: Hirosaki shishi hensan iinkai 編纂委員會 , 1963.

HITS: Han'guk immyŏng taesajŏn, see Yi Hŭi-sŭng.

Hsien-hsing hsing-lü 現行刑律 (The Statutes Currently in Force). Peking: Fang chü-chen pan 仿聚珍板, 1910 ed.

Hsing-an hui-lan 刑案滙覽 (Conspectus of Penal Cases). 40 ts'e. Shanghai: T'u-shu chi-ch'eng chü 圖書集成局 , fang hsiu-chen pan yin 仿袖珍板印 (Pocket ed.), ca. 1886. Reprinted Taipei: Ch'eng-wen ch'u-pan-she 1968. This ed. contains the Hsing-an hui-lan and its first two supplements, listed below; for the Third Supplement, see Hsing-an hui-lan hsü-pien, below. Contents of this edition:

- Hsing-an hui-lan (HAHL). Compiled by Chi Ch'ing-ch'i 祝慶祺 and Pao Shu-yün 鮑書芸 . 60 chüan, ts'e 1-28. Preface by Pao, 1834.
- Hsü-tseng 續增 Hsing-an hui-lan (HAHL, First Supplement). By Chu Ch'ing-ch'i and Pao Shu-yün. 16 chüan, ts'e 29-36. Preface by Pao, 1840.
- Hsin-tseng 新增 Hsing-an hui-lan (HAHL, Second Supplement). Compiled by P'an Wen-fang 潘文舫 and Hsü Chien-chüan 徐諫荃. 16 chüan, ts'e 37-40. Preface by Ho Wei-k'ai 何維楷 , 1886.

Hsing-an hui-lan hsü-pien 刑案滙覽續編 (HAHL; Third Supplement [HAHLHP]). By Wu Ch'ao 吴潮 and Ho Hsi-yen 何錫儼. 10 ts'e. Completed in 1871, published 1900. Reprinted Taipei: Wen-hai ch'u-pan-she 文海出版社, 1970.

Hsing-pu tsou-ting chang-ch'eng 刑部奏定章程 (Regulations Established Through Memorials of the Board of Punishments). Kwangsi, n.d.

Hsing-fa fen-k'ao 刑法分考 (Detailed Examination of the Criminal Law), see Shen Chia-pen.

Hsiang-shan hsien-chih 香山縣志 (Hsiang-shan District Gazetteer). 1827 ed.

Hsü Tao-lin 徐道鄰 [Hsü Dau-lin]. Chung-kuo fa-chih-shih lun-lüeh 中國法制史論略 (Brief Discussion of Chinese Legal History). Taipei: Cheng-chung shu-chü 正中書局, 1953.

_____ "Sung-lü chung te shen-p'an chih-tu" 宋朝的審判制度 (The Sung Trial System as Prescribed in the Fundamental Statutes of the Sung). Tung-fang tsa-chih fu-k'an 東方雜志復刊 (Eastern Miscellany New Series), Vol. 4, No. 4 (1970), pp. 18-28.

_____ "Chü-yen fen-ssu k'ao" 鞫獄分司考 (Note on the Separate Function of Investigation and Decision). Tung-fang tsa-chih fu-k'an, Vol. 5, No. 5 (1971), pp. 40-45.

_____ "Sung ch'ao te hsien-chi ssu-fa" 宋朝的縣級司法 (Administration of Justice at the District Level During the Sung Dynasty). Tung-fang tsa-chih fu-k'an, Vol. 5, No. 9 (1971), pp. 19-28.

_____ "Fan-i pien-k'an k'ao" 翻異別勘考 (A Study of the Principles of Repudiation of Confession and New Trials). Tung-fang tsa-chih fu-k'an, Vol. 6, No. 2 (1972), pp. 20-28.

Hsü tzu-chih t'ung-chien ch'ang-pien, see Li T'ao.

Hsüeh Yün-sheng 薛允升. Tu-li ts'un-i 讀例存疑 (Concentration on Doubtful Matters while Pursuing the Substatutes of the Ch'ing Code). Peking: Han-mao chai 翰茂齋, 1905. New ed. punctuated and ed. Huang Ching-chia 黃靜嘉 with pages and statutes numbered consecutively. Taipei: Ch'eng-wen ch'u-pan-she, 1970.

Hsün-tzu 荀子. Ssu-pu pei-yao ed. Shanghai: Chung-hua shu-chü, 1927.

HTSL, see Ta Ch'ing hui-tien shih-li.

Hu Chao-k'ai 胡肇楷 and Chou Meng-lin 周孟隣. Ta Ch'ing lü-li t'ung-tsuan chi-ch'eng 大清律例統纂集成 (Collected Thorough Compilation of Commentaries on the Ch'ing Code). Chekiang, 1811. 1814 and 1822 eds. available in Harvard-Yenching Library.

Huang-ch'ao hsü wen-hsien t'ung-k'ao 皇朝續文獻通考 (Compendium of Historical Records of the Ch'ing Dynasty, Supplement). Compiler Liu Chin-tsao 劉錦藻, compiler's preface dated 1921. Wan-yu wen-k'u ed. Shanghai: Commercial Press, n.d. (ca. 1935).

Huang-ch'ao wen-hsien t'ung-k'ao 皇朝文獻通考 (Compendium of Historical Records of the Ch'ing Dynasty). Wan-yu wen-k'u 萬有文庫 ed. Shanghai: Commercial Press, 1936.

Huang Ching-chia 黃靜嘉. Jih-chü shih-tai chih T'aiwan chih-min-ti fa-chih yü chih-min t'ung-chih 日據時代之臺灣殖民地法制與殖民統治 (The Colonial Legal System and Colonial Control of Taiwan during the Period of Japanese Occupation). Taipei: She-hui k'o-hsüeh ts'ung-k'an she 社會科學叢刊社, 1960.

Hung Hung-hsü 洪弘緒 , ed. Ta-Ch'ing lü chi-chu 大清律輯註 (The Great Ch'ing Code with Commentaries). Revision of Shen Chih-ch'i 沈之奇 , compiler, Ta-Ch'ing lü chi-chu, 1715, including his original preface. 1st published, 1740. 1755 ed., Chekiang, available in Columbia University Library.

Hung Mai 洪邁. Jung-chai san-pi 容齋三筆 (Jung-chai's Collected Essays, Third Collection).

Huang Ming T'ai-tsu shih-lu, see Ming shih-lu.

I-ching 易經 . Chou-i chu-shu 周易注疏 (Book of Changes), in Shih-san-ching chu-shu 十三經注疏 . Nanchang: 1815.

Inō Yoshinori 伊能嘉矩 . Taiwan bunka shi 臺灣文化史 (Cultural History of Taiwan). 3 vols. Tokyo: Tōkō Shoin 刀江書院 , 1929.

Inoue Kazuo 井上和夫 . Hampō bakufu-hō to ishin-hō 藩法幕府法と維新法(Domain Law, Shogunate Law and Restoration Law). 3 vols. 1st. printing, 1940. Reprinted Tokyo: Ganshodo 巌南堂 , 1965.

_____"Nihon kinsei hampō no seiritsu" 日本近世藩法の制立 (Establishment of Han Law of Pre-modern Japan). Shihō kenshujo-hō 司法研究所報 (Reports of the Legal Training and Research Institute), No. 14 (1955), pp. 88-153.

_____. Shohan no keibatsu 諸藩の刑罰 (Penalties of the Various Domains). Tokyo: Jimbutsu Ōraisha 人物往來社 , 1965.

Ishii Ryōsuke 石井良助 , ed. Nihon hōseishi gaisetsu 日本法制史概説(General Survey of Japanese Legal History). Tokyo: Kōbundō 弘文堂 , 1960.

_____ Edo no keibatsu 江户の刑罰 (Penalties of Edo). Tokyo: Chūō Kōronsha 中央公論社 , 1965.

______ *Kinsei hōsei shiryō sōsho* 近世法制資料叢書 (Compilation of Writings on Legal History in the Premodern period). 3 vols. 1st printed 1941.

______ *Tokugawa kinreikō bekkan* 徳川禁令考(別巻) (Notes on Tokugawa Regulations [Supplementary Volume]). Tokyo: Sōbunsha, 1961.

Ishio Yoshihisa 石尾芳久. "Kainan seiten, kainan ritsurei no kenkyū" 海南政典, 海南律例の研究 (Studies of the *Kainan seiten* and the *Kainan ritsurei* Codes [Tosa]). *Kansai daigaku hōgaku ronshū* 關西大學法學論集. Vol. 15 (1965), p. 57; Vol. 16 (1966), Nos. 1, 2, and 3.

______ *Kainan seiten no kenkyū* 海南政典の研究 (Study of the *Kainan seiten*). Osaka: Kansai University Press, 1969.

Jen Chen-to 任振鐸 and Ho En-t'ao 何恩濤. "Ju-ho chien-li Chung-kuo hsing-shih su-sung hsin t'i-hsi" 如何建立中國刑事訴訟新體系 (How to Establish China's New System of Criminal Litigation). *Chi-lin ta-hsüeh jen-wen k'o-hsüeh hsüeh-pao* 吉林大學人文科學學報 (Kirin University Journal of Humanistic Sciences), Vol. 2 (1959), p. 121.

"Jikki," Kokushi taikei, see *Yūtokuin dono go jikki.*

Kamata Hiroshi 鎌田浩. "Kumamoto-han ni okeru keisei no tenkai" 熊本藩における刑政の展開 (Development of Penal Administration in the Kumamoto Domain) in Harafuji Hiroshi 服藤弘司 and Koyama Sadao 小山貞夫, eds., *Hō to kenryoku no shiteki kōsatsu--Sera kyōju kanreki kinen* 法と權力の史的考察—世良教授還暦紀念(上) (Historical Considerations of Law and Authority--Commemoration of Professor Sera's 60th Birthday). 1:606-639 (1977).

Kaneda Heiichirō 金田平一郎. "Kumamoto-han 'Keihō sōsho' kō" 熊本藩「刑法草書」考 (Thoughts on the 'Draft Penal Law' of the Kumamoto Domain). Hōsei kenkyū 法制史研究 (Studies of Law and Politics), Vol. 12 (1942), pp. 135-205.

Kasai Sukeharu 笠田助治. Kinsei hankō ni okeru shuppansho no kenkyū 近世藩校に於ける出版書の研究 (Study of Books Published in the Han Schools of the Recent Era). Tokyo: Yoshikawa Kōbunkan 吉川弘文館, 1962.

Kawasaki Mitsunari 川崎光成. "The Attorney System," in Chūgoku no hō to shakai 中國の法と社會 (Chinese Law and Society). Tokyo: Shin Dokushosha 新讀書社, 1960.

Ketsugokuko 决獄考 (Thoughts on a Criminal Case of 1711), in Arai Hakuseki zenshū 新井白石全集 (Complete Works of Arai Hakuseki), Vol. 5. Tokyo: Kokusho Kankōkai 國書刊行會, 1907, pp. 272-275.

KI, Kukcho Immulchi, see Yi Chong-hwa.

Kim Chŏng-guk 金正國. Kyŏngminp'yŏn 警民編 (A Compendium to Warn the People). Photolithograph of 1658 woodblock ed. Taehak kugo kojŏn ch'ongsŏ series. Seoul: Sangmun'gak 尚文閣 Press, n.d.

Kim Paek-kan 金伯幹. Sasong yuch'wi 詞訟類聚 (A Compilation on Petitions). 16th century. Modern Korean tr. published Seoul: Pŏpchech'ŏ 法制處 (Legal Material series, No. 16), 1964.

Kim Yongsŏp 金容燮. Chosŏn hugi nongŏpsa yŏn'gu: nongch'on kyŏngje; sahoe pyŏngdong 朝鮮後期農 史硏究·農村經濟·社會變動 (Studies in the Agrarian History of the Late Yi Dynasty, with Emphasis on the Peasant Economy in the Changing Phase of Social Structure). Seoul: Ilchogak 一潮閣, 1970.

Kinreikō, bekkan, see Ishii Ryōsuke, Tokugawa kinreiko (bekkan).

Kinsei hampō shiryō shūsei, see Kyoto teikoku daigaku hōgakubu, ed.

Kobayakawa Kingo 小早川欣吾. "Min-ritsuryō no waga kinsei-hō ni oyoboseru eikyō" 明律令の我近世法に及ぼせる影響 (Ming Code Influences Extending Into Our Law of the Pre-Modern Tokugawa Period). Tōa jimbun gakuhō 東亞人文學報 (Report of Studies in East Asian Culture), Vol. 4 (1945), pp. 197-257.

_______ Meiji hōseishi-ron 明治法學史論 (Treatise on Meiji Legal History). 2 vols. Tokyo: Gonshōdo, 1940.

Kondō Iwao 近藤磐雄. Kaga Shōun-kō 加賀松雲公 (Lord Kaga Shōun). 3 vols. Tokyo: Hano Chiken 羽野知顯, 1909.

Ko pu-yüan t'iao-li ts'e 各部院條例冊 (A Compilation of Regulations Issued by Various Boards and Departments). Shansi, 1871.

Koryŏsa 高麗史 (History of Koryŏ). Photoreprint of a late 15th-century movable type ed.; some portions taken from woodblock eds. of a later date. Seoul: Asea munhwasa 亞細亞文化社, 1972.

KSJK, see Taian kanshū kiji.

KT, see Kyŏngguk taejŏn.

Kuang-hsü hui-tien shih-li, see Ta Ch'ing hui-tien shih-li.

Kukcho Immulchi, see An Chong-hwa.

Kuo Mo-jo 郭沫若. *Liang-Chou chin-wen tz'u ta-hsi t'u-lu k'ao-shih* 兩周金文辭大系圖錄考釋 (Inscribed Bronzes of Western and Eastern Chou). 1st printed 1935. Reprinted Peking: K'o-hsüeh ch'u-pan-she 科學出版社, 1957.

Kuo T'ing-i 郭廷以. *Chin-tai Chung-kuo shih* 近代中國史 (A History of Modern China). 2 vols. Changsha: Commercial Press, 1940.

Kuo-yü 國語 (Discourses of the States). *Ssu-pu pei-yao* 四部備要 ed. Shanghai: Chung-hua shu-chü, 1927.

Kyŏngguk taejŏn 經國大典 (Collected Statutes for National Administration) (*KT*). Reprinted Keijō [Seoul]: Chōsen sōtokufu chūsūin 朝鮮總督府中樞院, 1934.

Kyoto teikoku daigaku hōgakubu 京都帝國大學法學部 ed. "Kumamoto han go-keihō sōsho furei" 熊本藩御刑法草書附例 (The Draft Penal Law of Kumamoto Domain with Substatutes Appended), in *Kinsei hampō shiryō shūsei* 近世藩法資料集成 (Collection of Historical Materials on Domain Law of the Pre-modern Period), Vol. 2. Kyoto, 1943.

"Legal Treatise." For "Ch'ing legal treatise," see *Ch'ing-shih-kao hsing-fa chih chu-chieh*. For other dynasties, see *Li-tai hsing-fa chih*

Li-chi (Li Ki) 禮記 (Book of Rites). Nanchang: Shih-san-ching chu-shu ed., 1815.

Li Han-san 李漢三. *Hsien-Ch'in Liang-Han chih yin-yang wu-hsing hsüeh-shuo* 先秦兩漢之陰陽五行學說 (Theory of Yin-yang and the Five Elements in the Pre-Ch'in and Han Periods). Taipei: Chung-ting wen-hua ch'u-pan-she 鐘鼎文化出版社, 1967.

Li-tai hsing-fa chih 歷代刑法志 (Legal Treatises of the Various Dynasties). Ed. Ch'iu Han-p'ing 丘漢平. Changsha: Commercial Press, 1938. 2nd ed., Taipei: Commercial Press, 1965.

Li-tai ming-ch'en tsou-i 歷代名臣奏議 (Memorials Submitted by Famous Officials of the Various Dynasties). Originally published 1417. Reprinted Taipei: Hsüeh-sheng shu-chü 學生書局, 1964.

Li T'ao 李燾. Hsü tzu-chih t'ung-chien ch'ang-pien 資治通鑑長編 (Detailed Supplement to the Comprehensive Mirror for Aid in Government). Chekiang: Che-chiang shu-chü 浙江書局, 1881.

Li Yüan-pi 李元弼. Tso-i tzu-chen 作邑自箴 (Self-Exhortations of a Magistrate). Original preface dated 1117. Ssu-pu ts'ung-k'an hsü-pien 四部叢刊續編 ed. Shanghai: Commercial Press, 1934.

Liang-Che chin-shih chih 兩浙金石志 (Inscriptions on Stone and Metal in the Province of Chekiang). Chekiang: Che-chiang shu-chü, 1890. Reprinted Taipei: I-wen yin-shu kuan 藝文印書館, 1966.

Lü-shih ch'un-ch'iu 呂氏春秋 (Mr. Lü's Spring and Autumn Chronicle). Ssu-pu pei-yao ed. Shanghai: Chung-hua shu-chü, 1927.

Ma Shih-lin, see Ch'eng-an so-chien chi.

Ma Tuan-lin, see Wen-hsien t'ung-k'ao.

Maema Kyōsaku 前間恭作. Kosen sappu 古鮮冊譜. 3 vols. Tokyo: Tōyō Bunkō 東洋文庫, 1934, 1956, 1957.

Maki Kenji 牧健二. "Higo-han 'Keihō sōsho' no seiritsu; toku ni sono Minritsu sanshaku ni tsuite" 肥後藩刑草書の成立特にその明律参酌に就いて (The Establishment of the "Draft Penal Law" of the Higo Domain Especially Concerning Its Reference to the Ming Penal Code). Hōgoku ronsō 法學論叢 (Kyoto Law Review), Vol. 48 (1943), pp. 701-747.

Matsushita Chū 松下忠. "Dai-Minritsu kenkyū ni okeru Kishū-han to Ken'engaku-ha" 大明律研究における紀州藩と蘐園學派 (Studies of the Great Penal Code of the Kii Domain and the Ken'en Scholarly Group"). Wakayama daigaku gakugei gakubu kiyō jimbun kagaku (Wakayama University Reports of the Department of Arts and Cultural Sciences), Vol. 3 (1953), pp. 68-85.

_____ Kishū no hangaku 紀州の藩學 (Domain Scholarship in Kii Province). Tokyo: Hō Shuppan 法出版, 1974.

Meikun Kyōhō-roku 名君享保録 (Kyōhō Records of an Enlightened Lord). Handwritten copy, 8 fascicles. Kyoto, 1716-1735.

Min-shang-shih hsi-kuan tiao-ch'a pao-kao-lu 民商事習慣調查報告録 (Report of the Survey of Civil and Commercial Customs among the People), 1930. Reprinted Taipei: Chung-hua shu-chü, 1970.

Ming Code, see Ming-lü chi-chieh fu-li. For a Korean version, see Taemyŏngyul chikhae.

Ming Code and Commentary (Japanese version), see Uchida Tomoo.

Ming-lü chi-chieh fu-li 明律集解附例 (Annotated Ming Penal Code with Supplemental Statutes), 1908 ed. Reprinted Taipei: Ch'eng-wen ch'u-pan-she, 1969.

Ming shih-lu 明實録 (Veritable Records of the Ming Dynasty). Facsimile of National Peking Library Copy. Nankang, Taiwan: Institute of History and Philology, Academia Sinica, 1962-1968.

T'ai-tsu 太祖 Shih-lu (Hung-wu Emperor, r.1368-1399).

Miyazaki Ichisada 宮崎市定. "Sō-Gen jidai no hōsei to saiban kikō" 宋元時代の法制と裁判機構 (Law and Judicial System in the Sung-Yuan Period). Tōhō gakuhō 東方學報 (Journal of Oriental Studies), Vol. 24 (1954), pp. 115-225. Reprinted in Ajiashi kenkyū アジア史研究 (Studies in Asian History), Vol. 4 (Kyoto, 1964), pp. 179-305.

______"Ōanseki no rishi gōitsu saku" 王安石の吏士合一策 (Wang An-shih's Policy of Combining Officials and Clerks). Ajiashi kenkyū, Vol. 2 (Kyoto, 1957), pp. 311-364.

______"Shokin to kinsho" 書禁と禁書 (Prohibition on Books and Prohibited Books). Ajiashi kenkyū, Vol. 2 (Kyoto, 1959), pp. 232-254.

Miyazaki Michio 宮崎道生, ed. Teibon oritaku shiba no ki 定本折たく柴の記 (Autobiographical Notes of Arai Hakuseki). Tokyo: Shibundō 至文堂, 1964.

Mizumoto Narumi 水本成美, ed. Zōshū kunten Shin-ritsu isan 增輯訓點清律彙纂 (Enlarged Compendium of the Ch'ing Code with Diacritical Markings Added). 12 kan 巻. Tokyo: Meihōryō 明法寮, 1874.

Mo-tzu 墨子. Ssu-pu pei-yao 四部備要 ed. Shanghai: Chung-hua shu-chü 中華書局, 1927.

Muro Kyūsō 室鳩巣. Rikuyu engi taii 六諭衍義大意 (The Broad Significance of the Amplification of the Six Admonitions), in Nihon kyōiku bunko 日本教育文庫 (Library on Japanese Education), Vol. 2 (1910).

Nanki Tokugawa-shi 南紀徳川史 (History of the Tokugawa of Southern Kii). 17 vols. Wakayama: Nanki Tokugawa Shi Kankō kai 南紀徳川史刊行會, 1930-1933.

Nieh-ssu ting-li hui-pien 臬司定例彙編 (A Collection of Established Regulations by the Provincial Commissioner's Office), Kiangsi, 1905.

Niida Gendō 新井田玄道. "Shibata han kenkyū" 新發田藩研究 (Study of Shibata Han). Shigaku ronkō 史學論考 (Consideration of History), No. 4 (1961).

Niida Noboru 仁井田陞 . Chūgoku Hōseishi Kenkyū: Tochihō Torihikihō 中國法制史研究：土地法,取引法 (A Study of Chinese Legal History: Law of Land and Law of Transaction) Tokyo University Press, 1960. (Vol. 2 of 4 unnumbered volumes.)

_____ Shina mibunhōshi 支那身份法史 (History of the Law of Status in China). Tokyo: Zayubo kan kai 座右寶刊會 , 1943.

_____ "Shina ni okeru keibatsu taikei no henkan--toku ni jiyūkei no hattatsu" 支那における刑罰體系の變換—特に自由刑の發達 (Changes in the System of Penalties in China--Especially the Development of the Penalty [Against] Freedom). Hōgaku kyōkai zasshi 法學協會雜誌 (The Journal of the Jurisprudence Association), Vol. 57, No. 3 (1939), pp. 1-38.

_____ Tōryō shūi 唐令拾遺 (The T'ang Ordinances Re-Collected). Tokyo: Tōhō Bunka Gakuin, Tōkyō kenkyūsho 東方文化學院東京研究所 1933.

Ōba Osama 大庭修 . "Tokugawa Yoshimune to Ta Ch'ing hui-tien-kyōhō jidai ni okeru Nisshin kōshō no ippan" 徳川吉宗と大清會典(享保時代における日清交渉の一斑 (Tokugawa Yoshimune and the Ch'ing Code, An Aspect of Sino-Japanese Relations in the Kyoho Period, 1716-1735), Hoseishi kenkyū, 21:61-95 (1971), pp. 61-95.

Ogyu's Ming Code and Commentary, see Uchida Tomoo.

Oryun haengsilto 五倫行實圖 (The Five Virtues in Practice, Illustrated). Photolithograph of 1797 ed. Preface by Yi Man-su 李晩秀 , tr. Yi Min-su 李民樹 . Seoul: Uryu munhwasa, 1972.

PAHP, see Po-an hsin-pien.

Pak Che-ga 朴齊家. Pukhagŭi 北學議 (Essays on Northern [Ch'ing] Studies). Korean tr. Yi Ik-sŏng 李翼成. Ŭryu mun'go series. Seoul: Ŭryu munhwasa, 1971.

Pak Pyŏng-ho 朴秉濠. Han'guk pŏpchesago 韓國法制史考 (Studies in Korean Legal History). Seoul: Pŏmmunsa 法文社, 1974.

Pan-fa t'iao-li 頒發條例 (Regulations Issued by the Government). Shantung, 1874.

Pien-li, see Wang Chin-chih.

Po-an hsin-pien 駁案新編 (A New Collection of Reversed Cases). Ch'üan Shih-ch'ao 全士潮, et al., compilers. Peking: Hsing-pu 刑部 (Board of Punishments), 1782. Reprinted Taipei: Ch'eng-wen ch'u-pan-she (8 vols. with continuous pagination), 1968.

"Poetry Classic," see Karlgren, tr., The Book of Odes.

Reference Materials, see Rinji Taiwan kyukan chosakai. Taiwan Shihō furoku sankō shō.

Rikō Mitsuo 利光三津夫 and Kasumi Nobuhiko 霞信彦. "Hachigyaku rokugi o meguru sho-mondai" 八虐六議をめぐる諸問題 (Various Problems Revolving Around the Eight Abominations and the Six Considerations) in Meiji hōseishi seijishi no sho-mondai-Tezuka Yutaka Kyōju taishoku kinen rombunshū (Various Problems in Meiji Legal and Political History--A Collection of Articles in Commemoration of Professor Tezuka Yutaka's Retirement). Keio tsūshin 慶應通信 (1977), pp. 1081-1127.

Rinji Taiwan kyūkan chōsakai 臨時臺灣舊慣調查會 (Temporary Commission for the Survey of Traditional Customs in Taiwan). Taiwan kanshū taiyō 臺灣慣習大要 (An Outline of Old Customs in Taiwan), Tokyo: Rinji Taiwan kyūkan chōsakai, (n.d.).

______(Temporary Commission for the Survey of Traditional Customs in Taiwan). *Taiwan shihō* 臺灣私法 (The Private Law of Taiwan). 6 vols. Tokyo: Rinji Taiwan kyūkan chōsakai, 1910.

______(Temporary Commission for the Survey of Traditional Customs in Taiwan). *Keiji oyobi shokan bunruishū* 契字および書簡分類集 (A Collection of Contracts and Documents). Tokyo: Rinji Taiwan kyūkan chōsakai, 1916.

(Temporary Commission for the Survey of Traditional Customs in Taiwan). *Taiwan shihō furoku sankōsho* 臺灣私法附録参考書 (Supplementary Reference Materials for the Private Law of Taiwan). 7 vols. Tokyo: Rinji Taiwan kyūkan chōsakai, 1910.

Shang-yü t'iao-tsou 上諭條奏 (A Collection of Imperial Orders and Memorials). Place and date of publication not available. Covering 1861-1885.

Shen Chi-i hsien-sheng i-shu chia-pien, see Shen Chia-pen.

Shen Chia-pen 沈家本. *Shen Chi-i hsien-sheng i-shu, chia-pien* 沈寄簃先生遺書甲編 (Bequeathed Writings of Shen Chi-i, 1st Series). Originally published in Peking (N.d., *ca*. 1929) in 20 *chüan*. Reprinted Taipei: Wen-hai ch'u-pan-she,1964, in 2 vols with continuous pagination.

Shen Chih-ch'i 沈之奇 , compiler. *Ta Ch'ing-lü chi-chu* 大清律輯註 (The Great Ch'ing Code with Collected Commentaries) 1715. No place of publication.

Shen Kua 沈括. *Meng-hsi pi-t'an* 夢溪筆談 . *Ssu-pu ts'ung-k'an hsü-pien* ed. Shanghai: Commercial Press, 1934.

Shih-ching 詩經 (Poetry Classic). See Karlgren, tr., *The Book of Odes*.

Shih-liao hsün-k'an 史料旬刊 (Historical Materials Published Every Ten Days). 40 vols. Peiping: Palace Museum, 1930-1931.

Shih-lu: For Ch'ing, see *Ta-Ch'ing li-ch'ao shih-lu*. For Ming, see *Ming shih-lu*.

Shu-ching 書經 (Document Classic; "Book of History"), see Karlgren, tr., "*The Book of Documents*."

Shuo-t'ieh pien-li, see Wang Chin-chih.

Shuo-t'ieh chai-yao ch'ao-ts'un 說帖摘要抄存 (Copying Essential Memoranda from the Board of Punishments). By Ch'ing-nien 清年. Honan, 1831.

Simnirok 審理錄 (Records of Review Hearings; *SR*). 1801 ed., 2 vols. Reprinted Seoul: Pŏpchech'ŏ, 1968.

Sinbo sugyo chimnok 新補受教輯錄 (Newly Supplemented Collected Edicts), in *Jukyo shūyō* 受教輯要 (Collected Essential Edicts). Keijō [Seoul]: Chōsen sōtokufu chūsūin, 1943.

SLHK, see *Shih-liao hsün-k'an*.

Soktaejŏn 續大典 (*ST*). Originally published 1746. Chōsen sōtokufu chūsūin ed. Keijō [Seoul]: Chōsen sōtokufu chūsūin, 1938.

Sŏ Il-gyo 徐壹教. *Chosŏn wangjo hyŏngsa chedo ŭi yŏn'gu* 朝鮮王朝刑事制度의研究 (A Study on the Criminal Law and Procedure of the Chosun (Yi) Dynasty 1392-1910). Seoul: Han'guk Pŏmnyŏng p'yŏnch'an hoe 韓國法令編纂會, 1968.

SR, see *Simnirok*.

ST, see *Soktaejŏn*.

Sugyo chimnok 受教輯録 (Collected Edicts), in Jukyo shūyō 受教輯要 (Collected Essential Edicts). Keijō [Seoul]: Chōsen sōtokufu chūsūin, 1943.

Sung Code, see Sung hsing-t'ung.

Sung hsing-t'ung 宋刑統 (Compendium of the Penal Laws of the Sung Dynasty), 963 A.D. Reprinted Peking, 1918. Reprinted Taipei: Wen-hai ch'u-pan-she, 1964.

Sung hui-yao kao 宋會要稿 (Draft Summary of Sung Governmental Institutions), "Hsing-fa" 刑法 (Penal Law Section). 200 ts'e. Peiping: Ta-tung shu-chü 大東書局, 1936. Reprinted Peking: Chung-hua shu-chü, 1957, in 16 vols.

Ta Ch'ing hsien-hsing hsing-lü 大清現行刑律 (The Criminal Law of the Great Ch'ing Dynasty Currently in Force). n.p. 1910.

Ta Ch'ing Hsüan-t'ung hsin fa-ling 大清宣統新法令 (New Laws and Ordinances of the Hsüan-t'ung Period of the Great Ch'ing Dynasty). Shanghai: Commercial Press, 1910.

Ta Ch'ing hui-tien 大清會典 (Collected Institutes of the Great Ch'ing Dynasty), Kuang-hsü ed., 1899. Reprinted Taipei: Ch'i-wen ch'u-pan-she 啟文出版社, 1963.

Ta Ch'ing hui-tien shih-li 大清會典事例 (Collected Statutes of the Ch'ing Dynasty with Precedents). Kuang-hsü 光緒 ed., 1899. Reprinted Taipei: Ch'i-wen ch'u-pan-she, 1963.

Ta Ch'ing Kuang-hsü hsin fa-ling 大清光緒新法令 (New Laws and Ordinances of the Kuang-hsü Period of the Great Ch'ing Dynasty). Shanghai: Commercial Press, 1909.

Ta Ch'ing li-ch'ao shih-lu 大清歷朝實錄 (Veritable Records of Successive Reigns of the Great Ch'ing Dynasty). Tokyo: Okuna Shuppan Kabushiki Kaisha 大藏出版株式會社, 1937-1938. Reprinted Taipei: Hua-wen shu-chü 華文書局, 1964. Sheng-tsu 聖祖 Shih-lu (K'ang-hsi Emperor r.1662-1723). Shih-tsung 世宗 Shih-lu (Yung-cheng Emperor, r.1723-1736). Kao-tsung 高宗 Shih-lu (Chien-lung Emperor, r.1736-1795). Jen-tsung 仁宗 Shih-lu (Chia-ch'ing Emperor, r.1796-1820)

Ta Ch'ing-lü chi-chieh fu-li 大清律集解附例 (The Great Annotated Ch'ing Code, with Substatutes Appended). 1646.

Ta Ch'ing-lü chi-chu, see Shen Chih-ch'i.

Ta Ch'ing lü-li 大清律例 (Statutes and Substatutes of the Great Ch'ing Dynasty). Ch'ien-lung ed., 1740.

Ta Ch'ing lü-li an-yü 大清律例按語 (Compilers' Notes on the Ch'ing Code). Canton: P'an-shih hai-shan hsien-kuan k'an-pen 潘氏海山仙館刊本, 1847.

Ta Ch'ing lü-li chi-chu ("Chyi-chu"), see Wan Wei-han.

Ta Ch'ing lü-li ch'ung-ting hui-t'ung hsin-tsuan 大清律例重訂會通新纂 (New Complete Revised and Annotated Ch'ing Penal Code). 36 chüan. Peking, 1832.

Ta Ch'ing lü-li hui-t'ung hsin-tsuan 大清律例會通新纂 (Comprehensive New Edition of the Great Ch'ing Code), 1873 ed. attributed to Yao Yü-hsiang 姚雨薌. With original commentary by Shen Chih-ch'i 沈之奇 and added commentary by Hu Yang-shan 胡仰山, ed., Peking, 1873. Reprinted Taipei: Wen-hai ch'u-pan-she, 1964, in 5 vols. with continuous pagination.

Ta Ch'ing lü-li t'ung-tsuan chi-ch'eng, see Hu Chao-k'an and Chou Meng-lin, above.

Ta Ch'ing-lü tsuan-hsiu t'iao-li an-yü ts'e-kao, see Yang Yüeh-k'un.

Ta Ming hui-tien 大明會典 (Collected Institutes of the Great Ming). 1587 ed. Reprinted Taipei: Tung-nan shu-pao-she 東南書報社, 1965.

Ta Ming lü, see *Ming-lü chi-chieh fu-li*.

Tabe Hō 田部芳. "Kyū Tsugaru-han hōritsu ippan" 舊津輕藩法律一斑 (An Aspect of the Law of the Old Tsugaru Domain). *Hōgaku kyōkai zasshi* 法學協會雜誌 (*The Journal of the Jurisprudence Association*) Vol. 10 (1892), pp. 147-177, 265-271, 387-390, 477-480, 573-578, 668-677, 745-749, and 825-829.

T'aejo sillok, see *Chosŏn wangjo sillok*.

T'aejong sillok, see *Chosŏn wangjo sillok*.

Taemyŏngyul chikhae 大明律直解 (The Directly Translated Great Ming Code [*TMC*]), 1395. Korean tr., Seoul: Pŏpchech'ŏ, 1964.

Taiwan kanshū kiji 臺灣慣習記事 (Articles on the Customs of Taiwan). Monthly magazine, 80 issues. Taihoku: 1901-1907. Reprinted Taipei: ku-t'ing shu-wu 古亭書屋, 1969.

Tai Yen-hui 戴炎輝. *T'ang-lü t'ung-lun* 唐律通論 (A General Treatise on the T'ang Code). Taipei: Kuo-li pien-i kuan 國立編譯館 1965.

_____ Chung-kuo fa-chih shih kai-yao 中國法制史概要 (A Concise History of the Chinese Legal System), 4th printing. Taipei: San-min shu-chü 三民書局, 1966.

T'ang Code, see *T'ang-lü shu-i*.

T'ang-lü shu-i 唐律疏義 (Official Commentary to the T'ang Code). Kuang-hsu ed., 1890. Reprinted in Kuo-hsüeh chi-pen ts'ung-shu 國學基本叢書 ed. Taipei: Commercial Press, 1955.

TCLL, see Ta Ch'ing lü-li hui-t'ung hsin-tsuan.

Tezuka Yutaka 手塚豐. "Aizu-han 'Keisoku' kō" 會津藩「刑則」考 (Thoughts on the "Criminal Rules" of the Aizu Domain). Keiō Gijuku sōritsu hyakunen kinen rombunshū--(hōgakubu) 慶應義塾百年紀念論文集(法學部) (Commemorative Collection of Articles on the Centennial of Keio Gijuku). Tokyo: Keio University, 1958.

______ Meiji shoki keihō-shi no kenkyū 明治初期刑法史の研究 (Study of the History of Early Meiji Criminal Law). Tokyo: Keio daigaku hōgaku kenkyūkai 慶應大學法學研究會 (Keio University Legal Research Association), 1956.

______ "Nagaoka-han no yoseba to Matsuyama [Takahashi] han no tokeisho" 長岡藩の寄場と松山(高梁)の徒刑所 (Prisons of the Nagaoka and Matsuyama Domains). Hōgaku kenkyū 法學研究 (Studies in Jurisprudence), Vol. 31 (1953), p. 311.

______ "Wakayama-han 'Kokuritsu,' Murata-hon" 和歌山藩國律,村田本 (The "Provincial Penal Law" of the Wakayama Domain, Murata Copy). Hōgaku kenkyū (Studies in Jurisprudence), Vol. 26 (1953), p. 425.

T'iao-fa shih-lei, see Ch'ing-yüan t'iao-fa shih-lei.

TLTI, see Hsüeh Yün-sheng.

TMC, see Taemyŏngyul chikhae.

TMHT, see Ta-ming hui-tien.

Toksŏ Sinmun 讀書新聞 (Readers Weekly), Seoul, no. 123 (April 15, 1973), p. 12.

Torio, Tadasuke 鳥尾タダスケ "Chinese Lawyers," in Hōritsuka no mita Chūgoku 法律家の見た中國 (China as Seen by Lawyers). Tokyo: Nihon hyōron sha 日本評論社 , 1965.

"Train a Contingent of Theoretical Workers in Struggle," (Tsai tou-cheng chung p'ei-yang li-lun tui-wu) 在斗争中培養理论队伍 Jen-min jih-pao 人民日報 (People's Daily), June 18, 1974, p. 1. Tr. in Peking Review, Vol. 17, No. 26 (June 28, 1974), pp. 5-6.

Tso-chuan 左傳 , see Legge, tr., The Chinese Classics.

Tsuji Tatsuya 辻達也 . Tokugawa Yoshimune 德宗吉川 (Tokugawa Yoshimune). Tokyo: Yoshikawa Kōbunkan, 1958.

______ Tokugawa Yoshimune-kō den 德宗吉川公傳 (Biography of Tokugawa Yoshimune), Nikko Tōshōgu Shamusho 日光東照宮社務首, 1962.

______ Kyōhō kaikaku no kenkyū 享保改革の研究 (Study of the Kyoho Reforms). Tokyo: Sōbunsha, 1963.

Tu-li ts'un-i, see Hsüeh Yün-sheng.

Tung Chung-shu 董仲舒 , Ch'un-ch'iu fan-lu 春秋繁露 (Abundant Dew from the Spring and Autumn Annals). Ssu-pu pei-yao ed. Shanghai: Chung-hua shu-chü, 1929.

T'ung-k'ao, see Huang-ch'ao hsü-wen-hsien t'ung-k'ao.

TWSH, see Taiwan shihō.

Uchida Tomoo 内田智雄 and Hihara Toshikuni 日原利國 eds. Ritsurei taishō teihon, Min-ritsu kokujikai 律例對照定本 明例國字解 (Standard Text of the Ming Penal Code with Comments in Our Script; with Laws and Substatutes Cross-Referenced). Tokyo: Sōbunsha, 1966.

Ushijima Shōzō 牛島省三 . Richō hōtenkō 李朝法典考 (Studies in Yi Dynasty Legal Codes). Keijō [Seoul]: Chōsen sōtokufu chūsūin, 1936.

Veritable Records. For Ch'ing, see Ta-Ch'ing li-ch'ao shih-lu; for Ming, see Ming Shih-lu.

Wan Wei-han 萬維翰 . Ta Ch'ing lü-li chi-chu ("Chyi-chu") 大清律例集註 (Collected Commentaries on the Ch'ing Code). Chekiang, 1766; 2nd ed. 1769. Available in Ōki Library, Tokyo University.

Wang Chin-chih 汪進之 , compiler. Shuo-t'ieh pien-li 說例辨例 (Analyzing Substatutes of the Code Through the Study of Memoranda). 1836.

Wang Ch'ung 王充 . Lun Heng 論衡 (Disquisitions). Ssu-pu pei-yao ed. Shanghai: Chung-hua shu-chü, 1929.

Wang K'en-t'ang chien-shih 王肯堂箋釋 (The Chien-shih [Expository Commentary] of Wang K'en-t'ang). Preface, 1612; preface to rev. ed. by Ku Ting 顧鼎, 1689.

Wang Kuo-wei 王國維 . Ku-pen chu-shu chi-nien chi-chiao 古本竹書紀年輯校 (A Collated Collection of Passages from the Ancient Text of the Bamboo Book Annals). Ts'e 29 in Wang Chung-ch'üeh kung i-shu san-chi 王忠愨公遺書三集 (Collected Works of Wang Kuo-wei, Third Collection), 42 t'se. 1927.

Wang Shih-chieh 王世杰 . "Chung-kuo nu-pi chih-tu" 中國奴婢制度 (The Legal Existence of Slavery in the History of China), She-hui k'o-hsüeh chi-k'an 社會科學季刊 (Social Science), Vol. 3 (1925), pp. 303-328.

Wen-hsien t'ung-k'ao 文獻通考 (Compendium of Historical Institutions). Compiled by Ma Tuan-lin 馬端臨. Shih-t'ung 十通 ed. Shanghai: Commercial Press, 1936.

Yaezu Yōhei 八重津洋平. "'Keihō sōsho' wo chūshin to shita Kumamoto-han no keibatsu taikei ni tsuite" 「刑法草書」を中心とした熊本藩の刑罰體系について (Concerning the System of Penalties of the Kumamoto Domain Centering on the "Draft Penal Code"). Hō to seiji 法と政治 (Law and Politics), Vol. 8 (1957), pp. 451-481.

Yang Hung-lieh 楊鴻烈. Chung-kuo fa-lü fa-ta shih 中國法律發達史 (The History of Chinese Legal Development). Shanghai: 1930. Reprinted Taipei: Commercial Press, 1967.

Yang Yüeh-k'un 楊曰鯤, ed. Ta Ch'ing-lü tsuan-hsiu t'iao-li an-yü ts'e-kao 大清律纂修條例按語冊稿 (A Collection of Compiler's Notes on Substatutes of the Ch'ing Code). 1807.

Yao Yü-hsiang, see Ta Ch'ing lü-li hui-t'ung hsin-tsuan.

Yi Ch'un-hŭi 李春熙. Yijo sowon mun'gogo 李朝書院文庫考 (A Study of Confucian Academy Libraries). Seoul: Kukhoe Tosŏwon , 1969.

Yi Hŭi-sŭng 李熙昇, et al.,eds. Han'guk immyŏng taesajŏn 韓國人名大事典 (Great Dictionary of Korean Biography (HITS)) Seoul: Sin'gu munhwasa 新丘文化社, 1967.

Yü-chih hsing-lü shuo-t'ieh 諭旨刑律說帖 (The Memoranda of the Penal Code Published Under Imperial Auspices). Handwritten copy available at Harvard Law School, dated 1802.

Yūtokuin dono go-jikki 有徳院殿御實紀 (Chronicle of Lord Yūtokuin), in Shintei zōho kokushi taikei 新訂增補國史大全 (Revised and Supplemented Compendium of Japanese History), Vol. 46 (Kuroita Katsumi 黒板勝美, ed.). Tokyo: Kokushi taikei kai 國史大全刊行會, 1934.

Glossary

Ai (duke of Ch'i) 哀

Aizu (*han*) 會津

amhaeng ŏsa (secret censor) 暗行御史

an chiao-kuan ho-kuo (a case had been approved by the Statutes Commission) 案交館核過

an-fu shih (supervisor of military affairs) 安撫使

An-p'ing 安平

Ao-men (Macao) 澳門

azukarisho (land granted by the Shogunate to the daimyos) 預所

bakufu (Shogunate) 幕府

bakuhan taisei (Shogunal system) 幕藩體制

bugyo (judges) 奉行

Buke shohatto 武家諸法度

Bunka (1804-1817 code) 文化

cha-ch'i kuan-ssu ch'ü-ts'ai (fraudulently obtaining public or private property) 詐欺官私取財

cha-wei (deceptions and frauds) 詐僞

ch'a-ch'u (to search out) 查出

chaep'an hapsida ("Let's take it to court") 裁判 합시다

chan chien-hou (decapitation after the assizes) 斬監候

chan li-chüeh hsiao-shih (immediate decapitation and exposure of the head) 斬立決梟示

ch'an-shu (bind together) 纏束

chang-chih (whippers) 杖直

ch'ang-jen tao ts'ang-k'u ch'ien-liang (theft of public property by ordinary people) 常人盜倉庫錢糧

Chao-ch'ing (prefecture) 肇慶

chao i-fa chiu-pan (to punish the offender according to barbarian law) 照夷法究辦

chao i-fa ch'u-ssu (executed according to barbarian law) 照夷法處死

che (loss of limb) 折

Cheng (feudal state) 鄭

Cheng Ch'eng-kung (Koxinga) 鄭成功

cheng-hsiung (actual offender) 正兇

ch'eng-chao (confession) 承招

ch'eng-hsiung (vicious) 逞兇

Chenhai (county) 鎮海

chi hsi hua-wai-jen yu fan (an offense by a person from beyond the pale of Chinese civilization) 即係化外人有犯

chi-hsing ch'in-na sung so-tsai kuan-ssu chun so-fan ch'ing-chung ch'eng-ch'u (they should be immediately arrested and sent to the local authorities to be punished according to the gravity of the offense) 即行擒拿送所在官司准所犯輕重懲處

chi-ssu (state sacrifices) 祭祀

ch'i (abusive) 欺

ch'i-ling (abusive and bullying) 欺凌

ch'i-tzu (type of contract) 契字

ch'i-wu (abusive and insulting) 欺侮

ch'i-yüeh (contract) 契約

Chia-ch'ing (r.1796-1820) 嘉慶

chia-nu (domestic slaves) 家奴

chia-jen (bond servant) 家人

ch'iang-chan liang-chia ch'i-nü (abduction of a woman of a respectable family) 強占良家妻女

ch'iang-tao (armed robbery) 強盜

ch'iang-to sha-jen (murder during a robbery) 搶奪殺人

ch'iang-to (unarmed robbery) 搶奪

chiao (measure of value) 角

chiao-ch'u (surrender) 交出

chiao-so (instigate an appeal) 教唆

chieh-chi (assistant warden) 節級

chieh-tan (loan receipt) 借單

ch'ieh-tao (theft) 竊盜

chien (humble, base) 賤

chien-shou tzu-tao ts'ang-k'u ch'ien-liang (embezzlement of public property) 監守自盜倉庫錢糧

chien-tang (cabals and state intrigues) 姦黨

chien-tuan (application of the law) 檢斷

Chien-wu (reign period) 建武

Chien-yen (r.1127-1130) 建炎

Ch'ien (prefecture) 虔

ch'ien (unit of value) 錢

ch'ien-chai (moneylending) 錢債

ch'ien-hsü (preface) 前序

ch'ien-hui pen-kuo (to deport back to one's own country) 遣回本國

Ch'ien-lung (r.1736-1795) 乾隆

ch'ih (feeblemindedness) 癡

chih-chih (administrative regulations) 職制

chih-lü (mental capacities) 智慮

ch'ih (Sung dynasty imperial edicts) 敕

chin (compassion) 矜

Chin (state) 晉

chin-ken (unconditional contract) 盡根

chin-p'iao (gold certificate) 金票

chin-shih (doctorate) 進士

chin-wu (prohibited cargo) 禁物

chin yü yu p'ing (now we wish there to be proof) 今欲有憑

ch'in-k'uei (embezzlement of government funds) 侵虧

ch'in-shu hsiang wei jung-yin (knowingly assisting and concealing relatives who are criminals) 親屬相為容隱

Ch'ing-yüan (r.1195-1200) 慶元

Chiphyonjon (Academy of Worthies) 集賢殿

Chiu Kao (section of Shu-ching) 酒誥

chiu-mu (horses and cattle) 廄牧

chojong (royal ancestors) 祖宗

Chŏngjo (r.1776-1880) 正祖

<u>Chosŏn kyŏnggukchŏn</u> 朝鮮經國典

Chou (ancient capital) 周

chou (prefecture) 州

chū (loyalty) 忠

Chu Hsi 朱熹

chū-kō (loyalty and filial piety) 忠孝

chu-pu (record keeper) 主簿

chu-tien (chief warden) 主典

Ch'u (state) 楚

ch'u-ch'i (law of divorce) 出妻

ch'u-fen tse-li (laws of various boards) 處分則例

ch'u-men wu-jen-huo (once the goods are out the door, they are no longer recognized) 出門無認貨

chuan-yün shih (supervisor of finance) 轉運使

chuang-shih-chih (document containing a request for trial) 狀式紙

Chuang-tzu 莊子

Ch'un-hsi (r.1174-1189) 淳熙

Chung-lu fa (heavy salary act of Wang An-shih) 重祿法

Chung-ni (Confucius) 仲尼

chung-shu (cabinet ministers) 中書

chü-lu (adjudicate two cases together) 聚錄

Ch'üan-chou (Zayton) 泉州

ch'üan-t'i (whole structure) 全體

chüeh-i (extinguish the obligation) 絶義

chüeh pu shih-yen (he definitely will not eat his words) 決不食言

chün-cheng (administration of the armed forces) 軍政

Chün-chi-ch'u (Grand Council) 軍機處

Chün Shih (section of Shu-ching) 君奭

chün-tzu (true gentleman) 君子

chün-tzu yüeh (a true gentleman would say...) 君子曰

dai-bugyō (great commissioner) 大奉行

Dai min ritsu no taii (Broad Meaning of the Code of the Great Ming) 大明律の大意

daimyō 大名

dangoku ritsu (law on trial and imprisonment) 斷獄律

dentaku (field and houses) 田宅

dōshin (prison wardens) 同心

Echigo (province) 越後

Edo 江戸

eikin ritsu (imperial palaces and guards law) 衛禁律

en (favors) 恩

erh-pi kan-yüan (both parties are willing and honest) 二比甘愿

fa-chia (legalists) 法家

Fa-ching (Classic of Law) 法經

fa-chung (violation of a tomb) 發塚

fa-ling (laws) 法令

fa-lo (execution of punishment) 發落

fa-ssu (law office) 法司

fa-tsui (legal guilt) 法罪

fan-chien (sexual offenses) 犯姦

fan hua-wai-jen fan-tsui che ping i-lü ni-tuan (all aliens who commit offenses on Chinese soil shall be sentenced according to the Penal Code) 凡化外人犯罪者並依律擬斷

fan hua-wai lai-hsiang-jen fan-tsui che ping i lü ni-tuan (all aliens who come to submit themselves to the government of the empire shall, when they commit offenses on Chinese soil, be sentenced according to the Penal Code) 凡化外來降人犯罪者並依律擬斷

fan-i (recant one's own testimony) 翻異

fan-tsui (commit a crime) 犯罪

fang-shui-li (interest sent to sea) 放水利

fei-chi (infirmity) 癈疾

fei wai-kuo chi che (persons who do not possess foreign nationality) 非外國籍者

fen (unit of value) 分

feng-ping (mental illness) 瘋病

fo-yin (Mexican dollars) 佛銀

fu-chih (system of mourning) 服制

fu-chih ts'un chao (to hand over as proof) 付執存照

fudai (hereditary) 譜代

Fukui (daimyō) 福井

Fukushima 福島

fu-shun i-ch'ing (deferring to barbarian wishes) 俯順夷情

gisei ritsu (ceremonial regulations) 儀制律

Go-keihō-cho (Catalogue of Penal Law) 御刑法牒

Go-keihō meimokū (list of names for the Penal Law) 御刑法名目

goningumi (five-man group) 五人組

gosanke (branch houses) 御三家

goyōnin (chamberlain) 御用人

hachigi (eight considerations) 八議

han (domain) 藩

Han-fei-tzu 韓非子

Han-shu 漢書

han'gŭl 한글

hankan ritsu (law on sexual violations) 犯姦律

Hansŏng (Seoul) 漢城

hei-shui i-yang (the deep foreign sea) 黑水夷洋

hen (chapter) 編

Heng-ch'un (hsien) 恒春

Hidetada 秀忠

Hideyoshi 秀吉

Higo (han) 肥後

Hirosaki (han) 弘前

ho-fang (river conservancy) 河防

ho-hsi (agreement and settlement) 和息

Ho Shen 和珅

ho-yüeh-tzu (type of contract) 合約字

hobō ritsu (law on arrests and escapes) 捕亡律

hōritsuka (jurists) 法律家

Hosokawa 細川

Hou [Yao] 舀

Hou-Han-shu (History of the Later Han Dynasty) 後漢書

hou-jih k'ung-k'ou wu-p'ing (empty words on a later day will have no effect) 後日空口無憑

hsi (in sport) 戲

hsi-hsüeh jen (apprentice law clerks) 習學人

hsi-sha wu-sha kuo-shih sha-shang-jen (killing or wounding during roughhousing, by error, or by accident) 戲殺誤殺過失殺傷人

hsi-yang (western ocean) 西洋

Hsiang 襄

Hsiang-shan (hsien) 香山縣

hsiao-chu (official interlinear commentary) 小註

hsiao-jen (petty person) 小人

hsiao-yü (enlightening instructions) 曉諭

hsien (district) 縣

hsien-ch'eng (assistant magistrate) 縣丞

hsien-ch'ien chiao-kuan (sale for cash) 現錢交關

hsien-hsing ting-li (established substatutes that are currently applicable) 現行定例

hsien-wei (police commissioner) 縣尉

Hsin-chu (county) 新竹

hsin-fu (newly settled) 新附

hsing (penal law) 刑

hsing-fang (punishment section) 刑房

hsing-lü (penal law) 刑律

Hsing-pu (Board of Punishments) 刑部

Hsing-shu (Book of Punishments) 刑書

hsing-ts'ao (bureau of punishments) 刑曹

hsiu-ting fa-lü ta-ch'en (commissioner for the revision of the laws) 修訂法律大臣

hsiung-i (vicious barbarian killers) 兇夷

Hsü (surname) 徐

hsü-tui-tan (receipt for part delivery and advance deposit payment) 許兑單

hsün (interrogate) 訊

Hsün-tzu 荀子

Hukuang (Hunan and Hupei) 湖廣

Hunmin chŏngŭm 訓民正音

hu-i (family and corvee) 户役

hu-lü (civil law) 户律

Hu-pu (Board of Revenue) 户部

hua-lo-mi (a kind of grain) 花螺米

hua-wai (alien) 化外

hua-wai-jen (persons from beyond Chinese civilization; aliens) 化外人

hui-p'iao (bill of exchange) 滙票

hui-tan (acknowledgement of delivery) 回單

hun-yin (marriage) 婚姻

Hung (Commander of Ch'in) 弘

hung-pin (red petition) 紅稟

Hyakkajō (100 articles) 百箇條

hyangso (magistrate's advisory council) 鄉所

hyōjōsho (conference chamber) 評定書

i (appropriateness, righteousness) 義

i (barbarian) 夷

i-chia (one family) 一家

i-chih (ceremonial regulations) 儀制

I-ching 易經

i-chu (one property owner) 一主

i-mu (barbarian headman) 夷目

i-nu (devoted slave) 義奴

i-tsui liang-ni (to be punished twice for the same offense) 一罪兩擬

i-tzu (adopted son) 義子

idu (Sino-Korean proto-syllabary for clerks) 吏讀

Ienobu (Shōgun, r.1709-1712) 家宣

Ili (district) 伊犂

jen-i chiao-kuan (this is a just transaction) 仁義交關

jen-ming (homicide) 人命

jisha ritsu (temple and shrine law) 寺社律

Joken'in 常憲院

ju-ts'ang tan (warehouse receipt) 入倉單

ju-kung (bring tribute) 入貢

jūaku (ten abominations) 十惡

jukan (Confucian advisers) 儒官

jung-yin (toleration of concealment) 容隱

kabo (year designation, 1894) 甲午

kagen (added and subtracted) 加減

Kagoshima (han) 鹿兒島

Kainan ritsurei 海南律令

Kainan seiten 海南政典

kakei (burn at the stake) 火刑

Kaitei ritsurei (Statutes and Substatutes as Amended) 改定律令

kambun ("Japanized" Chinese) 漢文

Kameyama (*daimyō*) 龜山

kamon (Tokugawa rank) 家門

kan-chieh-chuang (consent bond) 甘結狀

Kanazawa (*han*) 金沢

K'ang-hsi (r.1662-1722) 康熙

K'ang Kao (section of *Shu-ching*) 康誥

K'ang-shu 康叔

Kansei ritsu 寛政律

kanshin ritsu (barriers and fords law) 關津律

kao (accuse) 誥

Kao Shou-chüeh 高壽覺

Kao-tsung (r.1127-1162, Sung dynasty) 高宗

kao-wei (document issued) 稿尾

kapsin (year designation; 1884) 甲申

Kari keiritsu (Provisional Criminal Law) 假刑律

karō (minister to a daimyo) 家老

karyō (restitutive copper) 過料

kasen (fine) 過錢

Keihō sōsho (Draft Penal Law) 刑法草書

keikokan (*han* school) 稽古館

Keisoku (Penal Rules) 刑則

keiyaku (contract) 契約

Kii (province) 紀伊

ko (regulations) 格

kō (filial piety) 孝

ko-sha (killing in self-defense; killing an offender who resists arrest) 格殺

ko wu fan-hui (each party is without regret) 各無反悔

k'o-ch'eng (taxes and tariffs) 課程

k'o-chü (academic degrees) 科舉

Kochi (*han*) 高知

kōgi onsadame (decisions of the Shogunate) 公儀御定

Kojong (r.1863-1907) 高宗

kōkei (beating) 敲刑

koku (4.96 bushels) 石

kokudaka (putative rice rating) 石高

Kokuritsu (Provincial Penal Code) 國律

Kokuritsu hojo (Provincial Code Supplement) 國律補助

Koyaku (family and corvee) 戸役

kon'in (marriage) 婚姻

Koryŏ (dynasty) 高麗

kōsatsu (bulletin board) 高札

Kōsai 公裁

kōshiki ritsu (law on standards of official behavior) 公式律

Ku Ming (section of *Shu-ching*) 顧命

ku-sha (intentional homicide) 故殺

k'u-shu ("treasury janitor") 庫書

kua-mai (sale on credit) 掛賣

kuan-chin (frontier guard posts) 關津

kuan-li shou-ts'ai (officials and clerks accepting bribes) 官吏受財

Kuan-tzu 管子

kuan yu cheng-t'iao, min yu ssu-yüeh (the officials have their regulations, the people have private contracts) 官有正條民有私約

k'uan-ch'u (leniency) 寬處

Kuang-hsü (r.1875-1908) 光緒

Kuang Wu Ti 光武帝

kuei (noble) 貴

kuei-fu (to attach one's self to the empire) 歸附

kuei-hua (naturalized Chinese, to naturalize) 歸化

kujikata (judicial officers) 公事方

Kujikata osadamegaki 公事方御定書

kujishi (Tokugawa lawyer) 公事士

Kukcho oryeui 國朝五禮儀

Kumamoto (*han*) 熊本

kung (goods) 供

kung-an (Chinese detective story) 公案

kung-ch'en (meritorious officials) 功臣

kung-ch'ü ch'ieh-ch'ü chieh-wei tao (an open and violent taking constitutes a robbery, and a private and concealed taking, a theft; both are called *tao*) 公取竊取皆為盜

kung-fan-tsui fen shou-ts'ung (distinguishing principles and accessories) 共犯罪分首從

kung-lü (public works law) 工律

kung-shih (standards of official behavior) 公式

kung-wei (imperial palaces and guards) 宮衛

kung yüeh-hu chi fu-jen fan-tsui (offenses committed by government artisans, musicians, or women) 工樂户及婦人犯罪

k'ung-k'ou wu p'ing (empty mouths cannot be depended upon) 空口無憑

kunten (diacritical marks) 訓點

kuo-fa (the law of the nation) 國法

kuo-shih sha (accidental homicide) 過失殺

Kurume (<u>han</u>) 久留米

kwammon (amount of money) 貫文

kyŏkko (striking the drum) 擊鼓

Kyŏnggi (province) 京畿

<u>Kyŏngguk taejŏn</u> (Dynastic Code) 經國大典

<u>Kyŏngminp'yŏn</u> (Book to Warn the People) 警民編

lai-hsiang (come to submit) 來降

lao-hsiao fei-chi shou-shu (redemption of punishment for offenders who are old, young, or mildly disabled) 老小廢疾收贖

Le Kao (section of <u>Shu-ching</u>) 洛誥

li (substatute; precedent) 例

li (measure of distance) 里

li (ceremony; correct social behavior) 禮

li-ch'ü (unreasonable) 理曲

Li-fan-yüan (Mongolian Superintendency) 理藩院

Li k'uei 李悝

li Li-fan-yüan che jeng chao yüan-ting Meng-ku li (cases which fall within the jurisdiction of the Mongolian Superintendency shall be decided according to the regulations enacted for the Mongol tribes) 隸理藩院者仍照原定蒙古例

li-lü (administrative law) 吏律

li-lü (ritual law) 禮律

Li Yüan-pi 李元弼

liang (measure of weight) 兩

Liang-Chiang (Kiangsu, Kiangsi, Anhwei) 兩江

liang-chih (emperor's advisers) 兩制

Liang-Kuang (Kwangtung and Kwangsi) 兩廣

liang-tsui chü-fa i chung lun (the heavier punishment applies when one commits concurrent offenses) 兩罪俱發以重論

liang wu tiao-nan (neither side is obstructive) 兩無刁難

lieh (unit of value) 寽

ling (administrative statute; ordinance) 令

ling-ch'ih (death by slicing) 凌遲

<u>Liu-yü yen-i</u> (Amplification of Six Admonitions) 六諭衍義

lo-mi (kind of grain) 螺米

lu (circuit) 路

Lu (state) 魯

Lu-kang (port in Taiwan) 鹿港

lu-shih (second clerk) 錄事

lu-shih ts'an-chün (secretary-general) 錄事參軍

lung (deaf) 聾

lü (statute) 律

Lü-hsing (Punishments of Lü) 呂刑

lüeh-jen lüeh-mai jen (kidnapping and sale of human beings) 略人略賣人

ma-li (abusive language) 罵詈

mai fu shui (purchase of goods on board ship) 買浮水

mai-huan-huo (present payment for future goods) 買緩貨

mallyujip'ye (corrupt practices of a degenerate age, future abuses) 末流之弊

mao (venerable greybeard) 耄

Matsushiro (han) 松代

Meng-mai-fu (Bombay) 孟買府

Meng-tzu (Mencius) 孟子

mi-ping (confidential reports) 密稟

ming-li lü (terms and general principles) 名例律

Ming T'ai-tsu (r.1368-1398) 明太祖

ming-tan (name list) 名單

mizurō (water prison) 水牢

Mo-tzu 墨子

Mongmin simsŏ (magistrates' handbook) 牧民心書

Monkei jōrei (Compilation of Substatutes) 問刑條例

Morioka (han) 盛岡

mou (6.6 mou=1 acre) 畝

mou-fan ta-ni (high treason) 謀反大逆

mou-p'an (disloyal activities) 謀叛

mou-sha (kill with premeditation) 謀殺

Mu Wang (King Mu. r.1001-947 B.C.) 穆王

Murata-bon (printed copy) 村田本

Mutsu (province) 陸奧

myōrei ritsu (terms and general principles) 名例律

nei-yang (inner sea) 內洋

nieh-ssu (provincial judicial commissioner) 臬司

nikkei (flesh punishment) 肉刑

Ningpo 寧波

Ohaengji (Treatise on the Five Elements) 五行志

Okayama (*han*) 岡山

Oryun haengsilto (Illustrated five virtues in practice) 五倫行實圖

Osadamegaki see *Kujikata osadamegaki*

ou tsu-fu-mu fu-mu (striking grandparents or parents) 毆祖父母父母

pa-i (eight considerations) 八議

pai-chou ch'iang-tuo (daytime unarmed robbery) 白晝搶奪

pai-pin (white petition) 白稟

pan-li pu-i (the cases were not decided consistently) 辦理不一

p'an (judgment writing) 判

p'an-kuan (adviser, judge) 判官

pao (village organization) 保

pao-chieh-chuang (guaranty bond) 保結狀

pao-i (hereditary slaves of Manchu princes) 包衣

pao-ku hsien (statutory 40-day period of responsibility for murder) 保辜限

pao-shang (security merchant) 保商

pei-lu (Wen Kung's laws) 被虜

p'ei-huo-tan (invoice) 配貨單

pen-jung (still in good physical health) 本榮

Pi Shih (section of <u>Shu-ching</u>) 費誓

pi-yu pu-te-i chih ch'ing (could not act otherwise) 必有不得已之情

p'iao (ticket, contract) 票

pien-ch'ih (collection of edicts) 編敕

pien-lu ssu (archives; law clerk) 編錄司

ping-lü (military law) 兵律

p'ing-fan (clearing the innocent of grave charges) 平反

Po Yü 伯輿

pu-ch'ü (semi-slave of T'ang period) 部曲

pu te i-yen (shall not speak different words) 不得異言

pu-wang (arrests and escapes) 捕亡

pu-ying-tsou (ought not to memorialize) 不應奏

pu-ying-wei (doing what ought not to be done) 不應為

<u>Pukhag-ui</u> (Essays on Northern [Ch'ing] Studies) 北學議

rei (substatutes) 例

renkyū ritsu (related guilt law) 連反律

<u>Rikuyu engi</u> (Amplification of the Six Admonitions) 六諭衍義

ritsu (Japanese penal code) 律

ritsurei (penal laws) 律令

ritsuryō (ancient law pattern; T'ang law format) 律令

rōjū (senior council) 老中

ryō (ancient law) 令

ryō (amount of money) 兩

sagi ritsu (deceptions and frauds law) 詐偽律

saishi ritsu (state sacrifices law) 祭祀律

San-fu pa-mu t'u (The mourning chart for 3 types of fathers and 8 types of mothers) 三父八母圖

sang'ŏn (petitioning) 上言

sata (sifted and strained) 沙汰

seiten (administrative laws) 正典

Sejong (r.1418-1450) 世宗

Sengoku jidai (Warring States period; 1467-1567) 戰國時代

sha i-chia san-jen (killing of 3 members of the same family) 殺一家三人

Shang Yang 商鞅

Shao Kao (section of Shu-ching) 召誥

she-chang (credit account) 賒賬

shen (physical appearance) 身

Shen Chih-ch'i 沈之奇

Shen-hsing yüan (Counsellors' Committee) 審刑院

Shen Pu-hai 申不害

Shen-tsung (r.1068-1085) 神宗

sheng yi fa (restraint by the law) 繩以法

sheng-yü (holy admonitions) 聖諭

Shibata (han) 新發田

shih (master) 師

shih (ordinance) 式

shih (measure of grain) 石

shih (kinship group) 氏

shih-ch'an (public markets) 市廛

Shih-ching 詩經

shih-o (ten abominations) 十惡

shih-p'u (hereditary slave) 世僕

Shih Wei 士蔿

shikei (death) 死刑

Shinritsu (New Penal Code) 新律

Shinritsu kōryō (1870 Code) 新律綱領

Shinritsu toriatsukai no oboe (memorandum on applying the New Penal Law) 新律取報の覺

Shioki ruiki (Collected and Classified Punishments) 仕置類寄

shin-shaku (spooned and ladled; consideration) 斟酌

shokudō (restitutive copper) 贖銅

shou-chin (detention) 收禁

shou-fen (ordinary clerk) 守分

shou-liu mi-shih tzu-nü (receiving stray children and women) 收留迷失子女

shou-tan (farm rent receipt) 收單

shou-tsang (bribery) 受贓

shu (calligraphy) 書

Shu-ching 書經

Shu-hsiang 叔向

shu-p'u (scrivener's shop) 書舖

shu-t'ung chih (restitutive copper system) 贖銅制

shuo-t'ieh (memorandum) 說帖

Shushigaku (Chu Hsi learning; neo-Confucianism) 朱子學

simni (review hearing) 審理

sŏgyŏng (clearance procedure for appointments to the bureaucracy) 署經

sojo bako (complaint box) 訴狀箱

Soktaejŏn 續大典

sōko (storehouses) 倉庫

sōko ritsu (government granaries and treasuries law) 倉庫律

Sŏnggyun-gwan 成均館

sŏnwang (former kings) 先王

soshō (complaints) 訴訟

soshō ritsu (accusations and suits law) 訴訟律

Ssu Ch'uan 駟歂

ssu-k'ou (director of crime) 司寇

Ssu-yen tsa-tzu (Four Character Proverb-law textbook) 四言雜字

su-sung (accusations and suits; complaints) 訴訟

Sugyo chimnok (Collected Edicts) 受教輯錄

Sukchong (r.1674-1720) 肅宗

sun-shang yü jen, yü wu pu-k'o p'ei-ch'ang (inflicting irreparable bodily injury upon a person or causing uncompensatable damage to articles) 損傷於人於物不可賠償

sung (to litigate) 訟

Sung (dynasty) 宋

Sung hsing-t'ung (Sung Code) 宋刑統

sung-kun (litigation tricksters) 訟棍

Sung T'ai-tsu (r.960-976) 宋太祖

sute-bumi ("dropped" letters) 捨文

Ta Kao (section of Shu-ching; copy of the law) 大誥

Ta-li ssu (Supreme Court) 大理寺

Ta Ming lü ta-i (Broad Meaning of the Code of the Great Ming) 大明律大意

taegang (institutional-moral fiber) 大綱

T'aejo (r.1392-1398) 太祖

tai-fu (great officer) 大夫

tai-mai (sale on consignment) 代賣

tai-shu (scrivener) 代書

taipan (senior Canton merchant) 大辦

tan (receipt, contract) 單

tan-shen (slaves who sell only themselves) 單身

Tanshui 淡水

t'an-ya (restrain) 彈壓

tang-p'iao (pawn ticket) 當票

T'ang (Shang king) 湯

T'ang-yin pi-shih (Parallel Cases from Under the Pear Tree) 棠陰比事

Tao-kuang (r.1821-1850) 道光

tao ma-niu ch'u-ch'an (stealing horses, cattle, and other domestic animals) 盜馬牛畜產

tao-so (scene of the theft) 盜所

tao-tsei (theft and violence) 盜賊

t'ao-mo (pickpocketing) 掏摸

Tengchou (in Honan) 鄧州

Teng Hsi-tzu 鄧析子

Teng Ssu-hsien (Sung law text) 鄧思賢

teng-wen ku (complaint drum) 登聞鼓

terakoya (temple schools) 寺小屋

ti-ming (pay with one's life) 抵命

t'i-chü ch'ang-p'ing (supervisor of agriculture) 提舉常平

t'i-tien hsing-yü (supervisor of punishment) 提點刑獄

t'iao-ch'u (mediation) 調處

t'iao-fa shih-lei (classified laws) 條法事類

t'iao-li (substatutes) 條例

t'ieh-ssu (apprentice clerk) 貼司

tien (mortgage, lawful) 典

tien-hao (store name) 店號

tien-k'uang (insanity) 癲狂

t'ien-chai (land and fields) 田宅

ting-wei (year designation; 1907) 丁未

To Fang (section of Shu-ching) 多方

to-kei (penal servitude) 徒刑

tō-ō (affrays and blows) 鬥毆

To Shih (section of Shu-ching) 多士

tojime (barred-door confinement) 戸メ

Tokushima 徳島

Tongguk chŏng-un 東國正韻

Tongguk saryak 東國史略

Tosa (province) 土佐

Tottori (han) 鳥取

tou-ou (affrays and blows) 鬥毆

tou-ou chi ku-sha-jen (killing in a fight and killing with intent) 鬥毆及故殺人

tou-ou sha-jen (homicide in a fight) 鬥毆殺人

tou-sha (kill in a fight) 鬥殺

Tozama ("outside" daimyo) 外樣

tōzoku ritsu (violence and theft law) 盜賊律

tsa-fan (miscellaneous offenses) 雜犯

ts'ai-huo-tan (order form) 採貨單

ts'ai-sheng che-ke jen (murder with intent to mangle and divide the body of the deceased for magical purposes) 採生折割人

ts'an-chün (bureau chief) 參軍

ts'ang-k'u (storehouses; government granaries and treasuries) 倉庫

tsao hsü ku-tu sha-jen (rearing venomous animals and preparing poisons) 造畜蠱毒殺人

ts'ao (bureaus of prefectural government) 曹

tse-ling (order) 則令

tsei-tao (violence and theft) 賊盜

Tso-chih yao-yen (Precepts for Local Administrative Officials) 佐治藥言

Tso-chuan 左傳

tso t'ui-k'an ssu (left inquiring office) 左推勘司

tsou-shu (memorial) 奏疏

tsuihō (banishment) 追放

tsung-chu (general commentary) 總註

tsung-li (local headman) 總理

tu-chi (incapacity) 篤疾

tu-pan cheng-wu ch'u (superintendency of political affairs) 督辦政務處

t'u (penal servitude) 徒

t'u-liu jen t'ao (escaping from a place where one serves the punishment of penal servitude or banishment) 徒流人逃

t'u-ts'ai mou-sha (murder for profit) 圖財謀殺

tuan-li (examples of judgment) 斷例

tuan-tsui pu-tang (improper execution of sentence) 斷罪不當

tuan-yü (trial and imprisonment) 斷獄

t'ui-kuan (advisor; judge) 推官

t'ung-chih (subprefect) 同知

T'ung-chih (r.1862-1874) 同治

t'ung-ch'u (pay together) 同出

t'ung-hsing (general circular) 通行

t'ung-p'an (assistant prefect) 通判

t'ung-shih (linguist) 通事

t'ung-tso i-ch'uan (served on the same ship) 同坐一船

tzu (measure of grain) 秭

tzu (type of contract) 字

Tzu-ch'an 子產

tzu-hsing shou-kuan (to take the offender into custody) 自行收管

tzu-ni tzu-ho (reviewing an opinion which the Board itself had drafted on behalf of a lower court) 自擬自覈

tz'u-sung (litigation) 詞訟

Tzu Ts'ai (Section of *Shu-ching*) 梓材

uich'ŏp (ratification of new legislation) 依牒

ukagai (refer the question to Edo) 伺

Urumchi 烏魯木齊

Uwajima (*han*) 宇和島

wai-i (outer barbarians) 外夷

wai-yang (outer sea) 外洋

wairo (bribery) 賄賂

Wakayama (<u>han</u>) 和歌山

wakun (simple Japanese translation) 和訓

Wan-li (r.1573-1619) 萬曆

wan-mi (kind of grain) 萬米

wan-tan (final receipt) 完單

wang-ch'i (royal domain) 王畿

Wang ts'an men (Royal Comparison Office) 王參門

Wei (state) 魏

wei-chih fa-tu (not yet familiar with the laws) 未知法度

wei-pi jen chih-ssu (causing the death of an individual by violent and fearful threats) 威逼人致死

wei-tsui (afraid of punishment) 畏罪

Wen Hou Chih Ming (Section of <u>Shu-ching</u>) 文侯之命

<u>Wen-hsing t'iao-li</u> (Compilation of Substatutes) 問刑條例

Wen Wang (King Wen) 文王

wu (to insult) 侮

wu (mischance) 誤

wu-ch'eng (divisions of the city and suburbs of Peking) 五城

wu-hsing (5 elements) 五行

wu-hsing (5 punishments) 五刑

wu-i-le (this transaction is without coercion) 無抑勒

wu-p'o-le (this transaction is without coercion) 無迫勒

wu-tsung (no erroneous acquittal of the guilty) 無縱

Wu Wang (King Wu; r.1122-1114 B.C.) 武王

wu-wang (no erroneous conviction of the innocent) 無枉

ya (dumb) 瘂

ya-i (yamen runner) 衙役

yamen (office) 衙門

ya-ssu (chief clerk) 押司

yangban 兩班

yao (a brief) 要

Yao (tribe) 猺

Yao [Hou] 舀

yao-ch'iu (trying the case) 要囚

yeh-i ping-ku, ying wu-yung-i (since the offender has already died from sickness, the matter need not be deliberated further) 業已病故應毋庸議

yeh i tzu-chin, ying wu-yung i (since the offender has already died from suicide, the matter need not be deliberated further) 業已自盡應毋庸議

yen (speech) 言

Yi (dynasty, 1392-1910) 李

yi yu (year designation; 1885) 乙酉

Yi Sŏng-gye (Yi T'aejo; r.1392-1398) 李成桂

Yin (alternate name for Shang dynasty) 殷

yin-p'iao (silver certificate) 銀票

ying-tsao (public construction) 營造

ying wu-yung-i (the case should not be further considered) 應毋庸議

yoin (toleration of concealment) 容隱

yŏlsŏng (successive sage rulers) 列聖

Yongbi ŏch'ŏn'ga (Song of the dragons ascending to heaven) 龍飛九天歌

Yŏngjo (r.1724-1776) 英祖

Yōrō ritsu (code of 718) 養老律

yotoku (given and gained) 與得

yu-i (postal services and transport) 郵驛

yu-shih i-ts'ai ch'ing-ch'iu (offering a bribe) 有事以財請求

yu t'ui-k'an ssu (right inquiring office) 右推勘司

yü (detention house) 獄

yü-ch'eng (material facts established after accused signs confession) 獄成

yü i-chia wu-i (deemed to be of one family) 與一家無異

yü-k'ung (the detention house is vacant) 獄空

yü-tzu (jailers) 獄子

yüan (unit of value) 元

yüan (office head) 院

yüan-an wu-ts'ung chien-ch'a (the original record of the case is unavailable) 原案無從檢查

yüan-nien ch'eng-an (precedent from a remote period) 遠年成案

yüan-tso (vicarious responsibility) 緣坐

yüeh-chü (contract) 約據

Yüeh hai-kuan chien-tu (Canton "Hoppo") 粵海關監督

yüeh-tzu (type of contract) 約字

Yung-cheng (r.1723-1735) 雍正

yup'ye (degenerate practices, abuses; see mallyujip'ye) 流弊

zappan ritsu (miscellaneous offenses law) 雜犯律

zatsuhan (miscellaneous offenses) 雜犯

INDEX

Studies in East Asian Law
Harvard University

1. *Law in Imperial China Exemplified by 190 Ch'ing Dynasty Cases (translated from the* Hsing-an hui-lan) *with Historical, Social, and Juridical Commentaries.* By Derk Bodde and Clarence Morris. Cambridge, Mass.: Harvard University Press, 1967.
2. *The Criminal Process in the People's Republic of China, 1949-1963: An Introduction.* By Jerome Alan Cohen. Cambridge, Mass.: Harvard University Press, 1968.
3. *Agreements of the People's Republic of China, 1949-1967: A Calendar.* By Douglas M. Johnston and Hungdah Chiu. Cambridge, Mass.: Harvard University Press, 1968.
4. *Contemporary Chinese Law: Research Problems and Perspectives.* Edited by Jerome Alan Cohen. Cambridge, Mass.: Harvard University Press, 1970.
5. *The People's Republic of China and the Law of Treaties.* By Hungdah Chiu. Cambridge, Mass.: Harvard University Press, 1972.
6. *China's Practice of International Law: Some Case Studies.* Edited by Jerome Alan Cohen. Cambridge, Mass.: Harvard University Press, 1972.
7. *The Internal Organization of Ch'ing Bureaucracy—Legal, Normative, and Communication Aspects.* By Thomas A. Metzger. Cambridge, Mass: Harvard University Press, 1973.
8. *People's China and International Law: a Documentary Study.* By Jerome Alan Cohen and Hungdah Chiu. Princeton, N.J.: Princeton University Press, 1974.
9. *The Chinese Communist Treatment of Counterrevolutionaries, 1924-1949.* By Patricia E. Griffin. Princeton, N.J.: Princeton University Press, 1976.
10. *The T'ang Code: General Principles, Volume I.* Translated and edited by Wallace Johnson. Princeton, N.J.: Princeton University Press, 1979.
11. *Chinese Legal Tradition under the Mongols: The Code of 1291 as Reconstructed.* By Paul Heng-chao Ch'ien. Princeton, N.J.: Princeton University Press, 1979.

Library of Congress Cataloging in Publication Data

Essays on China's legal tradition.
(Studies in East Asian law, Harvard University)
Includes bibliographical references and index.
1. Law—China—History and criticism—Addresses, essays, lectures. I. Cohen, Jerome Alan. II. Edwards, R. Randle, 1934- III. Chen, Fu-mei Chang. IV. Series: Harvard studies in East Asian law.
Law 340'.0951 79-3197
ISBN 0-691-09238-9